Entrepreneurship

History of Management Thought
Series Editor: Derek S. Pugh

Titles in the Series:

Entrepreneurship

Edited by

Sue Birley

The Management School
Imperial College of Science, Technology and Medicine

Ashgate

DARTMOUTH

Aldershot • Brookfield USA • Singapore • Sydney

Published by
Dartmouth Publishing Company Limited
Gower House
Croft Road
Aldershot
Hants GU11 3HR
England

Ashgate Publishing Company
Old Post Road
Brookfield
Vermont 05036
USA

British Library Cataloguing in Publication Data
Entrepreneurship. – (History of management thought)
   1. Entrepreneurship
  I. Birley, Sue
  658.4'21

Library of Congress Cataloging-in-Publication Data
Entrepreneurship / edited by Sue Birley.
      p. cm.
  Includes bibliographical references.
  ISBN 1–85521–966–2 (hb)
   1. Entrepreneurship. I. Birley, Sue.
HB615.E6233 1998
338'.04—dc21   97–45887
                                                 CIP

ISBN 1 85521 966 2

Printed in Great Britain by Galliard (Printers) Ltd, Great Yarmouth

Contents

Acknowledgements

The editor and publishers wish to thank the following for permission to use copyright material.

Academy of Management for the essays: Robert H. Brockhaus, Sr. (1980), 'Risk Taking Propensity of Entrepreneurs', *Academy of Management Journal*, **23**, pp. 509–20. Copyright © 1980 Academy of Management Journal; James W. Carland, Frank Hoy, William R. Boulton and Jo Ann C. Carland (1984), 'Differentiating Entrepreneurs from Small Business Owners: A Conceptualization', *Academy of Management Review*, **9**, pp. 354–59; Johannes M. Pennings (1982), 'The Urban Quality of Life and Entrepreneurship', *Academy of Management Journal*, **25**, pp. 63–79. Copyright © 1982 Academy of Management Journal; William B. Gartner (1985), 'A Conceptual Framework for Describing the Phenomenon of New Venture Creation', *Academy of Management Review*, **10**, pp. 696–706.

Administrative Science Quarterly for the essays: Stanley M. Davis (1968), 'Entrepreneurial Succession', *Administrative Science Quarterly*, **13**, pp. 402–16; Andrea Larson (1992), 'Network Dyads in Entrepreneurial Settings: A Study of the Governance of Exchange Relationships', *Administrative Science Quarterly*, **37**, pp. 76–104. Copyright © 1992 by Cornell University.

Blackwell Publishers for the essays: M.J.K. Stanworth and J. Curran (1976), 'Growth and the Small Firm – An Alternative View', *Journal of Management Studies*, May, pp. 95–110; M.F.R. Kets de Vries (1977), 'The Entrepreneurial Personality: A Person at the Crossroads', *Journal of Management Studies*, February, pp. 34–57.

California Management Review for the essays: AnnaLee Saxenian (1990), 'Regional Networks and the Resurgence of Silicon Valley', *California Management Review*, Fall, pp. 89–112. Copyright © 1990, by the Regents of the University of California; Murray Weidenbaum (1996), 'The Chinese Family Business Enterprise', *California Management Review*, **38**, pp. 141–56. Copyright © 1996, by the Regents of the University of California. Reprinted from the California Management Review, by permission of the Regents.

Elsevier Science Inc. for the essays: Thomas M. Begley and David P. Boyd (1987), 'Psychological Characteristics Associated with Performance in Entrepreneurial Firms and Smaller Businesses', *Journal of Business Venturing*, **2**, pp. 79–93. Copyright © Elsevier Science Publishing Co., Inc.; Rita Gunther McGrath, Ian C. MacMillan and Sari Scheinberg (1992), 'Elitists, Risk-Takers, and Rugged Individualists? An Exploratory Analysis of Cultural Differences Between Entrepreneurs and Non-Entrepreneurs', *Journal of Business Venturing*, **7**, pp. 115–35. Copyright © 1992 Elsevier Science Publishing Co., Inc.; Sue Birley (1985), 'The Role of Networks in the Entrepreneurial Process', *Journal of Business Venturing*, **1**, pp. 107–17. Copyright © 1985 Elsevier Science Publishing Co., Inc.; Harry J. Sapienza (1992), 'When Do Venture Capitalists Add Value?', *Journal of Business Venturing*, **7**, pp. 9–27. Copyright © 1992 Elsevier Science Publishing, Co., Inc.

Series Preface

The *History of Management Thought* is based on the assumption that a knowledge of the intellectual history of an academic field is vital for a present day understanding of it. In the past scholars of management as a discipline have tended to ignore or underrate the historical development of their subject. This ignorance has encouraged the 'reinventing the wheel' and 'old wine in new bottles' phenomena which have plagued the subject of management since its birth. The insight that those who ignore history are condemned to repeat it, is surely most true about the development of ideas.

This indifference now appears to be beginning to change, and the history of management and management thought is attracting greater interest. The *History of Management Thought* builds on this development by presenting a number of volumes which cover the intellectual history of the subject. It makes available to a wide range of academics contributions to management thought that have been influential over the years. The volume topics range across the whole field of management studies from early management thought through to post-modern management theory.

Each volume in the *History of Management Thought* is edited by a leading international scholar who gives an introductory analytical historical review of the development of the subject, and then presents a selection of key articles. Many of these articles have previously only been published in journals, often in early volumes which are not generally available. They are now conveniently presented in book form, with each chosen article reproduced in full. They offer an important resource for use by academics and advanced students in the field for increasing their knowledge and understanding of the historical development of the disciplines of management.

DEREK S. PUGH
General Editor
History of Management Thought
Visiting Research Professor of
International Management
Open University Business School, UK

Introduction

It is strange to reflect that entrepreneurial activity in all its various forms is as old as time, and yet it is only recently that academics have begun to think about it and to try to understand the factors which stimulate and drive it. This volume is concerned with the development of that thought and with some of the academic papers which have formed milestones in its pathway to date. Inevitably, the authors come from diverse backgrounds. After all, they are not developing a discipline but, rather, studying a phenomenon from their own academic perspective. Thus, we have working in the field, for example, economists, social scientists, economic geographers, statisticians, psychologists, historians, and population ecologists, all adding their own particular perspective to the developing story.

The aim of this volume is to provide a range of key articles that will be useful to students and academics working in the field. Inevitably choices were made. For example, there is nothing about the phenomenon of management buyouts[1] which has emerged in the literature over the past 15 years, nor about the special problems that beset those concerned with launching new technology-based businesses.[2] For simplicity, it is arranged under a number of topic headings, although the discussion within them is by no means mutually exclusive. They do, however, reflect both the focus and volume of research to date and, as far as possible, the preoccupations of those practitioners and policy-makers concerned to use the research findings.

As I am sure was the case for all my colleagues editing this series on the 'History of Management Thought', selecting the papers was a daunting task. For entrepreneurship, this was complicated by the fact that a number of the academics who have been central to the development of thought in the field have eschewed the traditional academic journal in favour of books or the more popular practitioner media. For many, their aim has been very clearly to stimulate discussion and to influence policy. For others, there was no obvious journal available. Indeed, it is only in the last 15 years that credible publications directly concerned with the field, such as the *Journal of Business Venturing*, have emerged. Therefore, I have indicated in the text those books which readers may find of value.

Entrepreneurial Supply

There are three capstone essays. The first is one of the classic pieces from Schumpeter, published in 1949 and reproduced here as Chapter 1. It is *the* root paper for the field. Interestingly, and contrary to the perception often promulgated in the subsequent literature, he does not define an entrepreneur as an 'innovator' but, rather, says he 'has no objection to some such expression'. Indeed he has some difficulty with the entrepreneurial function being 'embodied in a physical person' and would prefer to see a concentration upon the activity being one of 'creating an entire new set up at will', an 'act outside of the pale of routine' after which the 'industrialist ... will, in a typical case, settle down to a merely administrative activity'. This distinction is important as we try to understand the inherent conflict between the two roles of creating and, subsequently, managing a new business entity. Moreover, he makes the logical point that follows – that organizations can act entrepreneurially and, indeed, that these aptitudes can become part of the 'corporate personality'.

Schumpeter's essay is rich in research ideas and practical insights. However, that is for the reader to explore. I would simply point to two themes that are echoed in many of the essays in this volume. The first very clearly defines entrepreneurship as a process of gathering resources within an environment, and the research task of understanding both the critical elements of the process and the nature of environments where entrepreneurship is successful. The second point that he is at pains to emphasize is that entrepreneurs 'do not form a social class. They hail from all corners of the social universe.' Readers may care to reflect on the extent to which subsequent researchers and policy-makers have ignored this and have tried to homogenize (or characterize) this heterogenous group.

The second capstone essay (Chapter 2) explores further the question of whether organizations can act entrepreneurially. To illustrate his argument, Peterson quotes Gerald Zornow, Chairman of the Board of Eastman Kodak: 'Asking a large company to engage in entrepreneurship is like trying to get an elephant to ice-skate.' His essay '… confronts the beast, the skates and the ice' by examining Schumpeter's view that entrepreneurship is a process not a person and, consequently, relevant to all organizations.[3]

The third capstone essay, by Baumol and reproduced as Chapter 3, is a fascinating insight into entrepreneurial activity through the ages, from the early Roman Empire through medieval China to the Industrial Revolution. However, unlike most writers, who implicitly assume that it is 'a good thing' which, when successful, automatically leads to financial profits both for the individual and the economy, Baumol clearly demonstrates that this is not necessarily the case. Indeed, he presents graphic examples of both 'unproductive' and 'destructive' entrepreneurship as major elements in societies. His basic thesis from this is that both the supply of entrepreneurs and the nature of their activity (be it, for example, military or commercial) is determined by the 'rules of the game' – the social, political, technological and economic environment. In other words, he leans very clearly towards the nurture end of the nature–nurture debate. As such, he provides comfort to policy-makers in the conclusion that it is possible to change the rules in order to stimulate productive entrepreneurship.

The Entrepreneur

Despite a clear warning from Schumpeter, much of the early work in the field was, indeed, concerned with attempting to describe the motivations, skills, goals and characteristics of the entrepreneur. The obvious purpose for many was to refine ways to 'pick winners',[4] to find tools and techniques which would help to identify those in society who were most likely to start and grow successful businesses. This whole stream of research starts with McClelland and his book *The Achieving Society*[5] which is based on the thesis that everyone has a measurable level of achievement motive (*n* Ach) but that this can be changed through training and development to a level where entrepreneurial activity can be stimulated. This he demonstrates through empirical study in the essay presented as Chapter 4. However, whilst high *n* Ach may be a necessary condition, Liles argues in Chapter 5 that it is not sufficient and that factors such as readiness, restraints, and precipitating events are equally important, along with the notion of risk – financial, career, family, and psychic (fear of failure). On this latter issue, Liles is very clear that entrepreneurs are not '… people who like to take risks', a conclusion that is empirically supported later in Chapter 8 by Brockhaus who found '… that risk taking propensity may not be a distinguishing characteristic of entrepreneurs'. Yet, the myth that entrepreneurs are, by definition, risk takers rather than risk minimizers, lives on. Ask any new class of students!

Liles' essay is also an important milestone because it encapsulates much of the received wisdom that has dogged the field in subsequent years. First, he reports the widely quoted study by Collins, Moore, and Unwalla[6] which looked at 110 manufacturing firms started in Michigan between 1945 and 1958 and found their owners to be misfits – 'men who have failed in the traditional and highly structured roles available to them in society'. Whilst Liles argues persuasively that this is not always the case, the myth continued in the literature for many years. The second unchallenged and explicit assumption is that we are dealing exclusively with '… the male career life cycle'. This gender-based view[7] is certainly not valid either for other cultures or, indeed, for the USA in the 1990s!

Kets de Vries enhances the story in Chapter 7 by providing an extensive review of the literature on behaviour patterns and, in particular, on the impact of the family, to arrive at a conceptualisation of the 'entrepreneurial personality'.[8] Moreover, for the purposes of this volume, he introduces two further pieces into the research jigsaw. The first is the use of Rotter's 'locus of control' instrument as another way of identifying those with a propensity for entrepreneurship, and the second is Smith's[9] classification of entrepreneurs into 'craftsmen' and 'opportunistic' based on factors such as education, social awareness, and self-confidence. From this, he notes that Smith suggests that the craftsman will build a 'rigid' firm and the opportunistic an 'adaptive' firm. Interestingly, subsequent literature takes the literal definition of these labels and implies some relationship to attitudes to growth. Thus, it is assumed that the craftsmen are the self-employed and that the opportunistic are those who create the growing businesses.

Implicit in this early classification, and the attempt at characterization, is an assumption about the business and the lifestyle goals and aspirations of the person starting the business. Quite simply, not everyone wants to own a large corporation and, even if they do, not many achieve it. Yet, despite the fact that many academics recognized this conundrum, the empirical literature continued to be very confused. The essay by Carland *et al.* (Chapter 9) was an attempt to take the two terms 'small business' and 'entrepreneur' and provide a conceptualization of the differences. Interestingly, this was not a new idea but had already been suggested in another form in an earlier essay by Stanworth and Curran in the UK (Chapter 6). They identified three '… latent identities [which] occur with some frequency in relation to the small firm entrepreneur': an 'artisan' who was concerned with intrinsic satisfaction and not very concerned with growth; a 'classic entrepreneur [who] most closely resembles the classical economists' view of entrepreneurship'; and the 'manager … concerned with the recognition, by significant others, of managerial excellence'. It would not be difficult to class these as aspiring to own respectively, small, medium, and large businesses.[10] Interestingly, the reason that this essay was not referenced in the Carland essay is that, as for many new fields of study, academics have a strong tendency to ethnocentricity! However, it is important to note, as is evident from this volume, that most of the widely quoted papers in the field are written by American academics and based in the USA – the footprint for most of the literature.

In Chapter 10, Begley and Boyd bring all these various factors together by relating the most commonly researched psychological characteristics of *n* Ach – locus of control, risk-taking propensity, tolerance of ambiguity and Type A behaviour (for example, impatience, irritability, driving ambition) – to both entrepreneurial firms and small businesses. In so doing, the essay provides a useful summary of the five instruments. Their conclusion, that there are '… few connections between psychological attributes and corporate performance', is reinforced in subsequent literature and gives a resounding '*No*' to the question as to whether they can be used to 'pick winners' at the start. Yet researchers still continue down this unrewarding path.

The final essay in Part II by McGrath, MacMillan and Scheinberg (Chapter 11) is a cautionary tale of the very first, and courageous, attempt to conduct cross-cultural research in this field. I was part of this process and contributed the UK data. Suffice to say it was fraught with methodological difficulties, language being but merely one. Nevertheless, it is important because it reintroduces the concept suggested by Schumpeter of national culture as one defining characteristic in the entrepreneurial decision.

Start-up and Networks

We now turn from the person who starts a business to the process, and to the recognition that a business idea, or ideas, may incubate for many years before actual germination takes place. Indeed, it makes intuitive sense that the type of product, the nature of the business created, and the timing of the decision to start is likely to be influenced by past experiences. Cooper's model of the three influences – antecedent, incubator organization, and environmental factors – is both clear and simple and, consequently, very powerful (see Chapter 12). Pennings takes the last of these in Chapter 13 and finds evidence of the impact of the (urban) quality of life – the five dimensions of economic, political, environmental, health/educational and social – on the rate of formation of new ventures. Gartner then takes us through to the actual creation of the venture in Chapter 14. In this process, the entrepreneur is concerned to gather all the necessary resources at the least cost. In the final chapter of Part III Starr and MacMillan take us back to Baumol's essay and remind us that this process may indeed involve such activities as begging, borrowing and stealing – in their terms, 'resource co-optation'! To do this, entrepreneurs must draw on their own resource base – their personal credibility – which is, of course, usually greatest with people they know.

Obviously, this is not a new idea. The 'old boy network', the Mafia and the Triads are all well known business networks. Nevertheless, according to my colleagues, it wasn't until I stumbled into the topic during a study of new businesses in South Bend[11] that it began to form part of the entrepreneurship stream of literature. At the beginning of Part IV, I introduce the concept of 'formal' and 'informal' networks which I later discovered are actually called 'professional' and 'social'. Indeed, readers may be amused to note that one of the reviewers of the essay commented that '… this person knows nothing about the social network literature but …! Subsequently, I was introduced to a new and fascinating field of study and, although the review was anonymous, I suspect that I know the person who has subsequently become a good friend. I tell the story to illustrate the excitement of the field, the random nature in which themes emerge in the literature, and the willingness of journal editors, in this case Ian MacMillan, to take risks in order to explore new approaches.

The essay by Aldrich and Zimmer (Chapter 13) embeds the study of entrepreneurship in the theory of social networks and gives academic credence to the saying 'It is not just what you know but who you know'. In so doing, they introduce both the nature of resources to be found in the network – information, advice, sponsorship, support and control – and measurable characteristics such as density, diversity, and accessibility. In Chapter 18 Saxenian, in her fascinating description of the development of the phenomenon known as 'Silicon Valley' demonstrates this clearly. However, she also takes the story further. Not only does she highlight '... the dense social networks [which] ... foster the recombination of experience, skill, and technology into enterprise' but also, as businesses mature, the development of interorganizational networks. Larson examines this latter process in the final chapter of Part IV and concludes that there are usually three phases to the building of 'network dyads'. The first 'preconditions for exchange', is concerned with prior social relationships; the second, 'conditions to build', is the trial period where, for example, rules and procedures are established; and the third, operational, phase is 'integration and control'. Her conclusion is persuasive: '... an examination of social control factors and their interaction with economic exchange will reveal a more complete account of these network organisational forms ... .'

Venture Capital

The process of starting a business involves the assembly of all the necessary resources, but raising finance is often viewed as the most difficult. It is not my intention to argue this thesis but, rather, to note that the vast majority of new ventures have no involvement with venture capital. Instead, they rely on personal savings and loans from family and friends. Nevertheless, the formal venture capital industry in the USA has been subjected to intense scrutiny by academics over the past 15 years and so I have included in Part V two essays from this stream of literature.[12] The first, by Tyebjee and Bruno, explores what venture capitalists actually do in deciding on a new investment. In particular, they examine the process that they adopt and the investment criteria that they use. Their analysis produces five basic decision dimensions – market attractiveness, product differentiation, managerial capabilities, environmental threat resistance and cash-out potential. Whilst subsequent studies, both in the USA and Europe, have expanded the list and have found some variation in results, the overall findings have proved remarkably robust. The second essay by Sapienza (Chapter 22) explores the post-investment relationship between venture capitalist and the entrepreneurial business and poses the question 'When do venture capitalists add value?'.

Wetzel (Chapter 20) reminds us that family and friends and venture capital are two ends of a funding spectrum and that there is clear evidence of a capital, or equity, gap. Moreover, this gap is clearly being filled by some third party. These 'business angels' are individuals not connected to the entrepreneur, who are prepared to invest insignificant amounts of personal cash, or 'informal risk capital' in new ventures. Indeed, Wetzel suggests that they may well represent the 'largest pool of risk capital in the country'. Whilst this is intuitively obvious – and there are many examples of this type of activity which can be drawn from history – this essay represents the beginning of a new stream of research for the field.

Growth Stages

Although Edith Penrose[13] had produced a pioneering book on *The Theory of Growth of the Firm* in 1957, it was not until the publication of Alfred Chandler's[14] book that a body of research began to emerge – primarily from the Harvard Business School – which was relevant to entrepreneurship. Implicit in these studies was an assumption that a primary goal of any business was to grow. This is not surprising since they were almost exclusively based in large and/or publicly quoted companies. Explicit in most of these studies was the assumption that a generic model, which described a number of 'stages of growth', could be identified and described. In 1972, Greiner (Chapter 23) presented such a model to describe the life cycle of a business from youth to maturity, postulating that changes from one phase to another are triggered by a series of identifiable crises. Eleven years later, and in the same journal, Churchill and Lewis (Chapter 24) took this concept of a 'business development model' and produced the 'Five Stages of Small Business Growth' – a model which continues to endure in the literature. However, both these essays reflect but one approach, and readers may welcome the useful 'critical literature review' of other, 'Alternative Theories of Small Firm Growth' published by O'Farrell and Hitchens in 1988. These three essays are presented in Part VI of this volume.

Family

No set of essays on the study of enterprise would be complete without the inclusion of the family. After all, for many families throughout the world, business and family affairs are inextricably intertwined. Inevitably, this leads to conflict between personal and business goals, between family and employees, and between parents and children. Three essays, all more than 20 years old, describe these dilemmas graphically and clearly. I usually find that they provide real comfort to students from such situations – many discover for the first time, in the anonymity of the classroom, that they are not alone! Davis (Chapter 26) studied succession in family firms in Mexico and found three patterns of conflict – between the strong father and weak son, the conservative father and progressive son and between other branches of the family. He concludes, 'Despite differences about how family businesses should be operated, personal relationships often take precedence over maximum profits'. Despite this 'Bringing about entrepreneurial succession is essential for survival in a competitive market'.

In Chapter 27, Levinson expands on this inevitable 'discord between father and son and other rivalries among relatives [which] can paralyse the organisation unless they are confronted'. Barnes and Hershon are concerned with the thorny question of power and the transfer of both managerial control and equity across the generations. Their model of the pressures and interests inside a family business, presented in Chapter 28, is both powerful and enduring. However, it is based on experience in America, and family cultures and behaviours vary significantly by country and religion. The essay by Weidenbaum, which concludes Part VII, presents a fascinating and different perspective – a valuable insight into the impact of Chinese entrepreneurs and their families on business in South East Asia.[15]

Past Research and Future Challenges

Schumpeter and Baumol argued that the 'rules of the game' as well as the social, economic and political climate of a country were likely to affect the nature and quantity of the supply of new ventures. In the recent upheaval in Eastern Europe, these changes are massive along all dimensions. So great is the change that even casual empiricism highlights new social attitudes towards enterprise in particular and commercial activity generally. The literature which tracks these changes is only just beginning to emerge, not least because academics were also both repressed and ill-equipped to study the new phenomenon. The essay by Naor and Bod (Chapter 30), which pre-dates the fall of the Berlin Wall, illustrates the size of the task necessary to change a command economy to a market economy.

Not only is the final essay by Low and MacMillan a useful addition to this volume in that it offers a wider summary of the published research to 1988, but it also carries important messages for colleagues. In short, they remind us not to forget our responsibility to use sound research methodologies – to be clear about purpose, theoretical perspective, focus, level of analysis, and time frame. This is important. For entirely understandable reasons, many of the early essays in the field were based on relatively small samples, were solely descriptive, had no evident basis in theory, were based in single industries or locations, had no basis for generalization, were confused in their level of analysis, and were cross-sectional. It is partly for this reason that the majority of the essays in this volume are less than 20 years old, since it is only during this period that a coherent stream of analytical research has emerged, which gives form to the field. Consequently, it has finally gained both momentum and acceptance within the wider academic community. Witness the growing number of academic and practitioner journals and chairs in universities. Much of this is due to the pioneering efforts of academics willing to take risks with their own personal careers. They are too many to name but they were, and are, truly entrepreneurial. I salute them.

Notes

1   For a fascinating insight into one of the largest ever attempted at the time, see the story of Nabisco: Burrough, B. and Helyar, J. (1990), *Barbarians at the Gate*, London: Arrow Books.

2   Ed Roberts at MIT has tracked this literature for more than 20 years. See Roberts, E. (1991), *Entrepreneurs in High Technology: Lessons from MIT and Beyond*, Oxford: Oxford University Press.

3   This predates the current concept of 'corporate venturing' which, for reasons of space is not covered in this volume. However, useful references include: Block, X. and MacMillan, I.C. (1993), *Corporate Venturing: Creating New Businesses Within the Firm*, Boston, Mass.: Harvard University Press; Burgleman, R.A. and Sayles, L.R. (1986), *Inside Corporate Innovation: Strategy Structure and Managerial Skills*, London: Collier, MacMillan; Kanter, R.M. (1983), *The Change Masters*, Simon and Schuster: New York.

4   Insights into the lives of successful entrepreneurs can often be obtained by studying the biographies of, for example, Ford or Disney. See, for example, Brown, M. (1989), *Richard Branson: The Inside Story*, London: Headline.

5   McClelland, D.C. (1961), *The Achieving Society*, D. Van Nostrand Company Inc. Princeton.

6   Collins, O.F., Moore, D.G. and Unwalla, D.B. (1964) *The Enterprising Man*, East Lansing, Michigan: Division of Research, Graduate School of Business Administration, Michigan State University.

7   See, for example, Goffe, R. and Scase R. (1985), *Women in Charge: The Experiences of Female Entrepreneurs*, London: George Allen and Unwin; Hertz, L. (1986), *The Business Amazons*, London: Deutsch; El-Namaki, M.S.S. and Gerritson, J.C.M. (1987), *The Entrepreneurial Role of Women in Developing Countries: Entry and Performance Barriers*, RVB Research Paper, March.

8   See also Schumacher, E.F. (1973), *Small is Beautiful: A Study of Economics as if People Mattered*, London: Blond and Briggs.

9   Smith, N.R. (1967), *The Entrepreneur and His Firm: The Relationship Between Type of Man and Type of Company*, East Lansing, Michigan: Division of Research, Graduate School of Business Administration, Michigan State University.

10   This issue of growth and, in particular, the job generation capabilities of new and small firms has been of particular interest to politicians and policy-makers since the publication of Birch, D. (1979), *The Job Generation Process; MIT Program on Neighbourhood and Regional Change*, Cambridge, Mass.: MIT Press. This study was reported as concluding that small firms created the largest number of net new jobs in the USA. Subsequent studies have shown that this is due to a very small number of firms within the population.

11   Indiana, USA.

12   Since the formal venture capital industry in Europe is much younger than that in the USA, it is not surprising that these essays emanate from this source.

13   Penrose, E. (1957), *The Theory of Growth of the Firm*, Oxford: Basil Blackwell.

14   Chandler, A.C. (1962), *Strategy and Structure: Chapters in the History of American Industrial Enterprise*, Cambridge, Mass.: MIT Press.

15   For further reading in this area see Redding, S.G. (1990), *The Spirit of Chinese Capitalism*, Berlin: Walter de Gruyter.

Part I
Entrepreneurial Supply

[1]

ECONOMIC THEORY AND ENTREPRENEURIAL HISTORY

Reprinted from *Change and the Entrepreneur*, 1949, 63-84.

In the areas of economic theory and entrepreneurial history, I propose to deal with three topics. First, I shall present a brief survey of the history, within economic literature, of the notions that economists have formed at various times on the subject of entrepreneurship and economic progress (I). Secondly, I shall deal with some aspects of enterprise as it actually evolved through the ages (II). And, thirdly, I shall briefly comment on the possibilities of what might be termed "general economic history" as viewed from the standpoint of the phenomenon of economic enterprise (III). The first topic will also provide the conceptual apparatus to be used in the treatment of the other two.

I

In the field to be discussed, as in others, early economic analysis started from the notions evolved by common experience of everyday life, proceeding to greater precision and refinement of these notions as time went on. From the first, the businessman was a familiar figure that did not seem to call for elaborate explanation at all. The particular forms of business enterprise that every particular environment produced — the artisan, the trader, the money-lender, and so on — took a long time in merging into the general concept of businessman. But by the end of the 17th century this modest generalization was pretty much accomplished. It is, however, worth noting that at least from the beginning of the 15th century on, the scholastic doctors in their economics had a very definite idea of the businessman and his functions, and that in particular they distinguished clearly between the specific *industria* of the merchant and the *labor* of the workman. The same applies to the laic successors of the scholastic doctors, "the philosophers of natural law," and still more to all those pamphleteers of the "mercantilist" age that laid the foundations of classic economics. Cantillon's work, which is usually, though not quite correctly, described as the first systematic treatise on economics, then introduced the term "entrepreneur." It is worth our while to note that Cantillon defined this entrepreneur as the agent who buys means of production at certain prices in order to combine them into a product that he is going to sell at prices that are uncertain at the moment at which he commits himself to his costs. I think that this embryonic analysis was not infelicitous. Besides recognizing business activity as a function *sui generis*, it emphasizes the elements of direction and speculation that certainly do enter somehow into entrepreneurial activity. Like most of Cantillon's ideas, including the idea of the *tableau économique*, this one was accepted by the physiocrats as a matter of course. Since directly and through the physiocrats Cantillon's teaching continued to be known in France, it seems fair to say that J. B. Say only continued the French tradition by developing this analysis further. In this he was greatly helped by the fact that, knowing from experience what business practice really is, he had a lively vision of the phenomenon which most of the other classic economists lacked. With him, then, the entrepreneur is the agent that combines the others into a productive organism. It could be shown both that this definition might be expanded into a satisfactory theory of entrepreneurship by analyzing what this combining of factors really consists in, and that Say himself did not do much with it beyond stressing its importance. Let us note in passing, however, that he put the entrepreneur into the center of both the productive and the distributive theory which, though it is disfigured by many slips, first adumbrated the analytic structure that became fully articulate in the hands of Walras, Marshall, Wicksell, Clark, and the Austrians. Still more clearly the nature and importance of entrepreneurship were perceived by Jeremy Bentham. It is a curious fact (curious, that is, considering the tremendous influence that Bentham exerted in other respects) that his views on this subject — which were not fully given to the public until the posthumous publication of his collected works — remained almost unnoticed by professional economists.

In spite of the great influence of the physiocrats and of Cantillon upon Adam Smith, English thought took a quite different line. To be sure, Adam Smith repeatedly talked about the employer — the master, the merchant, and the undertaker — but the leading or directing activity as a distinctive function played a surprisingly small role in his analytic scheme of the economic process. His reader is bound to get an impression to the effect that this process runs on by itself. Natural law preconceptions led Adam Smith to emphasize the role of labor to the exclusion of the productive function of designing the plan according to which this labor is being applied. This shows characteristically in his turn of phrase that asserts that "capitalists" hire "industrious people," advancing them means of subsistence, raw materials, and tools, and letting them do the rest. What the businessman does in the system of Adam Smith is, therefore, to provide real capital and nothing else: the identification of the capitalist's and the entrepreneur's function was thus accomplished. Let us note: first, that this picture of the industrial process is entirely unrealistic; but that, considering the prevalence at Adam Smith's time of the putting-out system, and also for other historical reasons, this identification was then less absurd than it became fifty years later; and that Smith's authority explains why it survived so well into times that presented different patterns. Since capital, according to Adam Smith, is the result of saving, and since providing capital is the only essential function of the businessman, the latter's profits was essentially interest to be explained on the lines of either an exploitation or an abstinence theory. Adam Smith elaborated neither, but no doubt suggested both.

With Ricardo and Marx the processes of production and commerce are still more automatic. The designing, directing, leading, co-ordinating function has practically no place at all in their analytic schemata. To avoid misunderstandings, let me emphasize that there is no doubt but that, if pressed, both Ricardo and Marx (and this goes for a majority of the writers of the classic period) would certainly have recognized the importance of entrepreneurship or business management or however they would have called it, for the success or failure of the individual concern. But it is possible to recognize this and to hold, nevertheless, that for the social process as a whole individual differences in this respect are of no great moment. John Stuart Mill who, at an early age, had experienced the influence of Say, abandoned Ricardianism in this as he did in other points. He emphasized the function of direction in the productive process and went out of his way to say that very often it required "no ordinary skill." His perception of the importance of entrepreneurial activity shows among other things in the fact that he regretted that there is no good English word for the French "entrepreneur." But this was all. When we observe that he analyzed the entrepreneur's profits into wages of management, interest on owned capital, and premium of risk, we wonder why he should not have been content with the perfectly good English term "business management," which was in fact to satisfy Marshall. For, after all, his entrepreneur does a type of non-manual work that does not essentially differ from other types, and therefore reaps a return that is analogous to wages. There should be no need for a distinctive term.

Just as the understanding of the phenomenon of rent of land was facilitated by the English land system that showed up the distinction between the owner of land and the agricultural producer with unmistakable clearness, so the distinction between the entrepreneur and the capitalist was facilitated in the second half of the 19th century by the fact that changing methods of business finance produced a rapidly increasing number of instances in which capitalists were no entrepreneurs and entrepreneurs were no capitalists. Though the owner-manager remained for a time still the ruling type, it became increasingly clear that a link between owning and operating the physical shell of industry is not a necessary one. Economists accordingly began to emphasize distinctions between the two functions and to devote more attention to the specifically entrepreneurial one. Fundamental change in the analytic set-up was very slow, however. Among other things, this shows in the survival of the risk theory of entrepreneurial profit. If providing the capital is not the essential or defining function of the entrepreneur, then risk bearing should not be described as an essential or defining function either, for it is obviously the capitalist who bears the risk and who loses his money in case of failure. If the entrepreneur borrows at a fixed rate of interest and undertakes to guarantee the capitalist against loss whatever the results of the enterprise, he can do so only if he owns other assets with which to satisfy the creditor capitalist when things go wrong. But, in this case, he is able to satisfy his creditor because he is a capitalist himself and the risk he bears he bears in this capacity and not in his capacity of entrepreneur. To this point I shall return below. The economists, therefore, who went on to emphasize the entrepreneurial function more and more, such as Francis A. Walker in the U. S., Marshall in England, Mangoldt and others in Germany, added very little to its analysis.

Two lines of thought that issued in distinctive theories of entrepeneurial profits as distinguished from interest should not go unmentioned. Mangoldt, following up a generalization of the rent concept that may be traced to Samuel Bailey, defined the particular element of total receipts that goes to the entrepreneur as a rent of ability. The underlying idea is very plausible. All current disturbances of the economic process, the whole task of adaptation to ever changing situations, impinges primarily upon the heads of business concerns. Obviously this is a very personal task of which some people acquit themselves very much better than others. There is a common-sense impression to the effect that there is such a thing as a distinct business ability, which includes aptitude for efficient administration, for prompt decision, and all that sort of thing; and it is very generally recognized in spite of some votes to the contrary (in this country, mainly from economists of Veblenite persuasion) that successful survival of difficult situations and success in taking advantage of favorable situations is not merely a matter of luck. The concept of a rent of ability expresses the element involved quite well. Again the cognate idea that business decisions in a world that is full of uninsurable risks ("uncertainty") will in general produce results that diverge more or less widely from the expected ones and thus lead sometimes to surplus gains and sometimes to losses, is one that common experience presses upon us very strongly. This idea may be but need not be added to the element of business ability and is of course, still more obviously, not quite the same as the element of risk: but we need not stress these relations. So far as I know, Böhm-Bawerk was the first to make use of this notion for the purpose of explaining entrepreneurial profits as distinct from interest. But this line of thought culminates in the work of Professor Knight.

It does not seem far-fetched, however, to analyze the entrepreneurial function in a different direction which moreover leads to a result that comprises also some of the elements of other theories. I shall try to convey this analysis by starting from two different standpoints. The first standpoint to start from is given by Say's definition of the entrepreneurial function. If production in the economic, as distinguished from the technological, sense consists essentially in transforming or combining factors into products, or as I have put it above, in providing the design of production, then we certainly have in this combining or planning or directing activity a distinct function before us. But this function would be an exceedingly simple matter and essentially a matter of administration if the combinations that have been carried into effect in the past had to be simply repeated or even if they had to be repeated subject to those adaptations which common business experience suggests in the face of conditions that change under the influence of external factors. Administrative or managerial activity of this kind, however necessary, need not be distinguished from other kinds of non-manual labor; but if we confine Say's definition to cases in which combinations that are *not* inherited from the past have to be set up anew, then the situation is obviously different and we do have a distinctive function before us. Naturally, to some extent, even current decisions contain elements that have not been contained in inherited routine. There is, therefore, no sharp dividing line between entrepreneurial activity in this restricted sense and ordinary administration or management, any more than there is a sharp dividing line between the *homo neanderthalis* and the types which we recognize as full-fledged human beings. This does not, however, prevent the distinction from being possible and useful. And the distinctive element is readily recognized so soon as we make clear to ourselves what it means to act outside of the pale of routine. The distinction between adaptive and creative response to given conditions may or may not be felicitous, but it conveys an essential point; it conveys an essential difference.

The other standpoint from which to get a realistic understanding of the entrepreneurial function comes into view when we try to analyze the nature and sources of the gains that attend successful entrepreneurship. This can be done in many ways, for instance, by analyzing the sources of a sufficient number of industrial fortunes. We find immediately that industrial activity in established lines and by established methods hardly ever yields returns that are much greater than is necessary to secure the supply of the factors required. Furthermore, we find that the earning capacity of almost any industrial concern peters out after a time that varies from a few months to a few decades. And, finally, we find that the great surplus gains are in general made in new industries or in industries that adopt a new method, and especially by the firms who are the first in the field. These propositions await scientific investigations in order to be fully established, but are strongly suggested by universally known facts.

If then we have, on the one hand, a distinctive function and, on the other hand, a distinct return on the exercise of this function, we can start with the task of conceptualization. First, we need a

CHANGE AND THE ENTREPRENEUR 259

word. I have myself suggested that the word "entrepreneur" be harnessed into service, but it is quite clear, of course, that since this "entrepreneurial function" is not a neologism other meanings are bound to creep in. I should, therefore, have no objection to some such expression as "business leader" or simply "innovator" or the like. The essential thing is the recognition of the distinct agent we envisage and not the word.[1] Secondly, in applying our conception to reality we find, as we do in other such cases, that real life never presents the function in and by itself. Even the English landlord is not merely the owner of a natural agent but does various other things besides. In the case of the entrepreneur it is even difficult to imagine a case where a man does nothing but set up new combinations and where he does this all his life. In particular an industrialist who creates an entirely new set-up will, in a typical case, then settle down to a merely administrating activity to which he confines himself more and more as he gets older. On the other hand, the entrepreneurial element may be present to a very small extent even in very humble cases and in these the entrepreneurial function may be all but drowned in other activities. It will be seen, however, that while this makes it difficult to deal with entrepreneurship irrespective of the other types of activity of the same individual and while Professor Cole is therefore quite right in emphasizing the necessity of considering business activity as a whole, the distinctive element and its *modus operandi* should not and need not be lost from sight.

Thirdly, since entrepreneurship, as defined, essentially consists in doing things that are not generally done in the ordinary course of business routine, it is essentially a phenomenon that comes under the wider aspect of leadership. But this relation between entrepreneurship and general leadership is a very complex one and lends itself to a number of misunderstandings. This is due to the fact that the concept of leadership itself is complex. Leadership may consist, as it does in the arts, merely in doing a new thing, for instance, in creating a new form of pictorial self-expression, but in other cases it is the influencing of people by methods other than example that is more important. Take, for instance, the phenomenon that we call the ability of being obeyed. Here it is not so much

---

[1]The difficulty of naming our function is of course greatly increased by the fact that such words as "management" or "administration" from which we are trying to distinguish our function have with many authors also caught some of the meanings that we wish to reserve for the term "entrepreneur."

example as a direct action upon other people that matters. The nature and function of entrepreneurial leadership, its causes and effects, therefore constitute a very important subject of investigation for our group.

Fourthly, the distinctive return to entrepreneurship presents difficulties of its own. It is certainly a return to a personal activity. In this sense we might be tempted to call it a form of wages as has in fact been done in the past by many economists. Furthermore, it is clear that if all people reacted in the same way and at the same time to the presence of new possibilities no entrepreneurial gain would ensue: if everybody had been in a position to develop the Watt condenser, prices of products to be produced with the new steam engine would have adjusted themselves instantaneously and no surplus over costs would have arisen for the firm of Boulton and Watt. Therefore, entrepreneurial gain may also be called a monopoly gain, since it is due to the fact that competitors only follow at a distance.[2] But if we called it either wages or monopoly gains we should be obscuring very important characteristics that do not apply to other wages or to other monopoly gains. Moreover, the entrepreneurial gain does not typically consist, and in any case does not necessarily consist, in a current surplus *per se.* If a man, for instance, sets up a new industrial organization such as United States Steel, the value of the assets that enter into this organization increases. This increase no doubt embodies, at least ideally, a discounted value of the expected surplus returns. But it is this increase in asset return itself rather than the returns that constitute the entrepreneurial gain, and it is in this way that industrial fortunes are typically created — another subject to be investigated.

Finally, as has been often pointed out, the entrepreneurial function need not be embodied in a physical person and in particular in a single physical person. Every social environment has its own. ways of filling the entrepreneurial function. For instance, the practice of farmers in this country has been revolutionized again and again by the introduction of methods worked out in the Department of Agriculture and by the Department of Agriculture's success in teaching these methods. In this case then it was the Department of Agriculture that acted as an entrepreneur. It is

[2]The rate of speed at which competitors follow is another very important point for our research program, as are the means at the disposal of the successful entrepreneur for holding his own against would-be competitors (patents and other practices)

another most important point in our research program to find out how important this kind of activity has been in the past or is in the present. Again the entrepreneurial function may be and often is filled co-operatively. With the development of the largest-scale corporations this has evidently become of major importance: aptitudes that no single individual combines can thus be built into a corporate personality; on the other hand, the constituent physical personalities must inevitably to some extent, and very often to a serious extent, interfere with each other. In many cases, therefore, it is difficult or even impossible to name an individual that acts as "the entrepreneur" in a concern. The leading people in particular, those who carry the titles of president or chairman of the board, may be mere co-ordinators or even figure-heads; and again a very interesting field of research opens up into which I do not wish to go, however, since this problem is in no danger of being forgotten.[3]

We have now briefly to advert to the relation that exists between economic change (usually called economic progress if we approve of it) and the entrepreneurial activity. At present there is, as has been stated above, a whole range of differences of opinion on this subject that extends from a complete or almost complete denial of any importance to be attached to the quality of leading personnel to the equally reckless assertion that the creative individual is nothing less than everything. It need hardly be pointed out that most of these opinions carry the stamp of ideological preconception. It is no doubt part of our work to put provable results into the place of such ideologies. The fundamental question is one of fact, but the necessity of a theoretical schema to start with is nevertheless obvious. I submit that the material under observation may be classed into two masses: on the one hand, there are the given data of the physical and social (including political) environment and, on the other hand, there are the observable reactions to these environmental conditions. But it is better perhaps to include those

---

[3]It is extremely interesting to observe that for a long time and occasionally even now economic theorists have been and are inclined to locate the entrepreneurial function in a corporation with the shareholders. However little the individual small shareholder may have to do with the actual management or else with the entrepreneurial function in the corporation, they hold that ultimate decision still lies with them to be exerted in the shareholders' meeting. All I wish to say about this is first, that the whole idea of risk-taking in this way takes on a further lease of life and, second, that such a theory is about as true as is the political theory that in a democracy the electorate ultimately decides what is to be done.

facts that may be independently observed concerning the quality of leading personnel among the conditions in order to display the interrelation between this and the other factors and to emphasize from the first that on principle there are never any causal chains in the historical process but only mutual interaction of distinguishable factors.

We can then attempt to construct an analytic model of the mechanism of economic change or else, for different countries and periods, different such schemata or models. Let us, in order to visualize this method, consider for a moment the situation that existed in England around 1850. A unique set of historical conditions had produced a uniquely able political sector, the bulk of the members of which hailed from a distinct social class. This sector, while very efficient in certain respects, was entirely unfit and unwilling to undertake anything that we now call economic public management or economic planning. Neglecting for the rest the agrarian sector, we find industry, trade, and finance substantially left to themselves; and if we add a number of other unique historical circumstances we are pretty much able to draw the picture of economic change that is in fact drawn in the ordinary text-book of economic history. In this process of change it is possible to identify a number of factors and events that are entirely impersonal and in some cases random. But looking more closely we see not only that these factors do not determine outcomes uniquely but also that they do not tell us how the actual changes such as the tremendous increase in exports actually came about. In order to make headway with this problem we must investigate how the thousands of individuals actually worked whose combined action produced these results. And for this purpose it is useful as a first step to assume all the environmental factors to be constant and to ask the question what changes we might expect under this assumption. We immediately see that simple increase of population and of physical capital does not constitute the answer. It is not simply the increase of the existing factors of production but the incessantly different use made of these factors that matters. In fact much of the increase in factors and particularly of physical capital was the result rather than the cause of what we may now identify as entrepreneurial activity. What we observe is rather a behavior pattern, possibly supplemented by a schema of motivation; a typical way of giving effect to the possibilities inherent in a given legal and social system both of which change in the process; the effects of entrepreneurial activity upon the industrial structure that exists at any moment; the consequent process of destruction and reconstruction that went on all the time. All these things may be conceptualized in a more or less complicated schema, every item of which has to be nourished with facts and corrected and amplified under their influence. And this is all.

I shall add, however, that in investigations of this kind the notion of an economic process that merely reproduces itself and shows neither decay nor progress has been found to be of considerable use. It is called the stationary state, and plays two distinct roles in economic theory. On the one hand, economists, ever since Adam Smith and perhaps earlier times, have envisaged the possibility that the energetic advance they were witnessing would some day subside into what we now call a stagnating or mature economy. John Stuart Mill differed from Ricardo not in his expectation that a stationary state would one day emerge but in the optimistic view he took of its features — a world without what he considered an unpleasant bustle, a world much more cultured and at ease than the one he observed. Now, as everybody knows, this "stagnationist thesis" has emerged once more, but it has emerged with two differences. First, the stationary state is by some authors not looked upon as something that looms in the far future but as something on which we are actually about to enter. Let us note in passing that the experiences of the crises 1929-1932 may have a lot to do with the emergence of this frame of mind. Secondly, a problem has arisen which did not worry the classics at all. Smith or Ricardo did not anticipate any particular difficulties that would arise from the very process of settling down into stationality: rates of change would converge towards zero in a slow and orderly way. But our modern stagnationists anticipate difficulties in this process of settling down. Keynes in particular anticipated that habits of saving to which equally strong or still stronger propensities to invest corresponded would run on in spite of the fact that there would be no longer any investment opportunities left. With everything indicating now that a new period of unheard-of "progress" is at hand it might be thought that we need not greatly worry about this. But I do not think that we can entirely overlook the problem and history's contribution to it.

II

Whether we define the entrepreneur as an "innovator" or in any other way, there remains the task to see how the chosen definition works out in practice as applied to historical materials. In fact it might be argued that the historical investigation holds logical priority and that our definitions of entrepreneur, entrepreneurial function, enterprise, and so on can only grow out of it *a posteriori*. Personally, I believe that there is an incessant give and take between historical and theoretical analysis and that, though for the investigation of individual questions it may be necessary to sail for a time on one tack only, yet on principle the two should never lose sight of each other. In consequence we might formulate our task as an attempt to write a comprehensive history of entrepreneurship.

So far as the institutional framework is concerned we are, comparatively speaking, well off. The social, legal, technological, and other conditions in which entrepreneurship has run its historical course, from the primitive tribe to the modern large-scale corporation, have been on the whole satisfactorily worked out already. But until relatively recent times it is this framework only that is really known: the actual activity of the entrepreneur, what he really was and did at various stages of historical development, is largely construction. It is true that this construction is in many cases quite safe. For instance, when we know the trade routes in the Near East during the first ten centuries A.D., the commodities that were transported, the political history of the territories through which they were transported, it is not very difficult to imagine the kind of tasks and difficulties that the trader met on these routes and the kind of chap he must have been in order to overcome them. When we know the history of the later trading companies such as the Trading Company of Ravensburg, we again have little difficulty in complementing this by a picture of the kind of man that a member of this company must have been. And to a certain extent we might hope to answer the question directly how environment, public authority, corporate action, and individual initiative must have co-operated and what relative weight we are to attach to each. However, these are favorable cases. In others, much digging may have to be done before we arrive at reliable results. Let us then note that the forms of organization of trade and later on of manufacturing are an acquired asset all along. The same applies largely to the fields and methods of what provisionally we should call entrepreneurial activity. That is to say we know or readily understand that at some times under certain conditions entrepreneurial activity must have consisted largely in trading and transporting, in manufacturing and organizing and financing at others. Finally, the history of entrepreneurial types and of the nature of entrepreneurial performance, the action of these types on the social organization and the reaction of the social bodies on the entrepreneurial impulse should not be too difficult to analyze. Having thus adumbrated my ideas about what that history of entrepreneurship should do, I want now briefly to touch upon a number of problems and stumbling blocks that will inevitably be met with on this road.

The first of all these stumbling blocks is that most of us do not approach the material with a perfectly unbiased mind. In other words, every age and every social organization approaches these problems from an *apriori* of its own, that is to say, from a conviction (all the more dangerous if subconscious) that individual initiative in the matter of economic development counts for almost everything or else for almost nothing, and it is easy to see how such a conviction supplies the basic colors of the picture. For some of us the problem of economic development is all but solved so soon as natural and social conditions and political measures are stated — the rest follows automatically, and if entrepreneurs have anything to do with what actually happens they are a sort of beast of prey who withhold the fruits of technological advance from the community and sabotage progress in their own interest. It is needless to point out that this attitude is very prevalent in this country and that any attempt to take another view is for many a modern economist stigmatized as apologetics. Nevertheless, it should be clear from even a superficial survey of facts that this view is as wrong as is the exactly opposite one and that careful discussion of ever more numerous situations is the only method of arriving at a more tenable one.

Secondly, in connection with this we frequently meet with an attitude that is indeed a necessary prerequisite for the "theory" just alluded to. This attitude may be expressed by saying that the entrepreneur or money-maker simply does nothing but take advantage of technological progress, which therefore appears, implicitly or explicitly, as something that goes along entirely independently of entrepreneurial activity. Now how far is this true? It is perhaps not difficult to understand that technological progress, so obvious in some societies and so nearly absent in others, is a phenomenon that needs to be explained. For instance, it is necessary to find out whether the rational or rationalist attitude to life has or has not been formed by the type of mind that pervades bourgeois society. In this case technological progress would be related to entrepreneurial action in a way that may not always be obvious but would be very important all the same. I have always emphasized that the entrepreneur is the man who gets new things done and not necessarily the man who invents. As a matter of history, the entrepreneur is almost as often an inventor as he is a capitalist but it seems to me that analysis shows that neither of these capacities are essential to him. I can adduce plenty of examples by which to illustrate what seems to me to be the true relation, but only extensive research can present really reliable results.

Thirdly, let us consider a very old problem that has played more of a role in economic literature than it does now under the title of "original accumulation." Some command over physical and personal factors is no doubt necessary in order to start any enterprise: but how is such command acquired in the first place? The old classical answer, that resources came from savings, was understandably unpopular with socialists and is equally unpopular with modern radicals. And it is quite true that, however great the role of self-financing may be in the course of the development of an enterprise, the original nucleus of means has been but rarely acquired by the entrepreneur's own saving activity — which in fact is one of the reasons, and a significant one, for distinguishing the entrepreneur as sharply as I think he should be distinguished from the capitalist. One important source of the means for early enterprise is no doubt to be found in the fact that such means were available in the hands of extra-bourgeois strata and in particular in the hands of temporal and spiritual lords. As everybody knows, this source has been particularly stressed by Sombart and drew so much critical fire that Sombart himself practically surrendered it. But the last word has certainly not been spoken on this affair and if we command co-operation from medieval historians we might well ask them to go into the matter. Another explanation is in the fact that for many types of enterprise the minimum of means to start with was very small: a shack which a man could put up with his own hands, very simple tools, and very few assistants were sometimes all that was required. Means of that order of magnitude many people would possess for a variety of reasons. A third source was tapping the savings of other people and "created credit." The roles of these two last-mentioned sources, though in a general way obvious, also deserve further research. "Credit creation" introduces banks and quasi-banking activities. Here we meet with the difficulty that orthodox banking theory, emphasizing as it does current financing of current trade transactions as the main function of banks, did its best to obliterate all that banks had to do with bringing into existence new industries. French and German experience offers a rich field for the study of this phenomenon, and the common saying that in the United States enterprise developed so well because its banking system was so bad also indicates an important truth: after all, we should not simply shut our eyes or sanctimoniously disapprove when we find that in certain cases even railroad building was financed by the issue of bank notes. Fourthly, it stands to reason that a bank which finances the overhead of a new enterprise must at the very least supervise very closely the behavior of the enterprise founded. That is to say, the necessity of supervising customers which exists to some extent even for the most ordinary routine business acquired in the case envisaged a novel importance. In consequence, two phenomena are observable which are so essential for capitalist life that they are well worth our attention. On the one hand, banks have, though to a very different extent in different countries, established themselves as a social organ of entrepreneurial activity. What this supervision actually consisted in, what the means were by which it was actually carried out, and the success with which it was exerted, has been frequently discussed but quite inadequately, even if we neglect the fact that many social critics have seen nothing in this institution (and it is an institution of later capitalism) but abuse. On the other hand, entrepreneurs and industrialists generally have fought against the restrictions imposed upon their freedom of action by bankers' interference, and important features of modern industrial policy are precisely explainable by the wish of industrialists to free themselves from it. For instance, this has been an important feature of industrial policy in this country during the first World War and in the 1920's. But an entrepreneur can also gain freedom from interference by bankers by turning into a banker himself. John Law and the brothers Pereire are outstanding examples. They illustrate also something else, namely, the fact that the economic and social meaning of this kind of activity has been almost invariably misunderstood.

However, if we could poll business leaders, we should, I am convinced, establish that according to their opinion it is self-financing from earnings which constitutes the soundest method of providing the means for raising an enterprise to its full size. This method, too, is highly unpopular with modern economists and its investigation is a matter of urgent necessity — as is, by the way, the opposite phenomenon, namely, the phenomenon that expenditure on current replacement of equipment is very often financed on credit. The actual results of the method of self-financing, for instance, the question whether or not it involves malallocation of resources, are so much blurred by preconceptions that a reopening of the case promises to add considerably to our knowledge of how modern business works.

III

In the enterprise economy the entrepreneur will inevitably exert some influence on things in general; hence the study of his interests, positions, and so on necessarily constitutes one of the possible approaches to an understanding of economic history or even of history in general. A recent paper by Professor Cochran may be referred to for the general philosophy of this approach as against the approach embodied in what he calls the "presidential synthesis."[4]

It has been emphasized above that when we speak of the entrepreneur we do not mean so much a physical person as we do a function, but even if we look at individuals who at least at some juncture in their lives fill the entrepreneurial function it should be added that these individuals do not form a social class. They hail from all the corners of the social universe. For instance, if we list all the entrepreneurs mentioned in Mantoux's work on the Industrial Revolution we find among them the Duke of Bridgewater and we may, starting from him, go through practically the whole extent of the social ladder until we reach men who rose to entrepreneurship from the ranks of manual labor. This seems to me a very important fact. How important precisely it is can again be only said after extensive research. However, all the men who actually do fulfill entrepreneurial functions have certain interests in common and, very much more important than this, they acquire capitalist positions in case of success. The modern corporation has not entirely done away with inheritance of this capitalist position and so we may say that entrepreneurs do in the end land in the capitalist class, at first as a rule in its most active sector until they wind up in its less active and finally in its decaying sector. I believe that this statement can be supported successfully but I do confess to a wish to see it established.

Now the man whose mind is entirely absorbed by a struggle for

⁴Cochran, Thomas C., "The presidential synthesis in American history," *American Historical Review*, vol. 53 (1948), pp. 748-59.

entrepreneurial success has as a rule very little energy left for serious
activity in any other direction — some philanthropy and some more
or less well-advised collectors' interests usually fill the bill. What
then does the influence or the power consist in which most economists and historians attribute to him? I shall state frankly that I
consider power to be one of the most misused words in the social
sciences, though the competition is indeed great. So firmly en-
trenched in our popular psychology is the idea that entrepreneurs
or else the capitalist class into which they merge are the prime
movers of modern politics that it is very difficult to make headway
against it and to point out how very little foundation there is to
this opinion. Let me take an example that is far enough removed
from us to be looked at with something like detachment: Ehrenberg's book on the Fuggers.[5] There, the rise and decline of that
industrial, commercial, and financial family is in my opinion described in a perfectly responsible way. Among other things, the
report itself clearly shows that in the time of Charles V the two
Fuggers who came into contact with the imperial policy and especially its financial needs exerted no influence on this imperial policy
other than is implied in their getting various concessions, especially
mining concessions, in the Emperor's Latin territories. For the rest,
however, they were ruthlessly exploited, so much so in fact that
their wealth declined in consequence, and there is no sign whatever
that they influenced the Emperor's policy in such matters as his
attitude toward the Protestants, toward France, toward the Turks,
and so on. Although all this is quite clear from Ehrenberg's own
report, he is, nevertheless, so imbued with the idea that in a capitalist age the capitalists rule as to emphasize repeatedly what he
considers to be the proud position of power of that family. Now
this instance could be multiplied as everyone knows and at the
end of a long list of instances, if I could present it, I should mention
a conversation I had with an otherwise quite intelligent lawyer who
defended the legislation that was to subject the insurance companies
to federal control on the ground that "we cannot allow the insurance companies to run the country."

It seems to me that at the outset it is necessary to distinguish
two entirely different things. Naturally, as has been pointed out
above, the mere emergence of a quantitatively significant number of
entrepreneurs presupposes, and its existence contributes to, a certain
type of civilization and a certain state of the public mind. En-

---

[5]Ehrenberg, Richard, "Das Zeitalter der Fugger" (Jena, 1896), 2 v.

trepreneurs will be few and without great importance in situations
where this activity is despised and frowned upon, and entreprenurial
success in turn will tend to change such a situation. If I had space
to develop this point, I should end up by saying that to some extent
entrepreneurial activity impresses the stamp of its mentality upon
the social organism. In any cultural history, therefore, the entrepreneurial factor will have to come in as one of the explaining elements,
but this is not the same as saying that the wishes and interests of
entrepreneurs or even of the capitalist class into which they merge
is a political factor that counts by direct influence or else at the
polls. It is quite true that in individual cases, for reasons of self-
defense primarily, individual entrepreneurs need to acquire and
do acquire political positions of their own. But the importance
of these positions seems to be limited, and the way to show this is
to analyze the means at their disposal in order to exert influence,
such as contributions to politicians' war chests, or ownership of
newspapers, and so on. I think it can be shown that the influence
that can be acquired in these and other ways is much smaller
than it is usually supposed to be. In fact, little more is necessary
in order to convince one's self of this than to look at the modern
situation in practically all countries. Methodological questions of
great interest arise in the course of an attempt to investigate these
matters. To begin with, we should have to have a much more realistic theory of politics than any that has been developed so far, but
this is not enough. In order to see what entrepreneurs or the capitalist class as a whole can and cannot do, it is necessary to establish
facts which are extremely difficult to get at and the appraisal of
which requires a kind of experience of life which, even in those
cases in which it is present in a research worker, is confined to
individual environments, inferences from which may easily mislead.

The attitude of the state to entrepreneurial activity is a most fascinating study and raises questions of interpretation such as these:
what was the nature of that amphibial condition of society that
culminated in the state of Louis XIV? The court and the bureaucracy which ruled that state were no doubt alive to the fact that in
order to spend as they did they needed adequate objects of taxation
and that the most promising of these objects was a powerful community of traders and manufacturers. Thus a large group of
measures find a ready explanation in the wishes to further the
wealth and taxable capacity of the bourgeoisie. But what precisely
does this mean and how would all parties concerned fare as a result?

CHANGE AND THE ENTREPRENEUR   271

Colbert has had among historians his fervent admirers. To my immense amusement, I have also found that Sir John Clapham described him as a big, stupid, brutal fellow, who never had an idea in his life. Whatever else such judgments prove or do not prove they certainly establish one thing: that the nature and amount of influence exerted by public administration in the period in question really is no more than a big question mark; and if we leave the time of Louis XIV and transfer ourselves into our own I feel that the question mark is still bigger.

IV

Students interested in the history of economic thought and in the writings upon economic development will draw two important, though variant conclusions from their inquiries as far as entrepreneurship and entrepreneurial history are concerned. First, I believe that they would be justified in the view that theories of past economists relative specifically to entrepreneurship will not form a very firm support for future investigations of facts. New hypotheses and the marshalling of factual data, old and new, must proceed together.

Secondly, I would commend to economic historians — and, for that matter, to economic theorists, if they will interest themselves in the problem — that they examine the already available secondary literature for data upon entrepreneurial characteristics and phenomena. A miscellany of such writings — from general economic histories to biographies of businessmen, and from local histories to studies of technological change — all hold information, which sifted and arranged with definite hypotheses in mind will carry us a goodly distance toward our goal. New facts will doubtless be needed in the end, but already we have a multitude that have as yet not been digested.

In the handling of old and new facts, the historian will gain from keeping in touch with theorists. Neither group should ever be distant from one another — but here the promise from collaboration is particularly great for both parties. As I have said before, the study of economic change is an area of research where "economic historians and economic theorists can make an interesting and socially valuable journey together, if they will."[6]

---

[6]Cf. my "Creative Response in Economic History," *Journal of Economic History*, vol. 7 (1947), p. 149.

[2]

RICHARD A. PETERSON

Entrepreneurship and organization

The word entrepreneurship, like democracy, patriotism, freedom, and equality, often gains such an inclusive connotation that it comes to denote nothing in particular (Kilby, 1971; Palmer, 1971). Like these other terms, entrepreneurship has been caught up in ideological cant, more often lauded than practiced (Huber, 1971; Miller, 1952; Rischin, 1965; Sutton *et al.*, 1956; Wyllie, 1966).

The term entrepreneurship has often been applied to the founders of new businesses, and a large literature has developed on individual entrepreneurship ranging from academic studies to prescriptive blueprints for setting up new ventures (Baty, 1974; Bylinsky, 1977; Cooper, 1973; Deeks, 1976; Dible, 1971, 1976; Griffin, 1974; Havelock, 1969; Klatt, 1973; Liles, 1974; Mancuso, 1973; Sarachek, 1978; Shapero, 1975; Swayne and Tucker, 1973; White, 1977).

For these reasons it might be advisable for organization theorists to scrap the term, except that there is no other word in the English language—except the word mutation as it is used in biology—that calls attention to the process of unprogrammed innovative recombinations of preexisting elements of activity.

Such social mutation is important for all human collectivities, and especially so for organizations in the increasingly fluid post-industrial society. The question is then: How far can one plan for the unplanned? This has proved no easy task since, as classically defined from Weber (1947) to Thompson (1967), organization and entrepreneurship are antithetical principles of organizing activity (Rowe and Boise, 1974). As Gerald Zornow, Chairman of the Board of Eastman Kodak, has put it, "asking a large company to engage in entrepreneurship is like trying to get an elephant to iceskate" (Barmash, 1971: 9).

This chapter confronts the beast, the skates, and the ice in four stages. The first is devoted to defining entrepreneurship in such a way that it is not exclusively associated by definition with an individual self-employed entrepreneur. The second stage details the critical problems of facilitating entrepreneurship in the increasingly organization-bound advanced society. It shows that the crucial means of increasing entrepreneurship is not creating a larger supply of entrepreneurially oriented individuals, but increasing the demand and opportunity for entrepreneurship by manipulating social structures and rewards. The third stage describes four ways in which entrepreneurship can be designed into organizations. The chapter concludes by suggesting that the scope for entrepreneurship may be increasing in the next decades.*

Entrepreneurship is not management

Many different and contrasting claims have been made for entrepreneurship, and a convenient way of beginning to clear away this confusion is to examine the various meanings given to the term (Cochran, 1977; Ellis, 1975). The word entrepreneur derives from the French verb entreprendre, meaning to undertake. In the early sixteenth century, the Frenchmen who organized and led military expeditions were referred to as entrepreneurs. By 1700 the term was applied to road, bridge, harbor, and fortification contractors, and by the middle of that century, French economists used the term to designate persons in the economic sphere who made innovations bearing risk and uncertainty (de Farcy, 1973; Hoselitz, 1951).

There was no comparable development of any single term in English usage. Words such as adventurer, projector, undertaker, factor, enterpriser, and innovator were used more or less coterminously (Gough, 1969; Redlich, 1949). Each of these terms designated a person rather than a process. As late as 1897, the Oxford English Dictionary defined entrepreneur simply as "the director or manager of a public musical institution: one who gets up entertainments, especially musical performances" (Gough, 1969: 9).

To this day, much confusion derives from the compounding of person and process, entrepreneur and entrepreneurship. The problem derives from the fact that ownership and entrepreneurship may or may not be combined in a single individual (Deeks, 1976; Livesay, 1977; Palmer, 1971). An illustration from the Wall Street Journal (Morgenthaler, 1975) makes the point. For three generations before the American Civil War, the McIlhenny family grew sugarcane and extracted salt

*The author would like to thank the following for their useful information comments, and suggestions: Brian Beer, Ivar Berg, Arnold Cooper, Bernard Ellis, Martin Gerstel, Siman Hoff, John Meyer, Paul Nystrom, Anthony Oberschall, Johannes Pennings, Harold H. Peterson, Bruce Pharris, Richard Scott, Albert Shapero, William Starbuck, Robert Stern, Martin Whyte, and Mayer Zald. Claire Peterson made a most valuable literature search for the final revision.

on an island in the swamps of Louisiana near New Orleans. During the war, federal troops occupied New Orleans, the McIlhenny family fled to Texas, and the plantation was destroyed. When they returned, the family was penniless. Without slave labor, a return to sugarcane production was impossible. A few colorful Mexican pepper plants brought to the plantation by a friend of the family who had been on a military expedition in Mexico were found to have taken over the plantation's kitchen garden. Seeking to enliven the bland postwar diet, the enterprising Edmund McIlhenny experimented with making a sauce from the pungent peppers. Hitting on a tasty blend, he bottled the product in the only containers available, French-made cologne bottles quarried from the trash heap of the old estate. To merchandise the product more effectively, he took an exotic name from an old map of Mexico. In this way, Tabasco sauce was created. Although his innovation does not rival those of Rockefeller or Ford, Edmund was clearly an entrepreneur in this venture.

Like most entrepreneurs of the nineteenth century, McIlhenny contributed capital, labor, and innovation. Perhaps this is why many historians, neoclassical economists, and business-oriented scholars find it difficult to identify the distinctive component of entrepreneurship, and so tend to identify it with ownership or organizational management per se. The historian Cole (1946; 1959) is an outstanding exponent of this use of the term entrepreneurship. The equation of entrepreneurship with the routine tasks of managerial decision making is illustrated by the use of the term in the standard microeconomic text by Henderson and Quandt (1971: 52), who concluded their discussion by saying "an entrepreneur transforms inputs into outputs, subject to the technical rules specified by his production function." Others who have identified it with ownership or management include Aitken (1963), Bain (1959), Becker and Gordon (1966), Copulsky and McNulty (1974), Davis (1968), Murphy (1977), and Swane and Tucker (1973).

The problems inherent in this conception of entrepreneurship are illustrated in the tabasco-sauce business. The family firm, with eight million dollars in annual sales, is now run by Edmund's grandson, Walter McIlhenny. During the latter's presidency, the firm has grown at an annual rate of ten percent and has been continually profitable. This record of success was achieved by stringent quality and cost control, as well as by expanding foreign sales and successful trademark-infringement litigation. The only product diversification in over 50 years was adding tomato juice to Tabasco sauce and selling the product as a Bloody Mary cocktail mix. Like his grandfather, Walter is an owner-manager of the firm, but his contribution has been to supply sound managerial practices with a minimum of innovation. In fact, the transition from entrepreneurial innovation to steady growth through sound management was made by the elder McIlhenny. For reasons discussed below, this transition is often most difficult for entrepreneurs to make, but to designate Edmund in the later phase of his stewardship and his grandson as entrepreneurs is simply to grant an honorific title that adds nothing to an understanding of their activities as owner-managers and that robs the term entrepreneurship of any distinctive meaning (Palmer, 1971; Schreier, 1975: 24).

Although some authors have identified entrepreneurship broadly with management, others, most notably the classical economists from Adam Smith to Alfred Marshall, could specify no clear place for the process at all (Deeks, 1976: 4; Nafziger, 1977: 8). In hindsight at least, this seems singularly ironic since their work spans the era of most conspicuous entrepreneurship (Balabkins and Aizsilnieks, 1975: 117). As noted by Cochran (1968), Kirzner (1973) and Nafziger (1977), the myopia of classical economists derives not from deficient powers of observation, but from the structure of their theory (Hagen, 1975: 268). Classical economic theory assumed a state of perfect market equilibrium deriving from the competitive interchange between numerous business persons, consumers, property owners, investors, and workers. The effects of individual actions were assumed to cancel each other out or be eliminated by competition. They assumed that each actor would continually seek his or her own best interest. Within such conditions, entrepreneurship was not considered problematic. Rather, social policy was focused on those political, legal, and customary procedures which could foster or inhibit the operation of a perfectly competitive market.

Schumpeter's definition: process not person

Although the work of the institutional economists R. T. Ely and John R. Commons presaged the idea of entrepreneurship as a vital factor in economic development, this view was first fully elaborated in the work of Joseph Schumpeter (1934: 62–94, 1947, 1950: 131–134, 1965). His usage of the term is the foundation for the definition of entrepreneurship used in this chapter.

For Schumpeter, entrepreneurship was the novel recombination of preexisting factors of production where the outcome of this recombination cannot clearly be predicted (Nafziger, 1977). In this usage, entrepreneurship is contrasted both with routine decision making and with invention. In a loose sense, entrepreneurs take risks, but not in the sense that a gambler bets with known odds or an investor wagers in hopes of gain in a market. Although entrepreneurs may also be capitalists, managers, or inventors, as entrepreneurs they contribute nothing but a unique combination of available factors (Bylinsky, 1977; Kling, 1976: 82). As Kirzner (1973: 48) stated most clearly, "the pure entrepreneur owns nothing and does nothing except discover something obtainable for nothing at all." Such discoveries may succeed or fail, and they may be great or small (Hagen, 1975: 271). In extreme cases the recombination is highly original and historically important, as exemplified, for example, by Henry Ford's methods of financing, mass production, and mass marketing in the auto industry. Even small acts of recombination, such as those made by the Zambian businessmen described by Oberschall (1973), are important in the aggregate.

Entrepreneurship refers to a process, not a person. When Schumpeter used the term entrepreneur, it was as a shorthand linguistic device designating one acting in an entrepreneurial way. In formal terms, individuals are entrepreneurs only when, and in so far as, they carry out what is, in their experience, a new combination of the existing elements of production. In this connection, Schumpeter (1934: 82) noted that "It is just as rare for anyone always to remain an entrepreneur throughout the decades of his active life as it is for a businessman never to have a moment in which he is an entrepreneur, to however modest a degree."

Cases of ceaseless, lifelong innovative ventures are rare, but some do exist (Gregg, 1952). A transition from entrepreneurship to management—in which what is initially an innovation becomes routine—is most common. Numerous cases could be cited illustrating all possible sequential combinations of entrepreneurship, routine management, success, and failure (Aitken, 1965; Business Week, 1977; Kling, 1976; Livesay, 1977; Martin, 1976; Miller, 1952; Sueno, 1977).

Even more than the French economist Jean Baptiste Say (1816) who formulated the classic definition of entrepreneurship, Schumpeter saw in this factor the prime active force in economic development. Not only did entrepreneurial effort create something from nothing and open the way to imitators, but it tended to trigger a whole sequence of entrepreneurial efforts (Martin, 1976; Sobel, 1974). Schumpeter cited the examples of the early American railroad construction, auto industry, and various colonial adventures. Thus, he saw entrepreneurship as dislodging a prior economic equilibrium and setting off a sequence of boom and recession. Commenting on this idea, Kirzner (1973) noted that as entrepreneurs recombine available factors, they capitalize on disequilibrium, and move the economic system toward greater rationality and equilibrium. This may be the first-order consequence of each entrepreneurial act, but as Smelser's (1959) study of the early English textile industry exquisitely illustrated, each innovation which solved one problem in a sector of the industry tended to disrupt other parts of the productive process. Thus, each act of equilibrating entre-

preneurship has disequilibrating consequences as well (Nafziger, 1977: 10–11).

As noted above, the classical economists assumed a perfectly rational and competitive market where, in effect, each actor was entrepreneurial, but to a trivial degree. Schumpeter assumed quite a different political economy, one in which the routines of business practices, sunk costs in established processes, consumer habits, laws, values, and social conventions all conspired against the minute incremental entrepreneurship implicit in classical economics.

To overcome these barriers, Schumpeter asserted, it took a person with unusual traits of character, a combination of the will to found a private kingdom, a drive to overcome all obstacles whether human or physical, and a joy in creating, getting things done, and exercising one's ingenuity. Schumpeter assumed that this set of traits, though relatively rare, was distributed more or less equally throughout the entire human population. The psychologically oriented students of entrepreneurship, whose ideas are discussed below, have engaged in much ingenious research in an effort to discover the origins, prevalence, and distribution of the entrepreneurial trait.

Entrepreneurship without ownership

Though potential entrepreneurs are ever present in the population, Schumpeter asserted that the ability for them to practice entrepreneurship is a function of socioeconomic conditions. Although in earlier times, the disincentives to entrepreneurship may have been legal or cultural (Kling, 1976: 5), Schumpeter viewed the twentieth century as increasingly hostile to entrepreneurship because innovation itself was being reduced to routine, and technological change was increasingly becoming the business of teams of trained specialists. He concluded that "personality and will power must count for less in environments which have become accustomed to economic change" (Schumpeter, 1950: 132).

Even though the heroic age of entrepreneurs, like the heroic age of personal military leadership, may be practically at an end, the overorganized structure of contemporary society itself may call forth entrepreneurship in new forms (Balabkins and Aizsilnieks, 1975; Livesay, 1977; Zonana, 1978). The latter sections of this chapter explore this possibility. Suffice it here to point to several sorts of entrepreneurial activity in which improved market performance measured in economic terms is only a secondary consideration, if involved at all.

Schumpeter recognized that the entrepreneurial function is increasingly expressed by persons who are not self-employed, but are employees. A classical case of the entrepreneurial employee is provided by the later career of Theodore Newton Vail (Sobel, 1974: 196), whom Drucker (1974) has called one of the least known of the great American businessmen. Vail was one of the founders of the Bell Telephone Company, but was forced to resign in 1887 by the investment bankers who had come to control the firm. Twenty years later, the company was near financial ruin. It was threatened on the one hand by a proliferation of rapidly expanding independent telephone companies which pressed for antitrust action against Bell. It was challenged on the other hand by the very real possibility of governmental takeover of the entire telephone industry, as was then happening in many European countries.

Vail patterned his response to these problems on the then-recent resolution of the conflictual development of American railroads. After decades of cutthroat competition with some chance of great short-term profit and a more likely risk of loss, the railroads accepted governmental regulation—which meant more nearly predictable long-term costs and profits (Peterson, 1973: 34–41). Vail convinced his board of directors that it would be to Bell's advantage to cooperate with the independents by providing them with long-distance service and to accept regulation by local, state, and federal government agencies, figuring rightly that it would be possible to manipulate regulations to protect what he termed Bell's natural monopoly of phone services. Having established the policy of cooperation with rivals and the government, it was possible to forestall public demands for change by steadily improving service, and at the same time regularly increase corporate profit (Sobel, 1974: 197). Vail's actions not only saved the Bell Company financially in the short run but helped to set the pattern for maintaining corporate enterprise in other types of public utilities.

The Vail example illustrates one factor found in many cases of entrepreneurship but not explicitly recognized as a general factor by scholars. This factor may be defined as disjunctive imitation. Although the particular parallels are obvious today, in 1907 it was probably considered silly to say that a phone company was like a railroad. Yet Vail solved the corporate problem of the Bell Company by acting as if the telephone company were more like a railroad than like the other divisions of the Bell Company which were devoted to producing phonograph records and machines. Another telling instance of disjunctive imitation was Alexander Graham Bell's early decision that the home electric-lighting system should be modeled as exactly as possible on the gas-light system then prevalent rather than on the electric arc-light system then being introduced into large public halls (Passer, 1965).

Entrepreneurship outside business

While focusing on entrepreneurship in economic activities, Schumpeter noted that the art of recombina-

tion extends to a wide range of other domains beside the economic means of production. Following this lead, sociologists have used the term to denote innovation in a wide range of fields. Mills (1951: 94), for example, noted that the natural milieu of the contemporary "entrepreneur is those areas that are still uncertain and unroutinized. The new entrepreneur is very much at home in the less tangible 'business services'—commercial research, public relations, advertising agencies, labor relations, and the mass communication and entertainment industry." Mills also used the term new entrepreneur to refer to organizational employees who recombine elements within organizations that become stultified by their own procedural complexities.

Without using the term, Merton (1968: 72–82) described the entrepreneurial activities of political bosses in the major American cities during the first half of the twentieth century. They gained prominence by aggregating the elements of power that were dispersed by the theory of democracy and the workings of civic bureaucracy to provide services for a wide range of clients ranging from ethnic immigrants to business leaders. Lehner (1975) suggested that the era of this sort of political entrepreneur may be at an end, but Smith (1968) has noted the role of political entrepreneurs in developing African nations.

Becker (1963) used the term moral entrepreneurship to describe the ways the U.S. Federal Narcotics Bureau and its supporters recombined various value elements to form a new attitude about opiates in the first decade of the twentieth century. Protestant values of sobriety and self-control, the alcohol-prohibition movement, antipathy to foreigners, and newly discovered medical findings about drug use were combined with the interests of the medical profession and law-enforcement agencies of the federal government to take opiates off the American market for moral reasons.

Smith (1974) described the career of the complete dandy, Beau Brummel, as that of an entrepreneur of style because of the innovations he made in the decaying world of nineteenth-century English aristocratic fashion. Rand (1964) and Young (1971) described the educational and theological entrepreneurs. Further analysis of political, fashion, moral, and cognate forms of entrepreneurship is beyond the scope of this chapter, but they serve to show the wide range of entrepreneurship outside of industry.

Returning to the person-process problem, it is now possible to state one of the prime dilemmas of entrepreneurship in the organizational context. Although entrepreneurial innovation seems to require iconoclastic persons, it can be utilized only intermittently in organized human activity. This leads to a number of vexing policy questions of the following sort. Should entrepreneurs be sought out, and if so, how does one test for this attribute? If entrepreneurship is desirable, can it be fostered or taught? Is it better to structure a situation in which entrepreneurship can develop, or is it better to eliminate it through fostering expert planning and research? In so far as it is possible to do so, should entrepreneurship be aggregated in a few organizational roles along the lines of the bureaucratic-expert model, or should it be infused into all roles as in the Maoist model of organizations (Whyte, 1973)? These and cognate questions treated below can be encapsulated in the simple question: How far can one plan for the unplanned?

Not supply, but demand and opportunity

A great deal of research has been devoted to gauging the practical limits on the exercise of entrepreneurship. For the purposes of presentation here, it is convenient to divide these efforts into four groups: psychological, cultural, economic, and sociological. Studies are grouped on the basis of what their authors take to be most problematic about entrepreneurship.

Scholars in the psychological group—though not all are psychologists by any means—assume that entrepreneurship is relatively rare. They focus on developing measures of the trait and on means of fostering its development in people (Hagen, 1962, 1975; McClelland, 1961; McClelland and Winter, 1969; McClelland *et al.*, 1976). Scholars in the cultural group focus on both supply and demand in their studies of diverse societies around the world. They assume that both supply and demand are functions of a society's culture, and show how cultural codes foster or inhibit the supply and demand for entrepreneurship (Balabkins and Aizsilnieks, 1975; LeVine, 1966; Peterson, 1979). Scholars in the economics group assume that the entrepreneurial orientation is abundant and that entrepreneurial activity will emerge when there are sufficient economic incentives (Collins *et al.*, 1964; Deeks, 1976; Levy-Leboyer, 1976). In their view, demand creates its own supply (Kilby, 1971). Scholars in the sociological group also assume that an entrepreneurial orientation is abundant. They observe that even when there is an economic market demand for entrepreneurship, it will not emerge unless the requisite sociocultural opportunities are present (Hagen, 1975: 294; Palmer, 1971; Smelser, 1976). This section of the chapter reviews these studies, beginning with a critique of the psychological studies that focus on the problems of supply. The comparative cultural studies of demand and supply are dealt with next. For purposes of presentation, the economics focus on demand is absorbed into the broader sociological focus on opportunities for entrepreneurship. The section concludes by moving from the societal level of analysis and looking at several problems of opportunity for entre-

preneurship provided in the environments of contemporary organizations.

The problem of supply

McClelland and his associates have generated a wide range of studies to find the actual supply of entrepreneurial talent, persons with what they call a high need for achievement. Several measures of need for achievement were developed, but they all involve scoring symbolic productions—such as stories, songs, or drawings—for achievement imagery or forms to correlate with need achievement. Scores have been obtained not only for groups in contemporary industrial and nonindustrial societies, but also for fourteenth-century England, ancient Greece from 900 to 100 B.C., and pre-Incan Peru from 800 B.C. to A.D. 700. Most of the specific studies found that an increase in achievement imagery is followed by economic development.

Ingenious as these efforts may be, they have been challenged at every point, from the choice of measures to the final conclusions drawn. The problems are too extensive to be detailed here. The interested reader is referred to independent, exhaustive critiques by Brown (1965), Deeks (1976), Lavin (1965), Palmer (1971), Salancik and Pfeffer (1977), and Schatz (1971). Brown (1965: 470), himself a social psychologist, concluded, "work with the achievement motive done to date does not enable us either to create the motive or select for it." Kilby (1971) reviewed McClelland's research published subsequent to the earlier critiques. He showed that McClelland had altered some of his earlier views, but Kilby (1971) and Nafziger (1977) came to the same conclusion that the need-achievement measure has no great empirical power. Beyond these methodological criticisms, a final, practical negative test of the measure's potency is that it has not been adopted by business for personnel-testing purposes.

McClelland assumed that the entrepreneurial trait was learned in childhood from models provided by normatively loaded stories and the like; thus, entrepreneurs would come from conforming, adjusted persons in society. In sharp contrast, the other major psychologically oriented theory of entrepreneurship, that of Hagen (1962, 1975), assumed that the need for achievement was engendered in the shock of status withdrawal experienced in childhood. Although this shock may occur in any family in any society, Hagen reasoned that it would happen for whole classes of people in times of economic, political, or religious turmoil. Hagen postulated a long time lag—ranging in his examples from 250 to 800 years—between the shock of status withdrawal and widespread entrepreneurial behavior. He provided an interesting example of the transition to development in Columbia, but it is a wonder to this author that anyone

70   *Handbook of Organizational Design*

has taken his formal theory seriously. Perhaps Hagen
has been so widely read because questions about the
psychological roots of entrepreneurship remain as interesting as they are opaque.

The problem of cultural support

Another attack on the question of entrepreneurial
supply comes from the detailed comparative analyses
of societies exhibiting different degrees of entrepreneurship. These cultural studies are made in the
tradition of Weber's pioneering study of the Protestant
ethic and the spirit of capitalism. For example, Cochran
(1953, 1977) showed that the supply of entrepreneurship depends on supporting cultural values, by
comparing the flowering of entrepreneurship among the
early American railroad developers with the frustration
of entrepreneurial efforts in Argentina where economic
conditions were comparable (Cochran and Reina,
1962). An excellent example of truncated entrepreneurial development because of the blinders of traditional
values was reported by König (1975), who studied the
bakers of nunbreads in Afghanistan. Without using any
supporting mechanization, the bakers have subdivided
the process of loaf making and created a factory-like
assembly line composed of jobs with cycle times of ten
seconds. Working with great efficiency, the system
delivers a large volume of high-quality bread at a low
unit price. This system of production has existed for
at least two generations. The obvious advantages of
this minute division of labor over the forms of craft
production characteristic in other Afghani industries
have been recognized but have not spread to other fields
of production. When asked, people say that this is just
the way to make nunbread. The only Afghani who has
adapted the division of labor and assembly-line technique is a Western-trained research colleague of König's
on the bakery study, who has set up a shop to mass-
produce Afghani stools for the export trade—another
example of the process of disjunctive imitation mentioned above.

Following another aspect of Weber's analysis, Geertz
(1963), Hagen (1975), Nevaskar (1971), Stinchcombe
(1974), and Young (1971), among others, have shown
that when cultural values inhibit entrepreneurship, it
may still flourish in ethnic, cultural, or religious enclaves
within a larger society. Examples include the Quakers in
England, Jews in the Mediterranean region, Jains of
India, and the Chinese in Southeast Asia. Studies in this
cultural mode tend to contrast a tradition-bound preindustrial society with an industrial society valuing and
rewarding innovation. It is assumed that preindustrial
cultural systems are highly integrated and do not change
rapidly, except under conditions of catastrophic stress.
Lerner (1958) first systematically challenged this

dichotomous view of tradition versus modernity with
data from five Mideastern societies. Kunkel (1970) has
questioned the view that to increase the rate of entrepreneurial behavior, fundamental values must be
changed. A number of studies challenge the view of
cultural determinism (Peterson, 1979).

Seibel (1974: 13–16) reported on the Kran of eastern
Liberia, who mix a hunting technology with simple agriculture and who stress achievement. The only roles in
the society that are ascribed—allocated to individuals on
the basis of customary rules—are ritual and ceremonial
roles involving no entrepreneurially problematic decisions. Leadership in those roles involving problematic
situations—primarily involving food gathering and warfare—are allocated on the basis of personally achieved
past success. Furthermore, these achieved roles do not
carry authority into other spheres of activity, and are not
inherited. Thus, the Kran, and other primitive groups
like them, most closely fit the functional theory of
stratification ascribed to the United States by Davis and
Moore (1945), in which class status is proportional to
societal contribution.

There is further evidence that the primitive achievers
described by Seibel are not anomalous. In a remarkable
set of studies, LeVine (1966) has described four societies
in modern Nigeria which vary in their level of economic
development, entrepreneurial allocation of roles, and
scores on McClelland-type need-achievement measures.
Entrepreneurial allocation of roles is positively associated with high need-achievement scores, and both are
negatively related to the level of economic development
of the society. The Ibo, who are most like the Kran,
reward individual achievement and score highest on
need for achievement. At the other end of the Nigerian
continuum, the richer Hausa have been, since the
thirteenth century, one of the technologically and organizationally most complex societies in Africa, with a
centralized governmental bureaucracy and elaborate
stratification systems. The possibility of entrepreneurial
advancement is slight and the need-achievement scores
for individuals in this country are quite low. Taken
together, these studies suggest that the level of entrepreneurial supply, far from being randomly distributed
in stable societies, is roughly proportional to the opportunities for exercising entrepreneurship (Nafziger,
1977: 23)

The problem of opportunity

An older generation of sociologists and anthropologists
assumed that culture did not change rapidly. From this,
they concluded that short-term changes in the opportunities for entrepreneurship could not be accommo-
dated by a rapid increase in the supply of entrepreneurs.
Recent research brings this assumption of societal inflex-

ibility into question. Rosen (1973) has made a number of studies of the ways that families socialize their sons for achievement both in the United States and Brazil. In a study of Brazilian peasant city-migrants and those who did not migrate, Rosen (1973) found a significant association between the length of urban residence and achievement training of the sons. He interpreted this to mean that an urban environment increases achievement orientation, but it seems equally possible that the more innovative families move to cities first. In any case, his studies suggest that there is a substantial reservoir of achievement-oriented individuals being trained in developing societies. A similar conclusion can be drawn from DeBord (1969), Koo (1976), Nafziger (1977), and Peterson and DeBord (1966). Oberschall's (1973) study of Zambian small businessmen showed that groups of persons considered incapable of innovation are able to move rapidly into the business sector when blocks to their entry are eliminated. During the colonial period of Northern Rhodesia, business activities were in the hands of English and Asian immigrants. Native Africans were presumed to be incompetent in such fields. They were not given training and were discriminated against in custom, law, and administrative practice. With Zambian independence and economic reform, Africans rapidly and successfully moved into small-scale business of all sorts. What is particularly significant is that these instant entrepreneurs were not drawn from any cadre that had been conditioned beforehand. They were not marginal to the Zambian society, they were not disproportionately from one particular ethnic group, and they were not driven to achievement for its own sake. They were different from their fellow Zambians only in the range of their personal experiences that gave them skills and models upon which to draw.

In those countries composed of people from ethnic groups with backgrounds of quite different entrepreneurial experience, the ethnic-group factor does seem to play a part in the development of entrepreneurship in the postcolonial era. As LeVine (1966) showed, the economically backward and organizationally simple Ibo entrepreneurs fanned out all over the country of Nigeria, becoming involved in a wide range of business enterprises, the professions, and governmental administration. When their efforts were blocked by the traditional, bureaucratic Hausa–Fulani elite, the Ibo organized a political movement in the 1960s and fought a bloody civil war in an effort to set up their own independent state of Biafra (Nafziger, 1977: 73–74; Schatz, 1977).

The Nigerian case shows that ethnic groups with markedly different achievement versus ascription roles differentially contribute to the total national supply of entrepreneurial talent. This is not always the case. The studies by Garlick (1971), Marris and Somerset (1971),

Oberschall (1973), and Papanek (1971) all suggest that entrepreneurs in Ghana, Kenya, Zambia, and Pakistan, respectively, are not disproportionately drawn from one or two ethnic groups. Oberschall (1973) suggested that the degree of differential recruitment is a function of the social and cultural barriers to innovation. If the barriers are high, then the entrepreneurs will be drawn from special groups; if the barriers are low, entrepreneurs will be recruited from all sections of the population (Nafziger, 1977: 23). Further evidence for this hypothesis comes from a quite distinct research tradition. Reviewing a great deal of research dealing with the diffusion of innovations, Katz (1973) came to similar conclusions. Katz found that if the innovation is of a narrow technical sort, early adopters are among the most prestigious and influential members of the target population. If the innovation is seen as threatening group norms, the early adopters are marginal to the group. Although there is still some question about who will initiate innovations, all studies agree that the significant blocks to the expression of entrepreneurship are legal, administrative, political, economic, and social, rather than characterological.

A social psychologist came to the same conclusion about how to increase the rate of entrepreneurial behavior: "The point of maximal leverage at present is social structure rather than psychology" (Brown, 1965: 491).

Opportunity in the environment of organization

Any number of illustrations might be used to show how organizational environments shape the exercise of entrepreneurial activity (Baldridge and Burnham, 1975; Hagen, 1975: 291–294). Garlick (1971: 154–155) has provided an inventory. The career of James R. Hoffa in the International Brotherhood of Teamsters is a striking example. Without detracting from the man's obvious genius, it is possible to suggest that Hoffa's success in consolidating the power of the national union was facilitated by the particular structure of the trucking industry (Brill, 1978; James and James, 1965). To show this, comparisons will be made with the construction industry and its carpenters' union (Peterson, 1973: 75–76). In the United States both industries employ over a million workers, and neither is dominated by a small number of large corporations. Unlike most other major contemporary industries, no corporation accounts for even one percent of the business in either industry. Working conditions are comparable in the two cases—employees in trucking and on construction sites are skilled and work without close supervision. In both cases, the amount of work varies seasonally, so union job–protection helps to stabilize employment. Finally, in both industries, strategic work stoppages are very costly to companies and so are effective for the unions.

The two industries differ as well. A local strike in trucking affects all companies across the nation whose freight is being shipped to the area. There is no comparable snowball effect in the construction industry since a work stoppage on a construction site in Memphis has no appreciable effect on construction in other cities. Finally, trucking firms can, and in the past often did, change their base of operation to avoid strong union locals, whereas companies in the construction industry obviously do not have this mobility.

Before World War II, both the teamsters' and the carpenters' unions consisted of loose confederations of strong locals. The carpenters' union has retained this locally focused structure while the International Brotherhood of Teamsters has become strongly centralized. Hoffa did not begin this process nor did he invent the prime strategy that has made centralization possible, but he used it to great advantage in his efforts to bring standard rates to all American truck drivers.

When he began organizing, the teamsters' union was composed almost exclusively of local truck drivers, and intercity truck drivers were beyond union protection. They drove a prodigious number of hours for low wages; drivers who complained were simply replaced. Hoffa organized these drivers by getting city teamsters in a region to stop deliveries to highway shippers until the latter signed a union contract. Once a large area was organized, it was possible to extend the organization by freezing all traffic going to adjacent nonunion areas. With truck companies highly fragmented and extremely competitive, the union could always depend on some truckers signing union contracts to gain a temporary advantage over their rivals. This done, all truckers would sign because none had the financial resources necessary to weather a long strike.

Then Hoffa pressed for standard wage contracts which could be administered from the Washington, D.C., headquarters, thus taking autonomy and power away from local-city teamster officials. Through these and diverse other practices which depended upon the national, interlocking nature of trucking and the fragmentation of trucking companies, Hoffa welded an increasingly centralized teamsters' union. These union efforts greatly accelerated the rate of consolidation of trucking firms which, in turn, increased the need for a centralized national labor union (Brown, 1971).

It is interesting to ask what Hoffa's career might have been had he got into the Detroit carpenters' local rather than the teamsters'. Being bright, articulate, aggressive, and innovative, he might have built the Detroit local into a powerful private kingdom for himself. But, because of the wholly local nature of the construction industry, he would not have been able to exercise the leverage necessary to build a strong, centralized national union. Even though this is just a mental experiment, it suggests that

Jimmy Hoffa's entrepreneurial effort was conditioned, like that of Henry Ford, James Vail, Royal Little of Textron, and the producers of Tabasco sauce, by the environment in which he worked.

Ossification creates opportunity

One may argue that these men were the product of an era of more primitive organization which is fast being displaced. Indeed, Schumpeter, and most theorists from Galbraith (1967) and Thompson (1967) to socialist scholars, have asserted that the vastly increasing capacity for advanced planning reduces the demand for entrepreneurship, as innovation and adaptation become routinized. In practice, however, the procedures and instrumentalities which have been created by technical experts as a means to achieve some goals, tend to evolve into self-perpetuating ends in themselves (Kohn, 1971; Macrae, 1976; Merton, 1940; Meyer, 1977; Ritzer, 1975; Schatz, 1977; Starbuck, 1965; Thompson, 1965). This universal process may be defined as the iron law of ossification. It is today perhaps the single greatest creator of entrepreneurial opportunity in advanced industrial societies.

Numerous examples could be given to show the role of entrepreneurship in revitalizing ossified organizations, including Hoffa in trucking, Vail at Bell, Alfred Sloan at General Motors, and Robert McNamara in the Department of Defense. Seen in isolation, these instances are easily interpreted as unique innovations in organizations which face randomly changing environments. When the unit of analysis is an industry, rather than a single organization, however, a cyclical pattern of ossification and reorganization begins to emerge. The periodic demand for entrepreneurship is more apparent at the industry level of analysis because industries are much better able than individual firms and organizations to shape their own environments, at least in the short run.

Research on the changing structure of the American popular-music industry provides a convenient case of this ossification-induced periodic opportunity for entrepreneurship (Peterson and Berger, 1971, 1975; Peterson and White, 1979). In its earliest days, entry into the industry was restricted by exclusive patents held by a few leading firms, but by 1914 this impediment was removed, and numerous firms entered the market because of the low costs of manufacturing. The new firms were successful in part because they popularized and profited on the emerging jazz-based musical style. With the stimulus provided by the music business, this new popular music largely displaced the traditional singing and dancing styles (Peterson, 1975a, 1978; Peterson and DiMaggio, 1975).

This period of intense competition did not last long. A few firms garnered an ever larger share of the market over the next three decades. They were able to dampen the inherent competitiveness of the industry by gaining control at three points: (a) the creative factors of production—singers, orchestras, and song writers; (b) the means of merchandising—movies and radio; and (c) the channels of distribution.

The process of creating a new record became a matter of routine production in this oligopolistic atmosphere. Each new record was modeled on prior successful hits to capture as great a share of the total market as possible, and although novel elements of rhythm and orchestration were incorporated, they were tailored to offend no one. In consequence, the music became increasingly bland and homogeneous, focusing almost exclusively on the travails of romantic love in abstract, idealized terms. This pattern of oligopoly and increasing homogeneity survived through the Great Depression and World War II into the early 1950s. Patterning each new song after prior successes, the tunesmiths did not see that a great number of potential customers simply withdrew from the market, so that there was huge unsated demand for more expressive music, as Peterson and Berger (1975) showed.

In the early 1950s, the new technologies of television, transistors, and phonograph-record formats, broke the oligopolistic control the big companies had held on merchandising records through radio and movies. This in turn broke their hold over creative factors and distribution. Dozens of independent firms successfully entered the market in the next few years. Just how quickly and completely the leading firms lost oligopolistic control of the popular-music industry is shown by the following series: In 1949 the largest four firms had a 90 percent share of hit records, and by 1955 they still had 74 percent, but just four years later, in 1959, they held just 33 percent, and in 1962 only 25 percent of the hit records. Over the same span of years, the average annual rate of growth in total industry sales, discounting inflation, jumped from two percent to eighteen percent, strongly suggesting the extent of the unsated demand (Peterson and Berger, 1975: 160–161). This dramatic change reflected a greatly increased scope for entrepreneurship which commercialized several rock and soul-based musical, lyrical, and dance styles. In a very few years, oligopoly and homogeneous music were replaced by competition and heterogeneity in musical styles.

The years since 1962 have shown a gradual but continuing trend toward oligopolies again, a reduction in the scope of entrepreneurship, less variation in popular music, and increasing unsated demand. These factors have not reached their 1949 levels, but these data, together with others noted by Chapple and Garofalo (1977), Denisoff (1975), Hirsch (1972), and Peterson and Berger (1975), suggest a 35-year cycle consisting of a long phase of gradually increasing concentration,

ossification, and homogeneity followed by a brief burst of competition and entrepreneurial creativity. The first golden age of individual entrepreneurship may be at an end, but this example, drawn from the music industry, suggests that entire industries as well as organizations operate to generate periodically the demand and opportunity for entrepreneurship.

Designing entrepreneurship into organizations

Having defined entrepreneurship and found the blocks to its development, this chapter considers how to design entrepreneurship purposefully into organizations. The preceding analysis has shown that the best way to increase entrepreneurship is by fostering opportunities for it to emerge by manipulating social structures. But, as the discussion of organizational ossification suggests, this is not easily accomplished since in pure forms entrepreneurship and organization are polar opposites and most mixtures prove quite unstable. However, four different blends of entrepreneurship and organization are relatively stable and widely practiced in special situations. They are described in order from least to most entrepreneurial.

Franchising

The first, and most limited, sort of entrepreneurship in organization is the self-employed employee—the general designation given here to the wide range of exclusive franchise and dealership arrangements (Vaughn, 1974). This form of enterprise was pioneered in the retail auto and auto-related industries before World War I, but has spread widely in the service sector from illicit-drug distribution and Tastie Freeze outlets to motel chains and real-estate sales since 1950 (House, 1977; Langer, 1977). All are independently financed operations which are bound to buy from a single supplier, but sell a product or service in an open, and usually highly competitive market.

Organizations lose some degree of control and revenue by dealing through franchised outlets, but this means of harnessing the desire for entrepreneurship has three distinct advantages for an organization (Peterson, 1973:69–70). Firstly, a franchisee's investments in facilities, machinery, equipment, and inventory make it possible for a corporation to expand rapidly without depleting its own capital resources. Secondly, the arrangement shifts much of the risk of financial loss from a corporation to a dealer. For example, dealers may be forced to take articles they may not want in order to get those which are selling well. In particularly bad years, dealers may be forced to buy more items than they can sell at the full retail price in order to keep their dealerships, thus absorbing the cost of a corporation's mistakes. Thirdly, franchising may reduce the vulnerability of a corporation in a number of ways. Taxes, governmental regulations, and code enforcement are usually less stringent on small businesses than on large corporations. Wholesale unionization has been frustrated by the creation of franchise dealerships. What is more, legal and financial liability, as well as customers' complaints, are more likely to focus on a local dealer than on a large corporation (Langer 1977; Schreier, 1975).

In addition, the franchising arrangement is an excellent method of motivating key personnel through the lure of entrepreneurship. Since a dealer's income depends on his or her unit's profit or loss, there is no need for close supervision by the corporation. For these reasons, the franchise arrangements are likely to be found where work sites are widely scattered and small, where customers must be sought out and actively solicited, where personalized service to customers is important, where spoilage or wastage is an important factor of costs, and where a low-paid and semi-skilled work force requiring close supervision makes up a large part of operating costs.

Although franchising does successfully capitalize on the desire for entrepreneurship, most contractual arrangements are so restrictive that there is little scope for its exercise. There are few comparative studies of franchisees and employed managers in the same lines of activity, but the available evidence suggests that the former work much longer hours and worry much more for the same level of money compensation (Peterson and Elifson, 1968). What is more, these entrepreneurs most often start their ventures less from an enthusiasm for the prospects than because of blocked or foreshortened careers in organizations (Collins *et al*., 1964; Cooper, 1973; Kling, 1976; Levy-Leboyer, 1976; Peterson and Elifson, 1968).

The franchisees in some industries have organized to argue collectively their grievances against corporations (Macaulay, 1965; Penn, 1979). This suggests just how much these self-employed persons are really employees. In summary, this sort of structural arrangement seems to have clear benefits for an organization, but less for an entrepreneur and entrepreneurship.

Contracting

Contracting has long been used in the construction industry, but in recent decades many sorts of organizations have divested themselves of one or more of their departments and purchased these services from specialized contractors. These range from legal to janitorial services, from computer accounting and component manufacturing to research and governmental liaison.

Like franchising, contracting operates at a boundary of an organization, and provides many of the same financial and legal advantages to an organization. The two differ in that whereas franchisees receive the routine outputs from organizations, contractors provide specialized inputs to organizations. This different locus in the flow of activities has a number of consequences which condition the degree of entrepreneurship which is possible.

Whereas franchisees perform the routine task of retail selling, contractors provide a specialized technical service or offer a routine service in a novel way. The franchisee is granted an exclusive selling territory in a long-term arrangement with a single organization, but a contractor who is in competition with other bidders usually makes a short-term arrangement and often with more than one organization. These differences usually work together to give contractors wider scope for entrepreneurship, because they are less tied to organizational constraints than the typical franchisee.

In recent decades, private organizations have taken a leading role in creating contracting firms. Perhaps the oldest pattern is for an organization to guarantee a prospective contractor enough business to make it possible for the contractor to enter the field. Many specialty firms in the auto, music, and chemical industries got their start in this way. Another clearly related strategy is for an organization to allow one of its departments to offer its services on a contract basis to outside organizations. In this way, a number of organizations have been able to support much larger or more sophisticated facilities than they could afford on their own. A common example of this strategy is for an organization to contract its computer-based clerical and accounting capacities to outside organizations.

Beyond acquiring the use of facilities, organizations often create contractual arrangements in order to motivate key personnel and allow scope for their entrepreneurship. Again, this operates in two distinctly different ways. One strategy is for an organization to purchase a competing business or specialty supplier, but allow it to function as an autonomous subsidiary. The other strategy is to form an autonomous division within an organization, to be run by a rising talent who might otherwise leave to establish a rival organization. Numerous successful examples of these two strategies can be found in those industries that face turbulent environments requiring rapid adaptation to changing conditions. The commercial-music industry is a good case in point, but the experience there suggests that these arrangements face two hazards. Following quick success, the key personnel often leave the contracting unit to seek their careers in the parent organization. Alternatively, the organizational urge to bring all activities into line with central policies may squelch the opportunity for entrepreneurship that the contracting unit was created to encourage (Chapple and Garofalo, 1977; Denisoff, 1975; Peterson and Berger, 1971, 1975).

Entrepreneurial departments

Franchising and contracting place entrepreneurship at the boundary of an organization where the opposing logics of entrepreneurship and organization can be easily maintained separately. The problems of isolation and containment become of central concern, however, where entrepreneurial roles are structured into an organization itself. All too often, adequate supporting incentives are not provided in the numerous instances where all employees are exhorted to apply creativity and innovation to their jobs. In such cases, suggestion boxes literally—or at least figuratively—fill up with cigarette butts and remarks suggesting where an organization should relocate.

The most successful strategy for building entrepreneurship into organizations is to isolate it within special departments and roles. An illustrative case of this strategy of containment is drawn from the music industry (Peterson and Berger, 1971).

Depending as it does on the rapidly changing style preferences of millions of youthful buyers, the industry's marketing environment has been quite turbulent since the shift from oligopoly to competition discussed above. The large, integrated industry firms such as Radio Corporation of America, Capitol, Columbia Broadcasting System, and Warner Brothers, have tried to contain entrepreneurship in three ways. Firstly, the segment of an organization which interacts with the turbulent element of the environment is segregated from the other segments of the organization as completely as possible. Secondly, within this environmentally linked segment, entrepreneurship is isolated into a specific role. Thirdly, the financial risk of each entrepreneurial decision is minimized as far as possible. These three strategies will be described in turn.

A recording company is ordinarily divided into three divisions. The first is manufacturing; its inputs include master-stamping record plates and jackets. Records are manufactured and packaged on highly standardized machinery so that no matter what sorts of sounds are recorded, be they string quartets or disco-rock, the stamping and packaging routines are unaffected. Thus, the manufacturing division of a company is fully segregated from environmental turbulence, and this division is quite bureaucratic in organization.

Sales and promotion comprise the second division. It is organized on a territorial basis, and like most sales divisions, a large part of its organizational activities is focused on seeing that its own agents are performing their assigned tasks. The division has a flat organizational chart, depending on frequent telephone contacts, internal publications, and money-incentive plans to coordinate and motivate its far-flung agents. The most effective way of merchandising new records is through radio air play, but artificially inducing air play—by any one of a number of practices which collectively are termed payola—is illegal. To protect themselves from the negative consequences of being caught at this activity, the large firms contract for payola services when they are required.

The third division of a record company—production—contains the entrepreneurial activity and is completely separated from the other two divisions. The production division is expected to create a succession of hit records and is loosely organized to adapt to continuous changes in the turbulent market, much as in the construction industry (Stinchcombe, 1959) and theater groups (Goodman and Goodman, 1976). The division is typically headed by a corporate vice-president, but his or her task is primarily to maintain the semblance of financial order over the activities of different types of professionals, craftsmen, and artists, many of whom work on a job-contract basis. Recording studios are often rented. The personnel and equipment are retained only so long as they are needed.

Within the production division of an organization, the entrepreneurial function is isolated, as far as possible, into a specific role simplifying the organizational control over entrepreneurship. In the record industry, entrepreneurship is most often isolated in the artist and repertoire department in the role usually called the producer. In creating a record, a producer interacts with numerous kinds of technical specialists who make a specific contribution to the final product. In contrast to these specialists, a producer must be a generalist, making novel combinations of available resources at each stage—from selecting songs to mixing the final sound for the record—in hopes of achieving success in a turbulent market. Peterson and Berger (1971) showed that the scope of entrepreneurship exercised by producers varies directly with market turbulence.

Four different tactics have been developed in the recording industry to limit the liability of entrepreneurship. In some particulars, the tactics are unique to the industry, but many similar strategies can be found elsewhere. Firstly, the discretion of each entrepreneur is limited. Although corporation executives say they give producers a free hand with money to create hits, in practice they retain considerable control, with the degree of discretion given to individual producers depending on the success of their prior productions. Parallel criteria seem to operate for extending discretion to editors in book-publishing houses and for granting basic research funds to scientists.

The second organizational strategy for reducing entrepreneurial liability is increasing as much as possible the number of entrepreneurial decisions while minimizing the investment in each. Because no rational way has been found for predicting which recording will be successful in a turbulent market, a recording company employs a number of producers, each of whom records six or more artists. In this way, the number of entrepreneurial decisions is quite large and the investment in each is not great.

Thirdly, the risks of entrepreneurship are decreased by developing a means of rapidly monitoring the market success of each decision (Cochran, 1977:22; Nafziger, 1977:232). This is easily accomplished in the recording industry, for the market life of a single record is usually 60 days and is rarely over 120 days. Record sales can be even more rapidly projected because several industry magazines chart the weekly market success of current hit records by compiling data from retail stores, juke-box operators, and radio stations. Whether a producer is currently in touch with a potential audience can thus be known within a matter of weeks. This knowledge aids company executives in deciding whether to promote heavily, release without fanfare, or withhold from release, records similar to current offerings.

Finally, entrepreneurial liability is limited by rapidly rewarding or firing entrepreneurs on the basis of success in the turbulent environment. Producers are hired on their presumed ability to find and produce that elusive novelty sound which generates hit records. New producers are given short-term contracts, and a company retains a first option to renew their contracts. In this way, a company can keep the successful producer from going to a rival company and can quickly get rid of those producers who lose the magic touch with the turbulent environment.

Parenthetically it might be noted that entrepreneurship in the industry has varied as a direct function of the degree of turbulence of the market. In the era of oligopoly prior to the mid 1950s, producers were much like other craftsmen in the production line. In contrast, in the years of highest turbulence, the large integrated firms either withdrew from the most turbulent segments of the market, or employed one or another of the contracting devices described above to provide sufficient entrepreneurship to compete in the turbulent market.

Entrepreneurial organizations

Entrepreneurial organizations structure entrepreneurship into all levels and departments. This strategy is the opposite of the three discussed so far. Just as they isolate entrepreneurship at the organizational boundary or contain it in prescribed niches within an organization, entrepreneurial organizations isolate or contain, as completely as possible, all modes of organization that are not entrepreneurial.

Entrepreneurial organizations are concentrated in the rapidly developing, high-skill and new-technology sectors of a few industries, most notably the aerospace, electronics, and computer industries. Entrepreneurial organizations' prime product is the marketing of a good idea. Their characteristic form is called matrix management or grid structure, but few organizations retain this form for long. Many fail and most of the rest are transformed by their success as the organizational logic of profits from routine production displaces the logic of entrepreneurship.

Only a few are self-consciously structured in the hopes of permanently retaining their innovative thrust. One of these, the Alza Corporation of Palo Alto, California, will be used to exemplify the principles of entrepreneurial organization. The description which follows is based on interviews conducted by the author with Alza personnel (Peterson, 1975b), and company documents supplemented by several journalists' reports on this and similar firms (Bylinsky, 1973; Loehwing, 1974; Tannenbaum, 1976).

In an entrepreneurial organization, the prime orienting reference is not an organizational chart, but a single, general statement of mission that includes organizational growth and profit but subordinates them to specific social goals. The mission is known by all organizational members and is continually invoked as the basis for making decisions. Founded in 1968, Alza is a new entrant into the pharmaceutical industry, long dominated by a few large firms. To understand the Alza mission, it must be placed in the context of the industry.

Since World War II, success in the industry has depended on discovering medically useful and patentable new compounds through biochemistry. Ingested orally or inoculated, these drugs must be given in dosages many hundreds or thousands of times greater than required to ensure that sufficient amounts will get to the affected tissue. This pattern of irregular overdosage often involves the danger of serious side effects.

The mission of Alza is to find ways to deliver drugs directly into the affected tissue in only the sufficient, small amounts required, at a constant rate for weeks or years. The chemical contraceptive project is an excellent case in point. Whereas other pharmaceutical firms have developed an oral contraceptive which must be taken daily, the Alza approach to the problem is to insert a device that will continually release minute amounts of the contraceptive drug directly into the uterus for a period of several years. Just this one operationalization of the mission idea could have a great impact on world population and thus bring fame and wealth to those involved with the firm.

The final element of the Alza mission is to move projects to the market on a publicly announced timetable. Drawing jeers from knowledgable industry experts, this policy heightens the sense of single-purpose team effort and competition with other organizations in a hostile environment. Combining the elements of focus, good for mankind, profit, personal short-term sacrifice, and competition, the Alza mission is structurally similar to the goal that President Kennedy set for the National Aeronautical and Space Agency—placing an American on the moon before 1970.

The President of Alza, Alejandro Zaffaroni, is personally known by all of the company's 700 employees. He has identified the mission and generated 56 million dollars by 1975 toward the operation of Alza. He has freely delegated authority and remains aloof from day-to-day affairs. Considered a genius by all of his co-workers, he keeps control as the creator, personification, and authoritative interpreter of the Alza mission.

The mission is channeled through a limited number of discrete programs or project areas, each being an operationalization of the mission with a specific commercial product as its goal. The chemical-contraceptive team is one of nine such programs at Alza. Each program director has a specified time line in which to stage activities, and has a budget to pay for the services of all the sorts of Alza personnel required. These time and money budgets are the prime mechanisms of organizational control. Several management committees periodically review the progress of programs and adjust their budget allocations accordingly. Changes are made in a zero-sum framework, so each supplementary allocation must come from another program. This prevents the proliferation of promising projects which are tangential to the organizational mission.

While all personnel in Alza Research are assigned to one or more projects, each is also a member of one or another of the departments of technical expertise, such as biology, engineering, device development, and medical testing. Thus, all employees have a permanent disciplinary home as well as a project assignment. Only a project director works on a program from its inception to its final finished product. All the other personnel are assigned on a month-by-month basis and may be working on several projects simultaneously. This fluid, goal-oriented grid structure minimizes the chances of organizational ossification and maximizes the potential for innovation.

Alza has experienced a high rate of personnel turnover. In the open environment of ingenious problem solving, incompetents are quickly exposed. Others have not functioned well in an environment of shared ideas, free-flowing suggestions, and self-paced work, where decisions are made collectively but responsibility is individualized. The work environment requires a blend of

self-confidence, respect for the achievement of others, and self-effacement. This combination was neatly illustrated by one interviewee (Peterson, 1975b). Praising the achievements of his colleagues, this man noted that he was almost the last of his graduating class without a job when Mr. Zaffaroni invited him to join Alza, yet *Fortune* magazine identified this same man as one "of the three most gifted graduates of the Stanford University Graduate School of Business for the preceding five years" (Bylinsky, 1973:32).

As in the case of most entrepreneurial organizations, many key personnel do not work in the fields for which they were trained or had their experience prior to joining Alza. Rather, the current activity applies their experience to a quite different field. In justifying this pattern and exemplifying the entrepreneurial style identified above as disjunctive imitation, one of the interviewees remarked, "after all, xerography was not invented by people in the carbon-paper industry" (Peterson, 1975b).

Incentives to work in entrepreneurial organizations flow from the mission. At Alza, this means contributing to producing a product that significantly benefits the human race, proving to the doubters that the mission can be accomplished, and gaining personal wealth. This final element is welded to mission success by tying employee earnings to corporate success by keeping salaries low, eliminating periodic bonuses, and providing wide participation in stock options. At Alza's research division, over a quarter of all the employees participate in stock-option plans. With such inducements to goal-oriented behavior, the usual trappings of supervision are largely dispensed with. There are no set hours, paperwork is minimized, and there are no dress or behavior codes except that nothing can be done on company property that disobeys an enforced law.

Just as a formal organization defends itself against entrepreneurship, an entrepreneurial organization defends itself against formalization. The first line of defense is the mission, since each organizational structure is defined as temporary and must periodically justify itself in reference to Alza's mission. This process of continuous revolution works well in the research division. However, profits in the pharmaceutical industry come not through perfecting products, but through manufacturing and successfully marketing them. Alza has used two devices to contain and isolate the formalizing influences of routine manufacture and marketing. Firstly, Alza Pharmaceuticals has been established as a distinct division with its own base of operations—separate from Alza Research—to perform the functions of manufacture and marketing. Secondly, in several cases, final product development has been contracted out as a joint venture with another firm.

The mission gives great coherence to an entrepreneurial organization, but it is also a great source of instability over time. The National Aeronautical and Space Agency is a good case in point. The public statement of mission was defined so narrowly on the single goal of the moon landing that it was very difficult to generate resources for other space-exploration goals as the moon mission neared completion. To avoid this singularity, the Alza mission was defined in sufficiently broad terms to encompass a number of distinct product applications. Some of these build on each other, so Alza planners see enough research to occupy them for ten years. But by that time, most of the key personnel may want to take profits on their Alza stock and so will want the company to be cutting down on expensive speculative research and to be concentrating on high sales and profits to increase the price of Alza stocks, thus bringing to an end the entrepreneurial phase of the company.

Many entrepreneurial organizations, like Alza, were formed by individuals who found they could not develop their own ideas within a corporate context. Entrepreneurial organizations in turn are the breeding grounds for further entrepreneurial spin-offs (Cooper, 1971; Shapero, 1975). This tendency has been institutionalized at Alza. When Alza personnel developed an idea outside the organization's mission, a separately financed company was established—with Alza aid in facilities and personnel. In this way, Alza is designed to become a central unit in a set of linked but financially independent entrepreneurial organizations. Such schemes are continuously tested by the exigencies of the market, and few succeed as projected.

Coming entrepreneurial revolution

Macrae (1976) predicted that the next generation will see the end of the big multinational corporation and its contemporary analogue, state capitalism, as these forms are presently known. Both of these, he argued, are ingenious mechanisms for decision blocking, which cannot survive in the ever changing world of high technology, world economy, rapid development, and well educated employees. Rather than being violently overthrown, he suggested, they will dissolve in a process of organizational devolution.

Organizational devolution

Macrae (1976) looked to a new era of competition and entrepreneurship. Implicit in his discussion is the assertion, developed in the early sections of this chapter, that the level of entrepreneurship has to do with the demand and opportunity for the activity, and not with the supply of entrepreneurial talent. Macrae did not provide a blueprint for the entrepreneurial revolution. He did,

however, touch on each of the four mechanisms described above for designing entrepreneurship into organization: franchising, contracting, entrepreneurial departments, and entrepreneurial organizations. He also noted the flowering of entrepreneurship in pockets of opportunity created by the operation of laws and regulations (Zonana, 1978).

Two quite different lines of effort suggest a renaissance of entrepreneurial opportunity. These involve paradigm shifts (Peterson, 1979) in the idea of both entrepreneurship and organization. Discussions of entrepreneurship have viewed the process as embedded in, and helping to perpetuate, a competitive, free-market system (Kirzner, 1973). Insofar as free enterprise is replaced by what has been variously called technocratic, meritocratic, or organizational society, however, the scope for entrepreneurship should decrease (Livesay, 1977:418; Schumpeter, 1934). And yet, in addition to the entrepreneurial model based upon free enterprise, there exists another model—which has developed in this century. Moreover, this second model has developed in an authoritarian organizational framework. Still closely identified with its prime proponent, it is called Maoism.

The differences between Maoism and free enterprise are important and have received the most attention (Schell, 1977), but their similarities are striking as well (Whyte, 1973). First, and foremost, both counterpose themselves to the principles of organization, which include the need for clearly specified rules and procedures, unitary hierarchical chain of command, reliance on technical experts, strict separation of job and personal life, and motivations based on the desire for career advancement and job security. Free-market and Maoist critics identify the same pathologies of organization: bureaucratic irrationality and red tape, myopic self-serving technical experts, and dehumanizing, ritualistic uses of rules. Both believe that great amounts of intelligence and activity will be liberated as ordinary people are freed from the fetters of organization (Kirzner, 1973; Whyte, 1973).

The structuring of an entrepreneurial organization around a social mission, discussed above, shows an unwitting blending of the Maoist and free-market principles of entrepreneurship. More explicit borrowings from Maoism may provide ideas for future forms of entrepreneurship, placing Maoism on Main Street.

Not only are ideas about the sociopolitical context of entrepreneurship shifting, but the very definition of organization seems to be undergoing a major change as well. The new notion of organization seems to be much more hospitable to entrepreneurship. The various orthodox theorists of organization from Weber (1947) to Thompson (1967) stressed the formal rules, technology-bound structure, and deterministic environment. Given this image of organization, it was easy to posit organization as an enormous positive-feedback process (Meyer, 1977) tending always to become more centralized and rigid. Gouldner (1955) years ago identified this view as not so much a statement of empirical reality as an assertion of metaphysical pathos.

A number of recent studies consider formal structure as a permeable myth or ceremony (Biggart, 1977; Jenkins, 1977; Meyer and Rowan, 1977). In the light of these ideas, which are becoming popular in academic circles, numerous alternative ways of viewing organization are being proposed (Benson, 1977; Brown, 1978; Hedberg *et al.*, 1976). Although quite different from each other in a number of important ways, they all conceptualize organization as a dynamic and fluid process, and thus compatible with the forms of entrepreneurship described here.

This chapter has focused on four topics: defining the term entrepreneurship so it can usefully be applied in contemporary organizational contexts; reviewing the blocks to entrepreneurship, found to be demand and opportunity rather than the supply of entrepreneurial organizations; detailing four sorts of arrangements which allow for varying degrees of entrepreneurship; and, finally, noting that the scope of entrepreneurship may now be expanding. If it has not been a complete plan for teaching organizational elephants to use entrepreneurial ice skates, at least this chapter has been able to suggest what sorts of elephants may be able to accomplish the task.

References

Aitken, Hugh G. J. (1963). "The future of entrepreneurial research." Explorations in Entrepreneurial History, Second Series 1: 3–9.

—— (1965). Explorations in Enterprise. Cambridge, Mass.: Harvard University Press.

Bain, Joe S. (1959). Industrial Organization. New York: Wiley.

Balabkins, Nicholas, and Aizsilnieks, Arnolds (1975). Entrepreneur in a Small Country. Hicksville, N.Y.: Exposition Press.

Baldridge, J. Victor, and Burnham, Robert A. (1975). "Organizational innovation: individual, organizational, and environmental impacts." Administrative Science Quarterly, 20: 165–176.

Barmash, Isadore (1971). Welcome to Our Conglomerate—You're Fired! New York: Delacorte.

Baty, Gordon B. (1974). Entrepreneurship. Reston, Vir.: Reston.

Becker, Howard S. (1963). Outsiders. London: Free Press.

Becker, Selwyn W., and Gordon, Gerald (1966). "An entrepreneurial theory of formal organizations, Part I: patterns of formal organizations." Administrative Science Quarterly, 11: 315–344.

Benson, J. Kenneth (1977). "Organizations: a dialectical view." Administrative Science Quarterly, 22: 1–21.

Biggart, Nicole Woolsey (1977). "The creative-destructive process of organizational change: the case of the Post Office." Administrative Science Quarterly, 22: 410–426.

Brill, Steven (1978). The Teamsters. New York: Simon and Schuster.

Brown, Richard Harvey (1978). "Bureaucracy as praxis: toward a political phenomenology of formal organizations." Administrative Science Quarterly, 23: 365–382.

Brown, Roger William (1965). Social Psychology. New York: Free Press.

Brown, Terry P. (1971). "Many small truckers go out of business." Wall Street Journal, 177 (37, February 24): 32.

Business Week (1977). "Top managers try venturing." Business Week, No. 2482 (May 9): 101–103.

Bylinsky, Gene (1973). "Visionary on a golden shoestring." Fortune, 87 (6): 150–153, 226, 229, 230.

—— (1977). "New companies that beat the odds." Fortune, 96 (6): 76–84.

Chapple, Steven, and Garofalo, Reebee (1977). Rock'n'Roll is Here to Pay. Chicago: Nelson–Hall.

Cochran, Thomas C. (1953). Railroad Leaders, 1845–1890. Cambridge, Mass.: Harvard University Press.

—— (1968). "Entrepreneurship." International Encyclopedia of the Social Sciences, 5: 87–91. New York: Macmillan.

—— (1977). 200 Years of American Business. New York: Basic Books.

Cochran, Thomas C., and Reina, Ruben E. (1962). Entrepreneurship in Argentine Culture. Philadelphia: University of Pennsylvania Press.

Cole, Arthur Harrison (1946). "An approach to the study of entrepreneurship: a tribute to Edwin F. Gay." Journal of Economic History, 6 (Supplement): 1–15.

—— (1959). Business Enterprise in its Social Setting. Cambridge, Mass.: Harvard University Press.

Collins, Orvis F., Moore, David G., and Unwalla, Darab (1964). "The enterprising man and the business executive." MSU Business Topics, 12(1): 19–34.

Cooper, Arnold C. (1971). "Spin-offs and technical entrepreneurship." IEEE Transactions on Engineering Management, EM–18: 2–6.

—— (1973). "Technical entrepreneurship: what do we know?" R & D Management, 3: 59–64.

Copulsky, William, and McNulty, Herbert W. (1974). Entrepreneurship and the Corporation. New York: American Management Association.

Davis, Kingsley, and Moore, Wilbert E. (1945). "Some principles of stratification." American Sociological Review, 10: 242–249.

Davis, Stanley M. (1968). "Entrepreneurial succession." Administrative Science Quarterly, 13: 402–416.

DeBord, Larry W. (1969). The Achievement Syndrome among Negro and White Culturally Disadvantaged Boys. Doctoral dissertation. Vanderbilt University.

Deeks, John (1976). The Small Firm Owner-Manager. New York: Praeger.

de Farcy, Henri (1973). "Esprit d'enterprise et développement economique." Archives Internationales de Sociologie de la Coopération et du Développement, 33: 3–42.

Denisoff, R. Serge (1975). Solid Gold. New Brunswick, N.J: Transaction Books.

Dible, Donald M. (1971). Up Your Own Organization! Santa Clara, Cal.: Enterpreneur Press.

—— (1976). The Pure Joy of Making More Money. Santa Clara, Cal.: Entrepreneur Press.

Drucker, Peter (1974). Management. New York: Harper & Row.

Ellis, Bernard (1975). Entrepreneurship in Rough Seas. Working paper, Vanderbilt University, Department of Sociology and Anthropology.

Galbraith, John Kenneth (1967). The New Industrial State. Boston: Houghton Mifflin.

Garlick, Peter C. (1971). African Traders and Economic Development in Ghana. Oxford: Clarendon Press.

Geertz, Clifford (1963). Peddlers and Princes. Chicago: University of Chicago Press.

Goodman, Richard Alan, and Goodman, Lawrence Peter (1976). "Some management issues in temporary systems: a study of professional development and manpower—the theater case." Administrative Science Quarterly, 21: 494–501.

Gough, John W. (1969). The Rise of the Entrepreneur. New York: Schocken.

Gouldner, Alvin W. (1955). "Metaphysical pathos and the theory of bureaucracy." American Political Science Review, 49: 496–507.

Gregg, Dorothy (1952). "John Stephans, general entrepreneur, 1749–1838." In William Miller (ed.), Men in Business: 120–152. Cambridge, Mass.: Harvard University Press.

Griffin, Barbara C. (1974). A Successful Business of Your Own. Los Angeles: Sherbourne.

Hagen, Everett Einar (1962). On the Theory of Social Change. Homewood, Ill.: Dorsey.

—— (1975). The Economics of Development. Homewood, Ill.: Irwin Press.

Havelock, Ronald G. (1969). Planning for Innovation.

Ann Arbor: Institute for Social Research, University of Michigan.

Hedberg, Bo L. T., Nystrom, Paul C., and Starbuck William H. (1976). "Camping on seesaws: prescriptions for a self-designing organization." Administrative Science Quarterly, 21: 41–65.

Henderson, James M., and Quandt, Richard E. (1971). Microeconomic Theory (2nd ed.). New York: McGraw–Hill.

Hirsch, Paul M. (1972). "Processing fads and fashions: an organization-set analysis of cultural industry systems." American Journal of Sociology, 77: 639–659.

Hoselitz, Berthold F. (1951). "The early history of entrepreneurial theory." Explorations in Entrepreneurial History, 3: 193–220.

House, Douglas J. (1977). Contemporary Entrepreneurs. Westport, Conn.: Greenwood.

Huber, Richard M. (1971). The American Idea of Success. New York: McGraw–Hill.

James, Ralph C., and James, Estelle D. (1965). Hoffa and the Teamsters. Princeton, N.J.: Van Nostrand.

Jenkins, J. Craig (1977). "Radical transformation of organizational goals." Administrative Science Quarterly, 22: 563–586.

Katz, Elihu (1973). "Differential factors in the diffusion of innovation." International Social Service Review, 32: 9–28.

Kilby, Peter (1971). "Hunting the Heffalump." In Peter Kilby (ed.), Entrepreneurship and Economic Development: 1–40 New York: Free Press.

Kirzner, Israel M. (1973). Competition and Entrepreneurship. Chicago: University of Chicago Press.

Klatt, Lawrence A. (1973). Small Business Management. Belmont, Cal.: Wadsworth.

Kling, Blair B. (1976). Partner in Empire. Berkeley: University of California Press.

König, Rene (1975). The Nunbakers of Afghanistan. Working paper, Vanderbilt University, Department of Sociology and Anthropology.

Kohn, Melvin L. (1971). "Bureaucratic man: a portrait and an interpretation." American Sociological Review, 36: 461–474.

Koo, Hagen (1976). "Small entrepreneurship in a developing society: patterns of labor absorption and social mobility." Social Forces, 54: 775–787.

Kunkel, John H. (1970). Society and Economic Growth. New York: Oxford University Press.

Langer, John (1977). "Drug entrepreneurs and dealing culture." Social Problems, 24: 377–386.

Lavin, David E. (1965). The Prediction of Academic Performance. New York: Wiley.

Lehner, Urban C. (1975). "Classic political boss is facing, some say, classic last hurrah." Wall Street Journal, 185 (98, May 20): 1, 30

Lerner, Daniel (1958). The Passing of Traditional Society. Glencoe, Ill.: Free Press.

LeVine, Robert Alan (1966). Dreams and Deeds. Chicago: University of Chicago Press.

Levy-Leboyer, Maurice (1976). "Innovation and business strategies in nineteenth- and twentieth-century France." In Edward C. Carter, II, Robert Foster, and Joseph N. Moody (eds.), Enterprise and Entrepreneurs in Nineteenth- and Twentieth-century France: 87–135. Baltimore: Johns Hopkins University Press.

Liles, Patrick R. (1974). New Business Ventures and the Entrepreneur. Homewood, Ill.: Irwin.

Livesay, Harold C. (1977). "Entrepreneurial persistence through the bureaucratic age." Business History Review, 51: 415–443.

Loehwing, David A. (1974). "Alza to Zoecon: both Syntex spin-offs are breaking scientific ground." Barron's, 54 (40, October 14): 3, 8, 13, 18.

Macaulay, Stewart (1965). "Changing a continuing relationship between a large corporation and those who deal with it: automobile manufacturers, their dealers, and the legal system." Wisconsin Law Review, 1965 (3): 483–575; 1965(4): 740–858.

McClelland, David C. (1961). The Achieving Society. Princeton, N.J.: Van Nostrand.

McClelland, David C., and Winter, David G. (1969). Motivating Economic Achievement. New York: Free Press.

McClelland, David C., Atkinson, John W., Clark, Russell A., and Lowell, Edgar L. (1976). The Achievement Motive. New York: Irvington.

Macrae, Norman (1976). "The coming entrepreneurial revolution: a survey." The Economist, 261 (6956, December 25): 41–44, 53–65.

Mancuso, Joseph (1973). Fun and Guts. Reading, Mass.: Addison–Wesley.

Marris, Peter, and Somerset, Anthony (1971). African Businessmen. London: Routledge and Kegan Paul.

Martin, Albro (1976). "James J. Hill and the first energy revolution: a study in entrepreneurship, 1865–1878," Business History Review, 50: 179–197.

Merton, Robert K. (1940). "Bureaucratic structure and personality." Social Forces, 18: 560–568.

—— (1968). Social Theory and Social Structure. New York: Free Press.

Meyer, John W., and Rowan, Brian (1977). "Institutionalized organizations: formal structure as myth and ceremony." American Journal of Sociology, 83: 340–363.

Meyer, Marshall W. (1977). Theory of Organizational Structure. Indianapolis: Bobbs-Merrill.

Miller, William (1952). Men in Business. Cambridge, Mass.: Harvard University Press.

Mills, C. Wright (1951). White Collar. New York: Oxford University Press.

Morgenthaler, Eric (1975). "Walter S. McIlhenny makes Tabasco sauce in milieu of old South." Wall Street Journal, January 10: 1, 15.

Murphy, Thomas P. (1977). "Making it as an entrepreneur." Forbes, 120 (July 15): 92–93.

Nafziger, F. Wayne (1977). African Capitalism. Stanford, Cal.: Hoover Institution Press.

Nevaskar, Balwant (1971). Capitalists without Capitalism. Westport, Conn.: Greenwood.

Oberschall, Anthony (1973). "African traders and small businessmen in Lusaka." African Social Research, 16: 474–502.

Palmer, Michael (1971). "The application of psychological testing to entrepreneurial potential." California Management Review, 13(3): 32–38.

Papanek, Gustav F. (1971). "The development of entrepreneurship." In Peter Kilby (ed.), Entrepreneurship and Economic Development: 317–329. New York: Free Press.

Passer, Harold C. (1965). "The electric light and the gas light." In Hugh G. J. Aitken (ed.), Explorations in Enterprise: 210–220. Cambridge, Mass.: Harvard University Press.

Penn, Stanley (1979). "Franchisers are often on outs with outlets, especially in fast foods." Wall Street Journal, 56 (4, January 2): 1, 8.

Peterson, Richard A. (1973). The Industrial Order and Social Policy. Englewood Cliffs, N.J.: Prentice–Hall.

—— (1975a). "Single-industry firm to conglomerate synergistics: alternative strategies for selling insurance and country music." In James Blumstein and Benjamin Walter (eds.), Growing Metropolis: 341–357. Nashville: Vanderbilt University Press.

—— (1975b). Six Interviews at Alza, August, 1975. Unpublished transcriptions, Vanderbilt University, Department of Sociology and Anthropology.

—— (1978). "The production of cultural change: the case of contemporary country music." Social Research, 45: 292–314.

—— (1979). "Revitalizing the culture concept." In Alex Inkeles (ed.), Annual Review of Sociology, Vol. 5: 137–166. Palo Alto, Cal.: Annual Reviews.

Peterson, Richard A., and Berger, David G. (1971). "Entrepreneurship in organizations; evidence from the popular music industry." Administrative Science Quarterly, 16: 97–106.

—— (1975). "Cycles in symbol production: the case of popular music." American Sociological Review, 40: 158–173.

Peterson, Richard A., and DeBord, Larry (1966). Educational Supportiveness of the Home and Academic Performance of Disadvantaged Boys. Nashville:

Institute on Mental Retardation and Intellectual Development, George Peabody College for Teachers.

Peterson, Richard A., and DiMaggio, Paul (1975). "From region to class, the changing locus of country music: a test of the massification hypothesis." Social Forces, 53: 497–506.

Peterson, Richard A., and Elifson, Kirk (1968). Entrepreneurship as a Mechanism of Social Mobility in a Blue Collar Occupation. Working paper, Vanderbilt University, Department of Sociology and Anthropology.

Peterson, Richard A., and White, Howard G. (1979). "The simplex located in art worlds." Urban Life, 7: 411–439.

Rand, Christopher (1964). Cambridge, U.S.A. New York: Oxford University Press.

Redlich, Fritz (1949). "The origin of the concepts of 'entrepreneur' and 'creative entrepreneur.'" Explorations in Entrepreneurial History, 1: 1–7.

Rischin, Moses (1965). The American Gospel of Success. Chicago: Quadrangle.

Ritzer, George (1975). "Professionalization, bureaucratization and rationalization: the views of Max Weber." Social Forces, 53: 627–634.

Rosen, Bernard C. (1973). "Social change, migration and family interaction in Brazil." American Sociological Review, 38: 198–212.

Rowe, Lloyd A., and Boise, William B. (1974). "Organizational innovation: current research and evolving concepts." Public Administration Review, 34: 284–293.

Salancik, Gerald R., and Pfeffer, Jeffrey (1977). "An examination of need-satisfaction models of job attitudes." Administrative Science Quarterly, 22: 427–456.

Sarachek, Bernard (1978). "American entrepreneurs and the Horatio Alger myth." Journal of Economic History, 38: 439–456.

Say, Jean Baptiste (1816). Catechism of Political Economy. London: Sherwood, Neely, and Jones.

Schatz, Sayre P. (1971). "Achievement and economic growth: a critical appraisal." In Peter Kilby (ed.), Entrepreneurship and Economic Development: 183–190. New York: Free Press.

—— (1977). Nigerian Capitalism. Berkeley: University of California Press.

Schell, Orville (1977). In the People's Republic. New York: Random House.

Schreier, James W. (1975). The Female Entrepreneur. Milwaukee: Center for Venture Management.

Schumpeter, Joseph A. (1934). The Theory of Economic Development. Cambridge, Mass.: Harvard University Press.

—— (1947). "The creative response in economic history." Journal of Economic History, 7: 149–159.

—— (1950). Capitalism, Socialism and Democracy (3rd ed.). New York: Harper & Row.

—— (1965). "Economic theory and entrepreneurial history." In Hugh G. J. Aitken (ed.), Explorations in Enterprise: 45–64. Cambridge, Mass.: Harvard University Press.

Seibel, Hans D. (1974). The Dynamics of Achievement. Indianapolis: Bobbs–Merrill.

Shapero, Albert (1975). Entrepreneurship and Economic Development. Working paper, University of Texas, Graduate School of Business.

Smelser, Neil J. (1959). Social Change in the Industrial Revolution. Chicago: University of Chicago Press.

—— (1976). The Sociology of Economic Life (2nd ed.). Englewood Cliffs, N.J.: Prentice–Hall.

Smith, Ruth Arbitman (1968). Entrepreneurs and Movements of Protest in Transitional Societies. Working paper, Vanderbilt University, Department of Sociology and Anthropology.

Smith, Thomas Spence (1974). "Aestheticism and social structure: style and social network in the dandy life." American Sociological Review, 39: 725–743.

Sobel, Robert (1974). The Entrepreneurs. New York: Weybright and Talley.

Starbuck, William H. (1965). "Organizational growth and development." In James G. March (ed.), Handbook of Organizations: 451–533. Chicago: Rand McNally.

Stinchcombe, Arthur L. (1959). "Bureaucratic and craft administration of production: a comparative study." Administrative Science Quarterly, 4: 168–187.

—— (1974). Creating Efficient Industrial Administration. New York: Academic Press.

Sueno, Akira (1977). Entrepreneur and Gentleman. Rutland Vt.: Tuttle.

Sutton, Francis X., Harris, Seymour E., Kaysen, Carl, and Tobin, James (1956). The American Business Creed. Cambridge, Mass.: Harvard University Press.

Swayne, Charles B., and Tucker, William R. (1973). The Effective Entrepreneur. Morristown, N.J.: General Learning Press.

Tannenbaum, Jeffrey A. (1976). "Controlled delivery promises to improve efficacy of medicines." Wall Street Journal, 188(4, July 7): 1, 23.

Thompson, James D. (1967). Organizations in Action. New York: McGraw–Hill.

Thompson, Victor A. (1965). "Bureaucracy and Innovation." Administrative Science Quarterly, 10: 1–20.

Vaughn, Charles L. (1974). Franchising. Lexington, Mass.: Lexington.

Weber, Max (1947). The Theory of Social and Economic Organization. New York: Oxford University Press.

White, Richard M. (1977). The Entrepreneur's Manual. Radnor, Penn.: Chilton.

Entrepreneurship *41*

Entrepreneurship and organization 83

Whyte, Martin King (1973). "Bureaucracy and modernization in China: the Maoist critique." American Sociological Review, 38: 149–163.

Wyllie, Irvin G. (1966). The Self-made Man in America. New York.: Free Press.

Young, Frank W. (1971). "A macrosociological interpretation of entrepreneurship." In Peter Kilby (ed.), Entrepreneurship and Economic Development: 139–149. New York: Free Press.

Zonana, Victor F. (1978). "World Airways' Daly relishes coming battle with major airlines." Wall Street Journal, 59 (48, December 21): 1, 23.

[3]

Entrepreneurship: Productive, Unproductive, and Destructive

William J. Baumol

New York University and Princeton University

The basic hypothesis is that, while the total supply of entrepreneurs varies among societies, the productive contribution of the society's entrepreneurial activities varies much more because of their allocation between productive activities such as innovation and largely unproductive activities such as rent seeking or organized crime. This allocation is heavily influenced by the relative payoffs society offers to such activities. This implies that policy can influence the allocation of entrepreneurship more effectively than it can influence its supply. Historical evidence from ancient Rome, early China, and the Middle Ages and Renaissance in Europe is used to investigate the hypotheses.

> It is often assumed that an economy of private enterprise has an automatic bias towards innovation, but this is not so. It has a bias only towards profit. [HOBSBAWM 1969, p. 40]

When conjectures are offered to explain historic slowdowns or great leaps in economic growth, there is the group of usual suspects that is

I am very grateful for the generous support of the research underlying this paper from the Division of Information Science and Technology of the National Science Foundation, the Price Institute for Entrepreneurial Studies, the Center for Entrepreneurial Studies of the Graduate School of Business Administration, New York University, and the C. V. Starr Center for Applied Economics. I am also very much indebted to Vacharee Devakula for her assistance in the research. I owe much to Joel Mokyr, Stefano Fenoaltea, Lawrence Stone, Constance Berman, and Claudia Goldin for help with the substance of the paper and to William Jordan and Theodore Rabb for guidance on references.

[*Journal of Political Economy*, 1990, vol. 98, no. 5, pt. 1]

regularly rounded up—prominent among them, the entrepreneur. Where growth has slowed, it is implied that a decline in entrepreneurship was partly to blame (perhaps because the culture's "need for achievement" has atrophied). At another time and place, it is said, the flowering of entrepreneurship accounts for unprecedented expansion.

This paper proposes a rather different set of hypotheses, holding that entrepreneurs are always with us and always play *some* substantial role. But there are a variety of roles among which the entrepreneur's efforts can be reallocated, and some of those roles do not follow the constructive and innovative script that is conventionally attributed to that person. Indeed, at times the entrepreneur may even lead a parasitical existence that is actually damaging to the economy. How the entrepreneur acts at a given time and place depends heavily on the rules of the game—the reward structure in the economy—that happen to prevail. Thus the central hypothesis here is that it is the set of rules and not the supply of entrepreneurs *or the nature of their objectives* that undergoes significant changes from one period to another and helps to dictate the ultimate effect on the economy via the *allocation* of entrepreneurial resources. Changes in the rules and other attendant circumstances can, of course, modify the composition of the class of entrepreneurs and can also alter its size. Without denying this or claiming that it has no significance, in this paper I shall seek to focus attention on the allocation of the changing class of entrepreneurs rather than its magnitude and makeup. (For an excellent analysis of the basic hypothesis, independently derived, see Murphy, Shleifer, and Vishny [1990].)

The basic proposition, if sustained by the evidence, has an important implication for growth policy. The notion that our productivity problems reside in "the spirit of entrepreneurship" that waxes and wanes for unexplained reasons is a counsel of despair, for it gives no guidance on how to reawaken that spirit once it has lagged. If that is the task assigned to policymakers, they are destitute: they have no means of knowing how to carry it out. But if what is required is the adjustment of rules of the game to induce a more felicitous allocation of entrepreneurial resources, then the policymaker's task is less formidable, and it is certainly not hopeless. The prevailing rules that affect the allocation of entrepreneurial activity can be observed, described, and, with luck, modified and improved, as will be illustrated here.

Here, extensive historical illustrations will be cited to impart plausibility to the contentions that have just been described. Then a short discussion of some current issues involving the allocation of entrepreneurship between productive and unproductive activities will be of-

fered. Finally, I shall consider very briefly the means that can be used
to change the rules of the game, and to do so in a manner that
stimulates the productive contribution of the entrepreneur.

I. On the Historical Character of the Evidence

Given the inescapable problems for empirical as well as theoretical
study of entrepreneurship, what sort of evidence can one hope to
provide? Since the rules of the game usually change very slowly, a case
study approach to investigation of my hypotheses drives me unavoid-
ably to examples spanning considerable periods of history and encompassing widely different cultures and geographic locations. Here
I shall proceed on the basis of historical illustrations encompassing
all the main economic periods and places (ancient Rome, medieval
China, Dark Age Europe, the Later Middle Ages, etc.) that the economic historians almost universally single out for the light they shed
on the process of innovation and its diffusion. These will be used to
show that the relative rewards to different types of entrepreneurial
activity have in fact varied dramatically from one time and place to
another and that this seems to have had profound effects on patterns
of entrepreneurial behavior. Finally, evidence will be offered *suggesting* that such reallocations can have a considerable influence on the
prosperity and growth of an economy, though other variables undoubtedly also play substantial roles.

None of this can, of course, be considered conclusive. Yet, it is
surely a standard tenet of scientific method that tentative confirma-
tion of a hypothesis is provided by observation of phenomena that the
hypothesis helps to explain and that could not easily be accounted for
if that hypothesis were invalid. It is on this sort of reasoning that I
hope to rest my case. Historians have long been puzzled, for example,
by the failure of the society of ancient Rome to disseminate and put
into widespread practical use some of the sophisticated technological
developments that we know to have been in its possession, while in the
"High Middle Ages," a period in which progress and change were
hardly popular notions, inventions that languished in Rome seem to
have spread like wildfire. It will be argued that the hypothesis about
the allocability of entrepreneurial effort between productive and unproductive activity helps considerably to account for this phenomenon, though it certainly will *not* be claimed that this is all there was to
the matter.

Before I get to the substance of the discussion, it is important to
emphasize that nothing that follows in this article makes any pretense
of constituting a contribution to economic history. Certainly it is not
intended here to try to explain any particular historical event. More-

over, the analysis relies entirely on secondary sources, and all the historical developments described are well known to historians, as the citations will indicate. Whatever the contribution that may be offered by the following pages, then, it is confined to enhanced understanding and extension of the (nonmathematical) theory of entrepreneurship in general, and not to an improved analysis of the historical events that are cited.

II. The Schumpeterian Model Extended: Allocation of Entrepreneurship

The analysis of this paper rests on what seems to be the one theoretical model that effectively encompasses the role of the entrepreneur and that really "works," in the sense that it constitutes the basis for a number of substantive inferences.[1] This is, of course, the well-known Schumpeterian analysis, whose main shortcoming, for our purposes, is the paucity of insights on policy that emerge from it. It will be suggested here that only a minor extension of that model to encompass the *allocation* of entrepreneurship is required to enhance its power substantially in this direction.

Schumpeter tells us that innovations (he calls them "the carrying out of new combinations") take various forms besides mere improvements in technology:

> This concept covers the following five cases: (1) the introduction of a new good—that is one with which consumers are not yet familiar—or of a new quality of a good. (2) The introduction of a new method of production, that is one not yet tested by experience in the branch of manufacture concerned, which need by no means be founded upon a discovery scientifically new, and can also exist in a new way of handling a commodity commercially. (3) The opening of a new market, that is a market into which the particular branch of manufacture of the country in question has not previously entered, whether or not this market has existed before. (4) The conquest of a new source of supply of raw materials or half-manufactured goods, again irrespective of whether this source already exists or whether it has first to be

[1] There has, however, recently been an outburst of illuminating writings on the theory of the innovation process, analyzing it in such terms as *races* for patents in which the winner takes everything, with no consolation prize for a close second, or treating the process, alternatively, as a "waiting game," in which the patient second entrant may outperform and even survive the first one in the innovative arena, who incurs the bulk of the risk. For an overview of these discussions as well as some substantial added insights, see Dasgupta (1988).

created. (5) The carrying out of the new organization of any industry, like the creation of a monopoly position (for example through trustification) or the breaking up of a monopoly position. [(1912) 1934, p. 66]

The obvious fact that entrepreneurs undertake such a variety of tasks all at once suggests that theory can usefully undertake to consider what determines the *allocation* of entrepreneurial inputs among those tasks. Just as the literature traditionally studies the allocation of other inputs, for example, capital resources, among the various industries that compete for them, it seems natural to ask what influences the flow of entrepreneurial talent among the various activities in Schumpeter's list.

Presumably the reason no such line of inquiry was pursued by Schumpeter or his successors is that any analysis of the allocation of entrepreneurial resources among the five items in the preceding list (with the exception of the last—the creation or destruction of a monopoly) does not promise to yield any profound conclusions. There is no obvious reason to make much of a shift of entrepreneurial activity away from, say, improvement in the production process and toward the introduction of new products. The general implications, if any, for the public welfare, for productivity growth, and for other related matters are hardly obvious.

To derive more substantive results from an analysis of the allocation of entrepreneurial resources, it is necessary to expand Schumpeter's list, whose main deficiency seems to be that it does not go far enough. For example, it does not explicitly encompass innovative acts of technology transfer that take advantage of opportunities to introduce already-available technology (usually with some modification to adapt it to local conditions) to geographic locales whose suitability for the purpose had previously gone unrecognized or at least unused.

Most important for the discussion here, Schumpeter's list of entrepreneurial activities can usefully be expanded to include such items as innovations in rent-seeking procedures, for example, discovery of a previously unused legal gambit that is effective in diverting rents to those who are first in exploiting it. It may seem strange at first blush to propose inclusion of activities of such questionable value to society (I shall call them acts of "unproductive entrepreneurship") in the list of Schumpeterian innovations (though the creation of a monopoly, which Schumpeter does include as an innovation, is surely as questionable), but, as will soon be seen, this is a crucial step for the analysis that follows. If entrepreneurs are defined, simply, to be persons who are ingenious and creative in finding ways that add to their own wealth, power, and prestige, then it is to be expected that not all of them will be overly concerned with whether an activity that achieves these goals adds much or little to the social product or, for that matter, even whether it is an actual impediment to production (this notion goes back, at least, to Veblen [1904]). Suppose that it turns out, in addition, that at any time and place the magnitude of the benefit the economy derives from its entrepreneurial talents depends *substantially*, among other variables, on the allocation of this resource between productive and unproductive entrepreneurial activities of the sorts just described. Then the reasons for including acts of the latter type in the list of entrepreneurial activities become clear.

Here no exhaustive analysis of the process of allocation of entrepreneurial activity among the set of available options will be attempted. Rather, it will be argued only that at least *one* of the prime determinants of entrepreneurial behavior at any particular time and place is the prevailing rules of the game that govern the payoff of one entrepreneurial activity relative to another. If the rules are such as to impede the earning of much wealth via activity A, or are such as to impose social disgrace on those who engage in it, then, other things being equal, entrepreneurs' efforts will tend to be channeled to other activities, call them B. But if B contributes less to production or welfare than A, the consequences for society may be considerable.[2]

As a last preliminary note, it should be emphasized that the set of active entrepreneurs may be subject to change. Thus if the rules of the game begin to favor B over A, it may not be just the same individuals who switch their activities from entrepreneurship of type A to that of type B. Rather, some persons with talents suited for A may simply drop out of the picture, and individuals with abilities adapted to B may for the first time become entrepreneurs. Thus the allocation of entrepreneurs among activities is perhaps best described in the way Joan Robinson (following Shove's suggestion) analyzed the allocation of heterogeneous land resources (1933, chap. 8): as the solution of a jigsaw puzzle in which the pieces are each fitted into the places selected for them by the concatenation of pertinent circumstances.

III. Entrepreneurship, Productive and Unproductive: The Rules Do Change

Let us now turn to the central hypothesis of this paper: that the exercise of entrepreneurship can sometimes be unproductive or even

---

[2] There is a substantial literature, following the work of Jacob Schmookler, providing strong empirical evidence for the proposition that even the allocation of inventive effort, i.e., the directions pursued by inventive activities, is itself heavily influenced by relative payoff prospects. However, it is now agreed that some of these authors go too far when they appear to imply that almost nothing but the demand for the product of invention influences to any great extent which inventions will occur. For a good summary and references, see Abramovitz (1989, p. 33).

destructive, and that whether it takes one of these directions or one that is more benign depends heavily on the structure of payoffs in the economy—the rules of the game. The rather dramatic illustrations provided by world history seem to confirm quite emphatically the following proposition.

PROPOSITION 1. The rules of the game that determine the relative payoffs to different entrepreneurial activities *do* change dramatically from one time and place to another.

These examples also suggest strongly (but hardly "prove") the following proposition.

PROPOSITION 2. Entrepreneurial behavior changes direction from one economy to another in a manner that corresponds to the variations in the rules of the game.

A. Ancient Rome

The avenues open to those Romans who sought power, prestige, and wealth are instructive. First, it may be noted that they had no reservations about the desirability of wealth or about its pursuit (e.g., Finley 1985, pp. 53–57). *As long as it did not involve participation in industry or commerce,* there was nothing degrading about the wealth acquisition process. Persons of honorable status had three primary and acceptable sources of income: landholding (not infrequently as absentee landlords), "usury," and what may be described as "political payments":

> The opportunity for "political moneymaking" can hardly be over-estimated. Money poured in from booty, indemnities, provincial taxes, loans and miscellaneous extractions in quantities without precedent in Graeco-Roman history, and at an accelerating rate. The public treasury benefited, but probably more remained in private hands, among the nobles in the first instance; then, in appropriately decreasing proportions, among the *equites,* the soldiers and even the plebs of the city of Rome. . . . Nevertheless, the whole phenomenon is misunderstood when it is classified under the headings of "corruption" and "malpractice", as historians still persist in doing. Cicero was an honest governor of Cilicia in 51 and 50 B.C., so that at the end of his term he had earned only the legitimate profits of office. They amounted to 2,200,000 sesterces, more than treble the figure of 600,000 he himself once mentioned (*Stoic Paradoxes* 49) to illustrate an annual income that could permit a life of luxury. We are faced with something structural in the society. [Finley 1985, p. 55]

Who, then, operated commerce and industry? According to Veyne (1961), it was an occupation heavily undertaken by freedmen— former slaves who, incidentally, bore a social stigma for life. Indeed, according to this writer, slavery may have represented the one avenue for advancement for someone from the lower classes. A clever (and handsome) member of the lower orders might deliberately arrange to be sold into slavery to a wealthy and powerful master.[3] Then, with luck, skill, and drive, he would grow close to his owner, perhaps managing his financial affairs (and sometimes engaging in some homosexual activity with him). The master then gained cachet, after a suitable period, by granting freedom to the slave, setting him up with a fortune of his own. The freedmen, apparently not atypically, invested their financial stakes in commerce, hoping to multiply them sufficiently to enable them to retire in style to the countryside, thereafter investing primarily in land and loans in imitation of the upper classes.

Finally, regarding the Romans' attitude to the promotion of technology and productivity, Finley makes much of the "clear, almost total, divorce between science and practice" (1965, p. 32). He goes on to cite Vitruvius's monumental work on architecture and technology, in whose 10 books he finds only a single and trivial reference to means of saving effort and increasing productivity. Finley then reports the following story:

> There is a story, repeated by a number of Roman writers, that a man—characteristically unnamed—invented unbreakable glass and demonstrated it to Tiberius in anticipation of a great reward. The emperor asked the inventor whether anyone shared his secret and was assured that there was no one else; whereupon his head was promptly removed, lest, said Tiberius, gold be reduced to the value of mud. I have no opinion about the truth of this story, and it is only a story. But is it not interesting that neither the elder Pliny nor Petronius nor the historian Dio Cassius was troubled by the point that the inventor turned to the emperor for a reward, instead of turning to an investor for capital with which to put his invention into production?[4] . . . We must

---

[3] Stefano Fenoaltea comments that he knows no documented cases in which this occurred and that it was undoubtedly more common to seek advancement through adoption into an upper-class family.

[4] To be fair to Finley, note that he concludes that it is *not* really interesting. North and Thomas (1973, p. 3) make a similar point about Harrison's invention of the ship's chronometer in the eighteenth century (as an instrument indispensable for the determination of longitude). They point out that the incentive for this invention was a large governmental prize rather than the prospect of commercial profit, presumably because of the absence of effective patent protection.

> remind ourselves time and again that the European experi-
> ence since the late Middle Ages in technology, in the econ-
> omy, and in the value systems that accompanied them, was
> unique in human history until the recent export trend com-
> menced. Technical progress, economic growth, productivity,
> even efficiency have not been significant goals since the be-
> ginning of time. So long as an acceptable life-style could be
> maintained, however that was defined, other values held the
> stage. [1985, p. 147]

The bottom line, for our purposes, is that the Roman reward system, although it offered wealth to those who engaged in commerce
and industry, offset this gain through the attendant loss in prestige.
Economic effort "was neither the way to wealth nor its purpose. Cato's
gods showed him a number of ways to get more; but they were all
political and parasitical, the ways of conquest and booty and usury;
labour was not one of them, not even the labour of the entrepreneur"
(Finley 1965, p. 39).

B. Medieval China

In China, as in many kingdoms of Europe before the guarantees of
the Magna Carta and the revival of towns and their acquisition of
privileges, the monarch commonly claimed possession of all property
in his territories. As a result, particularly in China, when the sover-
eign was in financial straits, confiscation of the property of wealthy
subjects was entirely in order. It has been claimed that this led those
who had resources to avoid investing them in any sort of visible capital
stocks, and that this, in turn, was a substantial impediment to economic expansion (see Balazs 1964, p. 53; Landes 1969, pp. 46–47;
Rosenberg and Birdzell 1986, pp. 119–20; Jones 1987, chap. 5).

In addition, imperial China reserved its most substantial rewards in
wealth and prestige for those who climbed the ladder of imperial
examinations, which were heavily devoted to subjects such as Confucian philosophy and calligraphy. Successful candidates were often
awarded high rank in the bureaucracy, high social standing denied to
anyone engaged in commerce or industry, even to those who gained
great wealth in the process (and who often used their resources to
prepare their descendants to contend via the examinations for a position in the scholar bureaucracy). In other words, the rules of the game
seem to have been heavily biased against the acquisition of wealth *and
position* through Schumpeterian behavior. The avenue to success lay
elsewhere.

Because of the difficulty of the examinations, the mandarins
(scholar-officials) rarely succeeded in keeping such positions in their

own families for more than two or three generations (see Marsh 1961, p. 159; Ho 1962, chap. 4 and appendix). The scholar families devoted enormous effort and considerable resources to preparing their children through years of laborious study for the imperial examinations, which, during the Sung dynasty, were held every 3 years, and only several hundred persons in all of China succeeded in passing them each time (E. A. Kracke, Jr. in Liu and Golas [1969, p. 14]). Yet, regularly, some persons not from mandarin families also attained success through this avenue (see, e.g., Marsh [1961] and Ho [1962] for evidence on social mobility in imperial China).

Wealth was in prospect for those who passed the examination and who were subsequently appointed to government positions. But the sources of their earnings had something in common with those of the Romans:

> Corruption, which is widespread in all impoverished and backward countries (or, more exactly, throughout the preindustrial world), was endemic in a country where the servants of the state often had nothing to live on but their very meager salaries. The required attitude of obedience to superiors made it impossible for officials to demand higher salaries, and in the absence of any control over their activities from below it was inevitable that they should purloin from society what the state failed to provide. According to the usual pattern, a Chinese official entered upon his duties only after spending long years in study and passing many examinations; he then established relations with protectors, incurred debts to get himself appointed, and then proceeded to extract the amount he had spent on preparing himself for his career from the people he administered—and extracted both principal and interest. The degree of his rapacity would be dictated not only by the length of time he had had to wait for his appointment and the number of relations he had to support and of kin to satisfy or repay, but also by the precariousness of his position. [Balazs 1964, p. 10]

Enterprise, on the other hand, was not only frowned on, but may have been subjected to impediments deliberately imposed by the officials, at least after the fourteenth century A.D.; and some historians claim that it was true much earlier. Balazs tells us of

> the state's tendency to clamp down immediately on any form of private enterprise (and this in the long run kills not only initiative but even the slightest attempts at innovation), or, if it did not succeed in putting a stop to it in time, to take over

and nationalize it. Did it not frequently happen during the course of Chinese history that the scholar-officials, although hostile to all inventions, nevertheless gathered in the fruits of other people's ingenuity? I need mention only three examples of inventions that met this fate: paper, invented by a eunuch; printing, used by the Buddhists as a medium for religious propaganda; and the bill of exchange, an expedient of private businessmen. [P. 18]

As a result of recurrent intervention by the state to curtail the liberty and take over any accumulated advantages the merchant class had managed to gain for itself, "the merchant's ambition turned to becoming a scholar-official and investing his profits in land" (p. 32).

C. The Earlier Middle Ages

Before the rise of the cities and before monarchs were able to subdue the bellicose activities of the nobility, wealth and power were pursued primarily through military activity. Since land and castles were the medieval forms of wealth most highly valued and most avidly sought after, it seems reasonable to interpret the warring of the barons in good part as the pursuit of an economic objective. For example, during the reign of William the Conqueror (see, e.g., Douglas 1964), there were frequent attempts by the barons in Normandy and neighboring portions of France to take over each other's lands and castles. A prime incentive for William's supporters in his conquest of England was their obvious aspiration for lands.[5] More than that, violent means also served to provide more liquid forms of income (captured treasure), which the nobility used to support both private consumption and investment in military plant and equipment, where such items could not easily be produced on their own lands and therefore had to be purchased from others. In England, with its institution of primogeniture (the exclusive right of the eldest son to inherit his father's estate), younger sons who chose not to enter the clergy often had no socially acceptable choice other than warfare as a means to make their fortunes, and in some cases they succeeded spectacularly. Thus note the case of William Marshal, fourth son of a minor noble, who rose

---

[5] The conquest has at least two noteworthy entrepreneurial sides. First, it involved an innovation, the use of the stirrup by the Normans at Hastings that enabled William's warriors to use the same spear to impale a series of victims with the force of the horse's charge, rather than just tossing the spear at the enemy, much as an infantryman could. Second, the invasion was an impressive act of organization, with William having to convince his untrustworthy allies that they had more to gain by joining him in England than by staying behind to profit from his absence by trying to grab away his lands as they had tried to do many times before.

through his military accomplishments to be one of the most powerful and trusted officials under Henry II and Richard I, and became one of the wealthiest men in England (see Painter 1933).

Of course, the medieval nobles were not purely economic men. Many of the turbulent barons undoubtedly enjoyed fighting for its own sake, and success in combat was an important avenue to prestige in their society. But no modern capitalist is a purely economic man either. What I am saying here is that warfare, which was of course pursued for a variety of reasons, was *also* undertaken as a primary source of economic gain. This is clearly all the more true of the mercenary armies that were the scourge of fourteenth-century France and Italy.

Such violent economic activity, moreover, inspired frequent and profound innovation. The introduction of the stirrup was a requisite for effective cavalry tactics. Castle building evolved from wooden to stone structures and from rectangular to round towers (which could not be made to collapse by undermining their corners). Armor and weaponry became much more sophisticated with the introduction of the crossbow, the longbow, and, ultimately, artillery based on gunpowder. Military tactics and strategy also grew in sophistication. These innovations can be interpreted as contributions of military entrepreneurs undertaken at least partly in pursuit of private economic gains.

This type of entrepreneurial undertaking obviously differs vastly from the introduction of a cost-saving industrial process or a valuable new consumer product. An individual who pursues wealth through the forcible appropriation of the possessions of others surely does not add to the national product. Its net effect may be not merely a transfer but a net reduction in social income and wealth.[6]

---

[6] In saying all this, I must not be interpreted as taking the conventional view that warfare is an unmitigated source of impoverishment of any economy that unquestionably never contributes to its prosperity. Careful recent studies have indicated that matters are more complicated (see, e.g., Milward 1970; Olson 1982). Certainly the unprecedented prosperity enjoyed afterward by the countries on the losing side of the Second World War suggests that warfare need not always preclude economic expansion, and it is easy to provide earlier examples. The three great economic leaders of the Western world preceding the United States—Italy in the thirteenth–sixteenth centuries, the Dutch Republic in the seventeenth and eighteenth, and Great Britain in the eighteenth and nineteenth—each attained the height of their prosperity after periods of enormously costly and sometimes destructive warfare. Nevertheless, the wealth gained by a medieval baron from the adoption of a novel bellicose technique can hardly have contributed to economic growth in the way that resulted from adoption of a new steelmaking process in the nineteenth century or the introduction of a product such as the motor vehicle in the twentieth.

D. The Later Middle Ages

By the end of the eleventh century the rules of the game had changed from those of the Dark Ages. The revival of the towns was well under way. They had acquired a number of privileges, among them protection from arbitrary taxation and confiscation and the creation of a labor force by granting freedom to runaway serfs after a relatively brief residence (a year and a day) in the towns. The free-enterprise turbulence of the barons had at least been impeded by the church's pacification efforts: the peace and the (later) truce of God in France, Spain, and elsewhere; similar changes were taking place in England (see, e.g., Cowdrey [1970]; but Jones [1987, p. 94] suggests that some free-enterprise military activity by the barons continued in England through the reigns of the earlier Tudors in the sixteenth century). All this subsequently "gave way to more developed efforts to enforce peace by the more organized governments of the twelfth century" (Brooke 1964, p. 350; also p. 127). A number of activities that were neither agricultural nor military began to yield handsome returns. For example, the small group of architect-engineers who were in charge of the building of cathedrals, palaces, bridges, and fortresses could live in great luxury in the service of their kings.

But, apparently, a far more common source of earnings was the water-driven mills that were strikingly common in France and southern England by the eleventh century, a technological innovation about which more will be said presently. An incentive for such technical advances may have been the monopoly they conferred on their owners rather than any resulting improvement in efficiency. Such monopoly rights were alike sought and enforced by private parties (Bloch 1935, pp. 554–57; Brooke 1964, p. 84) and by religious organizations (see below).

The economic role of the monks in this is somewhat puzzling—the least clear-cut part of our story.[7] The Cistercian abbeys are generally assigned a critical role in the promotion of such technological advances. In some cases they simply took over mills that had been constructed by others (Berman 1986, p. 89). But the Cistercians improved them, built many others, and vastly expanded their use; at

---

[7] Bloch (1935) notes that the monasteries had both the capital and the large number of consumers of flour necessary to make the mills profitable. In addition, they were less likely than lay communities to undergo military siege, which, which, Bloch notes, was (besides drought and freezing of the waterways) one of the main impediments to adoption of the water mill, since blocking of the waterway that drove the mill could threaten the besieged population with starvation (pp. 550–53).

least some writers (e.g., Gimpel 1976, pp. 3–6) seem to suggest that the Cistercians were the spearhead of technological advance.

Historians tell us that they have no ready explanation for the entrepreneurial propensities of this monastic order. (See, e.g., Brooke [1964, p. 69] and also a personal communication to me from Constance Berman. Ovitt [1987, esp. pp. 142–47] suggests that this may all have been part of the twelfth-century monastic drive to reduce or eliminate manual labor in order to maximize the time available for the less onerous religious labors—a conclusion with which Bloch [1935, p. 553] concurs.) But the evidence suggests strongly that avid entrepreneurs they were. They accumulated vast tracts of land; the sizes of their domesticated animal flocks were enormous by the standards of the time; their investment rates were remarkable; they sought to exercise monopoly power, being known, after the erection of a water mill, to seek legal intervention to prevent nearby residents from continuing to use their animal-powered facilities (Gimpel 1976, pp. 15–16); they were fierce in their rivalrous behavior and drive for expansion, in the process not sparing other religious bodies—not even other Cistercian houses. There is a "record of pastoral expansionism and monopolies over access established by the wealthiest Cistercian houses . . . at the expense of smaller abbeys and convents . . . effectively pushing out all other religious houses as competitors" (Berman 1986, p. 112).

As with early capitalists, the asceticism of the monks, by keeping down the proportion of the monastery's output that was consumed, helped to provide the resources for levels of investment extraordinary for the period (pp. 40, 83). The rules of the game appear to have offered substantial economic rewards to exercise of Cistercian entrepreneurship. The order obtained relatively few large gifts, but instead frequently received support from the laity and from the church establishment in the form of exemptions from road and river tolls and from payment of the tithe. This obviously increased the *marginal* yield of investment, innovation, and expenditure of effort, and the evidence suggests the diligence of the order in pursuing the resulting opportunities. Their mills, their extensive lands, and their large flocks are reported to have brought scale economies and extraordinary financial returns (chap. 4). Puritanical, at least in earlier years, in their self-proclaimed adherence to simplicity in personal lifestyle while engaged in dedicated pursuit of wealth, they may perhaps represent an early manifestation of elements of "the Protestant ethic." But whatever their motive, the reported Cistercian record of promotion of technological progress is in diametric contrast to that of the Roman empire.

E. Fourteenth Century

The fourteenth century brought with it a considerable increase in military activity, notably the Hundred Years' War between France and England. Payoffs, surely, must have tilted to favor more than before inventions designed for military purposes. Cannons appeared as siege devices and armor was made heavier. More imaginative war devices were proposed: a windmill-propelled war wagon, a multibarreled machine gun, and a diving suit to permit underwater attacks on ships. A pervasive business enterprise of this unhappy century of war was the company of mercenary troops—the *condottiere*—who roamed Europe, supported the side that could offer the most attractive terms, and in lulls between fighting, when unemployment threatened, wandered about thinking up military enterprises of their own, at the expense of the general public (Gimpel 1976, chap. 9; see also McNeill 1969, pp. 33–39). Clearly, the rules of the game—the system of entrepreneurial rewards—had changed, to the disadvantage of productive entrepreneurship.

F. Early Rent Seeking

Unproductive entrepreneurship can also take less violent forms, usually involving various types of rent seeking, the type of (possibly) unproductive entrepreneurship that seems most relevant today. Enterprising use of the legal system for rent-seeking purposes has a long history. There are, for example, records of the use of litigation in the twelfth century in which the proprietor of a water-driven mill sought and won a prohibition of use in the vicinity of mills driven by animal or human power (Gimpel 1976, pp. 25–26). In another case, the operators of two dams, one upstream of the other, sued one another repeatedly at least from the second half of the thirteenth century until the beginning of the fifteenth, when the downstream dam finally succeeded in driving the other out of business as the latter ran out of money to pay the court fees (pp. 17–20).

In the upper strata of society, rent seeking also gradually replaced military activity as a prime source of wealth and power. This transition can perhaps be ascribed to the triumph of the monarchies and the consequent imposition of law and order. Rent-seeking entrepreneurship then took a variety of forms, notably the quest for grants of land and patents of monopoly from the monarch. Such activities can, of course, sometimes prove to contribute to production, as when the recipient of land given by the monarch uses it more efficiently than the previous owner did. But there seems to have been nothing in the structure of the land-granting process that ensured even a tendency toward transfer to more productive proprietors, nor was the individual who sought such grants likely to use as an argument in favor of his suit the claim that he was likely to be the more productive user (in terms of, say, the expected net value of its agricultural output).

Military forms of entrepreneurship may have experienced a renaissance in England in the seventeenth century with the revolt against Charles I. How that may have changed the structure of rewards to entrepreneurial activity is suggested by Hobsbawm (1969), who claims that at the end of the seventeenth century the most affluent merchants earned perhaps three times as much as the richest "master manufacturers."[8] But, he reports, the wealthiest noble families probably had incomes more than 10 times as large as those of the rich merchants. The point in this is that those noble families, according to Hobsbawm, were no holdovers from an ancient feudal aristocracy; they were, rather, the heirs of the Roundheads (the supporters of the parliamentary, or puritan, party) in the then-recent Civil War (pp. 30–32). On this view, once again, military activity would seem to have become the entrepreneur's most promising recourse.

But other historians take a rather different view of the matter. Studies reported in Thirsk (1954) indicate that ultimately there was little redistribution of property as the result of the Civil War and the restoration. Rather it is noted that in this period the "patrician élites depended for their political power and economic prosperity on royal charters and monopolies rather than on talent and entrepreneurial initiative" (Stone 1985, p. 45). In this interpretation of the matter, it was rent seeking, not military activity, that remained the prime source of wealth under the restoration.

By the time the eighteenth-century industrial revolution ("the" industrial revolution) arrived, matters had changed once again. According to Ashton (1948, pp. 9–10), grants of monopoly were in good part "swept away" by the Monopolies Act of 1624, and, we are told by Adam Smith (1776), by the end of the eighteenth century they were rarer in England than in any other country. Though industrial activity continued to be considered somewhat degrading in places in which industry flourished, notably in England during the industrial revolution there was probably a difference in degree. Thus Lefebvre (1947, p. 14) reports that "at its upper level the [French] nobility . . . were envious of the English lords who enriched themselves in bourgeois

---

[8] The evidence indicates that the wealth of affluent families in Great Britain continues to be derived preponderantly from commerce rather than from industry. This contrasts with the record for the United States, where the reverse appears to be true (see Rubinstein 1980, pp. 22–23, 59–60).

ENTREPRENEURSHIP   909

ways," while in France "the noble 'derogated' or fell into the common
mass if [like Mirabeau] he followed a business or profession" (p. 11).
(See, however, Schama [1989], who tells us that "even a cursory examination of the eighteenth-century French economy . . . reveals the
nobility deeply involved in finance, business and industry—certainly
as much as their British counterparts. . . . In 1765 a royal edict
officially removed the last formal obstacles to their participation in
trade and industry" [p. 118].) In England, primogeniture, by forcing
younger sons of noble families to resort to commerce and industry,
apparently was imparting respectability to these activities to a degree
that, while rather limited, may have rarely been paralleled before.

The central point of all the preceding discussion seems clear—
perhaps, in retrospect, self-evident. If entrepreneurship is the imaginative pursuit of position, with limited concern about the means
used to achieve the purpose, then we can expect changes in the structure of rewards to modify the nature of the entrepreneur's activities,
sometimes drastically. The rules of the game can then be a critical
influence helping to determine whether entrepreneurship will be allocated predominantly to activities that are productive or unproductive and even destructive.

IV. Does the Allocation between Productive and Unproductive Entrepreneurship Matter Much?

We come now to the third proposition of this article.

PROPOSITION 3. The allocation of entrepreneurship between productive and unproductive activities, though by no means the only
pertinent influence, can have a profound effect on the innovativeness
of the economy and the degree of dissemination of its technological
discoveries.

It is hard to believe that a system of payoffs that moves entrepreneurship in unproductive directions is not a substantial impediment
to industrial innovation and growth in productivity. Still, history permits no test of this proposition through a set of anything resembling
controlled experiments, since other influences *did*, undoubtedly, also
play important roles, as the proposition recognizes. One can only note
what appears to be a remarkable correlation between the degree to
which an economy rewarded productive entrepreneurship and the
vigor shown in that economy's innovation record.

Historians tell us of several industrial "near revolutions" that occurred before *the* industrial revolution of the eighteenth century that
are highly suggestive for our purposes (Braudel [1986, 3:542–56];
for a more skeptical view, see Coleman [1956]). We are told that two

of the incipient revolutions never went anywhere, while two of them were rather successful in their fashion. I shall report conclusions of some leading historians on these episodes, but it should be recognized by the reader that many of the views summarized here have been disputed in the historical literature, at least to some degree.

A.   *Rome and Hellenistic Egypt*

My earlier discussion cited ancient Rome and its empire as a case in which the rules did not favor productive entrepreneurship. Let us compare this with the evidence on the vigor of innovative activity in that society. The museum at Alexandria was the center of technological innovation in the Roman empire. By the first century B.C., that city knew of virtually every form of machine gearing that is used today, including a working steam engine. But these seem to have been used only to make what amounted to elaborate toys. The steam engine was used only to open and close the doors of a temple.

The Romans also had the water mill. This may well have been the most critical pre-eighteenth-century industrial invention because (outside the use of sails in transportation by water) it provided the first significant source of power other than human and animal labor: "it was able to produce an amount of concentrated energy beyond any other resource of antiquity" (Forbes 1955, 2:90). As steam did in more recent centuries, it offered the prospect of providing the basis for a leap in productivity in the Roman economy, as apparently it actually did during the eleventh, twelfth, and thirteenth centuries in Europe. Yet Finley (1965, pp. 35–36), citing White (1962), reports that "though it was invented in the first century B.C., is was not until the third century A.D. that we find evidence of much use, and not until the fifth and sixth of general use. It is also a fact that we have no evidence at all of its application to other industries [i.e., other than grinding of grain] until the very end of the fourth century, and then no more than one solitary and possibly suspect reference . . . to a marble-slicing machine near Trier."

Unfortunately, evidence of Roman technical stagnation is only spotty, and, further, some historians suggest that the historical reports give inadequate weight to the Roman preoccupation with agricultural improvement relative to improvement in commerce or manufacture. Still, the following quotation seems to summarize the weight of opinion: "Historians have long been puzzled as to why the landlords of the Middle Ages proved so much more enterprising than the landlords of the Roman Empire, although the latter, by and large, were much better educated, had much better opportunities for making technical and scientific discoveries if they had wished to do so"

(Brooke 1964, p. 88). It seems at least plausible that some part of the explanation is to be found in the ancient world's rules of the game, which encouraged the pursuit of wealth but severely discouraged its pursuit through the exercise of productive entrepreneurship.[9]

B. *Medieval China*

The spate of inventions that occurred in ancient China (before it was conquered by the barbarian Yuan dynasty in 1280) constituted one of the earliest potential revolutions in industry. Among the many Chinese technological contributions, one can list paper, (perhaps) the compass, waterwheels, sophisticated water clocks, and, of course, gunpowder. Yet despite the apparent prosperity of the Sung period (960–1270) (see, e.g., Liu and Golas 1969), at least some historians suggest that none of this spate of inventions led to a flowering of *industry*[10] as distinguished from commerce and some degree of general prosperity. And in China too, as we have seen, the rules did not favor productive entrepreneurship. Balazs (1964, p. 53) concludes that

> what was chiefly lacking in China for the further development of capitalism was not mechanical skill or scientific aptitude, nor a sufficient accumulation of wealth, but scope for individual enterprise. There was no individual freedom and no security for private enterprise, no legal foundation for rights other than those of the state, no alternative investment other than landed property, no guarantee against being penalized by arbitrary exactions from officials or against intervention by the state. But perhaps the supreme inhibiting

[9] It has been suggested by historians (see, e.g., Bloch 1935, p. 547) that an abundance of slaves played a key role in Roman failure to use the water mill widely. However, this must imply that the Romans were not efficient wealth seekers. As the cliometric literature has made clear, the cost of maintaining a slave is not low and certainly is not zero, and slaves are apt not to be efficient and dedicated workers. Thus if it had been efficient to replace human or animal power by the inanimate power of the waterways, failure to do so would have cut into the wealth of the slaveholder, in effect saddling him with the feeding of unproductive persons or keeping the slaves who turned the mills from other, more lucrative, occupations. Perhaps Roman landowners *were* fairly unsophisticated in the management of their estates, as Finley (1985, pp. 108–16) suggests, and, if so, there may be some substance to the hypothesis that slavery goes far to account for the failure of water mills to spread in the Roman economy.

[10] Also, as in Rome, none of this was associated with the emergence of a systematic body of science involving coherent theoretical structure and the systematic testing of hypotheses on the basis of experiment or empirical observation. Here, too, the thirteenth-century work of Bishop Grosseteste, William of Henley, and Roger Bacon was an early step toward that unique historical phenomenon—the emergence of a systematic body of science in the West in, say, the sixteenth century (see Needham 1956).

factor was the overwhelming prestige of the state bureaucracy, which maimed from the start any attempt of the
bourgeoisie to be different, to become aware of themselves
as a class and fight for an autonomous position in society.
Free enterprise, ready and proud to take risks, is therefore
quite exceptional and abnormal in Chinese economic history.

C.   Slow Growth in the "Dark Ages"

An era noted for its slow growth occurred between the death of
Charlemagne (814) and the end of the tenth century. Even this period
was not without its economic advances, which developed slowly, including the beginnings of the agricultural improvements that attended the introduction of the horseshoe, harness, and stirrup, the
heavy plow, and the substitution of horsepower for oxen, which may
have played a role in enabling peasants to move to more populous
villages further from their fields (see White 1962, p. 39 ff.). But, still,
it was probably a period of significantly slower growth than the industrial revolution of the eleventh–thirteenth centuries (Gimpel 1976),
about which more will be said presently. We have already seen that
this was a period in which military violence was a prime outlet for
entrepreneurial activity. While this can hardly pretend to be *the* explanation of the relative stagnation of the era, it is hard to believe that it
was totally unimportant.

D.   The "High Middle Ages"

A good deal has already been said about the successful industrial
revolution (and the accompanying commercial revolution sparked by
inventions such as double-entry bookkeeping and bills of exchange
[de Roover 1953]) of the late Middle Ages, whose two-century duration makes it as long-lived as our own (see Carus-Wilson 1941; White
1962; Gimpel 1976).

   Perhaps the hallmark of this industrial revolution was that remarkable source of productive power, the water mills, that covered the
countryside in the south of England and crowded the banks of the
Seine in Paris (see, e.g., Gimpel 1976, pp. 3–6; Berman 1986, pp. 81–
89). The mills were not only simple grain-grinding devices but accomplished an astonishing variety of tasks and involved an impressive
variety of mechanical devices and sophisticated gear arrangements.
They crushed olives, ground mash for beer production, crushed cloth
for papermaking, sawed lumber, hammered metal and woolens (as
part of the "fulling" process—the cleansing, scouring, and pressing of

woven woolen goods to make them stronger and to bring the threads closer together), milled coins, polished armor, and operated the bellows of blast furnaces. Their mechanisms entailed many forms of ingenuity. Gears were used to translate the vertical circular motion of the efficient form of the waterwheel into the horizontal circular motion of the millstone. The cam (a piece attached, say, to the axle of the waterwheel, protruding from the axle at right angles to its axis of rotation) served to lift a hammer and to drop it repeatedly and automatically (it was apparently known in antiquity, but may not have been used with waterwheels). A crank handle extending from the end of the axle transformed the circular motion of the wheel into the back and forth (reciprocating) motion required for sawing or the operation of bellows. The most sophisticated product of all this mechanical skill and knowledge was the mechanical clock, which appeared toward the end of the thirteenth century. As White (1962, p. 129) sums up the matter, "the four centuries following Leonardo, that is, until electrical energy demanded a supplementary set of devices, were less technologically engaged in discovering basic principles than in elaborating and refining those established during the four centuries before Leonardo."[11]

In a period in which agriculture probably occupied some 90 percent of the population, the expansion of industry in the twelfth and thirteenth centuries could not by itself have created a major upheaval in living standards.[12] Moreover, it has been deduced from what little we know of European gross domestic product per capita at the beginning of the eighteenth century that its average growth in the preceding six or seven centuries must have been very modest, since if the poverty of that later time had represented substantial growth from

[11] As was already noted, science and scientific method also began to make an appearance with contributions such as those of Bishop Grosseteste and Roger Bacon. Walter of Henley championed controlled experiments and observation over recourse to the opinions of ancient authorities and made a clear distinction between economic and engineering efficiency in discussing the advisability of substituting horses for oxen. Bacon displayed remarkable foresight when he wrote, circa 1260, that "machines may be made by which the largest ships, with only one man steering them, will be moved faster than if they were filled with rowers; wagons may be built which will move with incredible speed and without the aid of beasts; flying machines can be constructed in which a man . . . may beat the air with wings like a bird . . . machines will make it possible to go to the bottom of seas and rivers" (as quoted in White [1962, p. 134]).

[12] But then, much the same was true of the first half century of "our" industrial revolution, which, until the coming of the railways, was centered on the production of cotton that perhaps constituted only some 7–8 percent of national output (Hobsbawm 1969, p. 68). Initially, the eighteenth-century industrial revolution was a very minor affair, at least in terms of investment levels and contributions to output and to growth in productivity (perhaps 0.3 percent per year) (see Landes 1969, pp. 64–65; Feinstein 1978, pp. 40–41; Williamson 1984).

eleventh-century living standards, much of the earlier population would surely have been condemned to starvation.

Still, the industrial activity of the twelfth and thirteenth centuries was very substantial. By the beginning of the fourteenth century, according to Gimpel (1976), 68 mills were in operation on less than one mile of the banks of the Seine in Paris, and these were supplemented by floating mills anchored to the Grand Pont. The activity in metallurgy was also considerable—sufficient to denude much of Europe of its forests and to produce a rise in the price of wood that forced recourse to coal (Nef [1934]; other historians assert that this did not occur to any substantial degree until the fifteenth or sixteenth century, with some question even about those dates; see, e.g., Coleman [1975, pp. 42–43]). In sum, the industrial revolution of the twelfth and thirteenth centuries was a surprisingly robust affair, and it is surely plausible that improved rewards to industrial activity had something to do with its vigor.

E. The Fourteenth-Century Retreat

The end of all this period of buoyant activity in the fourteenth century (see the classic revisionist piece by Lopez [1969] as well as Gimpel [1976, chap. 9]) has a variety of explanations, many of them having no connection with entrepreneurship. For one thing, it has been deduced by study of the glaciers that average temperatures dropped, possibly reducing the yield of crops (though recent studies indicate that the historical relation between climatic changes and crop yields is at best ambiguous) and creating other hardships. The plague returned and decimated much of the population. In addition to these disasters of nature, there were at least two pertinent developments of human origin. First, the church clamped down on new ideas and other manifestations of freedom. Roger Bacon himself was put under constraint.[13] The period during which new ways of thinking brought rewards and status was apparently ended. Second, the fourteenth century included the first half of the devastating Hundred Years' War. It is implausible that the associated renewal of rewards to military enterprise played no part in the economic slowdown.

F. Remark on "Our" Industrial Revolution

It need hardly be added, in conclusion, that *the* industrial revolution that began in the eighteenth century and continues today has brought

---

[13] The restraints imposed by the church had another curious effect: they apparently made bathing unfashionable for centuries. Before then, bathhouses had been popular as centers for social and, perhaps, sexual activity; but by requiring separation of the sexes and otherwise limiting the pleasures of cleanliness, the church undermined the inducements for such sanitary activities (see Gimpel 1976, pp. 87–92).

to the industrialist and the businessperson generally a degree of wealth and a respect probably unprecedented in human history. The fact that this period yielded an explosion of output at least equally unprecedented is undoubtedly attributable to a myriad of causes that can probably never be discovered fully and whose roles can never be disentangled. Yet the continued association of output growth with high financial and respectability rewards to productive entrepreneurship is surely suggestive, even if it can hardly be taken to be conclusive evidence for proposition 3, which asserts that the allocation of entrepreneurship *does* really matter for the vigor and innovativeness of an economy.

V. On Unproductive Avenues for Today's Entrepreneur: A Delicate Balance

Today, unproductive entrepreneurship takes many forms. Rent seeking, often via activities such as litigation and takeovers, and tax evasion and avoidance efforts seem now to constitute the prime threat to productive entrepreneurship. The spectacular fortunes amassed by the "arbitrageurs" revealed by the scandals of the mid-1980s were *sometimes*, surely, the reward of unproductive, occasionally illegal but entrepreneurial acts. Corporate executives devote much of their time and energy to legal suit and countersuit, and litigation is used to blunt or prevent excessive vigor in competition by rivals. Huge awards by the courts, sometimes amounting to billions of dollars, can bring prosperity to the victor and threaten the loser with insolvency. When this happens, it must become tempting for the entrepreneur to select his closest advisers from the lawyers rather than the engineers. It induces the entrepreneur to spend literally hundreds of millions of dollars for a single legal battle. It tempts that entrepreneur to be the first to sue others before those others can sue him. (For an illuminating quantification of some of the social costs of one widely publicized legal battle between two firms, see Summers and Cutler [1988].)

Similarly, taxes can serve to redirect entrepreneurial effort. As Lindbeck (1987, p. 15) has observed, "the problem with high-tax societies is not that it is impossible to become rich there, but that it is difficult to do so by way of productive effort in the ordinary production system." He cites as examples of the resulting reallocation of entrepreneurship " 'smart' speculative financial transactions without much (if any) contribution to the productive capacity of the economy" (p. 15) as well as "illegal 'business areas' such as drug dealing" (p. 25).

In citing such activities, I do not mean to imply either that rent-seeking activity has been expanding in recent decades or that takeover bids or private antitrust suits are always or even preponderantly unproductive. Rather, I am only suggesting where current rent-seeking activities are likely to be found, that is, where policy designers should look if they intend to divert entrepreneurial talents into more productive channels.

The main point here is to note that threats of takeovers are sometimes used as a means to extract "greenmail" and that recourse to the courts as a means to seek to preserve rents through legally imposed impediments to competition does indeed occur, and to suggest that it is no rare phenomenon. This does, then, become an attraction for entrepreneurial talent whose efforts are thereby channeled into unproductive directions. Yet, to the extent that takeovers discipline inefficient managements and that antitrust intervention sometimes is legitimate and sometimes contributes to productivity, it would seem that it will not be easy to change the rules in a way that discourages allocation of entrepreneurial effort into such activities, without at the same time undermining the legitimate role of these institutions. Some promising proposals have been offered, but this is not a suitable place for their systematic examination. However, a few examples will be reported in the following section.

VI. Changes in the Rules and Changes in Entrepreneurial Goals

A central point in this discussion is the contention that if reallocation of entrepreneurial effort is adopted as an objective of society, it is far more easily achieved through changes in the rules that determine relative rewards than via modification of the goals of the entrepreneurs and prospective entrepreneurs themselves. I have even gone so far as to use the same terms to characterize those goals in the very different eras and cultures referred to in the discussion. But it would be ridiculous to imply that the attitudes of a wealth-seeking senator in Rome, a Sung dynasty mandarin, and an American industrialist of the late nineteenth century were all virtually identical. Still, the evidence suggests that they had more in common than might have been expected by the casual observer. However, even if it were to transpire that they really diverged very substantially, that would be of little use to the designer of policy who does not have centuries at his or her disposal and who is notoriously ineffective in engendering profound changes in cultural influences or in the structure of preferences. It is for this reason that I have chosen to take entrepreneurial goals as given and to emphasize modification in the structure of the rewards to different activities as the more promising line of investigation.

This suggests that it is necessary to consider the process by which those rules are modified in practice, but I believe that answers to even this more restricted question are largely beyond the powers of the historians, the sociologists, and the anthropologists into whose domains it falls. One need only review the disputatious literature on the influences that led to the revival of trade toward the end of the early Middle Ages to see how far we still are from anything resembling firm answers. Exogenous influences such as foreign invasions or unexpected climatic changes can clearly play a part, as can developments within the economy. But the more interesting observation for our purposes is the fact that it is easy to think of measures that *can* change these rules quickly and profoundly.[14]

For example, the restrictions on royal grants of monopolies imposed by Parliament in the Statute of Monopolies are said to have reduced substantially the opportunities for rent seeking in seventeenth- and eighteenth-century England and may have moved reluctant entrepreneurs to redirect their efforts toward agricultural improvement and industry. Even if it did not succeed to any substantial extent in reallocation of the efforts of an unchanged body of entrepreneurs from one of those types of activity to the other, if it increased failure rates among the rent seekers while not impeding others who happened to prefer productive pursuits, the result might have been the same. Similarly, tax rules can be used to rechannel entrepreneurial effort. It has, for instance, been proposed that takeover activity would be reoriented substantially in directions that contribute to productivity rather than impeding it by a "revenue-neutral" modification in capital gains taxes that increases rates sharply on assets held for short periods and decreases them considerably for assets held, say, for 2 years or more. A change in the rules that requires a plaintiff firm in a private antitrust suit to bear both parties' legal costs if the defendants are found not to be guilty (as is done in other countries) promises to reduce the frequency with which such lawsuits are used in an attempt to hamper effective competition.

As has already been said, this is hardly the place for an extensive discussion of the design of rational policy in the arena under consideration. The objective of the preceding brief discussion, rather, has been to suggest that there are identifiable means by which the rules of the game can be changed effectively and to illustrate these means concretely, though hardly attempting to offer any generalizations about their character. Certainly, the few illustrations that have just been offered should serve to confirm that there exist (in principle)

---

[14] Of course, that still leaves open the critical metaquestion, How does one go about changing the society's value system so that it will *want* to change the rules? But that is not the issue with which I am grappling here, since I see no basis on which the economist can argue that society *ought* to change its values. Rather, I am positing a society whose values lead it to favor productivity growth and am examining which instruments promise to be most effective in helping it to pursue this goal.

testable means that promise to induce entrepreneurs to shift their attentions in productive directions, *without any major change in their ultimate goals*. The testability of such hypotheses indicates that the discussion is no tissue of tautologies, and the absence of references to the allocability of entrepreneurship turned up in extensive search of the literature on the entrepreneur suggests that it was not entirely self-evident.

VII. Concluding Comment

There is obviously a good deal more to be said about the subject; however, enough material has been presented to indicate that a minor expansion of Schumpeter's theoretical model to encompass the determinants of the *allocation* of entrepreneurship among its competing uses can enrich the model considerably and that the hypotheses that have been associated with the model's extension here are not without substance, even if none of the material approaches anything that constitutes a formal test of a hypothesis, much less a rigorous "proof." It is also easy to confirm that each of the hypotheses that have been discussed clearly yields some policy implications.

Thus clear guidance for policy is provided by the main hypothesis (propositions 1–3) that the rules of the game that specify the relative payoffs to different entrepreneurial activities play a key role in determining whether entrepreneurship will be allocated in productive or unproductive directions and that this can significantly affect the vigor of the economy's productivity growth. After all, the prevailing laws and legal procedures of an economy are prime determinants of the profitability of activities such as rent seeking via the litigative process. Steps such as deregulation of the airlines or more rational antitrust rules can do a good deal here.

A last example can, perhaps, nail down the point. The fact that Japan has far fewer lawyers relative to population and far fewer lawsuits on economic issues is often cited as a distinct advantage to the Japanese economy, since it reduces at least in part the quantity of resources devoted to rent seeking. The difference is often ascribed to national character that is said to have a cultural aversion to litigiousness. This may all be very true. But closer inspection reveals that there are also other influences. While in the United States legal institutions such as trebled damages provide a rich incentive for one firm to sue another on the claim that the latter violated the antitrust laws, in Japan the arrangements are very different. In that country any firm undertaking to sue another on antitrust grounds must first apply for permission from the Japan Fair Trade Commission. But such permission is rarely given, and, once denied, there is no legal avenue for appeal.

The overall moral, then, is that we do not have to wait patiently for slow cultural change in order to find measures to redirect the flow of entrepreneurial activity toward more productive goals. As in the illustration of the Japanese just cited, it may be possible to change the rules in ways that help to offset undesired institutional influences or that supplement other influences that are taken to work in beneficial directions.

References

Abramovitz, Moses. *Thinking about Growth, and Other Essays of Economic Growth and Welfare.* New York: Cambridge Univ. Press, 1989.

Ashton, Thomas S. *The Industrial Revolution, 1760–1830.* London: Oxford Univ. Press, 1948.

Balazs, Etienne. *Chinese Civilization and Bureaucracy: Variations on a Theme.* New Haven, Conn.: Yale Univ. Press, 1964.

Berman, Constance H. "Medieval Agriculture, the Southern French Countryside, and the Early Cistercians: A Study of Forty-three Monasteries." *Trans. American Philosophical Soc.* 76, pt. 5 (1986).

Bloch, Marc. "Avènement et conquêtes du moulin a eau." *Annales d'Histoire Économique et Sociale* 7 (November 1935): 538–63.

Braudel, Fernand. *Civilization and Capitalism, 15th–18th Century.* Vols. 2, 3. New York: Harper and Row, 1986.

Brooke, Christopher N. L. *Europe in the Central Middle Ages, 962–1154.* London: Longman, 1964.

Carus-Wilson, Eleanora M. "An Industrial Revolution of the Thirteenth Century." *Econ. Hist. Rev.* 11, no. 1 (1941): 39–60.

Coleman, Donald C. "Industrial Growth and Industrial Revolutions." *Economica* 23 (February 1956): 1–22.

———. *Industry in Tudor and Stuart England.* London: Macmillan (for Econ. Hist. Soc.), 1975.

Cowdrey, H. E. J. "The Peace and the Truce of God in the Eleventh Century." *Past and Present,* no. 46 (February 1970), pp. 42–67.

Dasgupta, Partha. "Patents, Priority and Imitation or, the Economics of Races and Waiting Games." *Econ. J.* 98 (March 1988): 66–80.

de Roover, Raymond. "The Commercial Revolution of the 13th Century." In *Enterprise and Secular Change: Readings in Economic History,* edited by Frederic C. Lane and Jelle C. Riemersma. London: Allen and Unwin, 1953.

Douglas, David C. *William the Conqueror: The Norman Impact upon England.* Berkeley: Univ. California Press, 1964.

Feinstein, C. H. "Capital Formation in Great Britain." In *The Cambridge Economic History of Europe,* vol. 8, pt. 1, edited by Peter Mathias and M. M. Postan. Cambridge: Cambridge Univ. Press, 1978.

Finley, Moses I. "Technical Innovation and Economic Progress in the Ancient World." *Econ. Hist. Rev.* 18 (August 1965): 29–45.

———. *The Ancient Economy.* 2d ed. London: Hogarth, 1985.

Forbes, Robert J. *Studies in Ancient Technology.* Leiden: Brill, 1955.

Gimpel, Jean. *The Medieval Machine: The Industrial Revolution of the Middle Ages.* New York: Holt, Reinhart and Winston, 1976.

Ho, Ping-Ti. *The Ladder of Success in Imperial China, 1368–1911.* New York: Columbia Univ. Press, 1962.

Hobsbawm, Eric J. *Industry and Empire from 1750 to the Present Day.* Harmondsworth: Penguin, 1969.

Jones, Eric L. *The European Miracle: Environments, Economies, and Geopolitics in the History of Europe and Asia.* Cambridge: Cambridge Univ. Press, 1987.

Landes, David S. *The Unbound Prometheus: Technological Change and Industrial Development in Western Europe from 1750 to the Present.* New York: Cambridge Univ. Press, 1969.

Lefebvre, Georges. *The Coming of the French Revolution, 1789.* Princeton, N.J.: Princeton Univ. Press, 1947.

Lindbeck, Assar. "The Advanced Welfare State." Manuscript. Stockholm: Univ. Stockholm, 1987.

Liu, James T. C., and Golas, Peter J., eds. *Change in Sung China: Innovation or Renovation?* Lexington, Mass.: Heath, 1969.

Lopez, Robert S. "Hard Times and Investment in Culture." In *The Renaissance: A Symposium.* New York: Oxford Univ. Press (for Metropolitan Museum of Art), 1969.

McNeill, William H. *History of Western Civilization.* Rev. ed. Chicago: Univ. Chicago Press, 1969.

Marsh, Robert M. *The Mandarins: The Circulation of Elites in China, 1600–1900.* Glencoe, Ill.: Free Press, 1961.

Milward, Alan S. *The Economic Effects of the Two World Wars on Britain.* London: Macmillan (for Econ. Hist. Soc.), 1970.

Murphy, Kevin M.; Shleifer, Andrei; and Vishny, Robert. "The Allocation of Talent: Implications for Growth." Manuscript. Chicago: Univ. Chicago, 1990.

Needham, Joseph. "Mathematics and Science in China and the West." *Science and Society* 20 (Fall 1956): 320–43.

Nef, John U. "The Progress of Technology and the Growth of Large-Scale Industry in Great Britain, 1540–1640." *Econ. Hist. Rev.* 5 (October 1934): 3–24.

North, Douglass C., and Thomas, Robert Paul. *The Rise of the Western World: A New Economic History.* Cambridge: Cambridge Univ. Press, 1973.

Olson, Mancur. *The Rise and Decline of Nations: Economic Growth, Stagflation, and Social Rigidities.* New Haven, Conn.: Yale Univ. Press, 1982.

Ovitt, George, Jr. *The Restoration of Perfection: Labor and Technology in Medieval Culture.* New Brunswick, N.J.: Rutgers Univ. Press, 1987.

Painter, Sidney. *William Marshal: Knight-Errant, Baron, and Regent of England.* Baltimore: Johns Hopkins Press, 1933.

Robinson, Joan. *The Economics of Imperfect Competition.* London: Macmillan, 1933.

Rosenberg, Nathan, and Birdzell, L. E., Jr. *How the West Grew Rich: The Economic Transformation of the Industrial World.* New York: Basic Books, 1986.

Rubinstein, W. D., ed. *Wealth and the Wealthy in the Modern World.* London: Croom Helm, 1980.

Schama, Simon. *Citizens: A Chronicle of the French Revolution.* New York: Knopf, 1989.

Schumpeter, Joseph A. *The Theory of Economic Development.* Leipzig: Duncker and Humblot, 1912. English ed. Cambridge, Mass.: Harvard Univ. Press, 1934.

ENTREPRENEURSHIP 921

Smith, Adam. *An Inquiry into the Nature and Causes of the Wealth of Nations.* 1776. Reprint. New York: Random House (Modern Library), 1937.

Stone, Lawrence. "The Bourgeois Revolution of Seventeenth-Century England Revisited." *Past and Present,* no. 109 (November 1985), pp. 44–54.

Summers, Lawrence, and Cutler, David. "Texaco and Pennzoil Both Lost Big." *New York Times* (February 14, 1988).

Thirsk, Joan. "The Restoration Land Settlement." *J. Modern Hist.* 26 (December 1954): 315–28.

Veblen, Thorstein. *The Theory of Business Enterprise.* New York: Scribner, 1904.

Veyne, Paul. "Vie de trimalcion." *Annales: Économies, Societés, Civilisations* 16 (March/April 1961): 213–47.

White, Lynn T., Jr. *Medieval Technology and Social Change.* Oxford: Clarendon, 1962.

Williamson, Jeffrey G. "Why Was British Growth So Slow during the Industrial Revolution?" *J. Econ. Hist.* 44 (September 1984): 687–712.

Part II
The Entrepreneur

[4]

THINKING AHEAD

Achievement Motivation Can Be Developed

*In this article David C. McClelland challenges
the thinking behind current programs
to help the poor in depressed areas of our
own country and stimulate economic growth in
underdeveloped countries overseas.
These programs take for granted, he notes,
that it is enough to increase the
opportunities available to the people in
need of help. But often, he insists,
this is not enough. It is necessary to move
in and increase the aspirations for
achievement that the local leaders possess.
He cites recent experiments confirming
the feasibility of such achievement motivation
training. The author is Professor of
Psychology and Chairman of the Department
of Social Relations, Harvard University.*

• THE EDITORS

Americans are giving a good deal of thought, time, and money these days to programs of aid for depressed areas in this country and for underdeveloped nations overseas. For some time now, searching questions have been raised concerning the potential of these programs. If, as often seems to be the case, the recipients of aid lack ambition and motivation, can they really be expected to take full advantage of outside help?

I remember well talking to a very successful American businessman who had lived and worked for 40 years in the Mexican business community. He accepted with enthusiasm my research finding that the need for achievement is an essential ingredient for entrepreneurial success. (See the box on page 8 for an explanation of the achievement motive.) His own experience fully supported it. But then I asked him how he thought some people came to have more desire for achievement than others, and whether he thought this desire could be developed in Mexico. His answer was categorical. Some people had "drive" and some did not, he said. Americans in general had more of it than most peoples; very few Mexicans had it, and furthermore it could not be developed in Mexicans. He had tried for years to develop "drive" in Mexican managers working for him but with little or no success.

I have heard this sentiment expressed over and over again by other Americans about businessmen from various poor countries with which I am familiar — India, Tunisia, Mexico, and others. The universal feeling is that few businessmen from such countries have "it" —the real spirit of enterprise — and what is more, it cannot be developed in them.

But, granted that the need for achievement runs weaker among some people than others, can anything be done about it? Where motivation is weak, can it be made stronger? In short, can men's motives be changed so that aid programs will be more effective? On the basis of evidence recently acquired, I believe the answer in each case is *yes*. I shall discuss this evidence and its implications in this article.

MOTIVATION ESSENTIAL

As past research has made clear, the person with a high need for achievement is more self-confident, enjoys taking carefully calculated risks, researches his environment actively, and is very much interested in concrete measures of how well he is doing. Somewhat surprisingly, in terms of traditional American business and economic theory, he does not seem to be galvanized into activity by the prospect of profit; it is people with low achievement need who require money incentives to make them work harder. The person with a high need works hard anyway, provided there is an opportunity of achieving something. He is interested in money rewards or profits primarily because of the feedback they give him as to how well he is doing. Money is not the incentive to effort but rather the measure

of its success for the real entrepreneur.

Such a finding does raise some interesting questions about what might be called the classical approach to stimulating enterprise or economic growth in underdeveloped countries or in "pockets of poverty" in the United States. Most policy-makers have taken the view that what should be manipulated in such places is the environment — or, more specifically, the opportunities to make money. They have felt it is safe to assume that, on the average, an increase in opportunities will evoke an increased response from potential entrepreneurs who will come forward to take advantage of the openings, just as more investors will come forward if interest rates go up.

Like most assumptions, however, this one holds true only under certain conditions. Above all, it holds only if there is a certain minimum level of achievement need present in the group of people affected. As an illustration, let us take a recent study by H. L. Sheppard:

> Sheppard surveyed the attitudes, actions, and achievement needs of a fairly large sample of unemployed blue-collar workers in Erie, Pennsylvania. He wanted to find out what they did when they were laid off, what they believed about their situation, and how long it took them to find a job. What is of particular interest here is how the small number of men with high achievement needs behaved as compared with those who had low needs.
> The "highs" were much more active in looking for a job. They started looking sooner — practically the day they were laid off rather than a week later after having rested up a little,

as in the case of the "lows." They checked more companies; they were more apt to go out of town to look for work; they looked more often for a *really different* job; they used more techniques for finding a job — checking both at the U.S. Employment Service and at private employment agencies, making direct company applications, checking with friends or relatives, and trying political, religious, and union groups with which they were connected. And not surprisingly, they found a job sooner than those with low achievement needs.

The picture one gets of the "lows" is that many of them spent their time at home living on unemployment insurance, waiting for their old company to rehire them, or for the U.S. Employment Service to turn up a job just like the one they had held, which they could accept with the minimum adjustment in skills or living conditions. In fact, many of them said they would not under any circumstances take a job that meant moving away to another community.[1]

The situation in Erie is analogous to the problem found in the business sphere in many underdeveloped countries: opportunities for business which men with much "git up and go" would find are not exploited by local potential businessmen because they have low needs for achievement.

LIBERALS VS. CONSERVATIVES

Why have policy-makers been so slow to act on this knowledge to invest in programs that would develop people's motives rather than merely their opportunities to work? The answer lies in a curious alliance of "liberals" and "conserva-

[1] See "Psychological factors involved in job seeking behavior of blue collar workers" (mimeographed, Washington, D. C., Upjohn Institute, 1965).

THINKING AHEAD

tives" who have agreed that "character education" of this sort is off the target.

To oversimplify the picture a bit, let us say the liberals take the view that a man or a nation is poor because of adverse circumstances. Poverty involves a vicious cycle — low employment opportunities, low income, low consumption, low investment opportunities, low employment opportunities — which can only be broken by *changing the environment*, i.e., by creating employment opportunities by massive infusions of capital, building institutions like banks and schools, and so on. From this point of view, changing men is really of secondary importance: they will be activated automatically once they see the opportunities available.

The conservative businessman, on the other hand, has always been a little skeptical of this approach. He knows from his own experience that many businessmen and workers fail to take advantage of opportunities available. He knows that a lot of people are "lazy." So why does he not believe in trying to make them less lazy, trying to change their motives? Basically, because he does not think it is possible. He shares the convictions of the businessman described at the beginning of this article.

Thus everyone has taken a dim view of character education — the liberals because they do not think it is necessary, the conservatives because they think it cannot be done. The current confusion about the effectiveness of our foreign aid stems from this very problem.

The liberals point to the tremendous success of Marshall Plan aid in developing the economies of Western Europe. But even they are becoming increasingly upset by the apparent failure of a similar type of aid to underdeveloped countries in recent years. Their response so far has been to conclude that they must not be making massive enough changes in the environment to produce the necessary takeoffs in economic growth. (They overlook the possibility that achievement needs were higher in

THE ACHIEVEMENT MOTIVE

In this article I use the term "achievement motive" in the sense described in my HBR article, "Business Drive and National Achievement" (July-August 1962, p. 99), and my book, *The Achieving Society* (Princeton, D. Van Nostrand Company, Inc., 1961). The achievement motive — or *n* Ach, as it is referred to in technical discussions — is a measurable factor in groups and individuals. Briefly, it is measured by coding an individual's spontaneous thoughts, as in the imaginative stories he tells, for the frequency with which he thinks about competing with a standard of excellence, or doing something better than before. On a broader scale, the popular literature of a country can be used to ascertain the achievement motivation levels of the people among whom the literature is popular. As used here, therefore, the achievement motive is a precise term, much as "relativity" is in physics or "regression" in medicine or mathematics.

Western Europe.) In short, they stick to their position and simply ask for more aid on a longer term basis.

They are not likely to get it, partly because of general discouragement over the past record, and partly because the conservatives can argue with increasing effectiveness that people in poor countries "just don't have the mentality" to make good use of aid.

NEW EXPERIMENTS

Up to a point the conservatives have an irrefutable case. It is not *enough* to change the environment alone. The response of people to such changes is *not* quick or automatic. Many with low achievement needs *will* sit around and do nothing. But suppose the achievement motive is an acquired characteristic which can be developed by certain special training techniques, just the way a language skill can be acquired in adulthood?

If so, the policy consequences would be very great. A way would be opened to making poor people more active in finding and seizing opportunities available to them.

Most contemporary psychological theory takes the position that developing deep-lying drives like the achievement motive in adults is difficult — if not impossible. Freudians have long taught that the basic character structure is laid down before the child enters school, and that from then on one can only "rearrange," so to speak, the way deeper motives express themselves or conflict with each other. Such a "rearrangement" requires a thorough job of reconstructing one's emotions, starting

with early childhood and using a course of psychotherapy that would certainly require years.

American behavior theorists, for the most part, have assumed that what they call social or acquired motives — such as the need for achievement — are based also on very early learning of the connection between behaving, let us say, in an achieving way and satisfying certain basic biological needs like hunger and relief from discomfort. Since biological needs are not so prominent in adulthood, it is presumably difficult to construct new motives based on them.

Some associates and I once shared these preconceptions, on the whole, with other psychologists. Nevertheless, we decided several years ago to go ahead and try to develop the achievement motive in adults. We had a distinct advantage over previous investigators who had been trying to change people by psychotherapeutic methods: we knew exactly what it was that we wanted to change — the measurable need for achievement we called *n* Ach — and we knew a great deal about the particular beliefs and actions it led to.

U.S. Company Program. Our initial idea was simply to take whatever we had learned about the achievement motive and teach it to a group of executives who had reason to want to improve their performance as entrepreneurs. Our pilot experiment was with a large U.S. corporation which sponsored a number of training courses for its executives and was willing to let us try our course as an experimental variation in its regular educa-

THINKING AHEAD

tional program. The sessions lasted only a week and consisted largely of teaching 16 participants (1)
about the achievement motive —
what it was and how research had
shown it to be important for entrepreneurship, and (2) how to think,
talk, act, and perceive the world
like a person with a high need for
achievement.

The 16 participants were carefully matched with other executives from the company of comparable age, length of service with
the company, job type, salary level, and so forth, who had attended
one of the regular executive development courses given by the company. We did a careful follow-up
study two years later to find out
which group of men had done better in the company subsequent to
training. Unfortunately we lost
some of the original participants
in our course through illness or
resignation from the company, but
the 11 remaining had clearly done
better on the average — been promoted faster — than their matched
controls.

In part this appeared to be due
to the fact that those men who
had attended the regular company
course had slowed down somewhat; that is, they were advancing somewhat less rapidly after
the course than they had before,
whereas our participants had continued to forge ahead. So far as
we could tell, the reason the regular group slowed down was that
the company course had stressed
the importance of "not rocking the
boat," of representing the company
image as it was outlined for them
in the course.

The fact remains that the results
were encouraging and taught us
two things:

(1) Not all management training
programs automatically lead to improved executive performance. This
was important to know. There is a
viewpoint in psychology which states
that the positive effects of such
courses are largely due to suggestion,
or to the "power of positive thinking";
and according to this view it would
not be achievement motivation training as such that produced the effect
we secured; any training promoted
as convincingly would work as well.

THINKING AHEAD

Yet the participants in the company course did not do as well, despite the fact that, if anything, it had solider company support — all of which argued against that viewpoint.

(2) Our experiment showed its effects only in comparison with a course that seemed to slow people down. This strongly suggested that we ought to be trying it out in a less achievement-oriented environment if we wanted to find more dramatic effects. To a certain extent we were only "gilding the lily" in trying to make the executives of this high-pressure firm more achievement-oriented.

Overseas Program. Would our program work in an underdeveloped country? If so, would the results be positive enough to encourage U.S. officials to adopt such an approach when providing foreign aid? To answer these questions, we turned next to India, where we were able to give a fairly extensive field test to our training methods, thanks to the cooperation and help of a number of institutions, chief among which were the Carnegie Corporation and the Small Industries Extension Training (SIET) Institute, a Government of India Society located in Hyderabad and initially financed in part by a grant from The Ford Foundation.

It is worth recording, to illustrate the dominant viewpoint guiding U.S. foreign aid policy, that the Agency for International Development at first strongly supported the project but at the last moment reversed its decision because AID's Administrator, David Bell, learned that financing such work, even as a research effort, would be severely criticized by members of Congress. He, his advisers, and his potential Congressional friends and critics seem to have been influenced by the issue as defined above: the liberals (including most economic advisers) would regard direct attempts to change individuals as irrelevant (or of very low priority); the conservatives might regard character as more important for development, but they would feel that it was impossible to "develop character" in any such manner as proposed. AID's decision did, however, put it in the strange position of refus-

ing to support a project aimed specifically at developing the "spirit of enterprise" for fear of Congressional criticism at the very moment that Congress was pressing AID to favor the development of the private sector abroad!

Fortunately, the staff leadership at SIET Institute was willing to give the program a try; also, the Carnegie Corporation was willing to invest risk capital in it. We decided to try to achieve a more ambitious goal this time — to push a whole community into an economic "takeoff" by training a significant number of its business leaders in achievement motivation.

After careful study, a number of small cities were identified throughout India which were economically comparable — that is, they were of about the same size (100,000 population), with comparable percentages of people who were literate, working in industry, and so forth, and with similar rates of development over the past 10 years. Our research plan was to put concentrated motivational training programs in several of these cities, observe the effects on business activities and economic indicators over a number of years, and compare these results with those in cities where businessmen had not been trained.

Kakinada, port city in Andhra Pradesh, on the Bay of Bengal, was chosen for the first series of courses. In four batches of 12 to 15 members each, 52 men from Kakinada traveled 350 miles to Hyderabad during 1964 to participate in a 10-day residential course at SIET Institute. They were for the most part heads of small businesses — bicycle shops, retail stores, small foundries, and fiber exporting — but the groups included also some lawyers, bankers, and politicians.

TRAINING METHODS

I cannot describe in detail the nature of the program in Hyderabad. I shall only outline four main techniques employed in efforts of this kind.

1. *Goal Setting.* A program like that in Hyderabad involves considerable goal setting for the partici-

THINKING AHEAD

pants. For instance, the very fact that the men from Kakinada voluntarily decided to take time off to go some distance to attend the course at some expense to themselves signified that they had to some degree accepted the notion which was the basic goal of the course — namely, that they *could* change, that certain prestigious institutions (Harvard University, the SIET Institute) might have come up with a new technique which would make them better businessmen.

Extensive research on attitude change, psychotherapy, and other types of psychological influence points to the great importance of "prestige suggestion" — creating a strong belief that one can and should change. Hence, starting from the belief in the general possibility of change, a course like that in Hyderabad arranges for the individual to focus on his specific personal plans for change in the next two years. Late in the course he writes out a document describing his specific goals, how he plans to achieve them, what personal or other difficulties he is likely to encounter, how he will feel under various conditions, and so on.

Much of the success of such a training enterprise depends on getting the man to be specific, realistic, and practical in his goal setting, since he often starts out with general statements like "I want to increase production (or sales) by 20%," or "I want to start a new business." The specific goals he sets are then used as a target against which he can evaluate his progress every six months for two years by filling out a report form. Such record keeping is, of course, simply a method of keeping the goal salient or ever in front of the person, at least for two years.

2. *Language of Achievement.* A second major component of the program can be best described as the achievement syndrome. This part deals specifically with having the individual learn to think, talk, act, and perceive others like a person with a high achievement mo-

THINKING AHEAD

tive. The details of coding thoughts or fantasies for measuring achievement needs are taught so that a person can write stories that give him a high achievement score. He learns in a variety of games how to make moderate risks in action that will lead to maximum possibilities of payoff. He learns almost unconsciously how to rethink concrete business problems from his own experience or from case studies of others in terms of the achievement-need categories — i.e., setting achievement goals, searching for means of attaining them, overcoming obstacles, getting expert help, worrying about possible disasters in advance, and so on.

In short, the participant learns to use the language of achievement so that it colors his experience in everyday life. He further learns to distinguish achievement goals from other strivings that activate men which may masquerade as achievement but actually interfere with it — such as the lust for power and the need to maintain social prestige at all costs.

3. *Cognitive Supports.* A third part of the program deals with what might loosely be called cognitive supports. If one conceives of what we are doing as an attempt to introduce a new associative network into the everyday thinking of the course participants, it is obvious that what is new must somehow come to terms with other networks that are already there. Chief among these are one's network of assumptions about: (a) what is reasonable, logical, and scientific; (b) what kind of a person he thinks he is (his self-image); and (c) what is important and valuable in life.

To satisfy the demands of the "what is reasonable" network, the whole scientific basis for believing the achievement motive to be important for entrepreneurial success is presented, including data from many experiments.

Then there is the question of self-concept. A man may well ask: "Am I a person with a high achievement motive? If not, do I want to

be? Do I have other characteristics which make it difficult for me to behave as if achievement is what really counts? What kind of a person am I?" Group and individual sessions are run in which the person tries to get an honest picture of himself, his desires, and what he might reasonably expect to become. In this process, his own psychological test data are fed back to him.

In addition, some of the often unconscious value assumptions of the culture need to be discussed. For example:

In India there are several traditional assumptions that typically interfere with achievement: the stress the Gita and much traditional Hindu thought places on noninvolvement in this world so that too much concern with achievement means one is both selfish and bound to make himself unhappy; the extent to which the interests of various communities are seen as separate and conflicting so that disputes and factions arise; the tendency to exalt mind and spirit over matter to the point that realistic goals may not be set; and others. These value assumptions need to be worked through to make sure that the new achievement-oriented outlook is not endlessly sabotaged and undercut by older well-established associative networks.

4. *Group Supports.* The would-be achiever needs to feel emotionally supported as well as rationally supported in his attempts at self-change. Emotional support is given by the instructors who maintain throughout an accepting, nonmanipulative attitude. The message they attempt to convey by thought, word, and deed is: "Whoever you are, we accept you as worthy of our respect. Whatever you decide you want to be, we will respect your choice — including the possibility that you may decide the achievement motive is not for you." (In fact, several participants in the Indian programs *have* decided it was "not for them.")

Another source of emotional support is the experience of group living — of being involved in a rather disturbing but exciting new experience *together* with other potential leaders. In the case of Kakinada, the participants decided to

continued on page 20

THINKING AHEAD
continued from page 16

maintain their newfound solidarity by creating the Kakinada Entrepreneurs' Association, which is designed to keep their interest in community and self-development alive.

ACTION STIMULATED

What are the effects of the Hyderabad course? It is too soon to know what the long-range results will be, but between six and ten months after training, two thirds of the men had become unusually active in business in some readily observable way; e.g., they had started a new business, expanded their old business, greatly increased profits, or taken active steps to investigate a new product line. Only one third of these men had been unusually active in similar ways in the two years prior to taking the course. In short, the course would appear to have *doubled* the natural rate of unusual entrepreneurial activity in this group.

What are some concrete examples of actions taken that such statistics summarize? The following are representative:

❧ One man who owned a small radio shop decided to start a paint and varnish factory. It has succeeded, and he has opened another radio shop.

❧ A banker decided that he had been too conservative in making commercial loans because typically he had been concerned only about the security for the loan. In effect, this meant that only the wealthy landowners could get loans by putting up land as security, and by and large they did not need loans except for occasional heavy expenditures for weddings and other such ceremonial events.

The banker decided that in addition to security he should take into account the quality of the project and the quality of the man asking for the loan — two obvious criteria, perhaps, to a Western banker, but not much used at that time in Kakinada. As a result his banking business began to flourish — so much so that his superiors offered him better jobs elsewhere, first in Calcutta and then in Delhi. He has now left for Delhi. His loans have already begun to bear fruit for Kakinada in the form of new enterprises started and of a new spirit in the banking business there.

THINKING AHEAD

Many other men have taken small concrete steps to improve their businesses:

• One has decided to go to work daily instead of leaving his shop to his assistant.

• A photographer has ordered a lens-grinding machine so that spectacles can be ground locally.

• One man is arranging to make bicycle stands locally.

• A palmyra fiber exporter is seeking the know-how that will enable him to process his raw material into a finished state locally so he need not sell it so cheaply to the Japanese for processing.

• A wealthy family has started a new sugar mill.

The examples could be multiplied many times over. Whether in the long run all this activity will lead to a significant "growth spurt" for Kakinada as compared with other similar cities remains to be seen. All one can say now is that many more of the businessmen of Kakinada are doing the things that should lead to such a spurt.

PROGRAM IN BOMBAY

What about salaried executives? Does achievement training affect them as it does small business owners and professional men? We have run another pilot experiment in India, this one in Bombay, that helps answer the question. There, 32 salaried executives from a variety of small to large firms took achievement training in January and February of 1963. Two years later a follow-up revealed that, once again, two thirds of the men had become unusually active as compared with 20% to 30% who were quite active before the course. Here the sign of unusual activity shifted from "new business starts" or innovative activities to unusual salary raises, for the most part.

One alumnus of this program has been extraordinarily successful. Thus:

Previously he had been for many years a salaried executive for a large oil company in charge of employee relations for all of India. As he had enough money to live comfortably, he had been thinking of retiring at 47 and moving to England where his son lived. This was before he took the training. Instead of moving he decided rather dramatically, after the program, to resign his job, take his savings, and risk them in the construction business in India.

Because of his excellent standing in the business community he was able to raise over a million dollars in a few months to put up the tallest building in Bombay — to be named, appropriately enough, the Everest Apartments! He is an active, interested, and successful large-scale entrepreneur, already started on his second building. He has put what the banker from Kakinada calls "dead money" to work, supplying a great demand for housing and creating employment for hundreds of workers.

Obviously, no shift in opportunities alone would induce men like this one to become unusually active. Most of them already are well-to-do and see no reason to work harder just to make money. As one traditional moneylender in Kakinada said to me: "Why should I go into business when I can make 2% a month with absolute security on personal loans?" He would not begin to get his return for several years; he would risk not getting it at all; and he probably would not make as much as 24% a year. But the fact is that the man just quoted is now seriously contemplating plans for an industrial estate because his achievement motivation has been aroused — or so he says!

Could it be that we were getting increased rates of entrepreneurial activity after the courses in Bombay because general business conditions in India between 1963 and 1965 were better than they had been in 1961 through 1963? In 1965 we followed up on a number of businessmen who had applied to take achievement motivation training in Bombay in 1963 but who had not taken the program because there wasn't room. The percentage of them who were unusually active by our criteria was roughly the same in the 1963–1965 period as in the 1961–1963 period, namely, around 20% to 30% — just what it had been for our course participants before their achievement training. Our conclusion, therefore, is that an improvement in general business opportunities in 1963–1965 was not responsible for the increased activity of the men who had been specially trained by us.

INFLUENCE OF CLIMATE

Achievement motivation training must, of course, take place in

THINKING AHEAD

a certain psychological or social climate — whether it be national or local. We believe such climatic factors are of tremendous importance, but we have only begun to investigate them. It is widely believed that the general climate of confidence in the American business community has a tremendous impact on the decisions of individual businessmen to expand or contract. In India at present the climate of opinion is not particularly confident; there is not a widespread feeling that the country is expanding and "going places." Newspapers and public speeches do not yield much that can be coded as indicating the existence of a strong climate of achievement.

Will the climate of doubt and pessimism in Kakinada override the generally increased level of achievement needs among local businessmen and discourage them in the long run? We tried to create a climate of community confidence by putting a significant number of them through the training courses, but even this may not be sufficient to withstand the national climate of doubt and discouragement.

Certainly we know the climate at the company level is of crucial importance. For instance:

John Andrews studied two comparable Mexican business firms, one of which was progressive and achievement-oriented, the other of which was traditional and rather authoritarian.[2] The owner-president of the latter ran the business like an old-fashioned Mexican *patrón*, rewarding those who were loyal to him and tending to punish those who stepped out of line or challenged what he had been doing. Tests given some years before the study showed that nearly all the top executives in the progressive firm scored higher in achievement needs than did the executives in the traditional firm.

Furthermore, the men in the latter firm with high achievement needs at the outset had either left it or lost some of their motivation; the climate of the organization had discouraged them. On the other hand, the progressive firm became so interested in

continued on page 178

[2] See "The Achievement Motive in Two Types of Organizations," *Journal of Personality and Social Psychology*, in press.

THINKING AHEAD
continued from page 24

achievement training that it decided to put all of its executives through the course and train them to give the course to their subordinates, who in turn would give it to *their* subordinates, and so on, right on down the line to the foremen and the factory workers. In this way the company tried to create an achievement-oriented climate throughout the whole organization. It is too early to know how effective this move has been, but certainly the company's growth rate has been rapid and accelerating.

TENTATIVE CONCLUSIONS

To return to the policy questions raised at the beginning of this article, the implication of our research findings, though preliminary, seems clear. If a nation is interested in helping the poor, it is often not enough to change opportunities; there are plenty of opportunities around the poor that they are not exploiting because of their low achievement motives. (To emphasize a point made earlier, I use the term "achievement motive" in a technical way — what we call *n* Ach in our research.) It is necessary to move in and increase their needs for achievement. Preliminary studies strongly suggest that this can be done and done fairly economically — not with long-term expensive educational programs taking months or years, but in short intensive courses lasting ten days to two weeks, under optimal conditions.

It also seems clear that large sums of money can be wasted trying to retrain unskilled workers and give them more opportunities if at the same time motivation training is not undertaken so that the individuals will *want* to use their new opportunities or new skills.

This line of reasoning applies specifically to such projects as attempting to upgrade the Negro population economically. Certainly opportunities have to be increased by breaking down discriminatory practices, but we also know from a number of studies that lower class Negroes have very low needs for achievement.[3] There are plenty of historical reasons for this

fact, but they do not change in the least the obvious inference that such Negroes will often not exploit to the limit new opportunities made available to them in the way that was done, for example, by immigrant Jews and Greeks, who had very high achievement motives.

Undoubtedly one of the most important effects of Martin Luther King's efforts to rouse the Negro population is the boost he is giving to a kind of "achievement mystique" for the Negro. He is trying to create a climate of opinion among Negroes which strongly backs the notion that Negroes are "on the move," overcoming obstacles, and accomplishing things. This improvement in the general climate of achievement ought to be supplemented by motivation-training courses for specific groups of Negroes in the working force.

Aid to underdeveloped countries could be strengthened in the same way. Certainly it is necessary to provide grants and loans to create important institutions and new opportunities — industrial complexes, business and technical schools, dams to generate electric power, and so on. But such grants should not be made to most countries without provision at the same time for motivation training of key executives in the locality. This training will make them ready, willing, and eager to exploit the new opportunities provided.

Obviously, such an approach would mean a major shift in our usual policies of providing aid to underdeveloped countries or pockets of poverty in our own country. It would mean policy shifts for which neither Congress nor the administrators of our AID program appear to be ready. Yet enough people are intrigued by the possibilities of this approach to have created a demand for an organization which can supply on a regular basis the kind of motivation training with which we have been experimenting in India. In the classic pattern of the American free enterprise system, such an organization has now come into existence — the Human Resources Development Corporation in Cambridge, Massachusetts.

Research on the achievement motive must and will continue. Our knowledge at present is useful, but very crude from the theoretical point of view. We must discover far more precisely how to influence motivation and use that knowledge for human betterment, how to help the underachiever in school, and how to assist the struggling businessman, the unemployed worker, the mentally sick. Looking farther ahead, even the politically unwise are fair subjects to work on. For there is no theoretical reason why, once we understand the motives of participants in unstable governments such as South Vietnam or the Congo, we could not employ the same educational techniques to create a climate of political stability and enthusiasm for a country's future.

— *David C. McClelland*

[3] See, for example, B. Rosen, "Race, Ethnicity, and the Achievement Syndrome," *American Sociological Review*, February 1959, p. 47.

[5]

PATRICK R. LILES

Who Are the Entrepreneurs?

It's a game not everyone can play, but more people should be aware of this career alternative.

Most American businessmen have at some time in their careers thought about starting their own company. Some have envisioned their own enterprise as an avenue to personal wealth through large capital gains. To them, there is a beautiful formula for financial success: *(1) start a small company, preferably in a glamour industry; (2) generate rapid growth in sales and profits; (3) then sell out either to the public or to some large acquisitive conglomerate.*

Others have seen their own company as an opportunity to do what they really wanted to do: to get close to a sport by developing a ski area, or to reduce a new technology to practical use. Still others have sought an escape from stultifying large-company constraints, politics, or career impasses. In their dreams, their own venture would be a means to gain the top position in a business.

Despite dreams, wishful thinking, and even plans, few people actually take the step of trying to start a company. Why is this? Is there a special breed of man which is particularly inclined to become an entrepreneur? Are there special characteristics or conditions which stimulate entrepreneurial activities?

The basic questions we are asking here are classic ones: Are entrepreneurs born or are they made?

If they can be made, what are the ingredients? I have reached the conclusions that, given a degree of ambition and ability not uncommon to many individuals, certain kinds of experiences and situational conditions — rather than personality or ego — are the major determinants of whether or not an individual becomes an entrepreneur.

If we examine some of the attitudes in the subculture of American businessmen we find that there are significant connotations to starting a company as a career alternative. Almost everyone gets a glow — a tingle — at the idea of being an entrepreneur. To men in their thirties and forties the idea of starting a company means "free enterprise" and "opportunity," as reflected in Horatio Alger stories. In value terms of the younger generation, starting a company is a way to "do your own thing." For such businessmen and for many business school students, starting a successful company is a very attractive idea, yet only rarely do they seem to consider it a serious alternative. When a possible opportunity presents itself, there is somehow too little time to investigate it properly and too little time to determine whether or not the idea really makes sense. Thus, it appears that *most* would-be entrepreneurs stop before they get started. Unfortunately, there is very little information on

Patrick R. Liles is on the faculty of the Graduate School of Business Administration, Harvard University.

people who have had ideas about starting companies but never seriously pursued them.

We might think that we already know a lot about the entrepreneurs themselves — those who actually go ahead and start companies. Yet, do we really? We find that there are people who think of entrepreneurs being formed by school systems and child raising,[1] by rejecting fathers,[2] or by the business environment.[3] However, efforts to measure and predict entrepreneurial potential are, at best, still in the development stages.[4]

Perhaps one of the best broad-based studies on entrepreneurs was carried out by Orvis F. Collins and David G. Moore at Michigan State University in 1964. Using a series of personal interviews and psychological tests, they reached a number of rather unsettling conclusions regarding people who start their own company:

Throughout the preceding analysis, obviously we have been having difficulty deciding whether the entrepreneur is essentially a "reject" of our organizational society who, instead of becoming a hobo, criminal, or professor, makes his adjustment by starting his own business; or whether he is a man who is positively attracted to succeed in it. We have, perhaps without intention, regarded him as a reject.

Entrepreneurs are men who have failed in the traditional and highly structured roles available to them in the society. In this . . . entrepreneurs are not unique. What is unique about them is that they found an outlet for their creativity by making out of an undifferentiated mass of circumstances a creation uniquely their own: a business firm.

The men who travel the entrepreneurial way are, taken on balance, not remarkably likeable people. This, too, is understandable. As any one of them might say in the vernacular of the world of the entrepreneur, "Nice guys don't win."[5]

". . . efforts to predict potential are still in the development stages."

Several small-sample studies at Harvard and MIT have yielded results different from the Collins and Moore study.[6] Entrepreneurs were found not to be failures. Instead "most of the founders had experienced a generally higher than average level of success in their previous employment. Several had established outstanding records of achievement."[7] These entrepreneurs seemed more typical of the successful, hard-charging, young business executive or engineer than a reject figure.[8]

One possible explanation, of course, is that people in Michigan are very different from those in New England. It might be more helpful, however, if we categorized in some detail: (1) the kinds of business which are used in studies of small business fatality rates and in the Collins and Moore study, and (2) the kinds of business which might be started as alternatives to professional management or engineering careers. The survey-type studies are comprehensive in that they essentially look at *all* companies which are started within a particular period of time. This includes a wide range of business ventures: dry cleaners, retail shops, electronics manufacturers, computer software firms, gas stations, and so forth. Each of these is used in the computation of a wide range of statistics about the rise and demise of new companies. There should be no reason to doubt the aggregate figures or the results of in-depth studies made of these situations. The Collins and Moore study looked at 110 manufacturing firms started between 1945 and 1958 in Michigan but made no further distinctions as to the nature of the business, size, or potential.

If we consider kinds of ventures which might be of interest to a professional manager or an engineer, the vast majority of the enterprises started each year (and, therefore, the bulk of those considered in large, broad-based studies) would not be included. A dry cleaning establishment or a small metal fabricating shop is not the basis for the dreams of these people. From their perspective (and therefore the perspective of this article), we should label this subcategory of small business as *marginal firms*.

That leaves us with the task of considering the kinds of venture situations which are potentially attractive career alternatives. The first, which I have labeled the *high-potential venture*, is the company which "is started with the intention that the venture grow rapidly in sales and profits and become a large corporation."[9] In its planning stage the high-potential venture is the extreme of personal economic opportunity, the entrepreneur's big dream: such as Polaroid, Digital Equipment, Scientific Data System, Cartridge Television, Viatron, and so on.

Another type of enterprise, less obvious than the high-potential venture, also holds a strong interest for many would-be entrepreneurs. This type of venture we might call the *attractive small company*. In contrast to the high-potential venture, the attractive small company is not intended to become a large corporation, probably will never have a public market for its stock, and will not be attractive to most venture capital investors. However, in contrast to the marginal firms, attractive small companies can provide salaries of $40,000 to $80,000 per year, perquisites (company car, country club memberships, travel, and so forth) to its owner/managers, and often flexibility in life-style such as working hours, kinds of projects and tasks pursued, or geographical location. In this subcategory we find such businesses as consulting and other service firms and some specialized manufacturers.

Both the high-potential venture and the attractive small company are interesting beyond the scope of the benefits they may provide to their founder/owners. In the high-potential venture we find the genesis of the major corporations of the future and, therefore, the source of a growing number of jobs and other contributions to the economy. The attractive small companies provide less spectacular but stable inputs of a similar nature. Both of these kinds of companies must gain and maintain their position by providing competitive discomfort to the existing corporate giants through innovation, flexibility, and efficiency.

The marginal firms, on the other hand, provide support for their owners/employers but frequently at a lower level than might be obtained by employment if they could or would work elsewhere. However, these people are not likely to seek employment elsewhere because of their difficulties in functioning in larger and more structured organizations.[10]

Without question, some of the businessmen and engineers who start high-potential ventures or attractive small companies *are* compulsive entrepreneurs. They cannot function effectively in a large organization. They must be their own boss and they may have known this all their lives. It may seem as if they could have behaved in no other way. But what about the others who started companies? What about the entrepreneurs who are basically well-adjusted people and who had given little previous thought, if any, to the idea of their own company? How did these people happen to become entrepreneurs although most were already successful in the pursuit of a more conventional career? What factors play a leading role in determining who becomes an entrepreneur? Which factors might be largely fortuitous and which might be controlled by the individual?

A Basic Prerequisite: Achievement Motivation

Not all people are inclined to take on significantly more than they have to. A high-potential venture or an attractive small company is usually recognized as requiring a tremendous amount of determined effort and commitment. These kinds of activities are not attempted unless an individual is willing to expend more effort and energy than would be required in a more conventional career.

People high in achievement motivation are the people who strive to make things happen — in the laboratory, on the production floor, in the sales office, in the classroom.[11] Obviously this factor alone is insufficient to determine who starts companies and who does not. But it is a beginning. People without this kind of orientation are unresponsive to the other influences which might encourage starting a venture. However, people with achievement motivation together with other influencing factors may become entrepreneurs.

Achievement motivation can be developed.[12] It would appear unlikely, however, that someone would try to develop achievement motivation in himself in order to start a high-potential venture or an attractive small company. One would expect that it would take a highly achievement-motivated person to want to start either of these kinds of enterprises in the first place.

A Disqualifying Influence: Social Self-Image

The majority of people trying to do exceptionally well in their careers never seriously consider starting a company. Even among the professional man-agers or career businessmen the number is small. This is not to say that many of these people would not gladly *be* successful enterpreneurs in their own companies. They are unwilling, however, to take what they see as a backward or downward step necessary to achieve that success.

An acquaintance of the author's, a Yale graduate, has described the effect of his college experience on his own thinking about his career:

It all came clear one night when I was arguing and describing how Charlie had not been able to go to college, but instead after working in a restaurant had bought a second-hand dump truck. That's when it dawned on me that *because* I went to college I could *never* buy a second-hand dump truck, not even a brand new one with someone else to drive it. When I ran across an old friend, I could not afford to explain that I was the owner of a dump truck. No, I was "with" the ABC Corporation. Not necessary to explain that they are the largest producers of this and that in the world. I was "with" them, and my friend was "with" someone just like them.

Because of recent increasing sentiments favoring personal independence and relevance, we might expect to find in the future a greater general public acceptance of entrepreneurial activities and, there-fore, to discover less and less of a conflict between this kind of a career and a person's social self-image. In this sense, it may be becoming easier for some-one to decide to strike out on his own than it has been in the past. Perhaps we shall come to the point where becoming an entrepreneur is recog-nized as a socially legitimate, and even attractive, career alternative.

Influence on Entrepreneurial Careers

For the person who has achievement motivation and whose social self-image is not in conflict with starting a company, there are two kinds of con-ditions which become critical: (1) how *ready* he sees himself for undertaking such a venture, and (2) how many *distractions* or *obligations* he sees holding him back.

The reader will note that what an individual does depends upon how he perceives a situation rather than upon what the situation actually is. This is particularly critical in considering a person's readi-

ness or his restraints because there is no way for anyone to make direct, objective measurements of these characteristics. Instead, a personal assess-ment of readiness or restraints is going to be a combination of knowledge, insight, judgment, and personal values.

Readiness

In terms of his decision to initiate a company and to try to run it successfully, a person's own assessment of how ready he is probably is a good approximation of how ready he really is. One would not likely find a runner expecting to run a four-minute mile without having some objectively valid reasons behind those expectations. Similarly, an individual who believes that he is ready to start a company is probably reaching that decision from some background of experience, exposure, special skills, and industry knowledge. This is not to say that some people do not try to initiate businesses when they are totally unprepared. It would imply, however, that in most of such instances the indi-vidual himself knows very well that the odds are against his being able to make a go of it.

It might be useful to think of an individual's readiness in terms of levels of specific and general self-confidence. Specific self-confidence in this context represents an individual's feeling of mastery over the kinds of tasks and problems he would expect to encounter in starting a company and making it successful. General self-confidence would be his feeling of well-being and his universal assur-ance that he can accomplish things.

What people learn through a variety of business and related experience accumulates over time. Most people learn relatively more and learn rela-tively more rapidly early in their careers when much of what they do and see is new to them. And although the relative rate of learning may diminish over time, the cumulative effect is an increasingly competent individual. The evolution of a person's readiness as reflected in his specific self-confidence to master various elements of a venture is depicted graphically in Figure 1.

General self-confidence, which is necessary for someone to want to try something new, is an elusive idea. Most people can identify in their own

FIGURE 1

READINESS TO START A VENTURE

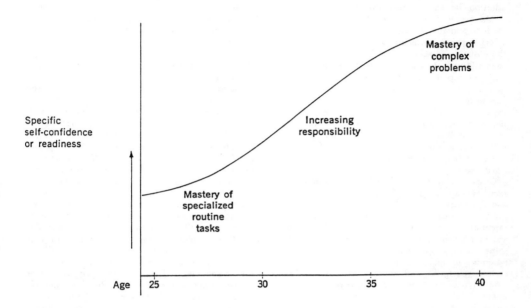

lives those periods when they were confident and up for doing big, new things. They can also recall other times when they were anxious, and uncertain — unwilling to get away from the sure and the known. Given the high degree of uncertainty for most people in starting a company, a high level of general self-confidence is necessary for them to be willing to try.

Restraints

Perhaps the most effective restraint on someone who otherwise might start a company is his continuing success and satisfaction in pursuing his present job. Why should anyone want to change if things are going well? Especially with the pas-

sage of time, increasing seniority for such people means a larger salary, greater responsibilities, and greater benefits. In addition, an individual develops a personal power base within an organization: key knowledge and skills, confidence and loyalty of associates, and so forth, which enables him to assert himself and to be effective. At some point, even in the face of a grave disappointment or disenchantment with the company, it becomes almost prohibitively "expensive" to resign and pursue another career direction.

A would-be entrepreneur's freedom to break away and start a company also becomes hindered by financial and other obligations typical of the U.S. male life-cycle development between the ages of twenty-five and forty years. A man gets married, buys a house, and starts to raise a family. He may immediately incur a sizable mortgage and heavy real estate taxes. With children he acquires the cost burdens for their future education. In addition, he assumes responsibility for his family in the event of his death or disability. These immediate and future costs tie him to a schedule of direct expense payments, a plan for savings, and the costs of insurance.

In addition, the usual pattern is for expenditures on living expenses to rise as a person receives promotions and increases in salary. He now has two cars instead of one, a larger house, and takes more expensive vacations. These costs, closely following if not sometimes overtaking income, as a practical matter are only adjustable upward. And until the children have finished school, it is unusual to find sufficient funds for anything approaching financial flexibility.

Other commitments created by marriage and families may do as much to restrict the freedom and flexibility of would-be entrepreneurs as do his financial obligations. Few women marry with the intention of becoming nurses and housecleaners for absentee husbands. Moreover, personal relationships among people take time, including even the minimum of spoken communication, the ritual of certain courtesies, and the recreational activities people pursue together. And some part of evenings, weekends, and holidays are expected by the family to be devoted to these activities. The family life cycle experience usually creates an increasing time requirement upon the husband until the children go away to school. As small children begin to lose physical dependence upon their mothers, the role of the father increases in both depth and scope. In the wisdom of everyday life, "This is the time when the children need a father."

Two other interesting phenomena frequently appear as part of the male career life cycle. The first is an evolution of values as the family, especially children, enters into his thinking. Their security is related to his career security and, therefore, his career security becomes more important to him. The time spent with wife and children is more than the minimal to satisfy physical or emotional obligations, but it is a part of a change in the importance he places on what he does — a transition from

preoccupation with a career to a realization of new interests in his life. The other aspect, closely related to a change of values, is a change of pace. The drive and physical and emotional energy expended by so many young executives in pursuit of a career do not lend themselves to the pursuit of many other interests. Perceived at the office, Joe at the age of forty is slowing down. Perceived by his wife, Joe is beginning to live. Perceived by himself, Joe is just doing other things — not necessarily enjoying himself more than when he was hotly pursuing his career interests, but enjoying himself in other ways.

For starting a company, an individual's self-perceived *effective capacity* can be derived from a combination of readiness and freedom from restraints and distractions. The results, depicted graphically in Figure 2, show that effective capacity for starting a company typically increases with age between twenty-five and thirty as the individual learns rapidly from his early experiences. As a person grows older, however, this trend is modified and then reversed as the marginal learning experience becomes less, and the influences of successful employment plus family-related interests and obligations are incurred. If we identify a certain level of capacity as being necessary for a person to be able to act, we can define a certain period — a *free choice period* — when the individual sees himself as able to act. During this period the capability, the self-confidence, and the career commitment on balance can be more of an influence than are his economic or emotional commitments and interests in other areas.

Precipitating Events

For some people, the combination of circumstances is such that they never attain sufficient capacity to start a company. They never reach a free choice period. Their other commitments become too large before they reach a point where they could strike out on their own. On the other hand, there probably are thousands and thousands of people who pass through a period when they could choose to start a company (when they have sufficient capabilities and few restraints) but they don't do it. It would appear that most people need

FIGURE 2

THE FREE CHOICE PERIOD FOR THE WOULD-BE ENTREPRENEUR

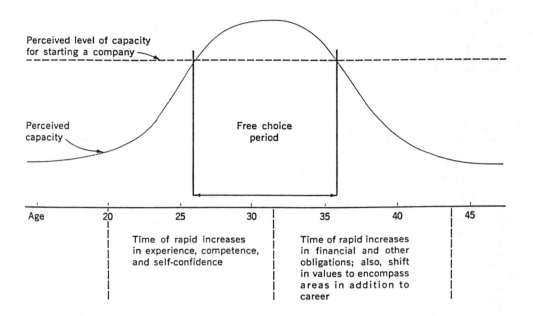

Perceived level of capacity
for starting a company

Perceived capacity

Free choice period

| Age | 20 | 25 | 30 | 35 | 40 | 45 |

Time of rapid increases
in experience, competence,
and self-confidence

Time of rapid increases
in financial and other
obligations; also, shift
in values to encompass
areas in addition to
career

something more: something to help break established ties, to create resolve, and something specific to pursue.

Three additional kinds of conditions appear to be major influences on decisions to start ventures. The first, *deterioration of job satisfaction*, disposes the individual to consider seriously other career alternatives. The second, *identifying a new venture opportunity*, helps to focus upon what might otherwise be a largely undefined possibility. The third, *encouragement to start a company*, helps an individual make what becomes a very subjective decision.

Dissatisfaction. This element — a negative outlook on his present and future job situation — ap-

pears to have a strong influence on the would-be entrepreneur. Relative to his expectations, something disturbs him. A budget for product development is cut back, the right promotion or salary increase does not occur, an addition to his staff is denied. Although entrepreneurs will cite such specific events or unfulfilled expectations as the triggering event which brought them to leave, the reasons usually are more complex. The last straw is but one of a number of disquieting and disappointing incidents which occurred over time and which produced a general feeling of dissatisfaction and, perhaps, resentment.

Job dissatisfaction — for whatever reasons — is not an unusual condition. Changing jobs in most instances is the easiest and more common occurrence. Frequently, it is the opportunity of another job that triggers a critical assessment of one's current employment situation. The transition from one job to another is relatively quick, and its results — it least in the short term — are predictable. In addition, it usually achieves direct use of special skills and knowledge accumulated in prior positions. The unusual thing is when an individual, instead of expressing his objections in the conventional way by changing jobs, elects to start a company.

Identifying a new venture opportunity. Opportunities for new ventures, like most other opportunities, usually emerge over time instead of suddenly appearing. In a technical area, an individual may find or learn of a solution to a particular kind of problem and see the potential for using this approach in areas where it has not been applied before. Or in dealing with his employer's suppliers, he may identify key features of purchased products or services which he believes he can handle better, or at less cost, than others in the business. Or he may discover that there are needs for particular products or services that no one else supplies.

An individual in any part of a business enterprise may see potential opportunities for new ventures related to areas in which he is active. The alternative of starting a company becomes possible only when an individual perceives the basis for a viable enterprise and can see himself playing a major role in it. Whether or not a person interprets a situation as an opportunity is determined to a large degree by his perception of his own ability to take advantage of it.

Encouragement and support. Today when most middle managers or engineers begin to think of leaving their jobs they never *seriously* consider the possibility of starting a company. Unlike the established training programs and junior positions created by major corporations, there are no recognized patterns or channels for getting into one's own business. A few individuals have the special insights from their fathers' having been entrepreneurs, but the majority do not. For many, any substantial encouragement or help in the direction of becoming an entrepreneur is happenstance or luck.

Inputs which expand an individual's thinking about starting a company may range from an encouraging word to assistance with a detailed plan and analysis. It may be offered in a casual way or directed toward achieving some specific objective of the helper. In any case, it frequently plays a significant initial role.

"A wife's reaction to the idea of starting a company usually is a major influence upon how long and how seriously an individual considers starting a company."

One source of support comes from other individuals who share in the feelings of job dissatisfaction and would like to join in pursuing a venture or to become part of a team that undertakes such an effort. These people may represent a logical combination of diverse talents and personalities needed to overcome the problems and inertia of getting the venture started and continuing it as a profitable operation. Moreover, they may be known to each other and therefore represent a degree of certainty about how specific tasks will get done. But at the outset, a key role for these people and for others outside the immediate founder group can be to provide psychological support and encouragement. At the initial stage, momentum for the venture originates from talking it up, proposing different ways to solve the problems of starting, and giving helpful criticism to each other.

A wife's reaction to the idea of starting a company usually is a major influence upon how long and how seriously an individual considers starting a company. Eventually, she will be directly affected. Her husband's happiness, her life-style and the family's financial future are at stake. I have seen wives who have responded with extreme anxiety at the prospect of their husband's starting a company, and I have seen those who have become a key part of the new venture. At either extreme the wife's role is critical.

Another source of support emerges from people to whom the would-be entrepreneur goes for help: potential suppliers, lawyers, bankers, other entrepreneurs, government officials, and so forth. These people can help an individual clarify his own thinking. They can assist in clarifying some of the specific uncertainties associated with starting the venture and can indicate their potential role in providing future information, assistance, or service should the venture be actively pursued. The existence of this kind of readily available help is part of the process of transforming an individual idea into a realistic alternative. If these sources of help are not apparent, then real and imagined problems of getting a venture going may appear insurmountable.

What About Risk?

Up to this point we have not dealt with risk as a factor *per se*. Entrepreneurs, in fact, have been described as people who *like* to take risks. (I believe the entrepreneurs I know would describe such people as fools.) There is more than a little difference between the person who likes risk and the person who finds risk to be a challenge. Risk covers a multitude of areas, all of which impinge in most instances upon entrepreneurial decisions.

Only when an individual considers starting a company as a serious alternative does his perception of risk become a key factor. Risk in this context has three elements: (1) the perceived "odds" of various good and bad events occurring, (2) the perceived consequences of these events, and (3) the perceived seriousness of these consequences. It should be noted that all three aspects of risk are subjective. The individual's assessment of the risk is what influences his decision.

When an individual is in a free choice stage of his career, and when he is considering starting a company as a specific alternative, the perceived risks in a situation will influence whether or not he goes ahead with it. Below are briefly described four critical risk areas.

FINANCIAL RISK

The problem most people would think of first is whether or not they can afford to work with little or no salary for a period of several months to several years while the venture is getting started. This is particularly significant for the successful young executive or engineer who has improved his stand-

ard of living as he received promotions and salary increases. What would happen to the family budget without the monthly paycheck? How many families are willing to take a severe cutback in their living expenditures?

But this is more a question of financial *sacrifice* than financial *risk*. In most new venture operations the individual will put a significant portion of his savings or other financial resources at stake. This money *is* risked and will in all likelihood be lost if the venture fails. The entrepreneur *may* also be required to sign personally on company obligations which far exceed his personal net worth. When such obligations significantly exceed the tangible net worth of the company, the individual exposes himself to the extreme condition of financial risk: personal bankruptcy.

CAREER RISK

A question raised by most would-be entrepreneurs is whether or not they will be able to find a job should they experience a failure in their own company. Obviously many people who are unsuccessful in their own firms *do* get jobs afterward with major corporations. The question, of course, is how difficult is it to get such a job and how will an employer look upon this kind of prospective employee?

FAMILY RISKS

As already mentioned, the requirements of starting a new venture frequently consume the energies, emotions, and time of the entrepreneur. As a result, he has little to give elsewhere, and his other commitments suffer. Entrepreneurs who are married, and especially those with children, expose their families, at best, to the risks of an incomplete family experience and, at worst, to permanent emotional scars from inattention, quarreling, and bitterness.

THE PSYCHIC RISK

An entrepreneurial effort by an individual has special features which subject a person to high psychic risk. First, everyone, including the entrepreneur himself, identifies the venture with one or two men. The company *is* these people. In addition, the magnitude of effort required to start a

"It probably is true that very successful entrepreneurs become men apart. But, at the beginning, when they make the decision to start an entrepreneurial career, they are . . . very much like other ambitious, striving individuals."

venture has given those activities priority over everything else in their lives — family, friends, and other interests. The greater the commitment, the more the identification with the venture is internalized.

If an individual fails, the experience can be shattering. In addressing the causes of a venture's failure, the entrepreneur himself is always one of the reasons. He planned poorly, he executed poorly, he followed through poorly, or in some way he did not allow sufficient margin for the unexpected. If an individual concludes that his failure in a particular effort was because of an inherent incapacity or inadequacy, he has lost his self-confidence. *The* risk to an individual is the risk of losing his self-confidence. The individual without self-confidence loses not only his abilities to function effectively in his career or profession but also loses his

ability to deal effectively in his personal life. Moreover, once begun, such a process gains momentum and tends to whirl into a relentless downward spiral.

Summary and Conclusions

We have examined the entrepreneur who is involved in substantial ventures and have considered what we found in light of traditional thinking that he is a special type or individual — somehow an unusual and uncomman man — a man apart. It probably is true that very successful entrepreneurs *become* men apart. But, at the beginning, when they make the decision to start an entrepreneurial career, they are in most respects very much like many other ambitious, striving individuals. It appears, moreover, that the entrepreneurial interests for those who elect that path are more a function of *external* differences than internal ones — more the result of practical readiness and cost/income constraints than of individual psychology or personality. This is not to suggest that starting a successful company is a game that anyone can play. It is, however, a statement that far more people could become entrepreneurs than ever do, and that the inclination of people to move in this direction could be increased by an increased awareness and recognition of this as a career alternative.

This article is adapted from a forthcoming book, *New Business Ventures and the Entrepreneur,* to be published by Richard D. Irwin, Inc.

1. William F. Whyte and Robert R. Braun, "Heroes, Homework, and Industrial Growth," *Columbia Journal of World Business,* Spring 1966.
2. Manfred F.R. Kets de Vries, "The Entrepreneur as Catalyst of Economic and Cultural Change" (Ph.D. diss., Harvard Graduate School of Business Administration, 1970).
3. Arnold C. Cooper, "Entrepreneurial Environment," *Industrial Research,* September 1970.
4. Michael Palmer, "The Application of Psychological Testing to Entrepreneurial Potential," *California Management Review,* Spring 1971.
5. Orvis F. Collins and David G. Moore with Darab B. Unwalla, *The Enterprising Man* (East Lansing, Mich.: Division of Research, Graduate School of Business Administration, Michigan State University, 1964), pp. 241, 243, 244.

6. Herbert A. Wainer, "The Spin-Off of Technology from Government Sponsored Research Laboratories: Lincoln Laboratory" (M.A. thesis, Massachusetts Institute of Technology, 1965); Paul V. Teplitz, "Spin-Off Enterprises from a Large Government Sponsored Laboratory" (M.A. thesis, Massachusetts Institute of Technology, 1965); and Patrick R. Liles, "The Use of Outside Help in Starting High-Potential Ventures" (DBA diss., Harvard Graduate School of Business Administration, 1970).
7. Liles, "The Use of Outside Help.
8. Walter Guzzardi, Jr., *The Young Executives* (New York: The New American Library, 1964).
9. Liles, "The Use of Outside Help."
10. Collins, Moore, and Unwalla, *Enterprising Man.*
11. David C. McClelland, "Business Drive and National Achievement," *Harvard Business Review,* July-August 1962.
12. David C. McClelland, "Achievement Motivation Can Be Developed," *Harvard Business Review,* November-December 1965.

[6]

GROWTH AND THE SMALL FIRM — AN ALTERNATIVE VIEW

BY

M. J. K. STANWORTH AND J. CURRAN

Introduction

FOR most of the 1960s, the small firm, if discussed at all in academic and business circles, tended to be regarded as a remnant of our industrial past inevitably doomed to disappear in an economy dominated by large-scale public and private enterprise. Since then, however, the Bolton Committee report,[1] various research studies,[2] and a growing disenchantment with the supposed virtues of large-sized economic units,[3] have all helped to refocus attention on the small firm.

One aspect of the small firm which has received some attention is its growth and development. The present paper seeks to offer a new perspective on the social processes involved here, and is backed by results from an in-depth longitudinal research programme carried out in a sample of small manufacturing firms from the Surrey area over a six year period.[4] Other research data, especially from American studies, is used to provide additional empirical support.[5]

The Small Firm: a Definition and Statistical Description

Defining the small firm is in itself no easy task. However, the Bolton Committee saw the small firm as a socio-economic unit with the following characteristics:

[1] See Bolton Committee, *Small Firms — Report of the Committee of Inquiry on Small Firms*, Cmnd. 4811, London: H.M.S.O., November 1971.

[2] See, for example, Wild, Ray and Swan, Kenneth, 'The Small Company, Profitability, Management Resources and Management Techniques', *Journal of Business Policy*, Vol. 3, No. 1, Autumn 1972, pp. 10–21; Deeks, John, 'The Small Firm — Asset or Liability?', *Journal of Management Studies*, Vol. 10, No. 1, February 1973, pp. 25–47; Stanworth, M. J. K. and Curran, J., *Management Motivation in the Smaller Business*, London: Gower Press, 1973.

[3] Instanced in discussions in Mishan, E. J., *The Costs of Economic Growth*, Harmondsworth: Penguin Books, 1969; Schumacher, E. F., *Small is Beautiful, A Study of Economics as if People Mattered*, London: Blond and Briggs, 1973; and in Wild, Ray and Swan, Kenneth, ibid.

[4] See Stanworth, M. J. K. and Curran, J., op. cit., where we have presented data on nine firms. However, our intention in the current article is not to present case material from the book, but rather to mount an argument concerning the whole issue of the way in which growth in the small firm is viewed. In doing this, we are building not only on data presented in our book, but also on additional data collected subsequently from the same research programme and data from a further ten firm study, the fieldwork of which has recently been completed.

[5] Readers will, of course, be aware of the caution required in applying United States data to the United Kingdom — see below our references to Mayer, Goldthorpe et al., Roberts and Warner, and Cooper.

THE JOURNAL OF MANAGEMENT STUDIES MAY

1. Economically, a small firm is one that has a relatively small share of its market.
2. Managerially, the small firm is administered by its owners or part-owners in a personalized way, rather than through the medium of a formalized management structure.
3. Finally, it is independent in the sense that it does not form part of a larger enterprise and owner-managers are free from outside control in taking their principal decisions.[6]

This definition may be criticized on several grounds. For instance, some small firms have quite large shares of their often specialized markets. A methodological drawback here is the lack of available data on ownership, management structures and market shares of firms which precludes any comprehensive operationalization of this definition. Instead, for manufacturing industry, the Committee was forced to adopt the less satisfactory statistical definition of '200 employees or less'. To maximize comparability between our own work and previous work on small firms, we have adopted the Bolton Committee's solution to this definitional problem, though not without reservations for, as our own research indicates, many of the significant social characteristics of the small firm become severely attenuated well before the number of participants reaches 200.

The 1968 Census of Production[7] states that there are 58,198 small manufacturing enterprises, employing nearly 1·4 million personnel and producing around £2,300 m. of goods. Small firms constitute approximately 94 per cent of all firms in manufacturing industry, though the average size of firm is very much smaller than 200 employees. In fact 44,635, or over 75 per cent, employ less than twenty-five personnel.

These figures suggest that small firms are an important element of the manufacturing sector, and a similar pattern emerges from an examination of other areas of the economy. In fact, the figures themselves understate the importance of the small firm. As the C.B.I. argues, if our small firms closed down tomorrow 'most of the large firms would grind quickly and painfully to a halt'.[8]

The small firm has declined in importance in our economy during this century but, in absolute terms, it remains highly significant and, what is

[6] The Bolton Committee Report, op. cit., pp. 1–2.
[7] Report on the Census of Production 1968, *Report 158*, Summary Tables: Enterprise Analysis, London: H.M.S.O., 1974, Table 42, pp. 158/10–11.
[8] Confederation of British Industry, *Britain's Small Firms: Their Vital Role in the Economy*, London: C.B.I., November 1970, p. 3.

more, the rate of decline appears to have been slowing down.[9] United States experience in recent years underlines this point. The Bolton Committee Report pointed out that the share of economic activity held by small firms in the U.S. is larger than in the U.K. Over 98 per cent of firms in the U.S. employ less than 100 people and between them they account for about 40 per cent of total employment.[10] Further, the decline of the small firm, in what may be considered the most advanced of industrial societies, appears to have halted and may even have been reversed.[11]

Previous Views of Growth in the Small Firm

A survey of the literature on growth and the small firm reveals several contributions to theory construction with certain close similarities between them.[12] Without discussing each in detail, and at the risk of some oversimplification, it can be argued that they reveal a dominant and a minor explanatory theme and a shared consistent overall theoretical perspective.

The dominant theme is that of a 'stage' model of growth. The number of stages offered varies, but typically there are three or four, though sometimes as many as ten.[13] The small firm here is seen as passing through a sequence of growth stages though there is little discussion on whether this is a necessary progression or whether, under certain conditions, one or more stages may be missed out or variations in the sequence occur. The absence of such qualifications almost certainly stems from a lack of empirical underpinning.[14] It is rare for samples of firms to exceed double figures; there is often a tendency

---

[9] Wood, Geoff, 'Where Have All the Small Firms Gone?', *The Financial Times*, 14th August 1974. Wood traces Census of Production data for manufacturing industry from 1935 to 1968 and concludes '. . . it appears that the rate of decline is slowing down'. Between 1963 and 1968 there was a further decline in the number of small firms (− 5 per cent), but the decline in the number of large firms during this period was even greater (− 13 per cent). Hence, the representation of small firms increased in percentage terms. It may well be the case that the current economic recession will take a high toll on small firms as against large, but it would be dangerous to extrapolate any long-term trend from this.

[10] Deeks, J., op. cit., p. 28.

[11] See the Bolton Committee Report, op. cit., Chp. 6, and Deeks, J., op. cit., pp. 26–8.

[12] Among the best known are Schumpeter, J. A., *The Theory of Economic Development*, Cambridge, Mass.: Harvard University Press, 1934; Urwick, L., 'Problems of Growth in Industrial Undertakings', *Winter Proceedings of the British Institute of Management*, No. 2, 1948–49; Penrose, E., *The Theory of the Growth of the Firm*, Oxford: Basil Blackwell, 1957; Collins, O. F., Moore, D. G., with Unwalla, D. B., *The Enterprising Man*, East Lansing: Michigan State University Press, 1964; Thomason, G. F. and Mills, A. J., 'Management Decision-taking in Small Firms', *European Business*, No. 14, October 1967, pp. 29–41; Lupton, Tom, 'Small New Firms and Their Significance', *New Society*, 21st December 1967, pp. 890–92; Matthews, T. and Mayers, C., *Developing a Small Firm*, London: B.B.C. Publications, 1968; Steinmetz, L. L., 'Critical Stages of Small Business Growth', *Business Horizons*, Vol. XII, No. 1, February 1969, pp. 29–34.

[13] As in, for example, Urwick, L., op. cit.

[14] Often the discussion appears to be entirely speculative but even where it has empirical backing the samples are frequently very small. For example, the theory offered by Thomason and Mills is apparently based on a sample of four firms.

to rely heavily on retrospective data or observations at a single point in time instead of longitudinal research strategies, and there is usually insufficient linking with data from other studies.

Stage models, regardless of the number of stages offered, also display certain further similarities. The initial stage, as we might expect, stresses the individual entrepreneur(s) with an idea for a product or service setting up in business. The next stage (or sometimes the next but one), is usually concerned with the division of managerial tasks.[15] The entrepreneur(s) can no longer exercise total managerial control and non-owner managers are recruited, often because they have skills lacking in the founder(s). The remaining stages tend to concentrate on organizational maturity and stability. The firm becomes more bureaucratic and rationalized and takes on the general character of the larger company. It evolves a board of directors who are essentially managers rather than entrepreneurs; it exploits a wide range of management, production and marketing techniques; and there is an acceptance that it must develop systematic working relations with other organizations in society such as trade unions and government departments.

These various approaches do contain a considerable element of truth but this derives at least partly from the definitional procedures used in theory construction. For instance, to define the first stage in terms of an individual or small group deciding to exploit a market for a product or service, is to go little beyond defining the coming into existence of a new independent economic entity.

Another curious aspect of these stage theories of growth is an implied disregard for the size distribution of firms discussed above. The Census of Production data show this to be highly skewed with over 94 per cent of manufacturing firms employing less than 200 people and the typical firm, in a statistical sense, employing less than 30. In other words, most firms do not grow to any considerable size in terms of workforce size (which we may assume is broadly correlated with other dimensions of growth) and that substantial growth is seemingly a rather *exceptional* process. This is reinforced by the data which suggest that the failure rate among small firms, especially in the years immediately following formation, is very high.[16]

Finally, an inspection of the implied characteristics of the firm's organizational and managerial structure contained within the later stages in most of the models strongly indicates that the authors concerned are discussing a firm which has long since entered the 6 per cent of large firms in our economy.

[15] Urwick, L., op. cit., and Thomason, G. F. and Mills, A. J., op. cit., provide examples of the division of managerial roles occurring in stage two while Lupton, T., op. cit., and Matthews, T. and Mayers, C., op. cit., appear to offer an example of this occurring in stage three.

[16] Exact data on the death rates of small firms is very difficult to come by but see the discussions in Deeks, J., op. cit., and the Bolton Committee Report, op. cit.

The minor theme present in theorizing on growth in the small firm is the so-called 's-curve hypothesis'[17] which can be seen as a special case of the stage theory. This suggests that the small firm will have a short formative period followed by a period of rapid growth perhaps reaching an exponential rate. The thinking behind this is that after the entrepreneur(s) have developed an idea for a product or service, there is an initial establishing period for the firm which ends with the clear demonstration of a market advantage. This leads to a high rate of investment, to further exploit the advantage, sometimes supplemented by outside capital attracted by the firm's performance in the establishing period. This investment fuels the high rate of growth in the next period of the firm's history.

This exceptional rate of growth, however, tails off as competition is offered by other firms who become aware of the market opportunities. A reduction in the rate of expansion further results from a lowering of investment to more conventional levels due to profit-taking by the owner-managers and a decline in the firm's attraction as an investment for outsiders due to the increased competition.

The consistent overall theoretical perspective which unites both the dominant and minor themes in current theorizing concerning growth in the small firm is a highly *positivist* one. The underlying paradigm for theoretical development is an idealized version of that used in the natural sciences. The small firm is seen here as a behaving entity whose elements are related in quantifiable, systematic and highly predictable ways and the object of theory construction is the generation of law-like propositions concerning the growth process.

However, theories of small firm growth, constructed upon this positivist view, fail to meet their self-imposed standards. They seldom, if ever, attain the level of precision required for the development of law-like propositions.[18] Nor are they adequately tested against acceptable samples of small firm histories necessary to define limits and boundaries to the relevance of such propositions. Finally, they appear to be inadequately articulated with our present knowledge of the structure of our economy, particularly with reference to the size distribution of firms. Since, in relative terms, so few small firms grow to become large sized, it might be expected that these

[17] A review of the literature on this view of growth in the small firm is provided in Mueller, D. C., 'A Life Cycle Theory of the Firm', *Journal of Industrial Economics*, Vol. XX, No. 2, July 1972, pp. 199–219. See also Steinmetz, L. L., op. cit., for one version.

[18] A fairly typical example is provided in Urwick, L., op. cit., p. 9, when he suggests that the limits within which a one-man business can work effectively are approached when the owner-manager has eight people directly reporting to him. The apparent precision here is not qualified by any reference to the kind of small firm the author has in mind; anyone with even the slightest research knowledge of small firms will know that even within a single branch of an industry small firms can display a considerable variation in management structure while remaining economically effective. Between industries such variations can be even greater.

theories should try to explain the rareness of the process they purport to explain. Their failure to do so suggests a blinkered approach.

The inadequacies of this general theoretical perspective have come in for harsh comment in recent years.[19] The main point made is that the assumption that natural and social phenomena belong to the same category of entities for purposes of theorizing and explanation is fundamentally mistaken. The crucial difference stems from the fact that social phenomena *understand* their own behaviour and can act *purposefully* while natural phenomena have neither of these properties.

The Entrepreneurial Spirit in Action Perspective

Our alternative, a *social action* view of the small firm, concentrates heavily on understanding the internal social logic of the small firm as a social grouping. We argue that the key to growth lies in the meanings attached to participation in the firm by the actors involved. The small firm, in this view, is an ongoing social entity constructed out of the meanings and actions of those who participate in the firm or who are 'outsiders' in relation to the firm as social grouping but nevertheless interact with the participants.

It should be stressed that this is *not* a psychological theory of the small firm. It takes the standpoint that definitions and meanings attached to situations are *socially generated*, *socially sustained* and, of special interest in the present context, *socially changed*. In other words, a social action perspective here links the meanings and actions of the small firm's participants with their wider social environment. Moreover, in order to achieve the necessary level of generality for a *social* view of the small firm, the view cannot be limited to specific individuals but is extended to cover tendencies for certain combinations of meanings and actions to recur after the fashion revealed in various studies of small firms in this country and the United States.

This creates a new dimension for analysis because the researcher cannot now simply adopt a theory which assumes that objects in the situation will behave in a relatively positivist and deterministic manner. Purposeful phenomena cannot be treated in this simplistic way. In seeking to interpret the situation, the researcher must now also endeavour to understand what participation means to those involved and the likely changes in these meanings. Only in this way is an adequate account possible.

The resulting interpretation also differs from positivist explanations in that it does not take the form of law-like 'predictions'. Instead, an interpretation

[19] For a discussion particularly relevant to economic organizations see Silverman, David, *The Theory of Organizations*, London: Heinemann, 1970, and more generally, Cohen, Percy S., *Modern Social Theory*, London: Heinemann Educational Books, 1968, and, Berger, Peter L. and Luckmann, Thomas, *The Social Construction of Reality*, London: Allen Lane, 1967.

of the social situation is provided based upon a knowledge of both internal and external forces[20] influencing the situation. This allows suggestions as to the probabilities of actors attempting certain lines of action, given their interpretation of the situation, and the social forces affecting the situation which originate from the wider social environment.

Given the very strong influence of the owner-manager on the small firm's organizational style, it is important to examine this key role in some detail. Of particular importance are the new owner-manager's reasons for going it alone. Understanding this aids an understanding of attitudes towards growth later on in the firm's life.

Individuals do not generate meanings in a vacuum for most of their social interactions, but rely on an available stock of meanings, 'culture', to make sense of specific social experiences and provide a framework for anticipated experiences aimed at achieving the actor's ends or avoiding certain outcomes. In our society there is a strong cultural bias favouring individualism, and this finds expression in many ways. Economic individualism, it may be argued, in the form of founding and operating a business of one's own, is one of the most legitimate of all culturally prescribed forms of individualism. Indeed, as Weber argued,[21] economic individualism, in this form, has been given divine sanction in our culture and in fact was closely associated with the genesis of modern industrial society itself. An American writer on the small firm claimed that starting one's own business has

> . . . always been considered an integral element of the American way of life. Our traditional concept of opportunity has carried and still carries, a heavy emphasis on 'freedom', on 'being on one's own', 'being one's own boss' and 'working for oneself'.[22]

While this cultural bias is not quite so highly emphasized in Britain's culture, survey data[23] show that the ideal of self-employment, in order to increase autonomy and personal self-esteem, is none the less widespread.

However, going into business for oneself is a difficult role transition if only because our educational system and vocational guidance processes operate to

---

[20] By 'external forces' we mean those factors which influence the structure of social relations in the firm but which originate from outside the firm. Actors in the firm may or may not be aware of these forces and their effects may be actual or potential.

[21] Weber, Max, *The Protestant Ethic and the Spirit of Capitalism*, London: Unwin University Books, 1965.

[22] Mayer, Kurt B., 'Business Enterprise: Traditional Symbol of Opportunity', *British Journal of Sociology*, Vol. IV, No. 2, 1953, pp. 160–80.

[23] See, for example, Goldthorpe, John H., Lockwood, David, Bechhofer, Frank and Platt, Jennifer, *The Affluent Worker: Industrial Attitudes and Behaviour*, Cambridge: Cambridge University Press, 1968, pp. 131–6.

minimize the practical consideration of this alternative.[24] Nevertheless, some people, albeit a very small minority, do take on the owner-manager role. It is important to know something about the social backgrounds and orientations of these people, especially first generation entrepreneurs, if we are to achieve an understanding of the small firm. It is also quite clear from the available data on entrepreneurship in this country and the United States that new entrepreneurs are far from randomly drawn from the population.

As a social category, entrepreneurs tend to share certain characteristics. For instance, they are not, on the whole, well educated. The Bolton Committee Report stated that nearly three-quarters of a sample of small manufacturing firms' chief executives had received no higher education and that only 1 per cent had a management qualification.[25] Other data support this claim for both Britain[26] and the United States[27] though there have been exceptions reported for the latter.[28] The more general conclusion, derived from the study of the backgrounds of new entrepreneurs, is that they tend to be people who consider themselves misplaced by the conventional role allocation processes of their society.

Our main point here of the special social character of those who embrace the entrepreneurial role is well supported in this quotation from the largest American survey on entrepreneurship:

> . . . Entrepreneurs are men who have failed in the traditional and highly structured roles available to them in the society. In this, as we have seen, entrepreneurs are not unique. What is unique about them is that they found an outlet for their creativity by making out of an undifferentiated mass of circumstance a creation uniquely their own: a business firm.[29]

We can use the term *social marginality* to refer to this situation in which there is a perceived incongruity between the individual's personal attributes — physical characteristics, intellectual make-up, social behaviour patterns —

[24] For instance, a recent survey of material on this topic, Williams, W. M. (Ed.), *Occupational Choice — A Selection of Papers from the Sociological Review*, London: George Allen and Unwin, 1974, contains no discussion of this occupational alternative.

[25] Bolton Committee Report, op. cit., pp. 8–9.

[26] Deeks, J., 'Educational and Occupational Histories of Owner-managers', *Journal of Management Studies*, Vol. 9, No. 2, May 1972, pp. 127–49.

[27] Collins, O. F., Moore, D. G., with Unwalla, D. B., op. cit., Chp. V.

[28] Roberts, E. B. and Warner, H. A., 'New Enterprises on Route 128', *Science Journal*, December 1968, pp. 78–83; Cooper, A. C., 'Entrepreneurial Environment', *Industrial Research*, September 1970, pp. 74–6; Liles, Patrick R., 'Who are the Entrepreneurs?', *MSU Business Topics*, Winter 1974, pp. 5–14. These sources seem, however, to refer to a special variety of entrepreneurship which emerged under conditions of a kind not frequently encountered in private enterprise societies. See the discussion below.

[29] Collins, O. F., Moore, D. G., with Unwalla, D. B., op. cit., pp. 243–4.

the role(s) he holds in society.[30] Social marginality is a common phenomenon due to the very nature of role allocation processes in society —
these are far from perfect in allocating individuals to social roles — and
also because individuals strive to maintain a sense of personal autonomy in
social roles in opposition to social pressures pushing towards conformity.
These common forms of social marginality are, however, unlikely to lead to
dramatic social responses.

But, for some individuals and in some areas of society, circumstances
combine to produce high levels of social marginality. The historical example,
par excellence, of a group displaying high social marginality has been the Jews.
Being a Jew has, regretfully, been something which has made a person an
'outsider' in non-Jewish society regardless of his personal and intellectual
characteristics. To some extent Jewish communities developed patterns of
social integration to counter these deprivations imposed from the wider
society but feelings of social marginality were likely to be present to an extent
rare in most other parts of society. For a Jew with only a weak commitment
to his religion and community, feelings of marginality were likely to be much
more pronounced.

Other common examples of social marginality are the intellectually gifted
manual worker and the fully acculturated second-generation coloured Briton.
Solutions to intense feelings of social marginality are varied. In some cases it
leads to adherence to 'extreme' political or religious ideologies which promise
to reconstruct social reality and thus 'solve' the individual's experiences of
social marginality. The gifted manual worker may choose to become a full-
time trade union official. For some, a solution is setting up their own firm.

Examples of the latter solution from our own research include some not
uncommon stories. We discovered social marginality resulting from a
promising academic career being shattered by domestic tragedy, or through
the war, sharply diminishing career prospects in conventional industrial/
commercial life. Or again, we came across social marginality occurring in
middle age when a successful career in the armed services could not be
matched by the attainment of a similarly responsible position in civilian life.
Other cases included instances of demonstrated talent being overlooked by
large employers due to the individuals' unorthodox attitudes and personal
idiosyncrasies.

An Action View of Growth in the Small Firm

Our previously published research, as well as that of others, indicates that
there is no one single, stereotyped entrepreneurial role and thus, by implica-

---

[30] For a comprehensive history of the concept of 'social marginality' see Dickie-Clark, H. P.,
The Marginal Situation, London: Routledge and Kegan Paul, 1966.

tion, no single simple pattern of growth. The classical economists offered a picture of the entrepreneur as a rational profit maximizer and this remains the popular stereotype despite little support from research. An American study for example, reported that, of a sample of 81 newly founded businesses, only six approximated to the classical economists' model of the entrepreneur.[31]

Rather, there are several possible constellations of meanings which may form the core of the entrepreneur's self-definition of the entrepreneurial role. We find it helpful, following Gouldner,[32] to distinguish these constellations of more personal role components from those which may be taken as basic cultural prescriptions by using the concept, *latent social identity*. Research on the small firm — both the research we have previously reported and studies by others — suggest that three such latent identities occur with some frequency in relation to the role of small firm entrepreneur:

1. *The 'artisan' identity*. Here the entrepreneurial role centres around intrinsic satisfactions of which the most important are personal autonomy at work, being able to pick the persons you work with, status within the workplace and satisfaction at producing a quality product backed with personal service.

   These are not the only meanings and goals attached to the role, but they are the ones which predominate. Thus, whilst income is important, as it must be for anybody who works and has no other source of income, it is secondary to intrinsic satisfactions.

2. *The 'classical entrepreneur' identity*. This latent social identity most closely resembles the classical economists' view of entrepreneurship. Earnings and profit become a core component in the entrepreneur's definition of his role and hence in the way he acts out his role. Again maximization of financial returns (consistent with the survival and possible expansion of the firm), is by no means the sole goal of the entrepreneur, but it is given great importance compared to the intrinsic satisfactions associated with the 'artisan' identity.

3. *The 'manager' identity*. Here the entrepreneurial latent social identity centres on meanings and goals concerned with the recognition, by significant others, of managerial excellence. The entrepreneur structures his role performance to achieve this recognition from fellow members of the firm but, and more especially, from outsiders such as other businessmen. Other goals and values stressed here are security and a

---

[31] Mayer, Kurt, B. and Goldstein, Sidney, *The First Two Years: Problems of Small Firm Growth and Survival*, Small Business Research Series, No. 2, Washington, D.C.: Small Business Association, 1961, reported in Deeks, J., 1973, op. cit.

[32] Gouldner, Alvin W., 'Cosmopolitans and Locals: an Analysis of Latent Social Roles', *Administrative Science Quarterly*, Vol. 2, No. 3, December 1957, pp. 282–92, and Vol. 2, No. 4, March 1958, pp. 444–80.

concern to ensure that the entrepreneur's children will eventually receive the benefits of his enterprise.

These identities are connected to other aspects of the firm's operations and to processes of growth although it should be stressed again that these links should not be seen in a positivist sense. The links occur through the internal social logic generated out of the ways in which the situation is perceived by those involved and the actions which follow on from these perceptions.[33]

The *'artisan'* identity is not very concerned with growth and is most frequently found among people who have only relatively recently adopted the entrepreneurial role. It reflects the feelings of social marginality common among entrepreneurs, and is greatly concerned with intrinsic satisfactions likely to minimize the psychological deprivations associated with recent social marginality. However, successful adoption of this identity must be tenuous. Given the data on the instability of new small firms, survival is always problematic. Equally, for the same reasons, it is unlikely that the goals and values associated with the other two identities will be given prominence at this stage.

On the other hand, a small firm which survives the formative period and enters a period of sustained profitability constitutes a social context conducive to the generation of a *'classical entrepreneur'* identity. The goals associated with the artisan identity will have been at least partially realized and the new social and economic situation of the firm is favourable to the possible emergence of a new self-definition for the entrepreneur.

But whether any dramatic take-off into sustained growth is likely, even when the external logic — the economic and market situation of the firm and social relations with outsiders — is highly favourable, is a matter for debate and even scepticism. The internal logic of the firm from the point of view of its chief actor contains certain contradictions. A sustained high rate of growth may change the firm from a solution to social marginality to a situation reinforcing it.

As a firm grows forces emerge, internally and externally, which push it towards a more rational and bureaucratic structure. Management functions have to be delegated as they become too complex and time consuming for a single person to handle. The need for certain skills, almost certainly not possessed by the entrepreneur, becomes crucial and specialists must be

---

[33] Some readers will note the similarity between this analysis and that of Smith, N. R., in *The Entrepreneur and his Firm: The Relationship Between Type of Man and Type of Company*, M.S.U., 1967. However, there are fundamental differences between our approach and that of Smith. He assumes a fixed and unchanging entrepreneurial personality type predating entry to the entrepreneurial role. This denies the interplay between role and social experience and the constant reinterpretation of social reality and self which occurs in any role performance. For a further discussion see Stanworth, M. J. K. and Curran, J., op. cit., pp. 171–6.

recruited. The social relations among participants can no longer be conducted on a highly personal basis but must be more systematically and bureaucratically ordered. From the entrepreneur's point of view, therefore, the firm comes increasingly to resemble previous social situations which produced the social marginality feelings the firm was established to minimize. Entrepreneurs in our own study, who took on the classical entrepreneur identity often claimed, despite financial success, that they were, 'beginning to feel like employees in their own firm'.

The emergence of these 'growth effects' depend on a variety of factors, and may not occur until the firm has grown to be of some size. But what is more important is whether the entrepreneur comes to perceive the likely outcomes of these changes and the decisions he makes concerning their desirability as well as his ability to cope with them in terms of the kind of person he has now become. So, again, we return to the internal social logic of the small firm, seen from the point of view of its main actor, and the possible outcomes which can develop.

Some small firm entrepreneurs will have little hesitation in deciding that growth is desirable or even necessary for survival. Having established that they can maintain a high profit growth company, they may come to redefine their entrepreneurial role in terms of the '*manager*' identity. In addition to the elements listed above, other behaviour patterns indicative of the presence of this identity are an increased interest in management training and development, employers' organizations, using management consultants, and attempts at taking over other firms and merging with larger companies or attempting to go public. Finally, it should be noted that the adoption of this new self-definition of the entrepreneurial role does not, of itself, give immunity against possible contradictions which may emerge as a result. The re-emergence of socially marginal feelings may occur but the entrepreneur, having embarked on a course of action, may find that it is extremely difficult to halt let alone reverse the outcomes.[34]

But this particular outcome, the rapid growth and expansion of the small firm, despite its important place in the social mythology of our society, is likely to be less frequent than many expect. The small entrepreneur may well make an assessment of the results of certain courses of action, and decide that, on balance the 'costs' (in social and psychological terms) of some of these are too high.

Adopting a conscious no-growth stance in our society is not easy. We live in a society with a strong growth ideology. Growth is 'progress' and businessmen are often judged by this criterion. It is not therefore surprising that small firm entrepreneurs are rather circumspect, even to the extent of self-

[34] For an example of this occurring see Stanworth, M. J. K. and Curran, J., ibid., Chp. 7.

deception, in not striving too hard for growth. One study of small firms in Britain summed up the attitudes among their sample as being:

> . . . roughly divided on this question (the amount of growth thought desirable). Rather more agreed that expansion was desirable than backed the maintenance of the *status quo*. But it was noticeable that they often tended to express their views in a somewhat generalized way, as if they were paying lip service to an absolute abstract ideal of growth.[35]

The reasons given for not growing were often difficult to accept at face value. Relatively minor administrative chores such as collecting insurance contributions and P.A.Y.E. were offered as 'barriers' to growth. Our view is that reluctance to grow has, in fact, much more to do with the consequences, in social terms, of growth than these vocalized reasons.

If this alternative view of the small firm growth patterns is accepted, a number of issues, not adequately covered by previous theories, are resolved. For instance, a social action view of the small firm and growth offers reasons as to why growth is, on the whole, much less common than the prevalent growth ideology would indicate. It explains why, given the data on the low level of rewards[36] (in material terms) of small businessmen the popularity of self-employment remains. It explains why the attractions of working for a large firm, with all that this implies in terms of security and material rewards, are rejected by certain people in our society. Also, it explains part of the highly skewed size distribution of firms in advanced industrial societies; it is not simply economic but social and psychological factors which also influence this distribution. Finally, this analysis also tells us something about the growth processes of those small firms who do join the 6 per cent of large firms in our economy.

Earlier theories of small firm growth, such as those discussed above, had, as one of their objectives, that of helping the owner-manager to better understand the growth process of his firm. Few theories in the social sciences would claim not to have practical implications, and ours is no exception. Our alternative approach to understanding the small firm has policy implications for small firm decision-makers, for government attempts to aid the small firm, and for consultants and others who seek to provide expert guidance. By taking a new starting point for analysis and a new theoretical stance, we see that much of the available effort here is likely to be ineffectual. In parti-

[35] Golby, C. W. and Johns, G., *Attitude and Motivation*, Committee of Inquiry on Small Firms, Research Report No. 7, London: H.M.S.O., 1971, p. 17.

[36] See Merrett Cyriax Associates, *Dynamics of Small Firms*, Committee of Inquiry on Small Firms, Research Report No. 12, London: H.M.S.O., 1971, p. 35, for data for the United Kingdom. Collins, O. F., Moore, D. G. with Unwalla, D. B., op. cit., suggest that a similar relatively low level of material rewards are received by small firm executives in the United States.

cular, our analysis and findings points up the fatuity of policies or advice uncritically taken from the experience or techniques of large firms.

Given a knowledge of the way the entrepreneur defines his role in relation to his self-identity, and accepting his decisive position in the firm, we can say quite a lot about how the firm is likely to operate in a wide variety of situations. Thus, the owner-manager with an 'artisan' identity places a high value on independence. This leads to an organizational climate founded on an autocratic leadership style, combined with a strong element of paternalism, which minimizes dependence on others whether they be inside or outside the firm.[37] He is likely to perceive the firm as a 'contented team', under-utilize the skills of subordinates and be blind to certain kinds of industrial relations problems. Awareness on the part of the entrepreneur of these possible results of a particular managerial style can help reduce unwanted side effects. Outsiders, wishing to aid the small firm, will be able to evaluate the likelihood of success of proposed strategies against their knowledge of social relations patterns within the firm dictated largely by the entrepreneurial self-identity.

Probably the most problematic situation identified by our research is that where the owner-manager attempts to make the transition from an 'artisan' to a 'classical entrepreneur' identity. Growth is a strategy normally associated with this transition and the anticipated consequences of this, we argue, are often instrumental in the transition not being made. Even where it is made, the full consequences are often not fully realized, and this results in problems and conflicts — both identity conflicts for the entrepreneur and structural conflicts within the firm.

The administrative necessity to use a more consultative leadership style, to delegate and 'negotiate' with professionally trained managers brought in from outside, is not easily reconciled with the owner-manager's desire for independence. To this extent, he is a captive of the new situation he has himself brought about to meet his changing goals. Problems of a similar nature are likely to arise out of the increasing likelihood of unionization. Entrepreneurs in our study were mostly aware of the positive correlation between organizational size and degree of unionization. However, it was not often that unionization was seen as an extension of the new order of things in a larger firm presenting management with benefits as well as problems. More commonly, a 'communications breakdown' or the actions of 'militants' among new workers were held responsible.

We are not arguing that all those who take on the owner-manager role are socially marginal. In some cases there are exceptional environmental circumstances which make entry into business comparatively easy. For example, an 'open' social and economic environment for entrepreneurship has apparently

---

[37] See the Bolton Committee Report, Chp. 2, p. 24, para. 2.47, on the attitude of many owner-managers towards sources of outside help and assistance.

occurred in many of the developing countries.[38] Similarly, within advanced industrial societies some areas of economic activity may also become highly favourable to entrepreneurship as seems to have happened in the U.S. defence and space industries in the 1960s.[39] In these circumstances, many people without feelings of high marginality will found firms, and may quite deliberately aim for high growth.

Finally, it must be remembered that much small firm growth results from the management of second and third generation owner-managers. Whether first generation owner-managed firms have lower rates of growth than their second and subsequent generation counterparts is unclear, as they start from different base lines making strict comparisons difficult. The Bolton Committee Report suggested that first generation owner-managed firms grew rather faster than those managed by subsequent generations, but this was based on a very small sample.[40] This was countered to some extent also by the further finding that fast growing firms relied to a great extent on borrowed funds. Our own research, and that of Collins *et al.* noted earlier, found that highly socially marginal owner-managers, who are, as we have argued, more likely to be first generation, were strongly opposed to external borrowing because of the threat posed to their personal autonomy.

We feel that second or third generation owner-managers, because they are more likely to have a conventional middle-class background and education are more likely to have a conventional 'managerial' view of economic activity. Their personal life situation is less likely to be one of strong discrepancy between personal attributes and social role, and their socialization will be toward the acceptance of the dominant business ideology of our society with its stress on growth and efficiency achieved through economies of scale. They will, therefore, be more receptive to ideas of expansion, merger and the professionally managed business.

The substantial differences between the view of the small firm growth process presented in this paper and previous views are, we hope, now readily apparent. We have argued against the previous positivist models of growth and our alternative view sees the small firm as a constructed social reality, derived from the meanings which have a central place in the cultures of many modern societies and the activities of individuals suffering role stress in such societies.

Our main focus of attention has been on the entrepreneur and his influence on the social character of the firm. For, although he only shares in the social

---

[38] This inference may be drawn from the data presented in Warren, Bill, 'Imperialism and Capitalist Industrialization', *New Left Review*, Vol. 81, September–October 1973, pp. 3–44.

[39] Roberts, E. B. and Warner, H. A., op. cit.; Cooper, A. C., op. cit.; and Liles, P. R., op. cit., all provide data on this type of entrepreneurship.

[40] The Bolton Report Committee, op. cit., p. 17.

construction of the firm and cannot achieve this without the cooperation of others, his influence is normally decisive. Small firms do grow though this may often be only to an extent that the firm still retains many of the social aspects associated with small size. Where growth proceeds beyond this point certain contradictions between the entrepreneur's self-identity and his participation in the firm are likely to result — at least in the case of a first-generation owner-manager.

Our interpretation is incomplete to some extent since it does not extend detailed attention to the social orientations of other participants in the firm and 'key' outsiders whose orientations and actions have important consequences for social relations within the firm. We have, however, previously discussed[41] some of the relations between owner-managers and wider society and are currently researching small firm worker orientations. This will enable us to greatly enhance our understanding of the firm as a whole and, of course, its growth processes.

---

[41] Stanworth, M. J. K. and Curran, J., op. cit., especially Chp. 6.

[7]

THE ENTREPRENEURIAL PERSONALITY:
A PERSON AT THE CROSSROADS

BY

M. F. R. KETS DE VRIES

'. . . Sometimes I have visions of myself driving through hell, selling sulphur and brimstone, or through heaven peddling refreshments to the roaming souls . . .'

Brecht, *Mother Courage*

Abstract

This paper reviews the concept of entrepreneurship and empirical studies of entrepreneurial behaviour patterns. In addition, it explores the social, economic and psychodynamic forces influencing entrepreneurship. A conceptualization of the entrepreneurial personality is proposed. Finally, the organizational impact of these entrepreneurial behaviour patterns on work environment and management succession is discussed.

Introduction

We quickly recognize an element of mythology and legend in the articles about entrepreneurship in such journals as *Fortune* magazine. This journal and others of its kind devote part of each issue to preaching the gospel of enterprise and business leadership. Not surprisingly these themes of individual success and failure are highly popular; they catch the readers' imagination and are empathy-provoking since they awaken the rebellious spirit present in each of us. We see that Prometheus and Odysseus have been replaced by that folk hero of the industrial world, the entrepreneur. He has become the last lone ranger, a bold individualist fighting the odds of the environment. He is that individual who after enduring and overcoming many hardships, trials and business adventures finally seems to have 'made it'. But frequently there is an epilogue added to these fairy tale endings whereby the 'and they lived happily ever after' theme is missing. As in Greek myths success may lead to hubris or excessive pride, and might come to fall. And as we can see in the case of many entrepreneurs success is a very fragile state, easily followed by failure.

Take for example the story of Bernard Cornfeld and Investment Overseas Services.[1] This tale tells us of a displaced person born in Istanbul of Jewish parents. We follow the family's emigration to America. The father, an

---

[1] Raw, Charles, Page, Bruce and Hodgson, Godfrey, *Do You Sincerely Want to be Rich?* New York: The Viking Press, 1971.

unsuccessful actor died when our hero was very young, leaving the mother to take care of the family, having to work extremely long hours. The story continues by describing how Bernard Cornfeld after many difficulties became an investment professional (thus ending his career as a social worker), and began to sell mutual funds overseas (not necessarily to the benefit of its investors) being extremely successful at it. But his fund of funds became like a chain letter game, financial controls were lacking and chaos prevailed in the company. Eventually Cornfeld was deposed leaving the remains of the company wide open to plunder by Robert Vesco.

Another entrepreneurial saga tells the tale of the rise and fall of Charles Steen, from an uranium millionaire to a pauper.[2] When we look at his family history we find a father who squandered all his money on 'loose living' and eventually divorced his wife. Charles Steen never saw his father again after this divorce. His mother on her part married a total of nine times. Further study of Charles Steen's personal background reveals that he seemed to have difficulties in holding on to a job. After his last dismissal, unsuccessful in finding a new position, he decided that the only choice left was to strike out on his own. The story continues by describing a period of extreme hardship and poverty finally broken by his uranium find. But his wealth did not last long; excessive spending and poor investments caused his bankruptcy. And now we can find him broke roaming the desert again.

These two stories are spectacular but not uncommon examples of the rise and fall of entrepreneurs. While other stories might be less dramatic and often limited to the successful part of the entrepreneur's endeavour, closer analysis of these various stories reveals that most of these tales of hardship and success contain a number of common, rather familiar themes. We are usually introduced to a person with an unhappy family background, an individual who feels displaced and seems a misfit in his particular environment. We are also faced with a loner, isolated and rather remote from even his closest relatives. This type of person gives the impression of a 'reject', a marginal man, a perception certainly not lessened by his often conflicting relationships with family members. The environment is perceived as hostile and turbulent, populated by individuals yearning for control, with the need to structure his activities. We observe an individual who utilizes innovative rebelliousness as an adaptive mode with occasional lapses toward delinquency, ways of demonstrating his ability to break away, to show independence of mind. Due to these reactive ways of dealing with feelings of anger, fear and anxiety, tension remains since 'punishment' in the form of failure may follow suit. Failure is expected and success is often only perceived as a prelude to failure.

[2] Becker, W. C., 'Consequences of Different Kinds of Parental Discipline', in Hoffman, M. L. and Hoffman, L. W. (Eds.), *Review of Child Development Research*, Vol. 1, New York: Russell Sage Foundation, 1964.

Interrelated with this strange pattern of elation and despair, of successes and failures, we also observe a kind of person who demonstrates a remarkable resilience in the face of setbacks, with the ability to start all over again when disappointments and hardships come his way.

The person we are describing, the entrepreneur or the 'creative destructor' to use Schumpeter's[3] terminology, is a highly complex individual, certainly not the simpleton or automaton which many economists would like us to believe he is. The entrepreneur is obviously not that 'lightning calculator of pleasures and pains', as Veblen[4] once cynically described him and bears no resemblance to that mythical creature of economic theory, the economic man. On the contrary, we are dealing with an individual often inconsistent and confused about his motives, desires and wishes, a person under a lot of stress who often upsets us by his seemingly 'irrational', impulsive activities.

Notwithstanding the multitude of articles written about entrepreneurship and the entrepreneurial organization, the entrepreneur has remained an enigma, his motivations and actions far from clear, a state of affairs aggravated because of contradictory theoretical and research findings. Consequently, the purpose of this article is a review of the concept of entrepreneurship and of empirical studies of entrepreneurial behaviour patterns. Subsequently, social, economic and psychodynamic forces influencing entrepreneurship will be explored. A conceptualization of the entrepreneurial personality will be presented largely based upon interviews and the life histories of a number of entrepreneurs. Finally the implications of these entrepreneurial behaviour patterns for entrepreneurial organizations will be discussed.

Entrepreneurial Roles

Economists have always looked at entrepreneurs with a great deal of ambivalence. The often unpredictable, irrational actions of entrepreneurs do not fit the economists' rational, logical schemes; they tend to disturb the implicit harmony of their models. Generally speaking their attitude toward entrepreneurship has been one of 'benign neglect'. Baumol's exasperated statement that 'the theoretical firm is entrepreneurless — the Prince of Denmark has been expunged from the discussion of Hamlet'[5] is not far from the truth. But some economists have shown interest in the entrepreneur. Beginning with Cantillon[6] and Say[7] who stressed respectively the uncertainty bearing and

[3] Schumpeter, Joseph A., *Theorie der Wirtschaftlichen Entwicklung*, 6ᵉ Aufl., München und Leibzig: Duncker und Humblat, 1931.

[4] Veblen, Thorstein, 'Why is Economics not an Evolutionary Science?', *The Quarterly Journal of Economics*, Vol. XII, No. 4, 1889, p. 389.

[5] Baumol, William J., 'Entrepreneurship in Economic Theory', *American Economic Review*, Vol. LVIII, No. 2, 1968, p. 66.

[6] Cantillon, Richard, *Essay sur la Nature du Commerce en Général*, Londres et Paris: R. Gyles, 1756.

[7] Say, Jean-Baptiste, *Catechism of Political Economy*, London, 1816.

coordinating functions, the entrepreneur has been discussed by various economists.

The term 'entrepreneur', derived from the French word *entreprendre*, to undertake,[8] has been defined and redefined by historians, economists and sociologists. Forgetting conceptual niceties, students of entrepreneurship usually define the entrepreneur as that individual instrumental in the conception of the idea of an enterprise and the implementation of these ideas. In this process the entrepreneur fulfils a number of functions which can be summarized as the innovation, the management-coordinating and the risk-taking functions.

The *innovation function* particularly, has been stressed by Schumpeter[9] who stated that '. . . entrepreneurship . . . essentially consists in doing things that are not generally done in the ordinary course of business routine'. Schumpeter's entrepreneur is an ideas man and a man of action who possesses the ability to inspire others, and who does not accept the boundaries of structured situations. He is a catalyst of change, able 'to carry out new combinations', instrumental in discovering new opportunities, which makes for the uniqueness of the entrepreneurial function. We notice that when a later student of entrepreneurship such as Drucker[10] summarizes the tasks of the entrepreneur as projection (forecasting the future), combination (of major new developments), innovation, and anticipation, he is actually doing nothing else than restating Schumpeter's original propositions.

Less spectacular but essential is *managing-coordinating* which is often regarded as a second function of entrepreneurship, but here the distinction between an entrepreneur and a business executive becomes blurred.[11] Some may even argue that the term manager and entrepreneur are actually mutually exclusive.[12] It raises the question of at what stage of an organization's development the more 'bureaucratically inclined' manager is taking over.

As a third function of entrepreneurship *risk-taking* is worth mentioning. After Cantillon this notion has particularly been proposed and developed by Knight[13] who views the entrepreneur as the taker of non-quantifiable

[8] Redlich, Fritz, 'The Origin of the Concepts of Entrepreneur and Creative Entrepreneur', *Explorations in Entrepreneurial History*, Vol. 1, 1949, pp. 145–66.

[9] Schumpeter, Joseph A., 'Economic Theory and Entrepreneurial History', in Aitken, Hugh, G. J. (Ed.), *Explorations in Enterprise*, Cambridge, Mass.: Harvard University Press, 1965, p. 51.

[10] Drucker, Peter F., 'Entrepreneurship in Business Enterprise', *Journal of Business Policy*, Vol. 1, No. 1, 1970.

[11] Hartman, Heinz, 'Managers and Entrepreneurs: a Useful Distinction', *Administrative Science Quarterly*, Vol. 3, No. 3, 1959, pp. 429–51.

[12] Schumpeter states that 'we maintain that someone is only then by definition entrepreneur if he "implements new combinations" — after which he loses this characteristic, when he then continues to manage the founded enterprise systematically'. See Schumpeter, J. A., 1931, op. cit., p. 116 (own translation).

[13] Knight, Frank H., *Risk, Uncertainty and Profit*, 5th edition, Boston: Houghton-Mifflin, 1940.

uncertainties. But with the division of ownership and management, the use of other than the entrepreneur's personal capital sources, the entrepreneur can be considered more a creator of risk than a taker of it. However, although the entrepreneur does not necessarily bear the financial risk of an operation, he is exposed to a considerable degree of social and psychological risks. More often than not a great decline in prestige and status income is a common phenomenon in the initial phase of entrepreneurship. The 'purgatory of entrepreneurship', *i.e.* the period preceding recognition of one's entrepreneurial abilities, can be a time of extreme hardship during which considerable sociopsychological sacrifices have to be endured. Naturally a certain tolerance for economic risk is necessary but a tolerance for psychosocial risks might be more important.

Testing Entrepreneurial Behaviour Patterns

After this brief description of entrepreneurial roles we will turn now to empirical studies of the entrepreneurial personality. Unfortunately, most of these studies have not excelled in conceptual clarity. Not only is there a recurring confusion in definition of differences between entrepreneurs and managers, but, in addition, many of these studies have focused exclusively on specific entrepreneurial sub-groups such as the high technology entrepreneur, or have concentrated on specific personality characteristics which might contribute to successfulness in company performance. Furthermore, the great diversity in test instruments has prevented or at least hampered the possibility of making more general comparisons. But in spite of these seemingly formidable handicaps we might be able to make some generalizations after reviewing a number of these empirical studies.

The major contributor to the empirical study of entrepreneurship has been McClelland as presented in his book *The Achieving Society*.[14] Using Thematic Apperception Tests[15] and specific games of skill he discovered that entrepreneurs scored high on need for achievement (n Ach). He defined this need as the desire to do well in competitive situations where the results of one's effort could be measured objectively. Not only did he find that entrepreneurs are high on n Ach but they also (1) desire to take personal responsibility for decisions, (2) prefer decisions involving a moderate degree of risk, (3) are interested in concrete knowledge of the results of decisions, and (4) dislike repetitive, routine work.

In his most recent study McClelland has shifted the emphasis from achievement to power.[16] He argues that for organizational effectiveness power

[14] McClelland, David C., *The Achieving Society*, New York: Van Nostrand, 1961.

[15] Murray, Henry A., *Manual for the Thematic Apperception Test*, Cambridge, Mass.: Harvard University Press, 1943.

[16] McClelland, David C., *Power: The Inner Experience*, New York: Irvington, 1975.

motivation is required. He concludes that high n Power combined with high self-control (socialized power) as opposed to high n Power and low self-control (personal power) makes for the greatest organizational effectiveness, particularly if n Affiliation is also low. Personal power men (power greater than affiliation, low self-control) characterized by a 'conquistador motive pattern' resemble the entrepreneur and represent those individuals who are difficult to organize in any kind of system. Their lack of inhibition or self-control limits their effectiveness as large institution builders in spite of their success in inspiring people in the initial stage of growth of the organization.

T.A.T.s were also used in a wider context (without the emphasis on n Ach and n Power) in the Collins and Moore study *The Enterprising Man*.[17] The major conclusions which Collins and Moore drew from the analysis of T.A.T.s was that entrepreneurs (1) suffer from a lack of problem resolution (to use their words: 'It is as though he panics at the idea of success or too much success,'[18] (2) prefer to have patriarchical relationships with their subordinates, (3) are uncomfortable with authority figures which explains their great need for autonomy, and (4) possess a high degree of anxiety and self-destructiveness.

Schrage[19] was influenced by McClelland's achievement study and the Collins and Moore study when he was looking at the successful R and D entrepreneur and the factors which contribute to successful company performance. His view of the successful R and D entrepreneur was that of a person high on n Ach, low in power motivation and high in awareness of self, market, and employees.

Roberts[20] and Waine and Rubin[21] who were also interested in successful R and D entrepreneurs and company performance, questioned Schrage's findings after discovering discrepancies when the same protocols of Schrage were rescored by the Motivation Research Group at Harvard. They concluded from their own study that the highest performing companies were led by entrepreneurs high on n Ach and moderate on n Power. In addition, they found that entrepreneurs who were high on n Ach and high on n Power performed less well than the sub-groups who demonstrated a moderate level of n Power. If n Ach is an ingredient for success, their findings give some

[17] Collins, Orvis F., Moore, David G. and Unwalla, Darab B., *The Enterprising Man*, East Lansing: Bureau of Business and Economic Research, Graduate School of Business Administration, Michigan State University, 1964.

[18] Ibid., p. 61.

[19] Schrage, Harry, 'The R and D Entrepreneur: Profile of Success', *Harvard Business Review*, Vol. 43, No. 6, November/December 1965, pp. 56–69.

[20] Roberts, Edward B., 'A Basic Study of Innovators: How to Keep and Capitalize on Their Talents', *Research Management*, Vol. XI, No. 4, 1968.

[21] Waine, Herbert A. and Rubin, Irwin A., 'Motivation of Research and Development Entrepreneurs: Determinants of Company Success', *Journal of Applied Psychology*, Vol. 53, No. 3, 1969, pp. 178–84.

notions about more or less effective entrepreneurial leadership styles. In
accordance with McClelland's findings the 'right' balance between need for
achievement, power and affiliation seems to be an important factor. They
felt that a 'democratic' style (characterized by a moderate level of n Power
combined with high n Ach or a moderate n Ach and a high n Affiliation)
makes for more effective and successful performance.

Litzinger[22] compared the motel entrepreneur with the motel manager
using as one of his instruments the Gordon 'Survey of Interpersonal Values'.[23]
He found that entrepreneurs are lower in 'support' than motel managers, *i.e.*
entrepreneurs placed a lower value of being understood, receiving encouragement, and being treated with consideration.

Lynn[24] found — after giving a group of entrepreneurs Eysenck's 'Personality Inventory'[25] — that entrepreneurs scored higher on neuroticism (a
concept closely linked to anxiety) compared to a group of general managers
(a finding which was statistically significant).

Hornaday and Aboud[26] were interested in racial differences among entrepreneurs and compared twenty black and twenty white entrepreneurs using
Kuder's 'Occupational Interest Survey',[27] Gordon's 'Survey of Interpersonal
Values'[28] and a questionnaire composed of three scales from Edward's
Personal Preference Scale.[29] In addition, they used data from a similar, earlier
study.[30] They found that compared to the population in general, entrepreneurs
scored significantly higher on scales reflecting need for achievement, independence, and effectiveness of leadership and low on the scale of need for
support. The differences between the black and white subgroups were
minor. Furthermore, they felt that the profile they developed of the entrepreneur did not distinguish between a successful one and the individual who
made an unsuccessful attempt at entrepreneurship.

Komives[31] studied the values of high technology entrepreneurs. In using

[22] Litzinger, William D., 'The Motel Entrepreneur and the Motel Manager', *Academy of Manage-ment Journal*, Vol. 8, No. 4, 1965.
[23] Gordon, Leonard V., *Manual for Survey of Interpersonal Values*, Chicago: Science Research Associates, 1960.
[24] Lynn, R., 'Personality Characteristics of a Group of Entrepreneurs', *Occupational Psychology*, Vol. 43, 1969, pp. 151-2.
[25] Eysenck, H. J., *The Dynamics of Anxiety and Hysteria*, London: Routledge and Kegan Paul, 1957.
[26] Hornaday, John A. and Aboud, John, 'Characteristics of Successful Entrepreneurs', *Personnel Psychology*, Vol. 24, No. 2, Summer 1971, pp. 141-53.
[27] Kuder, Frederic, *Manual for the Kuder Preference Record: Form DD*, Chicago: Science Research Associates, 1970.
[28] Gordon, L. V., op. cit.
[29] Edwards, Allen L., *Manual for the Edwards' Personal Preference Schedule*, New York: The Psychological Corporation, 1959.
[30] Hornaday, John A. and Bunker, Charles S., 'The Nature of the Entrepreneur', *Personnel Psychology*, Vol. 23, No. 1, Spring 1970, pp. 47-54.
[31] Komives, John L., 'A Preliminary Study of the Personal Values of High Technology Entre-preneurs', in Cooper, A. C. and Komives, J. L. (Eds.), *Technical Entrepreneurship: A Symposium*, 1972.

Allport–Vernon–Lindsey's 'Study of Values'[32] he discovered high aesthetic sense as the most meaningful indicator differentiating entrepreneurs from the general population. Entrepreneurs scored high on theoretical orientation and low on religious values. In using Gordon's 'Survey of Personal Values'[33] and Gordon's 'Survey of Interpersonal Values'[34] he found that entrepreneurs were high on achievement, leadership orientation and decisiveness but low on goal orientation, need for support, orderliness, comformity and practical mindedness. Moreover, entrepreneurs did not have high scores on economic values.

Litvak and Maule[35] looked at technical entrepreneurs in Canada using a simple questionnaire approach. The responses indicated that entrepreneurs wanted to have their own business because of (1) the challenge, (2) being one's own boss, (3) the freedom to explore new ideas.

Shapero[36] used Rotter's[37] 'Internal–External' scale to determine the 'locus of control' of entrepreneurs. Entrepreneurs tended to be on the 'internal' end of the scale. 'Internal' people were defined as individuals who felt that they have some influence on the course of events in their life (as opposed to 'external' people who felt dominated by outside forces such as luck or fate). For 'internal' people personal destiny comes from within and therefore they tend to be more self-reliant and more in need of independence and autonomy.

The psychological picture which emerges from this brief review is sometimes conflicting and confusing. It appears that particularly high achievement motivation is an important aspect in the entrepreneurial personality, but in addition, autonomy, independence and moderate risk taking are contributing factors. The entrepreneur also emerges as an anxious individual, a nonconformist poorly organized and not a stranger to self-destructive behaviour. Although power motivation is important, the degree of power motivation varies and has an influence on effective leadership style. Entrepreneurs seem to be 'inner directed', present themselves as self-reliant, and tend to de-emphasize or neglect interpersonal relations. And finally, entrepreneurs possess a higher than average aesthetic sense which may contribute to their ability to set up 'new combinations'.

Some Propositions About Entrepreneurial Types

A further refinement in the study of the entrepreneurial personality particularly

[32] Allport, Gordon W. and Lindsey, Gardner, *Assessment of Human Motives*, New York: Holt, Rinehart and Winston, 1964.

[33] Gordon, L. V., op. cit.

[34] Gordon, Leonard V., *Research Briefs on Survey of Interpersonal Values*, Chicago: Science Research Associates, 1963.

[35] Litvak, Isiaih A. and Maule, Christopher J., 'Profiles of Technical Entrepreneurs', *The Business Quarterly*, Summer 1974, pp. 40–9.

[36] Shapero, Albert, 'The Displaced, Uncomfortable Entrepreneur', *Psychology Today*, November 1975.

[37] Rotter, Julian B., 'External Control and Internal Control', *Psychology Today*, June 1971.

as it applies to testing entrepreneurial behaviour patterns might be in place. It is possible that entrepreneurs do not make up a homogeneous group. For example Smith[38] suggested two types of entrepreneurs: the craftsman-entrepreneur and the opportunistic-entrepreneur. He described the craftsman-entrepreneur as an individual narrow in education and training, low in social awareness and involvement, a lack of competence in dealing with the social environment and a limited or circumscribed time orientation. In contrast, the opportunistic-entrepreneur exhibits breadth in education and training, a high social awareness and involvement, a high confidence in dealing with the social environment and an awareness and orientation toward the future. Smith tries to relate these two 'ideal' constructed types to type of firm (defined as rigid *versus* adaptive). He then postulates that the craftsman-entrepreneur will tend to build a rigid firm while the opportunistic entrepreneur will create an adaptive firm (rigidity and adaptability depend on customer and product mix, production methods, dispersement of markets and production facilities, and plans for change). A main discriminating factor between these two types seems to be education. To go beyond this simple demographic differential (and establish what the reason for this difference is) a more in-depth analysis of personal history and non-work environment is necessary to see if there are distinctly different personality patterns. Only then are we on more solid ground to explore the possibility of two different types.

Most of the efforts at distinguishing entrepreneurial types have been directed at the spin-off, high technology, R and D or technical entrepreneur.[39] The common background of this 'type' of entrepreneur is usually previous work experience in high technology organizations or universities. What characterizes entrepreneurship of this nature most of all is the higher tolerance for formal education (average education a Master of Science degree). In addition, we see the regular use of entrepreneurial teams (a possible indication that interpersonal relations and control are less problematic) for this suggested subgroup.

Although it may very well be that the R and D entrepreneur is distinctly different in personality make-up, insufficient evidence exists at this point and more research is needed. Also the relationship between the opportunistic and R and D entrepreneur is not very clear. The type construction can be

[38] Smith, Norman R., *The Entrepreneur and His Firm: the Relationship Between Type of Man and Type of Company*, East Lansing: Michigan State University, Graduate School of Business Administration, 1967.

[39] Roberts, Edward B. and Wainer, Herbert A., 'Some Characteristics of Technical Entrepreneurs', *Research Program on the Management of Science and Technology*, Massachusetts Institute of Technology, 1966, pp. 145–66; Roberts, Edward B., 1968, op. cit.; Cooper, Arnold C., 'Technical Entrepreneurship: What Do We Know?', *Research and Development Management*, Vol. 3, Oxford: Basil Blackwell, 1973, pp. 59–64.

questioned. Overlap in types is very likely and the question of other types may be raised.

Naturally, the possibility exists that a new type of entrepreneur is emerging; an individual who is better educated, not as impulsive, less concerned about control and independence and more adaptive in his approach to the environment. If this is a trend in entrepreneurship, its impact on existing large companies (as far as internal entrepreneurship is concerned, creation of new product ventures and new technology divisions in existing companies) could be enormous. Perhaps 'internal' entrepreneurship in large bureaucratic organizations is the inevitable response to organizational decay and inertia. Which organizational parameters are important to create a work environment congenial to 'internal' entrepreneurship is another issue worth exploring, but will not be dealt with in this paper.

Patterns in Entrepreneurship

After this short interlude speculating about possible entrepreneurial types, we will continue this article by reviewing some of the social and economic factors which influence entrepreneurship. Many writers who have studied demographic patterns among entrepreneurs have indicated that entrepreneurs frequently belong to ethnic or religious minority groups.[40] Max Weber's 'Protestant Ethic thesis'[41] can be viewed as the starting point in the introduction of hypotheses of this nature. The *Santri* Moslems of Java, the Jains, Parsees, and Sikhs in India, Indians and Chinese in South-East Asia, Lebanese in North Africa, Ibos in Nigeria and the Jews in various parts of the world are only a few illustrations of the role minorities play.

The hypothesis is often put forth that the possession of, and belief in, different value systems from that of the mainstream of society will contribute to the development of unconventional patterns of behaviour–entrepreneurship being one of them. Hagen[42] postulates a cycle of events which culminates in the emergence of the entrepreneurial personality. In a society characterized by traditional values (as reflected in child-rearing practices) status deterioration of a particular segment of the population may cause a psychosocial disequilibrium leading to a situation of withdrawal of status respect and depletion of self-esteem. Anger, anxiety and suppression of traditional values follows eventually, contributing to a state of retreatism for this particular

[40] Roberts, Edward B. and Wainer, Herbert, A., ibid.; Hagen, Everett, *On the Theory of Social Change*, Homewood, Ill.: Dorsey, 1962; Kasdan, Leonard, 'Family Structure, Migration and the Entrepreneur', *Comparative Studies in Society and History*, Vol. VII, No. 4, 1965; Kets de Vries, Manfred, F. R., *The Entrepreneur as Catalyst of Economic and Cultural Change*, unpublished Doctoral Dissertation, Harvard University, Graduate School of Business Administration, 1970.

[41] Weber, Max, *The Protestant Ethic and the Spirit of Capitalism*, translated by Talcott Parsons, New York: Scribner, 1930.

[42] Hagen, Everett, op. cit.

group as reflected in the phenomena of normlessness, shiftlessness and anomie. However, this is an unstable state, and it may trigger off certain personality transformations. The existence of individuals who have gone through this process may be one of the contributing factors to the emergence of creative, innovative entrepreneurial activity. These changes in personality can be explained by the fact that the old patterns of behaviour of social group and family are not respected and acceptable any longer, therefore new innovative modes have to be found to integrate the individual with society. And according to Hagen four types of events can produce this process of status withdrawal: (1) displacement by force (*i.e.* by political upheavals and wars), (2) denigration of valued symbols (*i.e.* religion), (3) inconsistency of status symbols with changes of the distribution of economic power, and (4) non-acceptance of expected status of immigrant groups.

We can observe repeatedly how members of minority groups are exposed to discriminatory treatment in one form or another which prevents them from obtaining one of the more established, usually higher status bearing roles in society. As a consequence there is often no other choice open for these groups than doing something new, something which has not been done before.[43] We observe the creation of new roles out of necessity since many existing occupations are closed or barred to these individuals. Immigrants and political refugees who also have to deal with changes in original status position obviously fall into this category. They are another type of minority group suffering from displacement.

Besides the fact that entrepreneurs frequently come from ethnic, religious, or some other form of minority group, there is another pattern which stands out. Many entrepreneurs come from families where the father has been self-employed in one form or another.[44] The vicissitudes of self-employment, its ups and downs, its turmoil and other psychosocial uncertainties have a profound effect on the family situation and will influence career orientation at a later stage. Shakespeare's advice, 'better take the ills you have than fly to others that you know not of', seems very appropriate. It appears that in spite of the hardships so often experienced by the father, the son frequently follows his footsteps because, paradoxically enough, familiarity with the fact that obstacles have to be overcome in some way has an assuring quality. Moreover, early exposure to risk may increase one's tolerance to it.

But these conditions do not necessarily make for entrepreneurship. We can only postulate that — given these special background factors — individuals

[43] The alternative might be the establishment of ghetto areas in case of extreme hostility in the environment with a 'normal' distribution of vocations within the ghetto.

[44] Newcomer, Mabel, 'The Little Businessman: A Study of Business Proprietors in Poughkeepsie, New York', *Business History Review*, Vol. 35, No. 4, 1961; Collins, O. F., Moore, D. G. and Unwalla, D. B., op. cit.; Roberts, Edward B., op. cit.; Litvok, I. A. and Maule, C. J., op. cit.; Ket de Vries, M. F. R., op. cit.

originating from selected segments of society might have a greater disposition for developing entrepreneurial characteristics. We are not describing a causal relationship but probably only a part of a more complex phenomenon which contributes to the emergence of entrepreneurship. Changes in institutional patterns such as the legal system, infrastructure, technology, the political situation and resource availability will be other important dimensions.

As we have pointed out, environmental turbulence appears to be one of the dimensions responsible for the emergence of entrepreneurship. And this relationship is not only applicable to society at large but has some validity for individual industry segments. For example, Peterson and Berger[45] drew attention to the fact that in the popular music recording industry the emergence of entrepreneurship has been directly associated with the degree of turbulence in the industry. But, again we have to be careful not to arrive at simple causal relationships. These various studies point at an environmental turbulence–entrepreneurship loop, but the exact nature of these interrelationships is far from clear and extremely complex.

Entrepreneurial Family Dynamics[46]

In view of these frequently encountered general background factors of entrepreneurs and the importance of turbulence in the environment it follows that the childhood of many of them is portrayed as a very disturbing experience. Discussions with entrepreneurs are more often than not filled with images of endured hardships.[47] Desertion, death, neglect and poverty are themes which continue to be brought up in conversations with entrepreneurs. And in these conversations facts and fantasies about hardship intertwine and become indistinguishable. This pattern seems to belong to entrepreneurial mythology and the entrepreneurs usually oblige. It is worth realizing that as far as personality dynamics are concerned, the difference between perceived and real hardship is rather slim. For the impact on personality it is perception that counts, even if distorted.

In these 'memories of things past' the father appears to be the main villain in the life history of entrepreneurs. He is frequently blamed for deserting, manipulating, or neglecting the family. Death may be interpreted by a child as the ultimate form of desertion or rejection. What these conversations and

[45] Peterson, Richard A. and Berger, David G., 'Entrepreneurship in Organizations: Evidence from the Popular Music Industry', *Administrative Science Quarterly*, Vol. 16, No. 1, March 1971, pp. 97–106.

[46] Forty entrepreneurs were interviewed by the author, individuals who were operating in a wide range of industries. The interviews were of an open-ended nature to have maximum cooperation and a minimum of strain (no psychological tests were used). In addition, thirty life histories of entrepreneurs were studied (autobiographies, biographies and selected articles). Collins, Moore and Unwalla's study *The Enterprising Man* was also very influential in formulating concepts for this article.

[47] Collins, O. F., Moore, D. G. and Unwalla, D. B., op. cit.; Collins, Orvis, F. and Moore, David G., *The Organization Makers*, New York: Appleton–Century–Crofts, 1970.

study of life histories of entrepreneurs indicate is that a remote or absent father makes for a poor role model for the child.[48] The lack of familiarity and unpredictability of a remote father image makes the process of growing up not a very happy or harmonious one. It may leave the child and later the adult troubled by a burdensome psychological inheritance centred around problems of self-esteem, insecurity and lack of confidence. Repressed aggressive wishes towards persons in control are not strange to these individuals and the resulting sense of impotence and helplessness contributes to these feelings of rage, insecurity and low self-esteem.

Given the nature of family dynamics, the absence or remoteness of the father image in the family is often complemented by the mother who assumes part of the father's role. In conversations with entrepreneurs their mothers usually come across as strong, decisive, controlling women who give the family some sense of direction and cohesiveness.

A Conceptual Approach

One way of looking at the family dynamics of entrepreneurs and its role and emerging career orientations is by using a simplified conceptualization of basic personality dimensions. Here, referral is made to the polarities high control–low control, and acceptance–rejection, attitudes expressed by parents toward their children.[49] The way parents relate to these dimensions becomes extremely important for later personality development. The eventual personality make-up of the adult will heavily depend on the way in which these personality dimensions are emphasized and expressed by the parents, and eventually assimilated and internalized by the developing child. Combinations of these personality dimensions lead to four possible configurations for each parent. (Respectively: acceptance and high control, acceptance and low control, rejection and high control, rejection and low control.) Naturally the existence of siblings, the nature and intensity of intersibling rivalry, the competition for parental affection, and the latters' reactions, adds to the complexity of the dynamics of family life.

Consistency in childrearing assumes that parents will take a similar stand toward these personality dimensions. But given each person's unique psychological make-up, this situation will be rare, in spite of the fact that generally accepted childrearing practices encourage parents to make a concerted effort to appear as a 'closed front' to their children. It is obvious that the parents of entrepreneurs usually do not fall into the category of consistency in childrearing. At the risk of over-simplification, a possible configuration in the family of the potential entrepreneur (postulating a father who is remote

[48] Collins, O. F., Moore, D. G. and Unwalla, D. B., ibid.; Kets de Vries, M. F. R., op. cit.

[49] Becker, W. C., op. cit.; White, Robert W., *The Enterprise of Living*, New York: Holt, Rinehart and Winston, 1972.

or absent and a mother who is dominant but supportive) gives the impression of the father as low on control and basically rejective (in the child's fantasy world remoteness easily become synonymous with rejection) while the mother will be perceived as high on control and accepting. Naturally, the child's perception of the intensity of each dimension by parent will vary. And we can observe how, in spite of the limited integration of these perceptions by the child (the great dissonance between parental attitudes makes integration of the child's perceptions very difficult), some integration of these images will occur, to be assimilated and internalized by the child. We hypothesize that in the case of the potential entrepreneur a perception of high control and rejection usually becomes the predominant pattern.

The lack of integration of these parental configurations, in addition to each parent's stand on these two personality dimensions leaves the child with a feeling of inconsistency, confusion and frustration. On the one hand the child may submit to the control of the mother mainly with fear, anxiety and a sense of helplessness, while on the other hand the perceived rejection by the father is also resented and leads to aggressive retaliatory fantasies. A state of anger may be the legacy of this particular type of family dynamics, anger which may be directed toward the self or projected to others contributing to a sense of guilt and undermining of self-confidence. In a later state of personality development this tendency toward hostility and anger may injure relationships with peers.

In the case that the predominant attitudes of parents are rejection and high control, the psychologist White (a researcher of longitudinal life histories) comments that:

'. . . When combined with rejection, high control still exerts a pressure for docile compliance but there is now a problem connected with hostility. Rejecting parents offer the child a meagre ration of love in return for his sacrifices of freedom. He submits mainly out of fear, and with resentment. A variety of consequences follow, which are easily understood as different dispositions of the hostility. This may be directed at the self, creating a sense of guilt that eats away at self-confidence and that sometimes plays a part in the development of neurosis. It may injure the relation to other children, promoting either a quarrelsome tendency or, to avoid this, a withdrawal from contact. It may produce half-hearted compliance with authority in which socialized behaviour is performed with sour resignation. It may be displaced to more remote objects such as outgroups seen as enemies of sound values. It may finally come into focus on the parents or on authority in general, producing a belated and often difficult rebellion.'[50]

The combination of a dominant, controlling, somewhat nurturing mother

[50] Ibid., p. 53.

and a remote father, perceived as rejecting, can lead to problems in identity formation and career orientation, a process accentuated by the general inadequacy or unacceptability of the prevailing role models. A person with this type of family background may experience difficulties as an adolescent in deciding upon an occupational identity. Consequently he will not be a stranger to rebellious activities as a turnabout from originally half-hearted compliance toward authority figures. His confusion about career choice may not be a temporary one but may persist throughout his life.

The Reactive Mode

Before society at large recognizes his capabilities, the potential entrepreneur enters a period of disorientation, without apparent goals, but also during which he is testing his abilities and ascertaining his strengths. The future entrepreneur drifts from job to job, encounters difficulties in the acceptance of his ideas, in conceptualizing and structuring possible 'new combinations'. He is perceived by other people as a 'deviant', a person out of place, frequently provocative and irritating because of his seemingly irrational, nonconformistic actions and provocative ideas.

Collins, Moore and Unwalla particularly, point out this non-conformistic stand:

'. . . the way of the entrepreneur is a long, lonely and difficult road. The men who follow it are by necessity a special breed. They are a breed who cannot do well in the established and clearly defined routes available to the rest of us. The road they can follow is one that is lined with difficulties, which most of us could not even begin to overcome. As a group they do not have the qualities of patience, understanding and charity many of us may admire and wish for in our fellows. This is understandable. In the long and trying way of the entrepreneur such qualities may come to be so much excess baggage. What is necessary to the man who travels this way is great imagination, fortitude, and hardness of purpose.

'The men who travel the entrepreneurial way are, taken on balance, not remarkably likeable people. This too is understandable. As any one of them might say in the vernacular of the world of the entrepreneur, "Nice guys don't win" . . .'[51]

Non-conformistic rebelliousness becomes the entrepreneur's mode of behaviour, his way of exerting power and control over an environment perceived as dangerous and uncontrollable. The entrepreneur's actions do not derive from inner strength and self-assurance which a secure, consistent family upbringing would have provided. Instead, the confusing and dis-

[51] Collins, O. F., Moore, D. G. and Unwalla, D. B., op. cit., p. 244.

turbing family interactions forces the entrepreneur to react to situations out of inner insecurity. Optimism and resilience are the manifestations of a denial mechanism originating from a basic depressive conflict and become a form of characterological adjustment. Driving ambition may be viewed as a need to contradict strong feelings of inferiority and helplessness. Hyper-activity becomes a way of covering up passive longings. Passivity changes into activity as a reaction against anxiety.

The future entrepreneur *reacts* against the early demands imposed upon him by his family and immediate environment. If he originally perceives himself as being rejected, he will counteract his helplessness, seize control and do the rejecting himself. But it is behaviour without real conviction, not based on a secure sense of self-esteem and identity. No matter how strong his actions, doubt remains. Feelings of rejection, helplessness, and low self-esteem remain a haunting issue.

The 'reactive model' makes for a sense of impulsivity whereby speediness, abruptness and a lack of planning on a longer term basis determines the entrepreneur's actions. It is short-term, operational planning for the purpose of instant gratification which predominates and makes for success in actions. These people seem to be characterized by a low tolerance for frustration and tension and a low attention span, seemingly in pursuit of immediate gains and satisfactions. For the entrepreneur the initial impression, 'the hunch', often becomes the final conclusion without a further serious search and deliberation process. There seems to be an absence of concentration, of logical objectivity, judgement and reflectiveness, as if the process of cognition is impaired and does not fulfil its integrative function. A lack of analytical thinking, an absence of active search procedures and self-critical reflections becomes a predominant mode.[52]

The Paradox of Success

Thus, due to the frustrations and perceived deprivations experienced in the early stages of life, a prominent pattern among entrepreneurs appears to be a sense of impulsivity, a persistent feeling of dissatisfaction, rejection and powerlessness, forces which contribute to an impairment and depreciation of his sense of self-esteem and affect cognitive processes. The entrepreneur is a man under a great deal of stress, continuously badgered by his past, a past which is experienced and re-experienced in fantasies, daydreams and dreams. These dreams and fantasies often have a threatening content due to the recurrence of feelings of anxiety and guilt which mainly revolve around

[52] Many of David Shapiro's comments about the 'impulsive style' seem very applicable to the entrepreneur. He views as the essential feature of the 'impulsive style': the immediacy of experience and expression of impulse and the immediacy of cognitive response. See Shapiro, David, *Neurotic Styles*, New York: Basic Books, 1965, p. 155.

hostile wishes against parental figures or, more generally, all individuals in a position of authority. Distrust and suspicion of everyone in a position of authority forces the entrepreneur to search for non-structured situations where he can assert his control and independence. He is also an individual who tends to deny his hostile wishes and projects these on the outside world. And it is extremely hard, if not impossible for individuals with an entrepreneural disposition to integrate their personal needs with those of organizations. To design one's own organization, to create and structure organizations centred around themselves — often becomes the only alternative.

The 'reactive mode' which characterizes entrepreneurial behaviour makes for an extremely unstable personality make-up. Since prestige, power, and self-confidence are used as reassuring weapons to deal with low self-esteem, inferiority and related feelings of anxiety, any perceived depletion of these outward symbols may be the cause of a psychological disequilibrium and trigger off impulsive reactions. If self-confidence is weak and inner hostility provokes guilt feelings, punishment is expected unconsciously. Any sign of failure means that expected punishment is at hand, any sign of success may be interpreted as an achievement not really deserved, which again indicates that punishment is not far off. Although the entrepreneur fears failure, the 'irrational' unconscious notion prevails that punishment is deserved, be it only for hostile wishes against authority figures. Using the same kind of logic, success only means that punishment will follow immediately and therefore causes anxiety about future failures and punishments. Given the existence at an unconscious level of fear of success and fear of failure, combined with impulsivity of action and forgoing thorough deliberation and judgement, it is not surprising that the careers of many entrepreneurs appear to be a remarkable succession of business successes and failures. Actually, because of this psychological process the entrepreneur may feel at his best when he has reached 'rock bottom'. His feelings of guilt being 'paid off', he is 'free', unburdened, able to start all over again.

We notice how the entrepreneur emerges as a psychological risk taker subjected to a high degree of psychosocial risks. Due to intrapsychic transformations, original feelings of helplessness, dependency and rejection are replaced by a proactive style in which power, control and autonomy become predominant issues. What used to be an inclination toward submission and passivity becomes an active impulsive mode of behaviour. The entrepreneur may follow what is sometimes described as an 'identification with the aggressor' pattern.[53] The role of the passive, helpless victim is replaced by acting the role of the one in control. We have indicated before that the often self-employed father was frequently an undependable and terrifying influence to

[53] Freud, Anna, *The Ego and the Mechanisms of Defence*, London: Hogarth Press and the Institute of Psycho-Analysis, 1937.

the entrepreneur in his youth. Now the roles have changed; after having been continuously manipulated at an early age, the entrepreneur will do the manipulation himself (identify with the agressor) in a compensatory fashion, reliving these actions as a kind of 'protective reaction' against first his father and later authority figures in general. We see that the inability to function in structured situations makes it necessary for him to design his own organization where he is in control and at the centre of action. His achievements in setting up enterprises become important tangible symbols of prestige and power and a way of bolstering an easily depleted, insecure sense of self-esteem. But his achievements are not sufficient to ward off a persisting sense of anxiety and other stress indicators. Rejection, dissatisfaction and a sense of failure follow the entrepreneur like an inseparable shadow. (A summary of the various psychological forces working upon the potential entrepreneur is given in figure 1.)

The Entrepreneurial Work Environment

The preparatory period of entrepreneurship, as we have seen, is accompanied by authority conflicts, failures in organizational socialization, difficulties in adapting to organizational structure and predictable job-hopping behaviour, which has set the stage for the very unique relationship of the entrepreneur with his enterprise. Expectedly, the enterprise becomes the new setting where the entrepreneur's problems in adaptation and conforming to structure are accentuated and dramatized. Naturally, the enterprise itself becomes the tangible symbol to the entrepreneur of his success in 'overcoming odds' and assumes a much greater symbolic emotional significance than the reality of the situation may warrant. The enterprise is much more than merely a vehicle for profit maximization; it is not only the entrepreneur's contact with reality but, in addition, demonstrates his ability to create a new reality derived from confused internal images centred around conflict and frustration with authority figures. In a psychodynamic sense — using the defence reaction formation — the enterprise symbolizes the capacity of the entrepreneur in solving and compensating for endured childhood frustrations and hardships by creating an environment where, for a change, he is in control, not dependent on the whims and favours of undependable authority figures — a situation which was so resented in the past. Unlike the manager's relationship with organizations, the level at which an entrepreneur deals with his own organization is therefore far more intense and conflict ridden; this pattern cannot be explained merely by the higher financial risks at stake. While previously avoidance of structure and organizations was his way of coping with life, his own organization becomes the end of the road. For the entrepreneur there seems no other place to go, a development which contributes to the emotional significance of the enterprise.

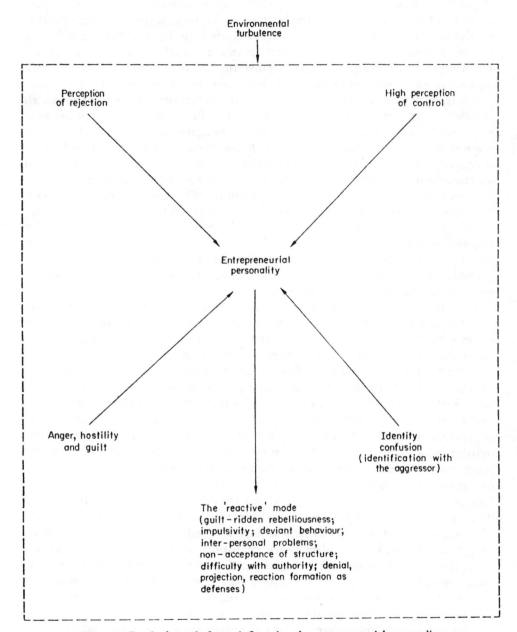

Figure 1. Psychodynamic forces influencing the entrepreneurial personality

But this very fact of complete psychological immersion of the entrepreneur — a factor which may have been a key ingredient for the initial success of the enterprise — can lead to serious dysfunctional developments in the future in the case of continued growth of the enterprise. What we frequently encounter in an entrepreneurial organization is an organizational structure and work environment completely dependent and dominated by the entrepreneur. The enterprise is run in a very autocratic, directive way whereby all the decision-making processes centre around the entrepreneur. We are also faced with an individual who refuses to delegate, is impulsive, lacks any interest in conscious, analytical forms of planning, and engages regularly in bold, proactive moves. Bold and proactive moves make for the initial successes and may contribute to the continued success of the enterprise, but due to the absence of a conscious planning effort also carry a high risk component. The entrepreneur makes no distinction between operating, day-to-day decision-making and more long-term strategic moves. The impulsivity of his style, his lack of deliberation and judgement, the importance of 'hunches' also makes for a rather limited time horizon. The entrepreneur has no sense of priorities and may spend equal time on the greatest trivia as on major strategic decisions.

Within the organization power depends on the proximity to the entrepreneur, is constantly changing and creates a highly uncertain organizational environment. This state of affairs contributes to a highly politically charged atmosphere where changing coalitions and collusions are the order of the day. The suprastructure is poorly defined, a formal organization chart is outdated by the time it is drawn, or non-existent. It basically resembles a 'spider's web' with the entrepreneur in the centre, who is constantly changing loyalties and keeping his subordinates in a state of confusion and dependence. The organization has usually a poorly defined or poorly used control and information system (no sharing of information); there is an absence of standard procedures and rules and a lack of formalization. Instead, we notice the use of subjective, personal criteria for the purpose of measurement and control. Job descriptions and job responsibilities are poorly defined or non-existent. This situation contributes to a high incidence of role conflict and role ambiguity leading to low job satisfaction, low self-confidence, a high degree of job-related tension, a high sense of futility and low confidence in the organization.[54] Withdrawal or avoidance behaviour and a reduction in communication among employees also becomes symptomatic. Information hoarding turns into a common practice and contributes to the general state of disorganization. In addition, given the 'spider's web' structure, the number of people reporting to the entrepreneur will be large, adding to a

[54] Kahn, Robert L., Wolfe, Donald M., Quinn, Robert P. and Snoek, G. Diedrick, *Organizational Stress: Studies in Role Conflict and Ambiguity*, New York: Wiley, 1964.

Table I. Entrepreneurial work environment

Leadership style	Autocratic Directive
Decision-making	Centralized Lack of delegation Impulsivity Lack of conscious planning Bold, proactive moves Mixture of operating and strategic decision-making
Time horizon	Short
Power	Proximity to entrepreneur
Organizational environment	High uncertainty Lack of sharing information
Suprastructure	Poorly defined Absence of formal organization chart 'Spider's web' structure

Infrastructure	Frequently poorly defined or poorly utilized control and
	    information system
	Absence of standard procedures and rules
	No formalized systems (use of subjective, personal criteria)
	Poor integration of activities
	Poorly defined job descriptions and job responsibilities (high
	    incidence of role conflict and role ambiguity)
	Large horizontal span of control

general sense of confusion. (See table I for a summary of the dimensions of the entrepreneurial work environment.)

Although the entrepreneur, in the initial stage of development of the enterprise, might have had the ability to inspire his subordinates, the mere fact of growth has complicated this process. His aversion to structure, his preference for personalized relationships and his reluctance to accept constructive criticism makes growth, with its implicit need for a more sophisticated infra- and suprastructure and greater decentralization, increasingly difficult to handle. Hoarding of information, inconsistencies in day-to-day interpretation of company policies, playing of favourites, and refusal or reluctance to let people really know where they stand does not contribute to an efficient and effective organization. And if this pattern becomes predominant and prevails, few capable subordinates will remain in the organization; the ones left will usually be of a mediocre calibre spending a great part of their effort on political infighting. It is the absence of actual responsibility with authority which causes capable people to leave while the yes-man — individuals who do not really challenge the entrepreneur's authority — will stay on.

What we are describing is the potential danger of the entrepreneurial mode; that given the nature of the entrepreneur's conflicts and his peculiar leadership style — useful as these qualities might have been initially — growth may lead to the eventual destruction of the enterprise. if the entrepreneur remains rigid in his attitudes and refuses to formalize the organization and change decision-making patterns. In case of continued growth of the enterprise, the effectiveness of the organization structure and the way of decision-making becomes increasingly insufficient in coping with the complexities of the external environment. The degree of environmental dynamism (change in technology, market behaviour and competitors' reactions), heterogeneity (differences in needs and behaviour of organizational constituents) and hostility (cut-throat competition, resource shortages, *etc.*) determines how long the entrepreneur will be successful in pursuing his old style.[55] Obviously in a very static industry segment the strain on the organization is not so quickly noticeable. And while the time period may vary before the organizational strains become intolerable, utter disorganization, the increasing necessity of coping with the environment and eventual financial losses will often be the inevitable outcomes of the entrepreneur's leadership style. It is this obsession with control, the unwillingness or inability to 'let go', which in the end leaves a rather unpleasant inheritance with the word bankruptcy written all over it. But as we have mentioned before, failure does not come as a surprise; it has been expected by the entrepreneur in a more unconscious sense.

Succession

Given the rigidity in attitudes, the inability to modify behaviour, abdication and succession is often the only alternative if the continued growth of the enterprise is a major goal, given the self-limiting nature of the entrepreneur's leadership style. But management succession is easier talked about than implemented if we take the emotional investment and symbolic meaning of the enterprise into consideration. Although from a rational point of view it may be better for both enterprise and entrepreneur if the entrepreneur distances himself and starts something new, from an emotional point of view this is not such an easy transition. Many rationalizations to prevent this type of transition are used by the entrepreneur. Usually we will hear the argument that there is no one good enough to take over, a statement with the implicit message that there is no alternative but to stay on, a demonstration of a rather insincere reluctance. The paradox of the situation is that the

---

[55] Danny Miller in his doctoral dissertation gives an elaborate description of these dimensions. He uses these dimensions in the formulation of organizational archetypes and the description of their strengths and weaknesses. (See Miller, Danny, *Strategy Making in Context: Ten Empirical Archetypes*, Doctoral Dissertation, McGill University, Faculty of Management, 1976.) For a conceptualization of pathways to success and failure of organizational archetypes including entrepreneurial variations see Miller, Danny, Friesen, Peter and Kets de Vries, Manfred F. R., *The Strategic Audit: and Why Your Organization Might Need It*, McGill University Working Paper, 1976.

entrepreneur has created a work environment of high dependency. He has always looked at any potential infringement upon positions of power and control with suspicion, and therefore it is naturally highly unlikely that a capable administrator has risen through the ranks, making his statements about the impossibility of stepping down a self-fulfilling prophecy.

And family members are certainly not excluded but are as suspect, or more so. They also fall into the category of possible intruders threatening the entrepreneur's position of control. As much as family dynamics are acted out in organizations, the presence of family members in these organizations seems only to intensify the eruption of these conflicts.[56] We can observe a confusion of roles between the social system of the family and that of the enterprise. At the base of these conflicts are feelings of rivalry, whereby the conflict-ridden relationship which the entrepreneur possessed toward his parents is transferred toward his son. What we frequently observe is a re-enactment of the old 'family romance', meaning that the son of the entrepreneur is exposed to the same treatment the entrepreneur felt he once endured. But now it is the entrepreneur who is in the position of authority and control and his son who is dependent on his whims, vulnerable to his erratic and unpredictable behaviour and kept in an infantile position. That the idea of abdication, of stepping down, is resented by the entrepreneur has become obvious, but that succession by his son is even more resented and traumatic has now become less mysterious in view of the reawakening of' these old feelings of rivalry with its connotations of frustration and despair.

Edsel Ford's relationship to his father, the first Henry Ford, is a good illustration of the abrasive dimensions these conflicts can reach and the destructiveness of this type of rivalry to the enterprise.[57] Henry Ford's refusal to change strategy, to make alterations to the Model T and his unwillingness to encourage Edsel Ford in his efforts to build an infra- and suprastructure brought the company to the edge of bankruptcy. Under extraordinary pressures changes were eventually made but at an extremely high cost in material resources and manpower. As was the case with the Ford Motor Company, old age or even death seem often the only times when control can be taken away from the entrepreneur. Unfortunately, at that point it might be too late to save the enterprise.

The successful entrepreneur who manages to guide the enterprise through the formative period of development into a stage of growth and maturity tends to follow a path which eventually may lead to his own functional self-elimination. He is a person at the crossroads, an enigma, on one hand

[56] Levinson, Harry, 'Conflicts that Plague Family Businesses', *Harvard Business Review*, Vol. 49, No. 2, March–April 1971, pp. 90–8.

[57] Jardim, Anne, *The First Henry Ford: a Study in Personality and Business Leadership*, Cambridge, Mass.: MIT Press, 1970.

highly creative and imaginative but, on the other hand, highly rigid, unwilling to change, incapable of confronting the issue of succession. Christensen[58] after studying over a hundred companies, came to a similar conclusion struck by the frequency in which he encountered a denial of the reality of the succession issue among the entrepreneurs.

Succession becomes identified with loss and losing out and therefore takes the meaning of a taboo. But the issue of succession is inevitable not only for reasons of age but also because of increasing maturation and growth of the company. The entrepreneur is no longer alone, other interest groups such as employees, family members, bankers, customers, suppliers and the government are getting involved. Depending on the strength of the entrepreneur's position they can have some influence on the policies of the enterprise. But change by this type of pressure is usually only of a modest character. A more drastic type of change is needed for continued growth and success of the enterprise apart from changes caused by old age or death. We imply here the attainment of a sense of psychological maturity on the part of the entrepreneur. This means a willingness to assess his personal strengths and weaknesses to master his conflict-ridden behaviour and overcome and surpass the problems of the past. But adaptation to present-day reality and foregoing the legacies of his personal history requires a considerable basis of self-awareness and insight. Important as this psychological state might be for the continued survival of the enterprise for overcoming rigid behaviour and greater flexibility in operating modes, adaptation of this kind is rare and hard to attain. More often than not, separation from the enterprise by the entrepreneur in one form or another turns out to be the only alternative for the purpose of survival. This development highlights the depressive facet of the entrepreneurial dimension. While the entrepreneurial spirit is one of the strong countervailing forces preventing decay and decline of the economy as a whole, in the final deliberation, the entrepreneur pays an extremely high price in an emotional sense in this process of economic growth.

---

[58] Christensen, C. Roland, *Management Succession in Small and Growing Enterprises*, Boston: Division of Research, Harvard University, Graduate School of Business Administration, 1953.

[8]

© Academy of Management Journal
1980, Vol. 23, No. 3, 509-520.

Risk Taking Propensity
of Entrepreneurs[1]

ROBERT H. BROCKHAUS, SR.
St. Louis University

The risk taking propensities of entrepreneurs of new ventures were objectively obtained using the Kogan-Wallach choice dilemmas questionnaire and were compared to those of managers and to normative data developed for the measurement instrument. The findings suggest that risk taking propensity may not be a distinguishing characteristic of entrepreneurs. They refute assumptions based on research that has been subjective and noncomparative and that used established entrepreneurs.

Palmer has suggested that psychological testing of entrepreneurs "be directed most toward the measurement of an individual's perception and handling of a risk" (1971, p. 38). The major purpose of the present research is to determine whether founders of new ventures and newly hired managers or newly promoted managers differ in their risk taking propensities. In order for this study to be understood completely, the varied definitions of the term "entrepreneur" must be presented and a functional definition for use in this study must be developed.

Webster's Third New International Dictionary (1961) defines an entrepreneur as "the organizer of an economic venture, especially one who organizes, owns, manages, and assumes the risk of a business." *Funk and Wagnall's Standard Dictionary* (1958) offers a similar definition. It states that an entrepreneur is "one who undertakes to start and conduct an enterprise or business, assuming full control and risks." Schumpeter (1954) credits J. S. Mill with bringing the term into general use among economists. Mill (1848) included as entrepreneurial functions direction, control, superintendence, and risk bearing. Mill appeared to believe that the inclusion of risk bearing distinguished the term "entrepreneur" from the term "manager."

[1]A version of this paper was presented at the annual Academy of Management meetings, Kansas City, 1976. The author would like to thank Walter Nord, Raymond Hilgert, Jerome Steinman, and Barry Anderson of Washington University for their helpful comments and advice.

510   *Academy of Management Journal*   September

In his own writings, Schumpeter stressed that the role of innovation was of major importance in defining the entrepreneur. He placed less emphasis on the role of risk because he believed that both entrepreneurs and managers are subject to the risk of failure.

McClelland (1961) was less restrictive and did not require that the entrepreneur be the owner of the business. He believed that an innovative manager who has decision making responsibility is an entrepreneur. Thus in McClelland's terms a manager in a corporation can be entrepreneurial.

However, Hartmann's (1959) thorough historical discussion of the differences between entrepreneur and manager found that a useful distinction can be made. He supported Weber's (1947) concept, which considered the entrepreneur the ultimate source of all formal authority within the organization. Such a definition, Weber stated, distinguished the entrepreneur from the manager.

Most present day writers would consider the owner-manager of a business to be an entrepreneur. Today, it is further generally accepted that a person who provides capital would not be considered an entrepreneur if he did not also manage the venture. However, many authors, such as Collins and Moore (1964) and Hornaday and Aboud (1971) are even more restrictive in their studies and have examined only business ventures that were successful.

Although it should be noted that different definitions do exist, the definition to be used in this study does not prevent the review of the findings based on somewhat different definitions. However, previous findings based on different definitions may not be true for those defined as entrepreneurs in this study.

In this study, an entrepreneur is defined as a major owner and manager of a business venture who is not employed elsewhere. Such a definition allows for a more distinct comparison of the entrepreneur with the manager than would be obtained if managers with entrepreneurial-like positions were considered as entrepreneurs rather than managers. However, distinction between successful and unsuccessful entrepreneurs will *not* be made. Respondents were selected who very recently had made the decision to become owner-managers. For this reason, the validity of this study will not depend upon a venture's degree of success as would a study based upon entrepreneurs in business long enough to be considered successful or unsuccessful.

ENTREPRENEURIAL RISKS

Liles (1974) speculated about what he believed is at risk in a new venture. He suggested that in becoming an entrepreneur an individual risks financial well-being, career opportunities, family relations, and psychic well-being. The personal financial obligations that the entrepreneur makes to an unsuccessful enterprise can result in major losses to the entrepreneur as an individual and could jeopardize his future standard of living. Moreover, because the entrepreneur is likely to have devoted himself to the venture at a personal level, the failure of the venture becomes, in effect, the failure of the individual and therefore can have major emotional consequences.

Realizing that the financial and emotional consequences of failure could be devastating, Liles suggested that the potential entrepreneur is well advised to analyze carefully the risks associated with his specific business proposal and then to determine whether or not he is willing to undertake them. Liles concluded that the decision depends to a great extent upon the potential entrepreneur's perception of the risk involved.

Risk Preferences

Expectance theorists, especially Atkinson (1957), have stimulated much study of risk preferences. Atkinson's risk taking model is derived from the relationship that McClelland found between need for achievement and preference for moderate probabilities of success. Atkinson's model involves six variables: the subjective probability (i.e., expectance) of success (P_s), the subjective probability of failure (P_f), the incentive value of success (I_s), the incentive value of avoiding failure $(-I_f)$, the achievement motive (M_s), and the motive to avoid failure (M_f). Atkinson assumed that I_s is a positive linear function of difficulty and can be represented by $(1 - P_s)$. He assumed further that $-I_f$ is a negative linear function of difficulty and can be represented by $-P_s$. The variables are combined multiplicatively in the following equation: Resultant motivation $= (M_s \times P_s \times I_s) + (M_f \times P_f \times -I_f)$. The resultant motivation function has a maximum at $P_s = .5$ if M_s is greater than M_f. Where M_f is greater than M_s, the resultant motivation function would be a maximum either at the lowest value of P_s or the highest value of P_s.

The major prediction that follows from Atkinson's theory is that performance level should be greatest when there is greatest uncertainty about the outcome (when subjective probability of success is .50). This prediction should be true regardless of whether the motive to achieve or the motive to avoid failure is stronger within an individual. However, persons in whom the achievement motive is stronger should prefer intermediate risk, and those in whom the motive to avoid failure is stronger should avoid intermediate risk, preferring instead either very easy and safe undertakings *or* extremely difficult and speculative ones. This preference is based on the theory that an individual with a stronger motivation to avoid failure will tend either to succeed with the safe task or will be easily able to explain failure of a very speculative task without assuming personal blame, which he finds particularly painful.

McClelland (1961) has stated that the situations in which an individual's degree of control or skill is most important are moderately risky situations rather than very risky or very certain ones. According to McClelland, the individual needs no more than average ability to perform successfully the functions that fall within the limits of the safe end of the continuum, but no amount of skill can help in the situation of pure chance.

Entrepreneurial Risk Preferences

These three levels of risk preferences—low, intermediate or moderate, and high—could affect an individual's decision to start a business venture. Mancuso (1975) stated that individuals who are considered established entrepreneurs tend to be moderate risk takers, but he did not provide empirical support for his viewpoint, nor did he suggest what the propensity for risk taking might have been at the time the entrepreneurial decision was made. Perhaps in some instances, as the entrepreneur becomes more aware of his business environment, he realizes that the venture has been more risky than he originally perceived it.

As noted earlier, no studies have considered the risk taking propensity of individuals whose business ventures failed before becoming reasonably well established. These individuals may have considered their ventures to involve moderate or low risks, or they may have recognized the highly speculative nature of their proposed ventures and even believed that there was a greater likelihood for failure than for success. As stated above, if their motivation to avoid failure was very strong, they may have preferred to fail in a high-risk environment where failure could be explained without assuming personal blame, instead of in a more moderate risk setting, where they might more likely be blamed personally for failure. Previous researchers who studied established (and, therefore, at least moderately successful) entrepreneurs may have eliminated from their studies those entrepreneurs who chose high-risk ventures and failed, as well as those who started what they considered to be low-risk ventures and failed.

Although previous research has not specifically compared the risk taking propensity of individuals who decided to start their own business venture with that of individuals not so inclined, research conducted by Meyer, Walker, and Litwin (1961), studied "managers" of shop operations in manufacturing plants and "staff specialists" to determine the relationship between measured motive patterns of individuals and their adjustment to particular job roles. The authors hypothesized that managers in jobs with definite entrepreneurial characteristics would score higher on a measure of need for achievement than would specialists whose jobs were nonentrepreneurial. Further, they hypothesized that in situations requiring decisions involving risk, the "entrepreneurs" would prefer risks with odds of success near 50-50, because previous research had shown this preference to be associated with achievement motivation. The study found that managers selected to represent the entrepreneurial role did show greater preference for intermediate risks on a risk preference questionnaire than did specialists of comparable age, education, and job level.

If managers holding positions with entrepreneurial characteristics have greater preferences for moderate level risks than do specialists whose jobs are nonentrepreneurial, then perhaps these findings can be generalized to include actual entrepreneurs. The writings previously referred to may suggest that actual entrepreneurs have a stronger preference for moderate risks. However, it is conceivable that the preference for moderate level risk is not associated with actual ownership of a business but rather with the managerial demands of any job. If this conjecture is true, then there should not be a significant difference in risk taking propensities between owner-managers and managers whose jobs are entrepreneurial with the exception of ownership.

Entrepreneurial literature since the writings of Mill has included risk bearing as a major distinguishing characteristic between the functions of a manager and those of an entrepreneur. Entrepreneurial risk can be divided into three components: the general risk taking propensity of a potential entrepreneur, the perceived probability of failure for a specific venture, and the perceived consequences of failure. Because the latter two components require intimate knowledge of the specific venture before they can be evaluated, a study based on them would be very difficult and very likely subject to uncontrolled independent variables. However, the general risk taking propensity of the entrepreneurs and managers can be compared empirically to determine whether this component of risk distinguishes entrepreneurs from managers.

Definition of Risk Taking Propensity

For the purpose of this study, the propensity for risk taking is defined as the perceived probability of receiving the rewards associated with success of a proposed situation, which is required by an individual before he will subject himself to the consequences associated with failure, the alternative situation providing less reward as well as less severe consequences than the proposed situation. Such a definition might best describe the situation that faces the potential entrepreneur when he decides to establish a new business venture.

METHOD

Participants

The study was conducted using three groups of participants. One group was composed of individuals who within the three months prior to the study ceased working for their employers and at the time of the study owned as well as managed business ventures. Because their businesses had not existed long enough to have failed, a broad spectrum of entrepreneurs is included, i.e., those who will be successful and those who will be unsuccessful.

The entrepreneurial group was compared with two groups of managers who were similar otherwise to the entrepreneurs. Members of both groups of managers also had changed positions within three months prior to the study. One group of managers had changed organizations, and the other had only changed positions within an organization.

This study initially involved only these three groups, and a comparison of the entrepreneurs with a more general population was not planned prior to the study. However, after the initial data analysis was conducted, comparison with a more generalized population seemed desirable. The normative data obtained by Kogan and Wallach (1964) was used as the best available data approximating the general population.

Measurement Instrument

Wallach and Kogan (1959, 1961) developed the choice dilemmas questionnaire (CDQ) to obtain probability preferences in everyday life situations. On this test a subject is presented with 12 hypothetical situations. Each item requires the respondent to choose between a safe alternative and a more attractive but risky one. In addition, the respondent is asked to indicate the probability of success sufficient for him to select the risky alternative. A typical item is:

> Mr. A, an electrical engineer, who is married and has one child, has been working for a large electronics corporation since graduating from college five years ago. He is assured of a lifetime job with a modest, though adequate, salary, and liberal pension benefits upon retirement. On the other hand, it is very unlikely that his salary will increase much before he retires. While attending a convention, Mr. A is offered a job with a small, newly founded company which has a highly uncertain future. The new job would pay more to start and would offer the possibility of a share in the ownership if the company survived the competition of the larger firms.
>
> Imagine that you are advising Mr. A. Listed below are several probabilities or odds of the new company's proving financially sound.
>
> Please check the lowest probability that you would consider acceptable to make it worthwhile for Mr. A to take the new job.
>
> _____ The chances are 1 in 10 that the company will prove financially sound.
> _____ The chances are 3 in 10 that the company will prove financially sound.
> _____ The chances are 5 in 10 that the company will prove financially sound.
> _____ The chances are 7 in 10 that the company will prove financially sound.
> _____ The chances are 9 in 10 that the company will prove financially sound.
> _____ Place a check here if you think Mr. A should *not* take the new job no matter what the probabilities.

The items contained in the CDQ are not in any respect a representative sample of all possible items in the universe. Therefore, instruments similar to the CDQ could readily be constructed. There is no basis known for the creation of any other possible scale as a measure of risk taking propensity. The CDQ score summarizes the responses made to a particular set of 12 choice dilemmas. A maximum score of 120 is possible, and 12 is the minimum score. Lower scores are associated with less conservatism in risk taking situations.

Kogan and Wallach (1964) reported reliabilities of .53 for the men and .62 for women using odd-even coefficients stepped up by the Spearman-Brown formula and considered to be adequate.

Items from the CDQ have been extensively used by researchers of risk taking propensity. Unfortunately, all reported research in the United States that utilized all of the items has used college students or elderly persons as subjects. Thus a comparison of the results of the present research with the results of previous research is necessarily of limited value.

However, after a thorough search of the literature, it was concluded that the most widely used and most appropriate instrument for the present research was the CDQ, despite its limitations. The limitations were determined to be of less importance because the primary purpose for inclusion of this instrument was to measure the relative differences between groups.

Procedure

The businesses whose owners served as participants were selected from the listing of businesses licensed by St. Louis County, Missouri, during the months of August and September 1975.

From this total listing of businesses, branch outlets of existing businesses were eliminated. Also eliminated were businesses that had been established previous to August but had recently relocated and were being licensed to do business at the new location. After this elimination procedure, the names of 93 businesses remained.

Each of these businesses received a letter informing the owner of a meeting to be offered at four different times at the School of Business and Administration of Saint Louis University. One purpose, stated in the letter for the meeting, was to gather information anonymously about the beliefs, attitudes, and background of the business owners. The second purpose mentioned was to allow the owners to meet one another socially and exchange information.

Each business was contacted by telephone to see if the owner would attend one of the meetings. If a business had more than one owner, the first one contacted by telephone was the only one who was considered for this study. Furthermore, if the owner was employed elsewhere he was eliminated from this study.

A total of 58 questionnaires were either provided during the meetings or mailed to those entrepreneurs unable to attend a meeting. Of these, 31 were completed in usable form. Five others were returned but were not completed as requested and therefore were disregarded.

The names of managers were obtained from St. Louis area newspaper articles that deal with personnel changes. Only one manager per organization was asked to serve as a participant. These managers received letters similar to those sent to the entrepreneurs except that these letters stated that managers were the focal point of the meetings.

A total of 106 questionnaires were either provided during the meetings or mailed to managers unable to attend any of the sessions. Of the 51 questionnaires provided to the promoted managers, 38 were returned but 3 were not correctly completed, leaving 35 in usable form for the study. Of the 55 managers who had joined a new organization, 40 returned questionnaires but 4 did not complete them correctly, leaving 36 in usable form.

To allow both managerial groups to be equal in size to the group of entrepreneurs, four questionnaires from individuals promoted within an organization and five questionnaires from individuals who had recently joined a new organization were randomly selected and eliminated from further data analysis.

It was necessary to determine whether significantly different results would have been obtained if all of the participants had responded. To make this assessment, two procedures were used.

First, the data provided by each primary group of respondents who attended the meetings was compared with the data for the same primary group of respondents who mailed in their responses. No significant differences were found to exist between either segment of any of the three groups. Second, the types of businesses and/or positions held by respondents of each primary group were compared with those of nonrespondents for each primary group. Once again no apparent differences were observed. However, these comparisons do not assure that similar results would definitely have been obtained had all participants responded.

RESULTS

The null hypothesis developed for this study is presented below:

Individuals who, within the past three months, have ceased working for their employers and now own as well as manage business ventures, will have the same risk-taking propensity as will

a) individuals who, within the past three months, have ceased working for their employers and now are managers for different employers, and

b) individuals who, within the past three months, have assumed new managerial positions with the same firms with which they have been associated for a year or more.

In order to test the hypothesis, data from the Kogan-Wallach CDQ were used. The mean CDQ score for the entrepreneurs was 71, while the transferred managers' mean score was 72.52, and the promoted managers' mean score was 66.97 (Table 1).

TABLE 1
Means and Standard Deviations on Kogan-Wallach
Choice Dilemmas Questionnaire

Group	Number of Respondents	Mean	Standard Deviation
Entrepreneurs	31	71.00	11.94
Transferred managers	31	72.52	12.19
Promoted managers	31	66.97	10.84

TABLE 2
Summary of Analysis of Variance on Kogan-Wallach
Choice Dilemmas Questionnaire

Source of Variation	df	SS	MS	F	Level of Significance
Between group	2	509.87	254.94	1.87	.1579
Within group	90	12262.71	136.25		
Total	92	12772.58			

If the range of differences among the three group means was similar to the range reported by Kogan and Wallach (1964), there is a 73 percent probability that it would have been discovered. This probability of detection or "power" of the statistical test was based on the range of means reported by Kogan and Wallach, 3 groups of 31 participants each and a Type I error of 5 percent. Although no generally accepted convention for significant power value exists, Cohen (1969) recommended 80 percent but noted that values larger than 60 percent should be considered acceptable. It therefore is concluded that if a difference in risk taking propensity had existed it probably would have been discovered.

A one-way analysis of variance test (Table 2) indicated that the CDQ scores of the three groups were not significantly different from each other. Therefore, the null research hypothesis was accepted in its entirety; the entrepreneurs appear to have the same risk taking propensity as managers.

In order to understand more fully the significance of risk taking propensity as it relates to the decision to start a business venture, additional exploratory analysis was conducted using the CDQ scores of the entrepreneurs together with the mean scores and standard deviations reported by Kogan and Wallach (1964) for 114 undergraduate male students and 103 undergraduate female students.

The chi-squared test of significance indicates that no significant difference exists at the .25 level of confidence between the distribution of the entrepreneurs' scores and those scores obtained from the Kogan-Wallach study, assuming normal distribution for the Kogan-Wallach data.

A Kolmogorov confidence band with a confidence coefficient of 95 percent was established using the data reported by Kogan-Wallach and assuming that the data were normally distributed. All individual scores for entrepreneurs were found to lie within this band, as illustrated in Figure 1. It therefore is concluded that the distribution of risk taking propensity held by entrepreneurs is the same as the distribution of risk taking in the general population, i.e., the population used by Kogan-Wallach to establish norms for the CDQ instrument.

DISCUSSION

The failure of risk taking propensity to distinguish entrepreneurs from managers appears to be a major deviation from the widely reported theory

FIGURE 1
Kolmogorov Confidence Band Based on Kogan-Wallach's CDQ Data
and Plot of Entrepreneurs' CDQ Scores

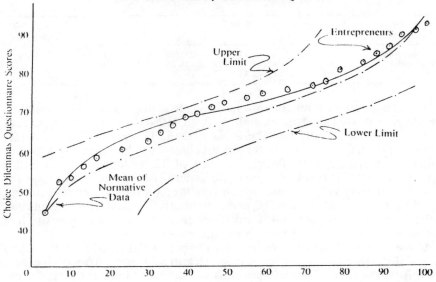

that entrepreneurs are the more moderate risk takers. However, the failure to find differences does not imply that entrepreneurs are not moderate risk takers. In fact, a comparison of the responses on the CDQ of the entrepreneurs and the managers who participated in this study with data from the original Kogan and Wallach (1964) study revealed that both groups were best described as moderate risk takers because their scores were clustered around the mean score reported by Kogan and Wallach.

However, if the *entire* range of scores obtained from entrepreneurs in this study are compared to the *entire* range of scores obtained in the Kogan-Wallach study an interesting comparison can be made: Figure 1 consists of a plot based on the scores obtained by entrepreneurs in this study compared with plots based on the Kogan-Wallach studies that were used to establish normative data. (The Kogan-Wallach plots were obtained by using the reported mean and standard deviations, and it is assumed that the Kogan-Wallach data were normally distributed.) This Kolmogorov confidence band indicates that the distribution of entrepreneurs' scores from this study and that of Kogan-Wallach subjects are not significantly different at the .05 level of confidence. In other words, the distribution of the risk taking propensity of the entrepreneurs of new ventures is similar to the distribution of risk taking propensity found to exist by Kogan and Wallach in a more general population. Thus, the data in this study indicate that the level of risk taking propensity does not distinguish new entrepreneurs either from managers or from the general population.

Just as the majority of the established entrepreneurs who were interviewed in earlier studies, such as Mancuso's (1975) study, expressed a desire for moderate levels of risk, over 64 percent of the entrepreneurs in this current study were found to have a propensity for moderate levels of risk, as indicated by their CDQ scores' being within one standard deviation of the mean for the Kogan and Wallach subjects. However, by definition, approximately 68 percent of the general population also would be expected to have scores in this range. Thus earlier studies concerned with the entrepreneurs' risk taking propensity may have *correctly* found the majority of entrepreneurs to have a tendency toward moderate levels of risk, but they may have failed to recognize that this same characteristic is also true of the population in general. Therefore, although a majority of the entrepreneurs of established ventures may in fact have preferred moderate levels of risk, this preference need not be a distinguishing characteristic. But even this statement must be followed with several cautions.

Because this study dealt with entrepreneurs of new ventures, it is possible that the risk taking propensity of established entrepreneurs might differ from that of a new entrepreneur. This difference might occur for several reasons. First, the process of being an entrepreneur may increase the desire for moderate levels of risk, thus causing a larger percentage of established entrepreneurs to appear to be moderate risk takers. Furthermore, those entrepreneurs who have a propensity for low or high levels of risk may tend to cease to be entrepreneurs at a greater rate than do those who have a propensity for moderate levels of risk. An additional source of error is introduced by certain difficulties already mentioned in using the data reported by Kogan and Wallach for comparison with data collected for this study.

Despite the limitations of this present study and the need for additional research, the finding that general risk taking propensity does not distinguish entrepreneurs from nonentrepreneurs, if confirmed by future research, would result in the revision of the importance of a variable that is widely accepted as an entrepreneurial characteristic.

REFERENCES

1. Atkinson, J. W. Motivational determinants of risk taking behavior. *Psychological Review*, 1957, 64, 359-372.
2. Cohen, J. *Statistical power analysis for the behavioral sciences.* New York: Academic Press, 1969.
3. Collins, D. F., & Moore, D. G. *The enterprising man.* East Lansing, Mich.: MSU Business Studies, Michigan State University, 1964.
4. *Funk and Wagnall's standard dictionary.* International Edition. New York: Funk & Wagnall's Co., 1958.
5. Hartmann, H. Managers and entrepreneurs: A useful distinction? *Administrative Science Quarterly*, 1959, 3, 429-451.

6. Hornaday, J. A., & Aboud, J. Characteristics of successful entrepreneurs. *Personnel Psychology*, 1971, 24, 141-153.
7. Kogan, N., & Wallach, M. A. *Risk taking*. New York: Holt, Rinehart, and Winston, 1964.
8. Liles, P. R. *New business ventures and entrepreneur*. Homewood, Ill.: Richard D. Irwin, Inc., 1974.
9. Mancuso, J. R. The entrepreneurs' quiz. In C. M. Baumback & J. R. Mancuso (Eds.), *Entrepreneurship and venture management*. Englewood, N.J.: Prentice-Hall, Inc., 1975.
10. McClelland, D. C. *The achieving society*. Princeton, N.J.: Van Nostrand, 1961, 226.
11. Meyer, H. H., Walker, W. B., & Litwin, G. H. Motive patterns and risk preferences associated with entrepreneurship. *Journal of Abnormal and Social Psychology*, 1961, 63, 570-574.
12. Mill, J. S. Principles of political economy with some of their applications to social philosophy. 1848. In J. A. Schumpeter (Ed.), *History of economic analysis*. New York: Oxford University Press, 1954.
13. Palmer, M. The application of psychological testing to entrepreneurial potential. *California Management Review*, 1971, 13 (3), 38.
14. Schumpeter, J. A. (Ed.). *History of economic analysis*. New York: Oxford University Press, 1954, 554-557.
15. Wallach, M. A., & Kogan, N. Sex differences and judgment processes. *Journal of Personality*, 1959, 27, 555-564.
16. Wallach, M. A., & Kogan, N. Aspects of judgment and decision-making: Interrelationships and changes with age. *Behavioral Science*, 1961, 6, 23-36.
17. Weber, M. *The theory of social and economic organization*. Edited and translated by A. M. Henderson & T. Parsons. New York: Free Press, 1947.
18. *Webster's third new international dictionary*. Unabridged. Chicago: Merriam Co., 1961.

[9]

Academy of Management Review, 1984, Vol. 9, No. 2, 354-359.

Differentiating Entrepreneurs from Small Business Owners: A Conceptualization

JAMES W. CARLAND
Western Carolina University
FRANK HOY
WILLIAM R. BOULTON
University of Georgia
JO ANN C. CARLAND
Western Carolina University

The literature of small business and entrepreneurship is explored. It is established that, although there is an overlap between entrepreneurial firms and small business firms, they are different entities. Using the 1934 work of Schumpeter and recognizing the additions to the field of current writers, a conceptual framework is established for the differentiation of entrepreneurs from small business owners.

Schumpeter (1934) was among the first to identify the entrepreneur as an entity worthy of study, distinct from business owners and managers. He described entrepreneurs as individuals whose function was to carry out new combinations of means of production. To Schumpeter, this function was fundamental to economic development. Entrepreneurs, therefore, warranted study independent of capitalists and business managers. Today there continues to be an implicit assumption that the entrepreneur contributes disproportionately to the economy of a nation, yet little has been done to isolate this individual for further analysis. Extending the theory of Schumpeter, who argued that an entrepreneur was distinguishable both by type and by conduct, two conceptualizations are proposed in this paper: one for differentiating entrepreneurs from small business owner/managers and the second for differentiating entrepreneurial ventures from small businesses.

Entrepreneurship: The Contribution

Because the definition of entrepreneurship denotes the creation of some combination that did not previously exist, entrepreneurship often is equated with small business ownership and management. The small business sector has received attention in the economic and management literature because of its significance to the economy. The Small Business Administration (U.S. Government Printing Office, 1982) has compiled a list of statistics that dramatically demonstrate the impact of small business on the nation's economy:

1. There are 14.7 million businesses in the United States, of which 3.2 million are farms.
2. Approximately 99.7 percent of these businesses are considered small by the SBA's size standards for loan applicants.
3. The small businesses identified above account for: 38 percent of the gross national product; 44 percent of the gross business product; and 47 percent of total U.S. business employment.
4. The small business sector identified above accounted for the vast majority of the net new jobs created by business between 1969 and 1976.

Although there is no uniform definition of a small firm, the statistics above relate to businesses that fall within SBA guidelines as being small. The Small Business Act states that "a small business concern shall be deemed to be one which is independently owned and operated and which is not dominant in

354

its field of operation" (U.S. Small Business Administration, 1978, p. 121.1).

As the SBA statistics demonstrate, small business research is justified because of sheer numbers. It must be noted that small firms are treated as a separate sector, not because they are cohesive and homogeneous, but because there are certain common management limitations due to extremely limited resources as compared with the "deep pockets" of resources of larger corporate organizations. Research often is directed toward the implications of public policy developments or the impact of environmental variables on the small business sector (Chilton & Weidenbaum, 1982; Goodman, 1981; Legler & Hoy, 1982; Robinson, 1982).

Although small business is a significant segment of the American economy, the entrepreneurial portion of that segment may wield a disproportionate influence. If entrepreneurship can be viewed as incorporating innovation and growth, the most fertile ground for management research may be entrepreneurs and entrepreneurial ventures. Entrepreneurship has been found to extend beyond small businesses: some large corporations have been described as engaging in entrepreneurial behavior (Ronstadt, 1982, Schollhammer, 1982, Shils, 1982). Additionally, a person who owns an enterprise is not necessarily an entrepreneur (Martin, 1982). Clearly, an overlap exists of entrepreneurship with the small business sector. The concern of this paper is: If entrepreneurs exist as entities distinct from small and large organizations and if entrepreneurial activity is a fundamental contributor to economic development, on what bases may entrepreneurs be separated from nonentrepreneurial managers in order for the phenomenon of entrepreneurship to be studied and understood?

Literature Review: The "Entrepreneur"

One of the earliest definitions of an entrepreneur was that of Cantillion (circa 1700) who described the individual as a rational decision maker who assumed the risk and provided management for the firm (Kilby, 1971). Schumpeter (1934) credited Mill (1848) with bringing the term into general use among economists. Mill, also, believed that the key factor in distinguishing a manager from an entrepreneur was the bearing of risk. Schumpeter, however, countered that risk bearing was inherent in ownership and that entrepreneurs, the combiners, were not necessarily owners; therefore, the risk bearing propensity would

not be a trait. Martin (1982) believes that capital risk is a function of the investor. Further, Brockhaus (1980) cast doubt on the validity of the risk taking propensity as an entrepreneurial characteristic with his descriptive work. Brockhaus found no statistical difference in the risk preference patterns of a group of entrepreneurs and a group of managers. It should be noted that Brockhaus used the establishment of a business as the criterion for inclusion of the participants in the entrepreneur group. Omitting business ownership as a designation of entrepreneurship permits both the inclusion of corporate entrepreneurs and the elimination of the risk bearing characteristic. However, many writers have asserted and continue to assert that risk bearing is a prime factor in the entrepreneurial character and function (McClelland, 1961; Palmer, 1971; Timmons, 1978; Welsh & White, 1981).

Numerous normative and descriptive studies have supported various sets of personality characteristics of entrepreneurship. Brockhaus (1982) has presented an excellent historic overview of the definitions of entrepreneurs. Perhaps the most important factor from a societal perspective is the characteristic of innovation. Schumpeter (1934) believed that innovation was the central characteristic of the entrepreneurial endeavor. His emphasis on this point is revealed in his declaration that one behaves as an entrepreneur only when carrying out innovations. McClelland (1961) stated that energetic and/or novel instrumental activity was a key factor in entrepreneurial activity. Martin (1982) stressed that entrepreneurial creativity is different from literary or artistic creativity in that the entrepreneur does not innovate by creating ideas but by exploiting the value of ideas. Table 1 displays a sampling of entrepreneurial characteristics appearing in the literature.

The characteristics listed in Table 1 represent attitudes and behaviors that may be manifested by entrepreneurs. Demographic characteristics such as birth order, sex, or marital status have been examined in certain of the studies cited and in various other investigations (Vaught & Hoy, 1981). They have been excluded from the present conceptualization because of the inability of a prospective entrepreneur to alter those variables in order to increase his/her probability of success.

Schein's (1974) work on career anchors clarifies some of the differences in individual approaches to careers. In studying M.I.T. graduates' careers, he

Table 1
Characteristics of Entrepreneurs

Date	Author(s)	Characteristic(s)	Normative	Empirical
1848	Mill	Riskbearing	×	
1917	Weber	Source of formal authority	×	
1934	Schumpeter	Innovation, initiative	×	
1954	Sutton	Desire for responsibility	×	
1959	Hartman	Source of formal authority	×	
1961	McClelland	Risk taking, need for achievement		×
1963	Davids	Ambition; desire for independence; responsibility; self-confidence		×
1964	Pickle	Drive/mental; human relations; communication ability; technical knowledge		×
1971	Palmer	Risk measurement		×
1971	Hornaday & Aboud	Need for achievement; autonomy; aggression; power; recognition; innovative/independent		×
1973	Winter	Need for power	×	
1974	Borland	Internal locus of control		×
1974	Liles	Need for achievement		×
1977	Gasse	Personal value orientation		×
1978	Timmons	Drive/self-confidence; goal oriented moderated risk taker; internal locus of control; creativity/innovation	×	×
1980	Sexton	Energetic/ambitious; positive reaction to setbacks		×
1981	Welsh & White	Need to control; responsibility seeker; self-confidence/drive; challenge taker; moderate risk taker		×
1982	Dunkelberg & Cooper	Growth oriented; independence oriented; craftsman oriented		×

found that five types of job directions were prevalent. He described these as career anchors that included managerial competence, technical/functional competence, security need, independence need, and creativity. The entrepreneurs made up his creative group.

> The group concerned with creativity is the most interesting in that it contains the entrepreneurs. Four of these men are successful in that they have been able to launch enterprises which have succeeded and have brought to their founders either fame or fortune or both. The kinds of activities vary greatly—but they all have in common that they are clear extensions of the person and his identity is heavily involved in the vehicle which is created (1974, p. 19).

It is difficult to sketch a profile of an entrepreneur from the attitudinal and behavioral characteristics listed in Table 1. It may be more appropriate to accept Vesper's (1980) view of a continuum along which several "types" of entrepreneurs exist. The question then becomes: Which characteristics and what level of intensity do the entrepreneurs possess at various points on the continuum? Vesper described the entrepreneur as an individual but implied that he or she could be found working with others in larger organizations. His first type, the "Solo Self-Employed Individual," is essentially what is treated here as the small business owner/operator, but not truly an entrepreneur in the Schumpeterian sense because a new combination is not created.

A major obstacle preventing the attribution of characteristics to entrepreneurs in firms along

Vesper's continuum is the great diversity of sources from which the authors cited in Table 1 derived the identified characteristics. Those citations that are indicated in Table 1 as normative are generally anecdotal, describing either the authors' personal impressions or conclusions drawn from reading the works of others. The empirical studies draw from quite diverse samples. McClelland's (1961) entrepreneurs were in fact business executives representing various functional specialities: general management, sales and marketing, finance, engineering, and personnel. Senior marketing managers were found to have the highest need for achievement. More frequently, samples of small business owners are chosen for study (Hornaday & Aboud, 1971; Pickle, 1964). The assumption underlying these selections is that the entrepreneur was the individual who brought the resources together and initiated the venture. Successful entrepreneurs are defined as those whose enterprises have survived some period of time, perhaps two years. The question then is: Are the characteristics listed in Table 1 those of entrepreneurs, of small business owners, or of some mixture that may or may not be capable of demonstrating the entrepreneurial function of economic development?

The Entrepreneurial Venture

A considerable body of literature has been built up treating the stages of organizational development

(Vozikis, 1979). This growth-orientation, in and of itself, would represent an entrepreneurial characteristic to some scholars (Dunkelberg & Cooper, 1982). Yet, as Vesper (1980) has pointed out in his continuum of venture types, many business owners never intend for their businesses to grow beyond what they consider to be a controllable size. It is necessary to go beyond the notion of corporate life cycles and stages to conceive of an entrepreneurial venture.

Glueck (1980) distinguished between entrepreneurial ventures and what he termed family business ventures by focusing on strategic practices. Strategic management in Glueck's family business must emphasize preferences and needs of the family as opposed to those of the business. When in conflict, the needs of the family will override those of the business. Glueck cited the oft observed family business strategies to remain independent and to provide outlets for family investment and careers for family members as an example of conflict. In contrast, an entrepreneurial strategist would opt for pursuit of growth and maintenance of the firm's distinctive competence through obtaining the best personnel available. Glueck's distinction is that strategic practices oriented toward the best interests of the firm are observed in entrepreneurial ventures.

An entrepreneurial venture can be identified by the strategic behavior of the firms. Schumpeter (1934) suggested that five categories of behavior can be observed that are characteristic of an entrepreneurial venture. These categories, listed below, are supported by Vesper (1980) and can be used as the basis for classification criteria.

1. Introduction of new goods
2. Introduction of new methods of production
3. Opening of new markets
4. Opening of new sources of supply
5. Industrial reorganization

Because of the ambiguity of criterion 4, it is not employed in this study. If any one of the remaining four criteria is observed in a firm's strategic actions, then that firm can be classified as an entrepreneurial venture. These criteria do permit the classification of a new small traditional firm as entrepreneurial if that firm represents an original entry into a market. Again, the determining factor would be whether organizational activity in any of the four criteria resulted in a new combination, indicating innovative behavior. Additionally, these criteria permit medium and large firms to be classified either as entrepreneurial ventures themselves or as the instigators of entrepreneurial ventures.

Schumpeter's criteria represent evidence of innovative strategies or innovative strategic postures. The criteria also emphasize the behavior of a firm consistent with its own best interests. This perspective is congruent with the development and pursuit of a distinctive competence prescribed by Vesper (1980) as a requirement for an entrepreneurial venture.

A Conceptual Distinction Between Small Business and Entrepreneurship

From the foregoing discussion, it can be seen that, although there is considerable overlap between small business and entrepreneurship, the concepts are not the same. All new ventures are not entrepreneurial in nature. Entrepreneurial firms may begin at any size level, but key on growth over time. Some new small firms may grow, but many will remain small businesses for their organizational lifetimes.

The critical factor proposed here to distinguish entrepreneurs from nonentrepreneurial managers and, in particular, small business owners is innovation. The entrepreneur is characterized by a preference for creating activity, manifested by some innovative combination of resources for profit. Drawing further on the characteristics outlined in Table 1, it is suggested that analyses of prospective entrepreneurial characteristics examine such traits as need for achievement (perhaps more appropriately labeled goal–orientation), internal locus of control, need for independence, need for responsibility, and need for power. Although a risk taking propensity is mentioned frequently in the literature, Schumpeter noted that it is inherent in ownership rather than entrepreneurship. Further, Brockhaus (1980) supported Schumpeter with empirical results demonstrating that risk taking behavior cannot be used as a distinguishing characteristic of entrepreneurship.

From this analysis, it is suggested that many published studies may be misleading in their conclusions. Economic theorists propose that the entrepreneur is essential to economic development (Schumpeter, 1934; Williams, 1981). Yet studies of entrepreneurship neglect to distinguish adequately between entrepreneurs and other business managers, primarily small business owners. Erroneous descriptions of entrepreneurs can jeopardize investigations in a variety of ways. Specifically, analyses of how entrepreneurs make their fundamental contributions to economic development cannot draw sound conclusions if the case studies are not entrepreneurial.

To guide future studies, the following definitions are proposed to distinguish among the entities discussed in the paper:

Small business venture: A small business venture is any business that is independently owned and operated, not dominant in its field, and does not engage in any new marketing or innovative practices.

Entrepreneurial venture: An entreprenuerial venture is one that engages in at least one of Schumpeter's four categories of behavior: that is, the principal goals of an entrepreneurial venture are profitability and growth and the business is characterized by innovative strategic practices.

Small business owner: A small business owner is an individual who establishes and manages a business for the principal purpose of furthering personal goals. The business must be the primary source of income and will consume the majority of one's time and resources. The owner perceives the business as an extension of his or her personality, intricately bound with family needs and desires.

Entrepreneur: An entrepreneur is an individual who establishes and manages a business for the principal purposes of profit and growth. The entrepreneur is characterized principally by innovative behavior and will employ strategic management practices in the business.

References

Borland, C. *Locus of control, need for achievement and entrepreneurship.* Unpublished doctoral dissertation, University of Texas at Austin, 1974.

Brockhaus, R. H. Risk taking propensity of entrepreneurs. *Academy of Management Journal,* 1980, 23(3), 509-520.

Brockhaus, R. H. The psychology of the entrepreneur. In C. A. Kent, D. L. Sexton, & K. H. Vesper (Eds.), *Encyclopedia of entrepreneurship.* Englewood Cliffs, N.J.: Prentice-Hall, 1982, 39-57.

Chilton, K. W., & Weidenbaum, M. L. Government regulation: The small business burden. *Journal of Small Business Management,* 1982, 20(1), 4-10.

Davids, L. E. *Characteristics of small business founders in Texas and Georgia.* Athens, Ga.: Bureau of Business Research, University of Georgia, June 1963.

Dunkelberg, W. C., & Cooper A. C. Entrepreneurial typologies. In K. H. Vesper (Ed.), *Frontiers of entrepreneurship research.* Wellesley, Mass.: Babson Center for Entrepreneurial Studies, 1982, 1-15.

Gasse, Y. *Entrepreneurial characteristics and practices: A study of the dynamics of small business organizations and their effectiveness in different environments.* Sherbrooke, Quebec: Rene Prince, 1977.

Glueck, W. F. *Business policy and strategic management.* New York: McGraw-Hill, 1980.

Goodman, J. P. *An exploratory investigation of some effects of mergers on selected organizations.* Unpublished doctoral dissertation, University of Georgia, 1981.

Hartman, H. Managers and entrepreneurs: A useful distinction! *Administrative Science Quarterly,* 1959, 3, 429-451.

Hornaday, J. A., & Aboud, J. Characteristics of successful entrepreneurs. *Personnel Psychology,* 1971, 24, 141-153.

Kilby, P. *Entrepreneurship and economic development.* New York: Free Press, 1971.

Legler, J. B., & Hoy, F. *Building a comprehensive data base on the role of small business in the U.S. economy.* Policy Paper 2. Chicago: Heller Institute for Small Business Policy Papers, 1982.

Liles, P. R. *New business ventures and the entrepreneur.* Homewood, Ill.: Irwin, 1974.

Martin, A. Additional aspects of entrepreneurial history. In C. A. Kent, D. L. Sexton, & K. H. Vesper (Eds.), *Encyclopedia of entrepreneurship.* Englewood Cliffs, N.J.: Prentice-Hall, 1982, 15-19.

McClelland, D. C. *The achieving society.* Princeton, N.J.: D. Van Nostrand, 1961.

Mill, J. S. *Principles of political economy with some of their applications to social philosophy.* London: John W. Parker, 1848.

Palmer, M. The application of psychological testing to entrepreneurial potential. *California Management Review,* 1971, 13(3), 38.

Pickle, H. B. *Personality and success: An evaluation of personal characteristics of successful small business managers.* Small Business Research Series No. 4. Washington, D.C.: U.S. Government Printing Office, 1964.

Robinson, R. B., Jr. The importance of outsiders in small firm strategic planning. *Academy of Management Journal,* 1982, 25, 80-93.

Ronstadt, R. *Entrepreneurship 1982.* Dover, Mass.: Lord Publishing, 1982.

SBA rules and regulations. Washington, D.C.: Small Business Administration, 1978.

Schein, E. H. *Career anchors and career paths.* Industrial Liaison Program, Massachusetts Institute of Technology, May 1974.

Schollhammer, H. Internal corporate entrepreneurship. In C. A. Kent, D. L. Sexton, & K. H. Vesper (Eds.), *Encyclopedia of entrepreneurship.* Englewood Cliffs, N.J.: Prentice-Hall, 1982, 209-223.

Schumpeter, J. A. *The theory of economic development.* Cambridge, Mass.: Harvard University Press, 1934.

Sexton, D. L. *Characteristics and role demands of successful entrepreneurs.* Paper presented at the meeting of the Academy of Management, Detroit, 1980.

Shils, E. Commentary on internal corporate entrepreneurship. In
C. A. Kent, D. L. Sexton, & K. H. Vesper (Eds.), *Encyclopedia
of entrepreneurship*. Englewood Cliffs, N.J.: Prentice-Hall,
1982, 224-229.

Sutton, F. X. Achievement norms and the motivation of entrepreneurs. In *Entrepreneurs and economic growth*. Cambridge,
Mass.: Social Science Research Council and Harvard University Research Center in Entrepreneurial History, 1954.

Timmons, J. A. Characteristics and role demands of entrepreneurship. *American Journal of Small Business*, 1978, 3, 5-17.

U.S. Government Printing Office. *State of small business: A report
of the President*. Washington, D.C.: U.S. Government Printing Office, 1982.

U.S. Small Business Administration. *SBA rules and regulations*.
Washington, D.C.: U.S. Small Business Administration, 1978.

Vaught, B. C., & Hoy, F. Have you got what it takes to run your
own business? *Business*, 1981, 31(4), 2-8.

Vesper, K. H. *New venture strategies*. Englewood Cliffs, N.J.:
Prentice-Hall, 1980.

Vozikis, G. S. *A strategic disadvantage profile of the stages of
development of small business: The experience of retail and service small business in Georgia*. Unpublished doctoral dissertation, University of Georgia, 1979.

Weber, M. *The theory of social and economic organization* (A.
M. Henderson & T. Parsons, Eds. and Trans.). New York:
Scribner's, 1917.

Welsh, J. A., & White, J. F. Converging on characteristics of entrepreneurs. In K. H. Vesper (Ed.), *Frontiers of entrepreneurship research*. Wellesley, Mass.: Babson Center for Entrepreneurial Studies, 1981, 504-515.

Williams, E. C. Innovation, entrepreneurship and brain functioning. In K. H. Vesper (Ed.), *Frontiers of entrepreneurship research*. Wellesley, Mass.: Babson Center for Entrepreneurial
Studies, 1981, 516-536.

Winter, D. G. *The power motive*. New York: Free Press, 1973.

*James Carland is Assistant Professor of Management,
School of Business, Western Carolina University.*

*Frank Hoy is Associate Professor of Management in the
College of Business Administration and Director of Re-
search and Experiential Education in the Small Business
Development Center, University of Georgia.*

*William Boulton is Associate Professor of Management in
the College of Business Administration, University of
Georgia.*

*Jo Ann Carland is Assistant Professor of Management in
the School of Business, Western Carolina University.*

[10]

PSYCHOLOGICAL CHARACTERISTICS ASSOCIATED WITH PERFORMANCE IN ENTREPRENEURIAL FIRMS AND SMALLER BUSINESSES*

THOMAS M. BEGLEY and DAVID P. BOYD
Northeastern University

EXECUTIVE SUMMARY

This article examines the prevalence of five psychological attributes in a sample of established entrepreneurs. These attributes are need for achievement, locus of control, risk-taking propensity, tolerance of ambiguity, and Type A behavior. These characteristics are widely regarded as hallmarks of the entrepreneurial personality.

The focus of the study is twofold: 1) Do these attributes distinguish entrepreneurs (founders) from small business managers (nonfounders)? 2) Does the presence of these "entrepreneurial" attributes relate to the financial performance of the firm?

Survey questionnaires were completed by 239 members of the Smaller Business Association of New England. Founders in this sample score significantly higher than nonfounders for three of the five dimensions: need for achievement, risk-taking propensity, and tolerance of ambiguity. Both groups manifest an internal locus of control: that is, they share a perception that they can influence events in their lives and are thereby free from external forces such as destiny or luck. In terms of Type A behavior, founders and nonfounders alike score 60% above the midpoint on the Type A scale. Such Type A persons tend to be competitive, restless strivers who constantly struggle against the limitations of time.

The relationships between psychological attributes and financial performance are few, but suggestive. Among founders, internal locus of control relates to a low liquidity ratio. Among nonfounders, high tolerance of ambiguity associates with high return on assets (ROA), and high need for achievement associates with a high liquidity ratio. A test for curvilinearity reveals a "threshold effect": in three instances, a psychological attribute associates with corporate performance only to a certain point. Beyond this optimal level, the psychological pattern appears to become dysfunctional and

*The research was supported in part by grants from the Center for Entrepreneurial Studies at New York University and from Northeastern University's College of Business Administration and Research and Scholarship Development Fund. We thank Barbara Kane and Ellen Balber for their assistance in the project. We also acknowledge the cooperation of Lewis Shattuck and Julie Scofield of the Smaller Business Association of New England. Reprint requests should be sent to Thomas M. Begley, College of Business Administration, Northeastern University, Boston, MA 02115.

Journal of Business Venturing **2**, 79–93(1987)
© 1987 Elsevier Science Publishing Co., Inc., 52 Vanderbilt Ave., New York, NY 10017

0883-9026/87/$3.50

80   T.M. BEGLEY AND D.P. BOYD

*financial returns falter. In the founders, for example, moderate risk-taking is associated with increased
ROA. However, the ROA of these firms decreases when risk-taking becomes excessive. In similar
fashion, founders may see their firms' ROA flourish if this attribute is present to a moderate extent.
When too pronounced, the profitability of the firm may decline. The same pattern exists between
tolerance of ambiguity and growth rate in the nonfounder group. Excessive ambiguity tolerance may
lead to a lack of response mechanisms for dealing with environmental change. In assessing the
leadership of established ventures, it might be prudent for bankers, investors, and entrepreneurs
themselves to pay heed to the mix of these characteristics.*

INTRODUCTION

In studies of entrepreneurial characteristics, attributes such as the following recur with
regularity: need for achievement, internal locus of control, moderate propensity for risk
taking, tolerance of ambiguity, and more recently, Type A behavior (Begley and Boyd 1985;
Borland 1974; Boyd 1984; Hornaday and Aboud 1971; Liles 1974; Sexton and Bowman
1978; Timmons 1978; Welsh and White 1981).

Yet these empirical studies are marked by diverse and disparate results, perhaps due
to problems in testing instruments and sample sizes (Sexton and Bowman 1983). As a
consequence, more research is required before the salient features of the entrepreneurial
personality can be persuasively proclaimed (Hoy and Carland 1983).

Accordingly, the first purpose of this study will be to construct a psychological profile
of small business entrepreneurs and then determine how closely this profile applies to small
business managers. Much of the existing literature uses the general population as a comparison point and thus circumvents the question we propose to address.

Previous research has also failed to isolate psychological dimensions which might
differentiate successful from less successful entrepreneurs (Sexton and Bowman 1984). Are
these characteristics identical to those which distinguish entrepreneurs from managers? To
answer these questions, the present study will explore the relationship between the psychological attributes of entrepreneurs and the financial performance of their firms.

Given the diverse definitions of entrepreneurship in the literature (Begley and Boyd,
in press), we propose a simple distinction in this study: an entrepreneur is a person who has
founded his or her own enterprise. The comparison group of nonentrepreneurs we propose
to examine is neither the general population nor large-company managers; rather we will
focus on chief executives who are running smaller business firms which they did not found.

An elementary distinction is often made between the founder of an enterprise and the
person who later becomes chief executive officer (Carland, et al. 1984). According to our
definition, the founder is considered an entrepreneur but the successor is not. This simple
classification avoids dependence on subjective distinctions such as strategic preference and
orientation toward innovation. In this definition, entrepreneurship and new venture creation
(Timmons, Smollen, and Dingee 1985) are synonymous.

In the following section, we develop hypotheses on 1) the psychological profile of
founders versus successors, and 2) the relationship between psychological characteristics and financial performance among founders. In examining financial performance, we
concentrate on founders since the dearth of literature on nonfounders limits hypothesis
generation.

NEED FOR ACHIEVEMENT

Since the pioneering work of McClelland (1961), the need to achieve (n ach) has been
associated with entrepreneurial behavior. High achievers set challenging goals and value

feedback as a means of assessing goal accomplishment. They compete with their own standards of excellence and continuously seek to improve their performance.

Although a study of business students by Hull, Bosley, and Udell (1980) found that n ach was a weak predictor of prospective entrepreneurs, most studies support the prevalence of high n ach among practicing entrepreneurs (Sexton and Bowman 1985). For example, Hornaday and Aboud (1971) as well as DeCarlo and Lyons (1979) found that entrepreneurs score higher than normative groups. Both studies used the Edwards Personal Preference Test (EPPS), which appears more reliable than the Thematic Apperception Test (Entwistle 1972).

Based on research to date, the authors propose to test this hypothesis:

> Hypothesis 1(a). In a sample of small business CEOs, founders will manifest a higher achievement orientation than nonfounders.

If the achievement drive is pronounced among founders, it should propel them toward high performance. In studies of successful entrepreneurs, a high achievement orientation seems invariably present (Sexton and Bowman 1983). This finding obtains despite variance in the measures employed. Komives (1972), for example, used Gordon's Study of Personal Values to assess the achievement drive of 20 successful high-technology entrepreneurs. He found that high n ach values were characteristic of his sample. Similarly, Smith and Miner (1984), using a new projective technique, reaffirmed the correlation between the achievement proclivity of entrepreneurs and the growth rate of their firms.

Given the unremitting aspiration of high achievers, corporate financial performance is an important indicator of goal accomplishment. Profit and growth data are objective ways of providing feedback (Timmons et al. 1985).

Accordingly, as a second hypothesis, the authors postulate that:

> Hypothesis 1(b). Among small business founders there will be a positive relationship between need for achievement and corporate financial performance.

LOCUS OF CONTROL

The Locus of Control Scale measures subjects' perceived ability to influence events in their lives. Internal persons believe in the efficacy of their own behavior and give little credence to "external" forces such as destiny, luck, or "powerful others." In contrast, externals reject the credo that personal effort is the primary determinant of outcomes. One person wields little influence over the varied contingencies of life (Seligman 1975).

Rotter (1966) submitted that an internal control locus was consonant with a high achievement orientation. Subsequent research has confirmed this relationship (Brockhaus 1982). The tie is logical, since the internality of high achievers persuades them that their actions can affect relevant outcomes. This is not, of course, tantamount to the naive belief that individuals can ordain the final configuration of environmental events; rather internals believe that judicious efforts can moderate external impacts (Kobasa, Maddi, and Kahn 1982).

While control disposition may be useful for distinguishing entrepreneurs from the general population, it is not a valid discriminator of entrepreneurs and managers (Brockhaus and Nord 1979). Entrepreneurs seem to be characterized by internality, but so do managers. Nevertheless, the two groups may be differentiated by degree of internality. As an hypothesis, the authors postulate that:

> Hypothesis 2(a). In a sample of small business CEOs, founders will manifest higher internal locus of control than nonfounders.

Even if the total sample under study is typified by an internal locus of control, variation among internal scores may serve as a useful predictor of corporate financial performance. In a longitudinal study by Brockhaus (cited in Brockhaus 1982), owners of surviving ventures manifested higher internality than their cohorts who had failed. Since internals are imbued with self-confidence and possess a penchant for action, they may be more likely to affect the outcome of events (Brockhaus 1974; Durand and Shea 1974). Conversely, extremely high external scores might denote a sense of detachment from one's distinctive skills and sentiments. In line with this reasoning, Maddi, Kobasa, and Hoover (1979) found that external locus of control showed a positive correlation with powerlessness. This may explain why externals often experience more job alienation than internals (Mitchell 1977; Seeman 1967; Wolfe 1972).

Other studies substantiate the tie between locus of control and a variety of performance indicators. For example, internal beliefs have been related to task orientation and academic achievement (Lefcourt 1965). Effective groups tend to be led by internals (Anderson and Schneider 1978). Internal small business CEOs are also more resilient in the face of environmental stressors (Anderson 1977; Anderson, Hellriegel, and Slocum 1977).

Factors besides energy and resilience may contribute to the success of internals. In a study by Julian, Lichtman, and Ryckman (1968), internals were less likely to engage in risky behaviors than were externals. Achievement performance might obviously be facilitated for those selecting high-probability outcomes. According to other studies, however, internal executives are less conservative than their external counterparts. Since internals are sanguine about the possibility of influencing the firm's direction, they do not recoil from bold and imaginative strategies. In a study of 33 business firms, Miller and Friesen (1982) found that the more internal the top executive, the more innovative the firm.

Whatever the causal dynamic might be, an internal control disposition appears to be associated with corporate financial performance (Anderson 1977). The authors propose to test Brockhaus' suggestion that "this internal belief and the associated greater effort . . . hold promise for distinguishing successful entrepreneurs from the unsuccessful" (Brockhaus, 1982). Specifically, we suggest that:

> Hypothesis 2(b). Among small business founders there will be a positive relationship between internal locus of control and corporate financial performance.

RISK-TAKING PROPENSITY

McClelland observed that entrepreneurs exhibit moderate risk-taking propensities. While subsequent studies have substantiated this tendency in entrepreneurs (see Sexton and Bowman 1983, for a review), Brockhaus (1980) found that managers were similarly situated along the risk dimension. A subsequent study suggests that risk-taking propensity may in fact distinguish the two groups (Sexton and Bowman 1986). Since the present study will use an instrument similar to that of Sexton and Bowman, the authors propose the following hypothesis:

> Hypothesis 3(a). In a sample of small business CEOs, founders will manifest higher risk-taking propensity than nonfounders.

Brockhaus (1982) suggests that risk-taking propensity has no direct bearing upon financial performance. He renders this observation "tentatively" because his sample consisted of new ventures. Brockhaus cautions that established entrepreneurs might be characterized by a different risk profile. Several writers have indicated that the process of entrepreneurship might palliate the proclivity for risk. Timmons et al. (1985), for example, argue that risk taking decreases as net worth accumulates. Venturesome boldness may be tempered when there is an asset base to protect. In similar fashion, Smith and Miner (1985) note that risk avoidance is stronger among entrepreneurs heading fast-growing firms than among those heading slow-growth firms. Such suggestions accord with conceptual models of successful entrepreneurs. Palmer (1971), for instance, writes that the effective entrepreneur "can correctly interpret the risk situation and then determine policies which will minimize the risk involved." As entrepreneurs scan their environment, they simultaneously seek to exploit opportunity and to avoid threat (Welsch and Young 1982).

Therefore, among the established entrepreneurs who typify our sample, the authors hypothesize an inverse relationship between financial success of the firm and risk-taking propensity of the owner. Accordingly, we submit that:

Hypothesis 3(b). Among small business founders there will be a negative relationship between risk-taking propensity and corporate financial performance.

TOLERANCE OF AMBIGUITY

Individuals perceive ambiguity when they lack sufficient cues to structure a situation. According to Budner (1962), ambiguity may emanate from novelty, complexity, or insolubility. Budner defines intolerance of ambiguity as the tendency to perceive ambiguous situations as threatening; tolerance of ambiguity is the tendency to perceive such situations as desirable. MacDonald (1970) is even less circumspect when he claims that persons with high ambiguity tolerance deliberately seek unstructured situations. For these entrepreneurial individuals, goal accomplishment is not predicated on uniformity, stability, or predictability. The focal point is the product rather than the process (Lafond 1984).

Their internal locus may help entrepreneurs lessen dissonance and preserve equilibrium; their robust control orientation may preclude, or at least discount, the possibility of unfavorable outcomes (Gasse 1982). Among internals lack of structure does not seem to induce job ambivalence (Organ and Greene 1974).

Given the uncertainty inherent in the entrepreneurial environment, Scheré (1982) called the owner's role "an ambiguity-bearing role." Scheré found that entrepreneurs displayed more ambiguity tolerance than either top executives or middle managers. Accordingly, the authors hypothesize that:

Hypothesis 4(a). In a sample of small business CEOs, founders will manifest higher ambiguity tolerance than nonfounders.

Entrepreneurs may be energized by the diverse opportunities of a fluid environment (Timmons et al. 1985). As Gasse (1982, p. 59) observes, entrepreneurs may view uncertainty as "an exciting stimulus rather than a severe threat". If ambiguity tolerance serves as a motivational catalyst, it may foster entrepreneurial success. It has been linked, for example, to creative behavior (Budner 1962) and to superior performance in complex tasks (MacDonald 1970). Conversely, intolerance of ambiguity has been associated with stereotypic categorization of novel stimuli (Budner 1962). The views of rigid persons are often undifferentiated from situation to situation (Kounin 1948). Since such individuals are not prone to recast their response repertoire, they recognize fewer possibilities for action.

While high tolerance of ambiguity does not ensure successful resolution of environmental exigencies, we nevertheless expect ambiguity tolerance to be associated with entrepreneurial success. Accordingly, we propose that:

84   T.M. BEGLEY AND D.P. BOYD

> Hypothesis 4(b).   Among small business founders there will be a positive relationship
> between tolerance of ambiguity and corporate financial performance.

TYPE A BEHAVIOR

Friedman and Rosenman (1974) defined the Type A Behavior Pattern (TABP) as:

> an action-emotion complex that can be observed in any person who is aggressively
> involved in a chronic, incessant struggle to achieve more and more in less and less time,
> and if required to do so, against the opposing efforts of other things or other persons.

The TABP is thus an exaggerated stylistic response to environmental challenge. Major pattern
elements include impatience and irritability, time urgency, driving ambition, accelerated
activity, and generalized competitiveness.

For small business populations, a qualification should be made about definitional
criteria. Prior research (Begley and Boyd 1986) supports the assertion of Timmons et al.
(1985) that growth-minded entrepreneurs strive to surpass their own results; they compete
with themselves more than with others. Since small business CEOs have reached the apex
of their firms, they are largely exempt from hierarchical rivalry. TABP questionnaires,
however, are oriented toward intracompany competition; small business leaders might therefore score low on this facet of the global Type A construct.

Despite modest scores on the competitive dimension, various studies have documented
the prevalence of Type A behavior among small business owner-managers (Begley and Boyd
1985, 1986; Boyd 1984). The Type A scores in all these studies are significantly above
national norms. In the most recent study, smaller firm respondents had a higher Type A
mean score than any of the 35 managerial groups from whom the national norms were
originally derived (Begley and Boyd 1986). Even after external pressures have abated, the
TABP remains an enduring characteristic of small business CEOs (Boyd and Gumpert 1983).

Studies to date, however, have focused on small business owner-managers as a collective entity that includes but does not isolate founders. Only one study has used the
founder–nonfounder distinction as the basis for a TABP comparison. In that study (Boyd
and Gumpert 1983), the Type A mean of founders was higher than the Type A mean of
nonfounders. Therefore, the authors hypothesize that:

> Hypothesis 5(a).   In a sample of small business CEOs, founders will manifest more
> Type A behavior than nonfounders.

As a result of their orientation toward achievement, Type A executives may be more
likely to achieve success than their Type B colleagues (Shekelle, Schoenberger, and Stamler
1976). Some studies support this observation (Boyd 1984; Howard, Cunningham, and Rechnitzer 1977). In a study of 236 managers from 12 different companies, Howard et al. (1977)
found that Type A behavior was related to recent company growth rates. Yet an opposing
argument seems equally plausible. The hyperkinetic style of Type A executives may repel
associates. Type A bosses, with their demanding expectations, often create enormous stress
for subordinates. Moreover, Type As appear to be poor time managers, often substituting
speed for deliberation. Sheer hyperactivity replaces well-monitored progress (Friedman and
Rosenman 1974).

For a smaller firm, the CEOs arousal and alacrity might eventually become dysfunctional. In a recent study (Begley and Boyd 1986), Type A behavior of small business owner-

managers associated negatively with profitability. Based on this finding, the authors propose the following hypothesis:

> Hypothesis 5(b). Among small business founders there will be a negative relationship between Type A behavior and corporate financial performance.

The hypotheses on the relationships between psychological characteristics and financial performance predict linear relationships. However, the literature hints that for at least some of the psychological variables, the relationships may be curvilinear. For example, McClelland (1961) found the risk-taking propensity of successful entrepreneurs to be moderate rather than high or low. Further, an extremely high posture on locus of control or tolerance of ambiguity might be dysfunctional for an entrepreneur. Therefore, we will test for curvilinear relationships.

MEASURES

Achievement motivation was measured by a subset of items taken from the EPPS. Information on reliability and validity is reported in the EPPS manual (Edwards 1959). The manifest needs associated with the EPPS achievement variable include: to do one's best, to be successful, to accomplish tasks requiring skill and effort, to accomplish something of great significance, to do a difficult job well, and to be a recognized authority. One's response to these items reflects an active or passive attitude toward decision making and personal goal setting. Our response format utilized option categories of strongly agree, agree, neither agree nor disagree, disagree, strongly disagree. The five items selected for our scale had a coefficient alpha of 0.672.

Locus of control was measured by the familiar Rotter scale (Rotter 1966). Considerable research has shown this scale to be a reliable and valid index of one's belief in the relative efficacy of external forces (Phares 1976). In the present survey, ten items were presented in Rotter's forced choice format. The original wording was modified in several instances, so external–internal attribution focused on business issues rather than general life events. The coefficient alpha in our study was 0.702.

Propensity for risk-taking was assessed by the Jackson Personality Inventory (JPI) (Jackson 1976). Various studies have supported the validity of the JPI as a measure of generalized risk-taking (Jackson, Hourany, and Vidmar 1972). Acceptable internal consistencies have been reported for this instrument (Jackson 1977). The scale renders scores for the relatively independent components of monetary, physical, social, and ethical risk-taking. For purposes of the present research, the monetary risk-taking items were used, since these best approximate the reality of business situations. Eight items were selected. As with the EPPS, a five-point response format of disagreement/agreement was employed. The items had a coefficient alpha of 0.784.

The conceptual theme of the scale aligns with Palmer's definition of risk-taking as "the willingness to commit to a course of action which may result in rewards or penalties associated with success or failure" (1971:32). The high JPI scorer takes monetary chances and enjoys adventures having an element of peril. Low scorers, on the other hand, are unlikely to bet, even in situations where the potential gain is high. They avoid uncertain monetary outcomes and gravitate toward predictable settings. Specific items are as follows: "If I invested in stocks, it would probably be in safe stocks from well-known companies"; "If the possible reward was very high, I would not hesitate putting my money in a new

86   T.M. BEGLEY AND D.P. BOYD

business that could fail"; "I probably would not take the chance of borrowing money for a business deal even if it might be profitable."

Ambiguity tolerance was assessed by eight items from the Budner Scale of Tolerance–Intolerance of Ambiguity (Budner 1962). The Budner Scale represents a homogeneous dimension of self-report. The scale measures the willingness of an individual to deal with uncertainty. Sample statements include: "A good job is one where what is to be done and how it is to be done are always clear"; "It is more fun to tackle a complicated problem than to solve a simple one"; "A person who leads an even, regular life with few surprises really has a lot to be grateful for." The response format paralleled that of the EPPS and the JPI. The scale items in our study had a coefficient alpha of 0.616.

The Framingham Type A scale was used to measure Type A behavior (Haynes et al. 1978). Of the paper-and-pencil measures designed to assess Type A patterns in the workplace, this scale is recommended by the pioneer of the A/B typology (Chesney and Rosenman 1980). The Framingham scale has significantly predicted the incidence of coronary heart disease in both sexes after 8 years of follow-up (Haynes et al. 1980). It has also been related to self-reports of emotional lability, daily stress, tension, anxiety, and anger (Haynes et al. 1978). In the present study, 7 of the 10 scale items were used, a revision recommended by Haynes (Chesney et al. 1981). The Framingham scale asks subjects to indicate the accuracy of self-descriptive statements. Sample items include: "I am pressed for time"; "I am hard driving"; "I get restless when I have to wait for something." A five-point Likert format was used, with response options of very often, often, sometimes, rarely and never. The greater the agreement with the designated statements, the higher the Type A score. The coefficient alpha in the present study was 0.723.

Two indicators of company characteristics were included in this study: company size and company age. Size was measured by asking for the "company's sales revenues for the last compiled fiscal year." Eight response options were given, ranging from "0–199,000" to "20 million or over." Company age was measured in years.

Three financial performance indicators were used: growth rate, return on assets (ROA), and liquidity. Growth rate was assessed by the company's typical yearly trends in revenues over the past five years; the eight response options ranged from "decreased" to "increased 30% or more." The second indicator, annual ROA over the past five years, had options from "less than 5%" to "50% or more." Liquidity was assessed with the following question: "What is your company's ratio of current assets to current liabilities?": less than 1.0, 1.0–1.24, 1.25–1.49, 1.5–1.99, 2.0–2.49, 2.5–2.99, 3.0 or more.

For the financial measures, categories were used rather than open-ended responses. This procedure was followed because 1) the convenience of categorical options may increase respondent participation; 2) respondents might be reluctant to reveal precise financial data that could compromise anonymity; and 3) a sufficient number of response options can approximate continuous measures. In an earlier survey of SBANE members, open-ended response options to financial questions resulted in a substantial number of blank responses.

Return on assets (ROA) was used as one measure of profit. Information was also sought on liquidity since some researchers hold that this measure is more relevant to smaller businesses than ROA. Response categories for the financial measures were recommended by the Small Business Administration and the Smaller Business Association of New England.

SAMPLE

The sample consists of randomly selected members of the Smaller Business Association of New England. Questionnaires were sent in the fall of 1985 to 730 chief executives. Re-

TABLE 1 Means and Standard Deviations for the Study's Variables

	Mean	Standard Deviation
Need for Achievement (max = 25)	21.25	2.22
Locus of Control (max = 10)	7.74	2.05
Risk-Taking (max = 40)	28.30	4.64
Tolerance of Ambiguity (max = 40)	29.66	3.61
Type A (max = 35)	27.99	3.66
Revenue Growth (5 = 11-15%; 6 = 16-20%)	5.42	2.11
ROA (4 = 15-19%)	4.00	2.74
Liquidity (4 = 1.5-1.99; 5 = 2.0-2.49)	4.44	2.12
Revenue (3 = 500,000-999,999; 4 = 1,000,000-1,999,999)	3.85	2.09
Company Age	20.98	23.97

spondents were assured of anonymity. An accompanying letter from SBANE's executive director urged participation in the study. Three follow-up reminders were sent. Completed forms were received from 239 members, a 33% response rate. Founders numbered 147, nonfounders 92.

The demographic profile of the typical executive in our sample resembles membership information compiled by SBANE. It also parallels the profile of this same membership obtained in an earlier study by the authors (Begley and Boyd 1986).

RESULTS

Table 1 presents means and standard deviations for the variables included in the article. It also lists values for some categories of ordinal-level variables. For the five psychological variables, the means are high. Mean scores on need for achievement, locus of control, and Type A, in particular, are located on the high side of the possible range.

Hypotheses 1(a), 2(a), 3(a), 4(a), and 5(a) deal with psychological comparisons between founders and nonfounders. Table 2 presents the hypotheses and the results of difference of means tests between founder and nonfounder scores. The table also indicates whether these scores support or refute the hypotheses.

TABLE 2 Difference of Means Test of Psychological Attributes Between Founders (F: $n = 147$) and Nonfounders (NF: $n = 92$)

Attribute	Hypothesis		Mean	Standard Deviation	Probability	Hypothesis Status
n ach	1(a) F > NF	F	21.52	2.41	0.007[a]	Supported
		NF	20.84	1.83		
control	2(a) F > NF	F	7.78	2.09	0.863[b]	Rejected
		NF	7.73	1.97		
risk	3(a) F > NF	F	29.08	4.35	0.001[b]	Supported
		NF	27.00	4.86		
ambiguity tolerance	4(a) F > NF	F	30.13	3.37	0.004[a]	Supported
		NF	28.83	3.89		
Type A	5(a) F > NF	F	28.17	3.64	0.201[a]	Rejected
		NF	27.75	3.75		

[a] one-tailed significance test.
[b] two-tailed significance test.

88   T.M. BEGLEY AND D.P. BOYD

TABLE 3   Partial Correlations Between Psychological Attributes and Company Financial Performance Controlling for Company Size and Age Among Founders and Nonfounders

| | Founders | | |
	Growth	ROA	Liquidity
Need for Achievement	0.025	−0.038	0.018
Locus of Control	−0.014	0.026	−0.260**
Risk-Taking	0.090	−0.089ᵃ	−0.170*
Tolerance of Ambiguity	0.064	0.060ᵃ	−0.075
Type A	0.001	−0.002	−0.003
	Nonfounders		
	Growth	ROA	Liquidity
Need for Achievement	0.041	0.133	0.274*
Locus of Control	0.021	−0.003	0.005
Risk-Taking	−0.080	0.177	0.075
Tolerance of Ambiguity	−0.088ᵃ	0.341**	0.007
Type A	0.033	−0.053	0.086

*$P < .05$; **$P < .01$
ᵃA statistically significant curvilinear effect.

Three hypotheses are supported. Hypothesis 1(a) postulates that founders rank higher in need for achievement than do nonfounders. Hypothesis 3(a) predicts that founders score higher in risk-taking propensity. Hypothesis 4(a) predicts that founders have higher tolerance of ambiguity than nonfounders. Two hypotheses are rejected. Hypothesis 2(a) predicts that founders are more internal on locus of control than nonfounders. The results show that the two groups are similar on this dimension. Hypothesis 5(a) predicts that founders will have higher Type A tendencies than nonfounders. No such difference emerges. Overall, founders have higher need for achievement, risk-taking propensity, and tolerance of ambiguity than nonfounders. The two groups do not differ in locus of control and Type A tendencies.

Hypotheses 1(b), 2(b), 3(b), 4(b), and 5(b) postulate relationships between the psychological attributes of founders and the financial performance of their firms. The top half of Table 3 presents partial correlations to assess the nature of the relationships. Partial correlations are used to control for the effects that company size and age might have on the psychological variable—financial performance relationship. As the columns indicate, no statistically significant relationships emerge for growth and ROA variables. Two attributes associate with liquidity: locus of control and risk-taking. Risk-taking moves in the expected direction: lower risk-taking associates with higher liquidity. Locus of control, on the other hand, proceeds in an unpredicted direction: internality associates with lower levels of liquidity. To test the comparative contribution of the two psychological variables, the liquidity measure was regressed on these attributes by means of a simultaneous entry procedure. In the equation, the locus of control variable retained its statistical significance while the risk-taking variable did not. In summary, the "b" hypotheses are largely disconfirmed.

For comparative purposes, partial correlations were computed between the psychological attributes of nonfounders and the financial performance of their companies. This procedure tests whether the hypothesized relationships between psychological attributes and financial success might be more characteristic of small business managers than entrepreneurs. The bottom half of Table 3 presents the results. Again, no significant associations appear for growth. Tolerance of ambiguity associates with ROA. Need for achievement associates with liquidity. These findings for nonfounders provide scant support for any relationship between psychological attributes and financial performance.

As noted in the hypothesis section, the dearth of expected relationships could result from curvilinearity in the data. Examination of residuals in the relevant regression equations showed evidence of possible curvilinearity in some relationships. We tested for this possibility by constructing polynomial equations (Kerlinger and Pedhauzur 1973, pp. 208–209). In each equation, a financial performance measure was regressed on a psychological variable and the squared value of that psychological variable. The significance of the increment in variance explained by the squared variable was assessed with an F ratio. A statistically significant increment indicated the presence of curvilinearity.

Results indicate two instances of curvilinear effects among founders and one among nonfounders. For founders, ROA was predicted by polynomials for risk-taking and tolerance of ambiguity. Risk-taking has a positive effect on ROA up to a point. Beyond that point, increases in risk-taking begin to exert a negative effect on ROA. Similarly, tolerance of ambiguity is positive for ROA up to a point and negative beyond it. For nonfounders, tolerance of ambiguity positively affects growth to a certain level and then negatively affects it. These instances of curvilinearity are indicated by an "a" in Table 3.

Is it possible that psychological attributes might associate with company size and experience rather than with financial performance? If so, earlier studies of entrepreneurial success may have confounded the effects of psychological and nonpsychological variables. Faster growing companies might have also been the largest ones, and the most profitable companies might also have been the oldest ones (in samples with limited ranges for both variables). To test this possibility, we correlated psychological attributes with size and experience. The results are presented in Table 4. Among nonfounders, size and age have little relationship with psychological attributes. Among founders, however, several associations appear. Internal locus of control and higher risk-taking propensity associate with size. Internal locus of control, intolerance of ambiguity and low Type A tendencies associate with company age. These relationships suggest that size and experience might be more closely connected to psychological attributes than are growth and profits.

DISCUSSION

The article's two main objectives were to test for differences between entrepreneurs (founders) and small business managers (nonfounders) on psychological attributes and to examine connections between these psychological attributes and financial performance. Results indicate that founders score higher than nonfounders in need for achievement, risk-taking propensity, and tolerance of ambiguity. While the two groups differ on these psychological

TABLE 4 Pearson Correlations Between Psychological Attributes and Company Size and Age Among Founders and Nonfounders

	Founders		Nonfounders	
	Size	Age	Size	Age
Need for Achievement	− 0.048	− 0.026	0.128	0.050
Locus of Control	0.174*	0.149*	0.055	− 0.096
Risk-Taking	0.285***	− 0.009	0.108	− 0.001
Tolerance of Ambiguity	− 0.124	− 0.210**	0.043	− 0.039
Type A	0.015	− 0.155*	0.152	− 0.028

*$P \leq .05$; **$P \leq .01$; ***$P \leq .001$.

90   T.M. BEGLEY AND D.P. BOYD

dimensions, the absolute differences are not large. Results also indicate few connections between psychological attributes and corporate performance. The chief connection for founders is between internal locus of control and low liquidity. This unexpected relationship may indicate that internals feel in control of their asset to liability ratio, and therefore are less concerned about building a high ratio to protect themselves.

Why is there so little relationship between psychological attributes and financial performance? A number of previous studies, reviewed in the Hypothesis section, led us to predict relationships. The psychological variables used are ones that recur in the literature about entrepreneurs. Our results run counter to these earlier studies.

Several explanations are possible. Methodological concerns deserve consideration. Since results are based on a mailed questionnaire, poorly performing firms may be underrepresented. CEOs of such firms may lack both the time and inclination to record perceived shortcomings. The nature of SBANE itself may have affected the results. SBANE firms tend to be well established or at least sufficiently solvent to sustain membership in a fee-paying organization. Since our sample is comprised of relatively mature firms, the characteristics of the chief executive may not affect performance as acutely as in the formative stages.

The nature of the questionnaire itself may generate difficulties. Need for achievement is viewed as a deeply embedded dimension. Controversy has arisen over the efficacy of paper-and-pencil measures to assess this need; some researchers prefer projective techniques. Debate also surrounds the use of paper-and-pencil instruments to assess the Type A behavior pattern. Many authors claim that the original interview format is the most valid assessor (Rosenman 1978). Moreover, our shortened and amended versions of standard scales may introduce distortion. On the other hand, our alterations rendered the instruments more relevant to business situations. Focused modifications of this nature might reduce the distortion in earlier versions. Finally, subject scores on the psychological attributes tend to be skewed toward the high end of the scales. This uniform response pattern lessens the likelihood of differential associations.

Another explanation is that the curvilinear nature of some relationships is not detected by linear regression. Indeed, when we tested for curvilinear effects, three statistically significant curves appeared. When added to the significant linear relationships shown in Table 3, these three curves somewhat mitigate the paucity of results. In fact, these findings lead us to wonder if many studies of entrepreneurial characteristics might have reached different conclusions, had they tested for curvilinear effects.

Although methodological and statistical limitations may have influenced study findings, an alternative explanation is that the paper accurately reflects the negligible impact of psychological attributes on financial performance. As stated earlier, the restricted size and age ranges of previous studies may have confounded growth with size and profits with experience. Further, while the psychological variables included in this study are often used to describe entrepreneurs, various studies contest their prevalence. Even if one accepts the widespread existence of such "entrepreneurial" attributes, their effectiveness remains conjectural (see Brockhaus 1982; Gasse 1982, for reviews).

An intriguing possibility is that the characteristics contributing to success among the relatively experienced entrepreneurs in this sample may differ from success factors for early stage entrepreneurs. For example, achievement motivation and risk-taking propensity may be crucial for success only in the early stage companies. If this is so, it is apparent that more is known about early stage than later stage entrepreneurship. Among nonfounders, too, psychological predisposition has no appreciable bearing on financial performance. Non-founding small business managers and entrepreneurs in maturing firms constitute a considerable proportion of the small business population. Yet success factors associated with these two groups have received almost no attention in the literature. This article indicates that psychological features commonly linked to successful venture creation do not generalize to success in ongoing small business management. If this observation receives further support, the need to identify performance predictors in post-start-up stages will become compelling.

REFERENCES

Anderson, C.R. 1977. Locus of control, coping behaviors and performance in a stress setting: a longitudinal study. *Journal of Applied Psychology* 62:446–451.

Anderson, C.R., Hellriegel, D., and Slocum, J.W. Jr. 1977. Managerial response to environmentally induced stress. *Academy of Management Journal* 20:260–272.

Anderson, C.R. and Schneier, C.E. 1978. Locus of control, leader behavior and leader performance among management students. *Academy of Management Journal* 21:690–698.

Begley, T.M. and Boyd, D.P. In press. A comparison of entrepreneurs and managers of small business firms. *Journal of Management*.

Begley, T.M. and Boyd, D.P. 1985. The relationship of the Jenkins Activity Survey to Type A behavior among business executives. *Journal of Vocational Behavior* 27:316–328.

Begley, T.M. and Boyd, D.P. 1986. Executive and corporate correlates of financial performance in smaller business firms. *Journal of Small Business Management* 24:8–15.

Borland, C. 1974. Locus of Control, Need for Achievement and Entrepreneurship. Unpublished doctoral dissertation, University of Texas, Austin.

Boyd, D.P. 1984. Type A behavior, financial performance and organizational growth in small business firms. *Journal of Occupational Psychology* 57:137–140.

Boyd, D.P. and Gumpert, D.E. 1983. The effects of stress on early-stage entrepreneurs. In J.A. Hornaday, J.A. Timmons and K.H. Vesper, eds., *Frontiers of Entrepreneurship Research*. Wellesley, MA: Babson Center for Entrepreneurial Studies, pp. 180–191.

Brockhaus, R.H. 1975. I-E locus of control scores as predictors of entrepreneurial intentions. *Proceedings of the National Academy of Management*, pp. 433–435.

Brockhaus, R.H. 1982. The psychology of the entrepreneur. In C.A. Kent, D.L. Sexton, and K.H. Vesper, eds., *Encyclopedia of Entrepreneurship*. Englewood Cliffs, NJ: Prentice-Hall, pp. 41–56.

Brockhaus, R.H. 1980. Risk taking propensity of entrepreneurs. *Academy of Management Journal* 23:509–520.

Brockhaus, R.H. and Nord, W.R. 1979. An exploration of factors affecting the entrepreneurial decision: personal characteristics vs. environmental conditions. *Proceedings of the National Academy of Management*, pp. 364–368.

Budner, S. 1962. Intolerance of ambiguity as a personality variable. *Journal of Personality* 30:29–50.

Carland, J.W., Hoy, F., Boulton, W.R. and Carland, J.A.C. 1984. Differentiating entrepreneurs from small business owners: A conceptualization. *Academy of Management Review* 9:354–359.

Chesney, M.A. and Rosenman, R.H. 1980. Type A behavior in the work setting. In C. Cooper and R. Payne, eds., *Current Concerns in Occupational Stress*. London: Wiley, pp. 187–212.

Chesney, M.A., Black, G.W., Chadwick, J.H. and Rosenman, R.H. 1981. Psychological correlates of the Type A behavior pattern. *Journal of Behavioral Medicine* 4:217–229.

DeCarlo, J.F. and Lyons, P.R. 1979. A comparison of selected personal characteristics of minority and nonminority female entrepreneurs. *Journal of Small Business Management* 17:22–29.

Durand, D.E. and Shea, D. 1974. Entrepreneurial activity as a function of achievement motivation and reinforcement control. *The Journal of Psychology* 88:57–63.

Edwards, A.L. 1959. *Edwards Personal Preference Schedule*. New York: The Psychological Corporation.

92   T.M. BEGLEY AND D.P. BOYD

Entwistle, D.R. 1972. To dispel fantasies about fantasy-based measures of achievement motivation. *Psychology Bulletin* 77:377.

Friedman, M. and Rosenman, R.H. 1974. *Type A Behavior and Your Heart*. Greenwich, CT: Fawcett.

Gasse, Y. 1982. Elaborations on the psychology of the entrepreneur. In C.A. Kent, D.L. Sexton, and K.H. Vesper, eds., *Encyclopedia of Entrepreneurship*. Englewood Cliffs, NJ: Prentice-Hall, pp. 57–66.

Haynes, S.G., Feinleib, M. and Kannel, W.B. 1980. The relationship of psychosocial factors to coronary heart disease in the Framingham study: Eight-year incidence of coronary heart disease. *American Journal of Epidemiology* 111:37–58.

Haynes, S.G., Levine, S., Scotch, N., Feinleib, M. and Kannel, W.B. 1978. The relationship of psychosocial factors to coronary heart disease in the Framingham study: Methods and risk factors. *American Journal of Epidemiology* 107:362–383.

Hornaday, J.A. and Aboud, J. 1981. Characteristics of successful entrepreneurs. *Personnel Psychology* 24:141–153.

Howard, J.H., Cunningham, D.A. and Rechnitzer, P.A. 1977. Work patterns associated with Type A behavior: A managerial population. *Human Relations* 30:825–836.

Hoy, F. and Carland, J.W. Jr. 1983. Differentiating between entrepreneurs and small business owners in new venture formation. In J.A. Hornaday, J.A. Timmons, and K.H. Vesper, eds., *Frontiers of Entrepreneurship Research*. Wellesley, MA: Babson Center for Entrepreneurial Studies, pp. 180–191.

Jackson, D.N. 1976. *Jackson Personality Inventory*. Goshen, NY: Research Psychologists Press.

Jackson, D.N. 1977. Reliability of the Jackson Personality Inventory. *Psychological Reports* 40:613–614.

Jackson, D.N., Hourany, L., and Vidmar, N.J. 1972. A four-dimensional interpretation of risk taking. *Journal of Personality* 40:483–501.

Julian, J.W., Lichtman, C.M., and Ryckman, R.M. 1968. Internal-external control and need to control. *Journal of Social Psychology* 76:43–48.

Kerlinger, F.N. and Pedhazur, E.J. 1973. *Multiple Regression in Behavioral Research*. New York: Holt, Rinehart, and Winston.

Kobasa, S.C., Maddi, S.R., and Kahn, S. 1982. Hardiness and health: A prospective study. *Journal of Personality and Social Psychology* 42:168–177.

Komives, J. 1972. A preliminary study of the personal values of high technology entrepreneurs. In A.C. Cooper and J. Komives, eds., *Technical Entrepreneurship: A Symposium*. Milwaukee: Center for Venture Management.

Kounin, J. 1948. The meaning of rigidity: A reply to Heinz Werner. *Psychological Review* 55:157–166.

Lafond, J.F. April 1984. Understanding the entrepreneur. In Coopers and Lybrand, *Executive Alert Supplement*, pp. 2–7.

Lefcourt, H.M. 1965. Risk taking in Negro and White groups. *Journal of Personality and Social Psychology* 2:765–770.

Liles, P.R. 1974. *New Business Ventures and the Entrepreneur*. Homewood, IL: Richard D. Irwin.

MacDonald, A.P., Jr. 1970. Revised scale for ambiguity tolerance: Reliability and validity. *Psychological Reports* 26:791–798.

Maddi, S.R., Kobasa, S.C., and Hoover, M. 1979. An alienation test. *Journal of Humanistic Psychology* 19:73–76.

McClelland, D.C. 1961. *The Achieving Society*. Princeton, NJ: Van Nostrand.

Miller, D. and Friesen, P.H. 1982. Innovation in conservative and entrepreneurial firms: Two models of strategic momentum. *Strategic Management Journal* 3:1–25.

Mitchell, T.R. 1975. Expectancy models of job satisfaction, occupational preference and effort: A theoretical, methodological and empirical appraisal. *Psychological Bulletin* 81:1053–1077.

Organ, D.W. and Greene, C.N. 1974. Role ambiguity, locus of control and work satisfaction. *Journal of Applied Psychology* 59:101–102.

Palmer, M. 1971. The application of psychological testing to entrepreneurial potential. *California Management Review* 13:32–38.

Phares, E.J. 1976. *Locus of Control in Personality.* Morristown, NJ: General Learning Press.

Rotter, J.B. 1976. Generalized expectancies for internal versus external control of reinforcement. *Psychological Monographs: General and Applied* 80: Whole No. 609.

Scheré, J.L. 1982. Tolerance of ambiguity as a discriminating variable between entrepreneurs and managers. *Proceedings of the National Academy of Management,* pp. 404–408.

Seeman, M. 1967. On the personal consequences of alienation in work. *American Sociological Review* 32:973–977.

Seligman, M.E.P. 1975. *Helplessness: On Depression, Development, and Death.* San Francisco: Freeman.

Sexton, D.L. and Bowman, N.B. 1983. Comparative entrepreneurship characteristics of students: Preliminary results. In J.A. Hornaday, J.A. Timmons, and K.H. Vesper, eds., *Frontiers of Entrepreneurship Research.* Wellesley, MA: Babson Center for Entrepreneurial Studies, pp. 213–232.

Sexton, D.L. and Bowman, N.B. 1984. Personality inventory for potential entrepreneurs: Evaluation of a modified JPI/PRF-E test instrument. In J.A. Hornaday, F. Tarpley, J.A. Timmons, and K.H. Vesper, eds., *Frontiers of Entrepreneurship Research.* Wellesley, MA: Babson Center for Entrepreneurial Studies, pp. 513–528.

Sexton, D.L. and Bowman, N.B. 1985. The entrepreneur: A capable executive and more. *Journal of Business Venturing* 1:129–140.

Sexton, D.L. and Bowman, N.B. 1986. Validation of a personality index: Comparative psychological characteristics analysis of female entrepreneurs, managers, entrepreneurship students, and business students. In R. Ronstadt, J.A. Hornaday, R. Peterson, and K.H. Vesper, eds., *Frontiers of Entrepreneurship Research.* Wellesley, MA: Babson Center for Entrepreneurial Studies, pp. 40–51.

Shekelle, R.B., Schoenberger, J.A. and Stamler, J. 1976. Correlates of the JAS Type A behavior pattern score. *Journal of Chronic Diseases* 29:381–394.

Smith, N.R. and Miner, J.B. 1984. Motivational considerations in the success of technologically innovative entrepreneurs. In J.A. Hornaday, F. Tarpley, J.A. Timmons, and K.H. Vesper, eds., *Frontiers of Entrepreneurship Research.* Wellesley, MA: Babson Center for Entrepreneurial Studies, pp. 488–495.

Smith, N.R. and Miner, J.B. 1985. Motivational considerations in the success of technologically innovative entrepreneurs: Extended sample findings. In J.A. Hornaday, E.B. Shils, J.A. Timmons, and K.H. Vesper, eds., *Frontiers of Entrepreneurship Research.* Wellesley, MA: Babson Center for Entrepreneurial Studies, pp. 482–488.

Timmons, J.A. 1978. Characteristics and role demands of entrepreneurship. *American Journal of Small Business* 3:5–17.

Timmons, J.A., Smollen, L.E., and Dingee, A.L.M. 1985. *New Venture Creation,* 2nd. ed. Homewood, IL: Richard D. Irwin.

Welsch, H.P. and Young, E.C. 1982. The information source selection decision: The role of entrepreneurial personality characteristics. *Journal of Small Business Management* 29:49–57.

Welsh, J.A. and White, J.P. 1981. Converging on characteristics of entrepreneurs. In K.H. Vesper, ed., *Frontiers of Entrepreneurship Research.* Wellesley, MA: Babson Center for Entrepreneurial Studies, pp. 504–515.

Wolfe, R.N. 1972. Effects of economic threat on autonomy and perceived locus of control. *The Journal of Social Psychology* 86:233–240.

[11]

ELITISTS, RISK-TAKERS, AND RUGGED INDIVIDUALISTS? AN EXPLORATORY ANALYSIS OF CULTURAL DIFFERENCES BETWEEN ENTREPRENEURS AND NON-ENTREPRENEURS

RITA GUNTHER McGRATH,
IAN C. MacMILLAN,
University of Pennsylvania

SARI SCHEINBERG
Scheinberg Associates

EXECUTIVE SUMMARY

The objective here is to extend work that relates systems of belief to economic activity. This is done by assessing the response of a sample of individuals who have started their own businesses (called "entrepreneurs" in this study) with a contrast sample of non-entrepreneurs deliberately chosen to differ (called "career professionals" in this study) to a series of questions designed to operationalize underlying cultural values.

The concept of culture as used in this study is based on early work by Kluckhohn and Strodbeck, which posits that human problems and their solutions are limited in number. Group cultures in this approach reflect the dominant responses to these problems and solutions. Geert Hofstede expanded upon this basic idea in a landmark 1980 study. Hofstede found statistical evidence for four underlying dimensions of culture, together with "consequences" that reflect a given society's culture in the institutions and behaviors it maintains. Hofstede's dimensions are:

Power distance	Management of inequality between people
Individualism	Relationship between individuals and collectives
Uncertainty avoidance	Stance toward the future
Masculinity	Allocation of roles between the sexes

Address correspondence to Rita Gunther McGrath, The Sol C. Snider Entrepreneurial Center, The Wharton School, University of Pennsylvania, Vance Hall, 4th Floor, Philadelphia, PA 19104.

The authors wish to thank the Sol C. Snider Entrepreneurial Center of the Wharton School, and the Graduate School of Management of New York University for support.

Journal of Business Venturing 7, 115–135
© 1992 Elsevier Science Publishing Co., Inc., 655 Avenue of the Americas, New York, NY 10010

0883-9026/92/$5.00

Just as Hofstede's work on culture alludes to certain economic consequences as a result of the institutionalization of beliefs, research on entrepreneurship suggests a connection between entrepreneurial activity and underlying values. This literature reflects the following array of entrepreneurial beliefs:

Power distance	Entrepreneurs will exhibit higher "power distance" scores than career professionals, reflecting a tolerance for inequality.
Individualism	Entrepreneurs will favor individual rather than collective action.
Uncertainty avoidance	Entrepreneurs will be prepared to take risks and will value their personal time.
Masculinity	Entrepreneurs will tend to have a highly "masculine" orientation, will live to work, and treasure things and money.

From this array of likely entrepreneurial beliefs, a set of hypotheses was derived that posits high power distance, high individualism, low uncertainty avoidance, and high masculinity orientations for entrepreneurs, no matter what the orientation of the base culture.

These hypotheses were tested by performing a discriminant analysis on responses from 1,217 entrepreneurs and 1,206 non-entrepreneurs in eight countries. A stepwise discriminant analysis reduced the initial set of 83 variables to a more parsimonious 25. The SAS "DISCRIM" procedure yielded correct classifications for 73.96% of the entrepreneurs and 67.68% of the non-entrepreneurs, suggesting consistent differences in response for the two groups. In comparing responses to individual questions, the findings reported here suggest support for all of the initial hypotheses.

The initial study suggests the following directions for future research. First, the key finding that entrepreneurs share a common set of values should be tested and evaluated against a cross-cultural sample. Second, attention should be given to the time sequence in which such values are generated before making causal inferences. In other words, it would be necessary to know whether people become entrepreneurs because they have a given set of beliefs, or because the experience of business start-up affects their system of values. A question that this study does not address is whether or not there are distinctions between the founders of new businesses and successful managers of existing businesses. Further work that addresses this question would shed additional light into the interrelations between social structure, wealth creation, and cultural beliefs.

INTRODUCTION

There is little disagreement that social and economic revitalization are associated with entrepreneurship. Studies further suggest that not all societies foster entrepreneurial activity with equal effectiveness (Shapero and Sokol 1982; Birch 1987; Shapero 1985, Birley 1987). In recent years, researchers seeking to explain the genesis of entrepreneurship have broadened the scope of inquiry from one that was psychologically centered to one that incorporates a view of cultural beliefs and values (Huisman 1985; Peterson 1988; El-Namaki 1988, Alänge and Scheinberg 1988). These efforts have been hampered by lack of readily available and interpretable data, confusion about terminology, and lack of consensus among researchers on appropriate ways to assess and describe cultural variables.

This project is intended to contribute to the growing research stream relating value systems to entrepreneurship by interpreting data from a large cross-cultural database in light of existing frameworks for the understanding of culture. The research analyzes responses from business founders in nine different countries and contrasts them with the reported beliefs of a contrast sample of professionals from the same countries. The study is intended to be exploratory, in that the results are meant to suggest potentially fruitful areas for further inquiry into the culture/entrepreneurship nexus.

TOWARD A USEFUL CONCEPT OF CULTURE

Shapero and Sokol (1982) observed that business formation rates vary from society to society. They argue that this is so because different cultures carry different beliefs about the desirability and feasibility of beginning a new enterprise. These beliefs help determine which actions will be seriously considered (because they are desirable) and which will be implemented (because they are feasible). Thus, beliefs frame entrepreneurial activity.

A variety of studies lend support to this argument. Huisman (1985) conducted an extensive survey of entrepreneurial activity across cultures, and concluded that values influence entrepreneurial behavior. Wittmann (1989), Scully (1988), and Klundert (1986) each developed economic models that relate economic growth to cultural artifacts, such as democratic and open political structures, or with regional dynamism versus passivity. When it comes to new business and wealth creation, research seems to suggest that culture does make a difference.

How then are we to characterize this difference in terms of individual entrepreneurs? Is there indeed a predictable set of values more likely to be held by business starters than by others without regard to the home culture? Before proceeding to address this question, we must undertake a definitional pause.

There is no shortage of definitions for culture. An early, all-encompassing definition was offered by Kroeber and Kluckhohn (1952).[1] Their seminal work helped to establish a view of culture as having to do with the way human societies organize social behavior and knowledge. Culture as a useful concept for theory development in the social sciences remained elusive, however—more a description of bundles of attributes than an integrated whole with predictive power.

In 1961, Kluckhohn and Strodbeck conceived a promising approach. They argued that a national culture is a fairly consistent set of value orientations developed in response to two universal facts: first, that there are a limited number of common societal problems; and second that there are a limited number of known responses. Kluckhohn and Strodbeck identify five fundamental problems:

1. The nature of human nature
2. The relationship of man to nature
3. Orientations toward time
4. Orientations toward activity
5. The nature of relationship between people

While individuals will tend to reflect the "dominant value orientations" of their cultures' solutions, many possible solutions will be in evidence in a given culture.

This approach to culture offered several advantages over previous work. First, it offered a comprehensible and parsimonious framework for analysis, the formulation of a (short) list of universal human conditions. Second, it separated the framework (the problems) from the

---

[1]Culture, in their view, encompassed 164 different definitions, involving such components as knowledge, values preferences, habits, customs, traditions, implements, artifacts and so forth.

118   R.G. McGRATH ET AL.

responses to these problems, giving the concept flexibility. Finally, this view offered the promise of predictive power by suggesting knowable relationships between cultural variables and behavior.

HOFSTEDE'S CULTURAL DIMENSIONS

A major advance along the lines suggested by Kluckhohn and Strodbeck was made by Hofstede (1980). He sought not only to identify differences in cultural patterns, but also to understand the mechanisms that permit these patterns to remain stable over time. He carried out his research between 1967 and 1978, gathering 116,000 questionnaire responses from employees of one multinational company in 40 countries. Hofstede corroborated the theoretical work of his predecessors by finding that people from different countries did indeed tend to exhibit stable differences in values.

Culture, according to Hofstede, is "the interactive aggregate of common characteristics that influence a human group's response to its environment. Culture determines the identity of a human group in the same way personality determines the identity of an individual" (1980). With an individual, personality influences the choices made and the resulting outcomes. Culture similarly leads to sets of consequences for the society.

Cultural characteristics, he argues, are to be found in four dimensions, each of which has distinctive implications for behavior. Like Kluckhohn and Strodbeck, Hofstede suggests that cultural patterns arise from the ways in which different groups deal with fundamental human problems. He defines values as "a broad tendency to prefer certain states of affairs over others" (1980, p. 19). Values are determined early in life; they are in fact "programmed" into individuals. Long-lasting values are non-rational. We are probably not even conscious of them, because they form the framework for our view of the world. They are also not always consistent. We may, for example, value both freedom to go about our business without government interference and governmental intervention to protect our personal safety.

Hofstede's work suggests that shared values endure over time and are fairly consistent within cultures because they have been institutionalized in the "consequences" of any particular culture. Consequences both are created by and reinforce the underlying cultural conditions. Societies with high norms of individualism, for example, will tend to have greater occupational mobility, more press freedom, and "worship of the independent actor" (1980, p. 238). Societies with low individualism values will tend to have less occupational mobility and less press freedom, and value instead identity and roots in place. Consequences can also be seen in relatively enduring political, social, and technical systems. The type of religion prevalent in a society is a clear example of a cultural consequence. Taken together, the systems of value orientation and their consequences represent singular and enduring national characteristics. For the purpose of this study, we were anxious to identify which cultural characteristics were most likely to be associated with the consequence of entrepreneurial activity.

Like Kluckhohn and Strodbeck, Hofstede (1980) suggests that culture can be traced to responses to common human problems. Four dimensions create his underlying framework:

1. *Power Distance:* management of inequality between people
2. *Individualism:* the relationship between individuals and collectives

3. *Uncertainty Avoidance:* stance toward the future
4. *Masculinity:* allocation of roles between the sexes

Each dimension is related to specific values and to definable consequences.[2]

IN SEARCH OF AN ENTREPRENEURIAL CULTURAL PATTERN

The entrepreneurship literature is replete with discussions of characteristics and behaviors that differentiate entrepreneurs from everybody else (Gartner 1985; Low and MacMillan 1988). For the most part, past research has been inconclusive. Significant attention has been paid to the psychological characteristics of entrepreneurs (Hornaday and Aboud 1971; Gasse 1982; McClelland 1967) and to the environmental and circumstantial conditions in which they live (Collins and Moore 1970; Susbauer 1972; Shapero 1972). Researchers are now beginning to turn their attention to the effects of culture upon entrepreneurial outcomes (Huisman 1985; Huisman and de Ridder 1984; Peterson 1988; El-Namaki 1988).

Since rates of entrepreneurial activity differ consistently in different cultures, despite other similarities in economic and social development, it appears that some values may be consistently associated with increased entrepreneurship, no matter what the home culture. Non-entrepreneurs therefore ought to respond differently than business founders to questions about value orientation. We will now utilize Hofstede's framework to review past research on entrepreneurship in order to develop testable hypotheses about the relationship between entrepreneurial behavior and cultural beliefs.

Power Distance: Differences in Approach to Inequality

Human inequality is unavoidable. People are different in their native abilities and in the circumstances into which they have been born. Some cultures accentuate these differences. Hofstede calls such cultures "high power-distance index" societies (1980, p. 92). A culture whose members score high on this dimension will tend to have institutions that are hierarchical, will have "zero-sum" theories of power, and will believe in large differences in the compensation or living standards of its members. Low power-distance index cultures in contrast will tend to have flatter organization pyramids, will believe in minimizing power differences between people, and will have tax systems that redistribute wealth.

One might expect that entrepreneurs would tend to exhibit higher power-distance values than career professionals in the same culture, regardless of whether the culture is high or low on power-distance scores. Entrepreneurship is one route to a mobility and a higher position. In a society oriented toward equality, entrepreneurial activities could gain the business owner an advantage that could be obtained in no other way or overcome disadvantages that could be overcome in no other way. In either case, it makes intuitive sense that the entrepreneur would tend to endorse a greater amount of differentiation between himself and others. Similarly, it seems logical that entrepreneurs would be less likely to endorse having a low power position in which others have authority.

This view has been somewhat corroborated by research. Hagen (1962) found that entrepreneurs "cannot accept authority." Collins et al. (1964) argue that negative previous

---

[2]It should be noted that although Hofstede's work has come under a great deal of criticism, its parsimony and broad operationalization make it uniquely useful among current cultural theories.

120   R.G. McGRATH ET AL.

work experiences are major factors influencing the decision to start one's own business. Draheim (1972), Susbauer (1972), and Shapero (1975) report related data that support the position that dissatisfaction with previous work is a major factor that contributes to the decision to found one's own business. It thus appears that entrepreneurs are prepared to assume power as a way of overcoming hindrances imposed on them by others, a high power-distance approach.

Other research suggests that societies in which large power distances are the norm may create particular incentives for entrepreneurial activity by blocking other routes to attain success. Hofstede, for example, notes that high power-distance differences tend to be associated with large differences in wealth (1980, p. 125). To the extent that entrepreneurship is perceived as a way out of poverty, the more extreme the differences in wealth, we might expect a greater incentive to start a business. Such a linkage is implied in Hagen's 1960 work, which pointed to such factors as lower-class group membership as an incentive to change the existing state of things.

Individualism: Differences in Orientation

Culture in part determines whether one is oriented towards personal action or prefers to act in concert with others. Hofstede associates high individualism scores with an emphasis on individual initiative and achievement, on leadership rather than membership. High individualism societies, he argues, socially encourage individual initiative. High individualism is also associated with a belief that everyone has a right to privacy, and that one must form one's own opinions. Rewards are couched in such terms as autonomy, variety, pleasure, and financial security, rather than expertise, order, duty, and security through social relationships.

From the popular view of entrepreneurs as highly independent loners, we would expect that they score higher than career professionals in their individualism scores. A stream of entrepreneurship research supports this view. McClelland's well-known ideas, for example, depicted the entrepreneur as someone with a personal high need for achievement, who preferred to take responsibility for decisions and set goals and accomplish them through his own effort (McClelland 1967). Sexton and Bowman (1985) concluded that entrepreneurs need autonomy, independence, and dominance and are not strongly absorbed by needs for support from others or conformity to the norms of others. Hornaday and Aboud (1971) reported that in comparison with men in general, entrepreneurs had stronger needs for achievement (measured by the Edwards Personal Preference Scale) and higher scores on independence and effectiveness of leadership scales in Gordon's Survey of Interpersonal Values. Brockhaus (1979) reported positive relationships between internality as measured by Rotter's Internality/Externality scale and the decision to become an entrepreneur. Throughout the psychological commentary in the literature on entrepreneurship, there is thus a common thread of "autonomy" or "desire to be independent."

A second perspective of the entrepreneur as individual actor cautions us not to overlook his social relationships. Aldrich and Zimmer (1986) and Birley (1985) emphasize the critically important nature of the entrepreneur's personal network. Such networks act as conduits to resources, opportunities, and guidance, expanding by far the capacities of any individual player. No matter how much we may come to know about the entrepreneurs as an individual, such research suggests, we will not know very much about the process without understanding the role played by social relations.

Differences in Uncertainty Avoidance

One unalterable problem of human existence is that of time. Since time runs only one way, we cannot undo what has been done, nor can we predict what is to come. Hofstede proposed that this leads to the question of how different cultures cope with future uncertainty. Some, the "low uncertainty avoidance index" societies, accept rather easily the notion of ambiguity and risk, teaching their members that they must learn to live with it. Other societies, the high uncertainty avoiders, try to cope with the unknown future by imposing increased stability upon their environment. In low uncertainty avoidance countries, values favor more risk-taking, smaller organizations, strong motivations for individual achievement, and more optimism. Personal time is felt to be of great value. High uncertainty avoidance systems, in contrast, believe in less risk-taking, larger organizations in which managers are selected on the basis of seniority, less individual ambition, and more pessimism.

A strong tradition in the entrepreneurship literature links entrepreneur's beliefs with low uncertainty avoidance. They have been posited to thrive on situations of moderate risk. McClelland (1967) found that extreme risk or complete safety did not provide entrepreneurs with an incentive. He theorized that entrepreneurs function best in situations offering moderate risk of failure, presumably because they believe that such risk can be reduced by increased effort or skill. Entrepreneurs also were found to work no harder than others on routine tasks or tasks that do not deviate from traditional methods. He thus posited the entrepreneur as a moderate risk-taker. Webster (1977) also concluded that entrepreneurs are moderate risk-takers, but pointed out that this characteristic does not differentiate them very much from other kinds of managers, a point that was reinforced by Sexton and Bowman (1985).

Several writers (Schere 1982; Sexton and Bowman 1985) assess the willingness of the entrepreneur to participate in an environment that is uncertain, changes frequently, and does not offer clear guidance for action, and conclude that entrepreneurs are far more willing to cope with ambiguity than are the less enterprising. Entrepreneurs are thought to believe that their own behavior and abilities shape events, not arbitrary fate. Brockhaus (1982), among others, identified this characteristic as "internal locus of control." Since they believe that they have the capacity to change the external environment, it stands to reason that entrepreneurs are more willing to venture out on their own without the protection of a large organization.

Masculinity: Allocation of Roles Between the Sexes

The final unavoidable dilemma of human life identified by Hofstede is that of differentiation between the sexes. Indisputedly, there are two sexes with different biological roles to play. From this fundamental difference in physical structure, human societies may erect strong parallels in social structure, or they may be more flexible about the roles men and women take. According to Hofstede, cultures with a high masculinity orientation tend to be oriented toward things and money, tend to value independence, tend to "live to work" and to value decisiveness. Cultures with low masculinity orientations "work to live," esteem service, are oriented towards people, and emphasize intuition rather than decision-making on observable fact. Achievement in a high-masculine oriented society is associated with wealth and position, rather than with human contacts and living environment. It is unfortunate that Hofstede chose to describe this dimension as "masculinity," as the phrase tends to evoke strong feelings that have little to do with the concepts the construct is intended to communicate. This confuses the concepts.

One such easily confused concept is the distinction between people's gender and their cultural beliefs. Women in a "masculine" culture might well have a more "masculine" set of beliefs than men in a "feminine" culture. Although there is a growing literature on female entrepreneurs (see for example, Birley 1989), researchers have not dealt extensively with the concepts as Hofstede defined them. Kets de Vries' 1985 report on the negative aspects of the entrepreneurial personality hinted that highly masculine traits, such as the need for control and focus on work, could have seriously dysfunctional consequences. It seems plausible that higher degrees of "masculine" beliefs would be associated with entrepreneurship, whereas higher degrees of "feminine" beliefs would be associated with work within the context of an organization.

Summary and Hypotheses

Not all people become entrepreneurs. Higher proportions of people in some countries become entrepreneurs than in others. We argue that cultural values play an important role in accounting for those differences. In other words, a given constellation of beliefs will tend to be associated with entrepreneurship, no matter what culture the individual entrepreneur is from. Hofstede (1980) provides us with a parsimonious model for comparing cultural differences. He argues that a distinctive culture can be categorized along four dimensions: power distance, individualism, uncertainty avoidance, and masculinity.

The following hypotheses derive from this discussion:

H1:   No matter what the overall cultural values of the home society are, its entrepreneurs will tend to exhibit a characteristic array of beliefs.

H2:   Entrepreneurs will tend to have higher power-distance scores than career professionals.

H3:   Entrepreneurs will tend to have higher individualism scores than career professionals.

H4:   Entrepreneurs will tend to have lower uncertainty avoidance scores than career professionals.

H5:   Entrepreneurs will tend to have a more "masculine" orientation than career professionals.

METHODOLOGY

This study is an outgrowth of a 13-nation study of entrepreneurship conducted under the auspices of The Center for Entrepreneurial Studies at New York University Graduate School of Business, the Snider Entrepreneurial Centers at the Wharton School of the University of Pennsylvania, and the affiliates of international collaborators. Collaborators from the following countries have contributed information to the entire database:

Australia	Canada
Denmark	England
Finland	Italy
Kenya	Norway
Portugal	China (People's Republic)
Sweden	Taiwan
United States	U.S.-Puerto Rico

Only eight of the collaborators were able to obtain a comparison sample for career professionals in their nations. This study utilizes data only from those countries in which both an entrepreneurial and a career professional sample are available. These countries are:

Australia	Canada
Finland	Italy
Portugal	China (People's Republic)
Sweden	United States
U.S.-Puerto Rico	

The entire database now contains over 3,000 responses. The countries in our sample represent 81% of the total ($n = 2423$). For this study, responses from 1,217 entrepreneurs and 1,206 non-entrepreneurs from the same countries were used. Where a response was not computed, the entire response was dropped, resulting in a lower n for the analysis as a whole. This was done in order to reduce response bias in developing the discriminant function.

Entrepreneurs in our sample were defined along the lines suggested by Gartner (1985) and Brockhaus (1987) as individuals who initiated an entrepreneurial event, starting a venture. In the context here, the term "entrepreneur" should be considered equivalent to "founder of a new business." To ensure maximum clarity in a cross-cultural context, the sample of entrepreneurs was chosen from people who had begun stand-alone businesses, not people who began new ventures associated with existing businesses. Founders themselves were requested to fill out the questionnaire. Criteria for inclusion were that the business be at least two years old, that it have at least one other person employed, and that the founder devotes a major portion of his or her time to this business.

A major focus of this exploratory study is to determine whether or not certain values are likely to be held consistently by entrepreneurs. This could only be accomplished by comparing entrepreneurs, not only with each other, but with people on entirely different career trajectories. We felt it important to use for comparison people who have factors such as base culture, social class, opportunity, and income level in common with the entrepreneurial sample. Other requirements were that every country in the survey must have contrast sample members, and that the roles of these individuals be reasonably consistent from country to country.

Within these constraints, the contrast sample was deliberately chosen to differ from the entrepreneurial sample as much as possible. The non-entrepreneurial sample was thus developed from three groups: (1) school teachers; (2) bank branch managers, and (3) government officers or employees. The roles of these three groups are reasonably consistent across countries, and all countries have representatives of one or more of these groups. In this study, we have referred to this group as "career professionals."

124   R.G. McGRATH ET AL.

TABLE 1   Summary of Classifications Using Full Set of 83 Variables

		Classification	
From category	N	Entrepreneur	Career professionals
Entrepreneur	657	86.61%	13.39%
Career professional	418	33.01%	66.99%
Prior probability		0.6112	0.3888

We are not so much interested here in the variation of response from country to country as in comparing the overall pattern of response in the two groups. It should be noted that inclusion of responses from only these countries must necessarily limit the generalizability of our conclusions, in particular since resource constraints prevent broader representation of countries that are not Western industrialized democracies. Furthermore, we have not touched upon the question of whether or not entrepreneurs running businesses of their own differ from private-sector managers in the same cultures. It may well be that organizational "entrepreneurs" have more in common with business founders than they do with school teachers, but that is not a question this research program can address.

The questionnaire was designed to operationalize cultural influence (Hofstede 1980; Kluckhohn and Strodbeck 1961; Lodge 1975). A series of questions seeking to identify the values of the respondents on 14 cultural variables was developed, and each respondent answered on a Likert-type scale. Possible answers were: 1 = strongly agree; 2 = agree; 3 = neither agree nor disagree; 4 = disagree; 5 = strongly disagree. The 14 general categories were associated with from 4 to 10 individual questions, for a total of 83 variables.[3] We used stepwise discriminant analysis for two purposes: (1) to determine if the self-reported beliefs of our respondents could be used to predict which of them would be most likely to have started their own businesses; and (2) to determine which of the 83 variables under consideration would have the greatest power to discriminate between the two groups.

Standard texts on discriminant analysis (see for example, Klecka 1980) recommend that a value of $p < 0.15$ be utilized to select variables for inclusion in such an exploratory analysis. Given that we had the luxury of a large number of variables from which to choose as well as a large number of degrees of freedom, we decided to perform the analysis at the $p < 0.05$ level. Despite this more stringent standard, 25 of our original 83 classification variables proved to have the power to discriminate between the two groups at a very stringent p level of < 0.05. We were able to correctly predict the category of 73.96% of the entrepreneurs and 67.68% of the career professionals in our sample. Given that the phenomena under consideration are generally recognized as being unusually difficult to predict and interpret, these are interesting results.

The SAS STEPDISC procedure was used to perform the stepwise analysis, and the DISCRIM procedure was used to do a subsequent discriminant analysis on the variables selected. Tables 1 to 8 summarize the results, comparing the full set of 83 variables (Table 1) with results obtained from selecting 25 variables (Table 2).

Unlike the population at large, entrepreneurs in our sample enjoyed a slight majority.

---

[3]The variable "Time", for example, was specified by four statements: (1) is a limited resource; (2) the private life and time of an employee is properly a matter of direct concern to his company; (3) never do tomorrow what you can do today; and (4) is best spent being planned for and organized to avoid surprises.

TABLE 2 Classifications Using More Parsimonious Set of 25 Variables

From category	N	Classification	
		Entrepreneur	Career professionals
Entrepreneur	868	73.96%	26.04%
Career professional	789	32.32%	67.68%
Prior probability		0.5238	0.4762

It was therefore necessary to adjust the discriminant function to take into account the difference in sample sizes of the two groups. We did this by using the SAS "priors proportional" program to accurately assess the power of the discriminating variables.

A fairly common problem with most statistical procedures lies in determining their vulnerability to a change in sample. To ensure that our solution would be both robust and reliable, we used the following test procedures. We randomly divided our sample size in half, then ran the same discriminant procedure as we had for the entire sample on the half-sample. This procedure generated a discriminant function for the variables, which we then used to predict the group membership of respondents in the other half of the sample. The split-sample test did not reveal significant problems with the robustness of our measures (Table 3).

Discriminant analysis allows us to measure the relative importance of variables in separating two groups. Table 4 summarizes the results of our stepwise selection. Those variables at the top of the table have comparatively greater power to differentiate than those at the bottom. Means and significance levels for each of the two groups are also provided.

FINDINGS AND DISCUSSION

The central thrust of this study has been to determine whether or not there are underlying patterns shared by entrepreneurs despite the cultural diversity of their origins. The findings reviewed here suggest that such an underlying pattern, not only exists, but that it can be identified and replicated using split-sample statistical techniques. This in itself is an interesting conclusion, lending support to the argument that the cultural dimension is worth further exploration in investigation of the entrepreneurial phenomenon.

The remainder of the discussion fleshes out this overall finding by relating these data to Hofstede's cultural dimensions. Before we begin, the reader should be aware of the limitations of the techniques we have employed here. We have identified a group of variables,

TABLE 3 Classifications of Split-Sample Test

From category	N	Classification	
		Entrepreneur	Career professionals
Entrepreneur	436	76.38%	23.62%
Career professional	394	30.71%	69.29%
Prior probability		0.5253	0.4747

126   R.G. McGRATH ET AL.

TABLE 4 Stepwise Discriminant Analysis of Variables Differentiating Entrepreneurs from Career Professionals (1 = strongly agree   5 = strongly disagree)

Var ID	Step in	Mean entrepreneurs	Mean career prof'ls	p <	Variable (exact text of questionnaire item)
c100	1	2.6015	3.19617	0.0001	Success is owning your own company
c98	2	2.94548	2.61244	0.0001	Success is being promoted up through the ranks in a corporation
c136	3	3.8572	3.62201	0.0001	Work is more desirable if it's in a large organization
c42	4	3.66256	3.30790	0.0001	Having a lot of money means you come from an influential family
c28	5	3.59084	3.79904	0.0001	Change of jobs or residence is highly discouraged and very difficult
c2	6	1.94671	2.17255	0.0001	Time is a limited resource
c134	7	2.54061	2.40192	0.0003	Work means to develop your identity and self-respect
c96	8	2.83742	2.9689	0.0011	Being successful is associated with making a lot of money
c84	9	4.50256	4.36125	0.0021	Being an entrepreneur means not being able to find a job
c112	10	2.25294	2.51914	0.0028	There is a duty to uphold the values and reputation of your family
c154	11	3.40573	3.13619	0.0037	Starting a company means a risk of not getting past employment back
c164	12	2.46603	2.54306	0.0065	Starting a company means a risk of uncertainty, but adds to the excitement of your life
c4	13	3.3671	3.86125	0.0052	Private life of employee is properly of direct concern to his company
c62	14	3.21185	3.42823	0.0038	Power is giving complete and detailed instructions to others who should do their jobs
c38	15	3.81763	3.69857	0.0061	Having a lot of money means you have been an expert in your field
c66	16	3.533	3.67943	0.0083	Being an entrepreneur means being a technical expert
C132	17	2.96038	3.09982	0.0077	(1 = more authoritarian manager, 4 = more consensus-oriented manager)
c88	18	2.86177	2.69139	0.0100	Failure is associated with losing face/respect
C128	19	2.46584	2.65538	0.0169	There is a duty to give all clients and customers the same treatment
c150	20	2.73544	2.86364	0.0272	Equality is characterized by a stress on rewards based on merit
c148	21	2.90287	2.5311	0.0174	Equality is everyone's right
c104	22	3.05964	2.98086	0.0270	Being successful is associated with being well-educated
C76	23	2.32376	2.59477	0.0434	Entrepreneurs produce existing products in a more-efficient way
c26	24	2.93026	3.00957	0.0238	Change of social status is open to everyone
c16	25	3.27732	3.14427	0.0242	Having rights means that every citizen is able to influence political decisions

TABLE 5   All Variables Comprising the Discriminant Analysis

	Agreed more	Disagreed more
Entrepreneurs	Duty: uphold values of the family	Work in large org. more desirable
	Duty: treat clients/customers the same	Rights: all can influence politics
	Success: owning your own company*	Money comes from influential family
	Equality: rewards based on merit	Money comes from expertise
	I'm like a more authoritarian manager*	Start-up risks unemployment
	Change of social status open to all*	Entrepreneurs can't find a job
	Start-up means risk but also excitement	
	Time is a limited resource	
	Success: making lots of money	
	Entrepreneurs increase efficiency	
Non-entrepreneurs	Work develops identity, self-respect	Power: giving detailed instructions
	Success: promotion in a corporation	Entrepreneurs are technical experts
	Equality is everyone's right	Change is difficult, discouraged
	Success: being well-educated#	Private life of employee is properly
	Failure means losing face/respect	of direct concern to his employer

Variables have been abbreviated to save space. See Table 3 for the precise wording of each variable.
*Entrepreneurs *agreed* with this statement while non-entrepreneurs disagreed with it.
#Entrepreneurs *disagreed* with this statement while non-entrepreneurs agreed with it.

taken together, as important in differentiating one group from the other. Responses on these variables are by definition significantly different in a statistical sense. As the reader should be able to discern from Table 4, there are cases where the differences between entrepreneurs and career professionals are statistically significant, but relatively small. In the following discussion, we speculate upon the nature of the differences in a practical, managerial sense. It is important for the reader to be aware that both entrepreneurs and career professionals may share a central tendency, for example, to disagree with a given question. Our discussion is intended to provoke reflection on the reasons for the differences that do exist between the two groups and to suggest potentially fruitful areas for further inquiry.

Table 5 presents a simple taxonomy of the response means for the two groups according to which group agreed or disagreed with the survey statements. If Hofstede is correct, distinct patterns of cultural values are related to distinct consequences. We have already concluded that one such consequence appears to be associated with business start-up. The remainder of this discussion will focus on how our findings relate to Hofstede's cultural dimensions and to the entrepreneurship literature.

Power Distance

We would expect entrepreneurs to believe that they can achieve power. What is not clear is whether the entrepreneur is more likely to believe that his efforts should increase the power distance between himself and his fellows (high power distance set of values) or whether the entrepreneur tends to feel that large power inequalities are a bad thing. In general, we would expect entrepreneurs to believe in larger power distances than career professionals. Should he be successful, the entrepreneur should feel that he is entitled to reap larger rewards for his risks in a high power-distance culture (Table 6).

We found that although entrepreneurs like people to be treated fairly, they are not egalitarians. Career professionals agreed more with the statement "equality is everyone's

128   R.G. McGRATH ET AL.

TABLE 6   Power-Distance Variables

	Agreed more	Disagreed more
Entrepreneurs	Change of social status open to all*	Rights: all can influence politics Money comes from influential family Money comes from expertise
Non-entrepreneurs	Equality is everyone's right Success: being well-educated#	Entrepreneurs are technical experts Change is difficult, discouraged

*Entrepreneurs *agreed* with this statement while non-entrepreneurs disagreed with it.
#Entrepreneurs *disagreed* with this statement while non-entrepreneurs agreed with it.

right" than did entrepreneurs. One might speculate whether this has to do with the entrepreneur's actual experiences (facing societal inequality) or with a sense that those who are more capable (as the entrepreneur would consider himself, according to the locus of control theories) earn their rights, while others are not able to do so. For example, non-entrepreneurs were more likely to disagree that being an entrepreneur meant being a technical expert. They tended to downplay the importance of education (agreeing less than did non-entrepreneurs that being successful is associated with being well-educated). Arguably, this might be because equality of education was not available to them. This is somewhat supported by the fact that career professionals were slightly more likely to equate financial rewards with technical expertise.

The theory that entrepreneurship is in part a reaction to restrictive or adverse situations encountered in the past gains some support here. Entrepreneurs were less likely than career professionals to disagree that change of jobs or residence is highly discouraged and very difficult. Furthermore, they disagreed more that having rights means every citizen is able to influence public policy outcomes. Entrepreneurs, however, did not appear to be unduly put off by such limitations, tending to agree that change of social status is open to everyone, whereas career professionals *disagreed* that this was the case. Entrepreneurs further put less weight on family background in terms of income potential, disagreeing more than did the career professionals that money is equated with coming from an influential family.

In general, we found strong support in this study for the notion that entrepreneurs tend to have values higher on the power-distance dimension than career professionals. Although they believe that everyone should be able to change his social status, they believe in power distance. Provided that social distinctions are based on merit, they seem to believe in dominating their social structure.

Individualism

Not surprisingly, our study corroborates the view that entrepreneurs believe in individualism (Table 7). The entrepreneurs agreed far more than did the career professionals that "Success is owning your own company." This agrees closely with Hofstede's results, in which high individualism is associated with "emphasis on individual initiative and achievement" (1980, p. 235). Similarly, career professionals were far more likely to agree that "Success is being promoted up through the ranks in a corporation," a variable that is similar to Hofstede's finding that low individualism is associated with "emphasis on belonging to an organization." Entrepreneurs, not surprisingly, were more likely to disagree that work is more desirable in a large organization.

TABLE 7   Individualism Variables

	Agreed More	Disagreed More
Entrepreneurs	Duty: uphold values of the family Duty: treat clients/customers the same Success: owning your own company* Equality: rewards based on merit I'm like a more authoritarian manager*	Work in large org. more desirable
Non-entrepreneurs	Work develops identity, self-respect Success: promotion in a corporation	Power: giving detailed instructions

*Non-entrepreneurs *disagreed* with this statement while entrepreneurs agreed with it.

Hofstede suggests that high individualism is associated with identity being based "in the individual," whereas low individualism associates identity with the social system. Both our groups agree that work and self-identity are related, but entrepreneurs were less likely to agree that work develops identity and self-respect, indicating perhaps that the entrepreneur *is* more comfortable with developing these attributes on his own.

Similarly, high individualism is associated by Hofstede with a greater concern for one's family than with the larger community. Along these lines, entrepreneurs agreed more that there is a duty to "uphold the values and reputation of your family."

Our entrepreneurial respondents are themselves business owners, not workers. Interestingly, they tend to appear to be somewhat more authoritarian than career professionals. While both groups disagreed that power results from giving "complete and detailed" instructions to others, entrepreneurs disagreed less. Furthermore, they tended to compare themselves with a manager who "makes his decisions promptly and communicates them to his/her subordinates clearly and firmly, and who expects subordinates to carry out the decisions loyally and without raising difficulties." Career professionals were more likely to identify with a manager who "consults with his employees before he reaches a final decision" and who "accepts the majority viewpoint as the decision." This agrees with Hofstede's findings, in which low individualism scores were associated with belief in group (rather than individual) decisions.

According to Hofstede, high individualism scores should be associated with an emphasis on universal standards, rather than on special treatment for certain groups. This is supported by our research. Entrepreneurs appeared more likely than career professionals to agree with statements linking positive results to merit, or to conditions under which merit might emerge. They tended to agree more that there is a duty to give all clients and customers the same treatment (as a businessman) and that equality between people is related to rewards based on merit.

For the most part, entrepreneurs respond as we would expect them to, in a manner that appears consistent with a value system stressing individualism.

Uncertainty Avoidance

If they are nothing else, entrepreneurs are surely risk-takers. Any new business involves change and a risk of failure. People who are extremely risk-averse are unlikely to become entrepreneurs. Entrepreneurs should therefore be associated with those values Hofstede maintains are consistent with "low uncertainty avoidance." Low uncertainty avoidance, Hofstede suggests, is associated with less resistance to change, stronger achievement mo-

130   R.G. McGRATH ET AL.

TABLE 8   Uncertainty Avoidance Variables

	Agreed more	Disagreed more
Entrepreneurs	Start-up means risk but also excitement	Start-up risks
	Time is a limited resource	unemployment
	Entrepreneurs increase efficiency	
Non-entrepreneurs	Failure means losing face/respect	

tivation, more risk-taking, stronger ambition for individual advancement, tolerance of competition, and optimism. High uncertainty avoidance he associates with pessimism, reliance on formal structures, and the fear of failure (Table 8).

Questions about risk did evoke different patterns of response. Entrepreneurs were close to neutral on a question that equated failure with loss of face or respect, whereas career professionals tended to agree. Career professionals also appeared to be more concerned than entrepreneurs about permanently losing their source of security. Entrepreneurs disagreed more that starting a company means a risk of not getting your past employment back if it fails. Entrepreneurs agreed that starting a company implies risks, but agree that it "adds to the excitement of your life."

A tolerance for competition is also implied in differing responses to the question of what entrepreneurs do. Entrepreneurs were more likely to agree that they produce existing products in a more efficient way, by implication changing the competitive environment through their activities. This is consistent with Hofstede's theory.

Finally, the two groups differ quite significantly on their view of time. Hofstede suggests that the view of time and its changes is the foundation for the dimension of uncertainty, since we are always uncertain of the future. We would expect that high uncertainty avoidance is associated with a reluctance to value personal time, since the cultural orientation is to downplay the changes wrought by time's passage. We found some support for this idea, in that entrepreneurs were much more likely to agree that "time is a limited resource" than were career professionals.

Masculinity

Cultures high on the masculinity scale, argues Hofstede, are more likely to value individual achievement, independent success, and financial rewards. Research relates similar characteristics to the entrepreneur. We would expect entrepreneurs to score high on masculinity values. High masculinity is associated with the belief that success is associated with recognition and wealth. It is correlated with a "money and things" orientation, according to Hofstede. Unfortunately, only three variables in our study appear to map onto Hofstede's "masculinity" construct, which indicates that caution is in order in interpreting the responses to these items (Table 9).

Entrepreneurs did agree more that being successful is associated with making a lot of money. They disagreed far more than the career professionals that "being an entrepreneur means not being able to hold a job." This seems to relate to Hofstede's identification of "earnings, recognition, advancement and challenge" as important to high masculinity societies (1980, p. 288) as well as his notion that managers in such societies have leadership, independence, and self-realization ideals.

TABLE 9 Masculinity Variables

	Agreed more	Disagreed more
Entrepreneurs	Success: making lots of money	Entrepreneurs can't find a job
Non-entrepreneurs		Private life of employee is properly of direct concern to his employer

High masculinity is also associated with tolerating the company's interference in one's private life. In our study, entrepreneurs were less likely to disagree that the private life of an employee is properly of direct concern to his company. Of the three variables identified, two map rather neatly onto consequences Hofstede identifies with high masculinity.

Evaluation of Hypotheses

A reasonable degree of support for all five initial hypotheses was found.

H1: The discriminant procedure as a whole provided support for the idea that entrepreneurs share a predictable set of values, when compared with individuals who have followed a non-entrepreneurial trajectory.

H2: High Power Distance: Entrepreneurs appear not to mind social inequality, but expect to be at the top of any social hierarchy on the basis of their own merit.

H3: High Individualism: We found support for the idea that entrepreneurs favor independent action and separation from groups and clans.

H4: Low Uncertainty Avoidance: This study supports earlier work that suggests that entrepreneurs can tolerate risk and ambiguity.

H5: High Masculinity: Our results suggest that entrepreneurs are more highly motivated to obtain economic and recognition rewards than are their non-entrepreneurial counterparts.

Our findings support these hypotheses of the value systems of the entrepreneur.

IMPLICATIONS

Implications for Public Policy

In general, governments tend to view entrepreneurship as a good thing. Many variations on this basic economic development theme are echoed in countries throughout the world. Our results suggest that pervasive differences exist in beliefs between people who choose careers in organizations with a civil-service flavor versus those who start businesses. This analysis therefore supports the notion that two different worlds of people intersect in the economic development area: people who administer the policies and people who are targeted by them. An area of entrepreneurship research with public-policy implications would thus be to explore the impact of this difference and incorporate this learning into the design of programs intended to facilitate entrepreneurial activity.

Should entrepreneurs share a common set of values, it may for example be possible to transfer what has been learned from one setting to another, even if they do not share common cultural values. This could increase the chance of effective "technology transfer" in the area of fostering entrepreneurship.

The nature of entrepreneurial value orientation may imply new economic development interventions. As an example, let us consider the policy implications indicated by the finding that entrepreneurs appear to believe in high individualism (for example that success means owning a company). In many less-developed countries, it is more desirable to work for government or in the army, not in start-up businesses. The beneficial effects for the economy of entrepreneurial activity are at odds with dominant value systems. In this case, an intervention design might focus on creation of mechanisms to increase social recognition of entrepreneur's value. The challenge is to develop intervention models that take the cultural value factor into account.

Other Implications

As an exploratory project, a major goal of this study was to suggest directions for further inquiry. Two substantive implications for entrepreneurship research arise from our findings.

First, the results suggest that certain predictable beliefs can be identified in people who have begun businesses as compared with people who have not. On a micro level, this conclusion expands upon the work of past researchers into entrepreneurs' psychological characteristics and traits by including a cultural component. At a macro level, the study suggests that culture, as reflected in a given society's institutions and practices, may have a predictable relation with proclivity to begin new ventures. The findings thus relate to current research in several fields, which attempt to link environmental factors with wealth-creating activity. This study illustrates one way in which the cultural dimension can be operationalized, and provides a basis for further creation of testable cultural hypotheses.

A second idea of relevance to future research lies in determining the causal relationship of values to venture creation. In entrepreneurship, as in much of organizational theory, there is an ongoing debate about the role of individual choice as opposed to environmental influences in shaping entrepreneurial outcomes. This tends to be phrased as a distinction between environmental "pushes" (such as negative previous life experiences) and "pulls" (such as the recognition of a new opportunity) (Shapero and Sokol 1982; Aldrich and Zimmer 1986; Gilad and Levine 1986). Our finding that entrepreneurs appear to share a common set of values across countries can be interpreted to support either a "choice" perspective or an "ecology" perspective, depending upon where in the causal chain these beliefs relate to entrepreneurship. The question is thus whether differences in values shape life choices, or whether experiences such as starting a new business lead to significant change in values.

This indicates a direction for future inquiry. If further research provides evidence that entrepreneurs have beliefs that lead them to choose to be entrepreneurs, this lends support to a "choice" position. Thus, entrepreneurs are more like each other than they are different and more different from everyone else than they are from each other. Given a set of "entrepreneurial" values, they will intentionally seek out opportunities to engage in venture creation as most consonant with their personal belief structure. This view would suggest that entrepreneurship stems from more-or-less purposive behavior, and would argue against the role of environmental chance, except as the environment contributes to the formation of entrepreneurial values in the first place.

If we see a set of common beliefs as an outcome, rather than a cause, of business start-up, however, an entirely different set of implications arises. First, a more "ecological" approach to the determination of entrepreneurial outcomes would be warranted, since factors other than belief structures are causally related to entrepreneurship. Second, this suggests commonality in the experience of business starting, which tends to move individuals' value structures toward those that are "entrepreneurial," no matter what the culture of origin. In this event, the life-changing nature of the entrepreneurial experience, rather than the set of initial values of the entrepreneur, becomes important.

Several fruitful directions for further research seem to be indicated. First, the finding that entrepreneurs share common sets of values should be tested, ideally utilizing a broader cross-cultural sample. Second, understanding the temporal dimensions of values appears to be important to developing a theory of entrepreneurship with predictive power. Finally, a comparison of entrepreneurial with managerial values might well provide additional insight into the interrelations between social structure, wealth creation, and cultural beliefs.

SUMMARY

Our cross-cultural study was designed to add empirical data on cultural values to research in entrepreneurship. Discriminant analysis was used to distinguish the responses of entrepreneurs and career professionals in eight countries to questions on cultural values. From this analysis, we identified 25 variables, significant at the $p < 0.05$ level, which successfully classified 74% of the entrepreneurs and 68% of the career professionals.

The results suggest that entrepreneurs have a persistent and characteristic value orientation, irrespective of the values of their base culture. Furthermore, these values appear to be aligned along four dimensions first identified by Hofstede (1980) in his *Culture's Consequences*. The dimensions are: (1) individualism; (2) power distance; (3) uncertainty avoidance; and (4) masculinity. We found that in a number of quite different societies, entrepreneurship is associated with high individualism, high power distance, low uncertainty avoidance, and high masculinity scores. This corroborates Hofstede's analysis and some existing theoretical work on entrepreneurship.

Practical implications of the work lie in identifying value orientation as an issue that must be considered in the design of economic development policies aimed at entrepreneurs. Implications for research concern the genesis of the difference: are entrepreneurs really different, or do they grow to be different through the experience of starting a business? Future research should consider the question of value orientation and cultural beliefs in developing explanatory theories about the entrepreneurial phenomenon.

REFERENCES

Alänge, S., and Scheinberg, S. 1988. Swedish Entrepreneurship in a Cross-Cultural Perspective. Paper presented at the Eighth Annual Babson College Entrepreneurship Research Conference, Wellesley, MA, May, 1988.

Aldrich, H., and Zimmer, C. 1986. Entrepreneurship through social networks. In D.L. Sexton and R.W. Smilor, eds., *The Art and Science of Entrepreneurship*, pp. 2–23. Cambridge, MA: Ballinger Publishing.

134   R.G. McGRATH ET AL.

Birch, D.L. July 1987. Yankee Doodle Dandy. *Inc.* (8), pp. 33, 36.

Birley, S. 1985. The role of networks in the entrepreneurial process. *Journal of Business Venturing* 1(1): 107–117.

Birley, S. 1987. New ventures and employment growth. *Journal of Business Venturing* 2(2): 155–165.

Birley, S. January 1989. Female entrepreneurs: Are they really any different? *Journal of Small Business Management* 27(1) 32–37.

Brockhaus, R.H. 1979. An exploration of factors affecting the entrepreneurial decision: Personal characteristics vs. environmental conditions. In *Proceedings of the National Academy of Management,* The Academy of Management, Mississippi State, Mississippi, pp. 364–368.

Brockhaus, R.H. 1982. The psychology of the entrepreneur. In C.A. Kent, D.L. Sexton, and K.H. Vesper, eds., *Encyclopedia of Entrepreneurship.* New York: Prentice-Hall, Inc.

Brockhaus, R.H. July 1987. Entrepreneurial folklore. *Journal of Small Business Management* vol 25, no 3, 1–6.

Collins, O.F., Moore, D.G., and Unwalla, D.B. 1964. *The Enterprising Man.* East Lansing, MI: Michigan State University Business Studies.

Collins, O.F., and Moore, D.G. 1970. *The Organization Makers.* New York: Appleton-Century-Crofts.

Draheim, K.P. 1972. Factors influencing the rate of formation of technical companies. In A.C. Cooper and J.L. Komives, eds., *Technical Entrepreneurship: A Symposium,* pp. 3–27. Milwaukee, WI: Center for Venture Management.

El-Namaki, M.S.S. August 1988. Encouraging entrepreneurs in developing countries. *Long Range Planning (UK)* 21(4)98–106.

Gartner, W.B. 1985. A conceptual framework for describing the phenomenon of new venture creation. *Academy of Management Review.* 10(4):696–706.

Gasse, Y. 1982. Elaborations on the psychology of the entrepreneur. In C.A. Kent, D.L. Sexten, and K.H. Vesper, eds., *Encyclopedia of Entrepreneurship.* New York: Prentice-Hall, Inc.

Gilad, B., and Levine, P. October 1986. A behavioral model of entrepreneurial supply. *Journal of Small Business Management* 24(4):45–53.

Hagen, E.E. 1960. The entrepreneur as a rebel against traditional society. *Human Organizations* 19(4):185–187.

Hagen, E.E. 1962. *On the Theory of Social Change: How Economic Growth Begins.* Homewood, IL: Dorsey Press.

Hofstede, G. 1980. *Culture's Consequences: International Differences in Work Related Values.* Beverly Hills, CA: Sage Publications.

Hornaday, J., and Aboud, J. 1971. Characteristics of successful entrepreneurs. *Personnel Psychology* 24:141–153.

Huisman, D., and de Ridder, W.J. 1984. International Small Business Survey: A Picture of Entrepreneurial Climate in Different Countries. Rotterdam, The Netherlands. SKIM Industrial Market Research.

Huisman, D. 1985. Entrepreneurship: Economic and cultural influences on the entrepreneurial climate. *European Research (Netherlands)* 13(4, Special Section):10–17.

Kets de Vries, F.R. November-December 1985. The dark side of entrepreneurship. *Harvard Business Review,* pp. 160–167.

Klecka, J. 1960. *Discriminant Analysis.* Beverly Hills: Sage Press.

Kluckhohn, F., and Strodbeck, F.L. 1961. *Variations in Value Orientations.* Evanston, IL: Row Peterson.

Klundert, T. van de. 1986. Economic resilience: A two-country analysis. *Economist (Netherlands)* 134(1):25–41.

Kroeber A., and Kluckhohn, F. 1952. *Culture: A Critical Review of Concepts and Definitions.* Cambridge, MA: Peabody Museum.

Lodge, G.C. 1975. *The New American Ideology*. New York, NY: Alfred Knopf.

Low, M., and MacMillan, I.C. 1988. Entrepreneurship: Past research and future challenges. *Journal of Management* 14(2):139.

McClelland, D.C. 1967. *The Achieving Society*. Princeton, NJ: Van Nostrand, Reinhold.

Peterson, R. April 1988. Understanding and encouraging entrepreneurship internationally. *Journal of Small Business Management* vol 26, no 2, 1–7.

Schere, J. 1982. Tolerance of ambiguity as a discriminating variable between entrepreneurs and managers. In *Proceedings*, pp. 404–408. New York: Academy of Management.

Scheutz, C. 1986. Critical events for Swedish entrepreneurs in entrepreneurial spin-offs. *Technovation (Netherlands)* 5(1–3):169–182.

Scully, G.W. June 1988. The institutional framework and economic development. *Journal of Political Economy* 96(3):652–662.

Sexton, D.L., and Bowman, N. 1985. The entrepreneur: A capable executive and more. *Journal of Business Venturing* 1(1):129–140.

Shapero, A. 1972. The Process of Technical Company Formation in a Local Area. In A.C. Cooper and J.L. Komives, eds., *Technical Entrepreneurship: A Symposium*, pp. 63–95. Milwaukee, WI: Center for Venture Management.

Shapero, A. 1975. The displaced, uncomfortable entrepreneur. *Psychology Today* 9(6):83–88.

Shapero A. 1985. Why entrepreneurship? A worldwide perspective. *Journal of Small Business Management* 23(4):105.

Shapero, A., and Sokol, L. 1982. The social dimensions of entrepreneurship. In C.A. Kent, D.L. Sexton, K.H. Vesper, K.H., eds., *Encyclopedia of Entrepreneurship*, pp. 72–88. Englewood Cliffs, NJ: Prentice-Hall.

Susbauer, J.C. 1972. The technical entrepreneurship process in Austin, TX. In A.C. Cooper and J.L. Komives, eds., *Technical Entrepreneurship: A Symposium*, pp. 28–46. Milwaukee, WI: Center for Venture Management.

Webster, F.A. 1977. Entrepreneurs and ventures: An attempt at classification and clarification. *Academy of Management Review* 2:54–61.

Wittman, D. December 1989. Why democracies produce efficient results. *Journal of Political Economy* 97(6):1395–1424.

Part III
Start Up

[12]

Long Range Planning, Vol. 14, No. 5, pp. 39 to 45, 1981
Printed in Great Britain

0024 6301/81/050039-07S02.00/0
Pergamon Press Ltd.

39

Strategic Management: New Ventures and Small Business

Professor Arnold C. Cooper, Krannert Graduate School of Management, Indiana

This paper examines the factors influencing the formulation and implementation of strategy in new and small firms. Small businesses vary substantially in their resource positions, the goals of their founders and their potential. They also vary in stage of development: thus strategic management is examined separately in the start-up stage, the early-growth stage, and the later-growth stage. Intracorporate entrepreneurship in established firms is also considered. Despite this diversity, small firms create an environment for strategic management in which both the opportunities and constraints are different from those in large organizations.

New and small firms provide a distinctive environment for the formulation and implementation of strategy. This paper, based upon a review of the literature, examines the processes by which strategy is developed in such firms and the nature of the resulting strategies. Because new ventures within established firms have many of the characteristics of new and small businesses, strategic management within this context will also be considered.

Most firms in the United States, the United Kingdom, and other Western countries are small. For instance, about 95 per cent of all U.S. firms have fewer than 20 employees.[1] However, the diversity among these small firms is enormous, so that statements which are descriptive of some do not apply to others. They differ in types of founders, in management sophistication, in stage of development, and in performance. Vesper has suggested that small firms might be classified as 'mom and pop' companies, stable high-payoff companies, and growth-oriented companies.[2]

By far the majority of small businesses would be classified as mom and pop firms, particularly in retailing and service industries. Many have no hired

employees and rely only on the proprietor or members of the family. Their founders often lack formal managerial training, but may have technical skills, such as being able to sell real estate, cut hair, or do automobile repairs. Capital barriers to entry are usually low, management methods intuitive, and profits moderate or low. Start-ups and discontinuances are frequent and the founders often move from blue-collar or clerical jobs to entrepreneurship and back again. Some such places of business need revolving doors, not for the few customers, but for the entrepreneurs who come and go.

Some small retail and service firms and a higher percentage of small manufacturing firms might be classified as stable, high-payoff companies. Their founders often have more formal education and higher expectations than the mom and pop founders. Often they enjoy strong competitive positions deriving from specialized know-how, patents, or a virtual monopoly in a particular local market. Management methods, although informal by large company standards, may be very effective. Without the pressures of growth, the founder may be able to engage in civic activities or achieving a lower golf handicap, while maintaining a high standard of living.

Growth-oriented small firms offer the possibility of high payoff through selling out, through floating public issues of stock, or through controlling a large enterprise. They are started more often by groups, with the founders usually having had managerial experience. Their strategies usually position them in growing markets or involve innovative methods or products which give them clear competitive advantages. However, their growth may impose heavy demands on the founders, in personal commitments and the need to take risks. Capital requirements may bring outside investors and loss of control. Management methods may change to such a degree that the original founders must be replaced.

Arnold C. Cooper is a professor at the Krannert Graduate School of Management, Purdue University, West Lafayette, Indiana 47907, U.S.A.

These classifications are fluid and it is certainly possible for a firm to move from one category to another. However, in general, these types of firms start with different resources, follow different growth paths, and involve different internal environments for the formulation and implementation of strategy.

The context within which strategy is managed also varies by the stage of development of the small firm. In this paper, we shall think of three stages:

(1) *the start-up stage*, including the strategic decisions to found a firm and to position it within a particular industry with a particular competitive strategy;

(2) *the early-growth stage*, when the initial product-market strategy is being tested and when the president maintains direct contact with all major activities (many firms stabilize at this stage);

(3) *the later-growth stage*, often characterized by multiple sites for retail and service businesses and by some diversification for manufacturing firms; organizationally the firm usually has one or more levels of middle-management and some delegation of decision-making.

All of the types of firms just considered pass through the start-up stage and, if they are successful, move on to an early-growth stage. However, only the growth-oriented firms are likely to be found in the later-growth stage.

As a firm grows, at what point is it no longer small? Any answer to this question is somewhat arbitrary, but the focus here, even for firms in the later-growth stage, is upon organizations with less than 500 employees.

Strategic Management in the Start-up Stage

The decision to found a new firm is, in every sense, a strategic decision by the entrepreneur. It involves non-routine decisions to commit major resources to create a particular new business at a particular time and place. The new business then has a strategy (which may or may not have been carefully considered); it provides selected goods or services to particular markets and it emphasizes (whether wisely or not) particular policies to provide a way of competing.

The decision to found a new firm seems to be influenced by three broad factors.[3] They are:

(1) the entrepreneur, including the many aspects of his background which affect his motivations, his perceptions, and his skills and knowledge;

(2) the organization for which the entrepreneur had previously been working, whose charac-

teristics influence the location and the nature of new firms, as well as the likelihood of spin-offs; and

(3) various environmental factors external to the individual and his organization, which make the climate more or less favorable to the starting of a new firm.

Of these factors, the characteristics of the entrepreneur have been most extensively examined. Psychological research suggests that entrepreneurs have a high need for achievement and a belief that they can control their own fate.[4] One group of manufacturing entrepreneurs was characterized as having had poor relations with their fathers, their teachers and their employers. They seemed to be driven to entrepreneurship by their need to avoid being in a subordinate relationship to others.[5] A number of studies have shown that entrepreneurs often come from families where the father or a close relative was in business for himself.[6,7] Some sub-groups of societies have higher rates of entrepreneurship than others; young members of such sub-groups (such as the Chinese in South-East Asia or the Indians in East Africa) are surrounded by 'role-models' of entrepreneurship. They may also choose this career path because other career paths are closed to them in the larger society.[8] The thrust of these findings is that some people, by virtue of their family background and early childhood influences, are much more likely to start businesses. However, entrepreneurial inclinations, like musical talent, may or may not be capitalized upon. A number of other factors, discussed below, interact to create a climate more or less favorable to starting a new business.

The typical entrepreneur with technical or managerial training starts his business when he is in his thirties.[9,10] It is then that he has the track record, experience, and savings to make founding feasible, while still having the energy level and willingness to take risks which are necessary. Thus, the conditions which exist when potential technical entrepreneurs are in their thirties, including the organizations they then work for and the environmental climate then extant, determine whether they will be likely to found new businesses. However, evidence on the founders of mom and pop firms suggest a wider range of ages at the time of founding.[11]

A second major factor influencing whether a potential entrepreneur will start a new business is the nature of the organization for which he works. This organization, which might be termed an incubator, seems to play a particularly important role in the founding of high technology firms. It locates the potential founder in a particular geographic area which may or may not have a favorable entrepreneurial climate. (A number of studies have shown that most entrepreneurs start their businesses where they are already living and working; it is the rare founder who moves at the time he is starting a new business.)[12]

The incubator organization also provides the entrepreneur with the experience which leads to particular managerial skills and industry knowledge. Since industries vary widely in the extent to which they offer opportunities for new ventures, this means that the strategy of the incubator organization determines to a great extent whether its employees will ever be in a position to spin off and start their own businesses. Thus an established organization in a mature industry with little growth and heavy capital requirements is unlikely to have many spin-offs. Its employees, no matter how motivated, are not acquiring the technical and market knowledge which can easily be translated into the strategic decision to start a new business.

The policies of potential incubator organizations also appear to determine, to a marked degree, the motivations of the entrepreneur. In brief surveys such as questionnaires, founders tend to report the socially acceptable reasons as to why they became entrepreneurs; these include such factors as the desire for independence and financial gain. However, depth interviews often disclose that the founder was 'pushed' from the parent organization by frustration.[3] Studies of spin-off rates from established organizations show that internal factors influence spin-off rates, with internal problems being associated with high rates of spin-off and placid times being associated with low rates.[9] Thus, the extent to which the strategic and operating decisions of the established firm satisfy or frustrate its employees influences whether spin-offs occur.

A complex of factors external to the individual and to the parent organization also appears to influence entrepreneurship. Much of the research in this area is only suggestive, but it seems that climates can change over time and that past entrepreneurship makes future entrepreneurship more likely. The credibility of the act of starting a company appears to depend, in part, upon whether the founder knows of others who have taken this step.[7] Venture capital availability and particularly the existence of well-developed communication channels vary across geographic regions and help to determine the feasibility of entrepreneurship. The presence of experienced entrepreneurs also influences future entrepreneurship; they serve as sources of advice and venture capital and they sometimes do what they know best—start additional new businesses.[3,13] Their companies become excellent incubators for other spin-offs and also offer consulting opportunities for fledgling founders who are seeking income while trying to get started. It seems clear that past entrepreneurship influences the climate for future entrepreneurship. What is not so clear and what deserves additional research is how an area begins to become enterpreneurially active or how an area which has been active becomes less so.

The three broad factors just discussed influence the entrepreneurial decision as summarized in Figure 1.

The Competitive Strategy of the New Firm

The decision to start a new firm is clearly a strategic decision. However, also of interest here is the cluster of decisions which determine the nature of the new business, including the products of services to be offered, the markets to be served, and the policies to be emphasized. What has been learned about the influences upon these decisions in the new firm and about the relationship between particular strategies and performance?

Since the new business draws primarily upon the knowledge and skills of the entrepreneur, one might expect that the product/market choice would be closely tied to the experience gained in the incubator organization. For the most part this is true, although it varies by industry. New companies are closely related to the nature of the business of the parent firms for about 80–85 per cent of high technology firms; for nontechnical manufacturing and service firms, the corresponding percentages are 50–55 per cent.[9,11,14] For new franchises, the percentage is probably very low,

Antecedent Influences Upon Entrepreneur

1. Genetics Factors
2. Family Influences
3. Educational Choices
4. Previous Career Experiences

Incubator Organization

1. Geographic Location
2. Nature of Skills and Knowledge Acquired
3. Contact with Possible Fellow Founders
4. Motivation to Stay With or to Leave Organization
5. Experience in a 'Small Business' Setting

Environmental Factors

1. Economic Conditions
2. Accessibility and Availability of Venture Capital
3. Examples of Entrepreneurial Action
4. Opportunities for Interim Consulting
5. Availability of Personnel and Supporting Services; Accessibility of Customers

Entrepreneur's Decision

Figure 1. Influences upon the entrepreneurial decision

since the franchisor supplies the expertise rather than the founder.

Although there has not been much explicit research on how the founder decides upon a business strategy, we can draw some inferences from general descriptions of the process and from case studies. For larger, more professionally-based ventures, and particularly for those seeking venture capital, there typically is a new business plan. Such a plan describes the way in which the proposed firm is to compete and often reflects considerable thought. For that much larger group of new ventures which start without the discipline of seeking outside capital from professional sources, the process of deciding upon a basis of competition seems to be informal and intuitive. It may be based upon an excellent, first-hand 'feel' for the market. However, many new service businesses of the mom and pop type seem to be started opportunistically, with the availability of particular facilities or sites being important determinants.[11]

We don't know very much about the relationships between characteristics of founders, the strategies of their firms, and subsequent performance. There has been some research on high technology firms, though, which suggests that successful new firms are more likely to be started by multiple founders, have more initial capital, transfer more technology from the parent organization, are more likely to have a marketing function, show greater concern for personnel matters, and are more likely to have spun-off from large organizations than from small ones.[15,16] With regard to strategy, those new high technology firms whose strategies were related to the parent firms, in markets served and technology utilized, were more likely to be successful. In addition, longitudinal study of 95 new manufacturing firms indicated that those judged to be successful were more likely to have been started by two or more founders and more likely to have founders with both relevant experience and post high school education.[14]

Strategic Management in the Early Growth Stage

As the new firm becomes established, the founder typically continues to be in direct contact with all activities and decisions. Many businesses of modest potential stabilize at this point, often with no hired employees. Other firms continue to grow, adding employees and sometimes additional management. At this time the founder or founders may delegate operating decisions, but not strategic decisions. Management methods continue to be informal, with few policies and with control exercised primarily through direct contact.

As the new business gets started, it immediately begins to receive 'feedback' from the market.

Sometimes, the assumptions underlying the new firm's strategy prove to be faulty, and the firm seems likely to run out of cash before reaching the break-even point. It appears that founders often change their strategies at this point. Thus, an electronics component manufacturer switches to sub-contract work or an ice-cream shop becomes a steak-house. The entrepreneur has the opportunity to change quickly at this point; there is no organization to convince and there is little commitment to the status quo. However, much will depend upon how the entrepreneur perceives the environment, whether he perceives it as it really is or as he would like to see it.[17] Founders are sometimes stubborn people with a dream and not really amenable to dispassionate analysis of their plans.

As the new firm becomes established, the extent to which management confronts strategic decisions varies with the kind of firm and the characteristics of its industry. For the mom and pop business in a stable environment, the focus is usually upon operating decisions. Whether the strategy is re-examined and whether opportunities are then pursued appears to depend on the characteristics of management. In experiments conducted in India, owner-managers who had received achievement-motivation training frequently investigated or undertook changes in strategy.[18]

For those businesses which grow to become what we have classified as stable, high payoff firms or growth-oriented firms, there are decisions associated with evolving successful strategies. However, we lack systematic research to indicate whether these firms have high-potential strategies from the time of founding or whether these strategies evolve from the feedback of the market place. One study of 270 manufacturing firms indicated that companies which achieved annual sales of $100,000 or more in sales did so in their first 10 years; old small companies usually didn't grow.[19] The firms in this sample also showed great stability in their strategies, with only one in twelve making substantial product changes in a 9 year period.

There is substantial 'wisdom-based' literature analyzing the characteristics of small firms and suggesting the most suitable strategies. Small firms, particularly in the early stages, have limited financial and human resources. They have almost no reputation and little in the way of economies of scale or benefits from experience curves. There is a concentration of risk in one or a few products, markets, and people; there is usually no cushion to absorb the results of bad luck or bad decisions. The capabilities of the new firm are often uneven, reflecting the unbalanced experience of the entrepreneur.

Against these disadvantages, the new firm has no

ties to the past; it can innovate, without worrying about the effect on existing sales. This, coupled with the talents and drive of the founding group, is undoubtedly one reason why new and small firms have been such remarkably fertile sources of technical innovation, accounting for major new innovations all out of proportion to their R & D expenditures.[20] (Of course, most small firms are not particularly innovative; it is the growth-oriented small firms which are most likely to have this characteristic.) New firms also have the ability to move quickly; the chain of command is short and decision methods are informal and, if not carefully documented, at least timely. Management often has a first-hand 'feel' for the realities of customers and operations, based not upon the abstractions of reports, but upon day-to-day contact. Small firms also can avoid the departmentalization and co-ordination problems which characterize large, complex organizations. There may be a lack of staff specialists and formalized analysis, but there is the opportunity to focus the attention of the organization upon opportunities. The small organization, with its shared sense of the need to survive, can create a cost consciousness and dedication which are difficult to achieve in large, profitable firms where each individual knows that his contributions are only a small part of the whole. Of course, in all instances these are potential advantages which may or may not be realized, depending upon the competence and commitment of management.

To summarize the advice of most writers, it would be that the small firm should choose a 'niche' and avoid direct competition with larger companies. Some would modify this advice to say that direct competition is possible, but that the small firm should concentrate on where it has a competitive advantage or where the large firm is complacent or doing a poor job.[21–23] Thus, large firms tend to concentrate on mass markets, so small firms should concentrate on specialized markets. Large firms tend to be slow to react, so small firms should concentrate on opportunities arising from rapid market change. Large firms tend to be organized to produce in large production runs and to offer standardized service. Small firms can concentrate on short production runs, quick delivery and extra service. Large firms must be concerned about whether raw material supplies, work forces, and manufacturing and personnel policies are suitable for large volume operations. Small companies can use scarce materials, locate in areas with small labor forces, and utilize unique approaches, unconcerned about the implications if these were applied throughout a large corporation. Large firms must be concerned about government regulatory attitudes and their visibility to communities and unions. Small firms have a low profile and can move more quickly and be less concerned about the reactions of such groups. The evidence supporting these recommendations is anecdotal and based upon general observation. Much of it appears to be sound, but there is no systematic research examining the strategies of large number of firms and their performance over time.

The process of strategic planning in small firms has received attention in several articles.[24–27] The small firm environment makes heavy demands upon management for day-to-day operations and there are usually no staff specialists to provide support. Explicit efforts to set aside blocks of time for planning and to shield management from day-to-day pressures may be necessary. Structured approaches to the process of planning have been recommended by several authors. Unlike large organizations the emphasis is not upon deciding how to allocate resources among businesses or upon formal planning as a communication mechanism. The primary focus is upon mechanisms for identifying problems and for 'stepping-back' to look at the implications of current strategy. Recognizing the flexibility of small firms, particular emphasis should be placed on short-term planning.[28]

Strategic Management in the Later Growth Stage

Many small businesses stabilize and maintain an environment in which the president is in direct contact with the key activities, possibly with a small management team, each member of which is responsible for a key function. However, growth-oriented small businesses may continue to grow, adding additional levels of management.

The internal environment for management then begins to change, as the sheer volume of activities compels the founder to turn some duties over to others. Typically, the role of the founder changes, with 'doing' activities largely delegated and with the job becoming more managerial in character. Many operating decisions may be delegated, although the president continues to be deeply involved in strategic decisions. One of the distinguishing characteristics of the very small firm, the president's direct contact with employees, with products, and customers, begins to change. More formal ways must be developed to keep management informed and to control operations. Policies must be developed and increased formality occurs. Top management must try to develop new skills in managing through others and in developing an organization. Some entrepreneurs are not suited for this kind of managerial task and their shortcomings may prevent the firm from growing successfully or may lead to the entrepreneur's departure.

These changes in the internal environment both aid and hamper effective strategic management. The growth in the organization may give the president more time for planning. The growing firm may have more resources to pursue particular activities and to withstand competitors' challenges. However, growth may cause management to 'lose touch'; control of operations may suffer and management's feel for markets, competitors, and organizational capabilities may diminish. Implementation of strategy, which is typically one area where a small firm has a real advantage, becomes more of a problem as the organization grows.

Many growth-oriented small firms seem to be positioned in newly-developing industries. As such, management faces the challenges of adapting strategy to the changing demands of an evolving industry. The strategic implications of industry life cycles become particularly important for these firms.[29] It is widely believed that new industries are characterized by a high rate of new company formation and a high rate of entry by established firms, both small and large. Later, there is often a 'shake-out' as the stronger competitors enlarge their market shares. The extent to which small firms survive and prosper as an industry matures appears to vary widely, but the reasons for these differences have not been examined systematically.

Growth-oriented small firms sometimes owe their success to innovative strategies. A number of authors have commented on how the small firm environment is conducive to innovation, with its informal decision processes in which relatively few executives must be convinced, its lack of commitment to the status quo, its low sales requirements to be successful, and its low costs of development.[20,30] However, the small firm may sometimes pioneer and then be faced with severe competition. It is surprising that there has been very little research on the most appropriate strategies for small firms which have been successful in innovation, but then face severe competition in a growing market.

Strategic Management in Intracorporate Ventures

A number of writers have suggested that large firms seem to be better at developing existing businesses than at growing new ones.[31-33] The large firm can bring great resources to bear upon new opportunities and can absorb failures. However, performance measurement systems often penalize those divisions and executives who assume risks. New ventures can disrupt existing manufacturing and marketing activities. New ventures often require different kinds of people and facilities and an orientation toward working closely with customers, short production runs, and continually changing technology.[34]

An increasing number of corporations have

developed new venture departments to facilitate intracorporate entrepreneurship. Two surveys, both published in 1973, indicated that the number of new venture departments was increasing.[35,36] As might be expected, large firms have adopted formal intracorporate entrepreneurship programs to a greater degree than smaller firms. However, more recent research suggests that many new venture departments are short-lived.[34]

New venture department organizations may range from *ad hoc* task forces with no formal training, to departments with established budgets, to separate legal entities. Typically, these intracorporate entrepreneurial groups study proposed ventures and sometimes proceed to start new businesses—developing, producing, and marketing new products. They usually can call upon the resources of the larger organization, although this sometimes presents problems because of lack of authority over other departments. The performance measurement system may be modified to place less emphasis on short-run profits. If the product is promising or becomes firmly established, it may be transferred to an existing department or become the basis for a new department.

Practices vary in the extent to which new ventures are separate, the timing of when products are transferred to the regular organization, and how venture managers are rewarded. An extreme form of venture management might be termed 'sponsored spin-offs' in which, with the parent firm's blessing, a separate new enterprise is created, possibly with the parent company holding some of the equity.[37]

Some of the issues associated with organizing venture management departments include determining how managers are to be rewarded and how their careers are affected if they return to the main organization. Other issues relate to the extent to which they can call upon resources from the main organization and the degree of delegation—the extent to which they can act as if they were managing their own firms.

Research by Fast indicates that new venture departments usually evolve, becoming operating divisions, staff departments, or new venture departments which differ in size, objectives, and corporate impact from their earlier versions.[34] Sometimes the departments are disbanded. The two major influences upon the evolution of a new venture department appear to be the changing nature of the firm's strategy and its political support within the organization.

In general, these approaches have demonstrated some success, but many companies are experimenting with different ways of creating an environment for intracorporate entrepreneurship.

Conclusion

Small businesses differ greatly in their resource positions, the goals of their founders, their stages of development and their potential. Yet, within this diversity, we can note certain common characteristics. These result in an environment for strategic management which creates both constraints and opportunities different from those in large organizations.

Acknowledgements—This paper is adapted from a chapter in D. Schendel and C. Hofer (Eds.), *Strategic Management: A New View of Business Policy*, Little, Brown & Co., 1979.

References

(1) 1967 *Enterprise Statistics, Part 1*. U.S. Government Printing Office, Washington, DC (1972).

(2) LaRue Hosmer, Arnold Cooper and Karl Vesper, *The Entrepreneurial Function*. Prentice-Hall, Inc., Englewood Cliffs (1977).

(3) Arnold Cooper, *The Founding of Technologically-Based Firms*, The Center for Venture Management, Milwaukee (1971).

(4) David McClelland, *The Achieving Society*, C. Van Nostrand, Princeton (1961).

(5) Orvis Collins and David Moore, *The Organization Makers*, Appleton-Century-Crofts, New York (1970).

(6) Edward Roberts and H. Wainer, Some characteristics of new technical enterprises, *IEEE Transactions on Engineering Management*, EM-18 (3) (1971).

(7) Albert Shapero, Entrepreneurship and economic development, *Entrepreneurship and Enterprise Development: A Worldwide Perspective*, Proceedings of Project ISEED, Project ISEED, Ltd. and The Center for Venture Management, Milwaukee (1975).

(8) Everett Hagen, The Transition in Columbia, in *Entrepreneurship and Economic Development*, P. Kilby (Ed.), The Free Press, New York (1971).

(9) Arnold Cooper, Technical entrepreneurship: what do we know? *R & D Management*, 3 (2), February (1973).

(10) Patrick Liles, *New Business Ventures and the Entrepreneur*, Richard D. Irwin, Inc., Homewood (1974).

(11) Kurt Mayer and Sidney Goldstein, *The First Two Years: Problems of Small Firm Growth and Survival*, U.S. Government Printing Office, Washington, D.C. (1961).

(12) Jeffrey Susbauer, The technical entrepreneurship process in Austin, Texas, in *Technical Entrepreneurship: A Symposium*, A. Cooper and J. Komives (Eds.), The Center for Venture Management, Milwaukee (1972).

(13) Lawrence Lamont, What entrepreneurs learn from experience, *Journal of Small Business Management*, July (1972).

(14) William Hoad and Peter Rosko, *Management Factors Contributing to the Success or Failure of New Small Manufacturers*, University of Michigan, Ann Arbor (1964).

(15) Arnold Cooper and Albert Bruno, Success among high-technology firms, *Business Horizons*, 20 (2), April (1977).

(16) Edward Roberts, Influences upon performance of new technical enterprises, in *Technical Entrepreneurship: A Symposium*, A. Cooper and J. Komives (Eds.), The Center for Venture Management, Milwaukee (1972).

(17) Harry Schrage, R & D entrepreneur: profile of success, *Harvard Business Review*, 43 (6), November–December (1965).

(18) David McClelland, Achievement motivation can be developed, *Harvard Business Review*, 43 (6), November–December (1965).

(19) Joseph McGuire, *Factors in the Growth of Manufacturing Firms*, Bureau of Business Research, University of Washington, Seattle (1963).

(20) Robert Charpie and others, *Technological Innovation: Its Environment and Management*, U.S. Government Printing Office, Washington, D.C. (1967).

(21) Alfred Gross, Meeting the competition of giants, *Harvard Business Review*, 45 (3), May–June (1967).

(22) W. Arnold Hosmer, Small manufacturing enterprises, *Harvard Business Review*, 35(6), November–December (1957).

(23) Robert Katz, *Management of the Total Enterprise*, Prentice-Hall, Englewood Cliffs (1970).

(24) Frank Gilmore, Formulating strategy in smaller companies, *Harvard Business Review*, 49 (3), May–June (1971).

(25) Preston LeBreton, *A Guide for Proper Management Planning for Small Business*, Division of Research, College of Business Administration, Louisiana State University, Baton Rouge (1963).

(26) George Steiner, Approaches to long-range planning for small business, *California Management Review*, X (1), Fall (1967).

(27) S. C. Wheelwright, Strategic planning in the small business, *Business Horizons*, XIV (4), August (1971).

(28) Theodore Cohn and Roy Lindberg, *Survival and Growth: Management Strategies for the Small Firm*, Amacom, New York (1974).

(29) Charles Hofer, Toward a contingency theory of business strategy, *Academy of Management Journal*, 18 (4), December (1975).

(30) Arnold Cooper, Small companies can pioneer new products, *Harvard Business Review*, 44 (5), September–October (1966).

(31) Mark Hanan, Venturing corporations—think small to stay strong, *Harvard Business Review*, 54 (3), May–June (1976).

(32) Richard Hill and James Hlavacek, The venture team: a new concept in marketing organization, *Journal of Marketing*, 36 (3), July (1972).

(33) Russell W. Peterson, New venture management in a large company, *Harvard Business Review*, 45 (3), May–June (1967).

(34) Norman Fast, The evolution of corporate new venture divisions, unpublished D.B.A. dissertation, Harvard Graduate School of Business Administration, Boston (1977).

(35) Jeffrey Susbauer, U.S. industrial intracorporate entrepreneurship practices, *R & D Management*, 3 (3), June (1973).

(36) Karl Vesper and Thomas Holmdahl, How venture management fares in innovation companies, *Research Management*, XVI (3), May (1973).

(37) Arnold Cooper and Arthur Riggs, Jr., Non-traditional approaches to technology utilization, *Journal of the Society of Research Administrators*, VI (3), Winter (1975).

[13]

© *Academy of Management Journal*
1982, Vol. 25, No. 1, 63-79.

The Urban Quality of Life and Entrepreneurship

JOHANNES M. PENNINGS
Columbia University

This paper examines the influence of quality of life on entrepreneurial activity in 70 urban metropolitan areas. Economic and health/educational quality of life were found to have a positive impact and political and environmental quality of life to have a negative impact on the creation of new firms. The effects exist regardless of the size of the local industrial base.

The recent research and debate on entrepreneurship has shown an increased interest in the role of environment as a stimulant for the creation of new organizations. The development of geographical areas with highly visible expressions of entrepreneurial vigor induced many investigators to examine the environmental factors that contribute to the founding of new firms. Well known cases such as the San Francisco peninsula, Austin, Texas, and Route 128 in Boston triggered a number of authors to scrutinize those areas and to identify relevant factors (Cooper, 1971, 1973; Shapero, 1975; Susbauer, 1972; Vesper & Albaum, 1979). This new line of research contrasts rather sharply with investigations that have dealt with personality characteristics and other psychological attributes to account for entrepreneurial decisions (McClelland, 1965). Although individual characteristics of entrepreneurs might be important predictors, the new surge of environmental studies clearly suggests that factors beyond the realm of the founders of new firms should be considered in explaining interregional or interurban variations in entrepreneurship. This paper attempts to make a contribution to the knowledge on the environment of entrepreneurs by quantitatively examining urban correlates of new business start-ups.

Several environmental studies have shown that availability of economic resources is conducive to the creation of new ventures. Those resources include venture capital, land, real estate, transportation facilities, supporting facilities, and a technologically skilled labor force. These studies also revealed more intangible factors, such as proximity to centers of higher education, entrepreneurial climate, public attitudes, and the quality of living conditions (Bruno & Tyzoon, 1980).

64 *Academy of Management Journal* March

Economists have displayed a tendency to stress economic conditions to define the entrepreneurial favorableness of the environment (Carlton, 1978). Location theorists have indicated that entrepreneurs will establish themselves in environments that are most advantageous with respect to transportation and other cost considerations (Alonso, 1975). An interesting feature of the earlier mentioned studies is the inclusion of noneconomic factors in accounting for entrepreneurial activity. If environment is defined rather narrowly, as in the case of Standard Metropolitan Statistical Area, noneconomic factors such as public attitudes and attractiveness of living conditions might outweigh some economic factors, especially because the latter might have a regional or national scope and the former are a reflection of the *couleur locale* and vary widely among metropolitan areas. For example, markets or customer basis, capital availability, and taxation often pertain to territorial systems that far exceed the boundaries of such areas. Transportation cost considerations might be fairly insignificant in those industries for which the cost of inputs and value added are disproportionately high. Other economic factors might similarly have little location significance and cannot explain differences in entrepreneurial propensity in various metropolitan areas. Urban-metropolitan areas do vary considerably, however, in their quality of life, and this might account for intermetropolitan variations in entrepreneurial activity level.

Investigators of the environment of entrepreneurship do not discard the economic aspects but stress that living conditions carry a greater weight in the creation of new firms (Cooper, 1971, 1973; Shapero, 1972). Shapero concludes that living conditions are by far the most crucial determinant of location decisions. In his study he found conditions such as climate and cultural and recreational facilities to be pervasive:

> A community must become an exciting and attractive place if it is to attract and retain the technical professional work force that is the chief production factor in high technology industries. This highly trained body of workers is relatively young, highly mobile, in great demand and has a choice of places to work and live. It will not stay in a community that does not have within it a selection of amenities that are available elsewhere (1972, p. 95).

Similarly, Cooper (1971) suggested that living conditions might be an important incentive for potential founders of new firms. However, in a later paper (Cooper, 1973) he modified his position. In his investigation of Palo Alto, he found that new firms were created by native entrepreneurs. Unlike the economic argument (Alonso, 1975), which holds that the location decision gravitates to those areas that are most advantageous economically, he indicates that founders of firms are rarely attracted from other parts of the country when they proceed in establishing a new venture. Rather they start their venture in areas where they are already living. Economic factors and living conditions do not induce any mobility among them. In his later paper Cooper (1973) further indicated that although attractive living conditions might not determine the location decision, they might attract technical people to the area. Thus it would appear that although attractive urban areas do not attract founders of firms, they attract individuals upon whom the entrepreneurs are dependent for staffing their firms. Cooper's analysis disagrees therefore with Shapero (1972) and other investigators who stress the urban quality of life (Danilov, 1972; Mahar & Coddington, 1965). It remains to be seen, however, whether entrepreneurs would succeed if the unattractiveness of their urban area repelled individuals from accepting employment.

This issue is particularly important for regional development agencies and the Small Business Administration and other public policy agencies, which are often motivated to improve the attractiveness of the community to insure economic growth and development. Mahar and Coddington (1965) list five attraction requirements that communities must meet in order to enhance entrepreneurial vigor. They include: (1) high quality industrial space, (2) reasonable operating costs and supporting services such as air transportation and local governmental services, (3) better than average living conditions such as climate, taxes, and secondary schools, (4) proximity of colleges and universities, and (5) a well developed professional and cultural environment.

Although they do not say so explicitly, Mahar and Coddington (1965) are dealing primarily with technical entrepreneurs. This restriction applies also to most of the other literature discussed. It is not known whether their arguments should be extended to nontechnical entrepreneurs. The research to be reported here also revolves around high-technology ventures and the extent to which their creation is subject to attraction requirements as illustrated by Mahar and Coddington.

Presently there is no systematic, quantitative assessment of the relative importance of these factors in explaining entrepreneurship. Such an assessment would facilitate a focused public policy on stimulating the creation of new organizations. This paper examines the extent to which quality of life is conducive to the frequency of business start-ups in urban metropolitan areas. The examination is made of three selected industries that have shown a comparatively high level of entrepreneurial activity.

The Study

Economic conditions are not irrelevant when evaluating the quality of life. However, during the most recent times there has been a growing disenchantment with an exclusive reliance on economic indicators such as GNP and unemployment as a basis for measuring the achievement of goals at the public policy level. Economic indicators alone do not adequately reflect the well-being of members of society. Paradoxically, the increase in affluence has witnessed a concomitant greater awareness of noneconomic aspects such as social, educational, health, and ecological ones. Although still sometimes controversial, there is widespread consensus that the quality of life should be measured by both economic and noneconomic indicators. This also implies that quality of life is multidimensional.

The quality of life indicators used in this study incorporate both economic and noneconomic elements. Thus, it is recognized that quality of life is multidimensional. This approach also will permit conclusions about the relative importance of different classes of living conditions when accounting for the frequency of new business start-ups. In this study five quality of life indicators are related to entrepreneurship. The unit of analysis is the Standard Metropolitan Statistical Area (SMSA).

The quality of life information was obtained by Ben-Chieh (1975). He reviewed and selected 120 variables pertaining to the urban living conditions, including economic, political, criminological, ecological, climatological, educational, health, recreational, and social ones. All variables are archival and originated mostly from governmental publications. (A list of the 120 variables is available on request.) Archival data are attractive because they are sufficiently universal, possess a certain degree of objectivity, have clear policy implications, can be easily updated, and are sufficiently broad to allow for variations in life style (Ben-Chieh, 1975).

These quality of life variables can be construed as objective measures of living conditions because they are based on archival information. Unlike archival or objective measures of organizational effectiveness, which are often idiosyncratic and hence preclude interorganizational comparisons, these dimensions are the same across the 70 urban metropolitan areas. Nevertheless, their objectivity or uniformity should not be evaluated as superior. In spite of the widespread preference for objectivity in organizational measurement, one should concur with Campbell's statement that "conventional wisdom says objectivity is good but perhaps a more accurate wisdom says an objective criterion is a subjective criterion once removed" (1977, p. 45). Indeed, subjective judgments go into the choice of variables. There have been recent developments to construct subjective quality of life measures, but their measurement is too aggregative. Survey-conducting organizations, such as the National Opinion Research Center and the Institute for Social Research, have begun a program of research to compare objective quality of life indicators with subjective ones (Campbell, Converse, & Rodgers, 1976). They seek to assess how people perceive or experience the settings in which they live. Such surveys have a national focus and, unfortunately, cannot be decomposed to cities, counties, or other smaller units of analysis. Availability of such measures would allow an examination of the concurrent validity of quality of life indicators. Although objective and subjective quality of life indicators should covary, there might be discrepancies. For example, FBI statistics might be less germane to the experience of neighborhood safety than would the occurrence of a felony that received widespread local publicity. Such proximate instances of crime have a greater saliency and enter more prominently into people's awareness of their environment (Angrist, 1976). Such problems are recognized, but it is contended that objective quality of life indicators are the best measures available. They are easier to obtain, more amenable to standardization, and highly malleable to different levels of analysis.

The information on urban quality of life applies to the year 1970. The 120 variables were subjected to factor analysis. A 5-factor solution was obtained. For a detailed description of the data reduction procedures, the loadings of the variables on the five factors, and other measurement issues, the reader is referred to Ben-Chieh (1975). Ben-Chieh also presents the ranking of urban areas with respect to each of the five indicators. The five rankings are rather dissimilar, suggesting that the measures vary independently from each other.

The near-orthogonality of the quality of life indicators is revealed by the product moment correlations of Table 1. Most coefficients are close to zero. The economic indicator is independent of the other factors except for the health/educational factor. It appears that economically attractive areas also enjoy a superior educational climate and a benign health environment. In contrast, the environmental indicator correlates negatively with the health/educational measure ($r = -.357$, $p < .05$). The seemingly paradoxical inference is that urban areas with unsound ecological conditions are bestowed with attractive health and educational conditions. The implication is that some SMSAs are superior on one and inferior on another dimension. Such SMSAs thus might exert competing forces on potential entrepreneurs. In general, however, Table 1 reveals the indicators not to be redundant with respect to each other.

Table 1
Product Moment Correlations Between Five
Quality of Life Dimensions for Seventy SMSAs

	1	2	3	4	5
1. Economic dimension	1.0				
2. Political dimension	-.01	1.0			
3. Environmental dimension	.15	-.07	1.0		
4. Health/educational dimension	.25*	.16	-.36*	1.0	
5. Social dimension	.10	-.08	.08	.03	1.0

$*p < .05$

Severe redundancy or multicollinearity among predictors might impede the unequivocal interpretation of the effects of quality of life dimensions on the frequency of business start-ups (Blalock, 1964). As Table 1 shows, the covariation is sufficiently low to view the regression estimation to be described as efficient.

The entrepreneurial activity level was determined for three 4-digit SIC industries: fabricated plastic products (SIC 3079), communication transmitting equipment (SIC 3662), and electronic components (SIC 3679). These three industries can be classified as high technology industries. They have shown a comparatively high level of new business start-ups (Carlton, 1978). Information on these start-ups was ascertained from Dun and Bradstreet's annual files. The creation of new firms was determined by comparing entries from each pair of successive years. Whenever an entry appeared that did not exist in the previous year's file, it was classified as a new firm. In many cases, however, a firm had undergone a change in name, location, or ownership. A new entry was classified as a new firm only after it could be shown that it was not due to a change in name, legal status, ownership, location, or due to a file maintenance error. Even minor errors such as a mistake in the firm's postal zip code could lead to the erroneous conclusion that a new firm had been founded. Errors were found in approximately 50 percent of the observations. All pairwise inconsistencies were checked and corrected with alternative publications such as trade publications and telephone directories. In view of these procedures, the present data on entrepreneurship are felt to be highly accurate. The data apply to 70 SMSAs in the United States over the periods 1967-1971 and 1972-1975.

Apart from the quality of life indicators, also incorporated were two variables that should be statistically controlled when examining the problem of this study. Those variables are population and size of industry. Population is a measure of size of the urban metropolitan area. The size of industry was measured by the number of production man-hours of 1967 and 1972 for the pertinent industries as reported by the U.S. Bureau of the Census (1976, 1972). This variable can be construed as representing the pool of potential entrepreneurs or the size of the local industry base from which entrepreneurs are likely to originate. By including this variable in the regression analysis, the results may be interpreted in terms of business start-ups per capita or per unit of potential entrepreneurs. Indeed, the effect of the quality of life indicators can be interpreted as predicting the number of new firms per capita, or perhaps more precisely, the number of new firms per production man hour.

Naturally, the greater the area and the greater the size of the industry, the higher the number of new firms within that industry. Carlton (1978) found that the creation of new firms is highly dependent on the industry size or what he calls "agglomeration economics." Indeed, the size of the industry can be viewed as the aggregate pool of potential entrepreneurs, if it is assumed that the founders of new firms are recruited primarily from the labor force that is employed by the pertinent industry. It follows that the greater the pool of potential entrepreneurs—or for that matter the aggregate set of "incubator organizations" (Shapero, 1975)—the higher the number of business start-ups. The study on entrepreneurial conduciveness of urban areas thus can be construed as an attempt to explain variations in entrepreneurial activity that are due either to "agglomeration economics" or to the quality of life of the urban-metropolitan area. It is hypothesized that all these variables have a positive relationship with the frequency of new ventures.

Results

There are considerable differences in the frequency of new firms. New York and Los Angeles stand out in that they show an unusually high level

Table 2
Leading SMSAs for the Formation of New Ventures[a]

Period	Plastic Products (SIC 3079)	Telecommunication Equipment (SIC 3662)	Electronic Components (SIC 3679)
1967-1971	Chicago	New York	Los Angeles
	New York	Los Angeles	New York
	Los Angeles	San Jose	San Jose
	Detroit	Boston	Boston
1972-1975	Los Angeles	New York	Los Angeles
	Chicago	Los Angeles	San Jose
	New York	San Jose	Anaheim
	Detroit	Chicago	New York

[a]The lists of the top eight SMSAs for SIC 3662 and SIC 3679 differ by only one SMSA for each of the two periods. For the first period the top eight SMSAs in SIC 3079 differ from SIC 3662 by three SMSAs and from SIC 3679 by two SMSAs. For the second period SIC 3079 differs from SIC 3662 and from SIC 3679 by four SMSAs.

of entrepreneurial activity in each of the three industries. They also stand out if a distinction is made between 1967-1971 and 1972-1975, the two periods for which data were obtained. Table 2 shows for each of these two periods the most important SMSAs with respect to their entrepreneurial vigor in the three industrial categories.

It is apparent that those urban areas that were entrepreneurially prominent in the period 1967-1971 also stand out in the period 1972-1975. This observation applies particularly to the two electronic industries: SMSAs that dominate in the first period also dominate in the second period. The rank correlations between urban areas are high for those involving the two periods and for those involving the two industries. Thus an SMSA's ranking for the first period is rather similar to its ranking in 1972-1975. There is a like correspondence in ranking involving telecommunication equipment and electronic components. In contrast, there are differences between electronics and plastic products. Not only is this noticeable from Table 2, but it also can be inferred from the relative lack of agreement between the two types of industries. Within the plastic products category there is substantial similarity in rank order across the two time periods.

As stated earlier, the three 4-digit industries show a high incidence of organizational births. For the period 1967-1972 the total number of new ventures was 1,232 (plastic products), 471 (telecommunication equipment), and 588 (electronic components). For the subsequent period, the number of new ventures was 1,453, 578, and 623, respectively. However, the somewhat larger size of the second set of numbers should not be construed as an upswing in entrepreneurial activity. For the two electronic industries, several of the smaller SMSAs had to be excluded from the first period data set because information on births was not accurate enough to be included in the study.

It should also be recognized that the standard industrial classification underwent some changes at the end of 1971. The definition of SIC 3662 (telecommunication equipment) remained unchanged, but the other two classes were redefined. In 1972 approximately 9 percent of the firms belonging to SIC 3079 (plastic products) were assigned to a different SIC code, and approximately 35 percent of the firms perviously coded SIC 3679 (electronic components) also were reclassified in 1972. It is virtually impossible to isolate the specific effect of reclassification—an effect that could be substantial for the last industrial class because 35 percent of the firms were eliminated.

The information available does not allow for disclosure of those firms that belonged to a different category prior to 1972. Thus it is not known whether the excluded ventures were more likely to have spawned in some SMSAs rather than in other ones. In view of the consistency of urban rankings across time periods, it may be cautiously assumed that reclassification did not systematically alter the results. Furthermore, when the two time periods are used for cross-validation purposes by performing separate analyses for each of the two periods, similar results are found. This lends further credence to the inference that reclassification did not fundamentally alter the distribution of observations. Nevertheless, the true effect of reclassification might be ascertained only with alternative data files. As with any other empirical study, the data could be more abundant and of a better quality. Despite these limitations, it is assumed that the present data set can be used to gain insights on the quality of life determinants of new locational activity.

An initial inference about the quality of life and entrepreneurship can be extracted from Table 2. It seems obvious that some of the strongest entrepreneurial areas do not evoke the imagery that authors such as Shapero (1972) mention in their discussion on attractiveness of the environment. SMSAs such as New York, Chicago, and Los Angeles have a notoriously bad reputation as to their environmental quality, although they are among the most superior on the political and health and educational quality of life indicators. Indeed, such a statement reveals that the multidimensionality of the quality of life precludes a simply binary conclusion on its relevance for the creation of new firms in certain metropolitan areas.

Table 3 shows the results of a correlational and regression analysis of organizational births. For each of the three industries the table lists the correlation coefficients in the first column with the regression coefficients and corresponding *t*-values in the second column.

The correlation coefficients indicate the bivariate relationships and can be contrasted with the regression coefficients. As is usually the case, the correlation coefficients are subject to omitted variable bias, that is, the relationships under consideration fail to reflect the simultaneous effects of other variables; hence the correlation coefficients are biased. Although the quality of life variables are fairly independent, as described in Table 1, their covariation, however small, should be considered. Furthermore, it is desirable to control for population and industry size to determine whether quality of life has effects on organizational births regardless of those two

Table 3
Correlation and Multiple Regression of Entrepreneurial Activity in Three Selected Industries[a]

Independent Variables	Plastic Products (SIC 3079)		Telecommunication Equipment (SIC 3662)		Electronic Components (SIC 3679)	
	r	b	r	b	r	b
Intercept		-58.84		-69.49		-59.31
		(-3.05)		(-5.51)		(-4.53)
Population	.54*	6.118	.54*	6.815	.43*	4.983
		(3.61)		(6.35)		(4.31)
Industry size	.43*	5.089	.52*	.52	.50*	2.198
		(14.50)		(5.92)		(10.48)
Quality of life:						
Economic	.15*	5.202	.07	2.889	.16*	3.816
		(2.069)		(1.74)		(1.85)
Political	-.02	-.83	.06	-.82	.02	-.31
		(-1.98)		(-2.92)		(-.94)
Environmental	.08	-5.971	-.04	-6.755	-.01	-.886
		(-1.45)		(-2.67)		(-.29)
Health/educational	.09	1.783	.17*	3.096	.23*	3.215
		(.92)		(2.41)		(2.05)
Social	-.02	.428	-.11	.307	-.02	.085
		(-.96)		(1.72)		(.24)
R^2		.844		.713		.766

[a]First entry in each of the regression columns is the raw regression coefficient. The second entry, between parentheses, is the corresponding t-value. The decimal point for the political and social variables has been moved four places to the right.
*$p < .05$

variables. Although many of the correlation coefficients involving quality of life dimensions are low, they might still be important predictors if one controls for population and industry size. As mentioned earlier, these controls have the effect of showing the quality of life effects on organizational births per capita. The correlation coefficients show the covariation between quality of life and total number of new ventures in each of the three industries. It therefore is more appropriate to consider the regression results.

The positive impact of urban size was expected. Larger urban areas are bound to show more new firms, and this is consistent with the view of regional economists (Pred, 1966; Thompson, 1966). Thompson specifies several reasons for what he calls the "urban size rachet." When cities increase in size their industrial base becomes more differentiated, which in turn might induce better than average growth rates. Larger cities also enjoy comparatively more influence over state and federal governments, and a greater proportion of their economic activity is oriented toward customers rather than toward sources of supply. Furthermore, larger urban areas are bound to show a greater degree of innovation; their sheer size alone will insure a steadier supply of invention and creativity.

It also is natural to find a strong and positive effect for industry size. Indeed, this variable appears to be the strongest predictor of organizational births. It can be viewed as describing the pool of potential entrepreneurs or the aggregate set of incubator organizations (Shapero, 1975). Shapero argued that most entrepreneurs originate from firms that frustrate their need for creativity and innovation. Those firms function as "incubators" and create a breed of potential entrepreneurs, some of whom eventually make the decision to leave the firm and start their own venture. One would surmise that the larger the industry, the greater the pool of potential entrepreneurs and the greater the likelihood that some of them will become real entrepreneurs. The results shown in Table 3 clearly corroborate this conclusion. It would be necessary, however, to disaggregate the data to determine whether indeed the new firms tend to be founded by native individuals previously employed by a local industry. It is quite possible that some individuals from elsewhere are attracted to urban areas whose pertinent industry has a sufficient amount of "critical mass." It seems more likely, however, that the new firms are founded by native individuals.

At a more general level the three coefficients can be described by referring to the term spin-off. A spin-off is a new organization whose creation typically is contingent on the presence of a conglomerate set of like-organizations. The regression effects show that the greater this set, the higher is the incidence of spin-offs.

The remaining five variables indicate the effects of quality of life on the frequency of organizational births. The results reveal that the effects of the different components are unequal. Furthermore, the effects are not similar across the three industries, although there is some agreement between the two electronic industries.

On global inspection several inferences can be made from the regression coefficients. First of all, not every coefficient reaches a statistically significant level. Only some of the quality of life indicators have a strong effect on entrepreneurship. Some of the other effects are significant only at the 10 percent level, and still some others have no effect at all. The effects also vary considerably among the three industries.

Second, some of the regression coefficients appear to be negative. Strictly speaking, one would have to conclude that the negative effects are not significant under a one-tailed test procedure. It had been hypothesized that the effects would be positive so that the significant negative effects ought to be discarded. Although the related correlation coefficients are negligible, those negative b coefficients should not be discarded. Their effects are strong and significant. A sequential review of all the coefficients will elaborate this issue further.

The economic component is pertinent to each of the three industries although its effect is most pronounced for plastic products ($b = 5.202$; $t = 2.07$). The regression coefficients in the other two columns are significant at the 10 percent level only. The greater dependence of plastic products entrepreneurs on economic well-being might be attributed to the horizons of the market domain, which tend to be much closer than for the electronic firms. They tend to have a more local customer base, perhaps because transportation cost considerations are stronger. The urban areas have a comparatively lesser importance for electronic ventures. Approximately 60 percent to 70 percent of their aggregate output is shipped over 300 miles; for the plastic product firms this percentage is closer to 50 percent. Although this evidence is circumstantial, it points to a greater dependence on proximate customers. Hence local economic activity should be more relevant.

The political component of quality of life has a significant effect on the entrepreneurship in plastic products and telecommunication equipment. However, the effects are *negative*. This effect was not expected, especially because a sophisticated, politically mature and well informed citizenry would form an ideal environment for entrepreneurs. Naturally, it is possible to provide a number of ex-post ad hoc reasons. One might, for example, speculate that politically healthy urban areas are better integrated, cohesive, and that they therefore discourage deviant and innovative behavior. Such urban areas spend also disproportionate amounts of funds on public assistance programs—an aspect that might be interpreted as a sign of urban decay. Furthermore, those urban areas have a disproportionately large administrative component: relatively many civil servants. This is likely to happen more frequently in larger and older SMSAs (Berry & Kasarda, 1977). Finally, the cost of labor, which might act as a disincentive for entrepreneurs, is comparatively high in those SMSAs that have relatively high wages for their civil servants. Although tentative, these speculations suggest that politically healthy SMSAs are not ideal location areas for entrepreneurs. Rather, entrepreneurs tend to be active in those areas where political participation is low, local government is light, public welfare is less, and civil servants are not numerous and are less well paid. Clearly, the effect of political quality of life is enigmatic, but it seems obvious that not every aspect of quality of life is conducive to entrepreneurship.

Similar inferences can be made about the third component, environmental quality. Its effect is particularly noticeable for entrepreneurs in the telecommunication industry ($b = -6.755$; $t = -2.67$). The cleaner the environment, the greater the amount of space, the less congested the streets, the more pleasant the temperatures, the lower the frequency of new business start-ups. The effects in the other two industries are not significant but their sign is in the same, unexpected direction. Clearly, this result is in conflict with the findings of Shapero (1972) and others, who argue that areas with a pleasant climate and high degree of tourist attractiveness are most conducive to entrepreneurship.

The reasons for this negative result are numerous and would require further research. Perhaps entrepreneurial vigor is incompatible with environmental quality of life. Urban metropolitan areas with an inferior environment show a high incidence of entrepreneurs. Such areas are "congested," have a higher proportion of vehicle registration, and are saddled with large amounts of solid waste. These symptoms of inferior environmental quality that correlate so strongly with some types of entrepreneurial activity seem to imply an incompatibility between entrepreneurship and uncontaminated environment. It seems that one cannot have both new ventures and a superior environmental quality.

It also is conceivable that there are offsetting effects. On the one hand, a high quality environment is an incentive for attracting potential entrepreneurs and for preserving the attachment of others. On the other hand, many tourist-appealing areas might not have the attraction requirements that Mahar and Coddington (1965) list as crucial for the "spinning off" of new firms. From the results of Table 3 it is rather evident that when one controls statistically for the presence of some of those requirements, the effects of environmental quality are mostly negative. More research is needed, however, to determine whether urban areas with many attraction requirements show higher degrees of organizational birth if their environmental quality is superior.

Consistent with the hypothesis is the positive relationship with the health and educational component. The association is particularly strong for the two electronic industries ($b = 3.096$; $t = 2.41$ and $b = 3.215$; $t = 2.05$, respectively). These findings corroborate the conclusions of the earlier mentioned studies on the need for a highly skilled labor force and the presence of an educational emphasis. Nevertheless, it is difficult to account for the absence of an effect for plastic products. Why would electronic entrepreneurs be more sensitive to the health and educational quality of life, while their chemical counterparts are not? The answer to this question might depend partly on the relative significance of the educational aspect of this quality of life component. The electronic industries are rather dependent on the accessibility of educational institutions and their output. For example, the proportion of scientists and engineers is much greater in the electronic industries than in the chemical industries (Scherer, 1970). One must therefore attribute a stronger inclination for electronic entrepreneurs to surface in educationally favorable urban areas.

Finally, the social component is not related to the entrepreneurial activity level of SMSAs. Controlling for the more specific quality of life indicators clearly does not leave much variance to be explained by the social quality of life. Naturally, this component might be crucial for an array of behaviors not considered in this study.

Altogether, the results discussed may not be as strong as was hypothesized, and other results are contrary to expectations. Nevertheless, they do indicate that quality of life can have an impact on the rate of business start-ups. Although population and "agglomeration economics" have an extremely strong effect, their inclusion in the regression equation does not remove or eliminate the quality of life effects on entrepreneurship. Indeed, some of its indicators have an effect over and beyond the effects of population and size of industry. The incremental variance due to the inclusion of quality of life indicators is substantial, with most of the incremental explained variance attributed to the economic and health/educational dimensions. In other words, their effects were not "suppressed" by including population and industry size in the regression equation. However, it is desirable not to invoke such stepwise regression results or to infer meaning from amputated regression equations. Such procedures are inappropriate (Johnston, 1972). The regression results of Table 3 lead to the conclusion that quality of life cannot be dismissed as marginal; quite the contrary, some of its dimensions appear to be empirically important predictors of entrepreneurship.

Conclusion

At the onset of this paper it was suggested that the debate on the importance of living conditions for entrepreneurship should recognize that they are multifaceted. This paper has shown that some of their dimensions are relevant in accounting for business start-ups. Both economic and noneconomic dimensions are significant, although the direction of their effects is not always positive. Most striking is the negative effect of the environmental dimension—an effect which can be explained away by suggesting that economically active SMSAs tend to have an inferior environment. This negative effect was one of the discrepant findings of the present study, along with the negative effect of the political quality of life. Those results indicate that the conditions that lead to a favorable assessment of living conditions are not necessarily coincident with entrepreneurial favorableness of the environment. Quality of life is a multidimensional construct and, as this study shows, some of its dimensions are positive and others are negative antecedents of entrepreneurship. It also is evident that the different quality of life dimensions have a differential impact on entrepreneurship in different industries. The size of the urban area as well as the pool of potential entrepreneurs—as inferred from the total number of production man-hours—were important predictors. But quality of life variables were predictors as well, although their weights were comparatively small and not nearly as significant. Also, their effects were not equally strong for the three industries of this study.

Because many of the hypothesized effects were nonexistent, there remains the vexing question about the true effects, if any, of quality of life. In view of the interindustry differences (whose detection was limited as only three industries were examined), it is desirable to investigate further the differential susceptibility among various kinds of organizational births. Perhaps this line of inquiry should be supplemented with a joint investigation of objective and subjective indicators of quality of life. As noted earlier, subjective perceptions of living conditions, regardless of whether they are veridical, might be more pervasive in entrepreneurial decision making. It also might be possible that various population segments within an SMSA have divergent experiences or espouse different values, such that aggregate SMSA indicators of quality of life are suspect. For example, some entrepreneurs might perceive the local political climate as highly favorable, even though other groups of individuals express an opposite perspective. As mentioned before, such information is not available at the present time. Nevertheless one could conduct surveys among distinct occupational groups, associations, or other homogeneous sets of individuals who are important "sources" of technical entrepreneurs and ascertain their shared assessment of the quality of life in all its dimensions. Such information might reveal whether objective SMSA quality of life measures are too aggregative. Such research also might reveal the extent to which objective quality of life measures have convergent and discriminant validity and thus allow a subsequent corroboration of the results of this study. It then also might reduce the gap between rhetoric and reality and forestall criticism that the importance of quality of life for organizational births is an expression of myths rather than a revelation of entrepreneurial decision making as a function of environmental favorableness.

One might also recast this question into a more encompassing framework and ask *how* quality of life promotes the environmental favorableness for entrepreneurship. Recent developments in organizational theory have led to two contrasting views of organizational environments. For brevity's sake, these might be labeled *resource dependence* (Bruno & Tyzoon, 1980; Child, 1972; Pfeffer & Salancik, 1978; Thompson, 1967) and *population ecology* (Aldrich, 1979; Hannan & Freeman, 1977; Pennings, 1980). The creation of new ventures would get a rather different treatment in each of these two approaches.

The first one views organizations as continuously adapting to actors in their environment, as negotiating attractive exchange relationships with them because they cannot generate all the necessary resources internally. Due to their dependence on external sources, they actively attempt to secure control over external sources of supply and will maneuver themselves into an environment such that outside interference is minimized and they can adjust their strategic postures whenever environmental conditions change.

This approach contrasts rather sharply with population ecology approaches. Firms are members of populations of organizations. The term population denotes a categorical demarcation of the inhabitants of the ecology, analogous to the biological "species." Like organisms in the world of biology, organizations and their populations are doomed to die unless they meet the environmental test of fitness. The key word for describing organization-environment relationships is selection: organizations survive depending on whether they are bestowed with the necessary characteristics that are isomorphic with those of the environment. However, this Darwinistic view has been softened (Aldrich, 1979), for example by postulating that organizations reveal mutations at a much faster rate than do their counterparts in biology, or that they sometimes can alter their ecology by manipulating its infrastructure such that they secure a better compatibility with the environment. Unlike the first framework—which depicts organizations as proactive, outgoing actors—this latter view ascribes a fairly passive, reactive organizational posture to the environment.

It seems reasonable to extrapolate these ideas to the environment of entrepreneurs. The resource dependence view would treat it as a pool of resources from which the entrepreneur can draw on in his initiative to create a new organization. The entrepreneur makes the strategic choices to secure the best transactional relationship with the environment. In the second view the entrepreneur's choices are predicated and molded by influences of the environment (ecology and population); it represents a set of influences that selectively permit some ventures to survive. Resource availability is crucial in that its variations determine the carrying capacity of the ecology (Hannan & Freeman, 1977).

Quality of life considerations seem to be compatible with each of the two frameworks. They might be more easily integrated into the population ecology framework, however. This framework seeks to identify the conditions that give rise to the creation and death of organizations. The resource dependence one is more amenable to the explanation of the behavior of existing organizations. Naturally this also holds for new ventures that have overcome the first, legendary years of their lives. Furthermore, the population ecology framework does acknowledge the importance of resources. Both richness of resources and ecological organization are relevant to growth and decline of populations of organizations.

The quality of life indicators of this study are primarily pertinent to the carrying capacity of the human ecology. Most of the variables in this study have a bearing on the extent to which an urban area has stretched its spatial, territorial capabilities. For example, parks per capita, medical facilities per capita, swimming pools and other recreational resources per capita, or motor vehicle registration per capita reflect the degree to which an urban-metropolitan area is congested, overloaded, or overextended. Especially a variable such as number of inhabitants per square mile might signal levels beyond which urban areas become less hospitable to new ventures. Indeed, these variables represent a more direct explanation of why growing metropolitan areas display decreasing growth in economic activities in general and decreasing new venture behavior in particular (Pred, 1966; Thompson, 1966).

Larger cities have higher levels of entrepreneurial activity than do smaller ones because larger cities enjoy more political clout, their economies are oriented more toward customers than to sources of supply, and because their sheer size alone insures a higher amount of innovation. However, beyond a certain size-imposed ceiling this urban size rachet (Thompson, 1966) dissipates. This diminishing activity is analogous to the phenomenon of organizational growth and the decreasing growth rate of its administrative component (Berry & Kasarda, 1977). SMSAs reach a point in their entrepreneurial activity level at which their growth rate declines, presumably because their infrastructure cannot accommodate new ventures at a rate that they enjoyed during the earlier stages of their life cycle.

Measures of quality of life permit a more direct explanation of declining entrepreneurial conduciveness of larger cities than does the size variable, because it does not require one to make the inference that some large cities have unfavorable quality of life. If the quality of life correlates of urban size can explain entrepreneurial conduciveness, insights have been gained that could not have been inferred from size alone.

Quality of life presents useful information on the carrying capacity of urban metropolitan areas, but it has little to say about ecological structure. Population ecology authors such as Aldrich (1979) and Hannan and Freeman (1977) have suggested that socioeconomic differentiation can explain organizational birth rates. It is the interaction among industries, or other populations of organizations, that ecological models invoke to account for growth and decline of populations of organizations. The results of this study cannot be linked to this argument. The present investigation was limited to three industries, two of which belonged to the broad category of electronics (SIC 36). Each of the three industries has witnessed a high level of organizational births. There probably is little or no feedback among them. Their entrepreneurial activity level cannot be related to waves of birth and bankruptcy in other industries; such information is not available. If such data were collected, it could be determined how new ventures and bankruptcies among different industries fluctuate cyclically around an ecological equilibrium and whether their levels vary with respect to the carrying capacity of the SMSA.

Considerable efforts are to be expended for a full understanding of the environmental factors of entrepreneurship. Such understanding is crucial not only for organizational theorists and regional or urban economists but also for urban planners who might benefit from knowing which factors are instrumental to entrepreneurial vigor so that they might formulate their public policies accordingly. The results of this study have revealed that both economic and noneconomic aspects have to be attended to when and if attempts are undertaken to improve the entrepreneurial conduciveness of urban-metropolitan areas.

References

Aldrich, H. E. *Organizations and environments*. Englewood Cliffs, N.J.: Prentice Hall, 1979.

Alonso, W. Location theory. In J. Freeman & W. Alonso (Eds.), *Regional policy*. Cambridge: The MIT Press, 1975, 35-63.

Angrist, S. S. Subjective social indicators for urban areas: How useful for policy. *Sociological Focus*, 1976, 9(3), 217-230.

Ben-Chieh, L. *Quality of life indicators in the U.S. metropolitan areas, 1970*. Kansas City, Ill.: Midwest Research Institute, 1975.

Berry, B. J. L., & Kasarda, J. D. *Contemporary urban ecology*. New York: Macmillan Publishing Co., Inc., 1977.

Blalock, H. M. *Causal inferences in non-experimental research.* Chapel Hill, N.C.: University of North Carolina Press, 1964.

Bruno, A. V., & Tyzoon, T. T. The environment of entrepreneurship. Paper presented at the Conference on Research and Teaching on Entrepreneurship, Baylor University, 1980.

Campbell, A., Converse, P. E., & Rodgers, W. L. *The quality of American life.* New York: Russell Sage Foundation, 1976.

Campbell, J. P. On the nature of organizational effectiveness. In P. S. Goodman, J. M. Pennings, & Associates (Eds.), *New perspectives on organizational effectiveness.* San Francisco: Jossey-Bass, 1977, 2-55.

Carlton, D. W. Models of new business location. Working paper, Department of Economics, Report 7756, University of Chicago, 1978.

Child, J. Organizational structure, environment and performance: The role of strategic choice. *Sociology,* 1972, 6, 1-22.

Cooper, A. C. *The founding of technological-based firms.* Milwaukee, Wisc.: The Center for Venture Management, 1971.

Cooper, A. C. Technical entrepreneurship: What do we know? *R & D Management,* 1973, 3, 59-64.

Danilov, V. J. Research parks and regional development. In A. C. Cooper and J. L. Komives (Eds.), *Technical entrepreneurship: A symposium.* Milwaukee, Wisc.: The Center for Venture Management, 1972, 96-107.

Hannan, M. T., & Freeman, J. H. The population ecology of organizations. *American Journal of Sociology,* 1977, 82, 929-964.

Johnston, J. *Econometric methods.* New York: McGraw Hill, 1972.

Mahar, J. F., & Coddington, D. C. The scientific complex—Proceed with caution. *Harvard Business Review,* 1965, 43(1), 140-163.

McClelland, D. S. Need achievement and entrepreneurship—A longitudinal study. *Journal of Personality and Social Psychology,* 1965, 1, 389-392.

Pennings, J. M. Environmental influences on the creation process. In J. R. Kimberly, R. H. Miles, & Associates (Eds.), *The organizational life cycle.* San Francisco: Jossey-Bass, 1980, 134-163.

Pfeffer, J., & Salancik, G. R. *The external control of organizations: A resource dependence perspective.* New York: Harper and Row, 1978.

Pred, A. *The spatial dimensions of U.S. urban-institutional growth: 1800-1914.* Cambridge: The MIT Press, 1966.

Scherer, F. M. *Industrial market structure and economic performance.* Chicago: Rand McNally, 1970.

Shapero, A. R. The process of technical company formation in a local area. In A. C. Cooper & J. L. Komives (Eds.), *Technical entrepreneurship: A symposium.* Milwaukee, Wisc.: The Center for Venture Management, 1972.

Shapero, A. R. The displaced, uncomfortable entrepreneur. *Psychology Today,* 1975, 9(11), 83-88.

Susbauer, J. S. The technical entrepreneurship process in Austin, Texas. In A. C. Cooper & J. L. Komives (Eds.), *Technical entrepreneurship: A symposium.* Milwaukee, Wisc.: The Center for Venture Management, 1972, 28-46.

Thompson, J. D. *Organizations in action.* New York: McGraw Hill, 1967.

Thompson, W. *A preface to urban economics.* Baltimore: Johns Hopkins University Press, 1966.

U.S. Bureau of the Census. *U.S. census of manufacturers.* Washington, D.C., 1967.

U.S. Bureau of the Census. *U.S. census of manufacturers.* Washington, D.C., 1972.

Vesper, K. H., & Albaum, G. The role of small business in research development, technological change and innovation in region 10. Working paper, University of Washington, Seattle, 1979.

Johannes M. Pennings is Associate Professor at the Graduate
School of Business at Columbia University

[14]

Academy of Management Review, 1985, Vol. 10, No. 4, 696-706.

A Conceptual Framework for Describing the Phenomenon of New Venture Creation

WILLIAM B. GARTNER
Georgetown University

A review of the entrepreneurship literature suggests that differences among entrepreneurs and among their ventures are as great as the variation between entrepreneurs and nonentrepreneurs and between new firms and established firms. A framework for describing new venture creation integrates four major perspectives in entrepreneurship: characteristics of the individual(s) who start the venture, the organization which they create, the environment surrounding the new venture, and the process by which the new venture is started.

The major thrust of most entrepreneurship research has been to prove that entrepreneurs are different from nonentrepreneurs (Brockhaus, 1980a, 1980b; Carland, Hoy, Boulton, & Carland, 1984; Collins & Moore, 1964; DeCarlo & Lyons, 1979; Hornaday & Aboud, 1971; Howell, 1972; Komives, 1972; Litzinger, 1965; McClelland, 1961; McClelland & Winter, 1969; Palmer, 1971; Schrier, 1975; Shapero, 1975) and that entrepreneurial firms are different from nonentrepreneurial firms (Collins & Moore, 1970; Cooper, 1979; Smith, 1967; Thorne & Ball, 1981). The basic assumption underlying this research is that all entrepreneurs and their new ventures are much the same. The present paper suggests that the differences among entrepreneurs and among their ventures are much greater than one might expect; in fact, the diversity may be larger than the differences between entrepreneurs and nonentrepreneurs and between entrepreneurial firms and nonentrepreneurial firms. Once the diversity among entrepreneurs and their ventures is recognized, the necessity for finding a way to classify them becomes apparent. Groups sharing

The research leading to this paper was supported in part by a grant from the National Science Foundation and is based on the author's doctoral dissertation. Additional support was provided by the Center for Entrepreneurial Studies, University of Virginia.

Requests for reprints should be sent to William B. Gartner, Center for Entrepreneurship Studies, School of Business Administration, Georgetown University, Washington, D.C. 20057.

similar characteristics must exist within the universe of entrepreneurs and their ventures. How are these groups revealed? Many different characteristics have been employed in past research to describe entrepreneurs and their ventures. Do the characteristics themselves fall into groups? In other words, does one subset of characteristics describe a single aspect of new venture creation, such as the environment surrounding the new venture, or the features of the organization that results?

This paper attempts to organize the many variables that have been used in past research to describe entrepreneurs and their ventures into a comprehensive framework. Far from being reductive, this new view of the entrepreneurship literature should provide valuable insights into the process of new venture creation by showing it to be a complex and multidimensional phenomenon. Once a clear retrospective analysis of the literature is provided, future research can proceed on more solid footing. Instead of many different researchers palpating different parts of the elephant and reaching reductive conclusions, at least all will know the name, if not the nature, of the beast with which they are dealing.

Much past research has been unidimensional, focusing on a single aspect of new venture creation, and its main purpose has been to show how entrepreneurs or their firms differ from nonentrepreneurs or nonentrepreneurial firms. (In fact, it might be said that unidimensional research goes hand in hand with the attitude that all entrepreneurs and their firms are alike, the task of the unidimensional research being to prove how all things entrepreneurial differ from all things nonentrepreneurial.) It has been consistently pointed out, however, in reviews of literature on entrepreneurs, for example, (Brockhaus, 1982; Glueck & Mescon, 1980; McCain & Smith, 1981) that variables that are assumed to differentiate entrepreneurs from nonentrepreneurs (managers, for instance) frequently do not bear up under close scrutiny. Yet the search for these elusive variables continues, and entrepreneurs and prospective entrepreneurs are subjected to batteries of psychological tests in attempts to isolate the single spring that makes them tick differently from others. As with other aspects of new venture creation, attempts are made to isolate key variables that separate entrepreneurial situations from nonentrepreneurial ones. Pennings (1980, 1982a, 1982b) has explored environments that support new venture creation; Van de Ven (1980) and Kimberly (1979) have focused on the process of venture creation.

This search for key variables is a motivation for research only if the task of entrepreneurial research is taken to be the distinction of entrepreneurs and things entrepreneurial from nonentrepreneurs and nonentrepreneurial situations. If a much different perspective is taken, the perspective that there are many different kinds of entrepreneur and many ways to be one and that the firms they create vary enormously as do the environments they create them in, then the burden shifts. How is each new venture creation different from another? Researchers need to think in terms of a combination of variables that make up each new venture creation (Van de Ven, Hudson, & Schroeder, 1984). The creation of a new venture is a multidimensional phenomenon; each variable describes only a single dimension of the phenomenon and cannot be taken alone. There is a growing awareness that the process of starting a business is not a single well-worn route marched along again and again by identical entrepreneurs (Hartman, 1983). New venture creation is a complex phenomenon: entrepreneurs and their firms vary widely; the actions they take or do not take and the environments they operate in and respond to are equally diverse — and all these

elements form complex and unique combinations in the creation of each new venture. It is not enough for researchers to seek out and focus on some concept of the "average" entrepreneur and the "typical" venture creation. New organizational forms evolve through variation, and this variation in new venture creation needs to be studied (Aldrich, 1979; Hannan & Freeman, 1977; Pfeffer & Salancik, 1978; Weick, 1979). This insistence on variation can be seen, for example, in Vesper (1979), who posits 11 different kinds of entrepreneur, and in a recent study by Cooper and Dunkelberg (1981), which reveals that entrepreneurs in certain industries can be very different from those in other industries.

Once the variation and complexity in new venture creation is recognized, it then is necessary to find a framework for systematically discovering and evaluating the similarities and differences among new ventures (McKelvey, 1982). Once it is no longer assumed that all entrepreneurs and their ventures present a homogeneous population, then other homogeneous subsets within the entrepreneurial universe must be sought out in order that entrepreneurial research can produce meaningful results. A primary value of the framework for describing new venture creation presented here is that it provides a systematic means of comparing and contrasting complex ventures; it provides a way to conceptualize variation and complexity.

A Framework for Describing New Venture Creation

Definitions of key words such as entrepreneur are often various and always a problem in the study of entrepreneurship (Brockhaus, 1980b; Komives, 1969; Long, 1983). Because the entrepreneur is only one dimension of this framework, it seems more important in this paper to define the term "new venture creation." Such a definition can be outlined here with less trepidation, if only because there is less precedent.

New venture creation is the organizing (in the Weickian sense) *of new organizations.* "To organize is to assemble ongoing interdependent actions into sensible sequences that generate sensible outcomes" (Weick, 1979, p. 3). The definition of new venture creation is synonymous with the definition of the new organization developed by the Strategic Planning Institute (1978, p. 1-2):

a new business venture launched as one of the following:
1. an independent entity
2. a new profit center within a company which has other established businesses, or
3. a joint venture which satisfies the following criteria:
   1. Its founders must acquire expertise in products, process, market and/or technology.
   2. Results are expected beyond the year in which the investment is made.
   3. It is considered a new market entrant by its competitors.
   4. It is regarded as a new source of supply by its potential customers.

The importance of this definition should not be overlooked, because it recognizes the multidimensional aspects of new venture creation. First, it emphasizes that individuals with expertise are a key element of the new venture. At the same time that it recognizes the new venture as an organizational entity, it stresses that the new venture is not instantaneously produced, but evolves over time (beyond a year). The new venture is seen further within the context of its environment: it is forced to seek out resources, and it competes in the market place. All these aspects of the new venture must be kept in mind if it is to be adequately described and classified.

Figure 1 presents a framework for describing the creation of a new venture across four dimensions: (a) individual(s)—the person(s) involved in starting a new organization; (b) organization—the kind of firm that is started; (c) environment—the situation surrounding and influencing the new organization; and (d) new venture process—the actions undertaken by the individual(s) to start the venture.

Any new venture is a gestalt (Miller, 1981) of variables from the four dimensions. No new venture creation can be comprehensively described, nor can its complexity be adequately accounted for, unless all of its four dimensions are investigated and an attempt is made to discover how variables from each dimension interact with variables from other dimensions.

This framework is the first to combine the four dimensions of venture creation, though other researchers have sought to combine two or more of the dimensions. This "thinking across dimensions" is especially apparent in the work of those theorists and researchers who have developed entrepreneurial classification schemes. Classifications of entrepreneurs themselves are often based on two dimensions: individual characteristics plus new venture process considerations — the word often used is "style." Danhoff (1949) based his scheme on the entrepreneur's openness to innovation; Cole (1959) on the sophistication of the entrepreneur's decision making tools; and Dailey (1971) according to bureaucratic or entrepreneurial style. Smith (1967) divided entrepreneurs by a stylistic orientation — craftsman or opportunistic. Filley and Aldag (1980) used management orientation. Vesper (1979, 1980) in two similar classifications differentiated among entrepreneurs by the activities involved in business formation and operation, and in another scheme (1980) by competitive strategy. In Cooper (1979) entrepreneurs are linked to particular environments, and, as cited previously, Cooper and Dunkelberg's (1981) study matches different entrepreneurs and their characteristics to the types of firms they are likely to start. In Vesper's (1979) classification the entrepreneur's type of firm is also a factor, as it is in several other classification studies (Braden, 1977; Filley & Aldag, 1980; Smith, 1967). Recently, Van de Ven et al.'s (1984) empirical study examined educational software firms on the basis of three dimen-

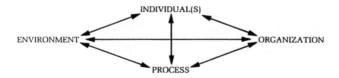

Figure 1. A framework for describing new venture creation.

sions: entrepreneurial—background characteristics and psychological attributes of the founding entrepreneurs; organizational—planning and
organizational activities undertaken before and
after company startup; and ecological—support
and resources made available to influence the
development of the industry. These classification schemes and frameworks are ways of stepping back to get an overall picture, a process like
model-building, which involves integration and
synthesis.

Individual(s)

Whether an entrepreneur is viewed as a "cap-
tain of industry," a hard-headed risk bearer (Mill,
1848), risk taker (Palmer, 1971) or a "rapacious
risk avoider" (Webster, 1976); whether he merely
metamorphoses into an entrepreneur at certain
moments and is something else the rest of the
time (Danhoff, 1949), or whether his need for
achievement (McClelland, 1961) and capacity for
innovation (Schumpeter, 1934) are always tick-
ing away; whether he is a "displaced person"
(Shapero, 1975), something close to a juvenile
delinquent (Gould, 1969), or a "man apart" (Liles,
1974) with an absolutely clear-headed (veridical)
perception of reality (Schrage, 1965), an aberrant
"artist" with an "innate sense of impending
change" (Hill, 1982); or whether he is, indeed,
that completely political animal, a community
builder (Schell & Davig, 1981), the entrepreneur
is overwhelmingly perceived to be different in
important ways from the nonentrepreneur, and
many researchers have believed these differences
to lie in the background and personality of the
entrepreneur.

One often pursued avenue has been the attempt
to develop a psychological profile of the entrepreneur and to measure such psychological characteristics as need for achievement (DeCarlo &
Lyons, 1979; Hornaday & Aboud, 1971; McClelland, 1961; McClelland & Winter, 1969;
Schwartz, 1976). However, other researchers have
not found need for achievement useful in describing entrepreneurs (Brockhaus, 1980b; Litzinger,
1965; Schrage, 1965); still others have questioned
the value and validity of using psychological
characteristics of any kind to describe entrepreneurs (Brockhaus, 1982; Glueck & Mescon,
1980; Jenks, 1965; Kilby, 1971; McCain & Smith,

1981; Van de Ven, 1980). However, the following
psychological characteristics have been used in
many studies and may have some validity in differentiating among types of entrepreneurs (Brockhaus, 1982):
1. Need for achievement
2. Locus of control
3. Risk taking propensity

Some researchers have found it fruitful to look
at the entrepreneur's background, experience, and
attitudes. Some individual characteristics that
may be of value in describing entrepreneurs are:
1. Job satisfaction (Collins & Moore, 1970; Komives, 1972)
2. Previous work experience (Cooper, 1970; Lamont, 1972; Susbauer, 1972)
3. Entrepreneurial parents (Collins & Moore, 1970;
   Roberts & Wainer, 1968; Schrier, 1975; Secrest,
   1975; Shapero, 1972; Susbauer, 1972)
4. Age (Komives, 1972; Liles, 1974; Roberts &
   Wainer, 1968; Secrest, 1975; Thorne & Ball,
   1981)
5. Education (Brockhaus & Nord, 1979; Collins &
   Moore, 1964; Howell, 1972; Roberts, 1969;
   Susbauer, 1969)

Process

In 1949 Danhoff wrote, "Entrepreneurship is
an activity or function and not a specific individual or occupation . . . the specific personal entrepreneur is an unrealistic abstraction" (p. 21).
Other theorists have pursued this idea of function and have tried to differentiate the entrepreneurial function from other more routine
functions such as the managerial function (Baumol, 1968; Cole, 1965; Hartmann, 1959; Leibenstein, 1968; Schumpeter, 1934). This "dynamic"
aspect of the entrepreneur has been acknowl-
edged in the work of eight researchers who have
enumerated certain actions that an entrepreneur
performs in order to create a new venture. Except
for Peterson and Berger (1971), who described
the entrepreneurial activities of record producers,
these studies were theoretical, that is, based on
general observation rather than systematic research. The similarities in their views are summarized here; six common behaviors are listed
(the order does not imply a sequence of actions):
1. The entrepreneur locates a business opportunity (Cole, 1965; Kilby, 1971; Maidique, 1980;
   Schumpeter, 1934; Vesper, 1980).
2. The entrepreneur accumulates resources (Cole,
   1965; Kilby, 1971; Leibenstein, 1968; Peterson &
   Berger, 1971; Schumpeter, 1934; Vesper, 1980).

3. The entrepreneur markets products and services (Cole, 1965; Kilby, 1971; Leibenstein, 1968; Maidique, 1980; Peterson & Berger, 1971; Schumpeter, 1934; Vesper, 1980).
4. The entrepreneur produces the product (Kilby, 1971; Maidique, 1980; Peterson & Berger, 1971; Schumpeter, 1934; Vesper, 1980).
5. The entrepreneur builds an organization (Cole, 1965; Kilby, 1971; Leibenstein, 1968; Schumpeter, 1934).
6. The entrepreneur responds to government and society (Cole, 1965; Kilby, 1971).

Environment

Much of the current concern (Peters & Waterman, 1982) over how to design organizations that keep and encourage innovative individuals is an indirect acknowledgment that entrepreneurs do not operate in vacuums — they respond to their environments. The existence of highly supportive regional entrepreneurial environments (Cooper, 1970; Draheim, 1972; Pennings, 1982b; Susbauer, 1972) — including "incubator organizations" — can, from one perspective, be said actually to *create* entrepreneurs. The idea of "pushes" and "pulls" from the environment has found its way into many studies of entrepreneurship (Shapero & Sokol, 1982).

In organization theory literature, two different views of the environment have been developed. One perspective, environmental determinism, sees the environment as an outside set of conditions to which the organization must adapt (Aldrich, 1979; Aldrich & Pfeffer, 1976; Hannan & Freeman, 1977). The other perspective, strategic choice, sees the environment as a "reality" that organizations create via the selectivity of their own perceptions (Child, 1972; Starbuck, 1976; Weick, 1979). In the entrepreneurship literature, both perspectives on the environment have been taken. In the present paper those characteristics that are viewed as relatively fixed conditions imposed on the new venture from without are called environmental variables. Variables over which the organization has more control (strategic choice variables) are more readily viewed as characteristics of the organization itself and are treated as such.

In an overview of 17 research papers on environmental variables that influenced new venture creation, Bruno and Tyebjee (1982) found 12 factors that they judged stimulated entrepreneurship:

1. Venture capital availability
2. Presence of experienced entrepreneurs
3. Technically skilled labor force
4. Accessibility of suppliers
5. Accessibility of customers or new markets
6. Governmental influences
7. Proximity of universities
8. Availability of land or facilities
9. Accessiblity of transportation
10. Attitude of the area population
11. Availability of supporting services
12. Living conditions

Another study of environmental influences on new venture creation was Pennings' studies of organization birth frequencies (1980, 1982a, 1982b). Pennings found that organization birth rates were high in areas with: high occupational and industrial differentiation; high percentages of recent immigrants in the population; a large industrial base; larger size urban areas; and availability of financial resources.

Another field of research has taken the deterministic perspective regarding the environment and new ventures: industrial economics. Oliver Williamson (1975) explored the process by which the failure of markets to coordinate efficiently the production and distribution of goods and services often resulted in the start-up of organizations to coordinate the production function through administration. Porter (1980) focused on the competitive environment that confronts firms in a particular industry. Porter's work provides five environmental influences on organizations: barriers to entry, rivalry among existing competitors, pressure from substitute products, bargaining power of buyers, and bargaining power of suppliers.

Organization

Despite a bold early attempt by Stauss (1944) to direct the focus away from the entrepreneur and toward his created organization (by claiming, somewhat tortuously, that the firm is the entrepreneur), most subsequent studies of new venture creation have neglected to comment on or even communicate certain characteristics of the organizations on which they focused. The assumption behind this seems to derive from two other assumptions: (a) if all entrepreneurs are virtually alike and (b) they all go through the same process to create their ventures, then (c) the organizations they create must, like widgets, not be of any interest in themselves.

Many research samples in entrepreneurship studies are selected, for example, without regard to type of firm (i.e., manufacturing, service, retail, wholesale). Of the studies that have indicated the type of firm, Smith (1967), Cooper (1970), Collins and Moore (1970), Susbauer (1972), and Braden (1977) studied manufacturing firms, and most focused on high technology manufacturing firms. Litzinger (1965) studied motel firms, and Mescon and Montanari (1981) studied real estate firms. However, researchers in these studies made no attempts to compare the type of firm studied to other types of firm to determine what difference type of firm might make in the process of new venture creation. Cooper and Dunkelberg (1981), Gartner (1982), and Van de Ven et al. (1984) have begun to link type of firm across other dimensions, such as entrepreneurial background and response to environment.

The presence of partners is another firm characteristic suggested by Timmons, Smollen, and Dingee (1977) as a vital factor in starting certain types of firm, and some research has mentioned partners as a characteristic of the firms studied (Cooper, 1970; DeCarlo & Lyons, 1979).

Strategic choice variables are treated here as characteristics of the organization. Porter (1980) identified three generic competitive strategies that firms may "choose": (a) overall cost leadership, (b) differentiation, and (c) focus. Vesper (1980) identified 14 competitive entry wedges: the new product or service, parallel competition, franchise entry, geographical transfer, supply shortage, tapping unutilized resources, customer contract, becoming a second source, joint ventures, licensing, market relinquishment, sell off of division, favored purchasing by government, and governmental rule changes.

Conclusion

Listing each variable of new venture creation under the appropriate dimension of the framework illustrates the potential for a high degree of complexity in the interaction of these variables within the multidimensional phenomenon of venture creation (Figure 2).

The four dimensional conceptual framework can be seen as a kaleidoscope, as an instrument through which to view the enormously varying patterns of new venture creation. Past attempts

to differentiate the typical entrepreneur and his/her typical creation from all nonentrepreneurs and all nonnew ventures have, whether intentionally or not, advanced the notion that all entrepreneurs are alike and all new venture creation is the same. However, there clearly is a wide variation in the kinds of new ventures that are started. For example, are there similarities between the creation of a waterbed store by a 20-year old college student and the creation of a personal computer company by three engineers? Are the differences between them more important than the similarities? What is the value of comparing the creation of a pet store by two unemployed physical therapists to the creation of a 5,000-acre business park by four real estate developers? The goal is not to smooth over any differences that might exist among these new ventures or to throw these very different individuals into the same pot in order to extract the typical qualities of the typical entrepreneur. The goal is to identify the specific variables that describe how each new venture was created, in order that meaningful contrasts and comparisons among new ventures can be made.

First must come careful description with an eye to variation. The search for key variables, for general principles, for universally applicable laws of entrepreneurship that has characterized much of the entrepreneurship literature betrays an impatience with the slow methodical process of description. Attention to careful observation and description is the basis of good scientific research (McKelvey, 1982). In what does all this careful description of new ventures result? A collection of uniquely described ventures, each different from all the others? Once good description is achieved, then good comparisons and contrasts can be made, and subsets of similar ventures can be established. These homogeneous populations are needed before any general rules or theories of new venture creation can be postulated. The lack of such homogeneous samples in the past has led to conflicts in the results of research studies.

The conceptual framework presented here provides a way of analyzing past research studies. Each study can be broken down into the types of individuals, organizations, environments, and processes that were investigated. One way in which the framework can be useful is in identify-

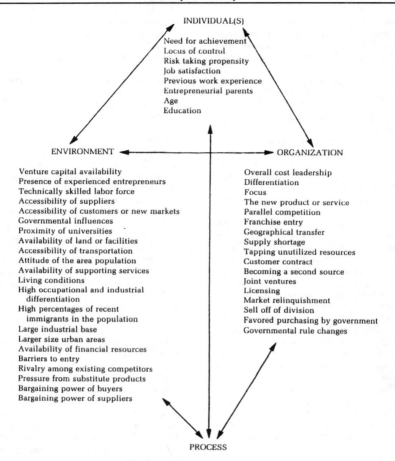

INDIVIDUAL(S)

Need for achievement
Locus of control
Risk taking propensity
Job satisfaction
Previous work experience
Entrepreneurial parents
Age
Education

ENVIRONMENT

Venture capital availability
Presence of experienced entrepreneurs
Technically skilled labor force
Accessibility of suppliers
Accessibility of customers or new markets
Governmental influences
Proximity of universities
Availability of land or facilities
Accessibility of transportation
Attitude of the area population
Availability of supporting services
Living conditions
High occupational and industrial
  differentiation
High percentages of recent
  immigrants in the population
Large industrial base
Larger size urban areas
Availability of financial resources
Barriers to entry
Rivalry among existing competitors
Pressure from substitute products
Bargaining power of buyers
Bargaining power of suppliers

ORGANIZATION

Overall cost leadership
Differentiation
Focus
The new product or service
Parallel competition
Franchise entry
Geographical transfer
Supply shortage
Tapping unutilized resources
Customer contract
Becoming a second source
Joint ventures
Licensing
Market relinquishment
Sell off of division
Favored purchasing by government
Governmental rule changes

PROCESS

The entrepreneur locates a business opportunity
The entrepreneur accumulates resources
The entrepreneur markets products and services
The entrepreneur produces the product
The entrepreneur builds an organization
The entrepreneur responds to government and society

Figure 2. Variables in new venture creation.

702

ing those aspects of new venture creation neglected by a particular study. New research may then be designed to account for these lacunae. For example, Brockhaus defines his sample of entrepreneurs as:

> Individuals who within three months prior to the study had ceased working for their employers and at the time of the study owned as well as managed business ventures. . . . The businesses whose owners served as participants were selected from the listing of businesses licensed by St. Louis County, Missouri during the months of August and September, 1975 (1980a, p. 39).

Although Brockhaus, unlike other researchers, attempts to close in on the actual entrepreneurial function by interviewing his entrepreneurs within a few months of the creation of their ventures, useful and necessary distinctions among the individuals and their new ventures are not made. One is not sure what types of firms were studied (retail, service, manufacturing, etc.) or whether the St. Louis environment was likely to influence certain types of individuals to create certain types of firms. Is the process of starting a venture in St. Louis different, or is the process different for certain types of businesses or certain kinds of individuals? Accounting for type of firm, environment, and process in this study would enhance comparison among the individuals in the study and individuals in other studies.

In analyzing results of research studies, a focus on differences in one of the four dimensions might explain conflicting results. For example, studies such as Collins and Moore (1970) suggest that individuals who start firms are social misfits who do not fit into most organizations. Yet other studies such as Cooper (1970) suggest that individuals who start successful firms are good team players. On closer examination it is seen that Collins and Moore studied manufacturing firms that were more like job shops in the 1950s, and Cooper studied high technology firms in the 1960s. High technology industries might require more skills than one individual would be likely to have, necessitating that individuals combine their abilities in teams in order to start an organization successfully.

In addition to providing a means by which past research can be analyzed, the framework outlines a format for future research methodologies and for reporting such research. More careful atten-

tion must be paid to the research sample. For example, women entrepreneurs are a popular research topic. If similarities are discovered among women who start firms, are these similarities a result of similar environments? Can differences be attributed solely to psychological or background characteristics? What is the value of research results that are based on such unexamined and possibly heterogeneous sample populations?

Even in a narrowly selected research sample, the framework might be useful in drawing the researcher's attention to considerations inherent in each of the four dimensions, in order that conclusions regarding the virtual sameness of all the members of the sample may not be made too hastily. For example, in a sample of new organizations in the micro-computer industry, a number of considerations might be made. What is the variation among the entrepreneurs in their work backgrounds, education, age? How do competitive strategies used by these new organizations vary? Are there regional or other subenvironments in the industry that cause variations in firms and strategies? What is the variation in the venture creation process: do all individuals devote equal time to financing the organization, hiring personnel, marketing? What differences exist between "new" and "old" firms in this industry?

The brief review of the literature provided earlier is only a running start at a comprehensive analysis and evaluation of the entrepreneurship literature. For example, in a study of individuals who start firms, who are the individuals? Are the individuals in McClelland's samples (McCelland, 1961; McCelland & Winter, 1969) similar to those in Brockhaus (1980a) or Schrage (1965)? More about the similarities and differences within and among past research samples needs to be known. There are many dimensions and variables across which these samples may be compared.

The framework also points up the importance of interactions of variables among dimensions in understanding new venture creation. How does an individual's background influence the type of activities undertaken to start an organization? Does the marketing individual devote his time to marketing instead of manufacturing, and are there some environments or firms that require more marketing? Is the process of starting a retail store similar to that of starting a steel mill? Are entry strategies used by new organizations in the robotics industry similar to those used in the brewery industry?

The framework for describing new venture creation provides the possibility of describing subsets within the unwieldy set of all entrepreneurs and all new ventures. Newly created ventures that display meaningful similarities across the four dimensions could be described and classified together (Gartner, 1982). Significant generalizations regarding some or all new venture creations might emerge, generalizations that do not, however, attempt to mask the variation in new venture creation.

This paper does not purport to answer specific questions about how new ventures are started or provide specific developmental models for new venture creation. No claim is made that the framework or the list of variables is comprehensive; the claim is only that the description of new ventures needs to be more comprehensive than it is at present. A great many more questions are asked here than are answered. However, the paper provides a means of making a fundamental shift in the perspective on entrepreneurship: away from viewing entrepreneurs and their ventures as an unvarying, homogeneous population, and towards a recognition and appreciation of the complexity and variation that abounds in the phenomenon of new venture creation.

References

Aldrich, H. E. (1979) *Organizations and environments.* Englewood Cliffs, NJ: Prentice-Hall.

Aldrich, H. E., & Pfeffer, J. (1976) Environments of organizations. *Annual Review of Sociology,* 76-105.

Baumol, W. J. (1968) Entrepreneurship in economic theory. *American Economic Review,* 58(2), 64-71.

Braden, P. (1977) *Technological entrepreneurship* (Michigan Business Reports, No. 62). Ann Arbor: University of Michigan.

Brockhaus, R. H. (1980a) The effect of job dissatisfaction on the decision to start a business. *Journal of Small Business Management,* 18(1), 37-43.

Brockhaus, R. H. (1980b) Risk taking propensity of entrepreneurs. *Academy of Management Journal,* 23, 509-520.

Brockhaus, R. H. (1982) The psychology of the entrepreneur. In C. A. Kent, D. L. Sexton, & K. H. Vesper (Eds.), *Encyclopedia of entrepreneurship* (pp. 39-56). Englewood Cliffs NJ: Prentice-Hall.

Brockhaus, R. H., & Nord, W. R. (1979) An exploration of factors affecting the entrepreneurial decision: Personal characteristics vs. environmental conditions. *Proceedings of the National Academy of Management,* 364-368.

Bruno, A. V., & Tyebjee, T. T. (1982) The environment for entrepreneurship. In C. A. Kent, D. L. Sexton, & K. H. Vesper (Eds.), *Encyclopedia of entrepreneurship* (pp. 288-307). Englewood Cliffs, NJ: Prentice-Hall.

Carland, J. W., Hoy, F., Boulton, W. R., & Carland, J.A.C. (1984) Differentiating entrepreneurs from small business owners: A conceptualization. *Academy of Management Review,* 9, 354-359.

Child, J. (1972) Organizational structure, environment and performance: The role of strategic choice. *Sociology,* 6, 1-22.

Cole, A. H. (1959) *Business enterprise in its social setting.* Cambridge, MA: Harvard University Press.

Cole, A. H. (1965) An approach to the study of entrepreneurship: A tribute to Edwin F. Gay. In H.G.J. Aitken (Ed.), *Explorations in enterprise* (pp. 30-44). Cambridge, MA: Harvard University Press.

Collins, O. F., & Moore, D. G. (1964) *The enterprising man.* East Lansing: Michigan State University.

Collins, O. F., & Moore, D. G. (1970) *The organization makers.* New York: Appleton-Century-Crofts.

Cooper, A. C. (1970) The Palo Alto experience. *Industrial Research,* 12(5), 58-61.

Cooper, A. C. (1979) Strategic management: New ventures and small business. In D. E. Schendel & C. W. Hofer (Eds.), *Strategic management* (pp. 316-327). Boston: Little, Brown.

Cooper, A. C., & Dunkelberg, W. C. (1981) A new look at business entry: Experiences of 1,805 entrepreneurs. In K. H. Vesper (Ed.), *Frontiers of entrepreneurship research* (pp. 1-20). Wellesley, MA: Babson College.

Daily, C. A. (1971) *Entrepreneurial management: Going all out for results.* New York: McGraw-Hill.

Danhoff, C. H. (1949) Observations on entrepreneurship in agriculture. In A. H. Cole (Ed.), *Change and the entrepreneur* (pp. 20-24). Cambridge, MA: Harvard University Press.

DeCarlo, J. F., & Lyons, P. R. (1979) A comparison of selected personal characteristics of minority and non-minority female entrepreneurs. *Journal of Small Business Management,* 17(4), 22-29.

Draheim, K. P. (1972) Factors influencing the rate of formation of technical companies. In A. C. Cooper & J. L. Komives (Eds.), *Technical entrepreneurship: A symposium* (pp. 3-27). Milwaukee, WI: Center for Venture Management.

Filley, A. C., & Aldag, R. J. (1980) Organizational growth and types: Lessons from small institutions. In B. Staw & L. Cummings (Eds.), *Research in organizational behavior* (Vol. 2, pp. 279-320). Greenwich, CT: JAI Press.

Gartner, W. B. (1982) *An empirical model of the business startup, and eight entrepreneurial archetypes.* Unpublished doctoral dissertation, University of Washington, Seattle.

Glueck, W., & Mescon, T. (1980) *Entrepreneurship: A literature analysis of concepts.* Paper presented at the annual meeting of the Academy of Management, Detroit, MI.

Gould, L. C. (1969) Juvenile entrepreneurs. *American Journal of Sociology,* 74, 710-719.

Hannan, M. T., & Freeman, J. (1977) The population ecology model of organizations. *American Journal of Sociology,* 82, 929-964.

Hartman, C. (1983) Who's running America's fastest growing companies? *Inc.,* 5(8), 41-47.

Hartmann, H. (1959) Managers and entrepreneurs: A useful distinction? *Administrative Science Quarterly,* 3, 429-457.

Hill, R. (1982) The entrepreneur: An artist masquerading as a businessman? *International Management,* 37(2), 21-22, 26.

Hornaday, J., & Aboud, J. (1971) Characteristics of successful entrepreneurs. *Personnel Psychology,* 24(2), 141-153.

Howell, R. P. (1972) Comparative profiles—Entrepreneurs versus the hired executive: San Francisco Peninsula semiconductor industry. In A. C. Cooper & J. L. Komives (Eds.), *Technical entrepreneurship: A symposium* (pp. 47-62). Milwaukee, WI: Center for Venture Management.

Jenks, L. (1965) Approaches to entrepreneurial personality. In H. G. J. Aitken (Ed.), *Explorations in enterprise* (pp. 80-92). Cambridge, MA: Harvard University Press.

Kilby, P. (1971) Hunting the heffalump. In P. Kilby (Ed.), *Entrepreneurship and economic development* (pp. 1-40). New York: Free Press.

Kimberly, J. R. (1979) Issues in the creation of organizations: Initiation, innovation, and institutionalization. *Academy of Management Journal,* 22, 437-457.

Komives, J. L. (Ed.). (1969) *Karl A. Bostrum seminar in the study of enterprise.* Milwaukee, WI: Center for Venture Management.

Komives, J. L. (1972) A preliminary study of the personal values of high technology entrepreneurs. In A. C. Cooper & J. L. Komives (Eds.), *Technical entrepreneurship: A symposium* (pp. 231-242). Milwaukee, WI: Center for Venture Management.

Lamont, L. M. (1972) The role of marketing in technical entrepreneurship. In A. C. Cooper & J. L. Komives (Eds.), *Technical entrepreneurship: A symposium* (pp. 150-164). Milwaukee, WI: Center for Venture Management.

Leibenstein, H. (1968) Entrepreneurship and development. *American Economic Review,* 58(2), 72-83.

Liles, P. R. (1974) *New business ventures and the entrepreneur.* Homewood, IL: Irwin.

Litzinger, W. D. (1965) The motel entrepreneur and the motel manager. *Academy of Management Journal,* 8, 268-281.

Long, W. (1983) The meaning of entrepreneurship. *American Journal of Small Business,* 8(2), 47-59.

Maidique, M. A. (1980) Entrepreneurs, champions and technological innovation. *Sloan Management Review,* 21(2), 59-76.

McCain G., & Smith, N. (1981, Summer) A contemporary model of entrepreneurial style. *Small Business Institute Review,* 40-45.

McClelland, D. (1961) *The achieving society.* Princeton, NJ: Van Nostrand.

McClelland, D., & Winter, D. G. (1969) *Motivating economic achievement.* New York: Free Press.

McKelvey, B. (1982) *Organizational systematics—Taxonomy, evolution, classification.* Berkeley: University of California Press.

Mescon, T., & Montanari, J. (1981) The personalities of independent and franchise entrepreneurs: An empirical analysis of concepts. *Journal of Enterprise Management* 3(2), 149-159.

Mill, J. S. (1848) *Principles of political economy with some of their applications to social philosophy.* London: J. W. Parker.

Miller, D. (1981) Toward a new contingency approach: The search for organization gestalts. *Journal of Management Studies,* 18, 1-26.

Palmer, M. (1971) The application of psychological testing to entrepreneurial potential. *California Management Review,* 13(3), 32-39.

Pennings, J. M. (1980) Environmental influences on the creation process. In J. R. Kimberly & R. Miles (Eds.), *The organization life cycle* (pp. 135-160). San Francisco: Jossey Bass.

Pennings, J. M. (1982a) Organizational birth frequencies. *Administrative Science Quarterly,* 27, 120-144.

Pennings, J. M. (1982b) The urban quality of life and entrepreneurship. *Academy of Management Journal,* 25, 63-79.

Peters T. J., & Waterman, R. H. (1982) *In search of excellence.* New York: Harper & Row.

Peterson, R. A., & Berger, D. G. (1971) Entrepreneurship in organizations: Evidence from the popular music industry. *Administrative Science Quarterly,* 16, 97-107.

Pfeffer, J., & Salancik, G. R. (1978) *The external control of organizations.* New York: Harper & Row.

Porter, M. E. (1980) *Competitive strategy: Techniques for analyzing industries and competitors.* New York: Fress Press.

Roberts, E. B. (1969) Entrepreneurship and technology. In W. Gruber & D. Marquis (Eds.), *Factors in the transfer of technology* (pp. 219-237). Cambridge, MA: M.I.T. Press.

Roberts, E. B., & Wainer, H. A. (1968) New enterprise on Rte. 128. *Science Journal,* 4(12), 78-83.

Schell, D. W., & Davig, W. (1981) The community infrastructure of entrepreneurship. In K. H. Vesper (Ed.), *Frontiers of entrepreneurship research* (pp. 563-590). Wellesley, MA: Babson College.

Schrage, H. (1965) The R & D entrepreneur: Profile of success. *Harvard Business Review,* 43(6), 56-69.

Schrier, J. W. (1975) Entrepreneurial characteristics of women. In J. W. Schrier & J. Susbauer (Eds.), *Entrepreneurship and enterprise development: A worldwide perspective* (pp. 66-70). Milwaukee, WI: Center for Venture Management.

Schumpeter, J. A. (1934) *The theory of economic development* (R. Opie, Trans.). Cambridge, MA: Harvard University Press.

Schwartz, E. B. (1976) Entrepreneurship: A new female frontier. *Journal of Contemporary Business.* 5, 47-76.

Secrest, L. (1975) Texas entrepreneurship. In J. W. Schrier & J. Susbauer (Eds.), *Entrepreneurship and enterprise development: A worldwide perspective* (pp. 51-65). Milwaukee, WI: Center for Venture Management.

Shapero, A. (1972) The process of technical company formation in a local area. In A. C. Cooper & J. L. Komives (Eds.), *Technical entrepreneurship: A symposium* (pp. 63-95). Milwaukee, WI: Center for Venture Management.

Shapero, A. (1975) The displaced, uncomfortable entrepreneur. *Psychology Today*, 9(6), 83-88.

Shapero, A., & Sokol, L. (1982) The social dimensions of entrepreneurship. In C. A. Kent, D. L. Sexton, & K. H. Vesper (Eds.), *Encylclopedia of entrepreneurship* (pp. 72-90). Englewood Cliffs, NJ: Prentice-Hall.

Smith, N. (1967) *The entrepreneur and his firm: The relationship between type of man and type of company.* East Lansing: Michigan State University.

Starbuck, W. H. (1976) Organizations and their environments. In M. Dunnette (Ed.), *Handbook of industrial and organizational psychology* (pp. 1069-1123). Chicago: Rand McNally.

Stauss, J. H. (1944) The entrepreneur: The firm. *Journal of Political Economy*, 52(2), 112-127.

Strategic Planning Institute. (1978) *The startup data manual.* Unpublished manuscript. Cambridge, MA: Strategic Planning Institute.

Susbauer, J. C. (1969) *The technical company formation process: A particular aspect of entrepreneurship.* Unpublished doctoral dissertation, University of Texas, Austin.

Susbauer, J. C. (1972) The technical entrepreneurship process in Austin, Texas. In A. C. Cooper & J. L. Komives (Eds.), *Technical entrepreneurship: A symposium* (pp. 28-46). Milwaukee, WI: Center for Venture Management.

Thorne, J. R., & Ball, J. G. (1981) Entrepreneurs and their companies: Smaller industrial firms. In K. H. Vesper (Ed.), *Frontiers of entrepreneurship research* (pp. 65-83). Wellesley, MA: Babson College.

Timmons, J. A., Smollen, E, & Dingee, A. L. M. (1977) *New venture creation.* Homewood, IL: Irwin.

Van de Ven, A. H. (1980) Early planning, implementation and performance of new organizations. In J. R. Kimberly & R. Miles (Eds.), *The organization life cycle* (pp. 83-134). San Francisco: Jossey Bass.

Van de Ven, A. H., Hudson, R., & Schroeder, D. M. (1984) Designing new business startups: Entrepreneurial, organizational, and ecological considerations. *Journal of Management*, 10(1), 87-107.

Vesper, K. H. (1979) Commentary. In D. E. Schendel & C. W. Hofer (Eds.), *Strategic management* (pp. 332-338). Boston: Little, Brown.

Vesper, K. H. (1980) *New venture strategies.* Englewood Cliffs, NJ: Prentice-Hall.

Vesper, K. H. (1981) Scanning the frontier of entrepreneurship research. In K. H. Vesper (Ed.), *Frontiers of entrepreneurship research* (pp. vii-xiv). Wellesley, MA: Babson College.

Vesper, K. H. (1982a) Expanding entrepreneurship research. In K. H. Vesper (Ed.), *Frontiers of entrepreneurship research* (pp. vii-xx). Wellesley, MA: Babson College.

Vesper, K. H. (1982b) Introduction and summary of entrepreneurship research. In C. A. Kent, D. L. Sexton, & K. H. Vesper (Eds.), *Encyclopedia of entrepreneurship* (pp. xxxi-xxxviii).

Webster, F. A. (1976) A model for new venture initiation: A disclosure on rapacity and the independent entrepreneur. *Academy of Management Review*, 1(1), 26-37.

Weick, K. E. (1979) *The social psychology of organizing* (2nd ed.). Reading, MA: Addison-Wesley.

Williamson, O. E. (1975) *Markets and hierarchies, analysis and antitrust implications.* New York: Free Press.

William B. Gartner is Assistant Professor of Business and Director of the Center for Entrepreneurship Studies in the School of Business Administration, Georgetown University.

[15]

Strategic Management Journal, Vol. 11, 79–92 (1990)

RESOURCE COOPTATION VIA SOCIAL CONTRACTING: RESOURCE ACQUISITION STRATEGIES FOR NEW VENTURES

JENNIFER A. STARR and IAN C. MACMILLAN
The Wharton School, University of Pennsylvania, Philadelphia, Pennsylvania, U.S.A.

This paper examines the role of social contracting strategies by independent and corporate entrepreneurs in acquiring resources for new ventures. Venture managers in both independent start-ups and corporate ventures use social contracting as a means to resource cooptation— an approach to resource acquisition which is especially suited to the particular constraints of new ventures. The analysis highlights potential obstacles to social contracting strategies for the corporate entrepreneur and presents a set of formal testable propositions which emerge from this perspective.

INTRODUCTION

A scan of recent articles in the strategic management literature would reveal a trend which is highly encouraging—materials that are being published increasingly use a rigorous economic lens to study strategic issues. However, this could also be a disturbing trend to the extent that it begins to so dominate the focus on strictly economic transactions that it starts to exclude research on the social transactions that characterize a business. Nowhere would this be more disturbing than in the case of corporate ventures and entrepreneurial activities. The corporate venture is an intensely social endeavor as well as an economic one, and the interactions among venture managers and those that must support them are such that a strict focus on economic exchanges is inadequate.

The objective of the paper is exploratory. It will start to explore the application of social transactions concepts to both independent and corporate entrepreneurial start-ups in the hope that this will spur further research along these lines. To this end it draws on the literature and a number of case vignettes to systematically:

1. Demonstrate that social contracting by some entrepreneurs and intrapreneurs is critical to the process of resource acquisition for their ventures.
2. Identify two key areas where social contracting behavior can be critically useful in the start-up, namely in coopting legitimacy and particularly in coopting underutilized resources.
3. Explore why the targets of such social contracting behavior are prepared to tolerate their resources being coopted. We suggest that it is because some entrepreneurs and intrapreneurs employ social assets such as friendship, liking, trust, obligation, and gratitude to secure resources at prices far lower than the market price, to the significant benefit of their ventures.
4. Identify how some entrepreneurs and intrapreneurs build these social assets.
5. Explore why corporate venture managers seem to have more difficulty than independent entrepreneurs in doing this.

0143–2095/90/050079–14$07.00

80   *J. A. Starr and I. C. MacMillan*

6. Develop a set of formal testable propositions that relate social contracting behavior with corporate venture characteristics and venture performance.

In deciding what type of venture to study one is faced with the choice of whether to study just the intrapreneur or also the independent entrepreneur. We have ample evidence in the work of Weiss (1981) that, compared to the independent entrepreneur, firms are particularly poor at corporate start-ups. On average, corporate ventures take twice as long to reach profitability and end up half as profitable as independent start-ups. We suspect this has a lot to do with the way in which corporate venture managers go about acquiring resources, and the cost of such resources, and so we saw value in studying both independent and corporate entrepreneurs.

In one article there is no intent to be exhaustive. Rather we wish to provoke further study along social contracting lines by demonstrating evidence of its usefulness for start-ups and provide a framework for thinking about how to study start-ups from this perspective.

ECONOMIC VERSUS SOCIAL TRANSACTIONS

Interpersonal exchange theories generally are derivatives of the neoclassical economic model of market exchange. Individuals, like firms, invest their time and energy in social transactions based on their expectations of future profits and rewards (Homans, 1950, 1958, 1961; Blau, 1964; Swedberg, 1987). As defined by Homans:

> Social behavior is an exchange of goods, material goods but also non-material ones, such as the symbols of approval or prestige . . . . This process of influence tends to work out at equilibrium to a balance in the exchanges. For a person engaged in exchange, what he gives may be a cost to him, just as what he gets may be a reward, and his behavior changes less as profit, that is, reward less cost, tends to a maximum. Not only does he seek a maximum for himself, but he tries to see to it that no one in his group makes more profit than he does (Homans, 1958: 606).

Thus, individuals voluntarily enter social relationships, based on psychic profit-maximizing rational calculations.

The major distinction between economic and social transactions is that social transactions engender feelings of unspecified, diffuse, future personal obligations, trust, and gratitude (Blau, 1964). Social transactions agreements are rarely explicit. Although there are calculable extrinsic and intrinsic costs and benefits in social transactions, they do not carry exact price tags or reflect market-based utilities and preferences. Difficulties can arise in adjusting the balance of accounts and assessing the competing trade-offs of social and instrumental advantages of interpersonal relationships.

A recent advance in theoretical paradigm development, socio-economics, adds a further complication to social exchange transactions (Etzioni, 1988). This paradigm argues that constraints on rational choice are not only attributable to earlier criticisms of rational models—namely cognitive limits of human information processing, or political processes (Cyert and March, 1963; Allison, 1971; Janis and Mann, 1977; MacMillan, 1978; Quinn, 1980; Narayanan and Fahey, 1982), but in addition, individual choice is characterized by tension between rational choice factors and moral commitments. Etzioni suggests that in most cases the strictly self-interested 'rational' decision is inhibited by moral commitments of the individual to what seems 'fair' or 'right' or 'appropriate.' Individuals struggle to find a balance between these two separate, and often incompatible, bases of valuation. In this paradigm, emotions and values, 'shape to a significant extent the information that is gathered, the ways it is processed, the inferences that are drawn, the options that are being considered and the options that are finally chosen' (Etzioni, 1988: 94).

It is in the context of such 'messy' social transactions that the venture manager sets out to secure the resources needed to start the business. This is not to suggest that social transactions do not pervade other facets of business endeavor. What we shall argue below is that entrepreneurs and some intrapreneurs are particularly skilled at using social transactions to parsimoniously secure start-up resources, that this capability is particularly beneficial to the start-up and therefore deserves specific study.

NEW VENTURE START-UPS AND SOCIAL TRANSACTIONS

In the formative stage a new venture is no more than a commercial experiment; a set of assumptions or hypotheses about market needs, product specifications, resource availability and production, and organizational capabilities that needs to be tested by practice (Block and MacMillan, 1985). Since venture managers rarely possess all the resources and capabilities required to seize an opportunity, the vital entrepreneurial task of assembling the resources is often a 'trial-and-error' process because the exact resources that will be needed are unknown. Given the uncertainty, the resource constraints and the survival challenges inherent in new ventures, venture managers must seek 'asset parsimony,' deploying the minimum assets needed to achieve the desired business results and securing the resources to do this at minimum cost (Ansoff, 1979; Hambrick and MacMillan, 1984; Stevenson and Gumpert, 1985; Spann and Hudson, 1988).

As a result, both corporate and independent entrepreneurs build ventures that use intensely cooperative strategies, primarily by employing social transactions to secure the instrumental results they seek (Barnard, 1938; Lin, 1982; Coleman, 1988). Accounts of entrepreneurial activity in established corporations resound with tales of skunkworks, horsetrading, tincupping and resourceful bootstrapping. Corporate intra-preneurs corral resources, steal personnel time, appropriate materials, conceal development activities, and curry personal favors to secure the resources needed for their new ventures (Quinn, 1979; Kanter, 1983, 1988). Champions of new businesses mobilize informal, multifunctional, loosely structured networks of organizational and extra-organizational members to provide resources and support (Schon, 1967; Quinn, 1979; Maidique. 1980; Burgelman, 1983; Hutt, Reingen, and Ronchetto, 1988). Similarly, pre-vious working relationships, voluntary connec-tions, and kinship and community ties lay the groundwork for independent new ventures (MacMillan, 1983; Birley, 1985; Johannisson, 1987b).

Thus there is ample evidence from these studies that social transactions play a critical role in the acquisition of venture resources. Our interest lies in how this happens, in what resources the venture manager procures using social transactions, in how the venture manager goes about securing such resources so parsimoniously, in why the owners or fiduciaries of these resources are prepared to release them. Our objective is to open up these issues and lay out some preliminary findings that will hopefully spur further studies of these questions.

Two cases, one about a Cuban American in the United States, the second about a Swedish venture manager in a European miniconglomer-ate, illustrate social transactions at work in securing resources. Both of these cases will be used to illustrate a number of points throughout the remainder of the paper.

The Cuban American entrepreneur, starting a men's clothing import business from Brazil, needed to establish credibility with his Manhattan buyers. He identified a friend of his from business school who had just expanded, and moved into new offices on Fifth Avenue. They had extra office space in anticipation of growth. He persuaded his friend to rent him a piece of the office at far lower than the market rate rental prices. In addition, he persuaded the company to give him a telephone line which was answered by their receptionist. He used their secretary for typing, their delivery van, xerox machine, and computer equipment. He agreed to pay pro-rata for all the office equipment and personnel that he used. He received permission to use their conference room as well. Every time buyers came around, he rushed his samples from the basement downstairs and assembled the display in the conference room so that it looked as if it were an ongoing permanent display. Once the buyers left he dismantled his displays and returned the conference room to its original condition. This went on for about 6 months. Although he had originally offered to pay pro-rata for all the resources that he used each week, whenever he offered to settle up his account his friend told him to forget about it. The arrangement not only enabled the entrepreneur to save thousands of dollars of fixed expenses, but gave him access to resources that he could never have afforded as a start-up company.

Such imaginative resource acquisition strategies are not the sole realm of the independent entrepreneur.

Consider the case of a Swedish miniconglomerate that has started 30 businesses in the past decade. One of the venture managers in this conglomerate builds new businesses by deliberately cultivating a network of consultants and a network of university professors, and consciously using them to aid in the start-up of his new ventures. He learned from one of his consultant colleagues that in the foundry industry in Sweden there were serious problems with labor and automation. No sane Swede wanted to work in a foundry because of the poor operating conditions—dust, grit, heat, and humidity. The problem could not be exported, because foundry goods are so heavy that the transportaton costs/price ratio is not economical. Conventional automated equipment would not work under these operating conditions either, and none of the manufacturers were prepared to create a special line just for the foundries. The venture manager took this strategic problem into his network and asked his consultants to find out if this was a problem in the rest of Europe. The consultants in his network started to ask others in their networks to find the answer and provide the market information. The word came back through the network that a lot of foundries in northern Europe are having this problem. He then went into his second network, an extensive network of engineering professors and found one group with the technology that could solve this problem. It was not very difficult, but they needed $250,000 to develop a prototype. So he returned to his consultant network and accompanied each of the consultants on a visit to their foundry clients. To each client he said, 'I want to develop a piece of equipment for you. Here is your consultant, who will vouch for my credibility and reputation. From you I ask $10,000, which is less than you will pay for a secretary in this company. I shall collect $10,000 from a number of foundries in Europe to develop the prototype that will solve your problems.' Without giving any foundry a piece of the action he easily raised more than enough funds to develop the prototype. By using social networks he was able to fund the venture without spending any of his own capital. In addition, he uniquely positioned the product with the foundry managers by having them buy into the prototype development, and more importantly to buy into the lengthy and expensive process of *helping him debug the prototype in their production systems.*

The case of these two venture managers, one an independent and one a 'professional' intrapreneur, illustrate a certain type of venture manager, a type that secures critical resources at low to zero cost, using social transactions, rather than economic exchange. There are many others like these two venture managers. However, there are also many corporate venture managers that do not resort to such social transaction approaches, preferring, or resorting out of igno-

rance, to 'pay full fare' for the resources that they need—thus following the approach of the traditional administrative manager (Stevenson and Gumpert, 1985).

We argue that there are benefits to studying those who pursue a social transaction perspective, as evidenced by the two cases above. In order to clarify the contribution of this perspective and specifically highlight *its relevance for corporate venturing*, we will in the course of the paper develop a series of formal testable propositions, starting with the first below that is purely definitional, but systematically developing others that relate social transaction-oriented behavior with corporate venture performance.

Proposition 1: In any large sample of corporate ventures, the resource acquisition behavior of the venture managers will fall along a spectrum ranging from 'strictly administrative' at one extreme to 'strictly social transaction-oriented' at the other extreme.

This proposition allows us to posit two types of venture manager—an 'administrative' venture manager who favors economic exchanges at full fare and a 'social transactions-oriented' (STO) manager who favors social exchanges that capture resources at reduced fare.

In propositions 8 and 9 below, after we have explored the behavior of STO venture managers more fully, we will provide behavioral yardsticks for categorizing venture managers into these two groups.

Turning now to a discussion of the two case vignettes, the first observation we would like to make is that in both cases *cooptation* laid the groundwork for successful resource acquisition. A college chum provided prestigious office space, necessary equipment, and absorbed the administrative overhead, for free! A network of consultants and professors willingly functioned as the marketing and research and development departments. In both cases, participants consciously and willingly allowed the venture manager to coopt vital resources at well below market cost. In both cases the participants' active cooperation in this cooptation process was evident. The research issue that flows from this is what patterns of cooptation are prevalent, and why the participants allow cooptation to take place at all. These are discussed next.

RESOURCE ACQUISITION VIA COOPTATION

Cooptation is one of the most flexible and easiest mechanisms for gaining access to resources, exchanging information, exercising influence, developing interfirm commitments, avoiding conflicts and establishing legitimacy (Selznick, 1948, 1949; Thompson, 1967; Pfeffer and Salancik, 1979; Burt, 1980, 1983).

In the above cases at least two major types of cooptation took place: coopting legitimacy and coopting underutilized goods. These are common types of cooptation secured through social transactions.

Coopting legitimacy

Legitimacy, the institutional support of powerful external actors, is often a critical ingredient for new venture success because of the 'liabilities of newness' (Stinchcombe, 1965; Aldrich and Auster, 1986; Singh, Tucker, and Meinhard, forthcoming). Because the venture has no track record, there is a (justifiable) lack of confidence on the part of customers, distributors, and suppliers that the venture will survive and therefore little reason to provide patronage. Given the propensity for firms to terminate corporate ventures, there are even insiders who question the legitimacy of the corporate venture. Thus the venture faces a credibility crisis, and has somehow to create an impression of viability and legitimacy before it will receive support. Building legitimacy by systematically building a reluctant customer and distributor base can be an extremely slow, painstaking, and therefore costly process.

Our observation is that STO venture managers coopt legitimacy, rather than build it, and they do it in two ways: by association and by endorsement.

By capitalizing on his college friendship, the Cuban American entrepreneur obtained a Fifth Avenue address which, by association, conveyed the image of a fashionable, sophisticated, and especially, reputable clothing business. This association communicated a credibility to his customers which was a critical factor in securing his first few orders.

The Swedish intrapreneur, on the other hand, was able to coopt legitimacy by securing the endorsement of the consultants, thus piggybacking on the credibility of the consultants with their clients. Without such an endorsement no sane foundry manager would likely have given up $10,000 for a 'paper' prototype. In another example:

> A young intrapreneur, charged with the creation of a synthetic filter cloth business in a very conservative customer industry, which had always used canvas cloth, managed to break through by securing an 'order' from the leading firm in the industry. In reality the deal was nothing more than an agreement with the leading firm to try the cloth and pay for it only after it had demonstrated superiority, a process that would take about eighteen months. However, the young intrapreneur persuaded the purchasing agent in the leading firm to provide him with an offical order for the trial batch. This official order was used to persuade other firms in the industry to buy the cloth. In the eyes of the lesser competitors the 'order' was a *de facto* endorsement of the product by the leading firm.

Without coopted legitimacy the business may not be able to start at all, or only be able to start after debilitating delays experienced while building credibility and after bearing the crippling costs associated with such delays.

We suggest that the venture manager is more likely to pursue strategies to coopt legitimacy and consequently more likely to secure legitimacy at lower cost than the administrative venture manager.

Proposition 2: STO venture managers will coopt legitimacy for their ventures more than administrative venture managers will.

Proposition 3. As a result of successfully coopting legitimacy, those corporate ventures started by STO managers that are entering new market areas will have: earlier customer acceptance; earlier distributor acceptance; and earlier revenue streams.

Coopting underutilized goods

The other cooptation achieved in the case vignettes was cooptation of goods underutilized by others. This is in keeping with the literature—entrepreneurs are those who identify new uses for goods and services that are being underutilized

84   *J. A. Starr and I. C. MacMillan*

by others (Schumpeter, 1934; Kirzner, 1973, 1979; Casson, 1982). From our analysis of the works of Kanter (1983, 1988), Burgelman and Sayles (1986) and many case examples, there appear to be four major classes of cooptation strategies for taking advantage of underutilized resources, each with distinct characteristics that have to do with permanence of ownership of the resource and the perceived value of the resource in the eyes of the original owner. These strategies are: begging, borrowing, scavenging and amplifying.

Borrowing strategies are used to secure, temporarily or periodically, the use of assets or other resources, under the premise that they will eventually be returned. In our case vignettes the Cuban American entrepreneur's use of the delivery van illustrates this approach.

> A corporate intrapreneur who grew his division tenfold in a decade is even more aggressive in his 'borrowing.' He often tells his people to charge the early expenses for their new projects to accounts of other divisions of his firm. He has found that it takes at least a year before the corporate auditors discover the charges, and by that time the project has usually generated the revenues to repay those accounts.

Begging strategies secure resources appealing to the charity, honor, or goodwill of the owner of the resources. In this way venture managers gain access to the resources without needing to return them, despite the fact that the owner recognizes the assets have a value. The Cuban American entrepreneur obtained the use of the typist's time, computer equipment, and telephone lines using this method. Kanter (1983), in her research, identifies many cases of 'tincupping' where intrapreneurs beg or scrounge resources from the rest of the firm.

Scavenging strategies extract usage from goods that others eschew or do not intend to use.

> One venture manager needed catalogs of buyers for her mail-order business. While these are commercially available, they are very expensive. Using her charm and ability to make friends, this venture manager convinced one of the big firms who repurchase these catalogs annually to give her their old catalogs. Since only 10 percent of the addresses change every year, she recycled the old catalogs with only 10 percent error, and saved herself precious funds that could be deployed elsewhere for fledgling start-up.

In a similar vein a major business information firm which has grown profits fifty-fold via intrapreneuring has created several lucrative businesses simply by repackaging former online information into print form and selling it to new sets of customers who want cheaper, less timely information.

Amplifying, the fourth strategy, is exemplified by the Cuban American's use of his friend's conference room as an 'instant' permanent display. Amplification is the capacity to lever far more value out of an asset than is perceived by the original owner of the asset. It is a phenomenon that is particularly important in societies which are desperately poor, or firms that are in dire circumstances, and thus deserves considerable more study.

These four strategies of resource cooptation allow the entrepreneur to secure resources that would otherwise have to be secured by economic exchange at much greater cost. There are three critical implications of this: by appropriating underutilized resources venture managers reduce the *cost* of start-up, they reduce the *risk* of start-up by dramatically bringing down the initial investment, and they increase the return on assets of the venture (by reducing the denominator of ROA).

Proposition 4: STO venture managers will coopt more underutilized assets than administrative venture managers.

Proposition 5: As a result of resource and asset cooptation, STO venture managers will: suffer fewer resource setbacks and disappointments; suffer fewer resource shortages; have ventures with lower asset intensity; have ventures with lower fixed cost/revenue ratios; achieve cash and profit breakeven in shorter time; have greater survival rates; and have greater return on assets.

We do not claim that we have identified the full array of characteristics and mechanisms of coopting underutilized goods. Rather we have tried to demonstrate

1. that resource cooptation can dramatically influence the viability and performance of the venture;
2. that such cooptation is intimately linked to social transactions;

3. that there appear to be clearly different classes of cooptation, each with distinct characteristics.

We make no claim that we have identified all the possible classes of social assets, or the distinguishing characteristics of these assets—this should be the topic of more research, if we acknowledge the potential importance of cooptation to venture performance.

The key puzzle which arises from the above examples is why should any owner of an underutilized good be party to such cooptation?

SOCIAL CONTRACTING AND SOCIAL ASSETS

We suggest that resource cooptation is often the result of a process of social contracting whereby the venture managers exploit certain 'social assets' they possess. These social assets are a set of obligations, expectations, and mutually developed norms and sanctions which evolved from prior social interactions (Lin, 1982; Coleman, 1988). By 'social contracting' the venture manager 'cashes in' on the patterns of expectations, norms, and governance structures built out of these past relationships (Barnard, 1938; Zucker, 1983; Johannisson, 1987b).

In such *social* contracts the goods and services the venture manager needs are implicitly 'traded' for social commitments: favors are extracted or obligations are built (Homans, 1958, 1961; Blau, 1964). While the mental records may be ambiguous, each party knows that at some time in the future, on a completely different and totally unspecified transaction, the initial provider of the resource may ask a favor, recalling his 'loan' or 'cashing in' the obligation.

In our analysis of such social contracting between STO venture managers and owners of the resources needed by these managers, we observed a number of distinct types of social assets. These assets appear to lie along a spectrum that has to do with two distinguishing characteristics: (1) how formal the recognition is by both parties that a social 'debt' is owed; (2) the cost of 'maintaining' the asset.

At the one extreme of this spectrum lies *friendship*. Friendship is a social asset that can be used over and over again without exhausting the account or building a sense of indebtedness

(Ben-Porath, 1980). The act of helping a friend in need may even reinforce the friendship itself, so the asset could be used many times in different ways. As in the case of the Cuban American entrepreneur, friends may gladly give or lend assets, and actually derive pleasure from doing so. Allowing a friend to provide assistance may even deepen the friendship. However, friendship is rare, and to develop close friendships takes much nurturing and maintenance, so there are limited opportunities to deliberately construct these social assets (Gabarro, 1987).

Liking is less intense than friendship, but some of the same characterisics apply. However, there is less spontaneity of giving and more need for an accounting of the levels of favors and obligations owed or discharged with each transaction. The important thing about liking and friendship is that, within reason, they both are repeatedly deployable, and may even increase with usage as opposed to being discharged.

Gratitude is a case where there is some unspoken recognition that a favor may be repaid in the future, that the debt of gratitude may be discharged by the return of the favor if the occasion arises. It is much easier to generate gratitude than to generate liking or friendship, and this social asset does not require maintenance, whereas liking and particularly friendship requires maintenance.

In the case of *trust* we have a neutral point, where favors are granted, but these social transactions are more formally recognized as favors which must be returned some day. The favor is granted with the knowledge that the favor will eventually be returned. The role of trust in these transactions is to reduce the uncertainty that an appropriate repayment will take place in the future (Granovetter, 1985; Williamson, 1985; Zucker, 1986; Etzioni, 1988).

At the other end of the spectrum is *obligation*. With the building of obligation there is a clear, mutually perceived understanding that a debt is being incurred, and clear expectations that a return of the favor is required to release the debtor from obligation (Homans, 1958; Blau, 1964). Obligation is earned and discharged much like a commodity, and is the closest to the tangible assets of the economic transaction.

Once again, we do not claim that the above listing of the social assets is exhaustive, nor do we claim that the characteristics of these assets are comprehensive. Rather we have tried to

86   *J. A. Starr and I. C. MacMillan*

demonstrate:

1. that the key to resource cooptation appears to lie in social contracting processes;
2. that in these social contracting processes access to the tangible assets needed to start the venture is exchanged for certain social assets;
3. that there appear to be distinctly different types of social assets with very different usage and maintenance implications.

We recognize that the usage of social assets is not unique to entrepreneurs and new ventures—the use of interpersonal exchange is as ubiquitous in everyday life as the use of cash and credit in economic exchange. However, given their start-up challenges, venture managers typically do not have formal access to sources of power, authority, and influence, and must rely more heavily on the tactics described here to obtain the resources they need (Starr, 1989; Cohen and Bradford, 1990). Therefore we suggest that the study of social contracting and social assets is especially important in the context of corporate venturing.

> *Proposition 6:   STO ventures managers will, prior to the launch of the venture, have built more social assets in the form of friendship, liking, gratitude, trust and obligation than administrative managers.*
> *Proposition 7:   STO venture managers will make more use of social assets to procure resources than would administrative managers.*

Venture managers are motivated to use social contracting strategies primarily because they see an opportunity to secure the resources they need to start their businesses. However, this form of contracting has other interesting advantages for the new venture. Since these resources are secured with vague, diffuse, implicit agreements with indefinite payback schedules, the future value of the current transaction is fuzzy, imprecise, and accountable only in the minds of the participants. As a result the terms of the 'debt' are usually flexible and postponable.

There are also dark sides to social contracting. There is the danger that differential 'record-keeping' and 'mental balances' by both parties could give rise to grave problems of, and disagreements over, false expectations. There is also no formal commitment, which raises the uncertainty of future 'payments,' or the possibilities of opportunistic behavior. A business built on social contracts which initially enable the entrepreneur to avoid extensive resource commitments may backfire, leading to the eventual loss of a valuable friendship, particularly if the business dealings created by the social contracts sour (Gabarro, 1987; Starr, 1989).

Despite these dangers of social contracting, venture managers seem willing to live with the potential negative aspects of social contracting for the benefits—the opportunity to create a new business.

We have identified some of the assets that underpin social contracts, and have discussed some of the reasons why entrepreneurs are motivated to use social contracting. However, unless these assets can be developed, the mere recognition of these strategies is of no use to the corporate venturer. The normative issue in this paper has to do with whether social assets can actually be developed.

Building an inventory of social assets

The development of social assets is not unique to the study of entrepreneurship (Walton and McKersie, 1969; Kotter, 1985). In their classic chapter on attitude structuring, Walton and McKersie document dozens of strategies for building social assets (Walton and McKersie, 1969). Rather than reiterating their comprehensive work here, we will summarize the key approaches they suggest that are used by entrepreneurs to build friendship, liking, trust, gratitude, or obligation. There appear to be at least four major types of strategies to build social assets.

1.   Sharing information

By sharing information the venture manager may be able to build up an inventory of social obligations or social affinities which can be "spent" at a future date. For example:

> A corporate entrepreneur saw an opportunity to connect two of his major suppliers while developing a new medical products business. One manufacturer, in the south, had cheap labor costs and good employee morale, but was nonetheless losing money due to lack of business. The other, in the north, had high labor costs

and an employee shortage. By introducing these two manufacturers the venture manager reduced the costs of one and increased the sales of the other. As a result of this information the venture manager received years of better service, special attention and better terms from both suppliers, which greatly facilitated the development of his new business venture.

2. Solving and receiving help with problems

Solving problems for someone is an obvious way of developing social assets such as liking, gratitude or obligation. For example:

An intrapreneur manager starting a new pump business for an engineering supply company was at a distinct disadvantage competing with several established manufacturers for a fairly large contract from a refinery. Fortunately, the venture manager discovered that the refinery manager was having a problem with a newly installed cooling-tower system. The venture manager suggested that the plant manager call one of his other customers who had solved a similar problem the week before. The plant manager called this customer and got a solution in minutes. As a result he was quite willing to give the contract to the venture manager. By exploiting his network and providing sorely needed information, the venture manager created feelings of gratitude that secured the sale.

Having your problems solved by another is a less obvious but equally successful strategy. People often develop an intense affinity or a high sense of responsibility for the people that they assist. Venture managers who seek and follow advice are often able to engage other types of support as well. Senior managers who have proffered advice become champions of the corporate venture they have advised, and individuals who have given advice may also offer endorsements, recommendations, or even funding.

A venture manager charged with developing a margarine business appealed to the contract manager of an engineering equipment supplier to help him with the design of a particularly difficult and expensive piece of plant. In the end the contract manager was aggressively helping the venture manager drive down the price of the entire contract. This included a recommendation to use some second-hand equipment that was being freed up in another job that the contract manager's firm was executing. The

contract manager eventually took great pride in the fact that he had helped reduce the price of his firm's contract by 40 percent.

3. Giving and receiving favors

This strategy operates similarly to solving and getting help with problems, which was described above.

4. Creating opportunities for people to demonstrate their skills and competence

By creating or seeking opportunities which enable individuals to display their abilities and to appear competent in front of others can engender considerable social goodwill. The Swedish intrapreneur consistently provided this service to his consultant network and, as a result, reaped the benefits from his investment in this network. This strategy works extremely well for new ventures inside organizations, as demonstrated by the management information intrapreneur we interviewed who increased profits 50-fold. He ascribed much of his success to a policy of 'always accept the blame yourself, always give credit to others.'

By investing time and attention to the above strategies it is possible to build a social asset base that becomes the foundation for using the resource cooptation strategies discussed earlier.

Proposition 8: STO venture managers will, both prior to the venture and during the resource acquisition phase, spend more time than administrative venture managers on: sharing information with others, both inside and outside the firm; solving problems for others, both inside and outside the firm; seeking help on problems, both inside and outside the firm; giving and receiving favors, both inside and outside the firm; creating opportunities for others to demonstrate their competence.

Proposition 9: In contrast, administrative venture managers will spend more time than STO venture managers on: detailed budgeting and a priori estimates of specific resource needs; detailed and a priori specific resource planning; formally applying for resources; monitoring

88   *J. A. Starr and I. C. MacMillan*

*and accounting for resource utilization; using
'official' corporate resources; using conventional vendors and distributors; attempting to
adhere strictly to plan.*

Social assets, once developed, can be further
leveraged by building them into networks.

Building and utilizing networks

The network analysis literature has contributed
much to our understanding of the general
structure of social networks (Granovetter, 1973;
Tichy, Tushman, and Fombrun, 1979; Burt,
1980). Recent research has explored how social
networks might operate in the case of this
independent and corporate entrepreneur
(Granovetter, 1985; Aldrich, and Zimmer, 1986;
Mueller, 1986; Thorelli, 1986; Johannisson,
1987a,b; Aldrich, 1988; Jarillo, 1988; Hutt,
Reingen, and Ronchetto, 1988; Ring and Van -
de Ven, 1989; Hansen and Wortman, 1989). Use
of networks is commonplace among venture
managers. For instance, the Swedish intrapreneur
in our second vignette consciously and systematically nurtured several networks, two of which
(consultant and university) played a crucial role
in his robotics venture.

Leveraging networks

Furthermore, entrepreneurs can use networks to
leverage their social asset base by drawing
on the networks of *their* network contacts
(Granovetter, 1973; Aldrich and Zimmer, 1986;
Aldrich, 1988). The Swedish intrapreneur piggy-
backed on his consultants' networks to establish,
through their many contacts, the scope of the
market he was considering entering. This saved
him significant market research expenditures.

> *Proposition 10: STO venture managers will,
> both prior to the venture and during the
> resource acquisition phase, spend more time
> than administrative venture managers on build-
> ing, nurturing, and maintaining internal and
> external networks.*

> *Proposition 11: Corporate ventures managed
> by STO venture managers will be characterized
> by: broader and richer networks, both inside
> and outside the firm; greater stakeholder com-*

*mitment; more pervasive, positive sentiments
towards the venture; as a result of the above,
there will be more tolerance and forgiveness
for early setbacks, from both inside and outside
the firm; as a result of the above, there will
also be a greater willingness to help with
problems, from people both inside and outside
the firm.*

So far we have identified that social contracting
does influence start-ups, that it can be useful in
obtaining resources for start-ups, that this is
possible by deploying social assets, and that
these assets can be consciously developed. There
remains a final puzzle—why do corporate entrepreneurs seem less inclined and able to use STO
approaches in their efforts to start their business?

CORPORATE CONSTRAINTS ON STO BEHAVIOR

We now examine some of the reasons why only
a few intrapreneurs elect to pursue the STO
strategies of their independent entrepreneurial
counterparts. In general, corporate venturers
(and resource-constrained established firms in
general, i.e. organizations in decline) have more
difficulty using resource cooptation and social
contracting strategies than their independent
counterparts. Although corporate venturers have
a potentially extensive internal organizational
network of resources and many do make use of
them, there are also constraints on corporate
entrepreneurs which make it difficult to take
full advantage of intra- and interorganizational
network resources.

Established organizations do not have an asset parsimonious mindset

They often take too much time, overplan, and
overstaff; rather than make rapid small-chunk,
spontaneous commitments. This organizational
overkill can be hazardous to fragile new ventures,
where timing, action, and social interaction are
critical. Further, social network resources are
'soft,' affective, and emotionally charged, with
uncertain tangible value. The typical corporate
culture creates significant pressures to 'look'
organized, calculating, certain, and rational rather
than tolerating experimental, exploratory, and

emotional behavior (Dougherty, 1987). In order to 'keep up appearances,' excessive resources may be deployed. While independent entrepreneurs often err on the side of the casual, corporate entrepreneurs may be burdened with demands for formality, or actually be conditioned by the firm to eschew informal, unstructured agreements and commitments.

As Kanter suggests, to innovate there must be resources 'between the cracks' of the system and a means to access them (Kanter, 1983). But slack is in the mind of the beholder—managers may be conditioned to see resources in only one way, and will see them in no other way. So they are conditioned by their corporate experience to be incapable of amplifying, and trained to look with disfavor on begging, borrowing, or scavenging.

With a frugal investment strategy, STO venture managers are able to come out damaged but intact. Administrative managers facing a failing venture with high investment may be driven to escalation of commitment ('double their bets'), making it ever more difficult to exit, especially in firms which are unforgiving of failure.

Management procedures and techniques for established businesses are inappropriately enforced on new ventures

Established firms revere accomplishment of plans (Block and MacMillan, 1985), yet it is virtually impossible to 'plan' building social assets or exploiting underutilized resources. There is an organizational mindset that renders rapid reactive mutual adjustments based on social contracting agreements incomprehensible to the organizational beholder. Corporate entrepreneurs may be constrained by organizational policies which rigidly prescribe usage of the firm's existing resources. Resources available in the firm, particularly human resources, may not be appropriate, but corporate venturers feel obligated or compelled by the firm to use them. Alternatively, because they have access to these resources they do not conduct an opportunistic search for more applicable resources outside the firm. Therefore, corporate venturers spend time trying to adapt existing, inappropriate resources within the firm to the new business, rather than having the opportunity to go outside the firm on an informal basis to try to get those resources which are appropriate to the new venture. The prescribed

resources which are used may be 'taxed' with full cost accounting and charged for overheads the ventures really do not need or use and cannot afford.

Corporate entrepreneurs are not allowed to bend and break rules

Levels of accountability, likelihood of detection, and penalities for breaking the rules are greater for corporate entrepreneurs.

Implementation of interorganizational relationships is critical but often unplannable

Rational strategic planning techniques rarely recognize the realities of managing interorganizational collaborative efforts, which rely on interpersonal interactions which are dominated by trust, empathy, and personal feelings rather than contracts and formal agreements.

Intrapreneurs need time to build social assets and to develop networks

To tap network resources requires time and imagination, which may be in limited supply to corporate entrepreneurs. Time is the ultimate substitute for capital. Corporate venturers complain about the difficulties of getting staff time allocated and budgeted to new business development (Dougherty, 1987). Even when time is allocated, people may be distracted by other organizational demands which interrupt the concentrated effort and freedom to participate in cross-functional and interorganizational exchanges. In contrast, some independent entrepreneurs we interviewed remarked on experiencing unstructured time, which is inherent in the new venture process. Entrepreneurs are able to capitalize on this time availability to focus their imagination on social asset building and to develop networks of resources.

It is important to note that the above barriers are largely attributable to the climate, structure, and culture of the firm. Ultimately these barriers stem from the behavior of senior management and the systems that they put in place. This places a significant challenge on top management to find ways to break down the bureaucratic barriers to STO behavior when corporate ventures

90   *J. A. Starr and I. C. MacMillan*

are under way, or these barriers seriously
compromise chances of success.

In the light of the above difficulties and
obstacles to using STO strategies inside the firm,
it is not surprising that STO behavior is less
frequent than the more 'conventional' administrative type of behavior one encounters in firms,
particularly because, in the management of the
firm's *ongoing* operations, there is typically little
need for STO resource acquisition strategies.
However, as we have already mentioned, we
have ample evidence in the study of Weiss (1981)
that, compared to the independent entrepreneur,
firms are particularly poor at corporate start-ups.
We suggest that the discouragement of STO
behavior is partially responsible. Firms insist on
behavior that is not parsimonious, and with the
exception of the relatively rare STO intrapreneurs
observed in the work of Burgelman and Kanter,
and in our sample, most corporate ventures are
started by managers who handicap the venture
with the burden of fully priced assets and the
full fixed costs associated with an ongoing
business. It is small wonder, then, that the track
record of corporate ventures is so inferior to that
of the independent startups.

CONCLUSION

We set out to argue that in the case of corporate
ventures there is a real need to use a social
transaction lens for studying the resource acquisitions needed for start-up. The article has
highlighted the fact that social as well as economic
processes can be very important in securing two
types of support for the fledgling start-up—
securing legitimacy and securing resources. There
are surely other types of support worth identifying. The analysis suggests that such support is
secured by social contracting, using social assets
such as obligation, trust, gratitude, liking, and
friendship. This allows the venture manager to
secure resources at a lower cost than rational
economic exchange would permit. Further
research should be devoted to enhancing our
understanding of the characteristics of these and
other social assets. We need to begin untangling
the subtleties that distinguish these assets from
one another, and how each is used in social
contracting. The analysis drew from extant
literature on attitude structuring to show that it
is possible to build such assets and leverage

them via network building, demonstrating that
deliberate social asset building strategies are
feasible for both corporate venturing and independent start-ups. Further research can begin to
identify the full gamut of ways to build social
assets. Finally we discussed some of the reasons
why some corporate entrepreneurs may have
difficulty in using potentially valuable social
contracting principles in starting their ventures.
This opens the way to further research on how
to reduce these barriers.

ACKNOWLEDGEMENT

The comments of two anonymous reviewers are
greatly appreciated.

REFERENCES

Aldrich, H. 'I heard it through the grapevine: Network-
    ing among women entrepreneurs', National Sym-
    posium on Women Entrepreneurs. Baldwin-Wallace
    College, 7–9 April, 1988.
Aldrich, H. and E. Auster. 'Even dwarfs started small:
    Liabilities of age and size and their strategic
    implications', *Research in Organizational Behavior*,
    8, 1986, pp. 165–198.
Aldrich, H. and C. Zimmer. 'Entrepreneurship
    through social networks'. In D. Sexton and
    R. Smilor (eds), *The Art and Science of Entrepre-
    neurship*, Ballinger, Cambridge, MA, 1986,
    pp. 3–24.
Allison, G. *Essence of Decision*. Little, Brown, Boston,
    MA, 1971.
Ansoff, I. 'The changing shape of the strategic
    problem'. In D. Schendel and C. Hofer (eds),
    *Strategic Management: A New View of Business
    Policy and Planning*, Little, Brown, Boston, MA,
    1979, pp. 30–44.
Barnard, C. *Functions of the Executive*. Harvard
    University Press, Cambridge, MA, 1938.
Ben-Porath, Y. 'The F-connection: Families, friends
    and firms and the organization of exchange',
    Population and Development Review, **6**, March,
    1980, pp. 1–30.
Birley, S. 'The role of networks in the entrepreneurial
    process', *Journal of Business Venturing*, **1**, 1985,
    pp. 107–117.
Blau, P. *Exchange and Power in Social Life*. John
    Wiley, New York, 1964.
Block, Z. and I. C. MacMillan. 'Milestones for suc-
    cessful venture planning', *Harvard Business Review*,
    5, (September–October), 1985, pp. 184–197.
Burgelman, R. 'Corporate entrepreneurship and stra-
    tegic management: Insights from a process study',

Management Science. **29**(12), 1983, pp. 1349–1364.

Burgelman, R. and L. Sayles. *Inside Corporate Innovation*. Free Press, New York, 1986.

Burt, R. *Toward a Structural Theory of Action: Network Models of Social Structure, Perception and Action*. Academic Press, New York, 1980.

Burt, R. *Corporate Profits and Cooptation*. Academic Press, New York, 1983.

Casson, M. *The Entrepreneur*. Barnes & Noble, Totowa, NJ, 1982.

Cohen, A. and D. Bradford. *Influence without Authority*. John Wiley, New York, 1990.

Coleman, J. 'Social capital in the creation of human capital', *American Journal of Sociology* **94** (Suppl.), 1988, pp. S95–S120.

Cyert, R. and J. March. *A Behavioral Theory of the Firm*. Prentice-Hall, Englewood Cliffs, NJ, 1963.

Dougherty, D. 'New product development: Managing the merger of technological possibilities and market potentials.' Work-In-Progress, The Wharton School, University of Pennsylvania, 1987.

Etzioni, A. 'Entrepreneurship, adaptation and legitimation, *Journal of Economic Behavior and Organization*, **8**, 1986, pp. 175–189.

Etzioni, A. *The Moral Dimension: Toward a New Economics*. Free Press, New York, 1988.

Gabarro, J. 'The development of working relationships'. In J. Lorsch (ed.), *Handbook of Organizational Behavior*. Prentice-Hall, Englewood Cliffs, NJ, 1987.

Granovetter, M. 'The strength of weak ties', *American Journal of Sociology*, **78**, 1973, pp. 1360–1380.

Granovetter, M. 'Economic action and social structure: The problem of embeddedness', *American Journal of Sociology* **91**(3), 1985, pp. 481–510.

Hambrick, D. and I. MacMillan. 'Asset parsimony—Managing assets to manage profits', *Sloan Management Review*, Winter 1984, pp. 67–74.

Hansen, E. and M. Wortman. 'Entrepreneurial networks: The organization *in vitro,*' *49th Academy of Management Proceedings*, Washington, DC, 1989.

Homans, G. *The Human Group*. Harcourt, Brace & Co., New York, 1950.

Homans, G. 'Social behavior as exchange', *American Journal of Sociology*, **62**, 1958, pp. 606–627.

Hutt, M., P. Reingen and J. Ronchetto. 'Tracing emergent processes in marketing strategy formation'. *Journal of Marketing* **52**, 1988, pp. 4–19.

Janis, I. and L. Mann. *Decision-making: A Psychological Analysis of Conflict, Choice and Commitment*. Free Press, New York, 1977.

Jarillo, J. C. 'On strategic networks', *Strategic Management Journal*, **9**, 1988, pp. 31–41.

Johannisson, B. 'Beyond process and structure: Social exchange networks'. *International Studies of Management and Organization*, **17**, 1987a, pp. 3–23.

Johannisson, B. 'Anarchists and organizers: Entrepreneurs in a network perspective', *International Studies of Management and Organization*, **17**, 1987b, pp. 49–63.

Kanter, R. M. *The Changemasters*. Simon & Schuster, New York, 1983.

Kanter, R. M. 'When a thousand flowers bloom:

Structural, collective and social conditions for innovation in organizations'. In B. Staw and L. Cummings (eds), *Research in Organizational Behavior*, JAI Press, Greenwich, CT, Vol. 10, 1988, pp. 169–211.

Kirzner, I. *Competition and Entrepreneurship*. University of Chicago Press, Chicago, IL, 1973.

Kirzner, I. *Perception, Opportunity and Entrepreneurship*. University of Chicago Press, Chicago, IL, 1979.

Kotter, J. *Power and Influence: Beyond Formal Authority*. Free Press, New York, 1985.

Lin, N. 'Social resources and instrumental action'. In P. Marsden and N. Lin (eds) *Social and Network Analysis*, Sage, Beverly Hills, CA, 1982, pp. 131–145.

MacMillan, I. *Strategy Formulation—Political Concepts*, West Publishing, St Paul, MN, 1979.

MacMillan, I. 'The politics of new venture management', *Harvard Business Review*, Nov.–Dec. 1983, pp. 4–8.

Mueller, R. *Corporate Networking*. Free Press, New York, 1986.

Narayanan, V. and L. Fahey. 'The micro-politics of strategy formulation', *Academy of Management Review*, **2**(1), 1982, pp. 25–34.

Pfeffer, J. and G. Salancik. *The External Control of Organizations: A Resource Dependence Perspective*. Harper & Row, New York, 1978.

Quinn, J. B. 'Technological innovation, entrepreneurship and strategy', *Sloan Management Review*, **20**, 1979, pp. 19–30.

Quinn, J. B. *Strategies for Change: Logical Incrementalism*. Irwin, Homewood, Il, 1980.

Ring, P. and A. Van de Ven. 'Formal and informal dimensions of transactions'. In A. Van de Ven, H. Angle and R. S. Poole (eds), *Research on the Management of the Innovation*, Ballinger, Cambridge, MA, 1989, pp. 171–192.

Schon, D. *Technology and Change*. Delacorte, New York, 1967.

Schumpeter, J. *The Theory of Economic Development*. Harvard University Press, Cambridge, MA, 1934.

Selznick, P. 'Foundations of the theory of organizations', *American Sociological Review*, **13**, 1948, pp. 25–35.

Selznick, P. *TVA and the Grass Roots*, University of California Press, Berkeley, CA, 1949.

Singh, J., D. Tucker and A. Meinhard. 'Institutional change and ecological dynamics'. In W. Powell and P. DiMaggio (eds), *The New Institutionalism in Organizational Analysis*. University of Chicago Press, Chicago, IL, Forthcoming.

Spann, M. and R. Hudson. 'Resource acquisition by entrepreneurial firms: Another look'. University of Tennessee, Department of Management, 1988.

Starr, J. 'Powers of the powerless: A comparison of interorganizational power and influence tactics of entrepreneurs and non-entrepreneurs'. Working Paper, The Wharton School, University of Pennsylvania, 1989.

Stevenson, H. and D. Gumpert. 'The heart of entrepreneurship', *Harvard Business Review*,

92   *J. A. Starr and I. C. MacMillan*

March–April 1985. pp. 85–94.

Stinchcombe, A. 'Social structure and organizations'. In J. March (ed.), *Handbook of Organizations*, Rand McNally, Chicago, IL, 1965, pp. 142–193.

Swedberg, R. 'Economic sociology: Past and present'. *Current Sociology*, **35**(1), 1987, pp. 1–221.

Thompson, J. *Organizations in Action*, McGraw-Hill, New York, 1967.

Thorelli, H. 'Networks: Between markets and hierarchies'. *Strategic Management Journal*, **7**, 1986, pp. 37–51.

Tichy, N., M. Tushman and C. Fombrun. 'Social network analysis for organizations', *Academy of Management Review*, **4**, 1979, pp. 507–519.

Walton, R. and R. McKersie. *A Behavioral Theory of Labor Negotiations*, McGraw-Hill, New York, 1969.

Weiss, L. 'Start-Up businesses: A comparison of peformance', *Sloan Management Review*, Fall, 1981, pp. 37–53.

Williamson, O. *The Economic Institutions of Capitalism*, Free Press, New York, 1985.

Zucker, L. 'Organizations as institutions', *Research in the Sociology of Organizations*, **2**, 1983, pp. 1–47.

Zucker, L. 'The production of trust: Institutional sources of economic structure, 1840–1920', *Research in Organizational Behavior*, **8**, 1986, pp. 53–111.

Part IV
Networks

[16]

THE ROLE OF
NETWORKS IN THE
ENTREPRENEURIAL PROCESS

SUE BIRLEY
Cranfield School of Management

EXECUTIVE SUMMARY

The extent to which the entrepreneur interacts with the networks in his local environment during the process of starting a new firm was studied. This study was based on the premise that, during this process, he is seeking not only the resources of equipment, space, and money, but also advice, information, and reassurance. Consequently the help and guidance received from both the formal networks (banks, accountants, lawyers, SBA) and the informal networks (family, friends, business contacts) will influence the nature of the firm substantially.

The study was conducted in St. Joseph County, Indiana, a county that has experienced the same economic problems as many other towns in the midwest smoke-stack belt during the 1970s. In 1982, in response to this general decline in the business climate, a fund was raised to create and manage a new industrial strategy. Before this, there was no collective strategy for nurturing either the small firm or the new firm. Therefore, in order to determine the extent to which an interventionist strategy was appropriate, a research project was designed that posed three basic questions: what does the environment look like; does it need changing; and, if so, in what ways? This article reports part of that study—a survey of firms that had started in the county in the previous five years (1977–1982). It was concerned with two issues: the characteristics of the St.Joseph County entrepreneur and the usage of the formal and informal networks.

The results of the survey show that the aggregate characteristics of the St. Joseph County entrepreneur are similar to those found in other studies. The new firms were founded by local people from small firms who started their small firms in similar industries that were local in nature. Moreover, the majority (90%) not only started small, but also grew very little subsequently—firms that have been classified elsewhere as life-style ventures. It is to be expected that such people would have a strong local network, both formal and informal, particularly in a county with a population of only 220,000. However, the results of the second part of the study showed that the main sources of help in assembling

Address correspondence to: Sue Birley, 38 Ripplevale Grove, London NI, England.

Journal of Business Venturing 1, 107–117(1985)
© 1985 Elsevier Science Publishing Co., Inc., 52 Vanderbilt Avenue, New York, NY 10017

0883-9026/85/$03.30

the resources of raw materials, supplies, equipment, space, employees, and orders were the informal contacts of family, friends, and colleagues. The only institution that was mentioned with any regularity was the bank, which was approached towards the end of the process when many of the resources were assembled and the elements of the business set in the entrepreneur's mind. This was not because the formal sources were unwilling to offer guidance, but rather that the entrepreneur and his social network appeared to be unaware of what was available. Moreover, in using only business contacts, family, and friends, the entrepreneur was likely to re-create the elements of previous employment, even when he was starting business in an entirely new market. Further, there was no significant difference between growth and no-growth firms. It would appear that in this county, the formal network was uniformally inefficient.

This research shows that a major aim of the new strategy should be to increase the awareness of the community to the formal sources and types of help that are available. However, whilst most of the institutions are prepared to solve specific problems, they are not in the business of diagnosis or counseling. The network needs a hub or an enterprise office.

The data on the start-up process and the role of networks in relation to new firms are very sparse and often anecdotal. This study was conducted in one environment, a small midwest county with a jaded entrepreneurial tradition. Further studies are necessary. Research questions include the extent to which networking is crucial in the start-up process, the length of time it took for the sophisticated networks of Boston's Route 128 and California's Silicon Valley to develop, and the effect of different geographic, cultural, and economic conditions. Only in this way is it possible to determine the extent to which regional, regeneration strategies for new firm creation should be county specific rather than state or country wide.

A NY STRATEGY AIMED AT IMPROVING THE ENVIRONMENT FOR NEW FIRMS MUST, perforce, take into account the characteristics of the entrepreneur and his perceived needs. Moreover it must recognize that start-up is not a discrete event but a process that may take years to come to fruition. The strategy must, therefore, encompass not only the needs but also their timing. In the broadest sense, this leads to a discussion of economic, social, and educational environments, and is beyond the scope of this paper, except in the sense that they create the pool from which the entrepreneur emerges. Moreover, recent studies suggest that the characteristics that define the people in this pool define a wider group than simply the potential business owner and that there are two keys to understanding the supply of new firms. The first is in identifying the triggers that push the individual with the passive need to do his own thing into actively considering ownership. Such triggers are specific to the individual and to his environment. However, they all include an element of belief that it is possible to create a business out of an idea, skill, or product.

The second key, which is the focus of this article, is an understanding of the elements of this process of creation. It begins with a recognition that there may be many mechanisms by which an idea can be transformed into a business. For example, the manufacture of the product could be subcontracted, licensed, or brought in-house; the premises and equipment could be leased, rented, or purchased; the product could be sold through wholesalers, agents, an in-house sales force, or by mail-order; employees could be fulltime, part-time, or freelance; the strategy could be high growth or low growth. Each of these combinations will require different skills, resources, and timescales.

However, the entrepreneur is guided in his choices by two factors: his previous employment, which provides an initial role-model of the elements of a firm, and the advice and assistance he receives, which may enlarge his perceived options. So the process is iterative (see Fig. 1) with the entrepreneur seeking the following: information on what is

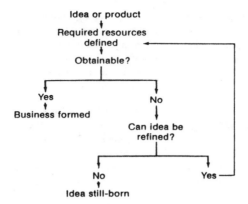

FIGURE 1 Idea still-born.

available; advice on how to best proceed; reassurance that it will work; and resources of equipment, space, and money.

It is during this process that the ability to build contacts and develop networks is fundamental. There are two networks on which he can draw: the formal and the informal. The formal includes all the local, state, and Federal agencies such as banks, accountants, lawyers, realtors, Chamber of Commerce, or the Small Business Administration (SBA). Because it is often seen as both expensive and time-consuming, all but the latter offer help to new firms as only a small part of their services. Moreover, in their interaction with the entrepreneur they are not usually in the business of diagnosing needs, but rather of satisfying them by responding to specific requests. The informal network includes family, friends, previous colleagues, or previous employers, a group which whilst it may be less informed about the options and schemes open to the entrepreneur, is more likely to be willing to listen and to give advice. Thus there are problems with both sources—the formal sources may or may not have their own established networks and may deter by their bureaucracy, and the informal may help to create a replica of previous employment. Nevertheless, both are important in helping the entrepreneur seek the optimum arrangement for his firm. The question posed in this study was the extent to which both were used by entrepreneur in assembling resources in a midwest county which, over the period studied, had suffered severe economic decline and had no new firm strategy.

PREVIOUS RESEARCH

The area of entrepreneurship that has recieved the most research attention is that of the characteristics and definition of the entrepreneur (Hull et al. 1980; Petrov 1980; Liles 1974). Classifications abound that range from those concerned with orientation (Cooper and Dunkelbery 1981; Carland et al. 1984), to those concerned with needs (Liles 1974), to those based upon industry (Webster 1977). Very rarely, however, is entrepreneurial skill itself defined other than as the process of creating a new business. Long (1983) defines it as "creative opportunism," a phrase that suggests an instinctive ability not only to recognize possibilities but also to make them happen. Combined with Vesper's (1983) findings that contacts are usually the main source of new firm ideas, this is an appealing definition. Indeed,

110 S. BIRLEY

MacMillan (1983) propounds the theory that building contacts and networks is the prime factor in determining the success of any firm. Beyond this, as Ambrose and Koepke (1984) note, the literature on networking in relation to small firms is very sparse. Vesper (1983) in his report on entrepreneurship and national policy refers to the need for adequate contacts and lists a number of formal "environmental helps," but comments that "just what stops a would-be entrepreneur from proceeding with a venture . . . has been given little or no formal study."

The literature on the entrepreneurial environment tends to concentrate upon the incubator organization, referring usually to the previous employment of the entrepreneur. Cooper (1981) summarizes the factors that relate the incubator to the entrepreneurial process as location, nature of business, type of organization, motivation, size, and team formation. The results of this and other studies conclude that entrepreneurs tend to come from smaller, for-profit organizations, and they tend to start similar businesses, in the same location, and with previous colleagues as partners. Clearly, for these firms, some form of local network is in place.

Beyond this, a few studies, notably those by Schell and Davig (1981), Bearse (1981), and Pennings (1982) have attempted to correlate community characteristics to the level of entrepreneurial activity. Each study isolated five distinct but different factors, all of which are quantifiable, for example, the proportion of immigrants (Pennings 1982), median family income (Schell and Davig 1981), or education levels (Bearse 1981). Bruno and Tyebjge (1982) suggest a further list, which concentrates on more subjective factors such as "favorable governmental policies." Building upon this, Schell (1983) proposes a model of community entrepreneurship, which refers to the role of both formal and informal networks in his components of "level of encouragement of entrepreneurship in the community by the macro-entrepreneurs" and "encouragement by Federal, state, and local government." He concludes his preliminary testing of this model by stating that the two most important research issues center around the relationship of the entrepreneurial pool of people to the power elite and the role of the informal venture capitalist in linking the entrepreneur to the power elite.

Thus research about the entrepreneurial process requires greater precision about the way in which the potential entrepreneur seeks to use the environment in creating the optimum business format out of his product idea. It is not merely that schemes should be created, but that they should be understood by those administering them and seen to be available by those wishing to use them.

BACKGROUND

This study was conducted in St. Joseph County in northern Indiana, and as is outlined in an earlier paper (Birley 1984) it may be viewed as reflecting in microcosm those patterns of unemployment and population shift experienced by most of the declining midwest states. It was in response to this general decline in business climate that a fund was raised by South Bend in 1982 (the main town in the county) to create and manage a new industrial strategy, called Project Future. There were three main goals: 1) to encourage existing companies to relocate within the area, or to open up new branches in the area; 2) to help existing firms to grow; and 3) to encourage the start-up of new firms.

Prior to 1982, there had been no collective small firm or new firm strategy in the area, and apart from an apparently dormant SBA branch office, little evident institutional activity. Moreover, whilst it was clear that entrepreneurs were active because new firms were evident, there were no data on the size or characteristics of the population nor of any difficulties encountered during the start-up phase. However, if the patterns discovered in studies elsewhere were repeated, entrepreneurs would be starting firms in industries related to their previous employment; in an area dominated by declining or failing engineering companies, this strategy could be a recipe for individual disaster. Therefore, before designing a strategy to improve the environment, it was first necessary to ask three questions: what does the environment look like; does it really need changing; and if so, in what ways? These questions formed the basis for the research, which was designed in two stages: stage 1—identification of population trends by studying all new firms started between 1977 and 1982 and analyzing their birth and death patterns, the industrial patterns, and job generation characteristics; and stage 2—questionnaire survey to those firms started during the period that had survived.

This paper deals with the results of stage 2. Stage 1 data are analyzed in earlier papers (Birley 1984a; 1984b). Three research questions were posited:

1. Would the St. Joseph County entrepreneur have similar characteristics to those found elsewhere? The factors studied included domestic environment, age, education, and previous job experience.
2. What was the extent of the usage of the formal and informal networks in the start-up process?
3. Was there any clustering of factors that discriminated between the use of formal and informal networks? In particular, would those companies starting in unfamiliar industries make more use of the formal networks?

RESEARCH METHODOLOGY

The major difficulty encountered in research into new firms is the lack of available reliable data. After exploring four possible sources—Dun and Bradstreet, Chamber of Commerce listings, the telephone directory, and Unemployment Security Statistics (ES202)—the latter was chosen as the most comprehensive. (For a full discussion of the reasons for this, see Birley 1984b.) A summary of the populations identified by three of the sources is seen in Table 1 below. The listings of the Chamber of Commerce were eliminated immediately because the nature of membership suggested a significant bias towards the larger firm or the professional firm.

TABLE 1 Number of New Firms by SIC Category (1977–1982)

	Data source		
SIC category[a]	ES202	Telephone directory	DMI files
Agriculture	22	20	1
Manufacturing	94	73	52
Service	479	407	31
Construction	153	97	14
Finance	97	69	6
Transport	61	37	6
Wholesale	a	a	23
Retail	a	a	70
Total	906	703	203

[a]Did not collect.

Unfortunately, the data on the ES202 listings does not include the address of the company and to preserve the integrity of the State sources, it was not made available. Therefore, for the purposes of the survey, company addresses were sought from the telephone directory, giving a population to be surveyed of 703 firms. Questionnaires were sent to all these firms, and 175 replies were received, of which 160 were usable.

The actual response rate is probably higher than the 25% shown here. In stage 1 of this research it was found that between 10% and 17% of firms in the county ceased trading during their first year, and a year had elapsed between collecting the data by ES202 and sending the questionnaire. Indeed, telephone interviews and visits to the premises indicated that a number of firms had already ceased trading. What was encouraging, however, was that the pattern of responses mirrored the distribution of SIC categories found in the original scan which gave the base population of 906 firms.

The questionnaire was designed as multiple choice for ease of completion, except for two questions that asked the entrepreneurs for reflections on their decision to start their own firms and upon the problems they encountered. It was piloted on a group of local small firm owners who did not participate in the survey. The results were analyzed using the SAS statistical analysis package.

THE RESULTS

The New Firm Characteristics

The aggregate pattern of entrepreneurial behavior in St. Joseph County was similar to that found in other studies (Gartner 1984; Cooper 1984). Thus it involved the following:

1. Local people—79% had lived in the county more than 10 years, with 39% having been born there.
2. From small companies—61% had previously worked in companies employing fewer than 100 people; only 9% were unemployed prior to starting.
3. Starting small companies—90% started with one or two employees, excluding the owners, and have subsequently grown very little.
4. In similar industries—66% had started a company that had some relationship to their previous employment, either as customer, competitor, or supplier.
5. Were local in nature—81% of customers were within a three-hour drive, with 51% being within St. Joseph County itself; 68% of all suppliers were within a three-hour drive.

Thus the process is essentially geographically constrained (see Fig. 2).

This process is very acceptable when the local economy is in balance, with the larger companies providing the necessary infrastructure for the new, small firms to start, survive,

FIGURE 2

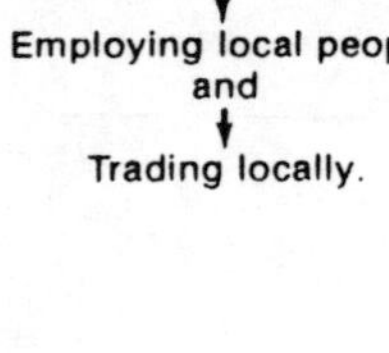

Local person
↓
Sets up small firm
↓
Employing local people
and
↓
Trading locally.

and grow. However, this was not the case in St. Joseph County, because over the period studied a number of key local firms both large and small had moved away, closed down, or contracted—a phenomenon seen in many "smoke-stack" areas in the US and Western Europe. Despite this, the pattern of firm births and deaths had remained consistent (Birley 1984a).

There were, nevertheless, a number of atypical firms, those that were either started by newcomers to the community, in specialist industry sectors, selling in wider markets, or growing. However, the results of subsequent multivariate analyses showed no apparent relationship between the factors described, with one exception. A small, but significant, number of service firms were started by people who had moved into the county in order to start their business. However, these firms were no larger, nor did they serve wider markets than the home-grown firms.

The Support Network

The main part of the study was concerned with the entrepreneur's use of networks: the extent to which he sought and received help from the various potential sources. If these were used currently, appropriately, and satisfactorily, the need for further systems would be questioned.

Available sources of help were listed and respondents were asked to rank the value of that source in assembling the resources of the firm. No ranking for a category indicated that as far as the entrepreneur was concerned, no help was received. The sources listed are shown in Table 2 as they were used in subsequent analysis. In the questionnaire not only were they mixed, but the order was changed for each question in order to prevent patterning by the respondent.

The results were startling. Despite the population of 220,000 St. Joseph County being relatively small, with a strong and active local community, the formal sources were hardly used. Table 3 lists those sources that were ranked as prime.

Whilst the start-up process is iterative, most entrepreneurs tentatively assemble the fixed costs of their business (group A) and identify potential revenue sources (group B) before seeking finance (group C). Dividing the data in this way highlights clear differences thus:

Informal contacts, mainly business contacts, are seen overall to be the most helpful in assembling the elements of the business.

Family and friends are the most useful where local issues are concerned, as with the seeking of location and employees. This applies to sales also and may explain in part the concentration upon local sales in most of the companies studied.

TABLE 2   Potential Sources of Help

Formal sources	Informal sources
Bank	Business contacts
Accountant	Other contacts
Lawyer	Family
Local government	Personal friends
Chamber of Commerce	
Realtor	
Small Business Administration	

114   S. BIRLEY

TABLE 3   Prime Source of Help: Number of Firms

	Formal sources	Informal sources			
		Contacts	Family or friends	Cold contact	No help
Group A					
Raw Materials/supplies	6	47	5	21	50
Equipment	16	75	7	27	35
Location/premises	7	64	35	40	14
Employees	5	57	34	39	25
Group B					
Sales	23	70	35	26	6
Group C					
Seeking finance	79	18	27	27	9
Finance source	53	6	79	7	15

The formal sources come to the fore when the elements of the firm are set and the entrepreneur is seeking to raise finance. It is hardly surprising, therefore, that the institution mentioned most of the time was the bank.

All other formal, declared sources of help, including the SBA, were mentioned on very few occasions.

However, these were the prime sources of help, not the sole source. It was expected that the efficient entrepreneur would seek help from a variety of sources in both types of network. Therefore, the primary, secondary, and tertiary ranked sources were weighted according to their ranks and a score computed for each type of resource needed. In only a few cases were more than three sources mentioned. The results are shown in Table 4. Using

TABLE 4   Sources of Help Ranked by Overall Usage

	Formal sources	Informal sources		
		Contacts	Family or friends	Cold contact
Group A				
Raw Materials/supplies	4	1	3	2
Equipment	3 =	1	3 =	2
Location/premises	4	1	3	2
Employees	4	1	3	2
Group B				
Sales	4	1	2	3
Group C				
Seeking finance	1	4	2	3
Finance source	2	3	1	4

sales as an example, the most used sources for help were the informal sources of business contacts, followed by family and friends. The least used were the formal sources.

These data further reinforce the reliance of the entrepreneur upon his network of informal contacts as a primary source of help when assembling the elements of his firm. Moreover, the second most used source was that of the cold contact, the direct approach. This involved, for example, newspaper advertisements for employees, mailshots, or letters to equipment manufacturers and raw material suppliers, and scanning the newspapers for available premises. Many of these activities could have been short-circuited had the formal network been approached earlier or used more.

We linked these results with those from the part of the survey that asked for the major difficulties encountered by the entrepreneur during the start-up process. Despite the form of an open-ended question, the overwhelming volume of replies concerned funding as the one area in which external help was most sought. Whilst it is not possible in this research to infer any causality for this, there are clues. The majority of the respondents came from skill-based or managerial backgrounds, but had little or no experience in finance. So the help that was sought was probably outside both their experience and their business contact network.

Multivariate analysis was conducted in an attempt to identify any patterns in the use of networks, but with one small exception, no significant patterns emerged. Those entrepreneurs who had moved into the area used and valued the services of the bank much more than those already living in the county. They did not, however, appear to have been subsequently fed into the local formal network when seeking the other resources of their business. Moreover, there was no significant difference between the growth and no-growth firms in any of the factors measured. It would appear that in this county, all types of entrepreneurs use their local networks in the same way.

CONCLUSION AND RECOMMENDATIONS

The data for this study were collected during a period when no strategy for encouraging the small firm sector existed. Each institution offered its normal services to all customers, but did not advertise any special help for small or new firms. Moreover, whilst in such a small community the formal system certainly had its own informal network, this was not promoted as a service to customers. Nevertheless, the formal and informal networks could be expected to be interlinked inextricably. It was from this base of nonintervention that the strategy for Project Future was to be formed: that strategy would include an objective of improving the supply of new firms in the area and of providing services that would support a healthier small firm sector. Ideally, the strategy would be focused on firms that were likely to survive and grow, and thus provide either more jobs or more wealth to the community.

This study was concerned with understanding the start-up process: the backgrounds of the people, the businesses they started, and the networks they used. Very clear results emerged. In St. Joseph County, firms tend to be started by local people using their own informal business and personal networks to form locally based firms.

The choice of networks is key in understanding the nature of the subsequent firm, because it is during the start-up process that the elements of the firm are set. Decisions are made upon what type of resources to use, sources for them, and what size the firm should be. In using only his business contacts and family, the entrepreneur is likely to re-create the elements of previous employment, even when he may be starting a business in a different market. Thus he may, for example, be unaware of leasing, or employing people on a freelance basis, or the need for manual rather than computer-based control systems. Moreover, in seeking his resources, the entrepreneur is, albeit subconsciously, seeking reassurance that the decisions are correct and the business viable. Whilst the informal contacts may be able to provide support, they may not be qualified to provide an unbiased judgement.

An efficient network is one in which, no matter where the entrepreneur enters the network, his needs are diagnosed and he is passed round the system until he gathers the necessary information and advice. This does not require that all entry points should provide diagnostic as well as counseling services, but rather that each should be clear on what services they and others are offering. Indeed, it may be very cost ineffective, for example, for the banks to do other than lend money; on the other hand, they should be aware of the services that, say, the local accountants provide, so that they can help the entrepreneur efficiently through the system. An inefficient use of the formal infrastructure can lead to poor advice and lack of use of the many schemes available.

From this research, the system is not working efficiently in St. Joseph County. The informal system appears to create a barrier to the formal system rather than acting as a conduit. It is unlikely that this is intentional, but either results from ignorance of the role that the formal system can play or because the formal system actively discourages the entrepreneur. However, because such networks are impossible to identify, strategies must be designed to increase the awareness of the community as a whole to the formal sources of help and advice that are available. There are two ways to approach this. First, the banks, accountants, lawyers, Chamber of Commerce, and all others in the formal system could exchange information on the various schemes and services they offer. Moreover, these services would be advertised regularly so that all in the community are aware that they exist. In this way the entrepreneur can enter the network at any point. The difficulty with this is the need for all the elements of the formal network to develop diagnostic and counseling skills—expensive and time consuming. For these reasons St. Joseph County has decided to adopt a second strategy. In this case, a central clearing house, an enterprise office offering information and advice has been set up so that the information exchange is kept to a minimum and those in the formal system stick to their own special skills.

Firms that sell only locally are vulnerable to local economic trends. However, many of the firms studied had potential to attack wider markets and appeared to be constrained merely by their local backgrounds and limited horizons. Unfortunately, they did not fall into any grouping that could be identified and thus targeted during the start-up process, nor is this necessarily appropriate until the firm has survived the initial period and has established a viable local base. The secondary role of an enterprise office would be to monitor these new firms, and to devleop strategies for finding new customers and new markets in new fields in the longer term.

This study was based on the premise that the process of testing the idea and assembling the necessary resources prior to the commencement of trading of a new venture can often be protracted. Consequently, a key factor in the process is the extent to which networks, both formal and informal, are used. Indeed, the creation of Small Business Development Centers, Business Technology Centers, and even the Small Business Administration itself, is partially based on this implicit assumption. Despite this, little evaluative work has been conducted. We do not know why or how the sophisticated networks of Boston's Route 128 or California's Silicon Valley have developed, although observers suggest that a necessary condition is a strong catalyst, such as the birth of Hewlett–Packard or the presence of a critical mass of a strong university group (*Economist* 1985). Perhaps the most important conclusion from this research, therefore, is that we need to know much more about the type and effectiveness of such networks in nurturing new businesses in different social and economic climates.

REFERENCES

Ambrose, D.M., and Koepke, G. February 1984. Networking: Building strength from the collective resources of small business. *Proceedings, the Small Business Institute Directors Association Conference.*

Bearse, S.J. 1981. *A Study of Entrepreneurship by Region and SMSA Size.* Philadelphia: Public/Private Ventures.

Birley, S.J. 1984(a). New firms and job generation in St. Joseph County. Babson, *Frontiers of Entrepreneurship Research.*

Birley, S.J. 1984(b). Finding the new firm. Boston, *Proceedings, 44th Academy of Management Conference.*

Bruno, A.V., and Tyebjee, T.T. 1982. The environment of entrepreneurship. In C.A. Kent, D.L. Sexton, and K.H. Vesper, eds. *Encyclopedia of Entrepreneurship.* Englewood Cliffs, NJ: Prentice Hall.

Carland, J.W., Hoy, F., Boulton, W.R., and Carland, J.A.C. 1984. Differentiating entrepreneurs from small business owners: A conceptualization. *Academy of Management Review* 9(2).

Cooper, A.C. 1981. Strategic management: New ventures and small business. *Journal of Long Range Planning* 14.

Cooper, A.C., and Dunkelberg, W.C. 1981. A new look at business entry: Experiences of 1805 entrepreneurs. Babson, *Frontiers of Entrepreneurship Research.*

Economist. March 16, 1985. Planting science parks in Britain.

Gartner, W.F. 1984. Problems in business start-up: The relationship among entrepreneurial skills and problem identification for different types of new ventures. Babson, *Frontiers of Entrepreneurship Research.*

Hull, D., Bosley, J., and Udell, G. January 1980. Renewing the hunt for the heffalump: Identifying potential entrepreneurs by personality characteristics. *Journal of Small Business Management* 18.

Liles, P.R. Winter 1974. Who are the entrepreneurs? *Business Topics.*

Long, W. Oct.–Dec. 1983. The meaning of entrepreneurship. *American Journal of Small Business* VIII(2).

MacMillan, I.C., Nov.–Dec. 1983. The politics of new venture management. *Harvard Business Review.*

Pennings, J.M. 1982. The urban quality of life and entrepreneurship. *Academy of Management Journal* 25:1.

Petrov, J.V. October 1980. Entrepreneurial profile: A discriminant analysis. *Journal of Small Business Management* 18:4.

Schell, D.W. 1983. Entrepreneurial activity: A comparison of three North Carolina communities. Babson, *Frontiers of Entrepreneurship Research.*

Schell, D.W., and Davig, W. 1981. The community infrastructure of entrepreneurship: A sociopolitical analysis. Babson, *Frontiers of Entrepreneurship Research.*

Vesper, K.H. 1983. Entrepreneurship and national policy. *Heller Institute for Small Business Policy Papers.*

Webster, F.A. January 1977. Entrepreneurs and ventures: An attempt at classification and clarification. *Academy of Management Review* 2(1).

[17]

1 ENTREPRENEURSHIP THROUGH SOCIAL NETWORKS

Howard Aldrich
Catherine Zimmer [1]

The formation of new businesses can be conceptualized as a function of opportunity structures and motivated entrepreneurs with access to resources. On the demand side, opportunity structures contain the environmental resources that can be exploited by new businesses as they seek to carve out niches for themselves. On the supply side, motivated entrepreneurs need access to capital and other resources so that they can take advantage of perceived opportunities. A cursory examination of this formulation reveals two essential issues that research on entrepreneurship must address: (1) entrepreneurship is a process and must be viewed in dynamic terms rather than in cross-sectional snapshots; and (2) entrepreneurship requires *linkages or relations* between key components of the process.

Entrepreneurs must establish connections to resources and niches in an opportunity structure, and at some point they must have been affected by relations with socializing agents who motivated them. Stevenson[2] noted that entrepreneurs are driven by opportunity-seeking behavior, not by a simple desire to "invest" resources. By contrast, managers are driven by a concern to invest the resources they manage, treating resources as an end in themselves rather than as a means to an end the way entrepreneurs do. Thus, for entrepreneurs the critical connection is to opportunities, whereas for managers it is to resources.

4   ENTREPRENEURSHIP CHARACTERISTICS

Traditional approaches to research on entrepreneurship neglect the relational nature of the process. Instead, they treat entrepreneurs either as atomized decisionmakers, operating as autonomous entities, or as prisoners of their cultural environment, predisposed to entrepreneurship. The approach we take, by contrast, focuses on entrepreneurship as embedded in a social context, channelled and facilitated or constrained and inhibited by people's positions in social networks. Our critique of traditional approaches and our proposed alternative are based on Mark Granovetter's thoughtful and thorough critique of explanations for "economic action."[3]

TRADITIONAL CONCEPTIONS OF ENTREPRENEURS

Traditional views of entrepreneurship have emphasized psychological and economic models, and a special kind of social-cultural model. In this paper we cannot do full justice to each model and so our objective is to highlight the deficiencies of each in dealing with the embedded nature of social behavior. (The embedded nature of social behavior refers to the way in which action is constrained or facilitated because of its social context.)

Following Granovetter, we have identified two undersocialized approaches to entrepreneurship that treat entrepreneurs as though they were "free agents," operating atomistically in an environment where their cognitions and beliefs drive their behavior.

Personality Theories

Personality-based theories of entrepreneurship posit that people's special personal traits make them prone to behaving and succeeding as entrepreneurs.[4] The list of traits is nearly endless but includes internal locus of control, low aversion to risk taking, aggressiveness, ambition, marginality, and a high need for achievement.

Problems with the Personality Approach

Three problems plague personality-based approaches to explaining entrepreneurship: empirical research does not find strong evidence supporting such approaches, similar approaches in the leadership field have made little progress in finding a generic "leadership" trait, and personality-based models underpredict the true extent of entrepreneurship in the United States.

First, rigorous empirical research has had trouble identifying any traits strongly associated with entrepreneurship, as Brockhaus and Horwitz pointed out at our conference. Most research on entrepreneurs suffers from selection bias—picking successful people and not evaluating their attributes against a comparison group. Research using appropriate comparison groups and other controls has uncovered inconsistent and weak relationships between personality characteristics and entrepreneurial behavior.

Second, a companion tradition in psychology studying leadership has foundered on a similar problem: After three decades of study, using a personality-based approach, investigators still have difficulty identifying leaders outside of the group context in which leadership is displayed. A fair summary would be that no one style of leadership is successful all the time—leadership is very much a contingent phenomenon, with different people exhibiting leadership in different situations.[5]

Third, the personality approach substantially underpredicts the extent of entrepreneurship in the United States as it overstates the extent to which entrepreneurs are different from others. Over their lifetimes, many people attempt, or at least strongly consider, setting up their own business. Hundreds of thousands try every year, and tens of thousands succeed in carrying through by establishing businesses that survive and prosper. All these people cannot be deviant, different, or special, possessing personality traits that the rest of us lack. Considering both the proportion of adults expressing an interest in self-employment and the proportion that actually attempt it, well over half the population must possess "entrepreneurial traits"!

Economic, Rational Actor Theories

Neoclassical economic theories view entrepreneurs as rational, isolated decisionmakers. These models assume that, with clear vision of one's goals and all the required information, a person makes a *decision* to enter self-employment. The motivated person scans the market and chooses the niche that will maximize his or her returns

6   ENTREPRENEURSHIP CHARACTERISTICS

on assets invested in the business. Recent modifications of the neo-classical approach take account of cognitive limits to rationality and information processing, recognizing the level of uncertainty involved in most economic decisions. However, even models of bounded rationality and satisficing behavior retain an emphasis on individual decisionmakers and fail to recognize the embedded nature of economic behavior.

Problems with Economic Approaches

Two problems confront investigators choosing economic, rational actor models of entrepreneurship: Cognitive limits on human behavior are much more stringent than typically recognized, and a strong research tradition in social psychology demonstrates the powerful influence of social factors on cognitions and information processing.

First, empirical research on cognition, perception, and decision-making by social psychologists has found that people do not behave the way atomistic models predict they should. A collection of papers edited by Kahneman, Slovic, and Tversky[6] has brought together a vast body of studies showing that people trying to make decisions have problems with (1) judging the representativeness of the information they receive; (2) making proper causal attributions; (3) limiting themselves only to information easily available, rather than searching for the information necessary to make informed decisions; (4) mistaking covariation for causal connections; (5) being overconfident; and (6) wildly overestimating their ability to make multistage inferences. Treated as isolated individuals, people do not measure up to the standards set by atomistic models.

Second, a person who behaved the way atomistic models describe would be an example of social pathology, not a rational decision-maker, as the person would have to reject all social contact. Ever since the original Sherif[7] autokinetic experiments, social-psychologists have been aware of the effect of social influence on decision-making. Persons do not make decisions in a vacuum but rather consult and are subtly influenced by significant others in their environments: family, friends, co-workers, employers, casual acquaintances, and so on.

American farmers are often cited as a classic example of how decisionmakers behave in a true competitive market, atomized and confined to taking individual actions that are futile in the face of unintended collective outcomes. However, the current predicament of American farmers is *not* because they made decisions as atomized individuals over the past decade but rather because they were influenced by their relations with significant others: bankers and commercial credit lenders, agricultural extension agents, and the farm-oriented business press. Farmers borrowed money to expand when they were advised to do so by persons whom they trusted. Paradoxically, we suspect that those farmers who are best off today are precisely those few who *were* most uninformed and socially isolated over the past decade, thus avoiding the influence of expansionist-oriented influentials!

Deterministic, Oversocialized Models of Entrepreneurship

Some theories posit a "propensity to entrepreneurship" based on national origins, culture, or religion. Certain groups are believed to possess beliefs, values, and traditions that predispose them to succeed in business, regardless of where they find themselves. At one time or another, various groups have been labeled this way, including the Jews, Chinese, Japanese, and Lebanese. Such models are deterministic and oversocialized because they presume the existence of a stereotypical standard that all members of the group display, and presume that behaviors are evoked regardless of the group member's situation.

Problems with the Sociocultural Approach

The major problem with this approach is that the groups alleged to possess a propensity to entrepreneurship display their predisposition only under limited, country-specific and historically specific conditions. Prior to immigration, persons originating from alleged entrepreneurial cultures are mostly indistinguishable from others around them, but in their new surroundings they take on entrepreneurial characteristics. For example, (1) Koreans in their native land versus

8   ENTREPRENEURSHIP CHARACTERISTICS

those migrating to Los Angeles, Atlanta, or Chicago[8] (2) Dominicans in their native land versus those migrating to New York City[9]; and (3) Indians on the Indian subcontinent versus those migrating to England, many of whom come from farming or peasant backgrounds.[10] Research findings strongly suggest that we should attribute the flowering of a group's predisposition to situational, rather than deterministic, conditions.

A strong case is often made for "American exceptionalism," alleging that America is "the land of opportunity" that socializes its citizens into becoming aggressive risk takers. Popular magazines and self-help manuals published today tout the entrepreneurial character of Americans and the rebirth of the entrepreneurial spirit. Were such arguments valid, we would expect the rate of business formation in the United States to be much higher than, say, in Western European nations, and the rate of failure to be lower. In fact, accumulating evidence shows that the rates of business formation and dissolution in Western European nations are much the same as in the United States. Pom Ganguly's research for the British government's Department of Trade and Industry has found that new businesses are being added to the British economy at a rate of about one for every ten existing businesses, and businesses are being dissolved at a rate of about one for every twelve existing businesses.[11] These rates are nearly the same as those found by the U.S. Small Business Administration, using the newly constructed Small Business Data Base.[12] Similar results are emerging for other Western nations.[13] "National character" arguments must give way to models based on an underlying similarity in the economies of all Western advanced industrial societies. Rather than posit overdeterministic models, we should turn our attention to the situational conditions under which entrepreneurs enter business.

THE EMBEDDEDNESS OF ENTREPRENEURIAL BEHAVIOR

As an alternative to under- and oversocialized models of entrepreneurship, we propose a perspective that views entrepreneurship as embedded in networks of continuing social relations. Within complex networks of relationships, entrepreneurship is facilitated or constrained by linkages between aspiring entrepreneurs, resources, and opportunities. We take a population perspective[14] on organizational formation and persistence, recognizing the interaction of chance, necessity, and purpose in all social action.

The Population Perspective

From the population perspective, net additions to populations of businesses reflect the operation of four evolutionary processes: variation, selection, retention, and diffusion, and the struggle for existence.[15]

Any kind of change is a *variation*, and the evolutionary process begins with variations that may be intentional or blind. Some entrepreneurs are driven by a single-mindedness of purpose as they attempt to adapt their plans to environmental exigencies. Other entrepreneurs stumble onto opportunities and resources by chance, perhaps never intending to create a new enterprise until an accidental conjuncture of events presents itself. The process of organizational creation depends only on the occurrence of attempted variations and not on the level of ambitions, foresight, or intelligence people bring to the process. (Of course, whether the attempts succeed is another matter.) The higher the frequency of variations, whatever their sources, the greater the chances of net additions to organizational populations.

Some variations—attempts at forming new enterprises—prove more beneficial than others in acquiring resources in a competitive environment and are thus positively selected. *Selection* criteria are set through the operation of market forces, competitive pressures, the logic of internal organizational structuring, and other forces usually beyond the control of individual entrepreneurs. Organizations founded through maladaptive variations in technology, managerial competence, or other attributes are likely to draw fewer resources from their environments and are therefore more likely to fail. Over time, populations of enterprises are more apt to be characterized by the attributes of surviving organizations than by the attributes of those that failed.

What is preserved through *retention* is the technological and managerial competence that all enterprises in a population use, collectively, to exploit the resources of their environment. The survival of a particular business is not terribly consequential to the survival of

10   ENTREPRENEURSHIP CHARACTERISTICS

the population as a whole, as the total population's survival depends on the total pool of technological and managerial competence. The variations possessed by a particular enterprise contribute to the total pool but do not determine its collective fate.

The competencies of a population are held by the entrepreneurs and their employees. Retained variations are passed on, with more or less variation, from surviving entrepreneurs to those who follow and from old to new employees, some of whom may leave to form their own businesses. Linkages between enterprises facilitate the *diffusion* of beneficial variations, whereas isolated organizations contribute little or nothing to future generations. Not all variations are diffused to new entrepreneurs (because of hostility, pique, mistakes, stupidity, unwillingness to learn, etc.), introducing a large element of uncertainty into the process.

A competitive *struggle over resources and opportunities* occurs, fueling the selection process. Sometimes opportunities are so diverse and resources so abundant that a high proportion of entrepreneurs are successful and the business population grows rapidly. In new industries, first movers have substantial advantages and enjoy rapid growth. As industries evolve, however, or resources become more scarce, shakeouts occur and competition increases the mortality rate, with populations stagnating or declining.

Using evolutionary principles, the population perspective explains how particular forms of organizations come to exist in specific kinds of environments. A specific environment constitutes an opportunity structure containing a resource pool uniquely suited to organizational forms that adapt to it or help shape it. A form well-adapted to a specific environment is probably not the fittest form imaginable and is vulnerable to entrepreneurial successes in founding new organizations with more adapted forms. Nonetheless, it is tolerably fit and probably more fit than previous failed forms.

The population perspective makes minimal assumptions about the cognitive capabilities of humans as information-processors and renders practically irrelevant any speculations about entrepreneurial personalities. People become entrepreneurs through the conjuncture of the four processes outlined above, and entrepreneurship takes on meaning only within the context of these processes. People are intentional or purposeful in their actions, but social conditions are such that we usually cannot attribute organizational formation to any particular, identifiable, intentional act or set of acts.

Environments, as opportunity structures, are diverse, uncertain, and imperfectly perceived, and it is seldom true that a particular individual will both have an accurate view and be aware of it. People are limited by bounded rationality, suffer from limited or biased information and poor communication, and are subject to processes of social influence and reconstructions of reality. Hence, comprehensive explanations of entrepreneurship must include the social context of behavior, especially the social relationships through which people obtain information, resources, and social support.

The Characteristics of Social Networks

The starting point for studying entrepreneurship through social networks is a relation or transaction between two people. Relations may be treated as containing: (1) communication content, or the passing of information from one person to another; (2) exchange content, or the goods and services two persons can exchange; and (3) normative content, or the expectations persons have of one another because of some special characteristic or attribute. The strength of ties depends on the level, frequency, and reciprocity of relationships between persons, and varies from weak to strong. Most research has focused on single content types of relations, and so there is a paucity of information about the effects of types of relations on one another and on the durability of relations composed of different combinations of relations.

Relations between pairs of individuals—entrepreneurs, customers, suppliers, creditors, inventors, and so forth—whatever their content and whatever a person's social role, could be extended and persons included in ways that would expand a unit of analysis indefinitely. A central interest of network theorists, therefore, has been to find ways to set meaningful limits to the scope of a social unit under investigation. The concept of role-set, action-set, and network provide us with some tools for setting such boundaries.

A *role-set* consists of all those persons with whom a focal person has direct relations. Usually the links are single-step ties, but indirect links can be considered by specifying how many steps removed an interacting person can be from the central focal person and still be treated as in the set. We have borrowed the concept of a role-set from Merton, who defined it as "that complement of role relation-

12   ENTREPRENEURSHIP CHARACTERISTICS

ships which persons have by virtue of occupying a particular social status."[16] Merton gave an example of the status of public school teacher and its role-set, relating the teacher to pupils, colleagues, school principal and superintendent, board of education, and professional organizations of teachers. For entrepreneurs, we could think of partners, suppliers, customers, venture capitalists, bankers, other creditors, distributors, trade associations, and family members.

One of the interesting issues highlighted by the role-set concept concerns conflict produced by divergent expectations from members of an entrepreneur's role-set. Entrepreneurs stand at the center of potentially conflicting demands and expectations from their role-sets, such as between expectations from spouses that some time will be spent at home versus demands from partners that weekends be used to catch up on paperwork. Business survival may depend upon the strategies entrepreneurs adopt to resolve such conflicts.

An *action-set* is a group of people who have formed a temporary alliance for a limited purpose. The concept of action-set has been used by anthropoligists, who have found a specific action or behavior, rather than status, helpful as a frame of reference in studying social change. Rather than the ego-centered analysis of role-set studies, action-set research examines the purposeful behavior of an entire aggregate of persons. Action-sets may have their own internal division of labor, behavioral norms vis-à-vis other persons, or clearly defined principles for the recruitment of new members. An action-set may be centered around the behavior of one individual, as in consortia of high-tech firms led by the enterprise with the most market power, but that is an empirical question.

A *network* is defined as the totality of all persons connected by a certain type of relationship and is constructed by finding the ties between all persons in a population under study, regardless of how it is organized into role-sets and action-sets. Given a bounded system, investigators identify all the links between people within the boundaries. Network analysis assumes that a network constrains or facilitates the action of people and action sets and thus is more than the sum of the individual links that comprise it.

Critical Dimensions of Networks

Before demonstrating the application of network concepts to the explanation of entrepreneurship, let us briefly review three dimensions of networks that are useful in social analysis: density, reachability, and centrality.

The *density* of a network refers to the extensiveness of ties between persons and is measured by comparing the total number of ties present to the potential number that would occur if everyone in the network were connected to everyone else. The simplest measures of density just consider the presence or absence of a tie, but more sophisticated measures take account of the strength of ties.

Reachability refers to the presence of a path between two persons, of whatever distance. Persons can be ranked by how many intermediaries a path travels before one person is indirectly linked with another. An example of the use of indirect ties in connecting distant individuals was provided by Travers and Milgram in their experimental study of communication channels, referred to as the small-world phenomenon.[17] Arbitrarily chosen persons in Nebraska were given letters to send to a target person in Boston, with the stipulation that the letters had to be channeled only through persons known to the senders. Out of 296 starts, 64 letters reached the target person, with the mean number of intermediaries being 5.2. The importance of linking pins was shown in that 48 percent of the completed chains passed through three central individuals before reaching the target.

The *centrality* of a person in a network is determined by two factors: (1) the total distance from a focal person to all other persons, and (2) the total number of other persons a focal person can reach. (For a comprehensive review of the centrality concept, and alternative definitions, see an article by Linton Freeman.[18]) The more persons that can be reached and the shorter the aggregate distance to these persons, the higher the centrality of a focal person. Persons who have extensive ties to different parts of a network can play a key role in entrepreneurial processes. Persons playing central roles may have ties to more than one action-set or other subset of a network, and they can serve three important functions: (1) they serve as communication channels between distant persons; (2) they may provide brokerage services linking third parties to one another by transferring resources; and (3) if they are dominant or high-status individuals, they may serve as role models for others or may use their position to direct the behavior of action-sets or individuals.

NETWORKS AND ENTREPRENEURSHIP

We turn now to four applications of network concepts to the study of entrepreneurship. The first application focuses on the effect of social forces that increase the density of networks, and the second application focuses on the role of "brokers" and other persons or organizations that increase reachability in networks. The third application applies Granovetter's discussion of the importance of linkage diversity to the question of which positions in networks are most likely to produce entrepreneurs.[19] The fourth application focuses on the importance of the social resources embedded in entrepreneurs' networks.

Increasing Density through Raising the Salience of Group Boundaries and Identity

Conditions that raise the salience of group boundaries and identity, leading persons to form new social ties and action-sets, increase the likelihood of entrepreneurial attempts by persons within that group and raise the probability of success. Increasing density can operate at two levels. First, at a local level, increasing density may lead to coalition formation between persons, thus enhancing their collective action capability. Repeated action-set formation, in turn, enhances the institutional infrastructure facilitating entrepreneurship. Second, if density increases not just at a local level but also at the system level—such as for an entire ethnic group or as a result of infrastructural development—then everyone is in a position to collect the combinations of resources necessary for successful ventures. The advantages of local action-sets would thus be eliminated and the entire group would have an advantage over outsiders.

Opportunities are irrelevant unless taken advantage of, and people vary widely in their ability to seize opportunities. Auster and Aldrich, Bonacich, Light, and others have argued that the possibility of exploiting opportunities is linked to a group's internal organizing capacity.[20] Ethnic groups with a high level of self-organization—a densely connected network—provide co-ethnics with a collective capacity for organizing new ventures. Indeed, the most salient feature of early business efforts by immigrant groups is their dependence on an ethnic community for support. Support is provided at two levels: informal support from the friends and relatives of aspiring business owners, and support from the larger network of ethnic institutions, including religious associations, fraternal organizations, and other small businesses. Strong community support, based on ethnic ties, allows small firms some degree of independence from the host community.[21]

Immigration, especially chain migration, may establish densely connected communities of co-ethnics who cooperate when confronted with host hostility.[22] The early opposition towards Japanese immigrants on the west coast of the United States by labor unions, who feared that Asians would replace them at lower wages, obstructed Japanese entry into the mainstream economy. In response, the Japanese pooled their resources and ultimately captured a significant portion of California's agricultural sector until their internment during World War II. The strong ethnic solidarity formed by union and public hostility generated ethnic networks that supported subsequent generations.[23]

Mutual aid, in the form of capital, credit, information, training opportunities, and the regulation of competition, gave Chinese and Japanese immigrants to the United States a strong base on which to develop small business. In contrast, black migrants from the South to Northern cities after World War I and continuing into the 1950s had few collective organizational traditions to follow, except for religion.[24]

Strong ties carry with them a history of past dealings in or out of a business setting that can form a basis for trust. Whereas banks and other formal institutions outside an ethnic group may have little or no objective credit history for an aspiring entrepreneur, within the group strong ties keep alive the memory of past experiences from which to infer trustworthiness, and these relationships may carry strong expectations of trust.[25] Another strength of strong ties is that "strong ties have greater motivation to be of assistance and are typically more easily available."[26]

Mutual benefit associations, cooperative housing and buying arrangements, joint capital raising activities, and other collective actions provide support for potential entrepreneurs. Recent groups in the United States who have followed this model include Cubans in Miami; Dominicans in New York City's garment trade; Koreans in Los Angeles's liquor, wig, and other retail stores; and Indians in Cali-

16   ENTREPRENEURSHIP CHARACTERISTICS

fornia's motel business. Most small firms are capitalized from the owner's savings, but other sources of funds are often sought. The Chinese *hui*, the Japanese *ko* and *tanomoshi*, and the Korean *kye* — rotating credit associations clothed in their respective cultural traditions — have provided simple mechanisms for immigrants to raise business capital.[27] In these cases, social conditions have raised the salience of group boundaries and identity, leading persons to form stronger ties with one another and often to the creation of effective action-sets.

Increasing Reachability and Connectedness Facilitate the Spread of Information and Resources in Networks

Broker roles are central positions in networks, resulting from people's attempts to minimize their transactions costs. Such positions exist because of their function of linking persons having complementary interests, transferring information, and otherwise facilitating the interests of persons not directly connected to one another. Many entrepreneurs enjoy a broker's position, and indeed Schumpeter's classic definition of an entrepreneur as someone who combines old resources in novel ways seems to equate the entrepreneurial with the broker role. However, we are interested in brokers who are not themselves entrepreneurs but who facilitate the actions of entrepreneurs. (Also, we believe many entrepreneurs do not themselves enjoy the advantages of a broker role.) For example, venture capitalists are as important for their broker role as for the funds they provide to struggling entrepreneurs because they bring together technical experts, management consultants, and financial planners to supplement the entrepreneur's limited knowledge and experience.

To illustrate the importance of broker roles, let us consider an example of a population divided into two major types of social roles — such as entrepreneurs and venture capitalists — where some method of interrole communication is desired by persons in each role. Communication is possible if all entrepreneurs are directly linked to all venture capitalists, thus creating a very complex set of relations. The total number of relations established would equal the number of entrepreneurs times the number of venture capitalists, assuming a link is established in each direction. If there were five entrepreneurs and five venture capitalists, the total number of links would be twenty-five.

Each new person added to either side would increase the number of required links linearly (e.g., if another entrepreneur is added, five more links are created). If another person were added to both sides, the number of linkages would increase as the square of the number added (e.g., if one pair is added, the number of ties jumps from twenty-five to thirty-six). In a large population, the maintenance of such a large set of linkages would be extremely costly, especially if the number of entrepreneurs and venture capitalists were increasing rapidly.

The evolutionary model from the population perspective would predict that any innovation or random variation that created a less costly solution to the problem would be quickly selected. Any cost-saving variation would give the entrepreneur using it a relative advantage, and thus a selective survival advantage, over other entrepreneurs in a resource-scarce environment. Similarly, any new organizational form that enabled entrepreneurs and venture capitalists to communicate with one another more quickly would be in a niche with an initially overwhelming advantage, as there would be a strong demand for its services.

If an intermediary or broker organization were created, linking entrepreneurs and venture capitalists—such as venture capital "fairs" or the joint seminars described by David Brophy[28]—the number of connections in the network would be reduced to the number of entrepreneurs plus the number of venture capitalists. That is, five plus five, joined by a central organization, rather than the five times five situation previously. Each person or organization would have one link to the broker, and the process of sorting out the various messages and information channels between them would be internalized by the broker. This is a complex task, but the broker specializes in the role and only a fraction of the ties would have to be active at any one time. Once introduced into a population, we would expect this function to persist, and the concept of the broker should become part of our industrial culture, passed on via imitation and tradition.

Voluntary associations, trade associations, public agencies, and other social units increase the probability of people making connections with one another. Rates of entrepreneurship should be higher in highly organized populations (i.e., populations with a high orga-

18   ENTREPRENEURSHIP CHARACTERISTICS

nizing capacity). The complex pattern of social organization described by Everett Rogers and Judith Larson in their book *Silicon
Valley Fever* illustrates the synergistic effects of brokers, central
meeting points—such as well-known "watering holes" and restaurants—and family and friendship networks that supported the high
start-up rate in the Silicon Valley.[29]

Social networks build slowly, and thus it could be years before an
area reaches a density threshold where reachability and hence entrepreneurship is facilitated. Formal studies are lacking, but it is our
impression that the time to maturity for the Silicon Valley and the
Route 128 complex in Boston was several decades. Accordingly, we
expect the Research Triangle of North Carolina to age another decade or so before any significant entrepreneurial activity occurs. At
present, the spin-off and new start-up rate appears very low.

The Importance of Diversity in an Entrepreneur's Network: Too Much Solidarity Stifles the Entrepreneurial Soul

Mark Granovetter has developed an argument linking the diversity of
ties in which a person is implicated to the scope of opportunities
open to that person.[30]

> The argument asserts that our acquaintances ("weak ties") are less likely to
> be socially involved with one another than are our close friends ("strong
> ties"). Thus, the set of people made up of any individual and his or her
> acquaintances will constitute a low-density network (one in which many of
> the possible relational lines are absent), whereas the set consisting of the same
> individual and his or her *close* friends will be densely knit (many of the pos-
> sible lines present).[31]

A potential entrepreneur may have a small group of friends he or
she knows well, each of whom knows the others quite well. He or
she may also have many casual acquaintances, each of whom also
has a circle of close friends. These close friends of his casual acquaintances are unlikely to be known to the potential entrepreneur, and
thus his or her only possible ties to them are through the casual
acquaintance. The weak tie between the potential entrepreneur and
his or her acquaintance is therefore "not merely a trivial acquaintance
tie, but rather a crucial bridge between the two densely knit clumps

of close friends. . . . It follows that individuals with few weak ties will be deprived of information from distance parts of the social system and will be confined to the provincial news and views of their close friends."[32]

Research in the Boston area by Granovetter has documented that lack of access to the information provided by weak ties puts people at a competitive disadvantage in the labor market, as such people will obtain only redundant information from close acquaintances, who travel in the same circles as the job seeker.[33] People with a more diverse role set, connected to distant others via brokers or other intermediaries, will have access to a wider range of information.

Following the logic of this argument, entrepreneurs are more likely to be found in positions whose centrality is high and which are connected to lots of diverse information sources. Entrepreneurs activate their weak ties for at least two purposes: to gain access to business information and to attract customers. First, information about new business locations, potential markets for goods and services, sources of capital or potential investors, innovations, and standard business practice is likely to be spread widely among individuals. Other things being equal, someone with a small role-set of overlapping ties is at a disadvantage when competing for information with someone who has a large role-set of divergent ties. There is also a disadvantage we might call the "weakness of strong ties," wherein those persons with whom we are tightly linked lead to the introduction of extraneous socio-emotional content into information exchanges, clouding their meaning.

Second, entrepreneurs ask both their strong and weak ties to become customers. Then, in turn, these new customers may tell their strong and weak ties about the new venture. It is the weak ties who can expand the pool of customers; strong ties deliver redundant information.

Perhaps these ideas are a way of rethinking the traditional relation posited between "marginality" and entrepreneurship. Marginality is important but as a characteristic of the social structure, not as a personal characteristic of entrepreneurs. Instead, marginality refers to the weak ties potential entrepreneurs have to diverse information sources and to potential customers, putting them in positions to capitalize on opportunities that remain unknown to the less marginal person.

20   ENTREPRENEURSHIP CHARACTERISTICS

Nine studies reviewed by Granovetter have tested the strength of the weak ties argument and have provided partial support for it.[34] None of these studies, however, focused on entrepreneurs or on persons classified as self-employed. The theoretical importance of weak ties would be broadened by specific research on how small businesses are founded and how they subsequently fare.

The Importance of Social Resources: It is not just What You Know but Who You Know

Lin and his colleagues have added a component to the strength of ties literature.[35] In his theory of instrumental action, Lin suggested that in a hierarchical social structure, a person in a "position nearer to the top of the structure has greater access to and control of valued resources not only because more valued resources are intrinsically attached to the position, but also because of the position's greater accessibility to positions at other (primarily lower) rankings."[36] He defined social resources as valued resources that are accessible through ties with others. Therefore, all weak ties are not equally useful for acquiring social resources. Weak ties to those contacts with the most social resources—that is, contacts as high in the social hierarchy as possible—will provide the greatest access to social resources. Lin's research on the status attainment of job seekers has weakly confirmed the social resources argument, but his research must be replicated before we can place high confidence in his results.

Extending the argument, successful entrepreneurs will be found in positions with weak ties to people who are in positions to provide timely and accurate information, to people with the resources to act as a customers, and/or to people with resources to invest.

Entrepreneurship is a social role, embedded in a social context. Investigators cannot treat entrepreneurs in isolation as autonomous decisionmakers or lump them together with others with similar social characteristics, without regard to context. It is the effects of social networks in facilitating or inhibiting the activities of potential entrepreneurs.

NOTES TO CHAPTER 1

1. We are deeply indebted to Valerie Haines and Peter Marsden, colleagues at the University of North Carolina, for their comments and suggestions.
2. Howard Stevenson, "A Perspective on Entrepreneurship," Harvard Business School, No. 9-384-131, November 1984.
3. Mark Granovetter, "Economic Action and Social Structure: A Theory of Embeddedness," *American Journal of Sociology* (forthcoming); see also Ronald S. Burt, "Tertius Gaudens, Structurally Autonomous Entrepreneur," Columbia University, 1983. (Unpublished.)
4. See Robert J. Brockhaus and Pamela S. Horwitz, "The Psychology of the Entrepreneur," in this volume.
5. Richard Hall, *Organizations: Structure and Process* (Englewood Cliffs, N.J.: Prentice-Hall, 1982).
6. Daniel Kahneman, Paul Slovic, and Amos Tversky, *Judgment under Uncertainty: Heuristics and Biases* (New York: Cambridge University Press, 1982).
7. M. Sherif, "A Study of Some Social Factors in Perception," *Archives on Psychology* 187 (1935). The autokinetic effect is a visual illusion—a fixed pinpoint of light shown to subjects in a totally darkened room appears to move, smoothly or erratically. Subjects' judgments of the extent to which the light moves are strongly influenced by the reports of others in the room—typically, persons who are confederates of the experimenter.
8. Pyong Gap Min and Charles Jaret, "Korean Immigrants' Success in Small Business: Some Cultural Explanations," Department of Sociology, Georgia State University, August 1984. (Unpublished.)
9. Roger Waldinger, "Immigrant Enterprise and Labor Market Structure," Working paper, Joint Center for Urban Studies, MIT and Harvard University, 1982.
10. Howard Aldrich, John Cater, Trevor Jones, and Dave McEvoy, "From Periphery to Peripheral: The South Asian Petite Bourgeoisie in England," in Ida Harper Simpson and Richard Simpson, eds., *Research in the Sociology of Work*, Vol. 2 (Greenwich, Conn.: JAI Press, 1983), pp. 1-32.
11. Pom Ganguly, "Births and Deaths of Firms in the UK in 1980," *British Business* 29 (January 29-February 5, 1982).
12. U.S. Small Business Administration, *The State of Small Business* (Washington, D.C.: USGPO, 1984).
13. Robert Brockhaus, personal communication,
14. See Howard Aldrich, *Organizations and Environments* (Englewood Cliffs, N.J.: Prentice-Hall, 1979); and Bill McKelvey and Howard Aldrich, "Populations, Natural Selection, and Applied Organizational Science," *Administrative Science Quarterly* 28: 1 (March 1983): 101-28.

22   ENTREPRENEURSHIP CHARACTERISTICS

15. See McKelvey and Aldrich, "Populations"; and Howard Aldrich, Bill McKelvey, and Dave Ulrich, "Design Strategy from the Population Perspective," *Journal of Management* 10: 1 (Spring 1984): 68–86.
16. Robert Merton, "The Role-Set: Problems in Sociological Theory," *British Journal of Sociology* 8 (1957): 106–20.
17. Jeffrey Travers and Stanley Milgram, "An Experimental Study of the Small World Problem," *Sociometry* 32 (1969): 425–43.
18. Linton C. Freeman, "Centrality in Social Networks: Conceptual Clarification," *Social Networks* 1 (1979): 215–39.
19. Mark Granovetter, "The Strength of Weak Ties," *American Journal of Sociology* 78: 6 (May 1973): 1360–80.
20. See Ellen Auster and Howard Aldrich, "Small Business Vulnerability, Ethnic Enclaves, and Ethnic Enterprise," in Robin Ward and R. Jenkins, eds., *Ethnic Communities in Business: Strategies for Economic Survival* (New York: Cambridge University Press), pp. 39–54; Edna Bonacich, "A Theory of Middleman Minorities," *American Sociological Review* 38 (October 1973): 583–94; and Ivan Light, *Ethnic Enterprise in America: Business and Welfare among Chinese, Japanese, and Blacks* (Berkeley, Calif.: University of California Press, 1972).
21. Kenneth Wilson and Alexandro Portes, "Immigrant Enclaves: An Analysis of the Labor Market Experiences of Cubans in Miami," *American Journal of Sociology* 86: 2 (September 1980): 295–319.
22. Bonacich, "A Theory of Middleman Minorities."
23. Edna Bonacich and John Modell, *The Economic Basis of Ethnic Solidarity* (Berkeley, Calif.: University of California Press, 1980).
24. See E. Franklin Frazier, *Black Bourgeoisie* (New York: The Free Press, 1957), and Nathan Glazer and Daniel Patrick Moynihan, *Beyond the Melting Pot* (Cambridge, Mass.: MIT Press, 1963).
25. Light, *Ethnic Enterprise.*
26. Granovetter, "Economic Action" (forthcoming), p. 14.
27. Mark Granovetter, "The Strength of Weak Ties; A Network Theory Revisited," in Peter V. Marsden and Nan Lin, eds., *Social Structure and Network Analysis* (Beverly Hills, Calif.: Sage, 1982), p. 113.
28. David Brophy, "Venture Capital Research," in this volume.
29. Everett Rogers and Judith Larson, *Silicon Valley Fever* (New York: Basic Books, 1984).
30. See Granovetter, "The Strength of Weak Ties," (1973); Mark Granovetter, *Getting a Job: A Study of Contacts and Careers* (Cambridge, Mass.: Harvard University Press, 1974); Granovetter, "The Strength of Weak Ties," 1982; and Granovetter, "Economic Action" (forthcoming).
31. Granovetter, "The Strength of Weak Ties," 1982, p. 105.
32, Ibid., p. 106.

33. Granovetter, *Getting A Job*. Scott Boorman has suggested that Grano-
     vetter's findings may apply only when jobs are scarce. Strong ties may well
     be more valuable in other labor market conditions, such as when one needs
     to have influence exercised on one's behalf. See Scott A. Boorman, "A
     Cominatorial Optimization Model for Transmission of Job Information
     through Contact Networks," *The Bell Journal of Economics* 6: 1 (Spring
     1975): 216–49.
34. Granovetter, "The Strength of Weak Ties," 1982.
35. See, for example, Nan Lin, W.M. Ensel, and J.C. Vaughn, "Social Re-
     sources and Strength of Ties: Structural Factors in Occupational Status
     Attainment," *American Sociological Review* 46: 4 (August 1981): 393–
     405; and Nan Lin, J.C. Vaughn, and W.M. Ensel, "Social Resources and
     Occupational Status Attainment," *Social Forces* 60: 59 (June 1981):
     1162–81.
36. Nan Lin, "Social Resources and Instrumental Action," in Marsden and
     Lin, *Social Structure and Network Analysis*, p. 131.

[18]

Regional Networks and the Resurgence of Silicon Valley

AnnaLee Saxenian

During the 1970s, the rapid growth, technological vitality, and entrepreneurial culture of Silicon Valley captured the imagination of policymakers and scholars around the world. This enchantment waned during the 1980s, however, as intensified Japanese competition left the region's leading semiconductor producers saddled with massive overcapacity and declining profits. Between 1984 and 1986, local chipmakers' sales fell 35%, forcing them to lay-off more than 7,000 employees while linked sectors eliminated another 20,000 jobs in the region.[1] Observers, drawing parallels with Detroit and Pittsburgh, were quick to predict the demise of Silicon Valley.

Despite this battering, more than 85 new semiconductor firms were started in Silicon Valley during the 1980s. This new wave of chipmakers represents the state-of-the art in semiconductor design and product innovation and has generated some 25,000 jobs and more than $2 billion in annual sales.[2] While the region's established producers struggle to stay in the black, several of these start-ups boast growth rates of 45-50% a year and only a handful have failed. Firms in the computer systems and related businesses are also flourishing and regional high-tech employment has surpassed pre-recession levels (see Table 1).

The dynamics of Silicon Valley's revitalization are reflected in this new wave of semiconductor start-ups. These firms, together with hundreds of neighboring technology firms, are forging a flexible model of production in the region. By building on the social networks and industrial infrastructure which were created and then abandoned by the established semiconductor

Special thanks to Paul Adler, Gary Herrigel, Charles Sabel, and especially Marty Manley for their comments, insights, and advice.

90   CALIFORNIA MANAGEMENT REVIEW   Fall 1990

Table 1. Santa Clara County High Tech Employment

Number of Employees, 1979-1989

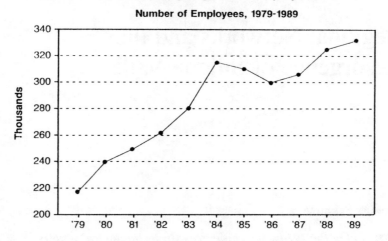

Source: California EDD, ES202 Series

firms, these small and medium-sized enterprises are pioneering a new Silicon Valley—one which fosters collaboration and reciprocal innovation among networks of specialist producers.

Although public attention is currently focused on trade policy and Sematech, the resilience of the Silicon Valley economy underscores the importance of regional economies to industrial competitiveness and the need for local industrial policy in the 1990s.

Reinterpreting Silicon Valley

The experience of Silicon Valley during the 1980s suggests that the current debate over the future of America's high-technology industry is miscast. Both advocates of national support for strategic industries, such as MIT's Charles Ferguson, and their free market adversaries, led by George Gilder, attribute the early growth of the American semiconductor industry to the entrepreneurial enterprises of Silicon Valley. They disagree only on the viability of such market-led growth in the 1980s—with the latter glorifying it and the former viewing it as inappropriate, even "pathological."[3]

For free marketeers such as Gilder, Silicon Valley's dynamism confirms the neoclassical vision of competitive markets as self-reproducing and suggests that increased entrepreneurship is the solution to America's industrial woes. Yet they cannot account for the current weakness of U.S. commodity producers relative to Japan's giant integrated firms. Nor can they explain the failure of regions around the world to replicate the Silicon

Valley experience, even after ensuring free flows of capital, skilled labor, and technology.[4]

National policy advocates such as Ferguson, by contrast, invoke the crisis of the semiconductor industry to argue that Silicon Valley's small and medium-sized enterprises are no longer appropriate to the dictates of global competition. Claiming that the fragmented structures of competitive capitalism are no match for the institutionalized coordination of America's Asian adversaries, these analysts advocate government support and consolidation of key technology sectors. Yet the resurgence of the Silicon Valley economy—particularly the flourishing of the 1980s start-ups—suggests the need to reconsider this approach as well.

Despite their differences, these opposing approaches place individual firms and national governments at the center of their analyses. As a result, neither can account for the resilience of the Silicon Valley economy: it is a product of the region's dense networks of social, professional, and commercial relationships, not simply of unfettered markets or national policy.

A more fruitful approach begins with the regional economy. Silicon Valley is best viewed as an American variant of the industrial districts of Europe—technologically dynamic regional economies in which networks of specialist producers both compete and cooperate in response to fast-changing global markets. In these districts, technical skill and competence are widely diffused, small and medium sized firms achieve external economies through complex supplier and subcontracting relations, and the region (not the firm) is the locus of production. The result is a decentralized system which is more flexible than the traditional vertically integrated corporation.[5]

While the resurgence of Silicon Valley demonstrates the adaptive capacities of this decentralized productive system, the semiconductor crisis also underscores the vulnerability of industrial districts in the American context. Although the new semiconductor producers are better organized to respond to volatile markets and technologies than their predecessors, they have yet to recognize the social basis of their dynamism and create institutions which allow them to respond systematically to shared challenges.

The New Wave of Semiconductor Start-Ups

The wave of semiconductor start-ups in the 1980s represented a collective revolt by Silicon Valley engineers against the established semiconductor firms.[6] Entrepreneurs like Cypress Semiconductors' T.J. Rogers and Chips & Technologies' Gordon Campbell quit jobs at the large semiconductor firms in frustration with their employers' growing isolation from customers and unwillingness to pursue promising technical leads. Complaining that the big firms had lost the agility which made Silicon Valley famous, these engineers "voted with their feet" and exposed the rigidities of the established semiconductor firms even before Japan did so.[7] They also created the

Table 2. U.S. Semiconductor Startups and Closings

Number of Firms, 1956-1987

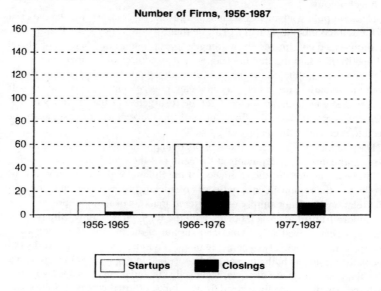

Source: Dataquest, Inc. 1988

largest wave of semiconductor start-ups in the industry's history (see Table 2).

These firms pioneered a flexible approach to semiconductor production—one well adapted to the market conditions of the 1980s. They unbundled production in order to remain focused and to share the costs and risks of developing new semiconductors, and they adopted flexible design and manufacturing technologies that have enabled them to introduce products rapidly and avoid the price wars which periodically plague commodity production.

While the region's established firms—such as Advanced Micro Devices (AMD), National Semiconductor (NS), and Intel—produced standard, general purpose semiconductors (such as commodity memories and microprocessors for mass markets),[8] the newcomers have focused on high-performance, high value-added components, including custom and semicustom chips as well as standard parts designed for narrow niche markets (semi-standard chips).[9] Specialist producers such as Cypress Semiconductor, Cirrus Logic, and Maxim Integrated Products emphasize product design, quality, and customer service—not simply low cost.

By 1987, for example, Cypress manufactured over 75 different high-performance products on a single flexible manufacturing line. While few of these individual products were large or stable enough to attract a major competitor, they collectively represented a $1.4 billion market—comparable to the market for 256K DRAMS. Today, the firm produces 159 products in seven distinct product areas, basic products, and its 50 packaging options yield close to 1000 distinct variants.[10] Maxim Integrated Products has similarly broken from industry tradition by developing an average of 67 new products every year since its founding in 1983.[11]

These specialization strategies were often the result of trial and error rather than foresight. Seeq Technology, for example, lost $35 million and was forced to lay off half of its work force in 1985 as a result of Japanese competition in EPROMs. It was only under these crisis conditions that Seeq withdrew from the commodity memory business and focused on specialty memory and logic products with electrically reprogrammable qualities (such as high-speed EEPROMs). By the end of 1987, the firm had completed an impressive turnaround, with annual revenues up 46% and three consecutive profitable quarters.

The new firms have achieved flexibility in manufacturing by avoiding the dedicated, high-volume production lines of their predecessors. In a move reminiscent of the mini-mills of the U.S. steel industry, they have pioneered the use of "minifabs" which process short runs (small wafer lots) of different designs quickly and economically on a single line. This is achieved through the use of modular fabrication lines, which rely on tiny equipment islands scattered throughout the plant to achieve maximum flexibility. While the traditional "mega fab"—optimized for very high throughput of a single design—can cost more than $250 million and take 2-3 years to build, a "minifab" can be built in 6 months for $20-50 million.[12] As a result, in 1985 Silicon Valley start-ups produced an average of 100-200 different types of chips on the same line with production runs ranging from 10 and 10,000 units. The large U.S. producers, by contrast, produced 10-20 different commodity memory or logic devices on a line, with runs of one millions units.[13]

The Cypress fab in Silicon Valley exemplifies flexible semiconductor manufacturing. The fab, which was built for a total capital investment of $36 million, manufactures over 100 different devices using 26 different process technologies. Its very short fab cycle times of about six weeks (compared to more than 16 weeks at a typical U.S. semiconductor manufacturer) allow the company to respond rapidly to changing market conditions. Moreover, by keeping assembly in the region, Cypress has maintained a four-day assembly cycle time (compared to six weeks for the large semiconductor firms which use offshore assembly.)[14]

Electronic design automation (combining advances in computer-aided design, engineering, and testing) further enhances the flexibility of the new producers as chip and systems designers are increasingly able to implement their ideas directly onto silicon. Custom and semi-custom integrated circuits now can be designed in weeks rather than months, while complex niche products at the very large scale integration (VLSI) level are being developed in months rather than years.

Finally, these start-ups have spread the prohibitive costs of chipmaking and further shortened their time-to-market by unbundling the production process. While the established firms designed, manufactured, and assembled integrated circuits in-house (and occasionally even ventured into systems production), the new firms tend to be highly focused. Many, such as Weitek, Altera and Chips & Technologies specialize in chip design alone and avoid the expense of a fabrication facility by subcontracting manufacturing. Others, including Cypress and Integrated Device Technology (IDT), specialize in leading-edge process technologies and design-process integration. Application specific integrated circuit (ASIC) producers such as LSI Logic and VLSI Technology assist systems firms to design semicustom chips which they in turn manufacture. And still others, such as Orbit Semiconductor, serve solely as quick turnaround, high-performance manufacturing foundries for chip and system houses.

This unbundling promotes technological upgrading. Each firm remains at the leading-edge of its particular expertise—be it chip design, fabrication processes, engineering and design services, or fast turnaround manufacturing —and has access to the products and services of equally sophisticated and specialized suppliers. Cypress founder T.J. Rodgers has even chosen to grow his company through internally funded start-ups rather than risk the loss of focus. Thus the $200 million company now consists of five relatively autonomous enterprises, each with a distinct technical mandate, which are linked by common strategy, vision, and management systems.

The successes of these 1980s start-ups demonstrate that neither scale nor vertical integration is necessary to survive in the increasingly capital-intensive semiconductor industry. These organizational and technological changes have allowed Silicon Valley's highly focused chipmakers to introduce state-of-the-art products faster than their more integrated competitors. While new product lead times in the industry traditionally exceeded 2 years, firms like Cirrus Logic have shortened development times to nine months.[15] This capability is crucial to compete in markets which require new product introductions every 12 to 18 months.

In short, while the region's established producers sought to mass produce general purpose, commodity devices, the new Silicon Valley chipmakers compete by getting to market first with a continuing flow of specialized products. These start-ups are organized to develop state-of-the-art products and processes and to target technological "windows of opportunity," rather than to pursue the high volumes required to move down the "learning curve" and reduce unit costs on standardized parts.

As they continue to introduce differentiated new products, the specialist chipmakers further fragment semiconductor markets. In the words of Weitek's Vice President of Marketing, John Rizzo:

> You've got to keep subdividing the market and making the niches smaller and smaller. A $1.5 billion market is not one product, it's one hundred products.[16]

And as fast-growing demand for semi-custom products such as gate arrays turns them into commodities, ASIC firms such as LSI Logic have responded by designing higher performance products for narrower, more specialized niches. Even the prototypical commodity market, standard memories, is being segmented by a proliferation of specialized niche products which are more tightly coupled to particular applications or systems.[17]

While commodity chips generated 80% of industry revenue in 1983, their share had fallen to 40% by 1988.[18] This change, referred to by one investment analyst as a "structural shift in the semiconductor industry away from a commodity-driven business," [19] is forcing the established producers to become more flexible. Even National Semiconductor, long known as a producer of commodity "jelly beans," is now replacing its standard, off-the-shelf parts with high-margin, proprietary devices. And while the attention of policy makers is focused on the declining share of U.S. producers in commodity markets, Silicon Valley's specialist chipmakers continue to dominate in high-performance, high value-added and customized semiconductors.

The Importance of Regional Networks

These strategies allowed firms such as Cypress and LSI Logic to grow profitably even during the semiconductor industry's worst downturn in 1985-86. But the success of these start-ups is not merely the work of individual entrepreneurs, nor is the region's continued vitality a demonstration of the intrinsic dynamism of free markets. These new firms have built on Silicon Valley's technical and institutional infrastructure and its dense networks of social and professional relationships. Their successes, like those of their predecessors, are inseparable from a regional environment that is not only rich in skill and know-how, but one which fosters new firm formation and collective learning.

Ironically, the region's established producers helped create this infrastructure during the 1950s and 1960s, but abandoned it in the 1970s as they shifted to high-volume production. They came to view regional traditions of information sharing and networking as signs of immaturity rather than sources of dynamism, and they distanced themselves from customers and suppliers as they standardized products and processes. The 1980s start-ups, by contrast, are formalizing collaborative relationships with customers and suppliers, both within and outside of the region.

Building on the Informal Networks—When Wilf Corrigan resigned as chairman of Fairchild Semiconductor in 1979, he began to sound out former customers and colleagues on the market for semicustom integrated circuits. Fairchild had abandoned its custom chip business in the early 1970s, but Corrigan sensed a renewed opportunity. He encountered a former employee, Robert Walker, who had recently completed research for an article on the state of the custom chip business. Walker joined Corrigan to write a business plan for a firm called LSI Logic Corporation (to focus on semicustom chips) and together they secured financing from some of Silicon Valley's leading venture capital firms, including former colleagues at Kleiner Perkins.

The two then recruited a team of engineers from the group that Walker had worked with on CAD and custom chips at Fairchild during the 1960s. Calling themselves the "over the hill gang," this new team relied on the region's extensive infrastructure of market research firms, public relations specialists, technical consultants, and trade associations for assistance. By 1985, when LSI Logic went public in one of the largest initial public offerings in the industry's history, it had created a burgeoning market for ASICs.

Similar entrepreneurial histories are commonplace in Silicon Valley, where dense social networks and local institutions foster the recombination of experience, skill, and technology into new enterprises. Several hundred new technology firms were formed annually in the region during the 1980s, including two out of every three of the nation's semiconductor start-ups.[20] These firms are unusually resilient. A recent study concluded that while only 75% of U.S. manufacturing start-ups survive their first two years, 90% of Silicon Valley manufacturing start-ups survive their first *six*.[21] As a result, by 1989 the region was home to 4,800 technology establishments, which employed more than 300,000 workers.[22]

It is not simply the concentration of skilled labor, suppliers and information that distinguish the region (as traditional economic accounts would have it).[23] A variety of regional institutions—including Stanford University, several trade associations and local business organizations, and a myriad of specialized consulting, market research, public relations and venture capital firms—provide technical, financial, and networking services which the regions' enterprises often cannot afford individually. By socializing costs and risks and pooling technical expertise, these institutions allow Silicon Valley's specialist firms to continue to innovate and react flexibly.

Venture capitalists are central to these networks. In fact, the venture capital industry in Silicon Valley was created by successful high-technology entrepreneurs who chose to reinvest their earnings in promising local start-ups— not the reverse, as frequently assumed. Today more venture capital is invested in Silicon Valley than elsewhere in the United States: in 1985, for example, local firms received $800 million in venture capital, compared to just over $300 million each in Massachusetts and Southern California, and under $200 million in Texas.[24] And because many of Silicon Valley's most prominent venture capitalists continue to come out of successful local companies, they are able to contribute not simply cash but also years of experience and contacts to new ventures.[25]

Equally important are the social relationships that develop with shared professional experiences and repeated interaction.[26] When John Gifford founded Maxim Integrated Products in 1983 he had already been involved in six different start-ups in his twenty-five year career.[27] This is not uncommon in Silicon Valley, where engineers are often more loyal to the industry and advancing technology than to an individual firm. In the words of LSI's Walker:

> Here in Silicon Valley there's far greater loyalty to one's craft than to one's company. . . . A company is just a vehicle which allows you to work. If you're a circuit designer it's most important for you to do excellent work. If you can't in one firm, you'll move on to another one.[28]

As individuals move from firm to firm in Silicon Valley their paths overlap repeatedly: a colleague might become a customer or a competitor, today's boss could be tomorrow's subordinate. Professional respect, loyalties, and friendships transcend this turmoil.

These networks defy sectoral barriers: individuals move easily from semiconductor to disk drive firms or from computer to network makers. They move from established firms to start-ups (or vice versa) and even to market research or consulting firms, and from consulting firms back into start-ups. And they continue to meet at trade shows, industry conferences, and the scores of seminars, talks, and social activities organized by local business organizations and trade associations. In these forums, relationships are easily formed and maintained, technical and market information is exchanged, business contacts are established, and new enterprises are conceived.

Moreover, these forums help to reproduce the "sense of community" which distinguishes the region. A shared commitment to advancing technology—derived originally from the common formative and professional experiences of engineers in the region—transcends inter-firm rivalries.[29] This social cohesion is reflected in the poster of the Silicon Valley "family tree" which hangs on many walls in the region (a genealogy of the scores of start-ups descended from Fairchild Semiconductor) and in frequent references to firms or individuals as "grandfathers" or "offspring."[30]

Although it is no longer true that "everyone knows everyone" in Silicon Valley, executives still regard the density and openness of the region's social and professional networks as a distinct advantage. Those who have worked elsewhere concur that the extent of informal exchange in Silicon Valley surpasses even other U.S. centers of technology industry such as Route 128 in Massachusetts and Austin, Texas.[31] Technical and market information thus diffuse rapidly among customers, suppliers, and competitors within the region, continually paving the way for new opportunities and enterprises.

This decentralized and fluid environment also promotes the diffusion of intangible technological capabilities and understandings. When individuals move between firms (and even sectors) in the region, they carry the tacit knowledge which is specific to a particular production process—and which cannot be bought or sold, or even written down. In fact, IDT's Larry Jordan claims that a distinct language has evolved in the region and that certain technical terms used by semiconductor production engineers in Silicon Valley would not even be understood by their counterparts in Boston's Route 128. The localization of technical know-how and skills encourages an ongoing process of learning by problem solving among the region's semiconductor and computer firms and the variety of linked industries.

This is not to suggest that conflicts are absent in Silicon Valley. It is the very intensity of competition among local producers that spurs the technological innovation for which the region is famous. In fact, competitive rivalries often become highly personalized, as status is defined by technical excellence and innovation as much as by market share. Lawsuits and conflicts over intellectual property are now commonplace. Yet even as these competitive pressures intensify, the sense of loyalty and shared commitment to technological excellence unifies the members of this industrial community.

Thus while Silicon Valley's high rates of inter-firm mobility and new firm formation may lead to losses for individual firms—as suggested by critics like Ferguson—it also fosters a dynamic process of industrial adaptation. The region as a whole benefits from an ongoing process of experimentation and collective learning as new ideas are continually recombined with existing skill, technology, know-how, and experience.

"Outgrowing" the Networks—The competitive difficulties of the region's established semiconductor producers—the "fathers" of Silicon Valley—demonstrate the importance of these networks. The companies which made Silicon Valley famous for their responsiveness and innovation withdrew from the networks in their shift to commodity production. Fairchild Semiconductor was not alone when it closed its computer-aided-design business in 1974: virtually all of the region's large firms rejected specialty and custom production in favor of standard products in the same period (thus infuriating small and medium-sized computer systems customers who depended on custom chips but could not afford to produce their own).[32]

By the late 1970s, the growing threat of low-cost Japanese producers led firms such as National Semiconductor, Intel, and AMD to invest heavily in dedicated, high-volume fab lines in order to reduce their unit costs. In fact, domestic semiconductor manufacturing capacity doubled between 1978 and 1980 as capital expenditures increased from eight to twenty percent of sales.[33] Silicon Valley's chipmakers quickly "matured"—changing from small, flexible enterprises into large and bureaucratic commodity-oriented corporations. This led many observers to predict an end to start-ups in the semiconductor industry.[34]

Failing to recognize the importance of the region and its relationships to their past successes, the merchant semiconductor firms chose an autarkic approach to mass production. As they standardized products and processes to achieve high-volume output and move down the "learning curve," they saw little need for the ongoing interaction with customers, suppliers, and competitors that had characterized specialty production.[35]

In 1979, Intel co-founder Andrew Grove articulated the industry consensus when he announced that the task for the 1980s was to "market pre-fabricated mass produced solutions to users."[36] Intel soon became infamous for its arrogant "take it or leave it" attitude toward its customers.[37] By 1987, a prominent venture capitalist observed that "the customer has become a distant entity to the merchant semiconductor producers."[38] As a result, firms such as NS, AMD, and Intel missed a series of key technical and market opportunities, including the CMOS process, ASICs, and chip sets. They also began losing customers to the more responsive Japanese producers.

Not only did the large chipmakers distance themselves from their customers, but they also antagonized their equipment suppliers, which tended to be small, undercapitalized firms. As they geared up for high-volume production, the merchants sought to shift the burden of increasingly severe business cycles onto their suppliers by double ordering during boom times and cancelling orders abruptly during downturns. Forced to minimize costs, they played key vendors against one another for price reductions. This reinforced the tendency of the financially weak equipment makers to ship products which were not fully debugged, and eliminated the trust needed to jointly refine and improve the complex process of manufacturing semiconductors. Recent research suggests that the inferior quality and lower yields of U.S. semiconductor producers relative to their Japanese competitors was a direct result of this arm's-length relationship.[39]

Even the informal cooperative practices of the 1960s and 1970s such as cross licensing and second sourcing were largely abandoned. Ignoring their own genesis, the merchants initiated lawsuits against former cross-licensees, suspected imitators and employees who left to start their own firms.

Finally, driven by the pressures of commodity production to minimize costs, Silicon Valley's merchants shifted manufacturing out of the region to lower-cost locations, both in the U.S. and overseas. While semiconductor assembly and test operations were shifted to Asia during the 1960s to exploit substantial wage differentials, during the late 1970s the merchant producers relocated wafer fabrication facilities to lower-cost areas within the U.S. It appeared that only high-level research, design and prototype production would remain in high-cost Silicon Valley.

This spatial separation of design, manufacturing, and assembly further undermined the ability of local semiconductor firms to improve products or to respond rapidly to market changes.[40] Although the problems created by distance can often be overcome by active management, this separation appears to have exacerbated a growing gulf between design and manufacturing.

By pursuing an autarkic version of mass production, Silicon Valley's leading chipmakers abandoned the flexibility and technological dynamism which had distinguished them in the past. In the words of one Intel vice president:

> Remember what Silicon Valley companies were good at to begin with: sensing new market opportunities, new market development, and prototype product development

. . . Until recently, the GNP of Silicon Valley was all new products. Silicon Valley simply hasn't been well positioned to handle the commodity market.[41]

This is not to suggest that the shift to mass production was necessarily mistaken. Silicon Valley's producers could have pursued a successful high-volume production strategy without abandoning the regional networks. Like the Japanese, they would have organized themselves to learn from their customers and equipment suppliers and maintained close ties between product development, manufacturing, and assembly.[42] By adopting an autarkic version of mass production just as the Japanese were refining a highly integrated approach however, Silicon Valley's merchant producers fell behind in customer relations, manufacturing improvements and product quality and quickly lost market share to Japanese competitors.

Formalizing the Networks—Silicon Valley's 1980s start-ups, by contrast, are not simply building on the region's social and professional networks—they are formalizing them. Firms such as Cypress, IDT, and Weitek have rejected the arm's-length relations of the commodity producers, and are building partnerships with customers and suppliers in order to monitor changing markets and jointly redefine products and processes.

The proliferation of strategic alliances in the industry is one clear indication of this reorientation. Semiconductor start-ups have forged more than 350 alliances since 1979, mostly involving technology sharing, subcontracting of chip fabrication, or joint product development.[43] In many cases, start-ups are collaborating with one another, as in the alliance between Cypress and Altera to jointly develop high-density EPLDs. In other cases a start-up teams up with a larger firm, as in the technology-licensing and manufacturing agreement between Seeq and National for high-density EEPROMS.

In a highly publicized case which typifies these partnerships, Hewlett-Packard opened up its state-of-the-art foundry for the first time to chip design specialist Weitek to manufacture a very high speed data-crunching chip. As a result, H-P now differentiates its workstations with a higher speed chip than it could have bought or designed in-house, while Weitek markets this sophisticated chip to other systems makers. Both firms see the relationship as paving the way for a succession of future joint efforts and technology exchanges.

These relations between chipmakers and their subcontractors are blurring the boundaries between independent firms. H-P sees itself as an extension of Weitek's manufacturing, in spite of the great differences in the size of the two firms. According to Jeffrey Miller, Vice President of Marketing at semiconductor producer Adaptec:

Our relationship with our vendors is not much different than my relationship was at Intel with our corporate foundry—except that now I get treated as a customer, not as corporate overhead. . . . It really is very hard to define where we end and where our subcontractors begin.[44]

Many start-ups are working closely with their equipment makers as well. Cypress engineers claim, for example, that it is critical that their supplier of ion implanters is located just across the parking lot because it allows them to confer, adjust complex processes, and trouble shoot easily. Others report collaborating with wafer stepper and automated test equipment producers to design and de-bug products which allow for rapid product change and reduced equipment set-up times. LSI Logic, for example, jointly develops automatic test equipment software for ASICs with local equipment maker Asix Systems.

Finally, the new chipmakers are building partnerships with customers in the computer systems industry. ASIC producers must work very closely with their customers in order to help them design semicustom circuits. But even producers of semistandard products like Cypress and IDT treat customers as extensions of their organizations in order to keep up with the accelerating pace of new product introductions and define products for highly focused applications. Alliances with trend-setting computer firms allow the chipmakers to stay apprised of fast-changing systems requirements and target emerging niches rapidly.

Design specialist Weitek is so committed to building close ties with customers that it maintains one applications engineer for every field salesman, compared with an engineer for every 16 salesmen at a traditional firm. The firm's Vice President of Marketing, John Rizzo, explains that he learned the importance of collaboration only after leaving Intel (where customers were largely ignored) to work for Apple Computers (where he gained the customer's perspective). At Weitek, he claims:

> We're trying to build an intangible emotional bond and loyalty between ourselves and the customer. Those intangible bonds are the hardest things for a competitor to break.[45]

Of course, all of these relationships are not within the region, or even within the U.S.; hundreds of alliances have been formed between domestic and foreign technology firms. One of Weitek's closest partnerships is with Texas-based Compaq and H-P is jointly developing its RISC microprocessor with Hitachi. In addition, many Silicon Valley semiconductor start-ups subcontract manufacturing to fabs in Japan, Taiwan, and Korea.[46] Yet proximity greatly facilitates the collaboration required for fast-changing and complex technologies which involve ongoing interaction, mutual adjustment, and learning.

The Creation of Regional Production Networks

The success of Silicon Valley's specialist semiconductor producers is inseparable from the growth of the computer systems producers that now dominate the region (see Table 3). New computer producers such as Silicon Graphics, Sun Microsystems, and Mips Computers, along with established

Table 3. Semiconductor and Computer Firms

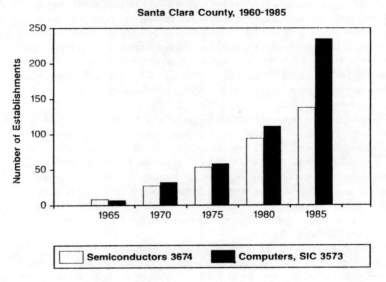

Santa Clara County, 1960-1985

☐ Semiconductors 3674   ■ Computers, SIC 3573

Source: County Business Patterns

firms such as Hewlett Packard, Tandem and Apple are now at the center of the region's emerging production networks.[47] As these systems firms rely increasingly on custom and specialized parts to differentiate their systems, they are being drawn into collaborative relations with networks of suppliers both within and outside of the region.

Sun Microsystems typifies the new systems firms: they design their own products and software and perform limited printed circuit board manufacturing and final assembly in-house; they subcontract or purchase the rest of their inputs, including ASICs, disk drives, terminals, power supplies, and networking hardware. Even the microprocessor at the heart of Sun's workstation is manufactured externally. By unbundling production and collaborating with subcontractors and suppliers, these systems firms share the costs and spread the risks of new product design and production, reduce their time to market, and increase the frequency of new product introductions. Sun, for example, introduced four major product generations in its first five years of business. This accelerating pace of new product introductions in turn has forced both start-ups and established systems producers to become more flexible.

Take the case of Mips Computer Systems. Mips was formed in 1984 to produce RISC-based microprocessors and computer systems. Despite its state-of-the-art microprocessor, Mips was nearly bankrupt by 1987, unable to sustain the cost of maintaining a semiconductor fab and innovating in chips, boards, and systems simultaneously. A new management team chose to focus solely on system-level design and to rely on independent semiconductor producers to manufacture, market, and support their RISC chips. According to the Vice President of Marketing at IDT (one of the subcontractors):

> The concept is that Mips is the hub and each of the partners are spokes on the wheel. . . .
> Each of the partners shares equally in the product knowledge and product evolution.[18]

Managers at other Silicon Valley firms similarly describe their relations with suppliers and subcontractors as partnerships, increasingly between equals. While some like H-P and Apple began by pursuing the cost reductions and quality improvements of just-in-time production, they are now building long-term and trust-based relationships—particularly with suppliers of technically complex and fast-changing components.

This represents a radical departure from past practices of seeking the lowest-cost supplier to meet pre-defined specs. Both customers and suppliers describe mutual commitments not to abandon each other during downturns or to exploit advantages during upturns. Many work to ensure that their suppliers survive hard times. For example, when several of Adaptec's major customers went out of business simultaneously, a key supplier extended credit to the firm, enabling it to stay in business. Other firms help identify new customers for their suppliers during tough periods.

The best of these partnerships evolve into highly interactive relationships with two-way flows of information, extensive technology exchange, and joint problem solving. Apple purchasing director Jim Bilodeau claims that good partnerships with key vendors involve not simply on-time delivery and quality control but continual extension of the relationship to new areas. He suggests that joint investment in new capital equipment, joint product development, shared funding of key engineering talent, and technology exchanges, are all ways to "build suppliers that you can keep healthy and they in turn will keep you healthy . . . The more you can get your vendors to think about you when building new products the better."[19]

In short, the process of solving problems and charting future directions in a technologically volatile environment is increasingly a cooperative effort by networks of linked firms. When Sun involves its contract manufacturer Solectron in the process of designing as well as producing the central processing units and peripherals for its workstations, or when a team of Sun and Cypress engineers collaborate in a shared facility to develop a high-performance version of Sun's RISC microprocessor, the boundaries of these firms begin to blur.

Despite this blurring of firm boundaries, however, both customers and suppliers make an explicit effort to avoid dependence and to preserve one another's autonomy. Most Silicon Valley companies today prefer that no customer, itself included, account for more than 20% of a supplier's output. These limits on dependence ensure that while firms benefit from collaboration in a shared goal, they do not become so tightly integrated as to loose the competitive spirit to innovate.

This is not to imply that all supplier relations in Silicon Valley are collaborative: computers still use large numbers of commodity semiconductors such as DRAMS and capacitors which are purchased in volume from the lowest-cost producers (often Asian). Moreover, there is a wide range of technologically unsophisticated parts—such as boxes and cables—which are competitively sourced without extensive relationship building.

However, as collaboration extends to a wider circle of firms, it generates a process of complementary innovation between networks of autonomous but interdependent producers in Silicon Valley. Not only do they spread their risk by serving a diversified customer base, but suppliers share the learning and know-how gained from serving a customer in one sector with customers in other industries. Collaboration thus both intensifies competitive pressures and contributes to the technological vitality of the region, ensuring that, in the words of Sun's purchasing director Scott Metcalf, "the world's best suppliers of technology products are in Silicon Valley."[50]

The process of reciprocal technological upgrading is clear in the transformation of the contract manufacturing industry. Flextronics, one of the region's largest contract manufacturers, grew explosively during the 1980s as it shifted from being a consignment assembler (a classic job shop) to a full turnkey assembler assisting with design and supplier selection as well as assembly and testing of printed circuit boards. As more systems firms subcontract manufacturing, the contract manufacturing industry is changing from low-skill, labor-intensive assembly to a high-skill, capital-intensive business. In fact, by investing in new technologies (such as surface mount technology) and serving customers in a variety of businesses, firms such as Flextronics and Solectron have achieved a level of manufacturing expertise unsurpassed among systems producers in the Valley.

Collaborative relations are by no means limited to Silicon Valley firms, yet there is little doubt that geographic proximity fosters the frequent interaction and personal trust needed to maintain these relationships. Robert Todd, CEO of Flextronics, claims that in his business, true collaboration cannot survive over great distances for long because of the continuous need to adapt jointly to unanticipated contingencies. As a result, Flextronics has built regional centers around the U.S. to serve localized clusters of customers. As Apple's Bilodeau notes:

> Our purchasing strategy is that our vendor base is close to where we're doing business. We like them to be next door. If they can't, they need to be able to project an image like they are next door.[51]

The need for continual interaction—particularly in a period of market volatility and rapid new product introduction—thus motivates firms to continue clustering in Silicon Valley, in spite of its exorbitant housing prices and high labor costs. Intensified regional concentration thus accompanies the ongoing internationalization of production.

Conclusion

Today, Silicon Valley is flourishing. While the performance of individual technology firms varied considerably during the 1980s, employment increased by more than 35%. The region's specialist producers continued to dominate growing markets for high-performance microprocessors, logic and memory chips, and computer systems. And as both new and established firms prosper, the geographic boundaries of the region expanded beyond Santa Clara County, spilling north into San Mateo, east into Fremont and south to Santa Cruz.[52]

Silicon Valley's resilience owes as much to its rich networks of social, professional and commercial relationships as to the efforts of individual entrepreneurs. The informal cooperation which promoted the diffusion of technology and know-how during the 1960s and 1970s was formalized through partnerships in the 1980s. Paradoxically, both cooperation and competition are intensifying as local firms organize themselves to learn with their customers, suppliers, and competitors about what to make next and how to make it.

However, the industrial fragmentation that is a source of Silicon Valley's flexibility and dynamism also represents its greatest vulnerability. There is no forum in the region for the administrative coordination and strategic planning which is achieved by the management of a vertically integrated firm. Individual firms cannot stay fully abreast of the rapid pace of market and technological change, nor can the evolving system of inter-firm supplier networks in Silicon Valley substitute for systematic, long-range planning.

The U.S. trade deficit in electronics has dramatized both the need for an industrial strategy in Silicon Valley and the absence of institutions to coordinate one. The region's venture capitalists, consulting firms, business organizations, and universities are largely private and narrowly specialized, and the local public sector is focused exclusively on providing the physical infrastructure for development. As a result, there is no vehicle for developing a regional response to shared challenges such as shortages of engineers or external technological shifts.

This institutional vacuum reflects the longstanding distrust of the public sector in Silicon Valley. The industry's early leaders were explicitly hostile toward the activities of large firms, banks, and government of any sort. In an environment of rapid and sustained growth, there was little need for collective action. Even today's entrepreneurs describe their successes in George Gilder's language of individualism and entrepreneurship, failing to recognize the importance of the region and its networks to their continued dynamism.

The semiconductor crisis did politicize a segment of Silicon Valley. In 1978, the region's commodity chipmakers formed the Semiconductor Industry Association (SIA) and, in response to heightened Japanese competition, abandoned their laissez-faire views. Unlike the established trade associations in the region, the American Electronics Association (AEA) and the Semiconductor Equipment Manufacturers International (SEMI)—which were oriented toward providing technical, educational and market services for small and medium-sized technology firms—the SIA devoted its attention exclusively to lobbying Washington for favorable trade and tax legislation and other federal support.

Although it represents only a handful of the region's technology firms, the SIA succeeded in establishing itself in the public eye as the representative of Silicon Valley—even of American technology industry. But once again, the established semiconductor firms overlooked the importance of the region's networks. The initial "victory" of the SIA in attaining the semiconductor trade agreement with Japan in 1986, for example, alienated the region's computer systems firms, who resented the dramatic price increases for memory chips and the subsequent memory shortages.[53] Nor did it win the support of the rest of the Silicon Valley community, including most of the semiconductor start-ups. Moreover, by the late 1980s, the AEA had accepted the SIA's definition of competitiveness as a sectoral problem which could be solved only at the national level, and redirected its resources away from local management education and training programs towards lobbying the federal government.

Sematech, the collaborative semiconductor manufacturing consortium, also has limited promise as an industrial strategy for Silicon Valley because its membership is severely restricted. Only 14 of the 293 semiconductor producers in the U.S. are members of Sematech and none of Silicon Valley's recent start-ups have joined the consortium because its prohibitive fees exclude all but the largest firms.[54] In addition, several of the region's equipment manufacturers have recently discontinued their participation in SEMI/ Sematech (which represents 84 U.S. equipment and materials vendors to Sematech), claiming that it favors large firms over small and is too expensive.[55] As a result, critics like Cypress's T.J. Rogers view Sematech as a bailout for aging semiconductor companies.[56] While carefully designed joint research projects could help to preserve the technological position of the U.S. semiconductor industry, a program which excludes so many of the industry's most innovative producers is unlikely to do so.

Silicon Valley needs public forums for debating regional industrial strategies and defining institutions to ensure the flexibility and dynamism of its networks of specialist firms. These institutions should preserve the openness of the region's social and commercial networks and ensure the continuing exchange of information, experience, and technology across industry boundaries and between firms of all sizes. They should enhance the ability of local firms to continually innovate, learn, and adapt to changing conditions—rather than protecting them or isolating them from change.

These institutions might ensure that the region's firms: have access to long-term financing and recent research findings; coordinate technical and managerial training programs and basic research projects; provide export and marketing assistance and global information-gathering services; organize data collection and analysis of the region's fast-changing industrial base; and establish forums for joint assessment of sectoral or regional problems. With time, they would provide a forum for defining and coordinating responses to external developments such as unanticipated technical advances and competitive challenges from outside of the region.

Trade associations in Silicon Valley already perform some of these activities. Local economic development agencies and business organizations could take on others. Others would require the creation of entirely new institutions, which can only develop out of public dialogue and debate.[57] To begin such a dialogue requires that Silicon Valley's entrepreneurs and managers overcome their deep-seated distrust of the public sector and recognize the social basis of their success.

The main challenge facing Silicon Valley today is to transcend the language of individual achievement and build a vocabulary which reflects a recognition of, and commitment to, the region as a key source of industrial competitiveness. Only a carefully considered public dialogue which defines appropriate regional institutions and moves beyond George Gilder's free markets and Charles Ferguson's national industrial policy can preserve the dynamism of the Silicon Valley economy.

Glossary

Application specific integrated circuit (ASIC): An IC designed by or with customers for a particular application. Includes full custom devices and semicustom gate arrays, standard cells, and programmable logic devices.

Central processing unit (CPU): The section of a computer system that controls interpretation and execution of instructions.

Chip set: A set of VLSI devices, designed using ASIC tools, which emulate the function of personal computer but are smaller and faster due to a radically reduced part count.

Complementary metal-oxide semiconductor (CMOS): A manufacturing process which allows ICs to function with far less power and than traditional metal-oxide semiconductors.

Dynamic random access memory (DRAM): The cheapest and least power consuming semiconductor memory which must be electrically refreshed periodically to retain memory.

Electrically erasable and programmable read-only memory (EEPROM): A memory device in which stored information can be erased and reprogrammed electrically while still in the circuit, e.g., from a keyboard.

Erasable programmable read-only memory (EPROM): A memory device in which the stored information can be erased and reprogrammed by exposure to ultra-violet light through a window in the package.

Erasable programmable logic device (EPLD): IC sold as a blank logic device which allows the user, typically a system designer, to customize it to a specific application.

Gate array: An ASIC in which an array of digital logic gates are interconnected to customer specifications to perform a specific function. Typically only the last one or two layers of the circuit are customized.

Integrated circuit (IC): A semiconductor circuit combining the functions of many electronic components in a single monolithic substrate which is usually silicon.

Metal-oxide semiconductor (MOS): Transistors and ICs that utilize metal (or silicon) gate devices insulated by an oxide layer from the semiconductor or silicon channel.

Microprocessor (MPU): A single chip large-scale IC which is the central processing unit of a small computer. It performs all logic and arithmetic operations and controls the operation of the other parts of the system, such as input, memory storage devices, and output devices.

Printed circuit board (PCB): Provides the hundreds of electrical interconnections between the components in a circuit through the flat, thin copper pathways on or embedded within an insulating base material (typically paper of fiberglass).

Programmable logic device (PLD): IC formed of digital logic gates connected together in a matrix and designed to be customized by the user, typically by "blowing" out fusable links.

Programmable read-only memory (PROM): A memory device in which information can be stored after the device is manufactured, but cannot be altered.

Random access memory (RAM): A memory device in which information can be entered into or retrieved quickly from any storage site and which is used to hold temporary information.

Read-only memory (ROM): A memory storage device in which the information is permanently wired into the device, and is used to store permanent instructions.

Reduced instruction set computing (RISC): Microprocessor which executes fewer, less complex instructions than the traditional microprocessor, thus streamlining and accelerating the entire chip.

Static random access memory (SRAM): The fastest and most expensive random access memory device which only loses its stored information when power is shut off.

Standard cell: An ASIC which is created using standard circuit cells arranged in a custom manner to perform specific functions. Closest of all ASICs to full custom.

Surface mount technology (SMT): Automated PCB assembly method in which devices are mounted directly onto the board surface, and which shrinks the board size significantly by allowing manufacturers to fit more devices into the same space.

Through-hole assembly: Conventional printed circuit board assembly method where component leads are pushed into holes through the board.

Yield: A measure of the efficiency of a production process determined by the ratio of acceptable parts completed to the number of parts attempted.

Very large scale integration (VLSI): A term applied to integrated circuit chips containing a minimum of 5,000 logic gates, or more than 16,000 bits of memory.

References

1. "The Chips Are Down," *San Jose Mercury News*, December 1, 1986.
2. Dataquest Inc., "Survey of Semiconductor Start-Ups" (Mountain View, CA: Dataquest, 1988).
3. C. Ferguson, "From the People Who Brought You Voodoo Economics," *Harvard Business Review* (May/June 1988), pp. 55-62; G. Gilder, "The Revitalization of Everything: The Law of the Microcosm," *Harvard Business Review* (March/April 1988), pp. 49-61.
4. See A. Saxenian, "The Cheshire Cat's Grin: Innovation, Regional Development and the Cambridge Case" *Economy and Society*, 18/4 (Winter 1989) for a critique of this free market approach (the "high-tech recipe").
5. These regions are modern counterparts of the 19th century Marshallian industrial districts. See C. Sabel, "Flexible Specialisation and the Reemergence of Regional Economies," in P. Hirst and J. Zeitlin, eds., *Reversing Industrial Decline* (Oxford: Berg, 1988); M. Piore and C. Sabel, *The Second Industrial Divide* (New York, NY: Basic Books, 1984).
6. The research for this project entailed over fifty open-ended interviews with Silicon Valley executives, managers, engineers, and venture capitalists that were conducted between 1988 and 1990.
7. See, for example, T. J. Rogers, "Return to the Microcosm," letter to the editor of the *Harvard Business Review* (July/August 1988), pp. 139-140.
8. While National was traditionally known for emphasizing low-cost production of commodity memories and AMD, Intel, and MMI specialized in design innovation (e.g., in microprocessors), all were oriented toward serving mass markets.
9. For a discussion of the various specialization strategies, see B. Cole, "ASIC Houses Revise Their Strategies," *Electronics*, August 6, 1987.
10. J. Corn and R. Rajaratnam "Cypress Semiconductor and Integrated Device Technology" Needham Investment Analysis, Needham & Co., Inc. April 4, 1990.
11. J. McCreadie and V. Rice, "Nine New Mavericks," *Electronic Business*, September 4, 1989.
12. M. Mehler, "Minifabs Reshape IC Production," *Electronics Business*, June 1, 1987; B. Cole, "Getting to the Market on Time," *Electronics* (April 1989).
13. M. Borrus, *Competing for Control* (New York, NY: Ballinger, 1988).
14. Corn and Rajaratnam, op. cit.
15. McReadie and Rice, op. cit.
16. Cited in V. Rice, "The Upstart Start-Ups," *Electronic Business*, August 15, 1987.
17. While in 1985 there were only half a dozen basic designs, there are now more than 100 standard memory architectures and options, and the process will continue. B. Cole, "By the Mid-90's the Memory Market Will Look Like the Logic Business," *Electronics* (August 1988).
18. M. Leibowitz, "ASIC Strategies for the Big Five," *Electronic Business*, October 15, 1988.
19. Investment report by Alex Brown & Sons, Baltimore. Cited in J. Goldman, "Nine Valley Chip Companies Recommended by R&D Firm," *The San Jose Business Journal*, October 30, 1989.
20. A. Scott and D. Angel, "The U.S. Semiconductor Industry: A Locational Analysis," *Environment and Planning D*, 19 (1987).
21. These are the results of a study of more than 400 Silicon Valley companies over a 20-year period (1967-1987) conducted by Professor Albert V. Bruno, University of Santa Clara School of Business. Cited in *The New York Times*, March 7, 1988.

22. *Rich's Business Guide to Silicon Valley and Northern California* (Los Altos, CA: Rich's Business Directories, 1989).
23. See, for example, P. David and J. Rosenbloom, "Marshallian Factor Market Externalities and the Dynamics of Industrial Localization,"Center for Economic Policy Research, Publication No. 118, Stanford University, 1987.
24. *Electronic Business*, 1987.
25. Silicon Valley's venture capitalists are typically intimately involved in the businesses they support: they advise entrepreneurs on business plans and strategies, help find coinvestors, recruit key people to fill out a management team, provide regular (even daily) management advice, and serve on boards of directors.
26. M. Granovetter, "Economic Action and Social Structure: The Problem of Embeddedness," *American Journal of Sociology*, 91/3 (1985).
27. D. Angel, "The Labor Market for Engineers in the U.S. Semiconductor Industry," *Economic Geography*, 65/2 (1986).
28. Interview, Robert Walker, Vice President and Chief Engineering Officer, LSI Logic Corporation, May 2, 1988.
29. Journalistic accounts of Silicon Valley capture this sense of social cohesion. See E. Rogers and J. Larsen, *Silicon Valley Fever* (New York, NY: Basic Books, 1984); M. Malone, *The Big Score* (New York, NY: Doubleday, 1985); E. Braun and S. Mac-Donald, *Revolution in Miniature* (New York, NY: Cambridge University Press, 1978).
30. A. Saxenian, "A High Technology Industrial District: Silicon Valley in the American Context," in P. Perulli, ed., *Citta della scienza e della technologia*, Quaderni della Fondazione Istituto Gramsci Veneto 6/7 (Venice: Arsenale Editrice, 1989).
31. See J. Weiss and A. Delbecq, "High Technology Cultures and Management: Silicon Valley and Route 128," *Group and Organization Studies*, 12/1 (March 1987).
32. As late as the early 1970s, the consensus of the industry was that the future lay in customization of large-scale integrated circuits and that the role of standard products would be small. The history is detailed in R. Wilson, P. Ashton, and T. Egan, *Innovation, Competition, and Government Policy in the Semiconductor Industry* (Lexington, MA: Heath, 1980).
33. *Business Week*, July 21, 1980.
34. See, for example, A. Robinson, "Giant Corporations From Tiny Chips Grow," *Science*, 208 (1980).
35. For the classic explanation of the "learning curve" in semiconductors, see R. Noyce, "Microelectronics," *Scientific American*, 237/3 (1977); R. Noyce, "Large-Scale Integration: What Is Yet to Come?" *Science*, 195 (March 1977).
36. Cited in *The San Jose Mercury News*, May 4, 1980.
37. A. Hayashi "The New Intel: Moore Mature, Moore Competitive," *Electronic Business*, November 15, 1987.
38. H. Jarrat, "A Look at the Semiconductor Industry in the 1990s," Speech presented to Robertson, Coleman and Stephens at The 1990 Semiconductor Conference, September 23, 1987.
39. J. Stowsky, "The Weakest Link: Semiconductor Equipment, Linkages, and the Limits to International Trade," Working Paper No. 27, Berkeley Roundtable on the International Economy, University of California, Berkeley, 1988.
40. C. Markides and N. Berg, "Manufacturing Offshore is Bad Business," *Harvard Business Review* (September/October 1988), pp. 113-120.
41. M. Schrage, "Hard Times Descend on Silicon Valley," *The Washington Post*, April 28, 1985.
42. E. Haas, "Applying the Lessons: Networking Semiconductor Companies," *Entrepreneurial Economy*, 6/1 (July/August 1987); M. Aoki, "The Japanese Firm in Transition," in K. Yamamura and Y. Yasuba, eds., *The Political Economy of Japan* (Palo Alto, CA: Stanford University Press, 1987).

43. Dataquest, op. cit., 1988.
44. Interview, Jeffrey Miller, Vice President of Marketing, Adaptec Corporation, May 10, 1988.
45. Cited in S. Jones, "Hewlett Packard Inks Major Chip Deal," *San Jose Business Journal*, May 18, 1987.
46. Observers often view this reliance on offshore foundries as a fatal vulnerability for the U.S. start-ups. They neglect, however, to recognize that manufacturing is only a minimal part of the total costs (typically less than 10%) of these highly specialized, design-intensive chips. Moreover, imitation is not the same threat that it is for a commodity chip maker: their design cycles are so fast that by the time a competitor had produced an imitation of a chip, their next generation would be available. Finally, it is worth noting that this dependence on foreign suppliers is a direct result of the autarkic behavior of the established U.S. semiconductor firms. Many start-ups report being driven to use Asian foundries by the refusal of domestic producers to provide them with manufacturing fab capacity.
47. A growing literature describes network forms of organization, which fall between market exchange and administered hierarchies. However, most scholars neglect the spatial aspects of these networks. See W. Powell "Neither Market Nor Hierarchy: Network Forms of Organization" *Research in Organizational Behavior*, 12 (1990): 293-336. For a more extensive discussion of the supplier relations of Silicon Valley computer systems firms, see A. Saxenian, "The Origins and Dynamics of Production Networks in Silicon Valley," Working Paper No. 516, Institute of Urban and Regional Development, University of California at Berkeley.
48. Cite in C. Koland, "Mips Chip Coalition Targets Leaders in Microprocessors," *San Jose Business Journal*, December 17, 1987.
49. Cited in M. Cohodas, "How Apple Buys Electronics," *Electronics Purchasing* (November 1986).
50. Interview, Scott Metcalf, Purchasing Director, Sun Microsystems, March 30, 1988.
51. "How Apple Buys Electronics," *Electronics Purchasing* (November 1986).
52. This geographic expansion means that the data presented here on Santa Clara County significantly understates the growth of employment in Silicon Valley, which now includes portions of three adjacent counties.
53. A. Pollack, "Chip Pact Falls Short of Goals," *The New York Times*, August 2, 1988. See also D. Mowery and N. Rosenberg, "New Developments in U.S. Technology Policy: Implications for Competitiveness and International Trade Policy," *California Management Review*, 32/1 (Fall 1989): 107-124.
54. Total entrance fees are about $2 million. Sematech requires a $1 million entry fee, and member firms must also join the Semiconductor Research Consortium for a $62,000 entry fee plus annual dues ranging from $65,000 to $2.4 million (depending on firm size). In addition a minimum of 5 engineers must be sent to participate in Sematech activities in Austin. These fees are high even for the established companies (equalling about 10% of their R&D budgets), but they are prohibitive for small firms; moreover, most start-ups can't afford to lose five of their best people. LSI Logic is the only Silicon Valley start-up that belongs to Sematech. It joined because it could afford to (being much larger than other start-ups) and because LSI founder Wilf Corrigan is a close personal friend of the founders of Sematech.
55. V. Rice, "The Decline of Chip Equipment Firms," *San Jose Mercury News*, December 4, 1989.
56. Cypress president T.J. Rogers claims that "Sematech is a carefully constructed lobby effort . . . to deliberately and systematically exclude smaller companies." Successful small firms like Cypress and IDT also claim that they are already ahead of Sematech technologically and thus would not benefit from it. S. Moran, "Sematech's Hefty Member

Fees May Bar Small Chip Makers," *San Jose Business Journal*, May 30, 1988; V. Rice, "Sematech: United We Stand?" *Electronic Business*, May 1, 1988.

57. Models might be drawn from Germany's Baden-Wurtemmburg, where public research institutes, regional governments, and trade associations support networks of innovative small and medium-sized machinery producers. G. Herrigel, "Industrial Order and the Politics of Industrial Change: Mechanical Engineering," in P. Katzenstein, ed., *Toward a Third Republic* (Ithaca, NY: Cornell University Press, 1988).

[19]

Network Dyads in
Entrepreneurial
Settings: A Study of the
Governance of
Exchange Relationships

Andrea Larson
University of Virginia

Social control in network organizational forms is
examined through an inductive field study of a sample of
dyadic relationships established by high-growth
entrepreneurial firms. The social dimensions of the
transactions are central in explaining control and
coordination in the exchange structures. A process
model of network formation is presented that highlights
the importance of reputation, trust, reciprocity, and
mutual interdependence. The network form is proposed
as an alternative to vertical integration for high-growth
entrepreneurial firms. The data also suggest that
studying the network form of governance can provide
insights into firm growth.[•]

INTRODUCTION

The recent proliferation of network organizational forms that
don't fit neatly into either the market or hierarchy
frameworks proposed by Coase (1952) to explain economic
exchange has resulted in some scrambling to explain how
such organizations are governed. The traditional transaction
cost approach also has not been very useful in
understanding the governance of such organizations.
According to the transaction cost approach (Williamson,
1975, 1985), the frequency, uncertainty, and specificity of
assets dedicated to a particular transaction influence the
costs associated with market contracts. When costs rise
sufficiently high, markets fail and transactions are absorbed
within the firm. Williamson (1991) has tried to come to
terms with these network forms in recognizing what he calls
the hybrid form of governance. Hybrids combine aspects of
market transactions and characteristics of hierarchies and fall
between the two alternatives on a continuum. While price
incentives, legal contracts, and administrative monitoring
play a role, cost minimization is the dominant control
mechanism that explains the hybrid organizational form.

The growing number of empirical studies of a variety of
hybrids, however, has challenged the cost-based view.
These exchange arrangements alternatively have been called
quasifirms (Eccles, 1981) and relational contracting
(Macaulay, 1963), as well as hybrids (Powell, 1987) and
networks (Powell, 1990). They have been described in a
variety of settings, including international business
(Contractor and Lorange, 1988), the U.S. construction and
publishing industries (Eccles, 1981; Coser, Kadushin, and
Powell, 1982), Japanese textiles (Dore, 1983), Swedish large
manufacturing companies (Hakansson, 1987), and
entrepreneurial firms (Johannisson, 1987; Jarillo, 1988;
Larson, 1988; Lorenzoni and Ornati, 1988). In contrast to the
efficiency and transaction cost explanation of control and
governance, these accounts point to reciprocity norms,
personal relationships, reputation, and trust as important
factors explaining the duration and stability of the exchange
structures.

As increasing numbers of these non-market and
non-hierarchy forms of organization have been documented,
Williamson's continuum notion of governance structures and
the categories themselves have come under question.
Powell (1990) has built an argument for the network form as

•
I wish to thank Walter Powell, Harrison
White, Eric Leifer, Mark Granovetter, and
R. Edward Freeman for their comments
and suggestions on earlier versions of
this paper. Acknowledgement is also due
William J. Goode, Robert Eccles, Howard
Stevenson, and Lenore Weitzman for
their early help in framing the issues
explored here. Thanks are due Marshall
Meyer, Linda Pike, and the three
anonymous reviewers, whose
recommendations were important in
focusing and refining the paper.

Network Dyads

a distinct organizational arrangement, as opposed to a hybrid
form that combines market and hierarchy. He defined
networks by a set of descriptive characteristics and critical
components. They are distinct from market or hierarchical
arrangements in their heavy reliance on reciprocity,
collaboration, complementary interdependence, a reputation
and relationship basis for communication, and an informal
climate oriented toward mutual gain. In contrast, market
governance arrangements rely primarily on price for control,
and hierarchical structures rely heavily on administrative
authority. According to Powell, firms more likely to engage in
network arrangements will be those needing to exchange
difficult-to-codify, knowledge-intensive skills that are best
transferred through processes of collaborative information
sharing. Powell also pointed to firms engaged in fast-moving
industries with short product cycles as likely to engage in
network partnerships in order to reposition products rapidly
and respond quickly to changing market conditions and
technological developments. Bradach and Eccles (1989)
mapped price, authority, and trust as control mechanisms
onto market, hierarchy, and network, respectively, and noted
that these are ideal types that in reality are often combined.
Such combinations have been documented by Stinchcombe
and Heimer (1985), who found hierarchical dimensions of
oil-exploration-project contracts, and Eccles (1985), who
described market forces and hierarchical authority at work in
transfer pricing within firms.

These alternative views on the nature of exchange
governance point to the need for more information on how
the network form is built and controlled. Existing studies
offer pieces of the picture. In a variety of settings,
investigators have reported social characteristics of network
exchange structures. Personal relationships that resulted in
allegiances were found to shape economic outcomes in the
publishing industry (Coser, Kadushin, and Powell, 1982).
Reciprocity, the importance of good personal relations, and
trust-based cooperation provided control and coordination
and enhanced the effectiveness of network forms in
international joint ventures (Walker, 1988; Doz, 1988;
Hakansson and Johanson, 1988). Looking at network
structures formed by Italian small to mid-sized textile firms,
Lorenzoni and Ornati (1988: 55) found "unconventional
mechanisms of coordination" guiding the collaborative
exchanges, including trust, reciprocity, and mutual
adjustment. In Japanese networked firms, trust and mutual
obligation enhanced information flows. These characteristics
were reinforced by a concern for reputation to give stability
and longevity to interfirm partnerships (Dore, 1987). In his
study of strategic networks and entrepreneurial firms, Jarillo
(1988) argued that trust and concern for reputation are
important in sustained cooperative exchange structures. The
findings suggest that these control mechanisms are
important, yet they have never been explicitly studied.

The purpose of this paper is to look at network structures in
entrepreneurial settings and to examine how control is
exercised in these settings. Field data are used to build a
model that accounts for control in these governance
structures. While economic control is present, social control

is crucial to the formation and maintenance of this form. Social control as understood here encompasses both self-regulation—with a moral dimension—the traditional view of social control as stated by Ross (1906) and restated by Janowitz (1976)—and a feedback process that is jointly determined by and diffused across multiple participants—the modern view of social control, as described by Leifer and White (1986). The specific question explored here is the extent to which social control, as opposed to contracts and formal agreements, governs transactions in entrepreneurial dyads. While Williamson (1991) emphasized the importance of contracts in governing exchanges in hybrid organizations, Macaulay (1963) and Dore (1986) have observed that written agreements and contracts can be relatively unimportant in economic exchange. Because early information from people I talked to in entrepreneurial firms indicated that legal-contractual aspects of exchange were less important than social dimensions, I focused the study on social control to gain a better understanding of its role in the transactions between networked organizations.

Given economists' predictions, one could ask why these transactions were not absorbed under single ownership, given the firms' intensity of mutual involvement. It is quite possible that the conditions present create a more effective control structure for exchange than the framework usually offered when vertically integrated units exchange products and services. In a formal organization, market prices are replaced with administrative coordinating and control mechanisms such as transfer pricing and employee incentives. A central authority mandates the terms of exchange, and negotiation and exit are administratively complex. The intricacies of these administrative challenges make it difficult to structure internal exchange processes efficiently and equitably (Fama and Jensen, 1983). A network structure avoids these problems while institutionalizing cooperation, shared information, and assured results, all of which are considered benefits of vertically integrated exchange.

The network form also offers advantages specific to entrepreneurial firms. The use of a network exchange structure represents a critical leveraging opportunity whereby resources can be gained and competitive advantages realized without incurring the capital investments of vertical integration. Most entrepreneurial companies are not in a sufficiently strong financial position to contemplate the acquisition of critical functions within a single hierarchy, nor would such a strategy necessarily fit with the product/service focus that defines their business. Entrepreneurial firms also need to maximize their adaptability to their environment. These network exchange structures can be seen as a flexible alternative to integration that provides entrepreneurial companies with many of the strategic benefits of vertical integration while avoiding the capital investments and bureaucratic inefficiencies of vertically integrated units.

RESEARCH DESIGN AND METHODS

This investigation was an exploratory ethnographic study for the purpose of understanding the processes by which a set

Network Dyads

of seven highly cooperative interfirm alliances were built and
preserved. The unit of analysis was the exchange
relationship between an entrepreneurial firm and its
partnered organization. What these seven case studies give
us that other research designs cannot is an intensive
investigation of developmental processes that reveals the
common evolutionary patterns among the alliances. The
limits of qualitative research involving a small set of cases
are obvious: We do not know if the results generalize to a
larger and more diverse population. The value of the
research lies, instead, in its capacity to provide insights
through rich detail, to produce a grounded model, and to
generate hypotheses for further testing.

This project did not begin as a study of interfirm alliances
but was the result of a pilot study designed to explore
factors enabling small, successful, high-growth firms to
sustain growth, adaptiveness, and innovation. This pilot
study was the outgrowth of my interest in understanding
how companies can remain entrepreneurial (defined as
adaptive and innovative) as they grow at a fast rate.
Successful rapid growth of small firms is statistically low,
and yet there has been little field investigation of those firms
that have run counter to this trend. The first step was to
identify a set of high-growth firms that had experienced
rapid growth between 1980 and 1986. Companies were
sought that also had 1985 revenues of at least $10 million
and revenue growth of 20 percent or more compounded
annually for five years. These criteria were selected to
ensure an established organizational base (e.g., beyond the
entrepreneur and a small team) and that companies had
experienced similar growth patterns. Sixteen firms were
identified through business contacts and venture capitalists,
and exploratory interviews were conducted with
management at each firm. Once at the firms, I found that
only nine companies met my selection criteria. Interviews at
the nine firms focused on a central question: "What, in your
opinion, explains your organization's rapid growth?" Although
responses varied across firms, and each respondent pointed
to internal factors such as decentralized decision making,
hiring policies, incentive systems, or technology, a pattern
emerged. Uniformly, respondents also reported that certain
critical external relationships with other companies
contributed significantly to the entrepreneurial firm's financial
success, rapid growth, adaptiveness, and innovation.
Although the existence of external ties was not surprising,
the consistency of this finding across the nine firms, and the
emphasis given them, was unexpected. Because very little
had been written about external relations and entrepreneurial
firms, I decided to investigate these external ties in more
detail through further exploratory research. My more focused
research questions were thus defined: What was the nature
of these external exchange relationships, and what enabled
them to operate?

Two of the remaining nine firms declined to participate in
further interviews because of the time it would have
required, and three others were eliminated from the sample
to avoid duplication of products, industry, and revenue size.
Upper management in each of the four remaining firms was

then asked to identify more specifically the sets of outside relationships seen as contributing significantly to growth and competitive success. In each company, sets of two to four alliances were described. From these networks, seven dyads were selected for in-depth study. Each had to be in existence for at least five years, indicating some measure of stability. A second criterion was that the entrepreneurial firm had to give a high rank to benefits derived from the alliance. This set was further culled by the willingness of the partnered organization to participate in the study.

The industries represented were telephone equipment, clothing, computer hardware, and environmental support systems. The latter included equipment to control air quality for sensitive electronic and clean-room processing environments. The companies are called here Telephone Distributor, Clothing Company, HiTech Computer, and Support Products, respectively. Two were manufacturing organizations (HiTech Computer and Support Products); one was a distribution company (Telephone Distributor); and the last was a combination of retail and catalog sales (Clothing Company). Each firm was operating in relatively turbulent competitive arenas. The telephone industry was experiencing deregulation, and Telephone Distributor and its partnered firm were attempting to carve out new market niches. Although the clothing company was in a mature market segment, it was actively growing its catalog business, an area of retailing that was experiencing very rapid growth in the mid-1980s. The computer hardware company was in a highly competitive environment characterized by rapid technology changes and new competition. Support Products, the manufacturer of environmental support systems, was the largest of the entrepreneurial firms and had reached that size very rapidly while having to stay abreast of fast-changing technologies in both manufacturing and product design. Support Products and Clothing Company were in slightly stronger competitive positions in their markets, having already established market niches through their product/service offerings.

The seven partnered organizations were suppliers, distributors, and final customers that linked the entrepreneurial firms backward and forward on the value chain. The partnered organizations varied from small, single-product-supplier businesses to large manufacturing units within even larger national and international firms. Although the scale and scope of these organizations varied considerably, their perspectives on the alliances under study were uniform: Each partner firm agreed that the alliance under study was an important one to both sides. The rewards to partnered firms for involvement in the alliances were different than those of the entrepreneurial firms, yet these companies shared the perspective that these exchange processes were unusual in their high levels of collaboration and cooperation.

In most cases, the primary economic transaction was the transfer of a product; however, one exchange was a subcontracting arrangement for labor only. Another was an unusual relationship with a sales organization. Most of the partnered organizations were tightly interlocked; others

Network Dyads

Figure 1. Dyadic ties and the relative size of the firms by revenue.*

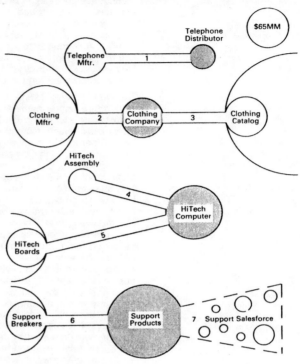

* Shaded circles are entrepreneurial firms.

appeared to be more loosely coupled. Some had very frequent, even daily contact; others communicated less often. The common features of this group of seven alliances were that each lasted for between five and eleven years, each was stable and cooperative, and each was evaluated by participants as having contributed significantly to the entrepreneurial firms' rapid growth and economic success. None of the relationships was terminated during the study period.

The firms partnered with entrepreneurial companies are identified in Figure 1 with the names: Telephone Manufacturer (manufacturer of telephone equipment for small to medium-sized businesses), Clothing Manufacturer (an apparel manufacturer), Clothing Catalog (a printing company), HiTech Boards (designer and manufacturer of complex printed circuit boards), HiTech Assembly (assembler, only, of printed circuit boards), Support Breakers (manufacturer of circuit breakers), and Support Salesforce (a specialized sales and service organization, neither in-house nor a separate organizational entity). The shaded circles are the entrepreneurial firms. The paths between circles, numbered one through seven, represent alliances. The size of each circle illustrates the relative size, by annual dollar

Table 1

Summary of Interviews

Firm	Interviews Number	Hours
Telephone Distributor	7	11
Telephone Manufacturer	4	6
Clothing Company	6	9
Clothing Manufacturer	3	5
Clothing Catalog	4	6.5
HiTech Computer	7	11
HiTech Assembly	5	7.25
HiTech Boards	4	6
Support Products	8	9.5
Support Breakers	3	5
Support Salesforce	2	3.75
Total	53	80

revenues in 1986, of the entrepreneurial companies and their partnered organizations using the $65-million measurement standard at the top right of the page. If an alliance organization was a subunit of a larger parent corporation, this is shown by lines that encircle the firm and move off the figure to the left or right.

While the research was not conceived as comparative at the outset, an implicit comparative method entered the data collection process early in the interview process. Respondents repeatedly contrasted these cooperative alliances with their more numerous and typical adversarial supplier and customer relationships. Most external links to other firms were arm's-length exchanges based on price. The pattern also emerged of respondents comparing these exchange relations with a theoretical organizational alternative, that is, vertical integration under single ownership. This allowed me to compare this organizational form with traditional market exchanges and hierarchically ordered transactions within formal organizations.

Individual, in-person interviews with founding entrepreneurs and top managers of the companies were conducted at the companies, using a two-part questionaire as a guide. The first section included questions designed to gather information on each company's history, products, and markets. The second section focused on the alliance, with the purpose of exploring its origins, the importance and impact of the relationship to each side, contracts and terms, the nature of routine interactions, and the benefits derived.[1] Informants were not asked to fill out a questionnaire; instead, the questionaire was used as a guide to direct and structure otherwise open-ended interviews. The questionaire is given in the Appendix. Interviews were tape-recorded and transcribed. Follow-up questions were explored through a combination of face-to-face interviews and telephone conversations. The data collection included fifty-three interviews, each averaging one and a half hours, for a total of eighty interview hours during the summer and fall of 1986 and the winter of 1986–1987. The number of interviews with each company and the length of interview times are summarized in Table 1. Interviews with

[1] See Larson (1991) for a detailed account of the significant benefits each side derived from participation in the sustained exchange structures.

Network Dyads

entrepreneurial company managers included discussions of one or two alliances, whereas partner-company interviews focused on one alliance. As a consequence, each alliance was discussed in anywhere from 11 to 16 full or partial interviews. Interviews were conducted with individuals on both sides of the alliance. Particular effort was made to locate and interview individuals originally involved in the formation of the alliances as well as those persons still actively managing the interfirm relationships. Annual reports, product descriptions, press releases, and other public sources of information about the companies also were reviewed.

THE NETWORK DYADS

The network dyads developed in three phases, each with particular and important social aspects. Figure 2 graphically

Figure 2. A process model of the formation of entrepreneurial dyads.

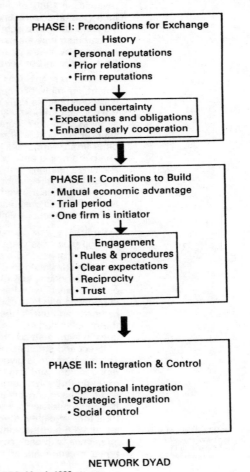

summarizes the formation process of the network dyads.
Preconditions for exchange were set out in Phase I. Prior
personal relationships and known reputations reduced
uncertainty and established expectations that enhanced early
cooperation between the organizations. A second phase
established conditions necessary to build the relationship.
While mutual economic advantage played a role, control in
the nascent exchange structure was the result of the
incremental growth of trust and the evolution of reciprocity
norms during a trial period, in which one of the partnered
firms took the role of initiator as rules and procedures and
expectations were established. In the third phase, the
organizations became operationally and strategically more
tightly integrated. But in lieu of cost considerations or legal
contracts, effective control and coordination were achieved,
and opportunism avoided, through the regulatory presence
of moral obligations, trust, and concern for preserving
reputations.

Phase I: Preconditions for Exchange

Personal reputations and prior relations. Personal
reputations, as well as histories and individual friendships,
were important factors in explaining the formation of ties.
Typically, a foundation for mutual trust was set down before
the two companies began their transactions. The founders of
Telephone Manufacturer and Telephone Distributor had
established good reputations in their industry in prior
positions. The two men who initiated the exchange knew
each other well, having worked together at the same
company. One explained how the partnership started, "It
was because of the trust and respect that had developed in
our prior relationships." This history of personal relations
shaped the context for the new exchange between
organizations by reducing the risks. That is not to say
economic incentives were absent but to point out what is
often missing in the study of economic exchange, that a
social context provides the environment within which
economic exchange can be initiated. In this case, concrete
personal relations provided a conducive frame for economic
exchange. Implicit obligations of fairness and honesty gave
structure and subtle control to this economic exchange from
its outset.

The importance of prior reputations, both of individuals and
companies, came up repeatedly in the interviews. Each
company, within the product markets it served, saw itself as
part of an industry that was better understood as a
community. Telephone Distributor's vice president
commented about his industry and what mattered in that
context, an account that was typical of the firms' outlooks:
"It is a very small community in which certain people have
established credibility and a reputation. The key is who you
know. You can put them all in our parking lot out there."
This quotation suggested an inner circle or network of
individuals within the broader industry circle. Credibility and a
positive reputation—for business practices and business
performance—were attributes of those in the inner circle. As
a consequence, affiliation with respected individuals and
organizations could lift new players into a higher status
group of top industry names. For entrepreneurial firms in

Network Dyads

particular, movement up the industry status hierarchy was one objective, if not often discussed in quite these terms. This was one side of the social context. There was also a negative side to working in community/industry environments where reputations counted and word traveled fast. If affiliation with a respected organization enhanced a second firm's reputation by earning it legitimacy and credibility, then the failure of a relationship could have a serious impact on reputation and status and, subsequently, on business. The president of HiTech Assembly talked about the risk of failure to maintain that company's relationship with HiTech Computer: "If we were to have a major breakdown in our relationship with HiTech Computer, within thirty days that would be well known throughout the industry in New England." He believed he would have difficulty explaining to existing and prospective customers why his company was not able to manage and sustain an alliance with a company known for its high product quality and the integrity of its business practices.

Knowing the people and knowing their capabilities were two prime considerations. The first is a social relations aspect, the second an economic aspect. The first reflects the conclusion that the entrepreneurial firm could work with this group (personal trust), the second that skill and performance (capabilities) could be relied upon (economic trust). With this type of description, the social and economic become very hard to separate. As one respondent put it, "We knew all the people [at the other firm]. They had worked together and we knew the software people. We knew the capabilities of the people that were putting together the organization and making it work. That has a lot to do with it [with starting the relationship]." Similarly, Support Products had worked with the individuals who became managers of that organization's independent local sales companies. Partnership agreements were proposed with people whose reputations had already been established.

Philosophy of partnership. Another example of prior relations setting the stage for exchange was provided by the entrepreneur who started Support Products, a charismatic individual who had learned early the importance of establishing relationships that went beyond immediate economic gain. Within the first year of his company's operations a fire destroyed much of the business. After the fire, friends and business acquaintances extended credit at very favorable terms so that the entrepreneur could rebuild his business. From this experience this individual came to believe in the power of strong relationships, not based solely on short-term economics but economics overlaid thickly with an ethos of friendship and mutual assistance. He established a reputation in local business circles for this philosophy and carried these values into the organization so that they became a strong part of the culture. As Support Products grew, prospective suppliers and customers knew that acceptance into the inner limited circle of preferred relationships involved a process heavily dependent on the intertwining of both economic and social factors. Commitment from each side, and regular demonstration of that commitment, was required.

This perspective continued as a dominant organizational value after the entrepreneur died and management passed to his son. Suppliers and customers sought partnership alliances with this firm in part due to the prospect of stable, mutually beneficial, and long-lived relationships. A manager at Support Breakers described the entrepreneurial firm's approach: "Support Products' attitude is different than the 30–40 other companies with which we do business in that they do everything they can to make it a mutually beneficial relationship. Support Products' procurement manager described the philosophy behind the firm's key supplier partnerships: "These people are extensions of your own organization, they are part of your family. Unlike more typical supplier relationships, we believe in a win-win relationship based on trust. Consequently our key suppliers have never treated us as just another company." It is clear that this entrepreneurial company had a philosophy that set preconditions for the formation of its alliances. This quotation also suggests that the philosophy of partnership and mutual gain was atypical in this industry. The two supplier linkages that were studied were established within this favorable context and could not be explained fully without this background.

Firms' reputations. In the case of the computer company and its two suppliers, company reputations for a high-quality product drew the prospective partners together. The entrepreneurial company assessed and rejected vertical integration of supplier functions and, instead, carefully chose a limited network of firms with which it linked itself. The decisions to enter the tight alliances that were studied were not based solely on short-term economic criteria but, rather, on multiple criteria, including long-term learning opportunities (e.g., what the entrepreneurial firm could gain from the expertise and innovative capacities of key suppliers and customers), ease of communications and working relationships, enhancement of reputation, and potential impact on growth.

The data suggest that reputation effects were especially important for the entrepreneurial firms. Individual entrepreneurs relied on their personal reputations to initiate alliances, since their company reputations were not well established. In addition, entrepreneurial firms sought partnerships with firms that had strong industry reputations because such alliances would give them product-quality benefits as well as enhance their own reputations. The data suggest that reputation is not only a crucial variable for entrepreneurship in ethnic communities (Light, 1972) but that it may have strong impacts in the context of entrepreneurial firms more generally. Individuals, and the activities and relationships they managed within and between organizations, became known, and reputations created the possibilities or could preclude the possibilities for future economic transactions. Within this social and inherently moral context, companies selected suppliers and customers. Obviously, short-run economic considerations were still factors in the formation of the interfirm ties, and this data in no way deny their importance, but it quickly became clear in interviews that companies and the

Network Dyads

individuals who made the decisions were predisposed to
connections with particular firms and people because of their
histories. It was these histories and the webs of trusted
connections that reduced uncertainty and improved the
likelihood of new transactions moving from arm's-length
relations to close collaborative alliances. The historical
preconditions thus set a context of expectations and
obligations with moral overtones that framed the actions that
would follow. At this point the two firms were poised to
make strong commitments at early cooperation.

The developmental phases that followed, and through which
each alliance advanced, were patterned. Each began as a
relatively arm's-length relation, in that no formal transactions
had occurred, and was transformed into a stable and
long-lived economic exchange, structured by the
expectations and obligations established in the first phase.

Phase II: Conditions to Build

The social aspects of economic exchange multiplied and
were magnified in the second phase to provide further
control over the expanding transactions. While multilayered
short- and long-term economic considerations played a role,
the building process for the network organization relied
heavily on trust and the development of reciprocity norms
during a trial period. Successful evolution also appeared to
require one side to initiate the iterative process toward
partnership.

Mutual economic advantage. The ties undeniably required
conditions of mutual economic advantage, but the data
strongly suggest that these were necessary but not
sufficient rationales. The primary economic exchange,
defined as the economic value of the annualized transaction,
was the most obvious incentive. In one case, the transaction
under study represented 10 percent of a partner firm's sales.
The same transaction accounted for 15 percent of the other
firm's cost of goods sold and 18 percent of sales. In another
case, 95 percent of one organization's dollar volume of sales
was attributed to the alliance. These percentages reflect
significant economic incentives. But not all the primary
transactions represented large economic values within their
firm context. One manufacturer's $3-million transaction with
a supplier accounted for only 2 percent of its cost of
production; that $3 million accounted for only 4.5 percent of
the supplier's outside sales. The economic values of the
primary transactions thus varied considerably in both
absolute and relative terms. As a consequence, simple
economic dependency as defined by the primary transaction,
while important in some cases, was not a definitive
economic factor.

The more important economic dimension was the growth of
the transaction as an incentive. For the established firms
that formed alliances with entrepreneurial firms, these
transactions represented among the fastest, if not the
fastest, sources of new revenue. One computer
subcontractor relationship grew from ten circuit boards
exchanged to over $500,000 worth of business six years
later, as an insignificant account became a key buyer.
Another relationship grew from nothing in 1980 to almost 25

percent of one partner's revenues by 1987. For the entrepreneurial firms, the rapid growth in the size of the economic exchange as their firms expanded allowed them to gain leverage with their partner organizations. Partners saw not only the current economic rewards but the promise of steadily increasing business volumes and returns. The growth of the transaction represented a more important resource dependency (Thompson, 1967; Pfeffer and Salancik, 1978).

These were the more obvious and purely economic conditions that fostered the alliances. However, the economic logic of partnering does not always translate into successful, long-term alliances. Equally important, but usually less visible and less well documented than purely economic motivations, were the interfirm and interpersonal dynamics that governed the day-to-day exchanges as the exchange relationships developed. These did not appear overnight. First, each alliance moved incrementally through a trial phase whose processes were consistent.

The trial period and the development of trust. The paired sets of companies moved successfully through a developmental trial period, at the conclusion of which a stable and predictable form network organizational form governed subsequent behavior. Certain relationships and actions in response to the environment (in this case, in response to specific suppliers and customers) came to be taken for granted. Representative accounts of the processes of the trial period follow:

You can't start out with a full-blown relationship. It's got to be incremental. You get closer as each side takes small steps. When I first started I didn't know whether I could believe what they told me, but experience, facts you collect, the transactions, build trust. [Support Breakers]

If it is going to be long-lasting, it doesn't happen overnight. It depends on the honesty of players at the outset. [Clothing Manufacturer]

We went through a trial and error period. We learned from mistakes and incrementally became part of their operation. Every relationship is unique so it takes time. It takes about a year—a minimum of one year. [HiTech Assembly]

Over time you build a history of situations, compromises, and solutions. You learn the unwritten rules and how they want to play the game, which makes it increasingly easier to do business. [HiTech Boards]

Thus the trial phase was characterized by incremental movement that edged organizations and individuals closer and closer. Time was required to develop what was called "the people interface and the systems and procedures." The partnered firms learned each other's businesses and their particular exchange dynamics over the first few months. Expectations were set, and in the process, explicit and implicit rules began to emerge. Through the steady exchange of information, communications became increasingly routinized, and procedures for coordinating activities were agreed upon. The integrity of participants, their honesty, and their continued efforts to improve the exchange process became important ingredients of the process as firms took incremental risks and invested more in

Network Dyads

the relationship. Only gradually did the two organizations become more closely integrated through the increasingly structured exchange process. The reality was one of an accretion of social processes (Granovetter, 1989) comprising actions and reactions, a layering of a richly textured game whose rules evolved slowly and whose success depended on dense social linkages.

A dominant image during the trial phase is a back-and-forth motion of reciprocity and risk taking. Action and reaction balanced the scale. Confidence grew as both sides won, so the game continued and the stakes grew. The following quotation illustrated this step-by-step movement forward as each side tested the waters:

It is like a balance, a scale—in return for commitment on their part we say we are committed to you and we prove it. So it's a quid pro quo. It's a balanced relationship that says you make investments, we make investments; you take risks, we take risks; you perform, we perform. That's the basis on which you build trust and everything that I would consider to be a strong successful relationship.

Initiator role. In each of these interfirm ties one side demonstrated an initiator proclivity, manifested in an initial willingness to engage in a more cooperative relationship. One manager at an entrepreneurial firm described this initiator role: "We initiate the step of going the extra distance for them. We respond to their requests. The effort to help is as important as the help itself. The relationship has to be attended to. You call them virtually every day to ask, 'How can I help?' " One side would frame the relationship as cooperative by actively working to build close relations. A marketing manager at Support Breakers described Support Products, the initiator firm:

Support Products works harder than anyone at making [key] vendors feel they are an important part of their business. They apologize for situations that become problematic; [they work hard to] ensure they are not part of the problem. Support Products is unique in its proactive program. They have taken the philosophy that says we are better off developing close relationships, personal relationships, with vendors.

Another example was provided by a manager at Clothing Catalog, who described Clothing Company's president's requests for meetings to improve the way the two companies worked together.

He would call a meeting for this purpose alone! He wants to know how his company can do a better job, how they can make our lives easier, how he can change his business to do a better job in any way. His attitude is, how can I help you do your job? A small number of companies pay lip service to this but [of the many other firms with which he worked] only Clothing Company really listens.

The president of Clothing Manufacturer described the trial period:

[the founder of the entrepreneurial catalog company] kept pushing us [saying], if you do this, I'll do that. We did, and he did. He would suggest that if we would work with this particular program then he felt sure that it would result in X amount of additional business. And it did. He always did what he said he would do. We needed to be encouraged because we had been operating in a slow-moving industry and were cautious about trying something different. This was how it grew from a very small beginning to a very significant relationship today.

These quotations underscore some important process characteristics that were shared across the seven exchange structures at this stage. The first was that firms eased into relationships incrementally and cautiously, giving and receiving signals. This was particularly true if one side of the exchange was accustomed to moving slowly because of the customers or markets it served. The second was that an active player, who took on the role of initiator for change and cooperation, could interrupt old patterns and restructure the behavior of the other side during a trial period, a pattern that has been observed before (Axelrod, 1984). Finally, reciprocity became an unwritten rule. If one side extended itself in a special effort to deliver on a promise, the other side responded in kind at the next opportunity. The results were perceived by both as beneficial (even if gains were small), and a cycle of reciprocity and mutual gain had begun.

This trial phase had two key dimensions, both of which were important to the ultimate viability of the evolving governance structures. The first dimension was the institution of rules and procedures that introduced into the exchange a predictable structure and a basis for performance and monitoring that provided stability and efficiency. These were based on implicit understandings and were adjusted as circumstances demanded. In much the same way that contracts provide control and reduce uncertainty by introducing hierarchical elements (Stinchcombe and Heimer, 1985), these understood contracts functioned to structure and stabilize the exchange processes.

A second key dimension of the trial phase was the evolution of clear expectations within each alliance. The processes of exchange established participants' reputations for fairness and credibility in both word and performance, confirming expectations set by top management in the precondition phase. This demonstrated the capacity and willingness of each side to participate in a cooperative, mutually beneficial, and sustained partnership. These expectations came to be taken for granted and shaped subsequent decisions and actions.

The trial period yielded an initial structure for the exchange. Implicit and explicit rules emerged and procedures were established. Clear expectations were now understood. A norm of reciprocity had evolved to govern the increasing number of communications and exchanges. But fundamental to the exchange structures at this point was the element of trust. The length of time for this process to evolve ranged from six months to a year and a half, but each alliance ultimately reached a stage at which the firms viewed themselves as trusted partners. A stable and predictable organizational structure for exchange had formed to govern present and subsequent transactions. Social relations and economic exchange were inextricably intertwined to govern behavior.

Phase III: Integration and Control

Three kinds of integration occurred between partners as relationships solidified. First, operational integration was

Network Dyads

required to enhance communication and connect the administrative apparatus of each firm. Second, the companies became increasingly interdependent strategically. This brought the future into the present to control and shape behavior. The third area is integration and control through social relations, or social control. As used here, social control encompasses self-regulation with a moral dimension in combination with control as jointly determined by and diffused across multiple participants. This form of control is not accounted for by the Williamsonian market-hierarchy continuum. In contrast with that perspective, social control can be seen here as a binding agent providing both the freedom and the control necessary for collaboration.

Operational integration. Operational integration of the partnered firms was accomplished through dense communications and administrative systems that set these exchanges apart from the other more typical market relationships in which the firms were involved. The extent and nature of communications also clearly distinguished the integration phase from the prior stage. Multiple communication linkages were established across the boundaries of the firms. One respondent gave this typical description of communications and administrative coordination in the third phase: "It takes a lot of work to maintain the relationship, including day-to-day communications across all levels of both organizations to constantly improve service. You need a breadth of relationships to catch problems immediately."

During this third phase, relationships began to resemble well-coordinated, vertically integrated units with established systems, procedures, and modes of communication. The president of HiTech Assembly said: "We communicate constantly as though we were part of their operations. Everyone has their contact at different steps of the ladder." Considering the extent of contact between HiTech Assembly and HiTech Computer, the latter's vice president of manufacturing made this comment: "We look at them as if they were another division, an extension of us. When I talk to them it is like calling someone who works for us directly. Both sides value the personal and business relationships highly." The marketing manager at Support Breakers described the tie with Support Products: "Here there is serious involvment together which differentiates it from more typical customer relations. Honesty and understanding makes the relationship different. We're in this together and the attitude is, here's what I need, what's that going to do to you?"

The depth of coordination had ripple effects across layers of economic decision making for a retailer and its supplier of finished articles of clothing: "They tell us their needs in excess of a year. We use that forecast information for our capacity planning and in working with our fabric suppliers so that we can support a particular need." This quotation revealed a network of connections across at least three firms: the entrepreneurial retailer (Clothing Company) with its manufacturer-supplier (Clothing Manufacturer) and through to the fabric suppliers that provided raw materials. At the time this project was underway these two firms were about to be linked through an expanded computer system that would enable them to exchange more planning, engineering, and test information, all of which was expected to result in technical improvements to the final product. These companies already were integrated through computers to enable the retailer to receive on-line transmissions from the manufacturer, who communicated shipping information before items arrived. The retailer in turn could access the partner's computer to determine the status of orders as they were processed through the manufacturer's production facility.

Achieving this kind of administrative integration through computers was common. In another case the partnered firms shared access to one side's MRP system, the computerized manufacturing planning system. A minimum of nine months' advance planning and scheduling information was relayed via computer to a handful of key suppliers to help them schedule their production runs. Within these dyads, the firms collaborated on ways to improve this coordination system for the benefit of both sides' respective operations. A vice president of HiTech Computer explained his company's approach to the two alliances under study, alliances that were part of HiTech's limited network of critical suppliers:

There has to be some kind of co-destiny type of relationship. It can't be just a call up, place an order and wait for it to come in. We want continuity. We're interested in his being a successful business so that we are successful together. You let the supplier know when orders are coming and you work out pricing ahead of time. It takes a lot of communication and trust.

This level of communication and coordination was routine between the firms after approximately one and a half years. It was not unusual for design, research and development (R&D), customer service, materials, control, purchasing, and shipping functions to communicate regularly and directly. The routine was described by one informant, "You could call it positive maintenance, reviewing to make sure everything is going well and that everybody is up to speed on where we are going so that there aren't any surprises."

Across the seven alliances both sides repeated that maintaining such relationships took continuous effort beyond that required by their more typical outside relations. The effort was based on mutual assistance and mutual gain. This typical quotation illustrated the point:

It is up to us to lessen the impact of constant changes, to make it easier for them, because making it easier for them brings benefits back to us. It means investing time. It comes down to allocating resources and getting information to them quickly so that they can better service us.

Strategic integration. Strategic integration extended beyond routine administrative coordination to new joint projects for the purpose of upgrading administrative coordination or to improve old or develop new products. Two companies that coordinated their shipping, warehousing, and inventory systems also developed a common computerized bar code controlled by jointly developed software so that boxes could move between firms and out to customers without being opened. Support Breakers, the circuit breaker manufacturer,

Network Dyads

used joint projects with its entrepreneurial partner firm to stay current on designs. As one informant told me, "They are the dynamic ones, so our long-term design engineers talk to theirs about future needs. The partnership has resulted in joint technology development and a coordinated R&D effort that has kept us a step ahead of the competition." Similarly, the telephone systems manufacturer and the distributor worked closely together on R&D, keeping both at the forefront of new technology: "Through joint engineering work and R&D collaboration we come up with new product features, then we field trial the new systems. They get our feedback and we get to work with state of the art technology." One firm's head of purchasing made this observation about product innovations and cost reductions resulting from combined efforts: "Close relations with our partners are strategically very important because the joint projects allow us to introduce new product features to the market before the competition."

It was clear that these exchange structures linked organizations in mutually beneficial, strategic ways. Equally clear was that the reward of immediate economic gain from the primary and initial economic transaction was dwarfed in comparison with a diffused set of potential rewards from long-term collaboration across a range of projects. These strategic stakes were not easily quantifiable but were nonetheless important. They were future oriented and defined as potential gains that carried with them the possibility of significant and positive impacts on the long-term competitive position of each company. The range of strategic motivations for cooperation that ultimately emerged was not necessarily obvious or even fully present at the beginning of the relationships. However, as each governance structure matured, strategic considerations became fundamental to the firms' willingness to commit to a long-term relationship and to invest in the costs of its maintenance.

Information exchange. Company representatives talked explicitly about the value of developing a cooperative pattern of information exchanges that extended beyond the primary economic transaction. What began as a single transaction became nested in a collection of exchanges, many of which had competitive and strategic relevance. The vice president of Clothing Manufacturer described it in this way:

There are a lot of things that evolve from vendor-customer relationships that help both parties beyond just a product or service. We look to them for direction on what may be important in the marketplace, and we share information about processing and shipping orders. There is a strategic advantage for us to share in that knowledge.

A respondent at Clothing Manufacturer described the information exchange this way: "The relationship is unusual and is based on mutual commitment and respect. But once established, we are privy to new product information from suppliers long before the rest of the world. We get information, technical data, and the first samples." Similarly, Support Products' partnership relationships with its locally owned salesforce organizations resulted in rapid market feedback that accounted for the steady innovations in products and services behind the upward sales growth between 1978 and 1987.

The partnership arrangements also gave firms access to a broader network of contacts that could open opportunities. An example was provided by an entrepreneurial firm using its larger partner organization to identify candidates for a top-management position. The larger company, through its extensive internal network, was able to find the individual who was eventually hired. In this way "weak ties" proved to be an important source of information (Granovetter, 1973).

Innovation and quality improvements. A more established company used one of the small high-growth firms as a source of technical and procedural innovation. A manager at Clothing Catalog, a larger and more bureaucratic partner firm, illustrated this dynamic:

We are constantly changing things to try to improve the way we do business together. We will experiment with new ideas, test new processes, try something different. Costs are incurred on both sides but we are willing to pay them. We have learned a lot from them. They have made us a better printing company because they are demanding, innovative, and willing to try things.

A representative from HiTech Assembly made a similar argument about the partnerships' effects on their competitiveness:

You have to look at the potential they offer you to develop your own internal capabilities. HiTech Computer designs a printed circuit board that is very complex. It is difficult to build so it keeps us on our toes. The experience filters down to other activities that we do to raise the overall quality of what goes out the door. It makes it possible to offer opportunities to other companies that we wouldn't be able to if it weren't for this work.

Other strategic motivations. All of the alliances studied had significant strategic importance for both organizations, yet, at the same time, each firm was motivated by distinctly different strategic considerations. In two cases the alliances were used by participants to gain access to new channels of distribution and new markets. In another case the entrepreneurial firm consciously used its larger supplier as a support system for its future growth and as a feedback mechanism. Other benefits with strategic implications included access to cost savings through a partner's economies of scale, consistent high-quality results, extra effort in a crisis, extended payment terms, and enhanced industry reputation through affiliation. Although the specific content of the strategic motivation and benefits varied among organizations, each partner firm looked to the other side for such strategic gains. This diverse range of strategic interests served by the integration of the two organizations demonstrated a clear message: the future had become important to these firms. When the relationships reached this phase, present economic transactions were seen in a context of future exchanges and long-term anticipated benefits. The single economic transaction that initiated the relationship had been expanded to a diverse set of ongoing joint projects and interrelated exchange processes. As a consequence, there were strong incentives to invest in and sustain the exchange process.

Network Dyads

Integration and control through social relations. Control in organizations needs to be "both flexibly strategic and reliably operational, and both on the same turf" (White, 1985: 191). The prior discussions of operational and strategic collaboration illustrate the centrality of these aspects of control. But flexibility and reliability cannot be accounted for without discussing the nature of control as it was fashioned through networks of social relations. This control is the common "turf" to which White refers. Together with control derived from the administrative and strategic links, this decidedly social control completes the picture and provides the linchpin.

Moral obligation and trust. When asked what protected the companies from opportunism by the other side in the absence of contracts, the interviewees repeatedly used the word "trust." The general manager at HiTech Assembly described his firm's alliance agreement and compared it to other outside economic transactions. He started with this summary of typical external transactions:

A purchase order; that's it. Take X [a nationally well-known computer company was named here], I have a contract that thick, and Y [another well-known computer company] has cover-your-tail type contracts. With HiTech Computer we don't have contracts. They aren't worth the paper they are printed on. Because the relationship, the day-to-day operating relationship is not managed by the verbiage contained in a contract. Contracts are used as a safety net in case the people relationship falls apart. I think trust is very basic to these relationships.

Other quotations from participants in the computer company alliances were representative of the emphasis on trust in shaping the economics of the partnerships. HiTech Computer's manager of supplier relations described the process: "It is like working with your own factory. There is full trust. When we call to say, 'Don't worry about cost,' they know what we mean. They trust us to pay and we trust them to give us a reasonable price." The head of manufacturing at HiTech Computer commented: "If trust weren't there we would have to have reserve orders placed with other vendors and would have to hold safety stock in inventory, none of which we do now." The fact that a firm did not hold inventory is a good example of economic decisions significantly influenced by trust. In reality, this firm was highly dependent on its partnered subcontractor, and this dependence represented a serious economic risk. Yet the risk was perceived to be manageable because the history of interactions between the two firms indicated that the probability of opportunism and malfeasance (predicted by economists) was low.

Honesty made trust possible and was therefore essential to the formation of a successful tie, and this differentiated these close alliances from the more typical links with which respondents compared these arrangements. One respondent talked about the confidence he had in the partner and suggested this level of trust was atypical: "Open communication and honesty is very important because we exchange confidential information on which we rely to plan for the future. It does not always work that way; I have many customers where I know what they are saying is not

100 percent true." This business style, of individuals communicating with consistent straightforwardness and honesty, encouraged each side to exert an effort to make each transaction opportunity mutually beneficial, although, as one respondent told me, it wasn't always easy: "If they ask for some cooperation we will do all we possibly can to accommodate their requests—and vice versa. But if we can't do something, then we say so, and that's OK. It's not as comfortable, but you do what you can."

Norms of fairness, honesty, and reciprocity were assumed and took on an invisible but powerful role during this third phase. They imposed expectations and obligations and referred to several aspects of behavior: confidence that the other side could be relied upon (for performance or for protecting proprietary information, for example); confidence that the relationship would not be exploited by the other side; confidence that extra effort would be made consistently; and, in return, that a partner would give the other side time and opportunity to adjust to changed circumstances rather than move abruptly to an alternative supplier or customer. The moral control imposed was inexpensive and flexible yet penetrating. It prevented certain acts through the pressure of its "immediate regulatory presence" (Ross, 1906: 95).

Reputation and identity as control. At the mature phase of the exchange the preservation of individual and organizational reputations and identities had become tightly intertwined with economic exchange. Individuals and firms became invested in the specific processes and relationships. Behavior reflected back on their integrity and identities. Individuals took on roles and became embedded in the personal and organizational relationships and were firmly invested in the ongoing social and economic exchanges. Participants indicated that deviation from the patterned routine of cooperation and the quid pro quo balance could call into question their individual integrity or the firm's performance capacities. This could cause outsiders to question the reliability of individuals or organizations.

The socially embedded and interrelated exchange processes made it difficult to separate out specific transactions for analysis. As a consequence, the isolation of any one transaction from its context distorted reality. Similarly, the separation of roles into principal and agent, one analytic approach to understanding business exchange (Pratt and Zeckhauser, 1985), was not a useful exercise. The principal-agent distinction was not helpful because the roles were not maintained, nor were the controls used that are thought to be necessary in economic transactions. Traditional controls and incentives are less relevant when objectives are jointly determined and implementation is accomplished through collaboration. The two sides were in daily interactions; they were equals who participated for individual and organizational gains but also for the social satisfaction of mutually constructing and reconstructing the contingent organizational domain.

What were the implications of these forms of social control? Support Products, an entrepreneurial firm, treated its select

Network Dyads

network of vendors well, including giving them recognition and awards, sharing information, and maintaining an attitude of "How can we help?" A manager from Support Breakers expressed an underlying sentiment that was shared among individuals participating in the exchange structures:

Am I going to react any differently, represent Support Products' interests in this business any differently than I am other important customers, some of whom do more business with us? Yes, there will be better service, extra effort, a sense of urgency difference. There's no doubt about it. Somehow they are always first to get the creative programs, the first with whom we had long-term development discussions. It's because they work very, very hard at developing the relationship that says we are still human beings, and as crass and straightforward as mature business can be, we are still driven by subjective things even though we may not want to admit it. The businesses are still run by people.

Another manager described the response once the social contract was set as, "We move more quickly for that company. They could call anyone in the organization and get a reaction because people enjoy working with them." The combination of assumed trust and the full involvement of each side, so that roles and identities became merged with the exchange process, resulted in self-regulation. Self-regulation solved the problem of control by dispersing it.

Intangible control also came from the ways in which the past and future influenced the present. The history of interactions set down mutual obligations and expectations that were organizationally structured: Individuals could come and go from particular positions and roles, but their behavior was framed and shaped by the history of exchange and the roles and identities of current participants. Equally important were the strategic stakes invested in activities that promised continued relations out into the future. Any single economic exchange could not help but be shaped by this rich context of past and future that reflected on current events. All of these dimensions accumulated to create a symmetry, not in every transaction but across a broad range of transactions within the alliance. The organizational form was a contingent control structure, patterned in its processes and architecture and reliably flexible due to the complex intersection of operational, strategic, and social controls.

Although I have been speaking in terms of the economic versus the social, this analysis strongly suggests that we cannot isolate economic transactions from the social world in which they take place. Neither the oversocialized conception of action (Wrong, 1961) nor the undersocialized model presented in idealized economic exchange is appropriate. Actors are oversocialized when portrayed as governed exclusively by values and norms and undersocialized when portrayed as isolated, rational economic units (Granovetter, 1985). A middle ground must be found. To reduce behavior and force it into these dichotomous categories would obscure the reality of these exchanges.

DISCUSSION AND CONCLUSIONS

A process model of the formation of entrepreneurial dyads was proposed. Three phases of dyad formation were specified: preconditions, conditions to build the exchange structures, and the final phase of integration and control. Field observations of four entrepreneurial firms and seven dyadic relationships linking the firms to key suppliers and/or customers were consistent with the model. Specifically it was found that the firms were engaged in relatively stable, sustained relationships characterized by multiple transactions and a high degree of cooperation and collaboration. They were governed in important ways by social controls arising from norms of trust and reciprocity. Governance was explained in large part by understanding the subtle control of interdependent and self-regulated players engaged in and committed to mutual gains. An explanation of governance is captured by certain aspects of institutional theory that acknowledge patterned histories of interaction that create mutual expectations. These social patterns "take on a rulelike status" (Meyer and Rowan, 1977: 341) to permit and/or constrain economic exchange. These rules control and coordinate behavior by defining what actions are appropriate (Scott, 1987). Furthermore, I suggest that these organizing modes constitute a distinct organizational form that is neither transaction governance through market (primarily controlled by price) nor governance by hierarchy (primarily controlled by administrative authority). Instead, this mode of exchange is best described as a network form of governance. Powell's (1990) definition of the network organizational form as applied to dyads was used. While Powell discussed networks of such relationships and referred to multiple relationships around a hub organization, the term was also used here to refer to the organizational form that constitutes and guides repeated exchanges between two firms. The alliances match Powell's characteristics of the network form in that they are long-term and recurrent exchanges that create interdependencies that rest on the entangling of obligations, expectations, reputations, and mutual interests. The initial transactions become embedded, not only in a larger set of economic exchanges but also in a rich and active network of social relationships that couple the two organizations strategically and administratively. These dyadic alliances are "a separate, different mode of exchange, one with its own logic, a network" form (Powell, 1990: 301).

Formal contracts, which might be expected to provide control, were only rarely discussed by the informants. Only four paired firms had formal agreements, and these varied considerably in length, complexity, content, and function. Uniformly, those firms that had written contracts discounted their relevance. In interviews, when asked about why and how these alliances functioned effectively, informants did not place emphasis on contracts, administrative controls, economic incentives, or market data; these were not the issues in the forefront of their minds. It became clear that to understand fully how the structures functioned on a daily and weekly basis required examination of informal and implicit social contracts. The relative unimportance of formal contractual aspects of exchange and, in contrast, the significance of trust and reciprocity norms appear to reflect the reality of economic exchange: it takes place within and is shaped by social controls.

Network Dyads

This analysis also provides information to begin to specify under what circumstances firms are able to construct alternative exchange governance structures that are not internalized through vertical integration and yet do not look like traditional market relations. Economic incentives and mutually beneficial strategic rewards obviously must be present. But the high failure rate of alliances with these economic and strategic characteristics suggests they are necessary but not sufficient conditions. Critical to the development of network forms is the history of prior personal relations and reputational knowledge that provides a receptive context for the initiation and evolution of economic exchange. Subsequent successful movement through a trial period provides mutually reinforcing economic incentives and social processes. One condition that allows for this progression is an organization's capacity to commit to a mutual orientation (Johanson and Mattsson, 1987). The mutual orientation requires sufficient commitment of resources and time to develop knowledge of the prospective partner's business and respect for the other's interests through a learning and adaptation process. Relations of this kind build through an accumulation of actions that create a system of social relations that transcends narrow self-interest and includes moral as well as economic motivations as fundamental to action (Etzioni, 1988).

It appears from the data collected that not all firms seek or are capable of engaging in such in-depth coordination and collaborative activities. In fact, the overwhelming majority of the entrepreneurial firms' interfirm relations did not involve this high a level of cooperation, integration, and trust. The question is why? One obvious answer is that less essential ties do not require this type of partnership arrangement. Price-based, arm's-length market exchange is sufficient in these cases. It seems clear, however, that some firms simply were not able to or were not strategically interested in establishing dense collaborative ties. Interviews revealed that some firms' cultures did not allow for the openness necessary for these ties to thrive. In addition, the staged evolutionary process described here strongly suggests that prospective partner firms must incrementally signal willingness to engage in this network form of exchange and that the technical, cultural, and performance capacities to embrace this staged process must consistently be present.

The relative stability of these ties should not obscure their inherent vulnerabilities. Despite the longevity of these network structures, risks were present. Soon after the conclusion of this field research two of the alliances were terminated. In one case, the smaller firm ended the alliance because its larger, more bureaucratic partner could not respond quickly enough to changing needs. The separation was amicable. In a second situation, after five years of successful collaboration, competitive forces in the rapidly changing deregulated telephone industry caused Telephone Manufacturer to violate its exclusive distribution agreement with its partner. This parting was less amicable. Two more alliances changed in character when Supports Products was acquired by a much larger corporation. The new parent imposed internal sourcing requirements on its newly acquired division that dramatically altered the terms and character of Support Products' supplier alliances. The partnership philosophy on which trust and loyalty was based was replaced by a short-term, cost-only focus. The Support Products purchasing manager explained that the exchange process was shifting to a more distant relationship in which collaboration and special treatment were increasingly unlikely. These termination stories suggest that subsequent research should include analyses of how and why these organizational forms disappear.

Threats to the alliances and, in four of seven cases, their dissolution or decline should be expected. Their demise underscored the fact that risk was built in. Changes in competitive conditions and strategic direction were legitimate and predictable reasons for the terms of a relationship to shift. In addition, while these arrangements offered a low-cost way for firms to gain resources and expertise, this strategy made them vulnerable because in-house capacities were not cultivated. Heavy reliance on a partner was an obvious risk. The exchange of proprietary information also represented a risk. Design specifications, new-product information, and scheduling timetables were all considered proprietary knowledge. Interestingly, on these issues, no violations of trust were found. Participants' concern for preserving the ongoing exchange and protecting reputations appeared to offer strong protection against this risk.

These partnerships cannot and should not necessarily last indefinitely. Instead, a more accurate picture is that of firms moving in and out of relatively stable networks of critical relationships over time. However, even short life cycles of three or four years should not undercut their importance or significance as alternative organizational forms that appear to contribute significantly to entrepreneurial firms' growth, adaptability, and effectiveness. Nor should their vulnerability to changing competitive circumstances detract from their stability and patterned predictability as an organizational form for the time they function.

One of the implications of this perspective on entrepreneurial firms is that it allows us to contemplate an alternative network model of firm growth. This paper provides insights into the processes and structure of sustained dyadic exchanges. But it should be kept in mind that the dyads were chosen for study because they represented constituent parts and archetypes of the network of dyadic alliances in which each entrepreneurial firm was involved. While the set of dyads, the network as a whole, was not the primary focus, this research, in combination with other reports (MacMillan, 1983; Birley, 1985; Aldrich and Zimmer, 1986; Lorenzoni and Ornati, 1988; Jarillo, 1988; Venkataraman, 1990; Larson and Starr, 1992) suggests an image of smaller companies using limited but dense networks of formal and informal exchange relationships as vehicles for growth. The key goal for resource-poor entrepreneurial organizations is to build network exchange structures with outsiders that are identified as critical resource suppliers, ones that can stabilize the new firm as a player in its targeted markets.

Network Dyads

The traditional picture of internally driven firm growth
(Greiner, 1972) is replaced by the creative use by
entrepreneurial organizations of networks to gain footholds
in markets and to serve as critical conduits to enhance
revenues, gain information and technology, and stimulate
innovation. The evidence gathered in this research argues for
considering that a model of growth via networks may help to
account for how and why successful small companies
persist (Larson and Starr, 1992).

The findings presented also have more general implications
for how network modes of economic exchange are studied.
Examples of these include R&D partnerships, cooperative
marketing agreements, and other forms of strategic
alliances and joint ventures. These interorganizational
forms have been receiving increased attention as their
numbers proliferate (e.g., Harrigan, 1985; Helper, 1987;
Doz, 1988; Contractor and Lorange, 1988; Kanter, 1989;
Badaracco, 1991). Strategic and transaction cost
approaches undoubtedly will reveal insights on these new
forms; however, these approaches emphasize short-term
economic costs and benefits (Auster, 1990), and they
examine the issue of control only from a relatively narrow
economic and financial perspective. The linkages studied
here between entrepreneurial firms and their suppliers and
customers undoubtedly share many of the exchange
characteristics of close collaborations between large firms.
Yet the social exchange aspects of large-firm transactions
are given little attention in these studies. This may be
because field-based process research is not commonly
associated with economic studies of organization. Yet the
contribution to our comprehension of economic activity that
can be made through understanding these dimensions of
exchange depends on detailed field studies of exchange
processes. The results of this study suggest that an
examination of social control factors and their interaction
with economic exchange will reveal a more complete
account of these network organizational forms in diverse
settings.

REFERENCES

**Aldrich, Howard, and
Catherine Zimmer**
1986 "Entrepreneurship through
 social networks." In Donald
 Sexton and Raymond Smiler
 (eds.), The Art and Science of
 Entrepreneurship: 3–23. New
 York: Ballinger.

Auster, Ellen R.
1990 "The interorganizational
 environment: Network theory,
 tools, and applications." In
 Frederick Williams and David
 Gibson (eds.), Technology
 Transfer: A Communication
 Perspective: 63–89. Newbury
 Park, CA: Sage.

Axelrod, Robert
1984 The Evolution of Cooperation.
 New York: Basic Books.

Badaracco, Joseph L., Jr.
1991 The Knowledge Link: How
 Firms Compete through
 Strategic Alliances. Boston:
 Harvard Business School
 Press.

Birley, Sue
1985 "The role of networks in the
 entrepreneurial process."
 Journal of Business Venturing,
 1: 107–118.

**Bradach, Jeffrey L., and
Robert G. Eccles**
1989 "Markets versus hierarchies:
 From ideal types to plural
 forms." In W. Richard Scott
 (ed.), Annual Review of
 Sociology, 15: 97–118. Palo
 Alto, CA: Annual Reviews.

Coase, Ronald H.
1952 "The nature of the firm."
 (Originally published in 1937.)
 In G. J. Stigler and K. E.
 Boulding (eds.), Readings in
 Price Theory: 386–405.
 Homewood, IL: Richard D.
 Irwin.

**Contractor, Farok J., and
Peter Lorange**
1988 Cooperative Strategies in
 International Business.
 Lexington, MA: Lexington
 Books.

**Coser, Lewis A., Charles
Kadushin, and Walter W. Powell**
1982 Books: The Culture and
 Commerce of Publishing. New
 York: Basic Books.

Dore, Ronald
1983 "Goodwill and the spirit of market capitalism." British Journal of Sociology, 34: 459–482.
1986 Flexible Rigidities: Industrial Policy and Structural Adjustments in the Japanese Economy 1970–1980. Stanford, CA: Stanford University Press.
1987 Taking Japan Seriously: A Confucian Perspective on Leading Economic Issues. Stanford, CA: Stanford University Press.

Doz, Yves L.
1988 "Technology partnerships between larger and smaller firms: Some critical issues." International Studies of Management and Organization, 17(4): 31–57.

Eccles, Robert G.
1981 "The quasifirm in the construction industry." Journal of Economic Behavior and Organization, 2: 335–357.
1985 The Transfer Pricing Problem: A Theory for Practice. Lexington, MA: Lexington Books.

Etzioni, Amitai
1988 The Moral Dimension. New York: Free Press.

Fama, Eugene F., and Michael C. Jensen
1983 "Separation of ownership and control." Journal of Law and Economics, 26: 327–349.

Granovetter, Mark
1973 "The strength of weak ties." American Journal of Sociology, 78: 1360–1380.
1985 "Economic action and social structure: A theory of embeddedness." American Journal of Sociology, 91: 481–510.
1989 "Society and economics." Unpublished book manuscript, Department of Sociology, State University of New York, Stony Brook.

Greiner, Larry E.
1972 "Evolution and revolution as organizations grow." Harvard Business Review, July-Aug.: 37–46.

Hakansson, Hakan
1987 Industrial Technological Development: A Network Approach. London: Croom Helm.

Hakansson, Hakan, and Jan Johanson
1988 "Formal and informal cooperation strategies in international industrial networks." In Farok J. Contractor and Peter Lorange (eds.), Cooperative Strategies in International Business: 369–379. Lexington, MA: Lexington Books.

Harrigan, Kathryn Rudie
1985 Strategies for Joint Ventures. Lexington, MA: Lexington Books.

Helper, Susan
1987 "Supplier relations and technological change." Unpublished Ph.D. dissertation, Department of Economics, Harvard University.

Janowitz, Morris
1976 Social Control of the Welfare State. New York: Elsevier.

Jarillo, Jose-Carlos
1988 "On strategic networks." Strategic Management Journal, 9: 31–41.

Johannisson, Bengt
1987 "Anarchists and organizers: Entrepreneurs in a network perspective." International Studies of Management and Organization, 17(1): 49–63.

Johanson, Jan, and Lars-Gunnar Mattsson
1987 "Interorganizational relations in industrial systems: A network approach compared with the transaction-cost approach." International Studies of Management and Organization, 17(1): 34–48.

Kanter, Rosabeth Moss
1989 When Giants Learn to Dance. New York: Simon and Schuster.

Larson, Andrea
1988 "Cooperative alliances: A study of entrepreneurship." Unpublished Ph.D. dissertation, Harvard Graduate School of Arts and Sciences and Harvard Business School.
1991 "Partner networks: Leveraging external ties to improve entrepreneurial performance." Journal of Business Venturing, 6(3): 173–188.

Larson, Andrea, and Jennifer Starr
1992 "A network model of organization formation." Entrepreneurship Theory and Practice, vol. 17 (1) (in press).

Leifer, Eric M., and Harrison C. White
1986 "Wheeling and annealing: Federal and multidivisional control." In The Social Fabric: 223–242. Beverly Hills, CA: Sage.

Light, Ivan
1972 Ethnic Enterprise in America: Business and Welfare among Chinese, Japanese and Blacks. Berkeley, CA: University of California Press.

Lorenzoni, Gianni, and Oscar Ornati
1988 "Constellations of firms and new ventures." Journal of Business Venturing, 3: 41–57.

Macaulay, Stewart
1963 "Non-contractual relations in business: A preliminary study." American Sociological Review, 28: 55–67.

MacMillan, Ian C.
1983 "The politics of new venture management." Harvard Business Review, Nov.–Dec.: 8–13.

Meyer, John W., and Brian Rowan
1977 "Institutionalized organizations: Formal structure as myth and ceremony." American Journal of Sociology, 83: 340–363.

Pfeffer, Jeffrey, and Gerald R. Salancik
1978 The External Control of Organizations. New York: Harper and Row.

Powell, Walter W.
1987 "Hybrid organizational arrangements: New form or transitional development?" California Management Review, 30(1): 67–87.
1990 "Neither market nor hierarchy: Network forms of organization." In Barry M. Staw and L. L. Cummings (eds.), Research in Organizational Behavior, 12: 295–336. Greenwich, CT: JAI Press.

Pratt, John W., and Richard J. Zeckhauser (eds.)
1985 Principals and Agents: The Structure of Business. Boston: Harvard Business School Press.

Ross, Edward A.
1906 Social Control. New York: MacMillan.

Scott, W. Richard
1987 "The adolescence of institutional theory." Administrative Science Quarterly, 32: 493–511.

Network Dyads

Stinchcombe, Arthur, and
Carol A. Heimer
1985 Organization Theory and
  Project Management:
  Administering Uncertainty in
  Norwegian Offshore Oil. Oslo:
  Norwegian University Press
  (distributed by Oxford
  University Press).

Thompson, James D.
1967 Organizations in Action. New
  York: McGraw-Hill.

Venkataraman, S.
1990 "Transaction set, architecture
  of complexity and new
  venture growth and
  stagnation." Working paper,
  The Wharton School,
  University of Pennsylvania.

Walker, Gordon
1988 "Network analysis for
  cooperative interfirm
  relationships." In Farok J.
  Contractor and Peter Lorange
  (eds.), Cooperative Strategies
  in International Business:
  227–240. Lexington, MA:
  Lexington Books.

White, Harrison C.
1985 "Agency as control." In John
  W. Pratt and Richard J.
  Zeckhauser (eds.), Principals
  and Agents: The Structure of
  Business: 187–212. Boston:
  Harvard Business School
  Press.

Williamson, Oliver
1975 Markets and Hierarchies:
  Analysis and Antitrust
  Implications. New York: Free
  Press.
1985 The Economic Institutions of
  Capitalism. New York: Free
  Press.
1991 "Comparative economic
  organization: The analysis of
  discrete structural
  alternatives." Administrative
  Science Quarterly, 36:
  269–296.

Wrong, Dennis
1961 "The oversocialized
  conceptions of man in modern
  sociology." American
  Sociological Review, 26:
  183–193.

APPENDIX: Interview Questionaire

The following questions were used during the interviews. They were used as a guide to gather factual information and generate discussion. The first set of questions resulted in general information on the company, including its history, products sold, markets, and general competitive environment. The second set of questions elicited detailed data on the alliances.

BACKGROUND
History

1. When was the company founded?
2. Describe your operations 5 years ago (10 years ago) and compare with today.
3. What has your revenue growth rate been over the last five years?
4. What were the primary drivers of that growth?
5. What role have alliances played?
6. Historically how important have they been?

Business description

1. What are the company's products/services?
2. In what markets and industries does the firm participate?
3. How competitive are these?
4. What does a firm have to do to be successful in these businesses?
5. Are alliances part of a strategy for success in these businesses?

ALLIANCE
History

1. How did this relationship first begin?
2. How did you hear about the alliance partner?
3. What kind of product/service were you looking for?
4. What factors caused you to enter into the alliance?
5. Are they the same factors that keep you involved today?
6. Is the history of this arrangement the same or different than that of other outside ties?
7. Is there, or was there ever, a written contract?
8. Were personal contacts a factor?
9. How important was the alliance to your business when it first began?
10. Has that changed over time?
11. Describe the exchange as it began and any important stages in its evolution.

Product/service exchanged

1. What is the product, how is it made, etc.?
2. What percentage of sales or cost of goods sold does this represent?
3. How has this changed over time?

4. How important is the exchange to your business?
5. Is the business run as a profit center?
6. What does it take to be successful?

Present situation

1. What is the present economic value of the exchange?
2. How important is the relationship to the company?
3. What is its strategic contribution?
4. How would you describe the benefits you get from this arrangement?
5. Are they economic only?
6. If other, were they always present or did they evolve over time?
7. Does your company have more or less leverage than your partner? Why?
8. Has this balance changed over time? How?
9. Has the relationship enhanced your competitive position?
10. Has it helped you to grow? How?
11. Do you see the alliance as a long-term commitment? How long?
12. Are there advantages/disadvantages of long- versus short-term commitment in this situation?
13. Describe communications between the two firms.
14. Who is responsible for the management of the relationship?
15. What are the costs of maintaining the tie?
16. How do you quantify those?
17. Have there been disputes? How handled?
18. Has it been easy/difficult to maintain this alliance?
19. What explains the stability over time?
20. What kinds of investments have you made in this alliance?

Contract

1. Is there a written contract?
2. How formal are your dealings with the other side?
3. Are there standard operating procedures?
4. Are there dispute-resolution mechanisms?
5. Do you use any non-market pricing variations?
6. How do you measure performance?
7. Have the terms changed over the course of the relationship?
8. How do you exercise control?
9. How does this arrangement compare with other outside relationships? How typical is it?

Subcontracting versus in-house

1. Why did you form an alliance instead of incorporating the activity in-house?
2. Are there advantages to this arrangement compared to vertical integration? Disadvantages?
3. How hard/easy would it be to replace this alliance?
4. What would be the gains/losses and costs?

Part V
Venture Capital

[20]

Sloan Management Review   Summer 1983   23

Angels and Informal Risk Capital

William E. Wetzel, Jr.   **University of New Hampshire**

Raising risk capital is always a challenging and difficult task. "Business angels" play a key role in the risk capital market by providing seed capital for inventors, and start-up and growth capital for small, technology-based firms. This article discusses the investment characteristics of a sample of angels active in New England, offers suggestions for entrepreneurs looking for angels, and recommends steps to improve the efficiency of the informal risk capital market. Ed.

The 1980s have been touted as an age of technological entrepreneurship in the United States. Success stories like DEC and Apple have stimulated expectations for an economy energized by technology and entrepreneurs. A growing body of research data documents the contribution of small, technology-based firms (STBFs) to job creation, technological innovation, and other economic benefits, such as productivity gains, price stability, and favorable trade balances. The Small Business Innovation Development Act of 1982 is testimony to the economic and technological virtues attributed to STBFs (and to the increasing political influence of small business). The Act provides for a federal investment of about $1 billion in research by STBFs over the next five years.

Risk capital investors play an essential role in the growth of the high-tech sector. However, despite tremendous growth in risk capital investments in STBFs, there is a continuing perception that "gaps" exist in the capital markets for smaller firms, and this raises questions about the vigor of any "age of entrepreneurship." Though such gaps have not been convincingly documented, the capital gap folklore maintains that there are shortages of product development financing for technology-based inventors, of start-up financing for STBFs that fail to meet the criteria of professional venture capital investors, and of equity financing for closely held STBFs that are growing at a faster rate than internal cash flows can support. Created by Congress in 1958, the Small Business Investment Company (SBIC) program was an early institutional attempt to fill such gaps. Following the 1980 White House Conference on Small Business, more recent efforts to deal with the gap include the Small Business In-

vestment Incentive Act of 1980 and the SEC's new Regulation D streamlining securities law for small business.

The capital gap folklore is based upon the observable behavior of financial institutions, including SBICs and professional venture capital firms. However, the data we have collected suggest that capital gaps may be more apparent than real. The folklore overlooks the investment record of informal risk capital investors — the "business angels." (Angels do not include founders, friends, or relatives.) Not only do these angels exist, they may represent the largest pool of risk capital in the country. According to our data, they tend to invest in precisely the areas that are cited as gaps in the capital markets for STBFs.

The effect of capital gaps can be created when markets fail to function efficiently. Modern financial theory rests upon assumptions of efficient capital markets where all relevant information about sources of funds and about investment opportunities is freely available to buyers and sellers of capital. Efficient risk capital markets require fully informed entrepreneurs and investors. Our data indicate that this necessary condition is not fulfilled in the angel segment of the risk capital markets. In the absence of efficient markets, the flow of capital from less productive to more productive uses will be impeded. The efficiency issue is a cause for concern, because angels play an essential role in the financing of many STBFs. Angels fill what would otherwise be a void in the risk capital markets by providing development funds for technology-based inventors, seed capital for STBFs that do not meet the size and growth criteria of professional venture investors, and equity financing for established STBFs. In 1980-81 Jeffry Timmons

William E. Wetzel, Jr.,
is Professor of Business
Administration at the
Whittemore School of
Business and Econom-
ics, the University of
New Hampshire. Mr.
Wetzel holds the B.A.
degree from Wesleyan
University and the
M.B.A. degrees from
Temple University and
the University of
Chicago. His research
interests include the
functioning of the risk
capital markets, the re-
lationships between
entrepreneurship and
economic develop-
ment, and financial
strategies for closely
held firms. Mr. Wetzel
has written for such
journals as *Business
Horizons* and *New En-
gland Journal of Busi-
ness and Economics*.

and David Gumpert conducted a survey of
fifty-one of the largest and most active professional venture capital firms. The survey
showed that the range of an individual investment was from $300,000 to $4 million
and that the size of a typical individual investment was $813,000. The figures were
similar for SBICs, but substantially higher
for corporate venture affiliates.[1] However, it
is clear that risk capital financing of between
$50,000 and $500,000 is primarily the domain of the angels and is a vital resource for
many inventors and STBFs.

Many entrepreneurs will confirm that,
once personal funds and "friendly money"
have been exhausted, raising the first piece
of external risk capital can be an enormous
obstacle to creating or expanding a small,
technology-based firm. STBFs tend to be
founded by technically skilled individuals;
although some of these founders may have
management experience and marketing
savvy, they seldom have had experience in
the capital markets, particularly in the risk
capital markets. The problem is compounded by the fact that the most likely
sources of risk capital for many STBFs are
the least visible — those mythical business
angels. They are a diverse, dispersed population of individuals of means; many have
created their own successful ventures and
will invest their experience as well as their
capital in ventures they support.

Informal Risk Capital
Any useful discussion of risk capital must
recognize the diverse nature of the commodity and its sources of supply. The market for
risk capital consists of at least three segments, each having a unique set of distinguishing characteristics:

— The public equity market,

— The professional venture capital market,
and

— The market for informal risk capital (business angels).

Although the boundaries separating these
segments are indistinct and often overlap,
nonetheless an appreciation of the distinctions is essential for entrepreneurs seeking
funds. A founder can waste much time talking to sources about deals that are unlikely to
occur.

The public equity market and the professional venture capital market are relatively
efficient and well understood. At the risk of
serious oversimplification, it can be said
that, if an entrepreneur is trying to raise from
$2 million to $5 million (or more) for a venture with sex appeal, the speculative new
issues market represents a potential source
of funds. The professional venture capitalist
is generally interested in ventures that require $500,000 (or more) of postrevenue
financing, that yield projected revenues of
more than $20 million within five to ten
years, and that can go public or sell out by
that time.

The informal risk capital market, on the
other hand, is virtually invisible, inefficient,
and often misunderstood. Yet searching for
an angel is appropriate for a technology-
based inventor looking for development
funds or an entrepreneur looking for less
than $500,000 to start or expand an STBF.
Inefficiency and the invisible nature of the
angel segment of the capital markets contribute to perceptions that funds for such
purposes are unavailable.

There is evidence to suggest that individual investors (despite their low profile) represent the largest pool of risk capital in the
country. In 1978 the organized venture capital industry invested approximately $500
million; in 1981 the industry invested an
estimated $1.2 billion. Although there are no
data documenting the total volume of risk
capital provided by individuals, clues can be
found. For example, in 1981 private placements reported by corporations to the SEC
under Rule 146 totaled over $1 billion. In a
1980 SEC survey of a sample of issuers who
filed Form 146, it was found that corporate
issuers were engaged primarily in high
technology or in other manufacturing or
nonfinancial services, and that they were
generally young companies employing few

workers. The survey indicated that 87 percent of those buying corporate issues were individual investors or personal trusts. The average amount invested by an individual in a corporate issue was $74,000. The $1 billion corporate financing reported under Rule 146 represents only a fraction of the total transactions that occurred in the informal risk capital market. Rule 146 private placements by noncorporate issuers engaged largely in oil- and gas-related activities or in the real-estate business totaled over $3 billion in 1981. Individuals and personal trusts represented 93 percent of the purchasers of noncorporate issues. Note also that Rule 146 private offering data exclude financings exempt from registration because of their intrastate nature (Rule 147) or financing by closely held firms under small-offering exemptions (Rules 240 and 242). Effective June 1982, Regulation D replaced the exemptive provisions that existed under Rules 146, 240, and 242.[2]

Other empirical data confirm the importance of angels in the financing of STBFs. In an examination of capital market imperfections, Charles River Associates, Inc. (CRA) excluded "individuals who act informally as providers of venture funds." Yet CRA commented that "they may represent the largest source of venture capital in the country." The CRA study looked at the composition of external funds received by STBFs prior to making initial public offerings. The study showed that between 1970 and 1974 "unaffiliated individuals" accounted for 15 percent of external funds while "venture capitalists" accounted for 12 percent. When the data were classified by stage (age of venture), unaffiliated individuals provided 17 percent of external capital during the start-up year, while venture capitalists provided 11 percent.[3]

A similar pattern can be found in David Brophy's study of financial support for new, technology-based firms that were incorporated and operating from 1965 to 1970. In a sample of Boston-area firms, private individuals (excluding founders, friends, and relatives) provided 14 percent of total financing and SBICs and private venture capital

firms provided 15 percent. The figures for a sample of Ann Arbor and Detroit firms were 16 percent from individuals and 2 percent from venture capitalists.[4]

Clearly, angels play a key role in the early financing of many STBFs: one or more wealthy believers will provide seed capital, help solve problems, and exploit the opportunities associated with commercializing an invention or innovation or with starting up a new enterprise. Most entrepreneurs have heard of business angels and some entrepreneurs have found them. However, no one has ever really found out where angels come from, how many there are, how to find them, or what angels look for in a venture proposal.

The Study of Angels

With the SBA's seed capital we undertook a hunt for business angels in New England in an attempt to learn more about this invisible segment of the risk capital markets.[5] Our search turned up 133 investors who fit the description of a business angel, a sample large enough to at least draw tentative conclusions about the characteristics of angels. However, much more study is required before definitive statements can be made about the functioning of the informal risk capital market. Our work focused on the role of informal investors as a source of funds for three types of investment situations:

— Financing for technology-based inventors,

— Start-up and early stage financing for emerging firms, and

— Equity financing for small established firms growing faster than retained earnings can support.

This article presents the results of our research and our perceptions of the lessons they offer for entrepreneurs.

It took nine months and the assistance of several professional organizations to identify and collect data from our sample of angels. We discovered that angels tend to be found in clusters that are linked by an informal network of friends and business associates. Finding one investor typically led to contacts with three or four more, a tedious but productive "snowball" search technique.

The total population of informal investors is unknown and probably unknowable. Our sample represents approximately ten investors per million population, or about 1 percent of the 1,000 per million incidence of "millionaires" based upon 1972 IRS data. Given ten years of inflation and the drop in capital gains tax rates, it is likely that the total population of angels in New England is substantially larger than our sample, perhaps by a factor of twenty or more.

Investment History

Our sample of angels reported risk capital investments totaling over $16 million in 320 ventures between 1976 and 1980, an average of one deal every two years for each investor. The average size of their investments was approximately $50,000, while the median size was about $20,000. Thirty-six percent of past investments involved less than $10,000, while 24 percent involved over $50,000.

In 60 percent of past financings, respondents participated with other individuals in larger transactions. It is clear that informal investors are accustomed to sharing investment opportunities with friends and business associates. Participation with other financially sophisticated individuals permits venture financing that approaches the $250,000 to $500,000 interest threshold of venture capital firms and equity-oriented SBICs.

Venture Life-cycle Preferences

The data developed by Gumpert and Timmons show that professional venture capital firms currently place from 25 percent to 35 percent of their funds in start-up situations; this is an increase from the mid-70s figure of approximately 15 percent.[6] While these professional investors appear to be increasingly willing to look at start-ups, their interest is generally limited to proposals from entrepreneurs with successful start-up track records or to investor-initiated start-ups in emerging technologies (e.g., genetic engineering and robotics). Even then their interest is only for ventures with enough growth potential to justify liquidation expectations through a public offering or acquisition by a larger firm within five to ten years of initial financing.

Historically, informal investors have been the principal source of external seed capital. The age distribution of ventures receiving financing from our sample of angels is consistent with this record. Forty-four percent of past financings were start-ups, and 80 percent involved ventures less than five years old. If the definition of start-up is tied to the achievement of break-even operations rather than age, 63 percent of past investments were in situations that had not achieved break-even performance. With respect to future investments, 78 percent of our sample expressed a "strong interest" in start-up and early stage financing for emerging firms. The lesson for entrepreneurs is clear: if you need less than $500,000 to launch a new venture, look for one or more angels.

For technology-based inventors the lesson is even more compelling to find an angel. One third of our sample of informal investors expressed a "strong interest" in financing technology-based inventors. An angel with technical and managerial experience in the commercialization of related technology can bring a "sense of the market" to the work of an inventor. When asked whether their interests were limited to specific fields of technology, the areas investors cited most frequently were electronics, computers, energy, and health care. However, the principal criterion cited by these investors was that the technology be in a field that they understood and could evaluate:

— "A field in which I have some technical competence."

— "Fields in which I am sufficiently experienced to permit evaluation."

— "Related to my background in organic chemistry and pharmaceuticals."

Sloan Management Review   Summer 1983   27

— "Those I know: electronics, physics, mechanics."

— "It is limited to what I know and understand myself, especially about the marketplace, or can get trustworthy opinions on."

Approximately one respondent in five expressed a "strong interest" in equity financing for established firms. Investors interested in established firms anticipated larger investments (approximately $75,000 per firm). In our sample of angels, the incidence of advanced technical training and start-up management experience was lower among investors interested in established firms than among investors interested either in technology-based inventors or in early stage financing for emerging firms.

Venture Relationships
Both informal investors and professional venture investors typically contribute more than capital to the situations in which they invest. They are active investors, generally playing a consulting role or serving on a working board of directors. The investors in our sample are no exception. They are a well-educated group and experienced in the management of start-up situations. Ninety-five percent hold four-year college degrees and 51 percent have graduate degrees. Of the graduate degrees, 44 percent are in a technical field and 35 percent are in business or economics (generally an MBA). Three-quarters of the sample had been involved in the start-up of a new venture.

The relationship between angels and their portfolio firms was tested by asking respondents about the nature of their contact with portfolio firms. Passive investors were defined as those whose contact consisted of receiving periodic reports and attending stockholder meetings. Active investors were defined as those whose relationship included one or more of the following roles: membership on the board of directors, a consulting role, part-time employment, or full-time employment. Eighty-four percent reported that they expect to play an active role, typically having an informal consulting relationship or serving on a board of directors. In addition to raising capital, the entrepreneur's task is to find investors with a combination of training and experience that will contribute to the venture's success. For first-time entrepreneurs this resource can be more valuable than capital.

Geographic Patterns
The tendency of informal investors to maintain close working contact with ventures they finance is reflected in the geographic distribution of their portfolios. Three-quarters of the firms financed by our sample of angels were located within 300 miles of the investor (roughly one day's drive). Fifty-eight percent were within 50 miles. The geographic distribution of portfolio ventures may also reflect the absence of systematic channels of communication between investors and entrepreneurs. The likelihood of an investment opportunity coming to an individual investor's attention increases, probably exponentially, the shorter the distance between the two parties. The lesson for entrepreneurs looking for angels is: "Look close to home."

Industry Preferences
Both professional and informal risk capital investors display a broad range of industry preferences. The fields that interest professional venture firms are described in Stanley Pratt's *Guide to Venture Capital Sources*, but information about the tastes of angels is very difficult to find.[7]

Our sample of angels reported a clear preference for manufacturing enterprises in general and for "high technology" manufacturing in particular. Fifty-seven percent of past investments were in manufacturing firms: 28 percent in high technology products, 20 percent in industrial products, and 9 percent in consumer products. Service firms were a distant second, attracting 12 percent of past investments. Reported investment objectives were more broadly distributed. At the top of the list, 64 percent of the respondents expressed "strong interest" in high technology manufacturing, 33 percent in industrial product manufacturing, and 30 percent in service firms. At the bottom of the list, only 5 percent expressed a "strong interest" in wholesale trade, 3 percent in retail trade, and 1 percent in transportation firms. Even in the least attractive categories (retail trade, wholesale trade, and transportation), one investor in three reported either a "moderate" or a "strong" investment interest. These patterns indicate two things to entrepreneurs: first, some types of ventures attract much more interest than others; and second, somewhere there is an angel interested in backing a viable opportunity in virtually any business or industry category.

Exit Expectations

Risk capital is "patient money." Returns take the form of long-term capital gains realized after an extended period during which an investment possesses little or no liquidity or marketability. Liquidation expectations with respect to timing and method are variables that influence risk capital investment decisions. Forty-seven percent of our respondents reported that provisions for liquidating their investment were "definitely" or "generally" included in the initial investment agreements.

The "patience level" of informal investors was tested in terms of expected holding periods. The median expected holding period of respondents was five to seven years. Entrepreneurs will be particularly interested that 24 percent of the respondents either consider the holding period unimportant or expect to hold their risk capital investments longer than ten years, a "patience level" well in excess of the typical expectations of venture capital firms and SBICs.

Patience and shared exit expectations are particularly critical for ventures with a five-to ten-year sales potential below $20 million (i.e., ventures with limited prospects for a public offering or acquisition by a larger firm within the typical exit horizon of risk capital investors). Patience is a virtue, and angels tend to be virtuous.

Rejected Proposals

Most entrepreneurial lessons come the hard way — by making mistakes — and the same can be said of venture investing. "Schools" for entrepreneurs and venture investors are out on the street, not on university campuses. However, some entrepreneurial lessons can be learned from the mistakes of others. In order to help guide future entrepreneurs, we wanted to discover the reasons our sample of investors had rejected past investment proposals.

The "typical" angel seriously considers and rejects two or three investment opportunities each year. The most common reasons cited for rejection were lack of confidence in management; unsatisfactory risk/reward ratios; absence of a well-defined business plan; the investor's unfamiliarity with products, processes, or markets; or the venture was a business the investor "did not want to be in." The following comments reflect the range of reasons for rejecting investment proposals:

— "Risk/return ratio was not adequate."

— "In most cases management did not seem adequate for the task at hand."

— "Simply not interested in the proposed businesses. Saw no socio/economic value in them."

— "Unable to agree on price."

— "Too much wishful thinking."

— "One of two key principals not sufficiently committed — too involved with another activity."

— "Unfamiliar with business."

— "Wife refused."

Entrepreneurs can learn several important lessons from this:

— Be realistic about the prospects for your venture and about the risks and costs of venture investing.

— Be sure all essential management func-

Sloan Management Review   Summer 1983   29

tions are staffed with experienced, committed individuals.

— If you cannot put your proposal in writing, you cannot finance it.

Risk Perceptions
The world is populated with risk-averse individuals, including venture investors. Risks and, consequently, required rewards vary substantially over the spectrum of risk capital investment opportunities. However, with the exception of a number of highly visible success stories, little is known about the past performance or future expectations of risk capital investors, particularly informal investors. The problem of dealing with risk/return considerations is compounded by the absence of generally accepted risk measurement criteria.

We addressed the question of risk by hypothesizing portfolios of ten investments of a given type, all of which met the investor's criteria regarding investment size, industry, location, and management qualifications at the time of the investment. Investors were asked to specify how many of the ten would probably turn out to be "losers." Losers were defined as investments in which eventual losses exceeded 50 percent of the original investment. This definition of risk was selected because it is representative of the way investors think about "downside risk."

We also asked risk-and-return questions for five types of investment portfolios:

— Technology-based inventors,

— Start-up firms,

— Infant firms about one year old and approaching break-even operations,

— Young firms less than five years old and entering a rapid growth stage, and

— Established firms growing too fast to finance from retained earnings.

By measuring risk and return for the five types of investments, it was possible to identify investors' risk/return tradeoffs — not only how expensive risk capital is in general, but also how much more expensive it is for inventors than for start-ups, established firms, etc.

As expected, venture investors perceive noticeable risk differences among the five types of portfolios. The median number of expected losers in a ten security portfolio covered the following range: seven for inventors, six for start-ups, five for infant firms, four for young firms, and two in a portfolio of ten established firms. The dispersion of expectations within each portfolio was also substantial. Informal investors do not have homogeneous perceptions of risk.

The range of loser expectations indicates that perceptions of risk drop dramatically over the developmental stages in the life of a new venture. Since risk and cost are directly related, entrepreneurs can conclude that the longer a venture can survive on personal funds, "sweat equity," and internal cash flow, the lower will be the cost of external risk capital — i.e., the lower the share of equity required to purchase any given amount of venture capital. A start-up venture that is at the frontier of some new technology can be an exception to this generalization. Having no track record may then be an advantage. In such a case the dreams (and sometimes avarice) of investors can lead to startling share prices. Recent examples of this include many genetic engineering firms and the Denver penny energy stocks. Selling romance instead of reality is a treacherous game, and is not recommended as a strategy for raising funds or for building lasting relationships with sophisticated investors.

Reward Expectations
Entrepreneurs who pursue venture capital are always concerned about the questions: "What will it cost?" and "How much of my venture will I have to give up to raise the capital I need?" The answers will depend upon a number of variables, including the amount of capital required and the rewards expected by investors. The other variables, however, are unique to the firm, its history, and its prospects, and this makes the answer

also unique to the firm. The methodology for arriving at mutually agreeable terms, however, is not unique, and every entrepreneur should become familiar with it before entering negotiations.[8]

Entrepreneurs are advised to think of fund raising as a process of "buying capital," rather than of "selling stock." The difference is subtle but important. Risk capital is a commodity that is available from a variety of sources on a variety of terms. For every venture some combination of sources and terms will be more appropriate than others, and will exert a powerful influence on the future performance of the venture. Besides the price, such factors as exit expectations, the availability of future growth funds, and the quality of management assistance available from an investor will all influence the choice of sources. The final deal should be a partnership of professionals with complementary resources and shared goals.

In our research we undertook an assessment of the reward expectations of informal investors. Within each risk category, we posed two questions dealing with rate-of-return expectations. The first dealt with the "upside potential" of the most successful venture in a ten investment portfolio. It was an attempt to identify the expectations of returns on individual investments. Presumably, all investments of a given type possess the upside potential of a "winner" at the time an investment is made. Expected returns on winners represent the cost of risk capital to successful inventors and entrepreneurs. This cost is substantially higher than the average cost of risk capital for a given type of investment. As the risk questions reveal, investors recognize that many expected winners turn into losers. Substantial returns on the real winners must offset the losers and provide an adequate return on a portfolio of risk capital investments. The second question dealt with portfolio rate-of-return expectations — the average cost of risk capital.

With respect to "winners," investor expectations ranged from median five-year returns of 50 percent per year and capital gains mul-

tiples of ten times for inventors and start-up firms, to 38 percent per year and six times for infant firms, to 30 percent per year and five times for young firms, to 23 percent per year and three times for established firms. Rate-of-return expectations were widely dispersed around these medians, again reflecting the diversity of the informal investor population. With respect to minimum acceptable portfolio returns, median expectations were a consistent 20 percent compound annual rate and a five-year capital gains multiple of three times for all portfolios except established firms, where minimum portfolio returns were 15 percent and capital gains multiples only two times in five years.

The data suggest several observations of interest to entrepreneurs. First, seed capital is expensive. Despite every entrepreneur's confidence in his or her "sure thing," investing in entrepreneurs is extremely risky, and investors must be paid to take risks. Remember that risk capital investors win only when a venture succeeds, i.e., only when the entrepreneur is an even bigger winner. Entrepreneurs and risk capital investors earn their financial rewards from creating ventures whose economic muscle (cash earning power) supports equity values many times the amount invested. Second, given the extraordinary risks inherent in risk capital investing, the overall level of both "winner" and portfolio expectations seems low when compared to the range of expectations usually attributed to professional venture capital firms. The relatively low cost of informal risk capital may be due in part to the nonfinancial rewards that often motivate informal investors.

Nonfinancial Rewards

The influence of nonfinancial factors is a characteristic that distinguishes angels from professional venture capitalists. Professional venture investors consider the financial risk/reward relationship to be paramount. Individual investors, on the other hand, often look for nonfinancial returns from their risk capital portfolios. These nonfinancial re-

Sloan Management Review   Summer 1983   31

turns fall into several categories; some of them reflect a sense of social responsibility of many informal investors and some seem to reflect forms of "psychic income" (or so-called "hot buttons") that motivate individuals. The influence of these motivators was explored through questions that posed a form of nonfinancial reward and asked investors which ones, if any, represented substitutes for financial returns. Investors responding affirmatively were then asked how large a reduction in the rate of return would be accepted in exchange for the nonfinancial reward. We recognized that tradeoffs may involve undertaking higher risks in situations exhibiting nonfinancial benefits, rather than accepting lower returns. Difficulties in quantifying risk precluded asking the question in this form.

The list of nonfinancial considerations included ventures creating jobs in areas of high unemployment, ventures developing socially useful technology (e.g., medical or energy-saving technology), ventures contributing to urban revitalization, ventures created by minority or female entrepreneurs, and the personal satisfaction derived from assisting entrepreneurs to build successful ventures in a free enterprise economy.

Nonfinancial considerations affect the decisions of a significant fraction of our sample of angels — 45 percent in the case of "assisting entrepreneurs." Between 35 percent and 40 percent of the respondents reported that they would accept lower returns (or perhaps assume higher risks) when risk capital investments create employment in their communities or contribute to the development of socially useful technology. Median rate-of-return reductions of 20 percent were associated with investments that create employment and that assist minority entrepreneurs. Entrepreneurs sensitive to the match between the characteristics of their ventures and the personal tastes of investors should be able to raise funds on terms that are attractive to both parties.

Referral Sources

In view of the difficulty entrepreneurs encounter in locating potential investors, we were particularly interested in discovering the channels through which angels most often learn of investment opportunities, and their level of satisfaction with these channels. Respondents were provided with an illustrative list of sources of investment opportunities, and asked to classify each as a "frequent source," an "occasional source," or "not a source" of proposals they had seriously considered during the previous five years.

The pattern of "frequent source" responses reveals that informal investors typically learn of investment opportunities through a network of friends and business associates. Fifty-two percent cited "business associates" as a frequent source, 50 percent cited "friends," and 41 percent cited "active personal search." The next most common source, "investment bankers," was cited as a frequent source by 15 percent of the respondents. All other sources, including business brokers, commercial bankers, attorneys, and accountants, were insignificant.

Tapping this informal network is not easy. Entrepreneurs can expect little guidance in finding their way through the maze of channels leading to informal risk capital. By the same token, angels continue to rely largely on random events to bring investment opportunities to their attention. There are no systematic techniques for identifying clusters of individual investors or for assessing their distinguishing investment objectives. The best advice for entrepreneurs seems to be: put your plan in writing and then look close to home for an angel familiar with the technologies and markets you plan to exploit.

The angels in our sample were asked if they were satisfied with the effectiveness of existing channels of communication between bona fide entrepreneurs seeking risk capital and investors like themselves. "Totally dissatisfied" respondents (34 percent) outnumbered "definitely satisfied" respondents (8 percent) by more than four to one. The opinions expressed by our sample of angels support a conclusion reached by Bean, Schiffel, and Mogee with respect to venture capital markets in general: "The issue of little knowledge of the venture capital/new technological enterprise is multi-faceted. Entrepreneurs and potential entrepreneurs seem to need better information on financial sources while capital suppliers seem to need better information on new venture/technological investment opportunities."[9]

Respondents were then asked to indicate their interest in an experimental referral service that would direct investment opportunities to their attention. Fifty percent reported a "strong interest" in such a service and 38 percent reported a "moderate interest." Timeliness, objectivity, and confidentiality appear to be essential ingredients of such an activity.

Conclusion

Business angels are often the most likely sources of funds for technology-based inventors looking for development funds and for small, technology-based firms looking for start-up and growth capital. Collectively, angels appear to represent the largest pool of risk capital in the country, and they finance perhaps five times as many ventures as the public equity markets and professional venture capitalists combined. Based upon our experience, entrepreneurs can expedite the search for informal risk capital by following some basic guidelines:

1. First, prepare a comprehensive, documented business plan, including a two- to three-page synopsis of the venture and its management.

2. Be realistic about the risks of and prospects for the venture.

3. Recognize that risk capital is and deserves to be expensive, and understand the process investors follow in structuring and pricing a deal.

4. Look for an angel with relevant experience as well as capital — i.e., look close to

home for an investor who understands the venture and will work with it.

5. Be prepared to discuss when and how an investor can cash in his or her chips. Shared liquidation expectations are especially critical for ventures with limited prospects for an eventual public offering or acquisition by a larger firm.

6. If the venture is likely to appeal to an individual investor's "hot buttons," exploit them for both sides will benefit.

7. Anticipate the need for substantial follow-on financing if the venture succeeds, and be sure that either the initial investors can provide it or they are themselves realistic about the cost of additional outside equity.

Public Policy Proposal

Since the end of World War II, the question of institutional gaps in the capital markets serving small firms has periodically been a topic for economic and political debate. The first serious study of capital gaps was conducted by the Federal Reserve Board and led to the Small Business Investment Act of 1958, which created the SBIC program. With the current interest in entrepreneurship and small business, capital formation is again a "hot topic" in and out of Washington. As examples of "capital gaps," the debate invariably cites problems in raising both seed capital for inventors and new ventures, and equity financing for expanding firms. While institutional gaps may well exist, our data suggest that effectively filling the gaps will depend more upon improving the efficiency of the private risk capital markets and the angel segment in particular, than upon creating new institutions or changing the behavior of old ones. With little or no recognition, successful entrepreneurs and other financially sophisticated individuals are filling the void in the institutional capital market. Eight out of ten investors in our sample would like to examine a broader range of

Sloan Management Review   Summer 1983   33

investment opportunities than they currently see.

Recent reductions in capital gains tax rates have enhanced the rewards for all risk capital investors. The impact of the reduction on the size of the professional venture capital pool is well known (increasing from roughly $2 billion in 1978 to over $7 billion today). There is no reason to believe that the impact on the pool of informal risk capital has been any less dramatic. The SEC's new Regulation D will also expedite the risk capital financing of small firms. Mobilization of the pool of "angel money" appears to be impeded by the absence of systematic, efficient channels of communication between entrepreneurs and investors.

The absence of private attempts to improve the efficiency of this market is due in part to the fragmented nature of the informal risk capital market and the existence of "external benefits" that cannot be captured by private investors. Public support for programs that improve the efficiency of private capital markets serving STBFs is justified by the benefits the public receives from STBFs: an enhanced flow of jobs, innovative technology, and tax revenues. Many STBFs will find access to informal risk capital essential to their ability to commercialize the federal investment in their research mandated by the Small Business Innovation Development Act: "To the extent that investment in small, technology-based firms produces external economies, too few resources will be allocated to all phases of investment in them, including generating information about investment opportunities."[10]

Our experience suggests that an experimental effort at expediting the private risk capital financing of emerging, technology-based ventures requires the efficient, systematic performance of four basic functions:

1. Identifying opportunities for risk capital investment in emerging, technology-based ventures and profiling their investment characteristics;

2. Identifying active informal investors and profiling their distinguishing investment objectives;

3. Providing a timely, confidential, and objective referral mechanism that will serve both investors and entrepreneurs;

4. Enhancing the networks of friends and business associates that link risk capital investors with each other, and expanding the flow of information through those networks.

The experimental venture outlined above would act as a clearinghouse of information for investors and entrepreneurs, and should be managed, in our judgment, by a respected but "disinterested" third party. No attempt would be made to evaluate the merits of investment proposals or the qualifications of investors. Given the characteristics of the informal risk capital market, it seems that such an activity should occur at the regional (rather than state or national) level (e.g., the six-state New England region). Professionally managed, such an activity should be at least partially self-supporting once the experimental stage is concluded, and data collection and referral techniques are refined.

At the request of committees of both houses of Congress, the Office of Technology Assessment is currently engaged in an eighteen-month study to "determine where high-technology firms are appearing and what factors influence their distribution and growth; [to] identify and evaluate the effectiveness of State and local initiatives to encourage innovation and high-technology development; [to] explore the changing opportunities presented by new and emerging technologies such as robotics and bioengineering; and [to] address the appropriate Federal role in affecting the conditions for such growth in the future."[11] Generating information about opportunities for private investment in STBFs is one federal role worth testing.

References

1
See D. E. Gumpert and J. A. Timmons. "Disregard Many
Old Myths about Getting Venture Capital." *Harvard
Business Review*. January-February 1982.

2
See *Report of the Use of the Rule 146 Exemption in
Capital Formation* (Washington, DC: Directorate of
Economic and Policy Analysis. U.S. Securities and
Exchange Commission. January 1983).

3
See Charles River Associates, Inc., *An Analysis of
Capital Market Imperfections* (Prepared for the
Experimental Technology Incentives Program. National
Bureau of Standards. Washington, DC: February 1976).

4
See D. T. Brophy, "Venture Capital Research."
Encyclopedia of Entrepreneurship (Englewood Cliffs,
NJ: Prentice-Hall. 1982). ch. IX.

5
The SBA's Office of Advocacy and Milton Stewart (then
Chief Counsel for Advocacy and now president of the
Small Business High Technology Institute) were our
believers. See W. E. Wetzel and C. R. Seymour, *Informal
Risk Capital in New England* (Prepared for Office of

Advocacy. U.S. Small Business Administration.
Durham, NH: University of New Hampshire. 1981).

6
See Gumpert and Timmons (January-February 1982).

7
See S. E. Pratt. ed., *Guide to Venture Capital Sources*,
6th ed. (Wellesley Hills, MA: Capital Publishing. 1982).

8
For a brief illustration of the technique, see Gumpert
and Timmons (January-February 1982).
For a more detailed discussion, see:
"Structuring and Pricing the Financing," in *Guide to
Venture Capital Sources*, 6th ed., ed. S. E. Pratt
(Wellesley Hills, MA: Capital Publishing, 1982);
W. E. Wetzel, "Technovation and the Informal
Investor." *Technovation*, Winter 1981.

9
See A. S. Bean, D. Schiffel, and M. E. Mogee. "The
Venture Capital Market and Technological Innovation."
Research Policy (4): 1975.

10
See Charles River Associates, Inc. (February 1976).

11
See *Technology, Innovation, and Regional Economic
Development* (Washington, DC: Office of Technology
Assessment. U.S. Congress. September 9. 1982).

[21]

MANAGEMENT SCIENCE
Vol. 30, No. 9, September 1984

A MODEL OF VENTURE CAPITALIST INVESTMENT ACTIVITY*

TYZOON T. TYEBJEE AND ALBERT V. BRUNO

School of Business, University of Santa Clara, Santa Clara, California 95053

The paper describes the activities of venture capitalists as an orderly process involving five sequential steps. These are (1) Deal Origination: The processes by which deals enter into consideration as investment prospects, (2) Deal Screening: A delineation of key policy variables which delimit investment prospects to a manageable few for in-depth evaluation, (3) Deal Evaluation: The assessment of perceived risk and expected return on the basis of a weighting of several characteristics of the prospective venture and the decision whether or not to invest as determined by the relative levels of perceived risk and expected return, (4) Deal Structuring: The negotiation of the price of the deal, namely the equity relinquished to the investor, and the covenants which limit the risk of the investor, (5) Post-Investment Activities: The assistance to the venture in the areas of recruiting key executives, strategic planning, locating expansion financing, and orchestrating a merger, acquisition or public offering. 41 venture capitalists provided data on a total of 90 deals which had received serious consideration in their firms. The questionnaire measured the mechanism of initial contact between venture capitalist and entrepreneur, the venture's industry, the stage of financing and product development, ratings of the venture on 23 characteristics, an assessment of the potential return and perceived risk, and the decision vis-à-vis whether to invest. The modal venture represented in the database was a start-up in the electronics industry with a production capability in place and seeking \$1 million (median) in outside financing. There is a high degree of cross-referrals between venture capitalists, particularly for the purposes of locating co-investors. Factor analysis reduced the 23 characteristics of the deal to five underlying dimensions namely (1) Market Attractiveness (size, growth, and access to customers), (2) Product Differentiation (uniqueness, patents, technical edge, profit margin), (3) Managerial Capabilities (skills in marketing, management, finance and the references of the entrepreneur), (4) Environmental Threat Resistance (technology life cycle, barriers to competitive entry, insensitivity to business cycles and down-side risk protection), (5) Cash-Out Potential (future opportunities to realize capital gains by merger, acquisition or public offering). The results of regression analyses showed expected return to be determined by Market Attractiveness and Product Differentiation ($R2 = 0.22$). Perceived risk is determined by Managerial Capabilities and Environmental Threat Resistance ($R2 = 0.33$). Finally, a discriminant analysis correctly predicted, in 89.4% of the cases, whether or not a venture capitalist was willing to commit funds to the deal on the basis of the expected return and perceived risk. The reactions of seven venture capitalists who reviewed the model's specification were used to test its validity.
(FINANCE—INVESTMENT CRITERIA; FINANCIAL INSTITUTIONS—INVESTMENT; RESEARCH AND DEVELOPMENT—PROJECT SELECTION; STATISTICS—REGRESSION—VENTURE CAPITAL)

Introduction

Venture capital has become an increasingly important source of financing for new companies, particularly when such companies are operating on the frontier of emerging technologies and markets. It plays an essential role in the entrepreneurial process. The purpose of this paper is to model the deal flow in a venture capital firm, namely the stages in the consideration, scrutiny and disposition of venture investment deals. The theory of equity markets is well developed in finance; it will not be reviewed here. These theories are typically oriented toward equity financing in publicly traded companies. Venture capital investments, however, differ in several important aspects (Poindexter 1976). First, venture capital is usually invested in new firms which have very little performance history. As a result, the investor cannot rely on historical performance data, as in the case of the stock market. Second, the investment is typically in small firms and the nature of the investor and investee relationship involves a higher degree of direct involvement as

* Accepted by Burton V. Dean; received June 13, 1983. This paper has been with the authors 1 month for 1 revision.

1052   TYZOON T. TYEBJEE AND ALBERT V. BRUNO

compared to the relatively inactive role of investors in publicly traded companies. Third, venture capital investments are illiquid in the short term because of the lack of efficient capital markets for equity shares of privately held companies. Long horizons of product and market development make valuation difficult. Moreover, the legal restrictions that apply to the resale of such investments lock the investor in for a certain period. Fourth, when a venture capitalist invests in a new startup, it is usually with the implicit realization that future rounds of capital infusion may have to be financed before the initial investment can bear fruit (Cooper and Carleton 1979).

The lack of capital markets for the financial instruments of small, new companies introduces considerable problems in studying venture capital investments within the paradigm of the capital asset pricing model. The absence of a clearing price determined by the market makes the valuation of an investment vulnerable to the subjective assessment procedures of the analyst. One study of 29 SBIC funds found that venture capital funds enjoy a rate of return 63% higher than Standard & Poor's market index returns. This premium, however, is offset by a higher risk; the variability of the firm's returns were higher than that of the market index return (Poindexter 1976). Poindexter concludes that venture capital markets are efficient since higher returns are offset by higher risk. Using a considerably different methodology, Charles River Associates (1976) reached the same conclusion.

The efficiency of venture capital markets is a central public policy concern because of the latter's goal of stimulating the flow of funds to new, small companies. However, the efficiency proposition provides little insight into the decision process of venture capitalists, other than the implication that they select investments with potential returns high enough to offset the higher risk. In the next section we develop a descriptive model of the activities or processes involved in managing a venture capital fund. Portions of the model are empirically tested on the basis of interviews with venture capitalists, and analyses of the characteristics and disposition of deals which they had recently considered. This methodology is not without its problems. In the experience of the authors, venture capitalists are reluctant to violate the confidentiality of their investees. Also they are not receptive to highly structured measurement instruments, which are perceived to be time consuming to complete. They view every deal and every venture capital fund to be peculiar to itself, and resist the generalizations which behavioral scientists wish to impose upon them. For this reason, research methodology which relies on the cooperation of venture capitalists in divulging data on their activities is likely to suffer from a high nonresponse bias and criticisms regarding the generalizability of small sample research. It is with this backdrop that we seek to model the activities of venture capitalists.

Model of the Venture Capitalist's Investment Activity

The investment activity of a venture capitalist is modeled as a sequential process involving five steps (see Figure 1). The first step is one of *deal origination* which describes how venture capitalists become cognizant of potential investment activities. The second step is a *screening* process by which venture capitalists seek to concentrate only on a manageable set of potential deals. The *evaluation* step involves an assessment of the potential return and risk of a particular deal. If the outcome of the evaluation process is a favorable one, the venture capitalist enters into a negotiating process with the potential investee so as to *structure the deal* in terms of the amount, form and price of the investment. Once a deal is consummated, the venture capitalist typically has close contact with the venture. These *post-investment activities* include setting up controls to protect the investment, providing consultation to the fledgling management of the venture, and, finally, helping orchestrate the merger, acquisition, or public offering which would create a public market for the investment.

On the basis of several previous studies (Dorsey 1977; Hoffman 1972; Poindexter 1976; Timmons and Gumpert 1982; Wells 1974) we can describe the salient features of each of these steps as follows:

Step 1—Deal Origination. The venture capitalist faces a very poorly defined environment within which to find prospective deals. The typical investment prospect is too small a company to be readily identifiable as a potential candidate. For this reason, we could expect that various intermediaries play an important role in matching venture capital investors with fledgling ventures with cash needs.

Step 2—Screening. Venture capital firms typically have small staffs. As a result, these firms must screen the relatively large number of potential deals available and consequently invest in only a fraction of the deals which come to their attention. Their screening criteria reflect a tendency to limit investments to areas with which the

VENTURE CAPITALIST INVESTMENT ACTIVITY 1053

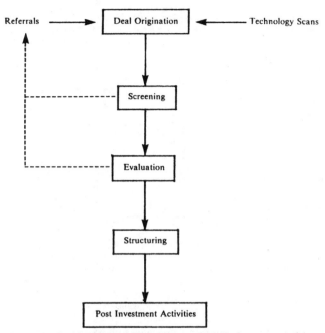

FIGURE 1. Decision Process Model of Venture Capitalist Investment Activity.

venture capitalist is familiar, particularly in terms of the technology, product and market scope of the venture.

Step 3—Evaluation. As noted before, most ventures in search of capital have very little, if any, operating history. The venture capitalist has to rely on a subjective assessment procedure based upon the business plan presented by the venture's management. Venture capitalists do weigh risk and return in their decision whether or not to invest in a particular deal, but few formalize this assessment into a computation of an expected rate of return or determine its sensitivity to future uncertainties. Instead, the evaluation procedure seeks to subjectively assess the venture on a multidimensional set of characteristics. Table 1 shows the characteristics found to be important in previous studies. Not surprisingly, these criteria are similar to those found in several new product evaluation models (Montgomery and Urban 1969; O'Meara 1961; Pessemier 1982). It is interesting to note, however, that none of these criteria reflects how a prospective deal may correlate with one already in the venture capitalist's investment portfolio.

Step 4—Deal Structuring. Once the venture capitalist has decided that a deal is acceptable, the deal will be consummated only if the venture capitalist and the entrepreneur are able to structure a mutually acceptable venture capital investment agreement. From the perspective of the venture capitalist, the agreement serves several purposes. First, it establishes the price of the deal, that is the equity share the entrepreneur will give up in exchange for the venture capital (Golden 1981). Second, it establishes protective covenants which limit capital expenditures and management

1054   TYZOON T. TYEBJEE AND ALBERT V. BRUNO

TABLE 1

Venture Evaluation Criteria

WELLS (1974) Sample: Eight Venture Capital Firms (Personally interviewed)		POINDEXTER(1976) Sample: 97 Venture Capital Firms (Mailed questionnaires)	TYEBJEE & BRUNO (Study I) Sample: 46 Venture Capitalists (Telephone survey, open-ended questions)	
Factor	Average Weight	Investment Criteria by Rank Order Of Importance	Factor	% of Respondents Mentioning
Management Commitment	10.0	1. Quality of Management	1. Management Skills & History	89
Product	8.8	2. Expected Rate of Return	2. Market Size/Growth	50
Market	8.3	3. Expected Risk	3. Rate of Return	46
Marketing Skill	8.2	4. Percentage Equity Share of Venture	4. Market Niche/Position	20
Engineering Skill	7.4	5. Management Stake in Firm	5. Financial History	11
Marketing Plan	7.2	6. Financial Provisions for Investor Rights	6. Venture Location	11
Financial Skill	6.4	7. Venture Development Stage	7. Growth Potential	11
Manufacturing Skill	6.2	8. Restrictive Covenants	8. Barriers to Entry	11
References	5.9	9. Interest or Dividend Rate	9. Size of Investment	9
Other Participants in Deal	5.0	10. Present Capitalization	10. Market/Industry Expertise	7
Industry/Technology	4.2	11. Investor Control	11. Venture Stage	4
Cash-Out Method	2.3	12. Tax Shelter Consideration	12. Stake of Entrepreneur	4

salaries. Covenants also establish the basis under which the venture capitalist can take control of the board, force a change in management or liquidate the investment by forcing a buy-back, a merger, acquisition or public offering even though the venture capitalist holds a minority position. The covenants may also restrict the power of the venture management to dilute the equity of the original investors by raising additional capital elsewhere (Cooper and Carleton 1979; Glassmeyer 1981). Third, through a mechanism known as the earn-out arrangement, where the entrepreneur's equity share is determined by meeting agreed upon performance objectives, the venture capitalist is able to assess the entrepreneur's expectations for the venture (Leland and Pyle 1977; Ross 1977).

Step 5—Post-Investment Activities. Once the deal has been consummated, the role of the venture capitalist expands from investor to collaborator. This new role may be via a formal representation on the board of directors or via informal influence in market, supplier and creditor networks. The intensity of involvement in the venture's operations differs from one venture capitalist to another. However, most of those interviewed agree that it is undesirable for a venture capital company to exert control over the day-to-day operations of the venture. If a financial or managerial crisis occurs, the venture capitalist may intervene and even install a new management team.

Finally, venture capitalists typically want to cash-out their gains five to ten years after initial investments. To this end, they play an active role in directing the company towards merger, acquisition or a public offering. Bruno and Cooper (1982) followed up on 250 startups of the sixties. They found that over half of these had either gone public, or had been merged or acquired.

The post-investment activities of venture capitalists vis-à-vis their portfolio companies have been ignored by the bulk of research on venture capital. In particular, the venture capitalist's decision-making process for second and subsequent rounds of financing for ventures already in his portfolio remains a fertile area of research.

Method

The results of two databases, referred to as Study I and Study II, are presented in the next section. These databases are described briefly below.

Study I

A telephone survey of 46 venture capitalists in California, Massachusetts and Texas. Of these, half were SBIC's. The telephone survey used a structured questionnaire which asked about how ventures are evaluated. The responses were open-ended and their analysis is based upon a post-hoc categorization of responses.

Study II

Venture capital firms listed in Pratt's directory (1981) of venture capital were contacted by mail to solicit their participation in a study of investment decision criteria. The mailing was restricted to the 156 venture capital firms in the states of California, Massachusetts, and Texas as these states account for a major portion of the venture capital industry, particularly as it applies to high technology startups. Forty-one venture capital firms agreed to participate in the study. For nonparticipants, the dominant reason for refusing to participate was the sensitivity of the information we requested. A second reason was the busy schedule of the venture capitalists. Finally, several firms disqualified themselves as participants in the survey as they were either inactive in new investments or only invested in deals put together by others. The 41 cooperating venture capital firms were mailed a structured questionnaire on which to evaluate deals under consideration. We asked that they indicate their decision vis-à-vis investing in that deal. Ninety completed evaluations were returned by the 41 participants, an average of 2.2 deals per participating venture capitalist. The industries represented in the 90 deals in our sample were computers, semiconductors and telecommunications (59.6%), energy (13.5%), consumer goods (10.1%) and miscellaneous industries including transportation, construction and biomedical (16.8%).

A major problem with the methodology used in this study for describing the evaluation step is that it may be biased in favor of the results obtained. In particular, the statistical relationships between subjectively assessed characteristics of deals and the venture capitalist's decision regarding them may reflect a post-hoc rationalization of the decision. To mitigate this problem, the methodology includes a validation component in which the key results described in the next section were presented to 7 venture capitalists and their reactions recorded. The validation component was administered by mail and its outcome is discussed following the next section.

Results

In this section, the results from Studies I and II are discussed within the context of the five-step model developed earlier. While the data and results are largely focused on the deal evaluation step of the model, results for the first two steps are also presented. The last two steps, namely deal structuring and post-investment activities, are not considered in this section, but will be discussed in the validation section which follows.

Step 1—Deal Origination

Potential deals are brought to the attention of venture capitalists from three sources. In Study II, 25.6% of the 90 deals in the sample originated as unsolicited cold calls from entrepreneurs. The typical response of the venture capitalist is to request the inquirer to send in a business plan. The second source is through a referral process. Sixty-five percent of the deals were referred to the venture capitalist. A third of the referrals came from within the venture capital community, 40% were referred by prior investees and personal acquaintances, 10% were referred by banks and the remainder involved an investment broker.

Of those deals referred by other venture capitalists, a substantial number represent the case of the referring venture capitalist acting as a lead investor and seeking the participation of other venture capital funds. This practice, known as a syndication, is becoming more prevalent as venture capital firms seek to diversify their portfolios over a larger number of deals. Syndication offers the capability of adding investments to the portfolio without adding to the administrative burden, the bulk of which is borne by the lead investor.

The third mechanism of deal origination is the active search for deals by the venture capitalist. The venture capitalist sometimes played an active role in pursuing companies at the startup stage or those at the critical point of needing expansion financing. The venture capitalist monitors the environment for such potential candidates through an informal network and attendance at conventions, trade shows and special conferences by groups such as the American Electronics Association. An extreme variant of this active role occurs when the venture capitalist first decides which technology markets he would like to add to his portfolio and uses executive search agencies to locate the management team for the venture. In such cases, the roles of venture capitalist and entrepreneur overlap considerably.

Step 2—Screening

The venture capital firm receives a large number of proposals; far more than they can possibly fund with the size of the staff and portfolio of the typical venture fund. Wells (1974) reports that in seven venture capital funds, the annual number of proposals received ranged between 120 and 1,000, with an average of about 450 per year. Broad screening criteria are used to reduce this set to a more manageable number for more indepth evaluation. The initial screening is based upon four criteria:

(1) *The size of the investment and the investment policy of the venture fund.* The lower limit of this policy is determined by the fact that a venture capital company is run with a lean staff and it cannot afford to spread its portfolio over too many small deals because the subsequent control and consultation demands placed on the venture capitalists are essentially the same regardless of the size of the investment. Brophy (1981) reports that of 73 venture capitalists surveyed in 1979 the average number of deals invested in was 5.6 and the average portfolio size was ten ventures. The upper boundary of the investment policy is determined by the capitalization of the portfolio and the desire to maintain an investment base which is diversified across several ventures. However, the upper limit to the investment policy is relatively flexible because a venture capitalist may consider larger deals with the intent of soliciting the participation of other venture capital funds. In fact, in our research we found that the venture capital community is highly inbred with a substantial amount of participation across funds, leading many entrepreneurs to conclude that the venture capital market involves substantially less competition between suppliers than is indicated by the mere count of number of funds in existence. Brophy (1981) estimates that approximately 80% of the venture capital deals struck in 1980 involved the participation of more than one venture capital fund and about a third of the deals involved five or more participants. Fifty-six percent of the deals analyzed in Study II involved the participation of more than one venture capital fund. In the case of two-thirds of the deals which were given a positive evaluation, the venture capitalist was himself willing to commit less than 75% of the amount requested, with the balance to be raised by inviting the participation of other venture capital funds.

The investment policy, in terms of the maximum and minimum amounts which will be considered, is quite heterogeneous across venture capital firms (Timmons and Gumpert 1982). The dollar amount requested in the 90 deals examined in Study II reflects this diversity. The amounts range from $30,000 to $7,500,000, with the median amount being $1,000,000. About a third of the deals were for less than $500,000 and another third were for amounts in excess of $1,500,000.

(2) *The technology and market sector of the venture.* Of 46 venture capitalists interviewed in Study I, 29 used this screening criterion. The venture capitalist is investing in more than a company. Implicitly, he/she is investing in the future of a particular technology or market. For this reason, the venture capitalist must have some familiarity with the technology or the market of the proposed venture. This leads to an implicit specialization in a few technology markets because of the inability of the venture capital fund's manager to be well-versed across a large number of technologies or markets. Also, venture capitalists tend to favor nascent technology industries over mature technologies, the industrial market over the consumer market, and products over services.

The 90 deals in Study II, which presumably had passed initial screening, demonstrated these preferences. More than three out of four were in technology-intensive industries, only a tenth were in the consumer goods sector, and over 90% were manufacturing companies. Sixty-four percent of the deals were described by the venture capitalist as involving either a new technology or a new application of an existing technology, 18% were described as improvements on current products, and the remaining 18% were described as me-too products.

(3) *Geographic location of the venture.* Of 46 venture capitalists interviewed in Study I, 9 used this screening criterion. When a venture capitalist invests in a company, he expects to meet regularly with the management of the new venture. To maintain travel time and expense at manageable levels, some venture capitalists limit their investment activity to major metropolitan areas with easy access. Sometimes, this screening criterion will be ignored if the venture capitalist can involve the participation of another venture capital fund which is close to the venture's location and which can oversee the venture with greater ease. Though most venture capital companies do not actively pursue a policy of restricting their investment activity to a specific geographic boundary, their portfolios often exhibit this specialization because of a tendency of entrepreneurs to search for capital close to their venture's home where their banking, legal and accountancy contacts are strongest.

(4) *Stage of financing.* Of 46 venture capitalists interviewed in Study I, 22 used this screening criterion. Venture capital infusions into a company occur at several points in the life cycle of the venture. Seed capital refers to funds invested before the venture exists as a formal entity. Venture capitalists rarely invest seed capital and entrepreneurs typically turn to informal sources for this money (Wetzel 1981). Startup capital refers to financing for establishing the operation; subsequent rounds of financing are used for expanding operations. Brophy (1981) reports that of 196 venture investments in 1978, 34.2% were for startups, 40.3% were for first round expansion and 19.4% were for second round expansion (6.1% were unclassified).

In Study II, the 90 deals showed a very similar profile to Brophy's data: 45.6% were startups, 22.2% were first round expansion deals and 21.1% were second round expansion deals. Described in another manner, in the case of 23% of the deals the product was still at the design stage, in the case of another 23% a working prototype had been developed and in the case of the remaining 54% the product was already in production.

These aggregate statistics, however, hide the fact that the risk preferences of venture capital funds differ. As a result, some funds will commit capital to later stage rounds only. Others will not commit to later stage rounds unless they have already invested in the venture in the prior rounds.

Step 3—Evaluation

We asked cooperating venture capitalists to rate several deals which had passed their initial screen and were under serious consideration. The deals were rated on 23 criteria

TABLE 2

Factor Structure of Evaluation Criteria

Evaluation Criteria	Factor 1	Factor 2	Factor 3	Factor 4	Factor 5
Management Skills (6.6%)*	0.15	− 0.07	0.85	0.16	0.10
Marketing Skills (8.9%)	0.31	− 0.06	0.80	− 0.07	− 0.03
Financial Skills (6.6%)	− 0.23	− 0.01	0.74	0.16	0.12
References of Entrepreneur (16.7%)	0.24	0.09	0.48	0.16	0.33
Technical Skills (7.8%)	0.11	0.72	0.01	− 0.12	0.27
Profit Margins (13.4%)	0.19	0.62	0.25	− 0.02	− 0.04
Uniqueness of Product (11.1%)	0.14	0.87	− 0.02	0.03	0.06
Patentability of Product (30.0%)	− 0.02	0.67	− 0.31	0.27	0.01
Raw Material Availability (31.1%)	0.12	0.18	− 0.07	0.05	− 0.07
Production Capabilities (30.0%)	0.11	0.11	0.06	0.04	− 0.03
Access to Market (12.3%)	0.66	0.07	0.14	0.13	0.24
Market Need for Product (12.2%)	0.79	0.07	0.00	0.12	0.04
Size of Market (10.0%)	0.84	0.03	0.00	0.10	0.07
Growth Potential of Market (13.3%)	0.66	0.35	0.06	− 0.20	0.20
Freedom from Regulation (16.7%)	0.09	− 0.09	− 0.20	0.07	0.41
Protection from Competitive Entry (12.3%)	− 0.01	0.36	− 0.12	0.77	0.24
Resistance to Economic Cycles (12.2%)	0.28	0.32	0.27	0.59	− 0.38
Protection from Obsolescence (17.8%)	0.10	− 0.19	0.12	0.75	0.17
Protection against Down-side Risk (13.4%)	0.02	− 0.13	0.09	0.70	0.18
Opportunities for Exit (15.6%)	0.28	0.15	0.12	0.24	0.76
Merger/Acquisition Potential (17.8%)	0.12	0.20	0.25	0.12	0.80
Hedge Against Current Investments (53.3%)	—	—	—	—	—
Tax Benefits (34.4%)	—	—	—	—	—
% Variance Explained	22.5	12.9	9.6	8.2	7.2

* Percentage of deals for which evaluation was not reported.

(see Table 2) using a four-point rating scale (Poor = 1, Adequate = 2, Good = 3, Excellent = 4). In addition to rating the venture on the 23 criteria, the participant also rated the venture on overall expected return and risk, respectively. A straightforward measure of expected return proved intractable because in 42% of the cases the venture capitalist was unable to assign a numerical estimate of the expected rate of return. For this reason, expected return was measured on a four-point scale (Low = 1, Moderate = 2, High = 3, Very High = 4). The perceived riskiness of the deal was measured by asking the venture capitalist to assign a subjective probability to the venture being a commercial failure. Finally, the venture capitalists indicated their decision regarding the deal. Of the 90 deals in the sample, 25 were rejected, 43 were found to be acceptable and thus fundable, 18 were pending further investigation, and in the case of 4 deals, the decision was not specified.

Table 2 lists the 23 items which served as the basis for evaluating deals under consideration. The number in parentheses next to each item reports the frequency with which deals received no evaluation at all on each of these criteria. A deal would not be evaluated on a particular criterion if it did not enter the decision-making process. The frequency of missing responses was particularly high in the case of five of the evaluation criteria. The patentability of the product was not evaluated in 30% of the cases. Manufacturing aspects such as raw material availability and production capabilities were not evaluated in almost one-third of the cases. The tax benefits of the investment were not evaluated in 34.4% of the deals. Finally, the extent to which the investment offset or hedged the risk of the existing portfolio was not evaluated in 53.3% of the cases.

Why do these five items sustain such a high nonresponse rate? Though the data themselves do not answer these questions, it is possible to speculate why this occurs. There is a disillusionment with the patent process and many entrepreneurs and venture capitalists feel that the public disclosure of the product design in the patent application leads to more competitive entry rather than less. Venture capitalists generally do not worry about raw material and production capabilities as these are technical problems easily solved if the product and its marketing are viable. Tax benefits are not relevant in evaluating many deals because venture capitalists see their mission as reaping capital gains rather than providing tax shelters for the investors in their fund. Finally, the fact that a deal's relationship to the existing portfolio is not evaluated in more than half the cases is consistent with the results of Study I. Of the 46 venture capitalists interviewed, 28 claimed that they evaluated each deal on its own individual merit. Only one of the interviewees claimed that impact on portfolio risk was formally analyzed.

All the scales, with the exception of the two which had the highest rate of missing data, namely the tax benefits and hedge against current portfolio, were factor analyzed.

The varimax factor loadings are given in Table 2. A five-factor solution explains 60.4% of the variation in the 21 rating items. Adding a sixth factor would have added an incremental 6.3% of the variance explained; however the interpretability of this sixth factor was poor (each factor was interpreted on the basis of the items which load most heavily on it).

Based upon the factor structure in Table 2, we conclude that venture capitalists evaluate potential deals in terms of five basic characteristics. The first characteristic which we labeled *Market Attractiveness* depends upon the size, growth and accessibility of the market and on the existence of a market need. The second characteristic reflects *Product Differentiation* which is determined by the ability of the entrepreneur to apply his technical skills in creating a product which is unique can deter competition through patents and enjoy a high profit margin. The third characteristic reflects the *Managerial Capabilities* of the venture's founders. This capability results from skills in managing several business functional areas and is associated with favorable references given to the entrepreneurs. The fourth factor represents the extent to which the venture is resistant to uncontrollable pressures from the environment. These pressures may result from obsolescence due to changing technology, from sensitivity to economic conditions or from low barriers to entry by competition. This factor was labeled *Environmental Threat Resistance*. The final factor represents the extent to which the venture capitalist feels that the investment can be liquidated or "cashed out" at the appropriate time. This is labeled as *Cash-Out Potential*.

The next step was to profile each deal in terms of the five dimensions. A score was computed for each deal on each factor as an average of the ratings of the items which loaded heavily on the factor.[1] For each factor, a Cronbach alpha was computed as an indication of the reliability of that factor. The Cronbach alpha values are reported on the diagonal of the matrix in Table 3. These range from 0.71 to 0.79. Table 3 also reports the intercorrelation of the factors.

A linear regression model was used to relate each deal's scores on the five dimensions to subjective estimates of its level of expected return and perceived risk, respectively. The expected return was estimated on a four-point scale. Risk was

---

[1] The items used in computing each factor score are those blocked in Table 1, with the exception of "Reference of Entrepreneur" and "Patentability of Product" which were excluded as they lowered the Cronbach alpha reliability.

TABLE 3

Cronbach Reliability and Intercorrelation of Evaluation Factors[1]

	Market Attractiveness	Product Differentiation	Managerial Capabilities	Environmental Threat Resistance	Cash-Out Potential
Market Attractiveness	0.79*	0.35*	0.20*	0.48*	0.39*
Product Differentiation		0.76	0.12	0.33*	0.25*
Managerial Capabilities			0.77	0.18	0.18
Environmental Threat Resistance				0.71	0.26
Cash-Out Potential					0.77[2]

[1] Cronbach alpha reliability is reported on the diagonal. The off-diagonal elements are Pearson correlation coefficients between the factors.

[2] The Cronbach alpha when only two items are used in constructing a scale is equivalent to the Pearson correlation between the two items.

* $p < 0.05$.

estimated in terms of the probability of commercial failure: the higher the probability of failure, the greater the riskiness of the venture.[2] Table 4 reports the results of the two regressions.

The evaluation scores are able to explain 33% of the variance in perceived risk and 22% of the variance in estimated rate of return. The R^2 values associated with the two regressions are significant at the 0.01 level.

Two aspects of the deal's evaluation have a significant impact on the risk associated with the deal. A lack of managerial capabilities significantly increases the perceived risk ($p < 0.05$). The relative magnitudes of the beta coefficients show that managerial capabilities have the strongest effect on reducing the riskiness of the deal and resistance to environmental threats has the next highest effect. Other characteristics of the deal do not influence the perceived risk at a significant level.

Two different aspects of the deal's evaluation influence the expected rate of return. Attractive market conditions have the strongest effect ($p < 0.01$) and a highly differentiated product has the next highest effect ($p < 0.05$). Other characteristics of the deal do not significantly influence the expected return.

Interestingly, the cash-out potential of a venture does not seem to influence either perceived risk or return. This is particularly surprising because without a merger, acquisition or public offering, the investor is severely constrained in realizing any gains.

TABLE 4

Determinants of Risk and Return Assessment

Dependent Variable	Market Attractiveness	Product Differentiation	Managerial Capabilities	Environmental Threat Resistance	Cashout Potential	Adjusted R^2
Risk	− 0.05	− 0.12	− 0.46[a]	− 0.23[b]	0.01	0.33[a]
Return	0.40[a]	0.26[b]	0.03	0.02	− 0.13	0.22[a]

[a] Significant at the 0.01 level.
[b] Significant at the 0.05 level.

[2] The correlation between expected risk and return was − 0.13. This relationship is not statistically significant.

In our sample of 90 deals, 43 were endorsed as acceptable investments, 25 were denied funds and the balance were either pending a decision or no decision was specified. Discriminant analysis was used to examine the ability of the perceived risk and return to distinguish between rejected and accepted deals. For this purpose, we analyzed only the 68 deals for which a definite decision was made.

The standardized discrimination function coefficients of the two predictor variables, expected return and perceived risk, are 0.52 and −0.87, respectively. The signs are as expected; namely, a high expected return increases the likelihood that the deal is accepted and a high perceived risk increases its likelihood of being rejected. The fact that the signs of the discriminant coefficients are different, i.e., one is positive whereas the other negative, indicates a trade-off relationship between risk and return, a lower expected return is acceptable if offset by a lower risk.

The predictive ability of the discriminant function can be evaluated in terms of the accuracy with which it can classify deals as accepted or rejected. 68.4% of the deals actually rejected were classified as such and 95.2% of the deals actually accepted were classified as such. Together, this represents 86.9% of the deals being correctly classified. The predictive ability of a discriminant function can be evaluated by comparing the percentage of cases correctly classified against two criteria (Morrison 1969).

Proportional Chance Criterion: $C_{pro} = \alpha^2 + (1 - \alpha)^2$,

Maximum Chance Criterion: $C_{max} = \max(\alpha, 1 - \alpha)$,

where α and $1 - \alpha$ are the proportions in each group.

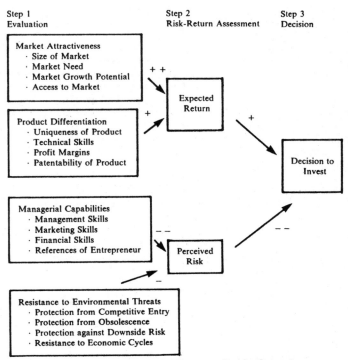

Step 1
Evaluation

Step 2
Risk-Return Assessment

Step 3
Decision

FIGURE 2. Venture Capital Investment Decision Process.*

*The + +, +, −, − − symbols indicate the direction and magnitude of the parameters describing the relationships of variables.

TABLE 5

Validation of the Model

	Venture Capitalist No. 1	Venture Capitalist No. 2	Venture Capitalist No. 3
DEAL ORIGINATION			
Most deals are referred to the venture capitalist rather than being cold contacts.	Agrees, but do get many cold contact deals. They tend to be considerably lower quality on average than "referred" deals.	Agrees.	Agrees.
A little less than half of the deals referred to the venture capitalist are referred by a former investee or a personal acquaintance; about a third are referred by other venture capitalists.	Agrees.	Agrees. In this case, "personal acquaintance" includes lawyers, auditors, and investment bankers that are well known to the venture capitalist.	Substantially true. A large number of deals come from personal or professional acquaintances. Number from other venture capitalists seems to be of less overall importance particularly for early stage deals.
Referrals by other venture capitalists are often in the form of an invitation to participate in a deal.	Agrees.	Agrees.	Not true in our experience. Often other venture capitalists invite us to examine a deal in conjunction with themselves. Their hope is to leverage our expertise and perspective in analyzing the deal. Quite often this may lead to a negative investment decision.
Sometimes a venture capitalist may select an industry of interest and set up a venture by searching out a management team. Such cases are rare. The more typical approach is when the venture capitalist lets the deal come to him.	Agrees.	Agrees.	Substantially true. Just as often as selecting an industry, however, we have more typically selected a management team and built a company around them.
DEAL SCREENING			
The most commonly used screening criteria are the size of investment, the technology and/or market, the stage of financing, and the geographic proximity	Interesting management team may be most important screening criterion.	Size of investment is not critical in the investment decision. Experience level of management group is the most important criterion.	The size of investment is often used as an excuse for turning a deal down but rarely would stand in the way of our participation if everything else seemed good. Technology and/or market are of interest but more particularly relate to barriers of entry achievable or ultimate size of the company achievable. Stage of financing has been a criteria for us in the past, i.e., we focus on first or second round deals. Geographic location has not been a concern. However, it is often used as an excuse to turn a deal down.
DEAL EVALUATION			
The decision to invest is based upon the expected return relative to the risk level. The best indicators of return prospect are		The capabilities of the management team is a better indication of expected return than risk level.	Overall, I believe your conclusions are correct. Factored into this, however, are issues such as portfolio diversification, other investors and the size of capitalization required.
(a) Market Attractiveness (size & growth potential, market used and ability of the venture to access the market).	Agrees.		Ability to develop a particular technology and bring it to market at a particular time represents a substantial risk in many deals.
(b) Product Differentiation (uniqueness of product, technical skills, profit margins/value added, patents). The best indicators of the risk level are:	Agrees.		Overall, it is very difficult to be comprehensive and succinct at the same time in stating all of the factors entering into a deal evaluation.
(a) Managerial Capabilities (management, marketing, financial skills, entrepreneur's background).	Agrees.		
(b) Protection from Uncontrollables (competition, obsolescence, economic cycles).	Agrees.		
DEAL STRUCTURING			
Convertible preferred stock is the typical form of financing.		Agrees.	With rare exceptions, all of our financing involve convertible preferred stock. Debt is used only in very rare instances for our partnership. A distinction should be made here between SBIC style financings versus more traditional mainstream venture capital financing; SBIC's are more prone to finance with debt instruments.
Equity share required is determined by pay-out expectations relative to rate of return objectives.			Price is determined largely by the quality of the opportunity as well as comparable opportunities which have recently been financed.
The entrepreneur's equity is determined by earn-out conditions.	In our experience, earn-out agreements are quite rare and counter productive for both the management team and venture capitalists.		In general we receive liquidity either through merger or public stock offering.
The negotiations regarding the earn-out agreement give insight into the entrepreneur's expectations for the venture.			
POST INVESTMENT ACTIVITIES			
The venture capitalist provides the venture with management guidance and business contacts. A representative of the venture capital firm generally sits on the board. The venture capitalist plays a significant role in orchestrating a merger, acquisition on public offering.	"Management guidance" can cover a lot of sins. Critical input most often comes in the areas of: (1) Recruiting key executives or managers to fill out the team. (2) Acting as a sounding board to CEO on self-evaluation and evaluation of other top management (3) Strategy development.	Agrees.	Management guidance and business contacts vary widely depending on the particular investment and our level of involvement. This level of involvement is tied directly to our participation on the board. However, we sit on the board in less than one-third of our portfolio companies, and typically only those deals in which we are lead investors. I would view our role in orchestrating a merger acquisition or public offering as relatively minor compared to our role as a management sounding board.

TABLE 5 (*continued*)

Venture Capitalist No. 4	Venture Capitalist No. 5	Venture Capitalist No. 6	Venture Capitalist No. 7
Agrees.	Founders have become very sophisticated. They develop relationship with lawyer and apprise bank contact of their intentions to start company. They also use their network, especially banks, lawyers and former associates who have started companies. This helps the targeting of vc potentials as well as providing introductions.	Agrees.	Agrees.
Agrees.		More than 1/2, 1/2 by other v.c.'s. Also past & present investees, corporate contacts & personal accounts	Agrees.
Agrees.			Agrees.
Agrees.			Agrees.
For us, I would rank in priority: (1) Management team (2) Technology/market (3) Stage of financing (4) Size (5) Location (only re being lead investor).	Missing is the most important... the people! I check the founders out before I will have first meeting.	We use potential return on capital as an early screening criterion.	Agrees.
Agrees. Agrees.	We don't actually use separate determinants of risk & return. Rather we use 3 evaluation criteria, weighted as follows: 40% - management quality/experience 40% - market (big wave can carry many surf boards) 20% - product niche, i.e., segmentation (performance/competition and many other implications)	Quality of management reflects return potential rather than the risk.	Managerial capabilities are an indicator of return prospects relative to the risk level.
Convertible preferred stock is typical for us; note that we discourage dividends.	One way to handle the question of performance is through a buy-back provision where the stock position of the entrepreneur is vested over a period of time. This allows for the replacement of poor/marginal performers and the ability to use repurchased (non-vested) stock to attract replacement in the management team. Past experiences in the realized valuation of comparable ventures which we have backed help determine the equity split between entrepreneur & us in future deals. For example, if we expect a company to have an upside potential of $10 million, we might put in $4 million and expect 40% equity in the venture.	Equity share is determined by the total equity valuation process; earn-out conditions are not used by our firm.	Converts were used more in the mid-seventies. They're still used by SBIC's but typically not by conventional VC partnerships. There hasn't been a convert in our last 40-50 investments. Equity share is determined by pay-out required expectations and by an assessment of the value currently represented by the business. Most VC's I know won't get involved in an earn-out. I haven't done one in 14 years in the business. You strike a deal with the management at the outset. Hopefully more equity is provided over time to successful management, but there's no way to take it away from them unless they leave or are fired. If you replace "earn-out" with "equity split," the statement would more accurately describe our reality.
For us, board seats for at least some venture investors. At least some of the venture capital investors, & especially the lead investor, should have representation on the board.	We agree. We especially contribute as follows: Help in recruiting key people Serve as sounding board to first time CEO Security check on strategy (OEM or direct sales, etc.)	We always serve on the board of our portfolio companies. We provide our portfolio companies with assistance in such areas as identifying legal counsel, performing compensation audits, focusing the product or service, recruiting management, locating additional capital and guiding acquisition/merger decisions.	Agree, but only one VC may be on the board even if there are 2-3 VC's in the deal, i.e., all of the investors don't go on the Board.

In our study, 43 of 68 deals were accepted ($\alpha = 0.63$) and 25 of 68 deals were rejected ($1 - \alpha = 0.37$). Thus $C_{pro} = 0.53$ and $C_{max} = 0.63$. Since the discriminant function classified 86.9% of the cases correctly, it performs considerably better than both the proportional chance criterion and the maximum chance criterion.

Figure 2 is a schematic representation of how evaluation criteria have an impact on the venture capitalist's decision to invest, as inferred by Study II. In summary, the attractiveness of the market and the product's differentiation are related to the expected return. A capable management team and resistance to environmental threats indicate a lower risk of commercial failure. Finally, the decision to invest is determined by the risk vs. return expectations vis-à-vis a venture. As expected, venture capitalists are risk-averse and profit-oriented in their decision and, moreover, they are willing to invest in risky deals if offset by the profit potential.

Neither Study I nor II collected any data relevant to the deal structuring (Step 4) or post-investment activities (Step 5) aspects of the model in Figure 1. These were addressed in a more general fashion in the validation component described in the next section.

Validation of the Model

Seven cooperating venture capitalists agreed to participate in a follow-up study to validate the model. The participants were selected to provide representation from the viewpoint of the various types of venture capital investors. Included in the set of cooperating venture capitalists were: a large venture capital firm which also participates in underwriting new equity issues; a small venture capital partnership composed of successful entrepreneurs who have sold their companies; a venture capital partnership with several generations of funds ranked in the top five in terms of number of deals made and dollars invested for 1982; a well-known venture capital firm which specializes in a narrow high technology industry segment; an SBIC; an individual venture capitalist investor; and a venture capital partnership substantially owned by a major banking institution. Each of the participating venture capitalists was asked to review the specification of the components of our model. These are summarized in the left-hand column of Table 5. Also the venture capitalists were asked to elaborate upon their reaction to the validity of the model. These responses are also shown in Table 5.

In general, there is agreement with the model's specification. Some of the comments elaborate upon the model specifications; others take exception with selected components of the model. The major departures from the model's specification are as follows:

(1) The model may have under-represented the extent to which venture capitalist's stress the quality of the management team as an early screening criterion. Also, the size of investment is not a screening criterion for several respondents.

(2) There was considerable disagreement with our statistical result that the quality of the management team influences risk but not expected return. Three of the seven respondents feel that management capabilities are an indicator of potential return rather than risk. A more fundamental issue is raised by VC5. This respondent does not formally distinguish between risk and return, as was implicitly assumed in our formulation.

(3) Earn-out arrangements are not extensively used in structuring deals. VC5 offers insight into a different type of deal structure which tries to achieve the same objective as an earn-out. In an earn-out arrangement, the share of the entrepreneur is determined by the venture's performance, thereby giving the investor control if the performance is poor. Instead, VC5 achieves much the same effect by the use of a "vesting" arrangement. Since the share of the entrepreneur vests over time, this gives the investor control in the early development of the venture even though his ultimate share may be a minority position.

VENTURE CAPITALIST INVESTMENT ACTIVITY 1065

Though the responses in Table 5 are in general agreement with our model's specification, there is a disturbing lack of common structure to the way the 7 venture capitalists reacted to the model. The diversity of the responses, both in content and style, demonstrates the heterogeneity in the practices of different venture capital firms. This heterogeneity cautions against too rigid a specification in any model describing venture capital management.

Conclusions

The purpose of this paper is two-fold. The first is to stimulate an interest in modeling the management of venture capital funds. The second is to provide entrepreneurs with insights which can help in their dealings with venture capitalists.

With respect to the first objective, the value of the study may perhaps be as much in what it did not achieve as in what it did achieve. A five-step model of the activities of venture capitalists has been developed. The model, however, is highly descriptive and lacks a theoretical basis. Moreover, the model is admittedly simplistic. A more rigorously specified model, however, could not capture the heterogeneity of practices across the many venture capital firms. Wells (1974) achieved a higher level of specificity in his modeling of venture capital fund management, but only at the expense of a unique model for each of the firms in his relatively small sample. Finally, the empirical portion of this paper has focused on the first three steps, and especially the third step, of the model. Most of the previous research on this topic share the same focus. In contrast, the fourth and fifth steps, namely deal structuring and post-investment activities, have not received much attention. In particular, the pricing of venture capital investments, in terms of the equity relinquished has not been modeled. Also, since most ventures involve several rounds of financing, the implications of future capital needs on investment decisions in earlier rounds of financing need to be explored. These limitations of the model presented in this paper are, hopefully, the stimuli for a continued interest in modeling venture capital investments.

The second objective of this paper is to provide potential entrepreneurs with insight into the way venture capitalists manage their funds. These insights are also valuable to managers in large companies who wish to improve their allocation of resources to internal ventures competing for new business development funds. First, professional relationships with CPAs, lawyers, bankers and successful entrepreneurs who have a high degree of credibility with the venture capital community is a help in locating capital. Second, the venture capital community is often smaller than it seems due to the high incidence of syndication whereby several venture capitalists co-invest in a venture. Third, venture capitalists differ in the screening criteria used to guide their investments. Most deals would have to match the investor's industry and geographic preferences, risk preferences for different financing stages, and investment policy in terms of the amount they will invest in a single deal. Finally, four aspects of the business plan are used to evaluate the riskiness and potential profit associated with a particular deal. These are (1) the marketing factors and the venture's ability to manage them effectively, (2) product's competitive advantages and uniqueness, (3) quality of the management team, particularly in its balance of skills, (4) exposure to risk factors beyond the venture's control, e.g., technological obsolescence, competitive entry, cyclical sales fluctuations. In presenting a deal to a venture capitalist, these four aspects should be used to favorably position the venture.[3]

[3] This research was funded by a National Science Foundation Grant NSF PRA-8006620-A01.

References

BROPHY, D. J., "Flow of Venture Capital 1977-1980," in *Frontiers of Entrepreneurship Research*, K. H. Vesper (Ed.), Babson College, Wellesley, Mass., 1981, 246–280.

BRUNO, A. V. AND A. C. COOPER, "Patterns of Development and Acquisitions for Silicon Valley Startups," *Technovation*, Elsevier Scientific Publishing Company, Amsterdam, Netherlands, 1982, 275–290.

CHARLES RIVER ASSOCIATES, "An Analysis of Venture Capital Market Imperfections," NTIS Report PB-254996, National Bureau of Standards, Washington D.C., 1976.

COOPER, I. A. AND W. T. CARLETON, "Dynamics of Borrower-Lender Interaction: Partitioning Final Payoff in Venture Capital Finance," *J. Finance*, 34 (1979), 517–529.

DORSEY, T. K., "The Measurement and Assessment of Capital Requirements, Investment Liquidity and Risk for the Management of Venture Capital Funds," unpublished doctoral dissertation, University of Texas, Austin, 1977.

GLASSMEYER, E. F., "Venture Financing Techniques," in S. E. Pratt (Ed.), *Guide to Venture Capital Sources*, Capital Publishing Corp., Wellesley, Mass., 1981, 64–66.

GOLDEN, S. C., "Structuring and Pricing the Financing," in S. E. Pratt (Ed.), *Guide to Venture Capital Sources*, Capital Publishing Corp., Wellesley, Mass., 1981, 67–76.

1066   TYZOON T. TYEBJEE AND ALBERT V. BRUNO

HOFFMAN, C. A., "The Venture Capital Investment Process: A Particular Aspect of Regional Economic Development," unpublished doctoral dissertation, University of Texas, Austin, 1972.

LELAND, H. E. AND D. H. PYLE, "Informational Asymmetries, Financial Structure, and Financial Intermediation," *J. Finance*, 32 (1977).

MONTGOMERY, D. B. AND G. L. URBAN, *Management Science in Marketing*, Prentice-Hall, Englewood Cliffs, N.J., 1969, 303–312.

MORRISON, D. G., "On the Interpretation of Discriminant Analysis," *J. Marketing Res.*, 6 (May 1969), 156–163.

O'MEARA, J. O., "Selecting Profitable Products," *Harvard Business Rev.*, 39 (1961), 84–85.

PESSEMIER, E. A., *Product Management: Strategy and Organization*, John Wiley, New York, 1982, 347–351.

POINDEXTER, J. B., "The Efficiency of Financial Markets: The Venture Capital Case," unpublished doctoral dissertation, New York University, New York, 1976.

PRATT, S. E. (Ed.), *Guide to Venture Capital Sources*, Capital Publishing Corp., Wellesley, Mass., 1981.

ROSS, S. A., "The Determination of Financial Structure: The Incentive Signalling Approach," *Bell J. Econom.*, 8 (1977), 23–40.

TIMMONS, J. AND D. GUMPERT, "Discard Many Old Rules About Getting Venture Capital," *Harvard Business Rev.*, 60 (1) (1982).

TYEBJEE, T. T. AND A. V. BRUNO, "Venture Capital Decision Making" in *Frontiers of Entrepreneurship Research*, K. H. Vesper (Ed.), Babson College, Wellesley, Mass., 1981, 281–320.

WELLS, W. A., "Venture Capital Decision Making," unpublished doctoral dissertation, Carnegie-Mellon University, 1974.

WETZEL, W. E., JR, "Informal Risk Capital in New England," in *Frontiers of Entrepreneurship Research*, K. H. Vesper (Ed.), Babson College, Wellesley, Mass., 1981, 217–245.

[22]

WHEN DO
VENTURE
CAPITALISTS
ADD VALUE?

HARRY J. SAPIENZA
University of South Carolina

**EXECUTIVE
SUMMARY**

*Venture capitalists functioning as lead investors and the entrepreneur-
CEOs of their portfolio companies responded to questionnaire surveys that
asked them to rate the venture capitalists' involvement in the ventures.
The perceived effectiveness of the investor's involvement weighted by its
perceived importance was used as a proxy for the investor's value to the
venture. The survey was administered in the early part of 1988. Eighty
percent of venture capitalists and 85% of entrepreneurs surveyed responded; in all, 51 matched pairs
of lead investor-CEO surveys were completed and returned. Over 50 hours of interviews were also
conducted to help clarify information derived through the surveys.*

*CEOs and venture capitalists rated the nature and intensity of their interaction as well as the
performance of the venture over a one-year period. CEOs also provided data on strategy, level of
innovation, environmental uncertainty, and their level of experience. Regression analyses indicated
that a significant portion of variation in the value of venture capitalist involvement was explained by
these factors. Specifically, the greater the innovation pursued by the venture, the more frequent the
contact between the lead investor and the CEO, the more open the communication, and the less conflict
of perspective in the venture capitalist-CEO pair, the greater was the value of the involvement. Neither
the stage of the venture nor the CEO's experience had a significant impact on value added. The value
of venture capitalists' involvement was also strongly positively correlated with venture performance.*

*The implications for the venture capitalists include the following: (1) the value of involvement
varies with circumstances; (2) the most effective venture capitalists are those who maintain frequent,
open communications while minimizing conflict; (3) opportunities exist for adding value in all venture
stages; and (4) both experienced and inexperienced CEOs can benefit.*

*For entrepreneurs, three key findings are: (1) because venture capitalists can add value beyond
the money supplied, choosing the right one at the outset is very important; (2) once in, it is important*

Address correspondence to Harry J. Sapienza, Department of Management, University of South Carolina,
Columbia, SC 29208.

The author would like to give special thanks to Jeffry A. Timmons for his insights and help in preparing
this manuscript.

0883-9026/92/$3.50

10 H.J. SAPIENZA

to keep communication channels open; and (3) high innovation ventures benefit most from venture capitalist involvement.

The results are important because they provide insight into controllable circumstances that impact the value of venture capitalist involvement in their portfolio companies. Given the general economic conditions now facing entrepreneurs and the degree of cut-throat competition in the venture capital industry, such information may prove extremely useful to both as they plan strategies for the 1990s.

INTRODUCTION

Despite the dramatic growth of venture capital in the U.S. over the last decade, the venture capital industry in the U.S. has been facing rough times, and no relief is currently in sight. The hard facts are that there is less money flowing into the industry than in 1987 and that rates of return have been dwindling since 1983 (Bygrave 1989). More venture capital is currently being raised in Europe than in the U.S., and alternative sources of financing for entrepreneurs have grown dramatically (Timmons and Sapienza 1990).

Though the prescience and sagacity of venture capitalists was being hailed in the mid-1980s, the tune has now changed. Some have argued that the best investment prospects do not generally consider venture capital when searching for financing sources (Amit et al. 1990), while others have charged that venture capitalists at times get in the way of a venture's progress (Rosenstein et al. 1990).

What has happened? In a meeting of the National Venture Capital Association, May 1990, Michael Porter, William Sahlman, and Howard Stevenson of Harvard argued that the influx of new domestic and foreign competitors, the increasing power of institutional investors, the growth of alternative financing sources such as strategic alliances and angels, and the increasing sophistication of entrepreneurs have undermined the structure of the venture capital industry and eroded returns. Because their limited partners have demanded less-risky investments and quicker returns, venture capital (VC) firms responded by making later-stage investments; meanwhile, entrepreneurs continue to seek better investment terms and to demand greater attention from their VC investors.

Timmons and Sapienza (1990) suggest that only those VC firms able to differentiate themselves from the more than 700 other domestic VC firms via value added involvement in their portfolio companies are likely to survive the impending shakeout in the VC industry. There has been little empirical research up to this point on the issue of how venture capitalists add value to the ventures they fund or on how much value is actually added. Such information is clearly of importance to suppliers of capital (limited partners), venture capitalists themselves, users of capital (entrepreneurs), and public policy makers.

EMPIRICAL EVIDENCE

Two general approaches have been taken by researchers on the issue of VC value added: one approach has been to look at early stock returns for VC-backed versus non-VC-backed initial public offerings; the other approach has been to survey entrepreneurs and venture capitalists on their perceptions of value added. We will review findings for each of these approaches.

Cherin and Hergert (1988) examined cumulative and risk-adjusted returns for a 24-month period after initial public offering (IPO) of 71 VC-backed ventures and 59 non-VC-backed ventures in the computer equipment and software industry. Using Compustat data, they found both sets to be realizing negative returns during this period, with no statistical difference between the two groups, and therefore rejected the notion that venture capitalists provide additional value. As they point out, however, this methodology fails to control for value that may have been added by venture capitalists in the approximately five-year-period before the IPO and which may have already been factored into the initial price.

Brophy and Verga (1988) compared initial stock price and the variability of stock returns for 20 days after IPO of 210 VC-backed and 1,053 non-VC-backed ventures, from 1977 to 1983. They hypothesized that if venture capitalists add value, the companies they back will be less underpriced at the outset than otherwise; further, their early returns would vary less than that of other ventures. This methodology attempts to take into account value that has already been supplied by venture capitalists; they also controlled for the presence of prestigious underwriters in their design. They concluded that: (1) ventures with VC backing outperform others; (2) ventures with VC backing do not gain substantially by adding a prestigious underwriter; and (3) non-VC-backed companies *do* benefit by having a prestigious underwriter.

Stein and Bygrave (1990) examined the returns of 77 VC-backed high-tech companies from the point of the original VC investment through four years after the IPO. They defined the "top 20 high tech venture capitalists" as those firms that held the most seats on the boards of directors of the sample companies (20 VC firms held 84 seats on 51 companies; the remaining 51 VC firms held 80 seats on 26 companies). Based on this split, they found that ventures with venture capitalists from the "top 20" enjoyed higher returns and concluded that venture capitalists from the "top 20" firms do indeed add value. One potential problem with this conclusion is that if these VC firms were among the elite, they may have been able to secure equity at a discounted price because of their reputation and prestige (Perry 1988). This again points up the difficulty of distinguishing the inherent value of the investment and the savvy of those arranging the investment deal versus additional value created through intervention by venture capitalists.

One problem with these studies is that they show only that the VC-backed ventures have (or have not) realized an initial stock price advantage. They do not investigate what actions are more or less valuable to the development of portfolio companies.

While the above studies treat value-added as a black box, other studies attempt to look at the activities of the venture capitalists in the ventures. Rosenstein et al. (1989) received questionnaire responses from 198 VC-backed ventures (26% response rate) in Massachusetts, California, and Texas. They found that the CEOs of these ventures did not perceive that venture capitalists on their boards added more value than did other board members; furthermore, they found no significant correlation between perceptions of value-added and venture performance. In a follow-up study, Rosenstein et al. (1990) conducted telephone surveys with 98 of the 162 companies in their first study. They found that CEOs rated venture capitalists as contributing about the same as other outside board members unless there was a venture capitalist on the board from the "top 20" VC firms (i.e., defined as in Stein and Bygrave 1990); when the "top 20" were represented, venture capitalists were rated as contributing *more* to the venture than outside board members. Rosenstein et al. concluded that venture capitalists add value *only* when there is one from the "top 20" present on the board. This conclusion appears to presume that other outside board members add no value to new ventures.

MacMillan et al. (1989) surveyed 62 venture capitalists about their input into strategic and operational activities relative to that of the top entrepreneurs in the ventures they funded. Using factor and regression analyses, they found that venture capitalists varied in their level of involvement and that high levels of some activities (e.g., negotiating employment terms) were associated with high performance, whereas high levels of other activities (e.g., re-

12   H.J. SAPIENZA

cruiting top management) were associated with poor performance, depending on the level of involvement of the lead investor. They found no evidence of systematic variation in involvement and concluded that activity levels depended on the personal preferences of the venture capitalists.

While this study begins to address the crucial question of *how* venture capitalists might add or detract value, the cross-sectional nature of the study clouds interpretation of activity-performance relationships. For example, poor venture performance may lead to high venture capitalist involvement in some activities (e.g., management recruiting) rather than resulting from these activities.

Sapienza and Timmons (1989) matched responses of CEOs of VC-backed ventures and lead investors to examine their assessment of the importance of individual roles assumed by venture capitalists. Three role-types emerged: strategic, supportive, and networking. Their results were consistent with those of MacMillan et al. (1989) and Rosenstein et al. (1989) with regard to important key roles (e.g., sounding board, financier, contact, management recruiter) and also identified the importance of non-instrumental roles such as mentor and confidant or friend. They found that venture capitalists' roles were assessed as being more important: (1) in early stage ventures; (2) for entrepreneurs who had less start-up experience; and (3) when venture capitalists held a larger equity position in the venture. Furthermore, the strategic roles were classified by both entrepreneurs and venture capitalists as most important, followed by social/supportive and networking roles, respectively. The study concluded that venture capitalists do add more than money; it did not, however, attempt to link the importance ratings with venture performance.

Gomez-Mejia et al. (1990) conducted 10 qualitative interviews with venture capitalists and 10 with CEOs and concluded that CEOs view the financial and networking activities as valuable, but give mixed reviews to the value of managerial involvement of venture capitalists, with many CEOs viewing managerial intervention as counterproductive.

Inconsistencies in findings can be attributed at least in part to differences in measures used to examine the value of venture capitalist input. Stock-price based measures enjoy the advantage of being objective and being tied to an economic outcome; the causes of the outcomes, however, remain shrouded in mystery. Perception based measures allow insights into the VC process but are potentially biased and do not adequately quantify value added or detracted. In sum, the evidence thus far suggests that in many circumstances venture capitalists do add value; however, key questions remain: When do venture capitalists most add (or detract) value? How much value? This study was designed to help answer the former question.

DIMENSIONS OF INTEREST AND HYPOTHESES

Researchers and practitioners have observed that venture capitalists provide value-added services to ventures (e.g., Kramer 1984; Timmons 1984), but few have examined the circumstances or methods that allow for substantial value creation. The following discussion focuses on context and venture capitalist-CEO (VC-CEO) relations variables expected to impact the value of venture capitalist involvement in the venture.

Context and Value-Added

Stage

The stage of a venture's development has long been seen as a critical variable. For example, venture viability has been observed to vary with stage (Stinchcombe 1965); some have claimed that venture needs, objectives, and management styles do or should vary with stage (e.g., Churchill and Lewis 1983). Bygrave's (1987) finding that VC firms tend to co-invest more extensively when funding early-stage ventures suggests that venture capitalists view such ventures as riskier than later-stage companies.

These risks result in part from venture newness itself. In the early stages, ventures are less likely to have established relationships with suppliers, distributors, buyers, and other business and professional help. Ventures may function with skeleton staffs, operating with positions unfilled and responsibilities as yet undefined; the CEOs may be untested in the industry or as leaders. For some of these reasons, Timmons and Bygrave (1986) concluded that venture capitalists made their greatest contributions to high-tech ventures in their earliest stages and that the important contributions tended to be managerial rather than strictly financial. Sapienza and Timmons (1989) provided some empirical support for this contention.

In summary, past evidence suggests that VC involvement is more critical to early than to late-stage ventures:

H1: The earlier the stage of the venture, the greater will be the value of venture capitalist involvement.

Innovation

Entrepreneurs seeking to gain market entry or competitive superiority through high innovation relative to competitors face severe information demands and impediments. If they seek to outpace competitors, they must keep abreast of competitor actions, and they must know what the market wants. The greater the number of dimensions upon which they seek to innovate (e.g., technology, marketing, service), the greater these demands become. While Porter (1985) has suggested that innovating along several dimensions of the value chain simultaneously can lead to sustainable superiority, achieving this can be especially problematic for developing businesses that do not have the resources or personnel to commit to the necessary boundary-spanning activities.

Gomez-Mejia et al. (1990) found that all of the entrepreneur-CEOs surveyed agreed that venture capitalists performed valuable boundary-spanning functions. As the number of dimensions in which a venture is attempting to innovate increases, the greater becomes the chance that venture capitalists can provide knowledge and service of value to the venture. Since innovative ventures can make great use of strategic input from outside advisors, such ventures appear to be the ones that can most benefit from lead-investor involvement:

H2: The higher the level of innovation pursued by the venture, the greater will be the value of venture capitalist involvement.

Competitive Strategy

Rosenstein (1988) found that venture capitalists play a major role in strategy formulation and implementation for their portfolio companies. Sapienza and Timmons (1989) also found that both venture capitalists and entrepreneurs attributed great importance to venture capitalists' strategic role in the venture. By functioning as sounding boards and advisors, venture capitalists provide additional perspectives on, and knowledge of, markets and external conditions.

Gupta (1987) argued that implementing a competitive strategy of differentiation re-

14   H.J. SAPIENZA

quires greater access to external information than does a low-cost strategy. Successful differentiation often depends upon information about the specific needs of suppliers and buyers, potential substitute products, and the attributes of competitor offerings. On the other hand, primary methods for achieving low cost often involve technical process innovation. While the information needed for differentiation is not necessarily any greater than that required for low-cost positioning, venture capitalists are much more likely to be able to contribute information on market conditions than on technical innovation. Thus, the value of venture capitalist input is apt to be greater when the venture is pursuing a differentiation strategy:

H3:   The farther the venture is toward the differentiation end of the strategy spectrum, the greater will be the value of venture capitalist involvement.

Environmental Uncertainty

The extent to which an entrepreneur can predict the future states of the environment will depend upon the knowledge he or she has about conditions, the skill in applying such knowledge, and the inherent volatility and instability in the environment. Perceived environmental uncertainty is high when entrepreneurs are unable to achieve a level of confidence in their forecasts. A savvy venture capitalist may be of some help when the primary cause of the uncertainty is from insufficient information or inappropriate application of the information available. When there is greater certainty about demand, supply, prices, and customer preferences, the value of outside input to forecasts is minimal. Therefore, one would expect the value of venture capitalist involvement to be greatest when perceived environmental uncertainty is high:

H4:   The greater the perceived environmental uncertainty, the greater will be the value of venture capitalist involvement.

Entrepreneur's Experience

The "quality" of the entrepreneur or entrepreneurial team has often been identified as a key component in venture capitalists' investment decision. An important practical question is, who benefits most by venture capitalist input, experienced or inexperienced entrepreneurs?

Inexperienced entrepreneurs stand to gain a great deal from venture capitalists' wealth of start-up experience; they can gain insights on what to expect at various stages, what to worry about and what not to, and on how they are progressing. This may be extremely valuable information. On the other hand, it may be that what venture capitalists do best is to complement and enhance the skills of experienced entrepreneurs. That is, such entrepreneurs may be more fully able to process and use outside advice, judge which is pertinent and which is not, and to take advantage of the connections and legitimacy afforded through the VC firms.

Therefore, it is unclear whether less experienced or more experienced CEOs are apt to derive greater value through venture capitalist involvement. Thus, no hypothesis can be advanced about the effect of the CEO's experience on the value of venture capitalist involvement. Nonetheless, the experience of the CEO could prove to be an extremely important variable in the potential for the venture capitalist to add value.

VC-CEO Interaction and Value-Added

Frequency of Interaction

A basic condition for venture capitalist involvement to add value beyond the financing provided is that an exchange of information take place in a timely manner. The more frequently interaction occurs, the greater the likelihood that problems and possible solutions are identified within the appropriate time frame.

Information exchange and contact are not costless; they incur opportunity costs and may slow implementation. However, both sides have cause to seek interactions in which the benefits exceed the costs. One would expect that interaction will occur primarily when one or both sides perceive the potential for gain through contact and communication in the VC-CEO dyad. If, in fact, venture capitalist involvement generally adds value to the venture, frequent involvement is likely to be more effective:

H5: The more frequent the interaction in VC-CEO dyads, the greater will be the value of venture capitalist involvement.

All of the above hypotheses are consistent with the information processing perspective (Galbraith 1973), which holds that effective organizations design their information processing structure for efficiency. Thus, when the organization's needs are high or its processing capacity low, more information must be processed or it must be processed with greater rapidity to function properly. In highly complex and unstructured environments such as those faced by entrepreneurial ventures, organic, informal coordinating mechanisms are held to be most efficacious. For example, Gupta (1987) found that in highly volatile environments, more openness in corporate-business unit relations leads to higher effectiveness of the cor- porate-business unit relations.

The risks, complexities, and uncertainties faced by new high-growth ventures create a highly volatile environment. The information processing perspective suggests that in such circumstances an atmosphere conducive to free exchange of information is apt to be more effective than relying on formal channels. This implies that informal and open relations are appropriate for intra- and interorganizational communications in new ventures. Therefore, one would expect that greater value will be derived from the involvement of the lead investors when communication is open and informal:

H6: The more open the interaction of VC-CEO dyads, the greater will be the value of venture capitalist involvement.

Divergence of Perspectives

The effects of a divergence or conflict of perspectives in the VC-CEO pair on the ability of venture capitalist involvement to add value are difficult to predict. On the one hand, different perspectives may prevent "group-think" in board meetings and thus lead to superior alter- native strategies. Given the need for creative and innovative solutions in ventures operating on the tightrope between success and failure, a variety of perspectives can be very useful. On the other hand, high divergence of opinion and approach may hamper implementation. Indecision can be especially dysfunctional in crisis situations when the entrepreneur must act quickly and receive timely financial support from the VC group. Furthermore, severe

16   H.J. SAPIENZA

divergence of opinion might lead to divisiveness, undermining the flow of information and the spirit of collaboration.

In sum, the level of divergence of VC-CEO perspectives may be an aid or a hindrance to a new venture. However, while it is unclear what relationship conflict will have with the value of venture capitalist involvement, it is potentially important.

Venture Performance and Value-Added

Ultimately, what is discovered about the factors influencing the value of venture capitalist involvement will be especially important if such value has a significant impact on venture performance results. It is not reasonable to expect that all ventures in which the lead investor has contributed significantly experience high performance or to expect that, where they have not, the ventures are failing. However, one would expect, ceteris paribus, that value added by lead investors would translate positively into venture performance. On average, then, ventures receiving greater value through venture capitalist involvement should be outperforming those receiving less:

H7: The value of venture capitalist involvement will be positively related to venture performance.

METHOD

The data collected for this study included questionnaire responses from the entrepreneur-CEOs of 51 venture capital-backed ventures in the U.S. matched with the responses from the lead VC investor in each of these portfolio companies. The response rates were 85% from entrepreneurs and 80% from venture capitalists. The ventures, geographically dispersed across the U.S., were primarily high-tech but also included service and low-tech firms. They ranged in sales from zero to $86 million with a median sales of $4 million; they were from 1 to 26 years since founding, with a median age of four years. Twenty-nine lead investors from 22 VC firms (primarily on the East Coast) participated; these firms ranged in size from $7 to $500 million with a median size of $49 million.

Measures

Table 1 presents summary statistics on the measures used in this study; the "Appendix" contains detailed descriptions of their construction. Unless otherwise indicated, higher values indicate a greater amount of the variable.

Stage of the Venture (STAGE)

The stage of the venture was measured by the venture capitalist's statement of the current financing stage of the venture. The range was from seed stage to bridge/acquisition, with the mean (3.57) falling about in the middle of the six-point scale.

Level of Innovation Pursued (INNOV)

The level of innovation pursued by the venture was measured as the entrepreneur's assessment on a five-point scale of the venture's level of innovation relative to competitors in each of

TABLE 1 Descriptive Statistics

Variable	Mean	S.D.	Min.	Max.	n
STAGE	3.57	1.65	1.00	6.00	51
INNOV	18.87	3.34	9.00	25.00	51
STRAT	17.04	3.33	8.00	25.00	48
UNCTY	17.76	3.17	12.00	26.40	51
FREQ	19.82	5.20	8.00	36.00	51
OPEN	3.00	0.68	2.00	4.75	51
DIVERG	22.45	4.28	14.00	31.00	51
T-EXP	6.70	5.40	0.00	33.50	47
S-EXP	1.82	0.90	1.00	3.00	50
DIST	112.70	126.22	5.00	600.00	46
VALUE	26.01	7.73	10.73	42.20	49
PERFORMANCE	3.11	0.90	1.30	4.89	51

six different dimensions. The possible range of responses was 6 to 30; the observed range was 9 to 25, with a mean of 18.9.

Competitive Strategy of the Venture (STRAT)

The competitive strategy pursued by each venture was measured as the entrepreneur's assessment of the venture's sources of competitive advantage along five categories, each evaluated on a 1 to 5 scale. These were combined to create a low cost-differentiation spectrum with a possible range of extreme low cost, 5, to extreme differentiation, 25; the observed range was 8 to 25, with a mean of 17.

Environmental Uncertainty (UNCTY)

Entrepreneurs' assessment of the unpredictability of seven aspects of the competitive environment (on a 1–5 scale) were summed to measure environmental uncertainty with a potential range of 7 to 35; the observed range was 12 to 26.4, with a mean of 17.8.

Frequency of Interaction (FREQ)

The frequency of contact in VC-entrepreneur (VC-CEO) dyads was measured as the frequency of contact face-to-face, by telephone, and in writing as assessed by both members of the dyad. The numbers in the table are difficult to interpret in the current form, but they indicate a range of contact from about four contacts per year to contact two to three times per week; the mean was contact about three times per month.

Openness in Interaction (OPEN)

Openness in interaction was measured as the average of four responses (two by each member of the dyad) on a 1 to 5 scale indicating the level of friendliness and social interaction outside

18   H.J. SAPIENZA

of work-related activities for the pair. The possible range was 1 to 5; the observed range was from 2 to 4.75, with a mean of 3.

Value of VC Involvement (VALUE)

The value of the venture capitalist's involvement in the venture was a weighted measure of both members' assessment of the VC's effectiveness in carrying out eight different roles in the venture. The possible range of scores was 1 to 50; the observed range was 10.7 to 42.2, with a mean of 26.

Venture Performance (PERFORMANCE)

Both members of the dyad rated venture performance using a multi-criterion measure (including 15 financial and nonfinancial dimensions); this measure was combined with each respondents' assessment of the overall performance of the venture. The possible range of scores was 1 to 5; the observed range was 1.3 to 4.9, with a mean of 3.1.

Other Variables of Interest

To allow for the possibility that divergence of perspective (DIVERG) in VC-CEO pairs, the CEO's task experience (T-EXP), or his/her start-up experience (S-EXP) account at least partially for differences in the value of venture capitalist involvement, variables measuring these constructs were created. The rationale for inclusion of these variables is explained above in the "Hypothesis" section. Geographic distance (DIST) is also included as a control variable because it may represent an impediment to the timely exchange of information or to the establishment of trust or familiarity necessary to create the proper channels of communication. The method of constructing these measures is described in the "Appendix."

Limitations of Measures in this Study

Because the measures in this study rely on the perceptions of the CEOs and the venture capitalists, caution must be exercised in their application and interpretation. Clearly, for many of the variables of interest (e.g., the nature of interaction, its frequency, and the performance of the portfolio company), no data are publicly available. Nonetheless, bias and inaccuracy are potential threats whenever perceptual measures are used. Accordingly, this study utilized assessments of both the CEO and the venture capitalist to measure the performance of the venture, the value of the involvement, and the interaction dimensions; the fact that these assessments were highly consistent with one another lends credibility to their validity (see the "Appendix" for details). Furthermore, the suggestion of John and Reve (1982) that measures be obtained from a knowledgeable "key spokesman" is followed by using the CEOs' assessment of innovation, strategy, and environmental uncertainty. That their assessments were relative to industry norms helped to control for variations by industry. Still, the possibility that the measures suffer from bias or inaccuracy must be taken into account in interpreting results.

RESULTS

Table 2 presents zero-order correlations among the independent variables, including the four additional control variables.

TABLE 2 Zero-Order Correlations: Independent Variables

Correlations:	1	2	3	4	5	6	7	8	9
STAGE									
INNOV	-0.08								
STRAT	0.05	-0.19							
UNCTY	0.19	-0.03	-0.11						
FREQ	-0.48^a	0.15	-0.17	-0.01					
OPEN	-0.11	0.12	-0.03	-0.01	0.36^b				
DIVERG	-0.20	0.27^c	-0.07	0.00	0.09	-0.28^b			
T-EXP	0.26^c	0.08	0.06	0.28^c	-0.40^a	-0.03	0.00		
S-EXP	-0.30^b	0.26^c	0.09	-0.08	-0.06	-0.17	0.28^c	-0.10	
DIST	0.35^b	-0.08	0.08	0.06	-0.34^b	-0.28^c	0.17	0.28^c	-0.27^c

$^a p < 0.01$.
$^b p < 0.05$.
$^c p < 0.10$.
These are two-tailed values.

As can be observed from Table 2, the independent variables are not highly intercor-related as a rule; this suggests that multi-collinearity will not pose severe impediments to the interpretation of the regression analyses. Some interesting observations can be derived, nonetheless, from an examination of Table 2. First, the fact that DIST and STAGE are positively related indicates a tendency for early-stage investments to be made primarily in ventures located near the lead investor. Second, the strong negative correlation between STAGE and FREQ confirms the many anecdotal reports that venture capitalists tend to be most heavily involved in the early stages of the venture's development. For the most part, the correlations are what one might well expect: FREQ and OPEN are positively related; FREQ is lower when the entrepreneur's T-EXP is high; DIVERG in VC-E pairs is negatively related to OPEN; entrepreneurs with greater S-EXP pursue higher INNOV.

Table 3 includes the results of two regression equations (one containing only the six hypothesized independent variables, and the other also containing the four control variables) testing Hypotheses 1 to 6; Table 4 presents the zero-order correlation between VALUE and PERFORMANCE used to examine Hypothesis 7. As can be seen, only one of the control variables have an impact on the value of venture capitalist involvement, less DIVERG is associated with a higher value of venture capitalist involvement (VALUE). Table 3 indicates that the addition of the control variables to the equation does not change the basic relationships

TABLE 3 Tests of Hypotheses^a

(H1) STAGE	(H2) INNOV	(H3) STRAT	(H4) UNCTY	(H5) FREQ	(H6) OPEN	DIVERG	T-EXP	S-EXP	DIST	R^2	F
-0.15	0.16^b	0.06	0.05	0.40^a	0.29^c					0.46	6.3^e
-0.17	0.22^d	0.06	0.08	0.36^c	0.25^c	-0.19^b	-0.15	0.05	0.01	0.51	4.2^e

^{a}Explaining VC value-added: results of regression analyses. Dependent variable VALUE (role effectiveness weighted by role importance).
$^b p < 0.10$.
$^c p < 0.05$.
$^d p < 0.01$.
$^e p < 0.001$.
For T-tests, these are one-tailed values.

20   H.J. SAPIENZA

TABLE 4   Test of Hypothesis 7[a]

	Performance
Value	0.44[b]

[a]Relationship between VC value-added and venture performance, zero-order correlation.
[b]$p < 0.001$, one-tail test.

between the predictors and VALUE; it can also be observed that neither T-EXP nor S-EXP has a significant impact on VALUE, though a lower level of T-EXP is moderately associated with greater VALUE of venture capitalist involvement.

Test of Hypothesis 1

Table 3 indicates that the predicted relationship between stage and the value of involvement is *not supported*. While the beta coefficients for STAGE are negative (as predicted), they are not statistically significant.[1]

Test of Hypothesis 2

Hypothesis 2 predicted that the value of lead investor invclvement would be greater in firms pursuing greater innovation relative to competitors. This hypothesis receives at least *moderate support* in both equations: betas for the effect of INNOV on VALUE = 0.16 ($p < 0.10$), and 0.22 ($p < 0.05$), respectively.

Test of Hypothesis 3

Hypothesis 3 predicted that ventures pursuing strategies toward the differentiation end of the low cost-differentiation spectrum would derive greater value out of venture capitalist involvement. This hypothesis is *not supported;* the betas for STRAT are in the expected direction, but are quite low.

Test of Hypothesis 4

Hypothesis 4 said that as uncertainty increased, the value of venture capitalist involvement would increase. This hypothesis is *not supported;* the betas for UNCTY are in the expected direction, but are quite low.

Test of Hypothesis 5

Hypothesis 5 predicted that the greater the frequency of interaction in the VC-CEO pair, the greater would be the value of the venture capitalist's involvement in the venture. This hypothesis is *supported* by the results: the betas for the effects of FREQ on VALUE = 0.40 ($p < 0.01$) and 0.36 ($p < 0.05$).

---

[1]The lack of a significant association between stage and value should not be construed as definitive evidence refuting the popular notion that venture capitalists' most important contributions are made in earlier stages of the venture's development. A separate analysis indicates that the zero-order correlation between STAGE and VALUE is -0.40 ($p = 0.003$). However, this association does not show up in the regression analyses that control for the frequency of interaction in examining association (recall that the correlation of frequency and stage is -0.48; see Table 2).

Test of Hypothesis 6

Hypothesis 6 held that the more open or informal the relations in the dyad, the greater would be the value of venture capitalist involvement. The results, positive and significant, *support* this hypothesis; the betas for the effects of OPEN on VALUE = 0.29 (p < 0.05) and 0.25 (p < 0.05).

Test of Hypothesis 7

Table 4 shows the zero-order correlation testing the notion that the value of venture capitalist involvement is positively associated with venture performance. The results *support* this view. As predicted, there is a positive relationship (r = 0.44, p < 0.001) between VALUE and PERFORMANCE; furthermore, this association is quite strong.

CONCLUSIONS AND IMPLICATIONS

This article set out to extend our understanding of the VC process by examining the circumstances under which venture capitalist involvement in portfolio companies contributes more versus less value in the eyes of two of the key stakeholders in the venture: its CEO and the lead venture capital investor. The most important findings are that the level of innovation pursued by the venture and the intensity and style of interaction have a significant impact on the value of venture capitalist involvement.

Conclusions

The connection identified here between high innovation and VC value-added is consistent with Timmons and Bygrave's (1986) observation that venture capitalists make significant contributions beyond the money provided to highly innovative technical ventures. In fact, the positive links between VC value-added and innovation, intensity, and openness of involvement fit perfectly with Perry's (1988) notion that the quality of the VC-E relationship is particularly crucial when the entrepreneur is what Perry calls an "innovator" type: "[Innovators] want a venture capital firm to provide them with money and counsel but, more importantly, they seek a long term partner" (p. 209). Perry also suggested that shared vision, interdependence, and collaboration are preferred conditions for relationships involving innovators. The finding that divergence of perspectives is associated with lower value-added suggests that shared vision may be important across the entire spectrum of entrepreneurial types, not just innovators.

What should be made of the strong positive correlation between value-added and venture performance? One possible explanation is that venture performance may influence perceptions. This possibility cannot be dismissed altogether in a cross-sectional study such as this. However, including ratings from both sides of the VC-E dyad on both measures provides a check on self-rating bias (i.e., we avoid the problem that entrepreneurs or venture capitalists might attribute high performance solely to their own efforts and low performance solely to the failings of the other member of the dyad). The alternative explanation is that, in fact, when venture capitalists are perceived as adding value, they do; and, this value is translated into superior venture performance.

Stein and Bygrave (1990) and Rosenstein et al. (1990) introduced the idea that entrepreneurs may derive value from VC presence only when a venture capitalist from an elite

22   H.J. SAPIENZA

set of firms ("the top 20") is present on the board of directors. They also suggested that the discrepancies in findings about value-added might be attributable to variations in samples: i.e., those studies that find significant value-added might be composed of VC firms from this elite set. In order to examine this possibility, we examined the available information. Only 4 of the 50 ventures in the current study had lead investors from the list of 14 of "the top 20," which was presented by Stein and Bygrave (1990). The fact that the median size of the VC firms in this study ($49 million) is well above the median for domestic VC firms in 1987 leaves open the possibility that the VC firms in this sample are "elite" (for instance, Bygrave (1987) presented information that suggested strong competitive advantages for the largest 61 VC firms in the U.S.). However, further investigation of our data revealed that the size of VC firms was not associated with the venture performance or with ratings of the value of venture capitalist involvement. Thus, while it does not refute the idea, this study does not support the notion that only an elite subset of VC firms add value to their investments.

This study has added to our understanding of the contingencies influencing venture capitalist value-added. Here are our conclusions based on this and previous studies: (1) the provision of money alone appears to play a necessary but far-from-sufficient condition to promote economic growth and resilience; evidence is mounting that venture capitalists do add value; (2) some "elite" VC firms *may be* better at this process than others; (3) venture capitalists provide assistance particularly useful for highly innovative ventures; and (4) the nature and style of VC-CEO interactions have a significant impact on the value of venture capitalist involvement; specifically, more involved, open relations appear superior.

Implications

For entrepreneurs of high potential ventures, the growing set of alternative sources of financing provide an attractive array of opportunities. The results here suggest that choosing VC can be particularly rewarding if the entrepreneur is planning to pursue high levels of innovation as a means of gaining competitive advantage. Furthermore, the results here suggest that entrepreneurs should be concerned not only with the money they receive as part of the deal structure but also the amount of assistance that the lead investor and his or her firm is planning to provide. Although venture capitalists may fall along a spectrum of styles from "laissez faire" to "close trackers" (as MacMillan et al. (1989) categorize them), entrepreneurs tend to credit those who are more deeply involved with the venture as being more valuable. Entrepreneurs should carefully assess how well they get along with the individual to be the lead investor and the reputation of the VC firms before committing. The findings also suggest that venture capitalists can add value regardless of the entrepreneur's level of prior experience; thus, entrepreneurs who presume that their experience precludes the possibility of gain through venture capitalist involvement may be doing themselves a disservice. Finally, the evidence suggests that CEOs who work toward an open, partnering atmosphere derive the greatest value from the venture capitalist's involvement.

For venture capitalists, this study suggests that, in general, more involvement is better than less. If this is so, firms that try to reduce risk though increasing diversification may be at a competitive disadvantage: providing value-added services across a wide range of investments and investment types is very difficult. VC firms seeking to differentiate themselves from the burgeoning set of domestic and international firms may do so most productively by focusing and seeking to provide value-added assistance to their portfolio companies. An earlier study found that conflict of perspectives between venture capitalists and entrepreneurs tended to be greatest in ventures seeking high technological innovation (Sapienza and Gupta

1989). The joint implication of that finding and this study is that venture capitalists who are particularly careful about managing the style and nature of their interactions with innovative entrepreneurs are apt to be most effective and valuable.

From a research perspective, several key challenges remain. Specifically, what other contingencies influence value-added? How much value is really added (i.e., controlling for the extra cost of venture capital)? How should value be measured? How long can it be sustained? On what does sustainability depend? What creative solutions for deal structuring exist? and, What public policy initiatives can foster the type of value-added investor involvement necessary for sustained value creation?

VC firms face severe competitive challenges as they enter the 1990s. Perhaps greatest among these will be the challenge of reversing the downward rates of return spiral that have been plaguing them since the early 1980s. At the same time, while new sources of financing developed in the late 1980s for entrepreneurs, the recent threats of recession do not bode well for the availability of capital in the near future. Both sides, important cogs in the development and creation of economic renewal, stand to benefit from further research that yields a deeper understanding of the forces that make their interaction more rather than less productive.

REFERENCES

Amit, R., Glosten, L.R., and Muller, E. 1990. Does venture capital foster the most promising entrepreneurial firms? *California Management Review* 32(3):102–111.

Brophy, D.J., and Verga, J.A. 1988. *More than Money? The Influence of Venture Capitalists on Initial Public Offering*. Paper presented at the Babson Entrepreneurship Conference, Calgary.

Bygrave, W.D. 1987. Syndicated investments by venture capital firms: A networking perspective. *Journal of Business Venturing*, 2:139–154.

Bygrave, W.D. 1989. *Venture Capital Industry: A Resource Exchange Perspective*. Doctoral dissertation, Boston University.

Cherin, A.C., and Hergert, M. 1988. *Do Venture Capitalists Create Value? A Test from the Computer Industry*. Paper presented at the Babson Entrepreneurship Conference, Calgary.

Galbraith, J.R. 1973. *Designing Complex Organizations*. Reading, PA: Addison-Wesley.

Gomez-Mejia, L.R., Balkin, D.B., and Welbourne, T.M. 1990. Influence of venture capitalists on high tech management. *Journal of High Technology Management Research* 1(1):103–118.

Guide to Venture Capital Sources. 1987. S.E. Pratt and J.K. Morris, eds. Wellesley, MA: Venture Economics.

Gupta, A.K. 1987. SBU strategies, corporate-SBU relations and SBU effectiveness in strategy implementation. *Academy of Management Journal* 30:477–500.

John, G., and Reve, T. 1982. Reliability and validity of key informant data from dyadic relationships in marketing channels. *Journal of Marketing* 19:517–524.

Kramer, D.J. 1984. The entrepreneur's perspective. In S.E. Pratt and J.K. Morris, eds. *Pratt's Guide to Venture Capital Sources*, 8th ed. Wellesley Hills, MA: Venture Economics, pp. 108–111.

MacMillan, I.C., Kulow, D.M., and Khoylian, R. 1989. Venture capitalists' involvement in their investments: Extent and performance. *Journal of Business Venturing* 4:27–47.

Perry, L.T. 1988. Venture capital connection: How relationships between founders and venture capitalists affect innovation in new ventures. *Academy of Management Executive* 2:205–212.

Porter, M.E. 1985. *Competitive Advantage*. New York: The Free Press.

Rosenstein, J. 1988. The board and strategy: Venture capital and high technology. *Journal of Business Venturing* 3:159–170.

Rosenstein, J., Bruno, A.V., Bygrave, W.D., and Taylor, N.T. 1989. Do venture capitalists on boards of portfolio companies add value besides money? In R.H. Brockhaus, Sr., N.C. Churchill, J.A.

24 H.J. SAPIENZA

Katz, B.A. Kirchhoff, K.H. Vesper, and W.E. Wetzel, eds. *Frontiers of Entrepreneurship Research*. Wellesley, MA: Babson College, pp. 216–229.

Rosenstein, J., Bruno, A.V., Bygrave, W.D., and Taylor, N.T. 1990. *How Much do CEOs Value the Advice of Venture Capitalists on Their Boards?* Paper presented at the Babson Entrepreneurship Conference, Boston.

Sapienza, H.J., and Gupta, A.K. 1989. Pursuit of innovation by new ventures and its effects on venture capitalist-entrepreneur relations. In R.H. Brockhaus, Sr., N.C. Churchill, J.A. Katz, B.A. Kirchhoff, K.H. Vesper, and W.E. Wetzel, eds. *Frontiers of Entrepreneurship Research*. Wellesley, MA: Babson College, pp. 304–317.

Sapienza, H.J., and Timmons, J.A. 1989. The roles of venture capitalists in new ventures: What determines their importance? *Academy of Management Best Papers Proceedings* pp. 74–78.

Stein, M., and Bygrave, W.D. 1990. *The Anatomy of High-tech IPOs: Do Their Venture Capitalists, Underwriters, Accountants, and Lawyers Make a Difference?* Paper presented at the Babson Entrepreneurship Conference, Boston.

Timmons, J.A. 1984. Venture capital: More than money? In S.E. Pratt and J. Morris, eds. *Pratt's Guide to Venture Capital Sources*, 8th ed. Wellesley Hills, MA: Venture Economics, pp. 39–43.

Timmons, J.A., and Bygrave, W.D. 1986. Venture capital's role in financing innovation for economic growth. *Journal of Business Venturing* 1:161–176.

Timmons, J.A., and Sapienza, H.J. 1990. *Venture Capital: The Decade Ahead*. Paper presented at the State-of-the-Art of Entrepreneurship Research Conference, Chapel Hill, NC.

APPENDIX

Stage

Data to measure the stage of the venture were obtained from venture capitalists. They indicated which of six definitions in Pratt's *Guide to Venture Capital Sources* described the venture's stage: 1 = "seed" financing; 2 = "start-up"; 3 = "first stage"; 4 = "re-start-up"; 5 = "expansion"; 6 = "bridge/acquisition." Measures collected from the CEOs were used for validation. As expected, the measure correlates positively with the following information about the venture provided by CEOs: the number of employees, $r = 0.59$, $p < 0.001$; the time since founding, $r = 0.41$, $p < 0.01$; the time since initial venture capital investment, $r = 0.40$, $p < 0.01$; and sales revenue level, $r = 0.27$, $p < 0.05$.

Innovation

Data on innovation pursued in the venture were obtained from the CEOs. They were asked to indicate, on a five point scale ranging from 1 = "to no degree" to 5 = "to a great degree," the extent to which they were seeking innovation relative to competition in processing technology, product design, management, packaging, distribution, and marketing/sales. These items were based on Porter's (1985) explication of the value chain. The summed score of these six items provided a measure of the level of innovation sought by each venture, with higher totals indicating a greater degree of innovation pursuit for the venture (alpha = .54). Because these dimensions are somewhat independent, a high alpha was not anticipated.

Competitive Strategy

Data on the venture's competitive strategy were obtained from the CEOs. Using a five-point scale ranging from 1 = "significantly lower" to 5 = "significantly higher," CEOs were asked to indicate their venture's position relative to competitors in terms of cost per unit, selling price (or intended selling price), product quality, R&D spending, and marketing spending. The sum of responses provided a measure of each venture's competitive strategy, with high values indicating differentiation positions and low values indicating low cost positions (alpha = 0.63). This multi-item scale was similar to the one devised by Gupta (1987) to examine the impact of competitive strategy on intra-organizational relations.

Environmental Uncertainty

Data on the uncertainty of the environment surrounding the venture were obtained from the CEO. They were asked to indicate their perceptions of how well they could predict facets of the environment on a five-point scale ranging from 1 = "highly predictable" to 5 = "highly unpredictable." They were asked to assess the predictability of input factors (raw material prices and raw material availability), throughput factors (process technology development and product attributes/design), and output factors (market growth rate, customer needs, and competitors' actions). Thus, a seven-item scale was created; the sum of the items provided a measure of perceived environmental uncertainty, with high values indicating relatively more uncertainty and low values indicating relatively less uncertainty (alpha = 0.57). Because these dimensions of the environment are relatively independent of one another, a high alpha was not anticipated.

Frequency of Interaction

Data to measure the frequency of interaction were obtained from *both* respondents. A seven-point scale (1 = "every day," 2 = "twice a week," 3 = "once a week," 4 = "twice a month," 5 = "once a month," 6 = "once a quarter," and 7 = "less often") was used to indicate the frequency of their contact face-to-face, by telephone, and in writing. A multi-item, multi-rater measure was obtained for frequency of interaction by combining the responses. To check for interrater reliability, the correlations between the responses of the CEO and the venture capitalist for each item was examined; for all three items (i.e., face-to-face, telephone, and written contact), the responses were positively correlated and were significant (at $p < 0.001$, $p < 0.001$, and $p < 0.01$, respectively). Because the responses were assigned lower numbers for greater frequency, the items were reverse scored; when summed, a measure of frequency of interaction was obtained; high values indicate greater frequency and low values indicate less frequency of interaction (alpha = 0.86).

Openness of Relations

Data to measure the openness of VC-CEO relations were obtained from *both* respondents. Using a five-point scale ranging from 1 = "strongly agree" to 5 = "strongly disagree," both members of the VC-CEO dyad were asked to indicate whether or not they agreed that: (1) "this [investor or CEO] and I are very friendly," and (2) "aside from work-related functions, this [investor or CEO] and I do not have frequent social interaction" (reverse scored). A multi-item, multi-rater measure was obtained for openness of interaction by combining the responses. To check for interrater reliability, the correlations between the responses of the CEO and the venture capitalist each item was examined; for each of the two items, the responses were positively correlated and were significant (at $p < 0.002$, and $p < 0.02$, respectively). The summed responses of the four items provided a measure of the relative openness of interaction in the VC-CEO dyad with higher values indicating more open, informal relations (alpha = 0.61).

26   H.J. SAPIENZA

Value of Venture Capitalist Involvement

Data on the venture capitalist's involvement in the venture were obtained from *both* respondents. They rated on a 1 to 5 scale the importance (1 = none at all to 5 = of great importance) of the lead investor's involvement in *eight key roles* (financier, source of professional contacts, source of industry contacts, business consultant, management recruiter, sounding board, coach/mentor, and friend/confidant) over the last one-year period; for each of these roles, both also rated on a 1 to 10 scale (1 = "very low effectiveness" to 10 = "very high effectiveness") the effectiveness of the venture capitalist in carrying out these roles. The product of the importance and effectiveness ratings of the two respondents were averaged for each role; then, the weighted average across the eight roles provided a scale of the "value" of the venture capitalist's involvement, with higher values indicating more value supplied. The possible range was thus 1 to 50. T-tests indicate no differences between raters, and correlations indicate high inter-rater reliability ($r = 0.67$, $p < 0.001$).

Venture Performance

Data on venture performance were obtained from both respondents. It was measured by (1) a multi-criterion scale and (2) an overall rating of performance. The multi-criterion scale was created by asking both respondents to rate the importance of 15 financial and non-financial dimensions of performance by distributing 100 points across these dimensions according to their estimated relative importance. Then, responding on a 1 to 5 scale, they both provided an assessment of his/her satisfaction with the venture's performance along that dimension (1 = "not at all satisfied," to 5 = "extremely satisfied"). A weighted average measure of performance was obtained for each respondent by multiplying the importance scores by the satisfaction scores and summing. The possible range was 100 to 500; converted to 1 to 5 by dividing by 100. T-tests indicate that the mean response provided by CEOs (2.99) is not significantly different from that provided by venture capitalists (3.25); thus, self-rating bias on the part of CEOs does not appear to be a problem on this measure. To check for interrater reliability, the correlations between the responses were examined; the responses were positively and significantly correlated ($r = 0.44$, $p < 0.001$). Both were also asked to rate the venture's "overall performance" on the same 1 to 5 scale used previously. The mean ratings provided by CEOs (3.12) and those provided by VCs (3.25) were not significantly different. To check for interrater reliability, the correlations between the responses of the CEO and the VC were examined; the responses were positively and significantly correlated ($r = 0.65$, $p < 0.001$). Finally, the four items (the weighted average multi-criterion response from both respondents plus the overall rating from both, were combined and averaged to produce a multi-item, multi-rater measure of venture performance on a five-point scale with higher values indicating relatively superior venture performance (alpha = 0.87).

CEO's Task Environment Experience

CEO's responses were used to measure their task environment experience. The task environment was conceptualized as having three dimensions: the market environment, the technological environment, and the managerial environment. Market experience was measured as the number of years experience the CEO had with the current industry, with current suppliers, and with current customers. Technology experience was measured as the number of years experience they had with the current process and with the current product technology. Their team experience was measured as the number of years they had worked on the current venture's management team and the number of years working with the current members of the venture's management team, whether or not such work occurred on this venture. The average of the three dimensions were summed to measure the CEO's overall task environment experience (alpha = 0.86).

CEO's New Venture Experience

Data on the extent of CEOs' new venture experience were obtained from the CEOs. CEOs were asked to indicate their new venture experience as: (1) no prior new venture experience; (2) worked in start-ups before but had never been a founder or co-founder of one; or (3) founded a venture prior to the current venture. These responses provided an ordinal scale measuring their new venture experience, with higher values indicating more and lower values less new venture experience.

Divergence of Perspective

Data to measure the divergence of views in VC-CEO interactions were obtained from *both* respondents who used a five-point scale ranging from 1 = "strongly agree" to 5 = "strongly disagree." Respondents were asked to indicate the extent they agreed that: (1) "this [investor or CEO] and I bring different perspectives to most work-related issues," (2) "striving for complete agreement between the two of us would slow down decision making considerably," (3) "this [investor or CEO] and I think alike on most issues" (reverse scored) and (4) "I am extremely satisfied with how well this [investor or CEO] and I are able to resolve conflicts" (reverse scored). Correlations between the responses in the dyad were examined as an indication of interrater reliability; all but one of the correlations were significant at $p < 0.001$. The eight responses were summed to create a measure of divergence of perspectives in the dyad (the possible range was 8–40), with higher values indicating relatively more divergence of perspectives in VC-CEO dyad (alpha = 0.63).

Geographic Distance

Data on the distance between the investor and the venture were obtained from investors. They estimated the time it took them to travel to the portfolio company (expressed as minutes in Table 1).

Part VI
Growth

[23]

Harvard
Business Review

July-August 1972

Larry E. Greiner

Evolution and revolution
as organizations grow

A company's past has clues for management
that are critical to future success

Foreword

This author maintains that growing organizations move through five distinguishable phases of development, each of which contains a relatively calm period of growth that ends with a management crisis. He argues, moreover, that since each phase is strongly influenced by the previous one, a management with a sense of its own organization's history can anticipate and prepare for the next developmental crisis. This article provides a prescription for appropriate management action in each of the five phases, and it shows how companies can turn organizational crises into opportunities for future growth.

Mr. Greiner is Associate Professor of Organizational Behavior at the Harvard Business School and is the author of several previous HBR articles on organization development.

A small research company chooses too complicated and formalized an organization structure for its young age and limited size. It flounders in rigidity and bureaucracy for several years and is finally acquired by a larger company.

Key executives of a retail store chain hold on to an organization structure long after it has served its purpose, because their power is derived from this structure. The company eventually goes into bankruptcy.

A large bank disciplines a "rebellious" manager who is blamed for current control problems, when the underlying cause is centralized pro-

Author's note: This article is part of a continuing project on organization development with my colleague, Professor Louis B. Barnes, and sponsored by the Division of Research, Harvard Business School.

Harvard Business Review: July-August 1972

cedures that are holding back expansion into new markets. Many younger managers subsequently leave the bank, competition moves in, and profits are still declining.

The problems of these companies, like those of many others, are rooted more in past decisions than in present events or outside market dynamics. Historical forces do indeed shape the future growth of organizations. Yet management, in its haste to grow, often overlooks such critical developmental questions as: Where has our organization been? Where is it now? And what do the answers to these questions mean for where we are going? Instead, its gaze is fixed outward toward the environment and the future—as if more precise market projections will provide a new organizational identity.

Companies fail to see that many clues to their future success lie within their own organizations and their evolving states of development. Moreover, the inability of management to understand its organization development problems can result in a company becoming "frozen" in its present stage of evolution or, ultimately, in failure, regardless of market opportunities.

My position in this article is that the future of an organization may be less determined by outside forces than it is by the organization's history. In stressing the force of history on an organization, I have drawn from the legacies of European psychologists (their thesis being that individual behavior is determined primarily by previous events and experiences, not by what lies ahead). Extending this analogy of individual development to the problems of organization development, I shall discuss a series of developmental phases through which growing companies tend to pass. But, first, let me provide two definitions:

1. The term *evolution* is used to describe pro-

longed periods of growth where no major up-heaval occurs in organization practices.

2. The term *revolution* is used to describe those periods of substantial turmoil in organization life.

As a company progresses through developmental phases, each evolutionary period creates its own revolution. For instance, centralized practices eventually lead to demands for decentralization. Moreover, the nature of management's solution to each revolutionary period determines whether a company will move forward into its next stage of evolutionary growth. As I shall show later, there are at least five phases of organization development, each characterized by both an evolution and a revolution.

Key forces in development

During the past few years a small amount of research knowledge about the phases of organization development has been building. Some of this research is very quantitative, such as time-series analyses that reveal patterns of economic performance over time.[1] The majority of studies, however, are case-oriented and use company records and interviews to reconstruct a rich picture of corporate development.[2] Yet both types of research tend to be heavily empirical without attempting more generalized statements about the overall process of development.

A notable exception is the historical work of Alfred D. Chandler, Jr., in his book *Strategy and Structure*.[3] This study depicts four very broad and general phases in the lives of four large U.S. companies. It proposes that outside market opportunities determine a company's strategy, which in turn determines the company's organization structure. This thesis has a valid ring for the four companies examined by Chandler, largely because they developed in a time of explosive markets and technological advances. But more recent evidence suggests that organization structure may be less malleable than Chandler assumed; in fact, structure can play a critical role in influencing corporate strategy. It is this reverse emphasis on how organization structure affects future growth which is highlighted in the model presented in this article.

From an analysis of recent studies,[4] five key dimensions emerge as essential for building a model of organization development:

1. Age of the organization.

1. See, for example, William H. Starbuck, "Organizational Metamorphosis," in *Promising Research Directions*, edited by R.W. Millman and M.P. Hottenstein (Tempe, Arizona, Academy of Management, 1968), p. 113.

2. See, for example, the *Grangesberg* case series, prepared by C. Roland Christensen and Bruce R. Scott, Case Clearing House, Harvard Business School.

3. *Strategy and Structure: Chapters in the History of the American Industrial Enterprise* (Cambridge, Massachusetts, The M.I.T. Press, 1962).

4. I have drawn on many sources for evidence: (a) numerous cases collected at the Harvard Business School; (b) *Organization Growth and Development*, edited by William H. Starbuck (Middlesex, England, Penguin Books, Ltd., 1971), where several studies are cited; and (c) articles published in journals, such as Lawrence E. Fouraker and John M. Stopford, "Organization Structure and the Multinational Strategy," *Administrative Science Quarterly*, Vol. 13, No. 1, 1968, p. 47; and Malcolm S. Salter, "Management Appraisal and Reward Systems," *Journal of Business Policy*, Vol. 1, No. 4, 1971.

2. Size of the organization.
3. Stages of evolution.
4. Stages of revolution.
5. Growth rate of the industry.

I shall describe each of these elements separately, but first note their combined effect as illustrated in *Exhibit I*. Note especially how each dimension influences the other over time; when all five elements begin to interact, a more complete and dynamic picture of organizational growth emerges.

After describing these dimensions and their interconnections, I shall discuss each evolutionary/revolutionary phase of development and show (a) how each stage of evolution breeds its own revolution, and (b) how management solu-

tions to each revolution determine the next stage of evolution.

Age of the organization

The most obvious and essential dimension for any model of development is the life span of an organization (represented as the horizontal axis in *Exhibit I*). All historical studies gather data from various points in time and then make comparisons. From these observations, it is evident that the same organization practices are not maintained throughout a long time span. This makes a most basic point: management problems and principles are rooted in time. The concept of decentralization, for example, can have meaning for describing corporate practices

Exhibit I. Model of organization development

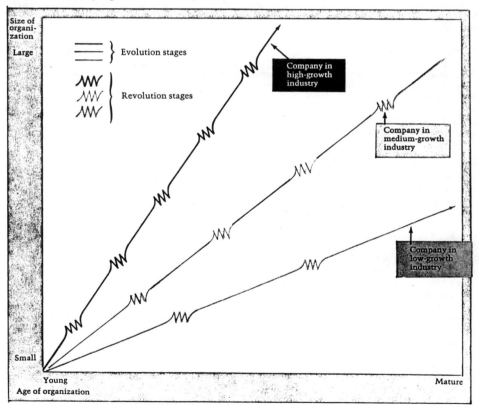

Harvard Business Review: July-August 1972

at one time period but loses its descriptive power at another.

The passage of time also contributes to the institutionalization of managerial attitudes. As a result, employee behavior becomes not only more predictable but also more difficult to change when attitudes are outdated.

Size of the organization

This dimension is depicted as the vertical axis in *Exhibit I*. A company's problems and solutions tend to change markedly as the number of employees and sales volume increase. Thus, time is not the only determinant of structure; in fact, organizations that do not grow in size can retain many of the same management issues and practices over lengthy periods. In addition to increased size, however, problems of coordination and communication magnify, new functions emerge, levels in the management hierarchy multiply, and jobs become more interrelated.

Stages of evolution

As both age and size increase, another phenomenon becomes evident: the prolonged growth that I have termed the evolutionary period. Most growing organizations do not expand for two years and then retreat for one year; rather, those that survive a crisis usually enjoy four to eight years of continuous growth without a major economic setback or severe internal disruption. The term evolution seems appropriate for describing these quieter periods because only modest adjustments appear necessary for maintaining growth under the same overall pattern of management.

Stages of revolution

Smooth evolution is not inevitable; it cannot be assumed that organization growth is linear. *Fortune's* "500" list, for example, has had significant turnover during the last 50 years. Thus we find evidence from numerous case histories which reveals periods of substantial turbulence spaced between smoother periods of evolution.

I have termed these turbulent times the periods of revolution because they typically exhibit a serious upheaval of management practices. Traditional management practices, which were appropriate for a smaller size and earlier time, are brought under scrutiny by frustrated top

managers and disillusioned lower-level managers. During such periods of crisis, a number of companies fail—those unable to abandon past practices and effect major organization changes are likely either to fold or to level off in their growth rates.

The critical task for management in each revolutionary period is to find a new set of organization practices that will become the basis for managing the next period of evolutionary growth. Interestingly enough, these new practices eventually sow their own seeds of decay and lead to another period of revolution. Companies therefore experience the irony of seeing a major solution in one time period become a major problem at a latter date.

Growth rate of the industry

The speed at which an organization experiences phases of evolution and revolution is closely related to the market environment of its industry. For example, a company in a rapidly expanding market will have to add employees rapidly; hence, the need for new organization structures to accommodate large staff increases is accelerated. While evolutionary periods tend to be relatively short in fast-growing industries, much longer evolutionary periods occur in mature or slowly growing industries.

Evolution can also be prolonged, and revolutions delayed, when profits come easily. For instance, companies that make grievous errors in a rewarding industry can still look good on their profit and loss statements; thus they can avoid a change in management practices for a longer period. The aerospace industry in its infancy is an example. Yet revolutionary periods still occur, as one did in aerospace when profit opportunities began to dry up. Revolutions seem to be much more severe and difficult to resolve when the market environment is poor.

Phases of growth

With the foregoing framework in mind, let us now examine in depth the five specific phases of evolution and revolution. As shown in *Exhibit II*, each evolutionary period is characterized by the dominant *management style* used to achieve growth, while each revolutionary period is characterized by the dominant *management problem* that must be solved before growth can continue. The patterns presented in *Exhibit II* seem to be

Exhibit II. The five phases of growth

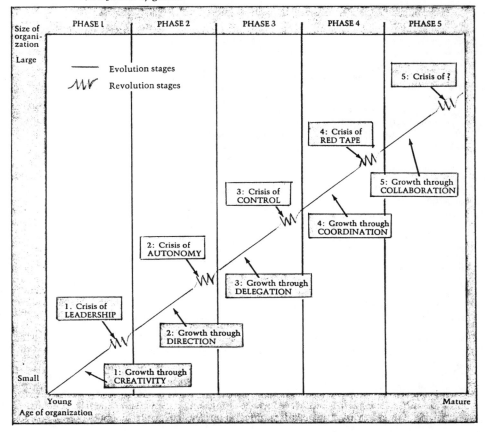

typical for companies in industries with moderate growth over a long time period; companies in faster growing industries tend to experience all five phases more rapidly, while those in slower growing industries encounter only two or three phases over many years.

It is important to note that *each phase is both an effect of the previous phase and a cause for the next phase.* For example, the evolutionary management style in Phase 3 of the exhibit is "delegation," which grows out of, and becomes the solution to, demands for greater "autonomy" in the preceding Phase 2 revolution. The style of delegation used in Phase 3, however, eventually provokes a major revolutionary crisis that

is characterized by attempts to regain control over the diversity created through increased delegation.

The principal implication of each phase is that management actions are narrowly prescribed if growth is to occur. For example, a company experiencing an autonomy crisis in Phase 2 cannot return to directive management for a solution—it must adopt a new style of delegation in order to move ahead.

Phase 1: Creativity . . .

In the birth stage of an organization, the emphasis is on creating both a product and a mar-

Harvard Business Review: July-August 1972

ket. Here are the characteristics of the period of creative evolution:

O The company's founders are usually technically or entrepreneurially oriented, and they disdain management activities; their physical and mental energies are absorbed entirely in making and selling a new product.

O Communication among employees is frequent and informal.

O Long hours of work are rewarded by modest salaries and the promise of ownership benefits.

O Control of activities comes from immediate marketplace feedback; the management acts as the customers react.

... & the leadership crisis: All of the foregoing individualistic and creative activities are essential for the company to get off the ground. But therein lies the problem. As the company grows, larger production runs require knowledge about the efficiencies of manufacturing. Increased numbers of employees cannot be managed exclusively through informal communication; new employees are not motivated by an intense dedication to the product or organization. Additional capital must be secured, and new accounting procedures are needed for financial control.

Thus the founders find themselves burdened with unwanted management responsibilities. So they long for the "good old days," still trying to act as they did in the past. And conflicts between the harried leaders grow more intense.

At this point a crisis of leadership occurs, which is the onset of the first revolution. Who is to lead the company out of confusion and solve the managerial problems confronting it? Quite obviously, a strong manager is needed who has the necessary knowledge and skill to introduce new business techniques. But this is easier said than done. The founders often hate to step aside even though they are probably temperamentally unsuited to be managers. So here is the first critical developmental choice— to locate and install a strong business manager who is acceptable to the founders and who can pull the organization together.

Phase 2: Direction ...

Those companies that survive the first phase by installing a capable business manager usually embark on a period of sustained growth under able and directive leadership. Here are the characteristics of this evolutionary period:

O A functional organization structure is in-

troduced to separate manufacturing from marketing activities, and job assignments become more specialized.

O Accounting systems for inventory and purchasing are introduced.

O Incentives, budgets, and work standards are adopted.

O Communication becomes more formal and impersonal as a hierarchy of titles and positions builds.

O The new manager and his key supervisors take most of the responsibility for instituting direction, while lower-level supervisors are treated more as functional specialists than as autonomous decision-making managers.

... & the autonomy crisis: Although the new directive techniques channel employee energy more efficiently into growth, they eventually become inappropriate for controlling a larger, more diverse and complex organization. Lower-level employees find themselves restricted by a cumbersome and centralized hierarchy. They have come to possess more direct knowledge about markets and machinery than do the leaders at the top; consequently, they feel torn between following procedures and taking initiative on their own.

Thus the second revolution is imminent as a crisis develops from demands for greater autonomy on the part of lower-level managers. The solution adopted by most companies is to move toward greater delegation. Yet it is difficult for top managers who were previously successful at being directive to give up responsibility. Moreover, lower-level managers are not accustomed to making decisions for themselves. As a result, numerous companies flounder during this revolutionary period, adhering to centralized methods while lower-level employees grow more disenchanted and leave the organization.

Phase 3: Delegation ...

The next era of growth evolves from the successful application of a decentralized organization structure. It exhibits these characteristics:

O Much greater responsibility is given to the managers of plants and market territories.

O Profit centers and bonuses are used to stimulate motivation.

O The top executives at headquarters restrain themselves to managing by exception, based on periodic reports from the field.

O Management often concentrates on making

new acquisitions which can be lined up beside other decentralized units.

O Communication from the top is infrequent, usually by correspondence, telephone, or brief visits to field locations.

The delegation stage proves useful for gaining expansion through heightened motivation at lower levels. Decentralized managers with greater authority and incentive are able to penetrate larger markets, respond faster to customers, and develop new products.

... & the control crisis: A serious problem eventually evolves, however, as top executives sense that they are losing control over a highly diversified field operation. Autonomous field managers prefer to run their own shows without coordinating plans, money, technology, and manpower with the rest of the organization. Freedom breeds a parochial attitude.

Hence, the Phase 3 revolution is under way when top management seeks to regain control over the total company. Some top managements attempt a return to centralized management, which usually fails because of the vast scope of operations. Those companies that move ahead find a new solution in the use of special coordination techniques.

Phase 4: Coordination ...

During this phase, the evolutionary period is characterized by the use of formal systems for achieving greater coordination and by top executives taking responsibility for the initiation and administration of these new systems. For example:

O Decentralized units are merged into product groups.

O Formal planning procedures are established and intensively reviewed.

O Numerous staff personnel are hired and located at headquarters to initiate companywide programs of control and review for line managers.

O Capital expenditures are carefully weighed and parceled out across the organization.

O Each product group is treated as an investment center where return on invested capital is an important criterion used in allocating funds.

O Certain technical functions, such as data processing, are centralized at headquarters, while daily operating decisions remain decentralized.

O Stock options and companywide profit shar-

ing are used to encourage identity with the firm as a whole.

All of these new coordination systems prove useful for achieving growth through more efficient allocation of a company's limited resources. They prompt field managers to look beyond the needs of their local units. While these managers still have much decision-making responsibility, they learn to justify their actions more carefully to a "watchdog" audience at headquarters.

... & the red-tape crisis: But a lack of confidence gradually builds between line and staff, and between headquarters and the field. The proliferation of systems and programs begins to exceed its utility; a red-tape crisis is created. Line managers, for example, increasingly resent heavy staff direction from those who are not familiar with local conditions. Staff people, on the other hand, complain about uncooperative and uninformed line managers. Together both groups criticize the bureaucratic paper system that has evolved. Procedures take precedence over problem solving, and innovation is dampened. In short, the organization has become too large and complex to be managed through formal programs and rigid systems. The Phase 4 revolution is under way.

Phase 5: Collaboration ...

The last observable phase in previous studies emphasizes strong interpersonal collaboration in an attempt to overcome the red-tape crisis. Where Phase 4 was managed more through formal systems and procedures, Phase 5 emphasizes greater spontaneity in management action through teams and the skillful confrontation of interpersonal differences. Social control and self-discipline take over from formal control. This transition is especially difficult for those experts who created the old systems as well as for those line managers who relied on formal methods for answers.

The Phase 5 evolution, then, builds around a more flexible and behavioral approach to management. Here are its characteristics:

O The focus is on solving problems quickly through team action.

O Teams are combined across functions for task-group activity.

O Headquarters staff experts are reduced in number, reassigned, and combined in interdis-

Harvard Business Review: July-August 1972

ciplinary teams to consult with, not to direct, field units.

O A matrix-type structure is frequently used to assemble the right teams for the appropriate problems.

O Previous formal systems are simplified and combined into single multipurpose systems.

O Conferences of key managers are held frequently to focus on major problem issues.

O Educational programs are utilized to train managers in behavioral skills for achieving better teamwork and conflict resolution.

O Real-time information systems are integrated into daily decision making.

O Economic rewards are geared more to team performance than to individual achievement.

O Experiments in new practices are encouraged throughout the organization.

. . . e) the ? crisis: What will be the revolution in response to this stage of evolution? Many large U.S. companies are now in the Phase 5 evolutionary stage, so the answers are critical. While there is little clear evidence, I imagine the revolution will center around the "psychological saturation" of employees who grow emotionally and physically exhausted by the intensity of teamwork and the heavy pressure for innovative solutions.

My hunch is that the Phase 5 revolution will be solved through new structures and programs that allow employees to periodically rest, reflect, and revitalize themselves. We may even see companies with dual organization structures: a "habit" structure for getting the daily work done, and a "reflective" structure for stimulating perspective and personal enrichment. Employees could then move back and forth between the two structures as their energies are dissipated and refueled.

One European organization has implemented just such a structure. Five reflective groups have been established outside the regular structure for the purpose of continuously evaluating five task activities basic to the organization. They report directly to the managing director, although their reports are made public throughout the organization. Membership in each group includes all levels and functions, and employees are rotated through these groups on a six-month basis.

Other concrete examples now in practice include providing sabbaticals for employees, moving managers in and out of "hot spot" jobs, establishing a four-day workweek, assuring job

security, building physical facilities for relaxation *during* the working day, making jobs more interchangeable, creating an extra team on the assembly line so that one team is always off for reeducation, and switching to longer vacations and more flexible working hours.

The Chinese practice of requiring executives to spend time periodically on lower-level jobs may also be worth a nonideological evaluation. For too long U.S. management has assumed that career progress should be equated with an upward path toward title, salary, and power. Could it be that some vice presidents of marketing might just long for, and even benefit from, temporary duty in the field sales organization?

Implications of history

Let me now summarize some important implications for practicing managers. First, the main features of this discussion are depicted in *Exhibit III*, which shows the specific management actions that characterize each growth phase. These actions are also the solutions which ended each preceding revolutionary period.

In one sense, I hope that many readers will react to my model by calling it obvious and natural for depicting the growth of an organization. To me this type of reaction is a useful test of the model's validity.

But at a more reflective level I imagine some of these reactions are more hindsight than foresight. Those experienced managers who have been through a developmental sequence can empathize with it now, but how did they react when in the middle of a stage of evolution or revolution? They can probably recall the limits of their own developmental understanding at that time. Perhaps they resisted desirable changes or were even swept emotionally into a revolution without being able to propose constructive solutions. So let me offer some explicit guidelines for managers of growing organizations to keep in mind.

Know where you are in the developmental sequence.

Every organization and its component parts are at different stages of development. The task of top management is to be aware of these stages; otherwise, it may not recognize when the time for change has come, or it may act to impose the wrong solution.

Exhibit III. Organization practices during evolution in the five phases of growth

Category	PHASE 1	PHASE 2	PHASE 3	PHASE 4	PHASE 5
MANAGEMENT FOCUS	Make & sell	Efficiency of operations	Expansion of market	Consolidation of organization	Problem solving & innovation
ORGANIZATION STRUCTURE	Informal	Centralized & functional	Decentralized & geographical	Line-staff & product groups	Matrix of teams
TOP MANAGEMENT STYLE	Individualistic & entrepreneurial	Directive	Delegative	Watchdog	Participative
CONTROL SYSTEM	Market results	Standards & cost centers	Reports & profit centers	Plans & investment centers	Mutual goal setting
MANAGEMENT REWARD EMPHASIS	Ownership	Salary & merit increases	Individual bonus	Profit sharing & stock options	Team bonus

Top leaders should be ready to work with the flow of the tide rather than against it; yet they should be cautious, since it is tempting to skip phases out of impatience. Each phase results in certain strengths and learning experiences in the organization that will be essential for success in subsequent phases. A child prodigy, for example, may be able to read like a teenager, but he cannot behave like one until he ages through a sequence of experiences.

I also doubt that managers can or should act to avoid revolutions. Rather, these periods of tension provide the pressure, ideas, and awareness that afford a platform for change and the introduction of new practices.

Recognize the limited range of solutions.

In each revolutionary stage it becomes evident that this stage can be ended only by certain specific solutions; moreover, these solutions are different from those which were applied to the problems of the preceding revolution. Too often it is tempting to choose solutions that were tried before, which makes it impossible for a new phase of growth to evolve.

Management must be prepared to dismantle current structures before the revolutionary stage becomes too turbulent. Top managers, realizing that their own managerial styles are no longer appropriate, may even have to take themselves out of leadership positions. A good Phase 2 manager facing Phase 3 might be wise to find another Phase 2 organization that better fits his talents, either outside the company or with one of its newer subsidiaries.

Finally, evolution is not an automatic affair; it is a contest for survival. To move ahead, companies must consciously introduce planned structures that not only are solutions to a current crisis but also are fitted to the *next* phase of growth. This requires considerable self-awareness on the part of top management, as well as great interpersonal skill in persuading other managers that change is needed.

Realize that solutions breed new problems.

Managers often fail to realize that organizational solutions create problems for the future (i.e., a decision to delegate eventually causes a problem of control). Historical actions are very much

Harvard Business Review: July-August 1972

determinants of what happens to the company at a much later date.

An awareness of this effect should help managers to evaluate company problems with greater historical understanding instead of "pinning the blame" on a current development. Better yet, managers should be in a position to *predict* future problems, and thereby to prepare solutions and coping strategies before a revolution gets out of hand.

A management that is aware of the problems ahead could well decide *not* to grow. Top managers may, for instance, prefer to retain the informal practices of a small company, knowing that this way of life is inherent in the organization's limited size, not in their congenial personalities. If they choose to grow, they may do themselves out of a job and a way of life they enjoy.

And what about the managements of very large organizations? Can they find new solutions for continued phases of evolution? Or are they reaching a stage where the government will act to break them up because they are too large.

Concluding note

Clearly, there is still much to learn about processes of development in organizations. The phases outlined here are only five in number and are still only approximations. Researchers are just beginning to study the specific developmental problems of structure, control, rewards, and management style in different industries and in a variety of cultures.

One should not, however, wait for conclusive evidence before educating managers to think and act from a developmental perspective. The critical dimension of time has been missing for too long from our management theories and practices. The intriguing paradox is that by learning more about history we may do a better job in the future.

An end to growth?

Jay W. Forrester,
World Dynamics,
Cambridge, Massachusetts,
Wright-Allen Press, inc.,
1971, pp. 2-3.

The battle between the forces of growth and the restraints of nature may be resolved in a number of ways. Man, if he understands well enough and acts wisely, can choose a path out of the conflict of world pressures that is more favorable than present actions, attitudes, and policies portend. Such a path must be toward a non-growing and balanced condition of the world system. . . .

Population, capital investment, pollution, food consumption, and standard of living have been growing exponentially throughout recorded history. Man has come to expect growth, to see it as the natural condition of human behavior, and to equate growth with "progress." We speak of the annual percentage growth in gross national product (GNP) and in population. Quantities that grow by a fixed percentage per year are exhibiting "exponential" growth. But exponential growth cannot continue indefinitely.

Pure exponential growth possesses the characteristic of behaving according to a "doubling time." Each fixed time interval shows a doubling of the relevant system variable. Exponential growth is treacherous and misleading. A system variable can continue through many doubling intervals without seeming to reach significant size. But then, in one or two more doubling periods, still following the same law of exponential growth, it suddenly seems to become overwhelming.

The psychological impact of exponential growth is seldom appreciated. Suppose that some ultimate physical limit stands in the way of a quantity that is growing exponentially. In all previous time before the limit is approached, the quantity is much smaller than the limit. The very existence of the limit may be unrealized. No clash between the growing quantity and the limit forces attention to the eventual pressures that must arise. Then suddenly, within one doubling interval, the quantity grows from half the limit to the limit. The stresses from overexpansion become highly visible; they can no longer be ignored. If the pressures created by approach to the limit are not great enough to suppress growth, then growth continues until the limit has been overstepped far enough to generate forces sufficient to inhibit growth.

Growing Concerns

Topics of particular interest to owners and managers of smaller businesses

Edited by
David E. Gumpert

The five stages of small business growth

Neil C. Churchill and
Virginia L. Lewis

Why is it that some business owners must work 15 hours a day to keep their businesses operating while other owners can go off and, say, run for political office as the business goes happily along on its own? Or how is it that some owners manage without any formal systems or overall strategies while others are driven to devote much attention to such approaches? While the style of the owner and financial circumstances of the business certainly are important, less noticeable factors are also at work, including business size, diversity, complexity, management style, and organizational goals. The authors have used such factors to build a framework consisting of five stages through which small companies pass. They have labeled the stages Existence, Survival, Success, Take-off, and Resource maturity. Owners who can assess the stage at which their companies are operating can use the framework to better understand existing problems and anticipate future challenges.

Neil C. Churchill is distinguished professor of accounting and

director of the Caruth Institute of Owner-Managed Business at Southern Methodist University. He has authored or coauthored three other articles for HBR, the most recent two being: "Don't Let Inflation Get the Best of You" (March-April 1982) and "Choosing and Evaluating Your Accountant" (with Louis A. Werbaneth, Jr., May-June 1979). Virginia L. Lewis is a senior research associate of the Caruth Institute at SMU.

Categorizing the problems and growth patterns of small businesses in a systematic way that is useful to entrepreneurs seems at first glance a hopeless task. Small businesses vary widely in size and capacity for growth. They are characterized by independence of action, differing organizational structures, and varied management styles.

Yet on closer scrutiny, it becomes apparent that they experience common problems arising at similar stages in their development. These points of similarity can be organized into a framework that increases our understanding of the nature, characteristics, and problems of businesses ranging from a corner dry-cleaning establishment with two or three minimum-wage employees to a $20-million-a-year computer software company experiencing a 40% annual rate of growth.

For owners and managers of small businesses, such an understanding can aid in assessing current challenges; for example, the need to upgrade an existing computer system or to hire and train second-level managers to maintain planned growth.

It can help in anticipating the key requirements at various points – e.g., the inordinate time commitment for owners during the start-up period and the need for delegation and changes in their managerial roles when companies become larger and more complex.

The framework also provides a basis for evaluating the impact of present and proposed governmental regulations and policies on one's business. A case in point is the exclusion of dividends from double taxation, which could be of great help to a profitable, mature, and stable business like a funeral home but of no help at all to a new, rapidly growing, high-technology enterprise.

Finally, the framework aids accountants and consultants in diagnosing problems and matching solutions to smaller enterprises. The problems of a 6-month-old, 20-person business are rarely addressed by advice

Authors' note: We thank Renato Tagiuri, professor of organizational behavior at Harvard Business School, for his participation in the construction and analysis of the questionnaires.

Harvard Business Review   May-June 1983   31

based on a 30-year-old, 100-person manufacturing company. For the former, cash-flow planning is paramount; for the latter, strategic planning and budgeting to achieve coordination and operating control are most important.

Developing a small business framework

Various researchers over the years have developed models for examining businesses. (See the first insert and *Exhibit I.*) Each uses business size as one dimension and company maturity or the stage of growth as a second dimension. While useful in many respects, these frameworks are inappropriate for small businesses on at least three counts.

First, they assume that a company must grow and pass through all stages of development or die in the attempt. Second, the models fail to capture the important early stages in a company's origin and growth. Third, these frameworks characterize company size largely in terms of annual sales (although some mention number of employees) and ignore other factors such as value-added, number of locations, complexity of product line, and rate of change in products or production technology.

To develop a framework relevant to small and growing businesses, we used a combination of experience, a search of the literature, and empirical research. (See the second insert.) The framework that evolved from this effort delineates five stages of development. (See *Exhibit II.*) Each stage is characterized by an index of size, diversity, and complexity and described by five management factors: managerial style, organizational structure, extent of formal systems, major strategic goals, and the owner's involvement in the business. We depict each stage in *Exhibit III* and describe each narratively in this article.

Stage I: Existence

In this stage the main problems of the business are obtaining cus-

Exhibit Growth phases
I

---- Evolution stages
- - - - Revolution stages

*Disengage
†Grow

Looking back on business development models

Business researchers have developed a number of models over the last 20 years that seek to delineate stages of corporate growth.

Joseph W. McGuire, building on the work of W.W. Rostow in economics,* formulated a model that saw companies moving through five stages of economic development:†

1
Traditional small company.

2
Planning for growth

3
Take-off or departure from existing conditions.

4
Drive to professional management.

5
Mass production marked by a "diffusion of objectives and an interest in the welfare of society."

Lawrence L. Steinmetz theorized that to survive, small businesses must move through four stages of growth. Steinmetz envisioned each stage ending with a critical phase that must be dealt with before the company could enter the next stage.§ His stages and phases are as follows:

1
Direct supervision. The simplest stage, at the end of which the owner must become a manager by learning to delegate to others.

2
Supervised supervision. To move on, the manager must devote attention to growth and expansion, manage increased overhead and complex finances, and learn to become an administrator.

3
Indirect control. To grow and survive, the company must learn to delegate tasks to key managers and to deal with diminishing absolute rate of return and overstaffing at the middle levels.

4
Divisional organization. At this stage the company has "arrived" and has the resources and organizational structure that will enable it to remain viable.

C. Roland Christensen and Bruce R. Scott focused on development of organizational complexity in a business as it evolves in its product-market relationships. They formulated three stages that a company moves through as it grows in overall size, number of products, and market coverage:‡

1
One-unit management with no specialized organizational parts.

2
One-unit management with functional parts such as marketing and finance.

3
Multiple operating units, such as divisions, that act in their own behalf in the marketplace.

Finally, Larry E. Greiner proposed a model of corporate evolution in which business organizations move through five phases of growth as they make the transition from small to large (in sales and employees) and from young to mature.‖ Each phase is distinguished by an evolution from the prior phase and then by a revolution or crisis, which precipitates a jump into the next phase. Each evolutionary phase is characterized by a particular managerial style and each revolutionary period by a dominant management problem faced by the company. These phases and crises are shown in *Exhibit I*.

*W.W. Rostow,
The Stages of Economic Growth
(Cambridge, England:
Cambridge University Press, 1960).

†Joseph W. McGuire,
*Factors Affecting the Growth of
Manufacturing Firms*
(Seattle:
Bureau of Business Research,
University of Washington, 1963).

‡C. Roland Christensen and
Bruce R. Scott,
Review of Course Activities
(Lausanne:
IMEDE, 1964).

§Lawrence L. Steinmetz,
"Critical Stages of
Small Business Growth:
When They Occur and
How to Survive Them,"
Business Horizons,
February 1969, p. 29.

‖Larry E. Greiner,
"Evolution and Revolution
as Organizations Grow,"
HBR July-August 1972, p. 37.

tomers and delivering the product or service contracted for. Among the key questions are the following:

> Can we get enough customers, deliver our products, and provide services well enough to become a viable business?

> Can we expand from that one key customer or pilot production process to a much broader sales base?

> Do we have enough money to cover the considerable cash demands of this start-up phase?

The organization is a simple one – the owner does everything and directly supervises subordinates, who should be of at least average competence. Systems and formal planning are minimal to nonexistent. The company's strategy is simply to remain alive. The owner *is* the business, performs all the important tasks, and is the major

supplier of energy, direction, and, with relatives and friends, capital.

Companies in the Existence Stage range from newly started restaurants and retail stores to high-technology manufacturers that have yet to stabilize either production or product quality. Many such companies never gain sufficient customer acceptance or product capability to become viable. In these cases, the owners close the business when the start-up capital runs out and, if they're lucky, sell the business for its asset value. (See endpoint 1 on *Exhibit IV.*) In some cases, the owners cannot accept the demands the business places on their time, finances, and energy, and they quit. Those companies that remain in business become Stage II enterprises.

Stage II: Survival

In reaching this stage, the business has demonstrated that it is a workable business entity. It has enough customers and satisfies them sufficiently with its products or services to keep them. The key problem thus shifts from mere existence to the relationship between revenues and expenses. The main issues are as follows:

☐   In the short run, can we generate enough cash to break even and to cover the repair or replacement of our capital assets as they wear out?

☐   Can we, at a minimum, generate enough cash flow to stay in business and to finance growth to a size that is sufficiently large, given our industry and market niche, to earn an economic return on our assets and labor?

The organization is still simple. The company may have a limited number of employees supervised by a sales manager or a general foreman. Neither of them makes major decisions independently, but instead carries out the rather well-defined orders of the owner.

Systems development is minimal. Formal planning is, at best, cash forecasting. The major goal is still survival and the owner is still synonymous with the business.

In the Survival Stage, the enterprise may grow in size and profitability and move on to Stage III. Or it may, as many companies do, remain at the Survival Stage for some time, earning marginal returns on invested time and capital (endpoint 2 on *Exhibit IV*), and eventually go out of business when the owner gives up or retires. The "mom and pop" stores are in this category, as are manufacturing businesses that cannot get their product or process sold as planned. Some of these marginal businesses have developed enough economic viability to ulti-

mately be sold, usually at a slight loss. Or they may fail completely and drop from sight.

Stage III: Success

The decision facing owners at this stage is whether to exploit the company's accomplishments and expand or keep the company stable and profitable, providing a base for alternative owner activities. Thus, a key issue is whether to use the company as a platform for growth – a substage III-G company – or as a means of support for the owners as they completely or partially disengage from the company – making it a substage III-D company. (See *Exhibit III.*) Behind the disengagement might be a wish to start up new enterprises, run for political office, or simply to pursue hobbies and other outside interests while maintaining the business more or less in the status quo.

Substage III-D. In the Success-Disengagement substage, the company has attained true economic health, has sufficient size and product-market penetration to ensure economic success, and earns average or above-average profits. The company can stay at this stage indefinitely, provided environmental change does not destroy its market niche or ineffective management reduce its competitive abilities.

Organizationally, the company has grown large enough to, in many cases, require functional managers to take over certain duties performed by the owner. The managers should be competent but need not be of the highest caliber, since their upward potential is limited by the corporate goals. Cash is plentiful and the main concern is to avoid a cash drain in prosperous periods to the detriment of the company's ability to withstand the inevitable rough times.

In addition, the first professional staff members come on board, usually a controller in the office and perhaps a production scheduler in the plant. Basic financial, marketing, and production systems are in place. Planning in the form of operational budgets supports functional delegation. The owner and, to a lesser extent, the com-

pany's managers, should be monitoring a strategy to essentially maintain the status quo.

As the business matures, it and the owner increasingly move apart, to some extent because of the owner's activities elsewhere and to some extent because of the presence of other managers. Many companies continue for long periods in the Success-Disengagement substage. The product-market niche of some does not permit growth; this is the case for many service businesses in small or medium-sized, slowly growing communities and for franchise holders with limited territories.

Other owners actually choose this route; if the company can continue to adapt to environmental changes, it can continue as is, be sold or merged at a profit, or subsequently be stimulated into growth (endpoint 3 on *Exhibit IV*). For franchise holders, this last option would necessitate the purchase of other franchises.

If the company cannot adapt to changing circumstances, as was the case with many automobile dealers in the late 1970s and early 1980s, it will either fold or drop back to a marginally surviving company (endpoint 4 on *Exhibit IV*).

Substage III-G. In the Success-Growth substage, the owner consolidates the company and marshals resources for growth. The owner takes the cash and the established borrowing power of the company and risks it all in financing growth.

Among the important tasks are to make sure the basic business stays profitable so that it will not outrun its source of cash and to develop managers to meet the needs of the growing business. This second task requires hiring managers with an eye to the company's future rather than its current condition.

Systems should also be installed with attention to forthcoming needs. Operational planning is, as in substage III-D, in the form of budgets, but strategic planning is extensive and deeply involves the owner. The owner is thus far more active in all phases of the company's affairs than in the disengagement aspect of this phase.

If it is successful, the III-G company proceeds into Stage IV. Indeed, III-G is often the first attempt [Continued on page 38]

38   Harvard Business Review   May-June 1983

Characteristics of small business
at each stage of development

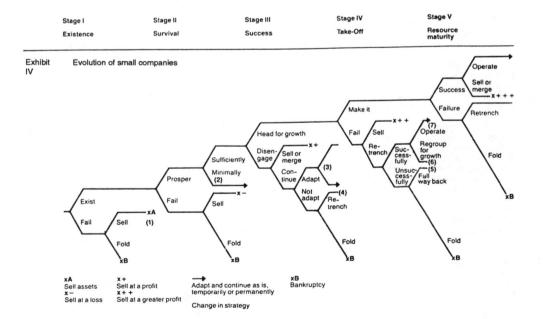

| | Stage I | Stage II | Stage III-D | Stage III-G | Stage IV | Stage V |
	Existence	Survival	Success-Disengagement	Success-Growth	Take-off	Resource maturity
Management style	Direct supervision	Supervised supervision	Functional	Functional	Divisional	Line and staff
Organization						
Extent of formal systems	Minimal to nonexistent	Minimal	Basic	Developing	Maturing	Extensive
Major strategy	Existence	Survival	Maintaining profitable status quo	Get resources for growth	Growth	Return on investment
Business and owner*						

Exhibit III

*Smaller circle represents owner.
 Larger circle represents business.

Stage I	Stage II	Stage III	Stage IV	Stage V
Existence	Survival	Success	Take-Off	Resource maturity

Exhibit IV   Evolution of small companies

xA	x +	→	xB
Sell assets	Sell at a profit	Adapt and continue as is, temporarily or permanently	Bankruptcy
x –	x + +		
Sell at a loss	Sell at a greater profit	Change in strategy	

40   Harvard Business Review   May-June 1983

at growing before commitment to a growth strategy. If the III-G company is unsuccessful, the causes may be detected in time for the company to shift to III-D. If not, retrenchment to the Survival Stage may be possible prior to bankruptcy or a distress sale.

Stage IV: Take-off

In this stage the key problems are how to grow rapidly and how to finance that growth. The most important questions, then, are in the following areas:

Delegation. Can the owner delegate responsibility to others to improve the managerial effectiveness of a fast growing and increasingly complex enterprise? Further, will the action be true delegation with controls on performance and a willingness to see mistakes made, or will it be abdication, as is so often the case?

Cash. Will there be enough to satisfy the great demands growth brings (often requiring a willingness on the owner's part to tolerate a high debt-equity ratio) and a cash flow that is not eroded by inadequate expense controls or ill-advised investments brought about by owner impatience?

The organization is decentralized and, at least in part, divisionalized – usually in either sales or production. The key managers must be very competent to handle a growing and complex business environment. The systems, strained by growth, are becoming more refined and extensive. Both *operational* and *strategic* planning are being done and involve specific managers. The owner and the business have become reasonably separate, yet the company is still dominated by both the owner's presence and stock control.

This is a pivotal period in a company's life. If the owner rises to the challenges of a growing company, both financially and managerially, it can become a big business. If not, it can usually be sold – at a profit – provided the owner recognizes his or her limitations soon enough. Too often, those who bring the business to the Success Stage are unsuccessful in Stage IV,

either because they try to grow too fast and run out of cash (the owner falls victim to the omnipotence syndrome), or are unable to delegate effectively enough to make the company work (the omniscience syndrome).

It is, of course, possible for the company to traverse this high-growth stage without the original management. Often the entrepreneur who founded the company and brought it to the Success Stage is replaced either voluntarily or involuntarily by the company's investors or creditors.

If the company fails to make the big time, it may be able to retrench and continue as a successful and substantial company at a state of equilibrium (endpoint 7 on *Exhibit IV*). Or it may drop back to Stage III (endpoint 6) or, if the problems are too extensive, it may drop all the way back to the Survival Stage (endpoint 5) or even fail. (High interest rates and uneven economic conditions have made the latter two possibilities all too real in the early 1980s.)

Stage V: Resource maturity

The greatest concerns of a company entering this stage are, first, to consolidate and control the financial gains brought on by rapid growth and, second, to retain the advantages of small size, including flexibility of response and the entrepreneurial spirit. The corporation must expand the management force fast enough to eliminate the inefficiencies that growth can produce and professionalize the company by use of such tools as budgets, strategic planning, management by objectives, and standard cost systems – and do this without stifling its entrepreneurial qualities.

A company in Stage V has the staff and financial resources to engage in detailed operational and strategic planning. The management is decentralized, adequately staffed, and experienced. And systems are extensive and well developed. The owner and the business are quite separate, both financially and operationally.

The company has now arrived. It has the advantages of size, financial resources, and managerial tal-

ent. If it can preserve its entrepreneurial spirit, it will be a formidable force in the market. If not, it may enter a sixth stage of sorts: ossification.

Ossification is characterized by a lack of innovative decision making and the avoidance of risks. It seems most common in large corporations whose sizable market share, buying power, and financial resources keep them viable until there is a major change in the environment. Unfortunately for these businesses, it's usually their rapidly growing competitors that notice the environmental change first.

Key management factors

Several factors, which change in importance as the business grows and develops, are prominent in determining ultimate success or failure.

We identified eight such factors in our research, of which four relate to the enterprise and four to the owner. The four that relate to the company are as follows:

1   Financial resources, including cash and borrowing power.

2   Personnel resources, relating to numbers, depth, and quality of people, particularly at the management and staff levels.

3   Systems resources, in terms of the degree of sophistication of both information and planning and control systems.

4   Business resources, including customer relations, market share, supplier relations, manufacturing and distribution processes, technology, and reputation, all of which give the company a position in its industry and market.

The four factors that relate to the owner are as follows:

1   Owner's goals for himself or herself and for the business.

2   Owner's operational abilities in doing important jobs such

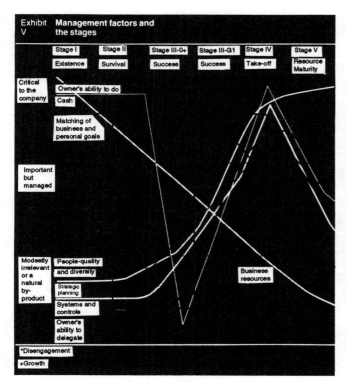

Exhibit V Management factors and the stages

as marketing, inventing, producing, and managing distribution.

3   Owner's managerial ability and willingness to delegate responsibility and to manage the activities of others.

4   Owner's strategic abilities for looking beyond the present and matching the strengths and weaknesses of the company with his or her goals.

As a business moves from one stage to another, the importance of the factors changes. We might view the factors as alternating among three levels of importance: first, key variables that are absolutely essential for success and must receive high priority; second, factors that are clearly necessary for the enterprise's success and must receive some attention; and third, factors of little immediate concern to top management. If we categorize each of the eight factors listed previously, based on its importance at each stage of the company's development, we get a clear picture of changing management demands. (See *Exhibit V.*)

Varying demands

The changing nature of managerial challenges becomes apparent when one examines *Exhibit V.* In the early stages, the owner's ability to do the job gives life to the business. Small businesses are built on the owner's talents: the ability to sell, produce, invent, or whatever. This factor is thus of the highest importance. The owner's

ability to delegate, however, is on the bottom of the scale, since there are few if any employees to delegate to.

As the company grows, other people enter sales, production, or engineering and they first support, and then even supplant, the owner's skills – thus reducing the importance of this factor. At the same time, the owner must spend less time doing and more time managing. He or she must increase the amount of work done through other people, which means delegating. The inability of many founders to let go of doing and to begin managing and delegating explains the demise of many businesses in substage III-G and Stage IV.

The owner contemplating a growth strategy must understand the change in personal activities such a decision entails and examine the managerial needs depicted in *Exhibit V.* Similarly, an entrepreneur contemplating starting a business should recognize the need to do all the selling, manufacturing, or engineering from the beginning, along with managing cash and planning the business's course – requirements that take much energy and commitment.

The importance of cash changes as the business changes. It is an extremely important resource at the start, becomes easily manageable at the Success Stage, and is a main concern again if the organization begins to grow. As growth slows at the end of Stage IV or in Stage V, cash becomes a manageable factor again. The companies in Stage III need to recognize the financial needs and risks entailed in a move to Stage IV.

The issues of people, planning, and systems gradually increase in importance as the company progresses from slow initial growth (substage III-G) to rapid growth (Stage IV). These resources must be acquired somewhat in advance of the growth stage so that they are in place when needed. Matching business and personal goals is crucial in the Existence Stage because the owner must recognize and be reconciled to the heavy financial and time-energy demands of the new business. Some find these demands more than they can handle. In the Survival Stage, however, the owner has achieved the necessary reconciliation and survival is paramount; matching of goals is thus irrelevant in Stage II.

About the research

We started with a concept of growth stages emanating from the work of Steinmetz and Greiner. We made two initial changes based on our experiences with small companies.

The first modification was an extension of the independent (vertical) variable of size as it is used in the other stage models – see *Exhibit I* – to include a composite of value-added (sales less outside purchases), geographical diversity, and complexity; the complexity variable involved the number of product lines sold, the extent to which different technologies are involved in the products and the processes that produce them, and the rate of change in these technologies.

Thus, a manufacturer with $10 million in sales, whose products are based in a fast-changing technical environment, is farther up the vertical scale ("bigger" in terms of the other models) than a liquor wholesaler with $20 million annual sales. Similarly, a company with two or three operating locations faces more complex management problems, and hence is farther up the scale than an otherwise comparable company with one operating unit.

The second change was in the stages or horizontal component of the framework. From present research we knew that, at the beginning, the entrepreneur is totally absorbed in the business's survival and if the business survives it tends to evolve toward a decentralized line and staff organization characterized as a "big business" and the subject of most studies.* The result was a four-stage model: (1) Survival, (2) Break-out, (3) Take-off, (4) Big company.

To test the model, we obtained 83 responses to a questionnaire distributed to 110 owners and managers of successful small companies in the $1 million to $35 million sales range. These respondents participated in a small company management program and had read Greiner's article. They were asked to identify as best they could the phases or stages their companies had passed through, to characterize the major changes that took place in each stage, and to describe the events that led up to or caused these changes.

A preliminary analysis of the questionnaire data revealed three deficiencies in our initial model:

☐ First, the grow-or-fail hypothesis implicit in the model, and those of others, was invalid. Some of the enterprises had passed through the survival period and then plateaued – remaining essentially the same size, with some marginally profitable and others very profitable, over a period of between 5 and 80 years.

☐ Second, there existed an early stage in the survival period in which the entrepreneur worked hard just to exist – to obtain enough customers to become a true business or to move the product from a pilot stage into quantity production at an adequate level of quality.

☐ Finally, several responses dealt with companies that were not started from scratch but purchased while in a steady-state survival or success stage (and were either being mismanaged or managed for profit and not for growth), and then moved into a growth mode.

Revision

We used the results of this research to revise our preliminary framework. The resulting framework is shown in *Exhibit II*. We then applied this revised framework to the questionnaire responses and obtained results which encouraged us to work with the revised model:

*John A. Welsh and Jerry F. White, "Recognizing and Dealing With the Entrepreneur," *Advanced Management Journal*, Summer 1978.

	Stage	Number of companies	Percentage
I	Existence	0	0.0 %
II	Survival	17	20.5
III	Success		
	Disengagement	15	18.1
	Growth	33	39.8
IV	Take-off	10	12.0
V	Resource-mature	1	1.2
	Unclassifiable		
	Lack of data	6	7.2
	Joint venture	1	1.2
	Total	83	100.0 %

A second serious period for goal matching occurs in the Success Stage. Does the owner wish to commit his or her time and risk the accumulated equity of the business in order to grow or instead prefer to savor some of the benefits of success? All too often the owner wants both, but to expand the business rapidly while planning a new house on Maui for long vacations involves considerable risk. To make a realistic decision on which direction to take, the owner needs to consider the personal and business demands of different strategies and to evaluate his or her managerial ability to meet these challenges.

Finally, business resources are the stuff of which success is made; they involve building market share, customer relations, solid vendor sources, and a technological base, and are very important in the early stages. In later stages the loss of a major customer, supplier, or technical source is more easily compensated for. Thus, the relative importance of this factor is shown to be declining.

The changing role of the factors clearly illustrates the need for owner flexibility. An overwhelming preoccupation with cash is quite important at some stages and less important at others. Delaying tax payments at almost all costs is paramount in Stages I and II but may seriously distort accounting data and use up management time during periods of success and growth. "Doing" versus "delegating" also requires a flexible management. Holding onto old strategies and [Continued on page 48]

48   Harvard Business Review   May-June 1983

old ways ill serves a company that is entering the growth stages and can even be fatal.

Avoiding future problems

Even a casual look at *Exhibit V* reveals the demands the Take-off Stage makes on the enterprise. Nearly every factor except the owner's "ability to do" is crucial. This is the stage of action and potentially large rewards. Looking at this exhibit, owners who want such growth must ask themselves:

Do I have the quality and diversity of people needed to manage a growing company?

Do I have now, or will I have shortly, the systems in place to handle the needs of a larger, more diversified company?

Do I have the inclination and ability to delegate decision making to my managers?

Do I have enough cash and borrowing power along with the inclination to risk everything to pursue rapid growth?

Similarly, the potential entrepreneur can see that starting a business requires an ability to do something very well (or a good marketable idea), high energy, and a favorable cash flow forecast (or a large sum of cash on hand). These are less important in Stage V, when well-developed people-management skills, good information systems, and budget controls take priority. Perhaps this is why some experienced people from large companies fail to make good as entrepreneurs or managers in small companies. They are used to delegating and are not good enough at doing.

Applying the model

This scheme can be used to evaluate all sorts of small business sit-

uations, even those that at first glance appear to be exceptions. Take the case of franchises. These enterprises begin the Existence Stage with a number of differences from most start-up situations. They often have the following advantages:

A marketing plan developed from extensive research.

Sophisticated information and control systems in place.

Operating procedures that are standardized and very well developed.

Promotion and other start-up support such as brand identification.

They also require relatively high start-up capital.

If the franchiser has done sound market analysis and has a solid, differentiated product, the new venture can move rapidly through the Existence and Survival Stages – where many new ventures founder – and into the early stages of Success. The costs to the franchisee for these beginning advantages are usually as follows:

Limited growth due to territory restrictions.

Heavy dependence on the franchisor for continued economic health.

Potential for later failure as the entity enters Stage III without the maturing experiences of Stages I and II.

One way to grow with franchising is to acquire multiple units or territories. Managing several of these, of course, takes a different set of skills than managing one and it is here that the lack of survival experience can become damaging.

Another seeming exception is high-technology start-ups. These are highly visible companies – such as computer software businesses, genetic engineering enterprises, or laser development companies – that attract much interest from the investment commu-

nity. Entrepreneurs and investors who start them often intend that they grow quite rapidly and then go public or be sold to other corporations. This strategy requires them to acquire a permanent source of outside capital almost from the beginning. The providers of this cash, usually venture capitalists, may bring planning and operating systems of a Stage III or a Stage IV company to the organization along with an outside board of directors to oversee the investment.

The resources provided enable this entity to jump through Stage I, last out Stage II until the product comes to market, and attain Stage III. At this point, the planned strategy for growth is often beyond the managerial capabilities of the founding owner and the outside capital interests may dictate a management change. In such cases, the company moves rapidly into Stage IV and, depending on the competence of the development, marketing, and production people, the company becomes a big success or an expensive failure. The problems that beset both franchises and high-technology companies stem from a mismatch of the founders' problem-solving skills and the demands that "forced evolution" brings to the company.

Besides the extreme examples of franchises and high-technology companies, we found that while a number of other companies appeared to be at a given stage of development, they were, on closer examination, actually at one stage with regard to a particular factor and at another stage with regard to the others. For example, one company had an abundance of cash from a period of controlled growth (substage III-G) and was ready to accelerate its expansion, while at the same time the owner was trying to supervise everybody (Stages I or II). In another, the owner was planning to run for mayor of a city (substage III-D) but was impatient with the company's slow growth (substage III-G).

Although rarely is a factor more than one stage ahead of or behind the company as a whole, an imbalance of factors can create serious problems for the entrepreneur. Indeed, one of the major challenges in a small company is the fact that both the problems faced and the skills necessary to deal with them change as the company grows. Thus, owners must anticipate and

50   Harvard Business Review   May-June 1983

manage the factors as they become
important to the company.

A company's development
stage determines the managerial factors that must be dealt with. Its plans
help determine which factors will
eventually have to be faced. Knowing
its development stage and future plans
enables managers, consultants, and
investors to make more informed
choices and to prepare themselves and
their companies for later challenges.
While each enterprise is unique in
many ways, all face similar problems
and all are subject to great changes.
That may well be why being an owner
is so much fun and such a challenge. ⊖

[25]

Environment and Planning A, 1988, volume 20, pages 1365-1383

Alternative theories of small-firm growth:
a critical review

P N O'Farrell
Department of Town and Country Planning, Heriot-Watt University, Lauriston Place,
Edinburgh EH3 9DF, Scotland
D M W N Hitchens
Department of Economics, Queen's University of Belfast, Belfast BT7 1NN, Northern Ireland
Received 8 June 1987; in revised form 11 December 1987

Abstract. This paper contains a review of alternative theories which have been developed in
order to explain growth and change in the small manufacturing firm. Models of small-firm
growth derived within the industrial economics literature are evaluated together with stage
models of growth and stochastic models. Social and psychological perspectives on growth are
reviewed and the spatial dimension is also considered. We argue that most previous theories
of small-firm growth place too little emphasis upon the difficulties which small owner-managed
firms have in meeting the competitive requirements of the marketplace.

Introduction

The implicit assumption underlying much of present concern to stimulate entrepreneurship, in general, and the foundation of new business in manufacturing, in particular,
is that as the UK Bolton Committee Report (DTI, 1971) contended small firms
provide the means of entry into business for new entrepreneurial talent and the
seedbed from which large companies will grow to challenge and stimulate the
established leaders of industry. However, empirical evidence [for example from
Ireland, where O'Farrell (1984, page 51) showed that of 2300 indigenous single-
plant firms which opened since 1967 and survived until 1981, only 1% employed
over 100 people] suggests, perhaps not surprisingly, that rapid and widespread
growth among new firms is not to be expected. Similar results have been obtained
by Storey (1981) for Cleveland County in England. In order to be able to establish
a link between the formation of new firms and employment growth, what is required
is a satisfactory theory of small-firm growth which takes account of the rarity of
the process it seeks to explain and the tendency for most firms, if they survive
infancy, to plateau and remain approximately the same size for many years. It is
important in order to improve policy design for the small-firm sector to understand
clearly how and why small firms grow and to examine alternative conceptualisations
which have been derived in order to explain growth and change. The purpose
here is to review some of the different approaches to this subject, and to contribute
to the development of a conceptual framework within which to analyse small-firm
growth. The thrust of the argument in this paper is that a detailed 'micro' approach is
required to explain growth in smaller firms and that most previous theories of
small-firm growth present frameworks which place too little emphasis upon the
difficulties which small owner-managed firms have in meeting the competitive
requirements of the marketplace[1]. Moreover, these theories do not identify
production problems as a fundamental constraint upon small-firm growth.

A major problem confronting the evaluation of the models of firm growth is the
different definitions of company size and the variable populations of firms that
have been used in empirical investigations. Furthermore, there is no consistency in

---

[1] The theory is outlined more fully in a subsequent paper.

1366   P N O'Farrell, D M W N Hitchens

the dimension of growth which theorists have used as the object of analysis: some
refer to employment; others to profits, value added, turnover, and total assets; and
a few theorists have not actually defined the parameter of interest. We shall try to
pinpoint these differences and to comment upon their implications for our understanding of the growth process, where relevant.

Small-firm growth: the industrial economics approach

Small firms in most cases commence production at a scale below the minimum
efficient size for their industry. If firms fail to achieve minimum efficient size for
their specific industry they will be potentially vulnerable and may eventually close
because of competition from other companies which are operating at or above the
minimum efficiency. Many small firms, even if they are not efficient, may reach
the minimum efficient size for their industry by selling to relatively uncompetitive
and partially protected local and regional markets. Given that the long-run average
cost curve is L-shaped rather than U-shaped (that is, costs per unit of current output
above the minimum efficient scale do not vary with the volume of output), subsequent
expansion will depend upon whether growth is a strategic goal for the firm, and
whether the firm can meet the varying demands of the marketplace. Clearly
distinctions need to be drawn between technological economies and managerial and
financial economies, although the concept of economies of scale is a static one and
our concern is with dynamic issues, namely the process of growth.

In reducing their costs, firms in an industry will be involved in a competitive
struggle, and, against a given industry demand, some firms will be forced out of the
industry as other firms grow to their minimum efficient scale (Hitchens, 1976,
page 32). The fact that firms exist at different sizes led to the rejection of the
perfect-competition model and to the development of the concept of imperfect
competition with falling demand curves to individual firms. Hence, some firms may
expand to the minimum efficient scale in their industry even if they are not efficient
producers.

A number of growth models have been developed in industrial economics but
primarily to explain the behaviour of large firms. For example, in their seminal
book on industrial economics, Hay and Morris (1979, page 277) introduce the
chapter concerned with the growth of firms by arguing that the theory of growth of
firms should be more 'realistic' and that the predominance of multiproduct firms of
very large size "suggests that there may be no limit to the size of a firm in the
long run. Only if there is a constraint on how rapidly a firm can expand would
there then be any limit on its size and then only in the short run". Size is, therefore,
simply a function of growth; it is not conceptualised as an influence upon the
growth rate. This implies that the owner-managed single-plant firm and the multinational corporation occupy different points along the same continuum of corporate
development (Taylor and Thrift, 1982, page 17). Furthermore, Hay and Morris
(1979, page 277) also assume that "the theory must partly focus on the firm itself
as an organisation able to manipulate to some extent the competitive environment
in which it finds itself, rather than as just a passive unit whose performance depends
on various structural characteristics of the market". For the great mass of small
manufacturing businesses, which must function largely as price-takers and in many
cases operate within a dependent relationship as suppliers to large firms who have
the power to squeeze their profit margins, this assumption is inappropriate except
insofar as small firms can adapt their product to suit markets of different
competitiveness. Hence, the unequal power relationships that occur between large
and small firms in such commercial arrangements as licensing, franchising, sub-

contracting, and access to venture capital need to be explicitly recognised in any theory of small-firm growth.

In one theory developed by Downie (1958) within the industrial economics paradigm, it is argued that the rate at which a firm grows depends upon financial and demand factors; the capital required to expand capacity; and the customers required to absorb production. Capacity varies directly with the rate of profit, whereas the rate of profit varies inversely with the rate of customer expansion and growth of demand. As a direct result, the model identifies an upper limit to the rate of expansion of a firm but no upper limit to the absolute size of the enterprise (Taylor and Thrift, 1982, page 16).

Andrews (1949) set forth a theory in which savings in unit costs provide a motive for growth. He noted that, because some costs are fixed and some are variable, "short run costs will normally be falling even if the long run cost curve is rising" (Andrews, 1949, page 59). This implies that business expansion is undertaken to obtain short-run cost savings. In the long run, however, the long-run cost curve reigns and the short-run cost savings sought by these businessmen are illusory (Starbuck, 1971, page 74). Businessmen differ in the degree of interest that they take in different aspects of their functions (that is, production, financial control, marketing, etc) and this may be important in influencing the size towards which a business is trying to grow.

Penrose (1959), conversely, placed a major emphasis upon the managerial constraints on growth (subsequently known as the 'Penrose effect'), arguing that there are at any time limits to the expansion that existing managers can achieve, but limits also to the rate at which management can expand its numbers and thereby its managerial capacity. The core of Penrose's theory was the supply of managerial services to the firm. As the firm grows, obtaining new managers, new abilities, and new information, there are increases in the maximum services that the resources can generate. Any limit on the scale of possible operations recedes and the issue becomes one of determining the limits on the rate at which the firm, in utilising those services in innovation, diversification, and the like, can in fact grow (Hay and Morris, 1979, page 300). Penrose rejected the notion that the long-run unit costs of a firm rise as the firm grows large:

"There may be an 'optimum' output for each of the firms' product lines, but not an 'optimum' output for the firm as a whole. In general, we have found nothing to prevent the indefinite expansion of firms as time passes." (Penrose, 1959, pages 98 – 99).

Hence, Penrose sees that only the growth rate of the firm is constrained and not its ultimate size. There are both theoretical and empirical reasons for believing that the Penrose effect is a major determinant of the growth of a firm: both case study and econometric analyses support this view. Richardson (1964) in a survey of managers found that availability of suitable management was the major check on expansion; and Shen (1970), in an econometric study, argued that growth to larger size at plant level, by permitting more economies of scale to be realised, higher profits to be made, and more advantage to be taken of the relative cheapening of capital in relation to labour, would tend to sustain growth. Although he verified this empirically, he found that overall growth in subsequent periods tended to reverse, with initially high-growth plants becoming low-growth ones, and vice versa. This result he attributed to Penrose-type effects which compelled fast-growing organisations to slow down and permitted slow-growing ones to catch up. O'Farrell and Crouchley (1985), for Irish data at establishment level, showed that the previous history of employment change was a more important predictor of recent change than was employment size, with the exception of plants in the 0 – 10 size group.

The notion of disequilibrium also plays a part in Penrose's theory of the growth of the firm. She referred to 'interstices' in an expanding economy—opportunities for growth which existing large firms, regardless of their competitive advantages over their small rivals, are not in a position to exploit because of their finite resources and greater opportunities elsewhere or because of imperfect knowledge. She argued that, if small firms cannot exploit the opportunities, there will be scope for the successful creation of new firms either in new industries or in existing ones which grow more rapidly than the capacity of their incumbent firms.

A formal integrated theory of growth of firms has been developed by Marris (1963), and the subsequently modified model (Marris, 1966) has become the standard one for the analysis of the managerially controlled firm. The Marris model is a steady-state one—that is to say it is formulated in terms of a steady-state system in which all characteristics of the firm (assets, employment, sales, profit, etc) are presumed to grow at the same constant exponential rate over time (Hay and Morris, 1979, page 279). In identifying the main determinants of the growth of demand, Marris recognised that firms are usually multiproduct and that diversification into new products is not just an important vehicle of competition, but the major engine of corporate growth. Again this is not a realistic assumption in the case of most small firms. There are significant costs attached to expanding by successful diversification and these costs of expansion all reduce the rate of return on capital (Hay and Morris, 1979, page 284). In addition, there are limits to the organisational and decisionmaking capacity of managers. Hence, Marris suggests that there are four major determinants of the rate at which firms grow: (1) the demand constraint that arises because costs of expansion reduce the profit margin and/or raise the capital–output ratio; (2) the managerial constraint that arises because of the deterioration in efficiency of managers as expansion becomes more rapid; (3) the financial constraint that arises because of the takeover threat that the sale of shares by shareholders creates or exacerbates; and (4) the objectives that a management pursues (for example, growth, sales, and so on). Hence, Marris recognised that a theory of the growth of the firm requires a theory of stock-market valuation in which shareholders will be concerned only with current and future dividends and with capital gains, whereas managers seek to maximise the rate of growth of the same enterprise. Resources for expansion can be obtained by borrowing, new share issues, or retained earnings. However, the extent of borrowing is limited because higher debt–equity ratios expose both the borrower and the lender to increased risk; there is also a limit to the finances that can be raised through new share issues; and, in the case of retained earnings, there is a trade-off with the dividends expected by shareholders (Taylor and Thrift, 1982, page 17). The depression of share prices which excess drawing on these sources brings about increases the threat of takeover. The essence of the model is the identification of pressures on the firm to sustain the maximum rate of growth, given the financial constraints, so that no limit is envisaged to the absolute size that the firm can attain (Taylor and Thrift, 1982, page 17).

This brief review has demonstrated that the proposition of a relatively unimpeded trajectory of growth is implicit in the array of models of corporate growth that has been developed in industrial economics for both national (Downie, 1958; Marris, 1966; Penrose, 1959) and multinational firms (Vernon, 1971) and in the geographical literature (Watts, 1981). Taylor and Thrift (1982) have questioned this proposition. Static, ahistorical models of corporate development cannot depict corporate development paths; on the basis of cross-sectional data for validation, Taylor and Thrift (1982, page 14) have argued that such models can describe only potential development sequences and not actual development paths. Drawing upon the work of Devine (1979), they suggest that there may be no single development sequence for all organisations, but rather a series of development sequences including: (1) the small-firm sequence, with size a historically variable factor; (2) a competitive sector sequence related to the smaller quoted companies that are most susceptible to takeover; and (3) an oligopolistic sector sequence related to the larger national and multinational corporations. Each of these groups of enterprises have different magnitudes of resources available and can exercise varying degrees of power in the networks of institutions and firms which constitute their operational environments. Movement of individual enterprises between these groups appears to occur predominantly by takeover and merger (Taylor and Thrift, 1982, page 15).

The industrial economics literature on the growth of the firm is, therefore, concerned primarily with large firms and their development, from the perspective of differentiated management structures which are not typical of owner-managed enterprises or small partnerships. The nature and scale of the impediments facing the small firm are fundamentally different and we shall have to look elsewhere for appropriate conceptual frameworks. For example, a shortage of working capital and a consequent inability to raise it from the banking sector, because of insufficient security or the absence of a track record, is a major factor constraining expansion of small firms, whereas it is unlikely to be a key bottleneck to the growth of larger companies. Yet small firms need to grow in order to reap economies of scale or they will be at a cost disadvantage. All such disadvantages must be taken into account in any satisfactory theory.

Stochastic models of firm growth
A casual inspection of the data on firm sizes suggests the development of market concentration over time. The size distribution of firms is highly skewed with a few large firms, and a large tail of small ones. Such a distribution is approximated by a number of skew distributions of which the lognormal is the most familiar. The common feature of these distributions is that they may be generated by a stochastic process in which the variate (the size of firms) is subjected to cumulative random shocks over time. The size distribution of firms at a given point in time is the product of a series of random growth patterns in the history of the market.

The process of random growth leading to a lognormal distribution was first formulated by Gibrat (1931) as the 'law of proportionate effect'. We may conceive the growth of a firm as being made up of three effects, the first of which is a constant growth rate (of the market) which is common to all firms. Let X_t be the firm size at time t, and let α be the constant growth rate. Then

$$\frac{X_{t+1}}{X_t} = \alpha . \tag{1}$$

The second element is a systematic tendency for the growth of a firm to be related to its initial size.

$$\frac{X_{t+1}}{X_t} = \alpha X_t^{\beta-1} . \tag{2}$$

The effect of initial size on growth is determined by the value of β. For $\beta = 1$, the exponent of X is zero and so size has no effect on growth. For $\beta > 1$, large firms grow faster than small ones, and vice versa for $\beta < 1$.

The third element is a random growth term, ε_t, which enters the growth equation multiplicatively:

$$\frac{X_{t+1}}{X_t} = \alpha X_t^{\beta-1} \varepsilon_t , \tag{3}$$

or

$$\log X_{t+1} = \log \alpha + \beta \log X_t + \log \varepsilon_t \,. \tag{4}$$

Gibrat then made two key assumptions: (1) that $\log \varepsilon_t$ is normally distributed with zero mean and variance σ^2, and that it is independent of the initial size of the firm; and (2) that the mean proportionate growth of a group of firms of the same initial size is independent of that initial size [in other words, that $\beta = 1$ in equations (2) and (3)].

The law is difficult to test and conflicting results have been produced by statistical analysis. However, Gudgin (1978, page 160) demonstrated that growth and size are inversely related for manufacturing firms in the East Midlands, indicating a general tendency for small firms to grow more quickly, results which were confirmed by O'Farrell and Crouchley (1985) in the case of Irish manufacturing establishments between 1973 and 1981. The empirical consensus also suggests that the variance of growth rates decreases with size of firm (Mansfield, 1962). The stochastic nature of the phenomenon of the law of proportionate effect suggests that many factors affect growth and, therefore, there is no dominant theory.

Stage models of growth

The models developed within the industrial economics framework have largely ignored the development sequence of the very small firm, an issue to which we shall now turn. The dominant explanatory framework in the case of small businesses has been that of a 'stage' model of growth (Churchill and Lewis, 1983). The small firm is conceptualised as passing through a sequence of growth stages; the number of stages postulated varies from three or four (Steinmetz, 1969; Velu, 1980) to five (Greiner, 1972) or as many as ten (Deeks, 1976). The first stage of these models typically stresses the individual founder or partnership setting up in business, with a simple organisation and a management style characterised by direct supervision, and with minimal formal planning. In the next stage the business has demonstrated a capacity to survive and is associated with the emergence of a division of management tasks and the need to raise capital to finance growth. Formal planning is rudimentary, at best cash forecasting, and the management style is one typified by personal supervision. Subsequent stages tend to focus initially upon the critical decision of whether to expand or keep the company stable and profitable. Organisationally the firm becomes more bureaucratic, recruiting functional managers to be responsible for certain duties; and basic marketing, financial, and production systems are installed. Key problems become how to grow rapidly and how to finance it. Can the owner delegate responsibility to others to improve managerial performance, a role many entrepreneurs do not perform effectively? Is the entrepreneur capable of developing the management skills necessary for long-term success? Will there be sufficient working capital to satisfy the demands that growth brings, a process that may require a willingness to tolerate high debt–equity ratios? Both operational and strategic planning are conducted. Hence, the nature of the tasks required for success will vary markedly from one stage to the next.

Churchill and Lewis (1983, page 31) proposed a five-stage development framework, with each stage being characterised by an index of size, diversity, and complexity, and described by five management factors: managerial style, organisational structure, extent of formal systems, major strategic goals, and the owner's involvement in the business. They have four factors relating to the enterprise, and four to the owner; these factors change in importance as the business develops. The four that relate to the company are: financial resources, including cash and borrowing power; personnel resources, relating particularly to the quality of staff; systems resources in terms of the degree of sophistication of information, planning, and control systems; and business resources, including customer and supplier relations, market share, process technology, distribution processes, and reputation. The four factors that relate to the owner are: the owner's goals for himself and his business; the owner's operational abilities in executing tasks such as production, management, and marketing; the owner's ability and willingness to delegate responsibility and to manage the activities of others; and the owner's strategic abilities for future planning. As the firm develops, the significance of these factors changes and the varying importance of the factors over time underlines the need for owner flexibility.

In discussing an alternative framework of organisational growth, Greiner (1972) suggested that there are five phases of growth: creativity, direction, delegation, coordination, and collaboration. According to Greiner, each stage, other than the first, is both an effect of the previous phase and a cause of the next, and all are heralded by signs of an impending crisis. The creative phase ends with a crisis of leadership; the direction phase with a crisis of autonomy; a crisis of control follows the delegation phase; and a crisis of red tape the phase to coordination. Velu (1980) simplified the hypothesis by reducing the five phases to three: namely, the pioneer, the differentiated, and the integrated stages. In the pioneer stage the founder tends to be autocratic, internal communications are easy and activities will be directed towards profitable sales. The differentiated stage begins with the introduction of a scientific professional approach to business management; planning and evaluation systems will appear and the organisation will expand to comprise many separate departments and divisions. For companies which enter the integrated stage, their principal concern will be to maintain a growth rate through the introduction of a succession of new products.

Gill (1985) has suggested that a 'loose' stage model combined with motivational and social factors linked to the owner-manager will make it possible to identify those owner-managers who are likely to succeed, as opposed to those who will simply survive or fail. However, much research is needed to establish the robustness and validity of these findings.

A second—albeit more minor—theme on the theory of small-firm growth is the so-called 's-curve hypothesis', a special case of stage theory (Mueller, 1972). This suggests that the small firm will have a short formative period followed by a phase of rapid growth because of initial market advantage. This rate of growth fades as competition is offered by other firms who become aware of the market opportunities (Stanworth and Curran, 1976, page 155). A similar approach was adopted by James (1973), who articulated the theory of the corporate life cycle which bears a striking resemblance to the concept of the product life cycle. He suggested that the progression of a company be analysed through four phases similar to those of the product life cycle—introduction, growth, maturity, and recycling/decline—and that, *within* these phases, the operation of four major functional areas of corporate activity be examined—finance, marketing, production, and administration. James (1973, page 73) argued that sales and profits are the only indices upon which a life-cycle curve can be based. The time interval between the various phases of the life cycle of a company or of the growth slope cannot be predicted with any great accuracy because the length of each phase is dependent upon a number of factors.

These stage theories of growth may be criticised on several counts. First, some of them seem little more than heuristic classification schemes rather than a conceptualisation of the processes underlying growth. Second, they implicitly assume that a small business will either grow and pass through all stages or fail in the attempt. Empirical evidence does not justify such an assumption. Consequently, the growth-or-fail hypothesis implicit in most stage models is unsatisfactory; an adequate theory of small-firm growth should be able to account both for the rarity of the process and for the tendency for most firms, once they have survived infancy, to plateau and remain essentially the same size for years. Are there important differences between the characteristics of founders who strive for and achieve growth, and of those who are content to let their firms remain among the mass of small 'living dead' enterprises? There appear to be three types of small firms: (1) fast growers; (2) satisfiers, who constitute the majority; and (3) those which attempt fast growth but which fail. Third, the models fail to capture the important early stages in the origin and the growth of a company (Churchill and Lewis, 1983, page 31). By and large, these approaches focus upon the growth of a company from a small unit to a large corporation; they do not attempt a detailed understanding of the process of change and growth of the small, independently owned firm itself (Gibb and Scott, 1985, page 599). Fourth, it is unclear whether the passage of a firm through a sequence of growth stages is a necessary progression or whether, under certain conditions, one or more stages may be missed out, or variations in the sequence may be allowed to occur. Stanworth and Curran (1976, page 154) consider that this reflects a lack of empirical evidence, a tendency to rely upon very small samples and to use cross-sectional data rather than a longitudinal approach. Fifth, these frameworks define company size typically in terms of annual sales (or number of employees) and ignore factors such as value added, product mix, and rate of innovation of new products and processes. Sixth, the models are aspatial and do not incorporate an explicit spatial dimension to take account of the range of advantages and disadvantages in various regional economies which may inhibit or facilitate small-firm growth (Hitchens and O'Farrell, 1985; O'Farrell and Hitchens, 1988). Seventh, this body of literature is primarily discursive and wisdom based; the models tend to reflect the symptoms of growth rates more than the processes underlying the phenomenon. For example, the development of a managerial division of labour may be both a consequence and an instigator of successful growth. Last, the stage models and corporate life-cycle theory both tend to *assume* the validity of a stage or corporate life-cycle model rather than to prove it by rigorous evaluation of counterfactual evidence. Whereas the economic theories tend to assume that production is largely a black box, the stage theories tend to ignore the economic environment.

Strategic model of small-firm growth
Hjern et al (1980) have developed a simple model of small-firm growth by relating the impediments to small-firm growth to the internal as well as external private and public resources available for overcoming the impediments. They also conceptualise the growth of small firms (assuming they are seeking to expand) as occurring in increments or stages, the stages being defined by the emergence and resolution of impediments (for example, lack of investment capital or skilled labour shortages). The model postulates that a new phase of growth cannot commence until the impediments which have brought the previous phase to a close have been overcome (Hjern et al, 1980, page 7). This simple incremental model accords with the findings of many studies that small firms are beset with managerial deficiencies; they are often undermanaged and those that close founder over problems which, in principle, are resolvable. It strategically highlights critical events upon which resources for fostering the development of a small firm might usefully be concentrated. It is the capability of the company to manage change which will largely determine its survival and/or growth (Gibb and Scott, 1985, page 600). We shall now turn to consider the strategic management perspective and the role of the owner-manager.

The strategic management perspective and small-firm growth

Some scholars—notably Milne et al (1982) at Glasgow University—have focused attention upon the strategic dimension of achieving sustained growth and the way in which the owner-manager responds to business and personal environmental indicators. Hence, they concentrate upon the identification of the owner-manager's policies and strategies for the conduct and development of the business and their subsequent translation into managerial action that will lead to sustained business development. These business strategies are thought to be determined by perceptions of what the owner-manager wishes to, or thinks he can, achieve through his business, in the light of the opportunities and constraints he sees (Milne et al, 1982, page 6). In turn, these aspirations and perceptions will be partly determined by personal characteristics.

Some researchers have emphasised that a key factor in sustaining the growth and development of a business is how quickly the owner-manager can adapt and learn from the experience of dealing with his environment (Milne and Thompson, 1982, page 12). There are two environments that establish the frameworks within which the firm does its business: *an external environment*, including suppliers, buyers, the strength of competition, potential entrants, interest rates, company taxation, degree of dependency upon a small number of customers, extent of complexity and uncertainty in the market served, sectoral trends, government policies, trends in exchange rates, and social, legal, and political conditions; and *an internal environment* consisting of the resources of the firm itself. These characteristics cover the range of the relationship that a firm has with the environment including interaction with the aid agencies and the existence of institutional or administrative impediments to progress such as delays in planning permission or in assessing external finance (Gibb and Scott, 1985, pages 602–603).

The important internal factors identified in the literature and summarised by Gibb and Scott (1985) include the personal and leadership characteristics of the owner-manager. Previous research has emphasised the influence of such factors as age and its effect on attitudes to growth (Deeks, 1976), occupational background, personal objectives, management style and decisionmaking, the level of the owner's education and training, and personal values and attitudes. The managers' value systems will influence whether a firm pursues the objective of growth or independence, diversifies, enters foreign markets, adopts an active or passive behaviour in the market, looks for technological leadership or is content to pursue a 'survival' policy. For the small business, the objectives of the firm are synonymous with those of the owner.

Other internal factors influencing growth include the extent of division of management labour and the proportion of highly qualified personnel; the control system and the extent to which planning is built into it (Gibb and Scott, 1985); the human potential of the organisation in terms of skills and flexibility of the work force; the financial situation of the company; the physical asset base of the company in terms of age and quality of machinery and equipment; availability of management time for coping with change; and awareness both of the wider 'macro' environment and of the task environment.

The management collects and evaluates only a portion of the information concerning characteristics, processes, opportunities, and constraints in both of these environments. The perceptions are interpreted and filtered, account having been taken of earlier experience, knowledge, and conceptions. Thus, as the business is subjected to pressures from the environment or from within, it will seek to adapt and cope, and it is partly by this means that procedures are formalised, systems are developed and new managerial tasks are created. Much small-firm growth is topsy-turvy and is reactive rather than pro-active (Gibb and Dyson, 1984, page 252).

In the early organisational literature, strategy was viewed as an activity in which the owner-manager would develop a plan of action that matched environmental opportunities and threats, internal strengths and weaknesses, and managerial values (Andrews, 1971; Chandler, 1962). The distinction between corporate-level strategy (what business should the organisation be in?) and business-level strategy (how should the organisation compete in a given business?) is of key importance. Strategy is conventionally seen to consist of four components: scope, distinctive competence, competitive advantages, and synergy (Hofer and Schendel, 1978). Scope is the extent of the interaction that a firm has with the environment, commonly defined by the product/market segments in which it will compete. Distinctive competences are those functions at which the firm is exceptionally skilled, as a result of the types, amounts, and deployment of its resources. Synergy is the joint effects of the scope, distinctive competence, and competitive advantages as they cut across markets and organisational units.

Numerous studies testify to a strategy–performance relationship, although the findings are significant more for establishing the importance of a strategy than for telling what strategies to follow under particular circumstances (Sandberg and Hofer, 1982, page 212). Harrigan (1980), for example, found that the performance of firms in eight declining industries could be explained by their adherence to (or violation of) certain strategic prescriptions.

Some writers have asserted that there is an association between long-range planning and small-firm development. For example, Bamberger has argued that "we can assume that there is a positive relationship between the existence of a more or less formalised strategic planning system and the firm's growth" [cited in Gibb and Scott (1985, page 598)]. There is, however, by no means universal agreement that planning is either necessary or desirable (Karger and Malik, 1975). Gibb and Scott (1985, page 598) suggest that the differences between writers on this issue almost certainly owe much to failure to agree over what constitutes planning, in addition to the failure to standardise on the size of small firms being studied. Hofer and Schendel (1978) argued that this concept of strategy applied to small or single-plant businesses as well as to the medium and large diversified firms on which they concentrated. The applicability of the concept of strategy to all firms, regardless of size or complexity, serves to emphasise that our knowledge of the relationships between the characteristics of founders, the strategies of their firms, and subsequent performance is inadequate and requires more research attention.

Porter (1980) has adapted the framework of industrial organisation economics to the strategies of individual firms. In examining the strategic decision of a firm to enter a new business, Porter analysed the problem from the perspective of an existing firm. He identified two major sources of deterrents to entry: structural barriers to entry, and the expected reaction of incumbent firms. As the combined effects of barriers to entry and retaliation can be substantial, Porter suggested that entry is attractive only if an industry is in such disequilibrium that above-normal profits will remain despite such effects. Porter (1985) argued that the fundamental basis of above-average performance in the long run is sustainable competitive advantage. He identified three generic competitive strategies available to all firms regardless of age or industry: overall cost leadership, differentiation, and focus. The focus strategy has two variants: cost focus, and differentiation focus. Each of the generic strategies involves a different route to competitive advantage, with the cost leadership and differentiation strategies seeking competitive advantage in a broad range of industry segments, and focus strategies aiming at cost advantage or differentiation in a narrow segment (Porter, 1985, page 11).

The growth imperative: is it a realistic assumption?
Any strategy to stimulate small-firm growth must explicitly recognise that many
small manufacturing companies (perhaps the majority) possess neither the
inclination, the expertise, nor the resources to grow. Whether their desire to
remain small is a rationalisation of their lack of capability and resources is not of
crucial importance; they are content to stay small, and policy instruments designed
to aid the process of growth in small businesses are likely to have little or no
impact upon such firms. A high proportion of small firms are more interested in
maintaining their current level of profit than in expansion. One reason for firms
wishing to stay small is that the ownership and the management reside in the same
person, or persons; so future company goals are determined not only by commercial
considerations but by personal life-styles and family factors. Independence is the
primary aim of most entrepreneurs (see O'Farrell, 1986a); it is not readily
relinquished. Consequently, a policy of survival is frequently preferred to one of
growth. Furthermore, a *growth strategy* almost inevitably involves dilution of
ownership through external equity investment, a price which many owner-managers
and partnerships are not prepared to pay in order to secure growth (O'Farrell,
1986a). Other factors which discourage many small firms from seeking growth
include the fear of takeover, and the possibility that expansion would attract
attention from larger competitors and unions. A further disincentive identified by
Scase and Goffee (1980) is the extent to which the owner feels personally competent
to deal with the organisation and supervision of labour. Many craftsmen-
entrepreneurs wish to continue to exercise their own trade skills and may be
reluctant or unable to become more heavily involved in administration and
paperwork (O'Farrell, 1986a).
    Expansion may also mean not only an increase in the number of customers but
a change in the *type* of customer; possibly a shift from old and well-established
clients, obtained through personal recommendation, to large-scale organisations.
Some may be reluctant to exchange their personal relationships with old customers
for more, anonymous interactions with companies and institutions (Scase and
Goffee, 1980, page 77). Hence, it is important to note that there is an inherent
preference and propensity *not* to expand in many small businesses, and there are
well-documented additional barriers to the growth of the small enterprise. However,
even if the firm achieves growth, it may lead to the eventual demise of the
enterprise if the entrepreneur remains rigid in his attitudes, refuses to formalise the
organisation, delegate authority, change decisionmaking patterns, and develop new
relationships with employees (Kets de Vries, 1977, pages 54–55). If the firm
continues to grow without any organisational change away from the 'spider's web'
model, with the entrepreneur at the centre, the effectivensss of this organisational
structure and mode of decisionmaking becomes increasingly insufficient to cope
with the complexities of the external environment. An obsession with control, an
aversion to structure, a preference for personalised relationships with employees,
and an unwillingness or inability to delegate may constitute major impediments to
long-term growth and may even threaten survival. Furthermore, the formulation
and implementation of a growth strategy requires a strategic planning capability
which lies beyond the range of expertise of many small-firm entrepreneurs. In
addition, the entrepreneurially oriented founder may not wish to take on new
specialised management staff; and indivisibilities may mean that it is not possible
to keep them fully employed.

A social perspective on small-firm growth

Stanworth and Curran (1976), in a seminal paper, offered a new perspective on the social processes involved in the growth and development of the small firm. Their social action view of the small firm concentrates on providing us with an understanding of the internal social logic of the small enterprise as a social grouping. They argue that the key to growth lies in the meanings attached to participation in the firm by the actors involved; a social action perspective links the meanings and actions of participants in the small firm with their wider social environment (Stanworth and Curran, 1976, page 157). Using the concept of latent social identity, they suggest that three such identities occur: the artisan identity, the classic entrepreneur, and the manager identity. These identities are linked to the processes of growth through the internal social logic generated out of the ways in which the situation is perceived by those involved and the actions which follow on from these perceptions. Reluctance to grow is viewed as much more to do with the consequences, in social terms, of growth than with the reasons frequently articulated by entrepreneurs in surveys; the social action perspective offers reasons why growth is, on the whole, much less common than the prevalent growth ideology would indicate (Stanworth and Curran, 1976, page 164). Stanworth and Curran's interpretation is incomplete insofar as it does not devote detailed attention to the social orientation of other participants in the firm and to the key outsiders whose orientations and actions have crucial implications for social relations within the firm. However, this work is an important contribution to improving our understanding of the small-firm growth process; and focusing upon the entrepreneur and his influence upon the social character of the firm may be justified because his role is normally decisive.

The entrepreneurial personality and growth

Empirical studies of the entrepreneurial personality have not excelled in theoretical clarity (Kets de Vries, 1977, page 36). There is confusion in the definition of entrepreneurs and managers (O'Farrell, 1986b). For example, some studies have concentrated on specific personality characteristics that might contribute to successful company performance. Kets de Vries (1977) has reviewed the sometimes conflicting evidence concerning attempts to link personality characteristics of founders and company performance, and he cites Hornaday and Aboud's (1971) study of successful entrepreneurs which found that, compared with the population in general, entrepreneurs scored higher on scales reflecting need for achievement, independence, and effectiveness of leadership, and low on the scale of need for support. Personal values may be effective in distinguishing successful entrepreneurs from the general population. However, Hornaday and Aboud's work does not distinguish between the general population and the entrepreneur who has made an attempt and failed; and the scales will not discriminate between successful and unsuccessful entrepreneurs.

There has been a considerable debate in the literature concerning the relationship between the concept of need for achievement and entrepreneurship, although much less attention has been focused upon the association (if any) between need for achievement and growth of firms. People who have high need for achievement tend to believe in their own ability to control the outcome of their efforts—a belief in an internal 'locus of control'. Although several scholars have attempted to relate entrepreneurship with beliefs in the internal locus of control, Brockhaus (1982) is one of the few authors to correlate the scores of the locus of control with success rates of businesses.

He found that this internal belief and the associated greater effort would seem to hold true both for successful entrepreneurs and for successful managers. Therefore, his study fails to distinguish uniquely entrepreneurs, but holds promise of distinguishing successful entrepreneurs from the unsuccessful ones (Brockhaus, 1982, page 45). He also tentatively concluded that general risk-taking propensity may not be related either to the entrepreneurial decision or to the success of the enterprise (1982, page 48).

Prior job dissatisfaction may also indirectly contribute to the success of the new venture: Brockhaus (1980) compared successful entrepreneurs with unsuccessful ones and found that the former were more dissatisfied with previous jobs at the time they started their business. They may have been more highly motivated to avoid returning to their previous or similar jobs.

The owner-manager's values directly influence the strategic decisions and the objectives and strategies of the firm. Studies on the influence of values on the performance of the firm are relatively rare. England (1975) has analysed the relationship between the personality of the manager and the performance of the firm, taking into account, particularly, the age of the manager. Bamberger (1983), reviewing German research on managers in agribusiness, concluded that the results are contradictory. This, in part, could be due to the choice of a 'personality' variable so that, at present, no firm conclusions can be drawn concerning the relationship between managerial values and performance.

The entrepreneur's personality and psychology have been examined mainly to determine what leads a person to entrepreneurship rather than to determine their effects upon his success (Sandberg and Hofer, 1982, page 217). However, Miron and McClelland (1979) have argued that training in achievement motivation significantly improves small-business performance and that it appears to be effective for manufacturing, retail, and service businesses. The research findings linking entrepreneurial personality characteristics and growth are highly tentative and therefore inadequate for the purposes of policy prescription. General studies on entrepreneurship are difficult to generalise; most involve specific groups of people and particular methodologies. Hence, all analysis of traits peculiar to the entrepreneur have resulted in equivocal findings with no clear evidence of any single trait which could distinguish successful entrepreneurs from unsuccessful ones (Chell, 1985, page 51).

The spatial dimension in small-firm growth

Mason and Harrison (1985, pages 4–5) have identified the "need for some detailed studies of the ... role and growth of new and small firms in contrasting regional environments" and have called for "an examination of the locational and structural characteristics of 'successful' small firms". They have also argued that, whereas there is now substantial research on the process of formation of new firms, equivalent research on the relative performance of small firms in different regions is virtually nonexistent. Small firms frequently need to address corporate-level strategic issues (what business should the firm begin?), and a wide range of functional area strategic problems (financial, marketing, personnel, production, etc), in addition to those of business-level strategy (for example, should the firm develop and launch a new product and gradually phase out an existing one?). The prescriptive literature on small-business planning emphasises the key role of 'outsiders' in improving the effectiveness of strategic planning in small firms. Hence, although managerial deficiencies may frequently cause problems in the development of small firms, many of these problems arise as a consequence of firm–environment relationships, for the growth of industrial concentration means that the external environment is increasingly structured by and for large firms. Furthermore, small firms, as a consequence of their limited managerial resources, are more dependent upon their external environment than are larger companies, and their growth may be constrained by the lower quantity and quality of public and private services available in peripheral regions.

The local milieu may be an important influence upon the prospects for small-firm growth and expansion; impediments to growth are likely to vary in nature and scale between different regions. Venture capital availability is more limited in peripheral areas owing to the centralisation of the lending institutions and the distorted perception of risk by banks. Lower rates of economic growth and lower levels of income inhibit the opportunities for small-firm expansion based upon local and regional markets. Small firms in peripheral regions also suffer technical impediments to growth, as reflected in the lower rates of innovation compared with similar sized firms in core regions (Oakey et al, 1980). Labour-supply bottlenecks —especially shortages of apprentice-trained craftsmen and managerial staff—vary between regional and subregional economies and may be a serious constraint upon growth. Hitchens and O'Farrell (1985) have reported that the quality of labour skills is the major factor underlying the poor performance of a sample of small firms in Northern Ireland—the region with the highest unemployment in the United Kingdom—compared with similar matched firms in the South East of England. Furthermore, peripheral economies such as South Wales, which are dominated by large firms such as the British Steel Corporation, BP, and Ford, are not an ideal source of skilled labour for small firms. Skilled personnel recruited from such enterprises tend to be more orientated towards maintenance than production, to be more narrowly specialised, and to lack the flexibility necessary for working in a small-firm environment (Hitchens and O'Farrell, 1986).

Gibb and Dyson (1984, page 25) have suggested that many independent entrepreneurs are closely in touch with the market, have many ideas for new products and processes, but lack the resources to take advantage of new developments as well as the knowledge of the best way to go about expanding the business. The resource shortage, argue Gibb and Dyson, is not that of cash but of management. Del Monte and Giannola (1986, page 282) have also argued that one of the major impediments to the expansion of small firms in peripheral regions is that the process of division of labour is constrained primarily through a restricted supply of managerial and organisational skills. As a firm grows it will need to change its organisational structure, for which it needs to employ the right people to implement the change. If the firm is not able to obtain the appropriate people because the skills are not available in the area it will not change its organisational structure, thereby constraining its growth. Hitchens and O'Farrell (1986) have also observed that, in South Wales, shortages of middle-management staff have impeded the growth of some small firms. Del Monte and Giannola (1986, page 286) also suggest that firms in less-prosperous areas will be more vertically integrated than those in developed regions and that this lack of specialisation reduces the competitiveness and rate of growth of local firms. O'Farrell and Hitchens (1988) have observed that subcontract engineering firms in peripheral areas such as South Wales, Scotland, and Northern Ireland are less specialised than in the South East. It is apparent that policies aimed at providing regional development grants and soft loans will in themselves not address impediments arising from supply-side shortages of appropriate skilled workers and management.

A further impediment to small-firm growth associated with economies in peripheral areas with high levels of external control is that branch plants purchase a smaller proportion of their inputs from local sources. Small independent firms are less well equiped than multiplant organisations to anticipate and avoid impediments and also to resolve them; not only are their own problem-solving resources fewer, but their limited management capacity may also constrain their access to external public and private resources; these latter resources may also be more scarce and of lower quality in peripheral areas. Such environmental impediments may have different impacts upon various kinds of business.

There is empirical evidence to demonstrate that firms are ignorant of external resources available to them and how difficult it can be for policy to reach them (O'Farrell, 1986a). It may be hypothesised that this problem will be greater in peripheral regions as a consequence of both the 'public – private services gap' (that is, the underrepresentation in certain regions of services which are important to locally based enterprises in promoting growth, innovation, productivity, effective control systems, more dynamic marketing, and so on) and the lower proportion of well-educated entrepreneurs who are better able to take advantage of aids, incentives, and advisory services. There is evidence that the knowledge possessed by small-firm entrepreneurs concerning the availability of assistance is frequently very limited; and where they have knowledge it is often distorted (O'Farrell, 1986a). The small-firm owner-manager's perception of the external environment is constrained by the limited amount of information the manager is able to draw from it and by his capabilities to assess it. This partly reflects the characteristic managerial weaknesses of many small firms and the magnitude of their ignorance may be compounded by the passivity of many agencies. This raises two fundamental questions. First, does the design of policy instruments and advisory systems address the key bottlenecks to the growth of small firms or is there a mismatch between the types of problems encountered and the policy measures and advisory services available? Second, do the ways in which policies are marketed and delivered ensure optimal take-up by small firms? As yet, there is no satisfactory answer to these questions; however, answers will be necessary in order to design and implement an appropriate set of policy instruments to stimulate small-firm growth.

Conclusion: towards a production-oriented theory of growth
As in so many aspects of the social sciences, it is easier to provide a critique of contemporary theories than to present a definitive new conceptual framework within which to study small-firm growth. We have argued that the stage models of growth focus primarily upon the internal dynamics of the firm and they tend to underestimate the importance of external factors in small-firm growth and development. Hence, factors such as the dependency of small firms upon large organisations, and the unequal power relationships that manifest themselves in such commercial arrangements as licensing, franchising, subcontracting and access to venture capital, need to be explicitly recognised within any theoretical framework of small-firm growth. The existence of a segmented or dualistic economy comprising unequal relationships between large business organisations, on the one hand, and the weaker, small-firm sector, on the other (with large retail chains, for example, having the power to squeeze the profit margins of small clothing manufacturers) is a fundamental reality in developed economies (Averitt, 1968).

In the industrial economics literature there is a tendency to assume implicitly that the small firm is a microcosm of the large enterprise in terms of organisation, behaviour, and strategy (in other words, that small enterprises are quantitatively but not qualitatively different from larger ones). We have argued that there are fundamental qualitative differences between large and small enterprises and that alternative conceptual frameworks are required in order to analyse small-firm growth.

It is clear that many factors need to be taken into account to explain small-firm growth and failure, and to this end there are lessons to be learned from several disciplines and conceptual approaches. At present an adequate explanatory framework within which to analyse the growth of the small owner-managed manufacturing enterprise has not been developed. We are still seeking a theory which will simultaneously explain the infrequency of the phenomenon and account for the major processes underlying growth, and we argue that this crucially depends upon the competitive framework and the ability of the firm to foresee and adjust to competition. The issue of the growth of small manufacturing firms needs to be viewed in terms of both the internal and external mechanisms which influence it.

In this paper we have reviewed the major theoretical contributions which have been made to our understanding of small-firm growth and have pointed to ways in which further research might be directed. We have also emphasised the importance of introducing a spatial dimension into the framework because small firms are much more dependent upon external factors operating in their local milieu than are large corporations. However, much work remains to be done for us to understand the mysteries that are contained within the small-business 'black box'.

Florence (1953, pages 64–65) wrote "Many small firms survive because they give the precise and reliable service required by customers, particularly in jobbing for producer customers ... . They promise firm delivery dates ... and keep their promise; they produce the exact unstandard quality and design (usually unreasonably) required". It appears that Florence, among many others, tended to assume implicitly that small firms are able to manufacture to the precise design, quality, and price required in specific market segments. Our recent research evidence (Hitchens and O'Farrell, 1985; 1986) suggests that such an assumption is unjustified and that the inadequate design, poor quality, and lack of price competitiveness are major factors constraining the growth and threatening the survival of many small firms. The key arguments in this paper is that a major reason (and possibly the most important one) why most small firms close or fail to expand is that they are manufacturing products that the market does not want; that is, they frequently do not optimise the price/quality relationship for the segments of the market towards which their products are targeted. This was especially true of firms in Northern Ireland in comparison with matched enterprises in the South East of England and South Wales.

All previous theories of small-firm growth implicitly assume that the production process is largely a 'black box' and that the firm can manufacture to the appropriate design, quality, and price for its specific market segment, and can, therefore, choose whether or not to grow. In short, these models underestimate the difficulties that small firms have in meeting the competitive requirements of the marketplace. If a firm can solve its production problems successfully it will have overcome a major constraint upon its potential for expansion.

Which firms achieve growth? Our thesis is that it will be those which can identify the key criteria upon which to compete in certain segments (for example, design, after-sales service, price, quality, delivery reliability, and so on) and can then build a competitive advantage based upon these criteria. It appears that small firms, even if they can identify the key criteria, have great difficulty in building a competitive edge. Other impediments may arise in the attempt to build a competitive advantage, such as need for venture capital, shortage of required skills, cash-flow problems, outdated machinery, and so on. However, the overcoming of these impediments may, in *some circumstances*, be a necessary but not a sufficient condition for successful growth. *The need to get the design and price/quality relationship correct for specific market segments is a necessary condition of growth for all firms.* Hence, for example, a firm may have up-to-date machinery and adequate working capital, but it will not achieve growth if it fails to meet the design and the price/quality requirements of the marketplace. Our ignorance of how small firms behave in response to certain stimuli is still too great for us to be confident in the design of policy instruments to encourage growth. Hence, the provision of capital grants for machinery and equipment in selected regions is predicated on the assumption that investment decisions are taken in a more or less rational manner related to market opportunities and competitive advantage. Yet Hitchens and O'Farrell (1986) have reported that small firms in Northern Ireland, where there are substantial capital grants, tended to invest in machinery first and then look for orders, in contrast to comparable London firms, with no grants available, which first obtained the work and then decided whether to upgrade the machinery. Policymakers clearly need a better understanding of how the factors they are seeking to influence in the small firms actually work, and this requires an improved conceptualisation of the processes of growth and change within the small firm.

Acknowledgements. The research upon which this paper is based is supported by a grant from the Economic and Social Research Council. We are grateful to Dr Colin Mason, University of Southampton, and Dr Ray Oakey, Heriot–Watt University, for many helpful comments upon an earlier draft. · The usual disclaimer applies.

References
Andrews D R, 1971 *The Concept of Corporate Strategy* (Dow Jones Irwin, Homewood, IL)
Andrews P W S, 1949, "A reconsideration of the theory of the individual business" *Oxford Economic Papers* **1** 54 – 89
Averitt R T, 1968 *The Dual Economy: The Dynamics of American Industry* (Jeffrey Norton, New York)
Bamberger I, 1983, "Value systems, strategies and performance of small and medium sized firms" *International Small Business Journal* **1**(4) 25 – 39
Binks M, Vale P, 1984, "Constraints on the new firm", Paper 3 from Nottingham University Small Firms Unit, University Park, Nottingham NG7 2RD, England; pages 1 – 34
Brockhaus R H Snr, 1980, "Psychological and environmental factors which distinguish the unsuccessful from the successful entrepreneur: a longitudinal study" in *Proceedings of the Academy of Management* pp 368 – 372; copy available from author
Brockhaus R H Snr, 1982, "The psychology of the entrepreneur", in *Encyclopedia of Entrepreneurship* Eds C A Kent, D L Sexton, K H Vesper (Prentice-Hall, Englewood Cliffs, NJ) pp 39 – 71
Chandler A D, 1962 *Strategy and Structure* (MIT Press, Cambridge, MA)
Chell E, 1985, "The entrepreneurial personality: a few ghosts laid to rest" *International Small Business Journal* **3**(3) 43 – 54
Churchill N C, Lewis V L, 1983, "The five stages of small business growth" *Harvard Business Review* **61** 30 – 50
Cooper A C, 1981, "Strategic management: new ventures and small business" *Long Range Planning* **14**(5) 39 – 45
Deeks J, 1976 *The Small Firm Owner Manager: Entrepreneurial Behaviour and Management Practice* (Praeger, New York)
Del Monte A, Giannola A, 1986, "Relevance and nature of small and medium sized firms in Southern Italy", in *New Firms and Regional Development in Europe* Eds D Keeble, E Wever (Croom Helm, Beckenham, Kent) pp 275 – 298
Devine P J, 1979 *An Introduction to Industrial Economics* 3rd edition (Allen and Unwin, Hemel Hempstead, Herts)
Downie J, 1958 *The Competitive Process* (Gerald Duckworth, London)
DTI, 1971 *Report of the Committee on Inquiry on Small Firms* Cmnd 4811, Chairman J E Bolton, Department of Trade and Industry (HMSO, London)
England G W, 1975 *The Manager and His Values: An International Perspective from the United States, Japan, Korea, India and Australia* (Ballinger, Cambridge, MA)
Florence P S, 1953 *The Logic of British and American Industry* (University of North Carolina Press, Chapel Hill, NC)

Gibb A, Dyson J, 1984, "Stimulating the growth of owner managed firms", in *Success and Failure in Small Business* Eds J Lewis, J Stanworth, A Gibb (Gower, Aldershot, Hants) pp 249–275

Gibb A, Scott M, 1985, "Strategic awareness, personal commitment and the process of planning in the small business" *Journal of Management Studies* 22 597–631

Gibrat R, 1931 *Les Inégalités Économiques* (Libraire de Recueil Sirez, Paris)

Gill J, 1985 *Factors Affecting the Survival and Growth of the Smaller Company* (Gower, Aldershot, Hants)

Greiner L E, 1972, "Evolution and revolution as organisations grow" *Harvard Business Review* July/August issue, pages 37–46

Gudgin G, 1978 *Industrial Location Processes and Regional Employment Growth* (Saxon House, Farnborough, Hants)

Harrigan K R, 1980, "Strategies for declining industries" *Journal of Business Strategy* 1(2) 20–34

Hay D A, Morris J, 1979 *Industrial Economics: Theory and Evidence* (Oxford University Press, Oxford)

Hitchens D M W N, 1976 *Business Efficiency in Ironfounding* Technology Ltd, Gloucester; copy available from author

Hitchens D M W N, O'Farrell P N, 1985, "Inter regional comparisons of small firm performance: the case of Northern Ireland and South East England", Working Papers in Economics, OP-24, Queen's University of Belfast. University Road, Belfast BT7 1NN, Northern Ireland

Hitchens D M W N, O'Farrell P N, 1986, "Small firm performance in the regions: a comparison of Northern Ireland and South Wales" *Omega* forthcoming

Hjern R, Hull C, Finlayson D, Gillespie A, Goddard J, 1980, "Helping small firms grow", Discussion Paper Series, International Institute of Management, Berlin

Hofer C W, Schendel D, 1978 *Strategy Formulation: Analytical Concepts* (West, St Paul, MN)

Hornaday J A, Aboud J, 1971, "Characteristics of successful entrepreneurs" *Personnel Psychology* 24 141–153

James B G, 1973, "The theory of the corporate life cycle" *Long Range Planning* 6(2) 68–74

Karger D W, Malik F A, 1975, "Long range planning and organisational performance—a cross validation study" *Long Range Planning* 8(6) 60–64

Kets de Vries M F R, 1977, "The entrepreneurial personality: a person at the crossroads" *Journal of Management Studies* 14 34–57

Mansfield E, 1962, "Entry, Gibrat's Law, innovation and the growth of firms" *American Economic Review* 52 1023–1051

Marris R, 1963, "A model of the managerial enterprise" *Quarterly Journal of Economics* 77 185–209

Marris R, 1966 *The Economic Theory of Managerial Capitalism* (Macmillan, London)

Mason C M, Harrison R T, 1985, "The geography of small firms in the UK: towards a research agenda" *Progress in Human Geography* 9 1–37

Miles R E, Snow C C, 1978 *Organizational Strategy: Structure and Process* (McGraw Hill, New York)

Milne T, Lewis J, Thorpe R, Thompson M, 1982, "Factors for predicting success in small companies", Management Studies Working Paper 1, University of Glasgow, Glasgow G12 8QQ, Scotland

Milne T, Thompson M, 1982, "The infant business development process", Management Studies Working Paper 2, University of Glasgow, Glasgow G12 8QQ, Scotland

Miron D, McClelland D C, 1979, "The impact of achievement motivation training on small businesses" *California Management Review* 21 13–28

Mueller D C, 1972, "A life cycle theory of the firm" *Journal of Industrial Economics* 20 199–219

Oakey R P, Nash P A, Thwaites A T, 1980, "The regional distribution of innovative manufacturing establishments in Britain" *Regional Studies* 14 235–253

O'Farrell P N, 1984, "Small manufacturing firms in Ireland: employment performance and implications" *International Small Business Journal* 2(2) 48–61

O'Farrell P N, 1986a *Entrepreneurs and Industrial Change* (Irish Management Institute, Dublin)

O'Farrell P N, 1986b, "Entrepreneurs and regional development: some conceptual issues" *Regional Studies* 20 565–574

O'Farrell P N, Crouchley R, 1985, "Employment change in permanent manufacturing plants: analysis and implications from an Irish case study" *Environment and Planning A* **17** 333 – 353

O'Farrell P N, Hitchens D M W N, 1988, "The relative competitiveness and performance of small manufacturing firms in Scotland and the Mid-West of Ireland: an analysis of matched pairs" *Regional Studies* forthcoming

Penrose E, 1959 *The Theory of the Growth of the Firm* (Blackwell Scientific Publications, Oxford)

Porter M E, 1980 *Competitive Strategy: Techniques for Analysing Industries and Competitors* (The Free Press, New York)

Porter M E, 1985 *Competitive Advantage: Creating and Sustaining Superior Performance* (The Free Press, New York)

Richardson G, 1964, "The limits to a firm's rate of growth" *Oxford Economic Papers* **16** 9 – 23

Sandberg W R, Hofer C W, 1982, "A strategic management perspective on the determinants of new venture success", in *Frontiers of Entrepreneurship Research* Ed. K H Vesper (Babson College, Babson Park, Wellesley, MA 02157) pp 204 – 237

Scase R, Goffee R, 1980 *The Real World of the Small Business Owner* (Croom Helm, Beckenham, Kent)

Shen T Y, 1970, "Economies of scale, Penrose-effect, growth of plants and their size distribution" *Journal of Political Economy* **78** 701 – 716

Stanworth M J K, Curran J, 1976, "Growth and the small firm—an alternative view" *Journal of Management Studies* **13** 152 – 171

Starbuck W H, 1971, "Organisational growth and development", in *Organisational Growth and Development* Ed. W H Starbuck (Penguin Books, Harmondsworth, Middx) pp 11 – 141

Steinmetz L L, 1969, "Critical stages of small business growth" *Business Horizons* **12**(1) 29 – 34

Storey D J, 1981, "New firm formation, employment change and the small firm: the case of Cleveland County" *Urban Studies* **18** 335 – 345

Taylor M J, Thrift N J, 1982, "Models of corporate development and the multinational corporation", in *The Geography of Multinationals* Eds M J Taylor, N J Thrift (Croom Helm, Beckenham, Kent) pp 14 – 32

Velu H A F, 1980, "The development process of the personally managed enterprise", copy from Proceedings of the 10th European Seminar on Small Businesses, European Foundation for Management Development, 1 – 21; copy available from author

Vernon R, 1971 *Sovereignty at Bay* (Basic Books, New York)

Watts H D, 1981 *The Branch Plant Economy: A Study of External Control* (Longman, Harlow, Essex)

Part VII
Family Business

[26]

Stanley M. Davis

Entrepreneurial Succession

This paper examines three patterns of entrepreneurial succession in private enterprise in developing countries. The process may be thought of as the succession from entrepreneurs to executives. The findings suggest significant variation in the adaptability of each type to the development of modern organizations in which the function *of management is distinct from the manager as a* person.

Stanley M. Davis is assistant professor in the graduate school of business administration at Harvard University.

MEN die, but organizations generally continue to exist beyond the life of their leaders. The dilemmas of succession in leadership are usually considered a potential source of danger and conflict.[1] In large and complex organizations, managers are expected to move around as they climb the corporate hierarchy, and this expectation greatly reduces the potentially disruptive aspects.[2]

[1] Two important case studies of succession are Alvin W. Gouldner, *Patterns of Industrial Bureaucracy* (Glencoe, Ill.: Free Press, 1954), and Robert H. Guest, *Organizational Change: The Effect of Successful Leadership* (Homewood, Ill.: Irwin-Dorsey, 1962). See also A. W. Gouldner, "The Problems of Succession in Bureaucracy," in his *Studies in Leadership: Leadership and Domestic Action* (New York: Harper, 1950), pp. 644–659; R. H. Guest, Managerial Succession in Complex Organizations; and Comment by A. W. Gouldner, *American Journal of Sociology*, 68 (July 1962), 47–56.

[2] For a discussion of this point, see Bernard Levenson's statement on *anticipatory succession*, in "Bureaucratic Succession," in Amitai Etzioni (ed.), *Complex Organizations: A Sociological Reader* (New York: Holt, Rinehart, and Winston, 1961), pp. 362–375. For discussions of the relation of organizational size to succession, see Oscar Grusky, Corporate Size, Bureaucratization, and Managerial Succession, *American Journal of Sociology*, 67 (November 1961), 261–269; and Louis Kriesberg, Careers, Organization Size, and Succession, *American Journal of Sociology*, 68

ENTREPRENEURIAL SUCCESSION   403

Although the problem of succession therefore can create strains
in an organization's structure, it seldom is severe enough to
destroy that structure.

While an organization may seem immortal, however, it does
have a beginning.[3] The first succession in leadership is crucial,
because it can determine whether the organization will continue
to exist beyond the life of its founders. This problem is inherent
to all forms of organization, whether religious groups, educational
institutions, and even nation-states.[4] Max Weber referred to it
as the institutionalization of charisma.[5] Generally, the problem
of succession refers to the separation of the functions of leadership
from the personage of the leader. In an industrial context, this
process may be thought of as the distinction between the *function*
of management and the manager as a *person*.

Although the succession from one manager to another may be
clearly marked, the separation of function and person does not
occur at any official or specific time. In traditional business
enterprises, it is particularly significant during the first transfer
of leadership, and the process may take several years, if not a
decade or more.

The succession from entrepreneurs to executives, as this process

(November 1962), 355–359; C. Roland Christenson, *Management Succession in Small
and Growing Enterprises* (Boston: Graduate School of Business Administration,
Harvard University, 1953); Donald B. Trow, Executive Succession in Small Companies, *Administrative Science Quarterly*, 6 (September 1961), 228–235. See also
O. Grusky, Administrative Succession in Formal Organizations, *Social Forces*, 39
(December 1960), 105–115; also his, Managerial Succession and Organizational Effectiveness, *American Journal of Sociology*, 69 (July 1963), 21–31; and Richard O. Carl-
son, Succession and Performance among School Superintendents, *Administrative
Science Quarterly*, 6 (September 1961), 210–226.

[3] The two case studies by Gouldner and Guest deal with succession in firmly
established organizations, *Patterns of Industrial Bureaucracy* (Glencoe, Ill.: Free
Press, 1954), and Robert H. Guest, *Organizational Change: The Effect of Successful
Leadership* (Homewood, Ill.: Irwin-Dorsey, 1962).

[4] Seymour Martin Lipset discusses the importance of George Washington's declin-
ing to run for a third term in office as a crucial decision because it institutionalized
presidential succession, which provided stability without stagnation; cf. *The First
New Nation* (New York: Basic Books, 1963). See also Nicholas J. Demerath, Richard
W. Stephens, and R. Robb Taylor, *Power, Presidents, and Professors* (New York:
Basic Books, 1967), pp. 148–178.

[5] See H. H. Gerth and C. Wright Mills (trans. and eds.), *From Max Weber: Essays
in Sociology* (New York: Oxford, 1946), pp. 262 ff.

may be called, is particularly relevant in developing economies. Because of the importance attached to the role of entrepreneurs in development,[6] their ability to resolve the succession problem in their own organizations has important consequences for the industrial growth of their country. The entrepreneur is important not only in his ability to take risks, innovate, and put together new organizations, but also in his ability to leave a successfully operating organization in which the function of management can be transmitted to other persons.

To study the problem of entrepreneurial succession, case studies were made of five family firms in Mexico, and focused interviews were obtained with twenty other Mexican entrepreneurs faced with the problem of succession. Mexico was selected as an excellent place to examine succession, because of its rapid rate of overall development in the last 25 years. The organizations varied from 50 to 1,200 employees, from ten to forty-five years old, and from labor-intensive textile companies to capital-intensive chemical companies. The research showed three recurrent patterns of conflict in organizational leadership, and found significant variation in the adaptability of each type to new organizational requirements. Before considering the patterns of conflict, however, it is important to understand the place of the family firm in the general process of industrial development.

FAMILY FIRM AND INDUSTRIALIZATION

The extended family is generally the most basic and stable unit of social organization in traditional society. It is the locus of all economic, political, social, and religious life. It provides companionship and protection, a common set of values, and highly

[6] The literature on entrepreneurs is too extensive to be catalogued here. Some of the earlier important statements on the role of entrepreneurs in economic development can be found in Arthur Cole (ed.), *Change and the Entrepreneur* (Cambridge: Harvard University, 1949). The journal, *Explorations in Entrepreneurial History,* is largely devoted to this subject; some of the most important articles from it may also be found in Hugh G. Aitken (ed.), *Explorations in Enterprise* (Cambridge: Harvard University, 1965). See also Joseph A. Schumpeter, *Capitalism, Socialism, and Democracy* (New York: Harper, 1942), and *The Theory of Economic Development* (Cambridge: Harvard University, 1951). Schumpeter's stress on entrepreneurship, rather than on the entrepreneur, reflects the importance of the separation of the function from the person.

ENTREPRENEURIAL SUCCESSION   405

proscribed means of fulfilling them. Early forms of commercial and industrial activity therefore represent an extension of the family system rather than a break with it. The intimate connection between family and business is considered natural and compatible, and with industrialization, the larger village community accommodates itself to the presence of a factory.[7] Writing of the agrarian heritage of the Puerto Rican businessman, for example, Thomas C. Cochran states:

The family-centered pattern was undoubtedly weakening among those who worked for wages in the larger industrial centers, but our evidence indicates that among the business elite it survived in an altered form. Close relatives were turned to for assistance in managing business properties. In this way, the extended family moved from a social system based on agriculture to a system of economic control based on the family firm.[8]

During early development, moreover, the control of the family firm is usually complete; investment rights, coincide with financial and managerial control.[9] Although the general trend of development shows a growing separation between ownership and management, the basic family foundation remains.[10]

The compatibility of family and business institutions, and of village life with factory life, requires social values in harmony with traditional economic activity. For an organization to survive for any length of time, this overlap of values of the family and the firm must occur at all levels of the social structure. In order for the small family firm to survive rapid industrial growth, the large corporation must continue to maintain strong family values. In other words, both the small family firm and the large corpora-

[7] For two studies of this process of accommodation, see A. F. A. Husain, *Human and Social Impact of Technological Change in Pakistan* (Dacca, Pakistan: Oxford University, 1956); and Manning Nash, *Machine Age Maya, The Industrialization of a Guatemalan Community* (Glencoe, Ill.: Free Press, 1958).

[8] Thomas C. Cochran, *The Puerto Rican Businessman* (Philadelphia: University of Pennsylvania, 1959), p. 118.

[9] Wilbert Moore uses this threefold scheme to describe the growth of the corporation and professional management in *Industrial Relations and the Social Order* (New York: Macmillan, 1951), pp. 41–64.

[10] W. Paul Strassmann, "The Industrialist," in J. Johnson (ed.), *Continuity and Change in Latin America* (Stanford: University of California, 1964), p. 168.

tion must follow these values, or else the former must ultimately succumb to the competitive power of the larger corporation. Such a family pattern survived in France, and David Landes described the typical French business in 1950 as, "family structured in a way that has generally been associated with precapitalist economies . . . the justification of survival lies not in the ability to make a profit, but in the correct performance of a social function."[11]

The family firm, then, is a positive impetus to entrepreneurial activity in early periods of modernization, which harmonizes with traditional patterns. It has also survived where goals and organization of large businesses maintain the characteristics of the modest family firm, and where social function takes precedence over economic profit. When a national ideology favors rapid economic development, however, this pattern is not likely to survive; traditional family-firm values of enterprise stability and perpetuity clash with new economic goals of sustained investment and expansion. The more competition invades the marketplace, the more vulnerable the traditional structures and the values associated with them become.[12] Under such conditions, the family firm must adapt to the requirements of modern industrial enterprise or ultimately face extinction. It cannot survive continuous and rapid industrial growth in its present traditional form. Or, by corollary, to the extent that this traditional form does perpetuate itself, industrial development will be impeded.

[11] David Landes, "Business and the Modern Businessman in France," in E. Earle (ed.), *Modern France* (Princeton: Princeton University, 1951), pp. 336, 348. In the same volume, see John E. Sawyer, "Strains in the Social Structure of Modern France," pp. 293–312. Also, see D. S. Landes, French Entrepreneurship and Industrial Growth in the Nineteenth Century, *The Journal of Economic History*, 9 (May 1949), 45–61; D. S. Landes, Observations on France: Economy, Society, and Polity, *World Politics*, 9 (April 1957), 329–350; J. E. Sawyer, "The Entrepreneur and the Social Order, France and the United States," in William Miller (ed.), *Men in Business* (Cambridge: Harvard University, 1952); and Charles Kindleberger, *Economic Growth in France and Britain, 1851–1950* (Cambridge: Harvard University, 1964), particularly chs. v, vi.

[12] Marion Levy speaks on this point in "Some Sources of the Vulnerability of the Structures of Relatively Non-industrialized Societies to Those of Highly Industrialized Societies," in B. Hoselitz (ed.), *The Progress of Underdeveloped Areas* (Chicago: University of Chicago, 1952), pp. 113–125.

Industrial trends in developing countries have in fact shown a reduction of both family ownership and family management. Moreover, the firms that have remained under family control and have flourished have been those that were able to adapt to the changing industrial requirements. Some of the adaptations have been providing employment on the basis of competence rather than family connection, employing non-related personnel at managerial levels and delegating authority to them, adapting technological innovations, specifying jobs, and maximizing profits. Changes such as these are likely to conflict with traditional organization and goals, which make little or no distinction between family and business, or between manager and management.

SUCCESSION

When Emerson said that an institution is the lengthening shadow of one man, he aptly described the intimate relation between the business firm and the person who heads it. A shadow is a fleeting thing, however, and if the firm is to persist beyond the lifetime of its founder, the leadership of the firm must pass from one generation to the next. Within a family firm, this pattern is obviously the succession of father to son, but only in theory do the two cast the same shadow. Typically, the father started his small business with a little capital, struggled, built it up through experience, and then sent his son to receive a formal education. The difference between experience and education often reflects different personalities, operating by different methods, and pursuing different goals. The task of management also differs. The founding father in one family firm said: "I had to work hard, but the management was easy"; while his son said, "I don't have to work too hard, but the management is much more difficult."

The separation of the managerial function from the individual is seldom a simple task of passing the authority from father to son. When the son enters the firm, he typically shares authority with his father, beginning in a slightly subordinate position and gradually assuming all responsibility. Several patterns repeatedly occur during this transitional period of shared authority among the two generations in the family firm. These patterns, of course, are abstractions of general tendencies; nevertheless, the evidence suggests that certain commonalities predominate, and it is these common aspects which are emphasized here.[13]

Pattern One: Strong Father and Weak Son

The first is the pattern of strong father and weak son. Here is the pioneer man of business who fought his way to the top. His case is a paradigm of all the clichés: sheer drive, stamina, judgment, risk, courage, and luck. He is typically proud of where he has "gotten" and is well aware of his importance, both in his family, his firm, and perhaps even in his community and society. He has a personal dynamism about him, knows every inch of his business, every man in his firm, and every trick in the book.

He runs his family and his business with the same iron hand, and his word is law. He is respected and often loved by his workers, and he is the epitome of a stern but benevolent *patrón* to them. Many of his workers have been with him for many years; they are loyal to him, would not want to work for anyone else, and will carry out almost any order—because it comes from him. Indeed, his relationship with his workers often *seems* more idyllic than his contact with his son. For the distinctions of class, status, and power between this *padre de familia* and his workers are clear and delimiting, while the distinction between father and son is not.

The fatal flaw in such a "man of iron" is that he cannot transmit his strength to his son. Often he only transmits the opposite: the father is all that the son is not. In terms of power, if the father rules like a tyrant, his son is often incapable of making and enforcing his own decisions. In terms of prestige, if the father considers social standing and refinement irrelevant to running a business, then his son is likely to emphasize prestige and gracious living to the exclusion of a concern with running the family business. Or, in less extreme cases, the father may

[13] Although the family firm seldom involves only one father and one son, these patterns do provide the outline for succession of a numerically more complex form. When more than one son is involved, it is usually the oldest who is most closely bound to the pattern, because of primogeniture. When more than one father is involved (say two brothers), then both may exhibit the same characteristics, or one may trigger one pattern of succession and the other set a second in process.

consider such factors necessary but not sufficient qualifications
for administering the family's interests, whereas his son will rely
on their sufficiency. Finally, in terms of wealth, where the father
wants to make money, the son wants to spend it; he is the first
family playboy.

The major focus of conflict between this father–son pattern
is in authority and responsibility. The father has made all the
major decisions and taken all responsibility for them. He is the
sole authority, and all employees and workers know this. Consequently, his son lacks any real power, has never become capable
of successfully wielding what power he does have, and is not likely
to make any appreciable gains in power in the foreseeable future.
The father simply cannot let go of his command; he cannot retire
himself. While outwardly he makes a display of pride in the
way his son is taking over the business, the son makes none of the
real decisions and is nothing but windowdressing.

Despite the father's overt pride in his son, he seems more to be
taking covert pride in his own abilities. In fact, the son may even
represent a threat of displacement to the father, which only drives
him further toward centralizing his control. When the son returns
with a degree in business administration, engineering, or the like,
he often has new ideas. Each time the son tries to act on his own,
however, he is either bridled or crushed by his father. With the
father's attitude that only he knows what is best, the son does
not have an opportunity to exercise his initiative as he waits to
receive his authority within the firm. This father–son relationship is a psychic struggle between generations and has an intense
undercurrent of conflict.

The virulence of this relationship in Mexican life makes it
especially relevant to patterns of organization within the family
firm. Psychologists of the Mexican personality have considered
this a reflection of the psychological and historical relation between father and son, with its roots in the family structure during
the Colonial period. In this setting, which observers feel has
influenced present-day family relations, the all-powerful Spanish
father and the powerless Indian mother have produced a *mestizo*
(hybrid) son who must endlessly search for his own identity. As
an adolescent he is caught in the dilemma of wanting to imitate

the manliness and freedom of his father, whom he loves but fears, and wanting to denigrate his mother, whom he loves but looks down upon because she is female, Indian, and weak. In consequence, his adult life is an endless search for his masculinity, that heroic and unreal power which he either lacks or feels that he lacks.[14]

Pattern Two: Conservative Father and Progressive Son

The second pattern that predominates in father–son relations in the family firms is less psychological. The differences in personality between father and son, and their consequences for the organization are more a function of age. In this pattern of conservative father and progressive son, the typical father is also a hard-driving man who began with nothing and gradually built up a solid and successful business. The unstable days and severe market fluctuations following the Revolution are still vivid in his mind, and he is no longer the young man of the early post-revolutionary days. He is tired of fighting and struggling; he wants to enjoy some of the fruits of his labor in his old age. By now he is a grandfather and he would like to devote himself more to his growing family. He has fulfilled his goal as far as the business is concerned.

In this second pattern, the son receives a formal education, often in the United States or in Europe, and returns to the family business full of "new ideas," but he is held back. The father, here, is willing to give more control to his son, but he still serves as overseer to all major decisions. He is very reluctant to make the major decisions that the son would like to make, and to any radically new suggestion he will say, "We knew nothing when we started, but we have made out all right, so why should we change? We've always done it this way." The contrast, here, is not so much between a traditional father and a modern son as

[14] For a fuller treatment of this theme, some of the better works are: Octavio Paz, *The Labyrinth of Solitude* (New York: Grove Press, 1961); Samuel Ramos, *El perfil del hombre y la cultura de méxico* (Mexico D. F.: Espasa-Calpe Argentina, 1951); Francisco González Pineda, *El mexicano: psicología de su destructividad* (Mexico D. F.: Editorial Pax, 1961); Santiago Ramirez, *El mexicano: psicología de sus motivaciones* (3rd ed.; Mexico D. F.: Editorial Pax, 1961).

it is a father who was modern for his time, but has become conservative with age.

The immediate focus of conflict between father and son in this second pattern often involves issues which develop as a result of the son's higher education. The son brings back many ideas about products and procedures, some of which can be imitated directly while others can be adapted to local requirements. The more general focus of conflict is in the area of the firm's change and growth, for technological adaptations seem more readily acceptable than administrative ones.[15] In this pattern, the son is given both authority and responsibility, but his mandate is to maintain the status quo. For the father, to continue the success of the firm is to follow in the same path; for the son, the same path in the future means failure. For the son, the family firm is a restraint as long as he is not free to build his own successful organization. He wants to do more than manage the family firm, but he is held back by respect for and obligation to his father. "I was offered a number of jobs," said one son, "but finally, after talking to my father, I decided that I couldn't abandon him and therefore I went into the family business."

In the first pattern, it appears to be the son who becomes the hanger-on in the management structure; in the second pattern it is the father who begins to get in the way of the son. For the son in the first pattern, the firm provides financial success, although the emotional relations may be difficult; whereas for the son in the second pattern the emotional problems are manageable, but the financial future worries him as long as he is not allowed to carry out expansion of the firm.

The fathers also differ in their personalities, in their family relations, and in their management goals and actions. In the extreme formulation of the first pattern, the father expresses the lone, aggressive, and invulnerable figure portrayed as the *macho*, the embodiment of masculinity, and summed up in the word power. [16] In the second pattern, however, the father is less tense

---

[15] This phenomenon has been given considerable attention in the past by anthropologists. It began with William F. Ogburn's notion of *cultural lag* in his book, *Social Change* (New York: Viking Press, 1922).

[16] Octavio Paz, *op. cit.*, p. 81.

and explosive; he is more willing to rely on his son as he begins to relax and withdraw. The first fears retirement and the second sees in it the fulfillment of his career. In the first pattern, the transfer of power will take the form of a contest in which, if the son rises to the struggle, leadership must be wrested away. In the second pattern, succession is a slow process of waiting out the natural change in generations.

The immigrant family is an important subcase of this second pattern, where the father in a family firm has migrated from another country, particularly to a different culture and one where he is of a minority group. The overriding value of such immigrant families is to "stick together," and family comes before business. Conflict is likely to arise when the second generation, which does not have the direct immigrant experience, begins to see the family enterprise as "just a business." Because of the insulation of the family, the son generally accepts the responsibility of taking over the firm, but begins to resist the restrictions involved in the transfer. He is less involved in the family experience. This pattern is especially characteristic of refugee families.[17]

Pattern Three: Branches of the Family

In addition to the conflict between father and son, conflict also occurs between various branches of a family. This third pattern may, therefore, be found in family firms where the first or second patterns are also present. The family branch groupings are highly correlated with the managerial division of labor, and are particularly related to the distinction between technical and administrative responsibilities. Where two brothers are involved, one will take charge of production while the other will concentrate on relations with the community. In time, and depending upon the closeness of the family and the size of the firm, these positions

[17] This runs somewhat counter to the interpretation offered by Strassmann that the immigrant father, as an outsider, has less to lose and is therefore more radical an innovator than his more assimilated son, who in turn becomes more conservative because of his greater stake in the existing social structure. Cf. *Continuity and Change, op. cit.*, pp. 164–166. See also, Louis Kriesberg, Entrepreneurs in Latin America and the Role of Cultural and Situational Processes, *International Social Science Journal*, 15 (1963). See also, Luis Bresser Pereira, Origenes Étnicas e Sociais do Empresário Paulista, *Revista de Administração de Empresas*, Vol. 2, No. 11 (1964), 83–106.

ENTREPRENEURIAL SUCCESSION   413

will be available for inheritance and succession among the younger generation. Each member of the founding generation is usually entitled to bring in at least one son to replace him in his position. If two brothers have started a business, with one having technical responsibilities and the other administrative responsibilities, then the succession of sons will parallel this distinction.

The closer the family relationship among the first generation, the less formal are the relations between family lines and organizational inheritance. When two brothers direct a firm, for example, the domain of one is still more open to his nephew than when two brothers-in-law or two cousins head a firm. Also, the smaller the firm, the less marked are these distinctions. Another variation in inheritance and succession is that the least educated and/or least ambitious of the sons more frequently assumes the technical responsibilities.

The division between in-plant (technical) and out-plant (administrative) management is important within the family firm, because of the prestige of the office within the enterprise. In Mexico, administrative personnel, at comparable levels, have more prestige than the technical personnel. The branch of the family in administration therefore has greater prestige; that is, the dominant family branch tends to go into administration rather than in the technical direction.

Although the distinction between technical and administrative roles is based upon the functional necessities of an organization, the separation of family groupings is not such a rational separation. The family firm, at least in its origins, is intimately linked to family values as well as business values. The connection between organizational roles and family groupings suffuses the requirements of the former with the values of the latter. Tension between two branches of a family, for example, may be reflected in the conflict between the technical and administrative tasks. Conversely, the different perspectives and requirements of the technical and administrative roles may cause dissension among family members. Conflict normally arising from differences between one set of roles is heightened by its confluence with the differentiation of roles from the other setting.

On the other hand, when neither the conflict between generations nor the conflict arising from family divisions along functional or nuclear lines is severe enough to destroy the family-firm bond, the overlapping of conflict may, in fact, prevent any one conflict from becoming so severe as to cause a complete rupture.[18] Ultimately, the decision must be made in each family firm between family relations and profit.

SUCCESSION AND THE FUTURE OF FAMILY FIRMS

At this point it is appropriate to ask what the patterns indicate about administrative change in industrial enterprises in developing economies. Because the traditional family firm is incompatible with rapid industrial advances, either the goals and organization of the family firm must change to meet the new industrial requirements,[19] or else the family firm will be superseded by the share-holding, executive-managed, corporate enterprise.[20]

To understand the direction of organizational development in a country, one must understand the typical family firm, the social relationships, and how these are affecting the development of the enterprise. Unless longitudinal studies are made of the same firm through time, it is difficult to make definitive statements about the future of an enterprise, but some hypotheses are possible.

The pattern characterized by the strong father and weak son seems likely to fail. The father is incapable of preparing anyone else to replace him, therefore the son is not apt to be prepared for the task of directing the enterprise. Although Harbison and Myers were not distinguishing between family patterns, they sum up this type, when they state:

The one-man ruler delegates too little, does too much himself, and thus has little time for effective organization building or for creative thinking. As a consequence, this type of management is likely to be defensive, enervated, and static. It breathes only at the top and when

[18] For an elaboration of this point, see Lewis Coser, *The Functions of Social Conflict* (New York: Free Press, 1956).

[19] Typical in Japan, and exemplified in Latin America by DiTella of Argentina, and until recently by Ford in the United States.

[20] The typical United States pattern. For recent and rapid changes in England toward the same pattern, see Anthony Sampson, *Anatomy of Britain Today* (London: Hodder and Stougton, 1965), pts. ii, iii.

the top disappears, the organization either collapses or must be completely rebuilt.[21]

The only question is the disposal of the firm, and two courses seem predictable. The weak son may attempt to direct the enterprise himself, in which case the enterprise is likely to fail; from Louis XIV to Louis XV within the family firm. The failure is predictable in the transition from the first to the second generation, but it is in the change from second to third generation that failure often occurs.[22]

The other alternative is public sale of the business. If the sale is made in time, the enterprise may be made profitable again. In the past three years since the field work was conducted, this has been a frequent solution. The buyer is often a foreign company, which retains the firm's original and already established name for advertising and public relations. Sometimes the buyer is a young native-born entrepreneur, who sees a financial opportunity in putting an ailing firm on its feet. A third possibility is that the government itself will take over the firm, which is especially likely to occur when the financial prospects are not very good, but the organization cannot be allowed to fail for social or political reasons. Each of these means the introduction of outside capital and management. Whether the business fails or grows, it will not remain within a traditional family form, and the distinction between managers and management will be instituted.

[21] Frederick Harbison and Charles Myers, *Management in the Industrial World* (New York: McGraw-Hill, 1959), p. 41.

[22] Observers report that the succession from second to third generation is the crisis period in the European family firm. Despite a few exceptions, most of the Mexican private enterprises are still owned and managed by the founding fathers, and the developing patterns of conflict, succession, and hence survival, with which we have dealt involve the change from first to second generation. It is therefore difficult to say which succession of generations is the more critical in the Mexican family firm. The change to third generation, however, is critical because of an overabundance of heirs. Unlike Europe, the Mexican birth rate, average family size, and extended family values create a critical proportion of sons and relatives pressing for privileged positions by the time of the first succession. And where crisis in the family firm is concentrated on how to maintain financial and managerial control, the patterns of succession have more relevance than the number of generations. This, of course, is conjectural until the succession to the third generation can be observed. See David Granick, *The European Executive* (New York: Doubleday, 1962), pp. 303–320.

In the pattern of conservative father and progressive son, the danger is that the son might get bored waiting. The father basically trusts his son and recognizes the need for transmitting authority to him; the son respects his father and does not push too hard. As the reins gradually change hands, so too does the entire character of the organization; the chances are good that such an enterprise can adapt to necessary change and still maintain the family trademark.

Such family firms can benefit from industrial growth and in turn contribute to it, to the extent that the transfer process gives the son an increasing freedom to institute expansion and change. If a family member is incapable of handling his job, then a school chum with the necessary training is brought in to replace him. If outside technical advice is required, then that too will be brought in. The firm will remain within the family, not because it resists outside influences, but because it incorporates them into its changing framework. In this second pattern, (as with the German family), "The good of the family enterprise is more likely to take precedence over the preferences of the individual family members."[23]

The future of the third pattern is related to the strength of conflict that develops between the various family factions and to the weight which expressive sentiments between relatives carry. The two are conversely related and have opposite effects on both the family and the firm. The deeper the internal strife, the more likely it is that one group will buy the other out and, in general, this will be advantageous for the firm.

Despite differences about how the family business should be operated, personal relations among relatives often take precedence over maximum profit. With this mixed pattern of social and business relationships, the firm can survive only as long as the market for its product is expanding more rapidly than its competitors can meet that demand. When family factions divide a firm, therefore, the change may be either in the direction of modernization within the family framework or into the nonfamily executive management enterprise. Bringing about entrepreneurial succession is essential for survival in a competitive market.

[23] Granick, *ibid.*, p. 313.

[27]

Harry Levinson

Conflicts that plague family businesses

Discord between father and son and other
rivalries among relatives can paralyze
the organization unless they are confronted

Foreword

The job of operating a family-owned company is often grievously complicated by friction arising from rivalries involving a father and his son, brothers, or other family members who hold positions in the business, or at least derive income from it. Unless the principals face up to their feelings of hostility, the author says, the business will suffer and may even die. He offers some advice on how relatives can learn to live with their peculiar situation. But he concludes that the only real solution is to move toward professional management.

Mr. Levinson is the Thomas Henry Carroll Ford Foundation Distinguished Visiting Professor of Business Administration, Harvard Business School, and is President of the Levinson Institute. He is the author of many previous HBR articles, including "On Being a Middle-Aged Manager" (July-August 1969) and "Management by Whose Objectives?" (July-August 1970). His latest books are *Executive Stress* (Harper & Row, Publishers, Inc., 1970) and *Organizational Diagnosis*, which is to be published next summer by the Harvard University Press.

In U.S. business, the most successful executives are often men who have built their own companies. Ironically, their very success frequently brings to them and members of their families personal problems of an intensity rarely encountered by professional managers. And these problems make family businesses possibly the most difficult to operate.[1]

It is obvious common sense that when managerial decisions are influenced by feelings about and responsibilities toward relatives in the business, when nepotism exerts a negative influence, and when a company is run more to honor a family tradition than for its own needs and purposes, there is likely to be trouble.

However, the problems of family businesses go considerably deeper than these issues. In this article I shall examine some of the more difficult underlying psychological elements in operating these businesses and suggest some ways of coping with them.

They start with the founder

The difficulties of the family business begin with the founder. Usually he is an entrepreneur for whom the business has at least three important meanings:

1. The entrepreneur characteristically has unresolved conflicts with his father, research evi-

[1.] For two thoughtful views of the subject, see Robert G. Donnelley, "The Family Business," HBR July-August 1964, p. 93; and Seymour Tilles, "Survival Strategies for Family Firms," *European Business*, April 1970, p. 9.

dence indicates. He is therefore uncomfortable when being supervised, and starts his own business both to outdo his father and to escape the authority and rivalry of more powerful figures.[2]

2. An entrepreneur's business is simultaneously his "baby" and his "mistress." Those who work with him and for him are characteristically his instruments in the process of shaping the organization.

If any among them aspires to be other than a device for the founder—that is, if he wants to acquire power himself—he is soon likely to find himself on the outside looking in. This is the reason why so many organizations decline when their founders age or die.

3. For the entrepreneur, the business is essentially an extension of himself, a medium for his personal gratification and achievement above all. And if he is concerned about what happens to his business after he passes on, that concern usually takes the form of thinking of the kind of monument he will leave behind.

The fundamental psychological conflict in family businesses is rivalry, compounded by feelings of guilt, when more than one family member is involved. The rivalry may be felt by the founder —even though no relatives are in the business— when he unconsciously senses (justifiably or not) that subordinates are threatening to remove him from his center of power. Consider this actual case:

☐ An entrepreneur, whose organization makes scientific equipment and bears his name, has built a sizable enterprise in international markets. He has said that he wants his company to be noted all over the world for contributing to society.

He has attracted many young men with the promise of rapid promotions, but he guarantees their failure by giving them assignments and then turning them loose without adequate organizational support. He intrudes into the young men's decision making, but he counterbalances this behavior with paternalistic devices. (His company has more benefits than any other I have known.)

This technique makes his subordinates angry at him for what he has done, then angry at themselves for being hostile to such a kind man. Ultimately, it makes them feel utterly inadequate. He can get people to take responsibility and move up into executive positions, but his behavior has made certain that he will never have a rival.

The conflicts created by rivalries among family members—between fathers and sons, among brothers, and between executives and other relatives—have a chronically abrasive effect on the principals. Those family members in the business must face up to the impact that these relationships exert and must learn to deal with them, not only for their own emotional health but for the welfare of the business.

I shall consider in turn the father-son rivalry, the brother-brother rivalry, and other family relationships.

Father-son rivalry

As I have indicated, for the founder the business is an instrument, an extension of himself. So he has great difficulty giving up his baby, his mistress, his instrument, his source of social power, or whatever else the business may mean to him. Characteristically, he has great difficulty delegating authority and he also refuses to retire despite repeated promises to do so.

This behavior has certain implications for father-son relationships. While he consciously wishes to pass his business on to his son and also wants him to attain his place in the sun, unconsciously the father feels that to yield the business would be to lose his masculinity.

At the same time, and also unconsciously, he needs to continue to demonstrate his own competence. That is, he must constantly reassure himself that he alone is competent to make "his" organization succeed. Unconsciously the father does not want his son to win, take away his combination baby and mistress, and displace him from his summit position.

These conflicting emotions cause the father to behave inexplicably in a contradictory manner, leading those close to him to think that while on the one hand he wants the business to succeed, on the other hand he is determined to make it fail.

The son's feelings of rivalry are a reflection of his father's. The son naturally seeks increasing responsibility commensurate with his growing maturity, and the freedom to act responsibly on his own. But he is frustrated by his father's intrusions, his broken promises of retirement, and his self-aggrandizement.

The son resents being kept in an infantile

2. See Orvis F. Collins, David G. Moore, and Darab B. Unwalla, *The Enterprising Man* (East Lansing, Michigan State University Bureau of Business Research, 1964).

Harvard Business Review: March-April 1971

role—always the little boy in his father's eyes—with the accompanying contempt, condescension, and lack of confidence that in such a situation frequently characterize the father's attitude. He resents, too, remaining dependent on his father for his income level and, as often, for

title, office, promotion, and the other usual perquisites of an executive. The father's erratic and unpredictable behavior in these matters makes this dependency more unpalatable.

I have observed a number of such men who, even as company presidents, are still being victimized by their fathers who remain chairmen of the board and chief executive officers.

Why don't you let me grow up?

Characteristically, fathers and sons, particularly the latter, are terribly torn by these conflicts; the father looks on the son as ungrateful and unappreciative, and the son feels both hostile to his father and guilty for his hostility.

The father bears the feeling that the son never will be man enough to run the business, but he tries to hide that feeling from his son. The son yearns for his chance to run it and waits impatiently but still loyally in the wings—often for years beyond the age when others in nonfamily organizations normally take executive responsibility—for his place on the stage.

If the pressures become so severe for him that he thinks of leaving, he feels disloyal but at the same time fears losing the opportunity that would be his if he could only wait a little longer. He defers his anticipated gratification and pleasure, but, with each postponement, his anger, disappointment, frustration, and tension mount. Here is a typical situation I know of:

☐ Matthew Anderson, a man who founded a reclaimed-metals business, has two sons. John, the elder, is his logical successor, but Anderson has given him little freedom to act independently, pointing out that, despite limited education, he (the father) has built the business and in-

tuitively knows more about how to make it successful.

Though he has told John that he wants him to be a partner, he treats John more like a flunky than an executive, let alone a successor. He pays the elder son a small salary, always with the excuse that he should not expect more because someday he will inherit the business. He grants minimal raises sporadically, never recognizing John's need to support his family in a style fitting his position in the company.

When John once protested and demanded both more responsibility and more income, his father gave Henry, the second son, a vice presidential title and a higher income. When Henry asked for greater freedom and responsibility, Anderson turned back to John and made him president (in name only). The father, as chairman of the board and chief executive officer, continued to second-guess John, excluded Henry from conferences (which of course increased John's feelings of guilt), and told John that Henry was "no good" and could not run the business.

Later, when John sought to develop new aspects of the business to avoid the fluctuations of the metals market, his father vetoed these ideas, saying, "This is what we know, and this is what we are going to do." He failed to see the possible destructive effects of market cycles on fixed overhead costs and the potential inroads of plastics and other cheaper materials on the reclaimed-metals business.

The upshot was that profits declined and the business became more vulnerable to both domestic and foreign (particularly Japanese) competition. When John argued with his father about this, he got the response: "What do you know? You're still green. I went through the Depression." Once again Anderson turned to Henry—making the black sheep white, and vice versa.

Angered, John decided to quite the business, but his mother said, "You can't leave your father; he needs you." Anderson accused him of being ungrateful, but he also offered to retire, as he had promised to do several times before.

Despite his pain, John could not free himself from his father. (Only an ingrate would desert his father, he told himself.) Also John knew that if he departed, he could not go into competition with his father, because that would destroy him. But John shrank from entering an unfamiliar business.

Nevertheless, from time to time John has explored other opportunities while remaining in the business. But each time his father has undercut him. For instance, John once wanted to borrow money for a venture, but Anderson told the bankers that his son was not responsible.

Now, when John is middle-aged, he and his father are still battling. In effect John is asking, "Why don't you let me grow up?" and his father is answering, "I'm the only man around here. You must stay here and be my boy."

'He's destroying the business'

The son also has intense rivalry feelings, of course. These, too, can result in fierce competition with his father and hostile rejection of him, or abject dependence on him. Sometimes the competition can lead to a manipulative alignment with the mother against him. Consider this actual case:

☐ Bill Margate, a recent business school graduate, knew that he would go into his father's electronic components business. But he decided that first he should get experience elsewhere, so he spent four years with a large manufacturing company. From his education and experience, he became aware of how unsophisticated his father was about running the business and set about showing the senior Margate how a business should be professionally managed.

Margate can do no right in Bill's eyes, at least not according to the books which he has read but which his father has never heard of. Bill frequently criticizes his father, showing him how ignorant he is. When Margate calls his son "green," Bill retorts, "I've forgotten more about managing a business than you'll ever know."

Bill's mother is also involved in the business; she has been at her husband's side for many years, though their relationship is less than the best. Mrs. Margate dotes on her son and complains to him about her husband, and she encourages Bill in his attacks on his father. When Bill undertook several ventures that floundered, she excused the failures as being caused by his father's interference.

But whenever the father-son battle reaches a peak, Mrs. Margate shifts allegiance and stands behind her husband. So the senior Margate has an ally when the chips are down, at the price of a constant beating until he gets to that point.

The struggle for the business has remained a stand-off. But as the elder Margate has grown older, his son's attacks have begun to tell on him. Bill has urged him to take long Florida vacations, but Margate refuses because he fears what would happen when his back is turned. For the same reason, he does not permit Bill to sign checks for the company.

Now Margate has become senile, and Bill's criticism of him continues, even in public. "He's destroying the business," Bill will say.

However, Bill cannot act appropriately to remove his father (even though he is now incompetent) because of his guilt feelings about his incessant attacks. That would destroy his father, literally, and he cannot bring himself to do it.

'The old man really built it'

The problem for the son becomes especially acute when and if he does take over. Often the father has become obsolete in his managerial conceptions. The organization may have grown beyond one man's capacity to control it effectively. That man may have been a star whose imagination, creativity, or drive are almost impossible to duplicate. He may also have been a charismatic figure with whom employees and even the public identified.

Whatever the combination of factors, the son is likely to have to take over an organization with many weaknesses hidden behind the powerful facade of the departed leader. For these reasons many businesses, at the end of their founders' tenure, fall apart, are pirated, or are merged into another organization.

The Ford Motor Company, at the demise of Henry Ford, was a case in point; a completely new management had to be brought in. Henry Ford II was faced with the uncomfortable task of having to regenerate a company that appeared to have the potential for continued success, but which, according to some, could easily have gone bankrupt.

While the son is acting to repair the organizational weaknesses left by his father, he is subject to the criticism of those persons who, envious of his position, are waiting for him to stumble. They "know" that he is not as good as his father. If he does less well than his father, regardless of whether there are unfavorable economic conditions or other causes, he is subject to the charge of having thrown away an opportunity that others could have capitalized on.

The scion cannot win. If he takes over a successful enterprise, and even if he makes it much more successful than anyone could have imagined, nevertheless the onlookers stimulate his feelings of inadequacy. They say, "What did you expect? After all, look what he started with." To illustrate:

Harvard Business Review: March-April 1971

☐ Tom Schlesinger, the president of a restaurant chain, inherited the business after his father had built a profitable regional network of outlets with a widely known name—a model for the industry.

Tom has expanded it into nearly a national operation. He has done this with astute methods of finance that allow great flexibility, and with effective control methods that maintain meal quality and at the same time minimize waste. By any standards he has made an important contribution to the business.

But those who remember his father cannot see what Tom has done because the aura of his father still remains. They tend to minimize Tom's contribution with such observations as, "Well, you know, the old man really built that business."

Tom cannot change the attitude of those who knew his father, and he feels it is important to keep lauding his father's accomplishments in order to present a solid family image to employees, customers, and the community. But he is frustrated because he has no way of getting the world to see how well he has done.

Brother-brother rivalry

The father-son rivalry is matched in intensity by the brother-brother rivalry. Their competition may be exacerbated by the father if he tries to play the sons off against each other or has decided that one should wear his mantle, as I showed previously. (In my experience, the greatest difficulties of this kind occur when there are only two brothers in the organization.)

The problem is further complicated if their mother and their wives are also directly or indirectly involved in the business. Mothers have their favorites—regardless of what they say—and each wife, of course, has a stake in her husband's position. He can become a foil for his wife's fantasies and ambition.

The rivalry between brothers for their father's

approval, which began in childhood, continues into adult life. It can reach such an intensity that it colors every management decision and magnifies the jockeying for power that goes on in all organizations. Consider this situation:

☐ Arthur, five years older than his sibling, is president, and Warren is an operating vice president, of the medium-sized retailing organization which they inherited. To anyone who cares to listen, each maintains that he can get along very well without the other.

Arthur insists that Warren is not smart, not as good a businessman as he; that his judgment is bad; and that even if given the chance, he would be unable to manage the business.

Warren asserts that when the two were growing up, Arthur considered him to be a competitor, but for his part, he (Warren) did not care to compete because he was younger and smaller. Warren says that he cannot understand why his older brother has always acted as if they were rivals, and adds, "I just want a chance to do my thing. If he'd only let me alone with responsibility! But he acts as if the world would fall apart if I had that chance."

Every staff meeting and meeting of the board (which includes nonfamily members) becomes a battle between the brothers. Associates, employees, and friends back off because they decline to take sides. The operation of the organization has been turned into a continuous family conflict.

The elder . . .

Ordinarily, the elder brother succeeds his father. But this custom reaffirms the belief of the younger brother (or brothers) that the oldest is indeed the favorite. In any event, the older brother often has a condescending attitude toward the younger. In their earliest years the older is larger, physically stronger, more competent, and more knowledgeable than the younger merely because of the difference in age, as in the case I just cited.

Only in rare instances does the younger broth-

er have the opportunity to match the skills, competence, and experience of the elder until they reach adulthood. By that time the nature of this relationship is so well established that the older brother has difficulty regarding the younger one as adequate and competent.

Moreover, the eldest child is earlier and longer in contact with the parents, and their control efforts fall more heavily on him. Consequently, older children tend to develop stronger consciences, drive themselves harder, expect more of themselves, and control themselves more rigidly than younger ones. Being already, therefore, a harsh judge of himself, the eldest is likely to be an even harsher judge of his younger siblings.

. . . and the younger

The younger brother attempts to compensate for the effects of this childhood relationship and his older brother's efforts to control him by trying to carve out a place in the business that is his own. This he guards with great zeal, keeping the older brother out so he can demonstrate to himself, his brother, and others that he is indeed competent and has his own piece of the action for which he is independently responsible.

If the brothers own equal shares in the organization and both are members of the board, as is frequently the case, the problems are compounded. On the board they can argue policy from equally strong positions. However, when they return to operations in which one is subordinate to the other, the subordinate one, usually the junior brother, finds it extremely difficult to think of himself in a subservient role.

The younger one usually is unable to surmount this problem in their mutual relationship. He tends to be less confident than his brother and considers himself to be at a permanent disadvantage, always overcontrolled, always unheeded. Since the older brother views the younger one as being less able, he becomes involved in self-fulfilling prophecies. Distrusting his younger brother, he is likely to overcontrol him, give him less opportunity for freedom and responsibility—which in turn make for maturity and growth—and likely to reject all signs of the younger brother's increasing competence.

If for some reason the younger brother displaces the older one, and particularly if the latter becomes subordinate to him, the younger brother is faced with feelings of guilt for having attacked the elder and usurped what so often is accepted as the senior brother's rightful role.

Intrafamily friction

The problems of the father and brothers extend to other relatives when they, too, become involved in the business. In some families it is expected that all who wish to join the company will have places there. This can have devastating effects, particularly if the jobs are sinecures.

The chief executive of a family business naturally feels a heavy responsibility for the family fortunes. If he does not produce a profit, the effect on what he considers to be his image in the financial markets may mean less to him than the income reduction which members of his family will suffer. So he is vulnerable to backbiting from persons whom he knows only too well and whom he cannot dismiss as faceless. Consider this case:

☐ Three brothers started a knitting business. Only one of the brothers had sons, and only one of the those sons stayed in the business; he eventually became president. The stock is held by the family. Two widowed aunts, his mother, his female cousins (one of whom was already widowed), and his brother, a practicing architect, depend on the business for significant income.

When business is off, the women complain. If the president wants to buy more equipment, they resist. If they hear complaints from employees or merchant friends, they make these complaints known at family gatherings. The president is never free from the vixens who are constantly criticizing and second-guessing him.

Perhaps more critical for the health of the business are the factional divisions that spring up in the organization as associates and subordinates choose the family members with whom they want to be identified. (Often, however, those who take sides discover that in a crisis the family unites against "outsiders," including their partisans, who are then viewed as trying to divide the family.)

If the nonfamily employees or board members decide not to become involved in a family fight and withdraw from relations with its members until the conflict is resolved, the work of the organization may be paralyzed. Worse yet, the dispute may eventually embroil the entire organization, resulting in conflicts at the

Harvard Business Review: March-April 1971

lowest levels, as employees try to cope with the quarrels thrust on them.

Now the business has become a battleground that produces casualties but no peace. Such internecine warfare constitutes a tremendous barrier to communication and frustrates adequate planning and rational decision making.

A business in which numerous members of the family of varying ages and relationships are involved often becomes painfully disrupted around issues of empires and succession. Its units tend to become family-member territories and therefore poorly integrated organizationally, if at all.

As for succession, the dominant or patriarchal leader may fully expect to pass on the mantle of leadership to other, elder relatives in their turn. He may even promise them leadership roles, particularly if he has had to develop a coalition to support his position.

But for both realistic and irrational reasons he may well come to feel that none of the family members is capable of filling the role. He cannot very well disclose his decision, however, without stirring conflict, and he cannot bring in outside managers without betraying his relatives or reneging on his promises. On the other hand, he fears what would happen if he died without having designated a successor.

He may decide that the only way out is to sell the business (at least each relative will then get his fair share). But that solution is costly—it signifies not only the loss of the business as a means of employment, but also the betrayal of a tradition and, inevitably, the dissolution of close family ties that have been maintained through the medium of the business.

Facing up to it

What can be done about these problems?

Most entrepreneurial fathers seem unable to resolve their dilemma themselves. They tend to be rigid and righteous, finding it difficult to understand that there is another, equally valid point of view which they can accept without becoming weaklings. Well-meaning outsiders who try to help the father see the effects of his behavior and think seriously about succession usually find themselves rejected. Then they lose whatever beneficial influence they may have had on him.

Several approaches have worked well. In some instances, sons have told their fathers that they recognize how important it is to the father to run his own business, but it is just as important for them to have the opportunity to "do their own thing." They then establish small new ventures either under the corporate umbrella or outside it, without deserting their father.

In a variant of this approach, a father who heads a retail operation opened a store in a different community for each of his sons. They do their buying together, with appropriate variations for each community, and maintain a common name and format, but each son runs his own operation while the father continues to run his.

In still another situation, the father merged his company into a larger one. Each of his two sons then became president of a subsidiary, and the father started a new venture while serving as a policy guide to his sons.

The son's role

Whether such alternatives can work depends in part on how the son conducts himself. He must be honest with himself and consider his paternal relationship candidly. He must take steps like these:

□ He must ask himself why he chose to go into the family business. Most sons will say it is because of the opportunity and the feelings of guilt if they had not done so. Often, however, the basic reason is that a powerful father has helped make his son dependent on him, and so his son is reluctant to strike out on his own.

He rationalizes his reluctance on the basis of opportunity and guilt. Struggling with his own dependency, he is more likely to continue to fight his father in the business because he is still trying to escape his father's control.

□ Having examined this issue, and recognizing whatever validity it may have for him, the son must realize how often his own feelings of rivalry and anger get in his way. The more intense the rivalry, the more determinedly he seeks to push his father from his throne and the more aggressively the latter must defend himself. The son must therefore refrain from attack.

□ He must quietly and with dignity, as a mature man, apprise his father of the realities—that he needs an area of freedom and an independent medium to develop skills and responsibilities. He can do so within the company framework or, if that is not feasible, outside it. In his own self-interest, as well as the company's, he must be certain that he gets the opportunity.

□ He must not allow himself to be played off against his brother, and he must not allow his guilt to be manipulated. By the same token, he himself must not become involved with others in manipulation.

□ He must honestly recognize and respect his father's achievement and competence. To build a business is no mean task, and usually the father still has useful skills and knowledge. Furthermore, the son should recognize the powerful psychological meaning of the business to his father and not expect him to be rational about his relationship to it.

If the son is still unable to make choices about what he wants to do, then, despite his pain and his father's reluctance to seek help, he himself must do so. Only he can take the initiative to relieve his anguish. Here is an example of how a group of sons has taken the initiative:

In Boston, a group calling itself son's (Sons of the Boss) has been formed to encourage men in that position to talk over common problems and share solutions. After educating themselves about the psychological dimensions of their situation, the group will make it a practice from time to time to invite their fathers as a group to discuss their problems openly. Then fathers and sons will get together separately.

This procedure may enable fathers and sons to realize that their particular problems are not unique to themselves, and to obtain support from those in a similar predicament.

Another approach for a son would be to ask his father to read this article and then discuss it privately with a neutral third party of their choice, to develop a perspective on their feelings and behavior. Having done so, a father is then in a better position to talk with his son, in the presence of the third party.

The third person must use his good offices to subdue recrimination. At the same time he must foster the father's expression of his fears over losing control, being unneeded, and suffering rejection, as well as the son's concerns about being overcontrolled, infantilized, and exploited.

If meeting with the third party fails to help, the next step is consultation with a psychologist or psychiatrist. There are rare instances, usually when conflict becomes severe, in which father and son are willing to go to a professional together or separately. In such cases it is often possible for the father to begin to make compromises, learn to understand his and his son's motivations, and work out with him newly defined, more compatible roles. Usually, however, such an effort requires continued supportive work by the professional and strong desire on the part of both men to resolve their differences.

If all these measures fail, those who work with patriarchs must learn to tolerate their situation until the opportunity arises for a change.

Fraternal spirit

With respect to the brother-brother conflict, it is important for brothers to see that in their relationship they recapitulate ancient rivalries, and to perceive clearly the psychological posture each assumes toward the other. Once they understand these two issues, they must talk together about them. They should try to discuss freely the fears, worries, anger, and disappointments caused by each other. They should also be able to talk about their affection for each other.

Since there is love and hate in all relationships, theirs cannot, by definition, be pure. They should not feel guilty about their anger with each other, but they do need to talk it out. Having done that, they then must consider how they can divide the tasks in the organization so that each will have a chance to acquire and demonstrate competence and work in a complementary relationship with the other.

A brother cannot easily be subordinate at one level and equal on another. If a brother is an operating executive subordinate to the other, he gets into difficulty when he tries to be an equal on the board of directors. If more than one brother is on the board, then only one, as a rule, should be an operating executive. Of course, such rules are unnecessary if the brothers work well together.

If the brothers still cannot resolve their conflicts, then it becomes necessary to seek professional aid. If that does not help, they should consider being in separate organizations. In such a case, the big problem is the guilt feelings which the departing brother is likely to have for deserting the other and the family business.

Toward professional management

Where there are multiple and complex family relationships and obligations in a company, and particularly problems about succession, the best

Harvard Business Review: March-April 1971

solution is a transcendent one. The family members should form a trust, taking all the relatives out of business operations while enabling them to continue to act in concert as a family.

The trust could allot financial support to every member who desires it to develop new business ventures on behalf of the family, thus providing a business interest that replaces the previous operating activity. This also helps maintain family cohesion and preserve the family's leadership role in the community.

In general, the wisest course for any business, family or nonfamily, is to move to professional management as quickly as possible. Every business must define its overriding purpose for being, from which it derives its objectives. Within this planning framework, the business must have a system for appraising the degree to which it and its components are achieving the goals that have been set.

All organizations need to rear subordinates in a systematic manner, thus creating the basic condition for their own regeneration. I know of no family business capable of sustaining regeneration over the long term solely through the medium of its own family members.

Where there is conflict, or inadequately rationalized territories, members of the family should move up and out of operations as quickly as possible into policy positions. Such movement recognizes the reality of ownership but does not confuse ownership with management.

It also opens the opportunity for professionally trained managers to succeed to major operating roles, instead of having to go to other organizations as soon as they are ready for major responsibility. The more competitive the business situation, the more imperative such a succession pattern is.

More than others, the family members need to have their own outside activities from which they can derive gratification equal to what they can obtain in the company. Otherwise they will be unable to let go and will continue to be barriers to others. Moreover, they will make it

difficult to recruit and develop young persons with leadership potential who, as they mature, will see the inevitable barriers.

A number of family businesses have handled these issues wisely and have become highly professional in their management. The Dayton-Hudson Corporation and E.I. du Pont de Nemours are examples. Family members in both organizations must compete for advancement on the same terms as nonfamily managers. This practice is reinforced, at least at Dayton-Hudson, by a thorough performance appraisal system which includes appraisal of the chairman and president by a committee of the board.

Concluding note

It is very difficult to cope with the problems of the family business. That does not mean, however, that one should merely endure them. There is no point in stewing in anger and guilt, since chronic irritation is only self-flagellation. It solves no problems; it only increases anger and hostility and paves the way for explosion, recrimination, and impaired relations.

The family member can do something about such problems, as he can with any other. If reasonable steps to solve the problems do not work and he continues to feel bound to the organization, his problem is largely psychological. To free himself to make choices about what he wants to do, he must talk his feelings out with his rival in the organization, which is best done in the presence of a neutral third person. Sometimes professional help is necessary.

This will reduce sufficiently the intensity of the emotions generated by the problem, so that he can see possible alternatives more clearly and make choices more freely. That is better than the years of agitation that usually accompany such problems, unless of course the rival needs to expiate his guilt by continuing to punish himself. In that case, it is his problem and not necessarily that of the family business.

You love the daylight: do you think your father does not?

Euripides, 485-406 B.C.
Alcestis

[28]

Transferring power in the family business

*For the company to grow
it is essential to remove the reins
from the old man's hands*

*Louis B. Barnes and
Simon A. Hershon*

Should a family business stay in the family? The question is really academic, since families appear to be in business to stay. But, when the management moves from one generation to the next, the transition is often far from orderly. In addition, as the company develops, there is a need for a management style that goes beyond survival thinking, and entrepreneurs tend not to be reorganizers. In fact, while a sometimes bitter power struggle is peaking, the fortunes of the company may be sliding downhill. In other cases, power struggles are part of a healthy transition. According to these authors, family and company transitions will be more productive when they are simultaneous. The eternal problem involves the older generation's making use of the flexibility and new ideas of the succeeding generation. Third party involvement may help to prevent irreparable family rifts and company stagnation. Dialogues between all the parties—family

managers, relatives, employees, and outsiders—can also help.

Louis B. Barnes will be familiar to readers of HBR as coauthor of "Putting Judgment Back into Decisions," March-April 1970, and "Power Networks in the Appraisal Process," May-June 1971. He is professor of business administration at Harvard Business School, and is at present on leave as president and professor, Iran Center for Management Studies, Tehran. Simon A. Hershon is currently on active duty with the United States Navy. His fieldwork at Harvard Business School provided much of the material for this article.

One of the most agonizing experiences that any business faces is the moving from one generation of top management to the next. The problem is often most acute in family businesses, where the original entrepreneur hangs on as he watches others try to help manage or take over his business, while at the same time, his heirs feel overshadowed and frustrated. Paralleling the stages of family power are stages of company growth or of stagnation, and the smoothness with which one kind of transition is made often has a direct effect on the success of the other.

Sons or subordinates of first generation entrepreneurs tell of patient and impatient waiting in the wings for their time to take over the running of the company. When the time comes, it usually comes because the "old man" has died or is too ill to actively take part in management, even though still holding tightly to the reins of the family business. Often this means years of tension and conflict as older and younger generations pretend to coexist in top management.

As one second generation manager put it, speaking of these problems: "Fortunately, my father died one year after I joined the firm." Concerning another company, a prospective buyer said: "The old man is running the company downhill so fast that we'll pick it up for nothing before the kids can build it back up."

The transition problem affects both family and non-family members. Brokers and bankers, professional

Authors' note: The authors gratefully acknowledge the help and sponsorship they received from the Smaller Company Management Programs at the Harvard Business School

managers, employees, competitors, outside directors, wives, friends, and potential stock investors all have more than passing interest as a company moves from one generation to the next. Some of these transitions seem orderly. Most, however, do not. Management becomes racked with strife and indecision. Sons, heirs, key employees, and directors resign in protest. Families are torn with conflict. The president-father is deposed. Buyers who want to merge with or acquire the business change their minds. And often the company dies or becomes stagnant.

The frequency of such accounts and the pain reflected in describing the transfer of power from one generation to the next led us to begin a more formal research inquiry into what happens as a family business, or more accurately, a family *and* its business grow and develop over generations. Specifically, what happens in the family and company between those periods when one generation or another is clearly in control but both are "around"? In addition, how do some managements go through or hurdle the family transition without impeding company growth? And can or must family and company transitions be kept separate?

The research project on these questions began in June 1974 and is still continuing. It has included interviews with over 200 men and women and multiple interviews in over 35 companies, not all of which went beyond the first crucial transition test. This article contains some of the initial findings and conclusions.

Professional or family management?

Some observers and commentators on family business believe that the sooner the family management is replaced by professional management in growing companies, the better. The problems just described can lead to disruption or destruction of either the family or the business, sometimes both, in the long run. Furthermore, the argument goes, an objective, professional management will focus on what is good for the business and its growth without getting lost in the emotions and confusions of family politics.

This rational argument for professional management in growing companies has many strong ad-

vocates. It has even been suggested that the family members should form a trust, taking all the relatives out of business operations, thus enabling them to act in concert as a family.[1]

Like any argument for objectivity, the plea for professionalism has logic on its side. It makes good business sense, and in a way, good family sense as well. It guides a business away from mixing personal lives with business practices, and it helps to avoid the evils of nepotism and weak family successors who appear so often to cause transition crises.

Historically, the main problem with this rational argument is that most companies lean more heavily on family and personal psychology than they do on such business logic. The evidence is overwhelming. There are more than one million businesses in the United States. Of these, about 980,000 are family dominated, including many of the largest. Yet most of us have the opposite impression. We tend to believe that, after a generation or so, family businesses fade into widely held public companies managed by outside managers with professional backgrounds. The myth comes partly from a landmark study of big business by Adolph Perle and Gardner Means, who maintained that ownership of major U.S. companies was becoming widely diffused and that operating control was passing into the hands of professional managers who owned only a small fraction of their corporation's stock. This widely publicized "fact" was further used by John Kenneth Galbraith to build a concept which he called the "technostructure" of industry, based in large part on the alleged separation of corporate ownership from management control.[2]

There is evidence to the contrary, though. A study reported in *Fortune* by Robert Sheehan examined the 500 largest corporations on this question. Sheehan reported that family ownership and control in the largest companies was still significant and that in about 150 companies controlling ownership rested in the hands of an individual or of the members of a single family. Significantly, these owners were not just the remnants of the nineteenth century dynasties that once ruled American business. Many of them were relatively fresh faces.[3]

The myth is even more severely challenged in a study of 450 large companies done by Philip Burch and published in 1972. By his calculations, over 42% of the largest *publicly* held corporations are controlled by one person or a family, and another 17%

are placed in the "possible family control" category. Then there is one other major category of large "privately" owned companies—companies with fewer than 500 shareholders, which are not required to disclose their financial figures. Some well-known corporate names are included in this category: Cargill, Bechtel Corporation, Hearst Corporation, Hallmark Cards, and Hughes Aircraft, among others. Burch notes that contrary to what one might expect, the rather pervasive family control exercised is, for the most part, very direct and enduring. It is exercised through significant stock ownership and outside representation on the board of directors, and also, in many cases, through a considerable amount of actual family management.[4]

When one thinks more closely about families in big as well as small businesses, some well-known succession examples also come to mind, suggesting that family transition and corporate growth occur together even though there may be strain in the process. For example:

□

H. J. Heinz was founded by Henry J. Heinz to bottle and sell horseradish, and today H.J. Heinz II, a grandson, heads the billion dollar concern.

□

Triangle Publications owns the *Morning Telegraph*, *TV Guide*, and *Seventeen*. It was founded by Moses Annenberg. He was succeeded by his son, Walter, and a daughter, Enid, is now editor-in-chief of *Seventeen*.

□

The Bechtel Corporation was begun by Warren A. Bechtel, for building railroads. His son, Steve Sr., directed the firm into construction of pipelines and nuclear power plants. Today, Steve Jr. heads the $2 billion company, which is now further diversified.

□

Kaiser Industries, built by Henry J. Kaiser, includes Kaiser Steel, Kaiser Aluminum and Chemical, Kaiser Cement and Gypsum, Kaiser Broadcasting, Kaiser Engineering, and Kaiser Resources. The present industrial giant is headed by Henry's son, Edgar, now over 65 years old. An obvious successor is Edgar Jr., president of Kaiser Resources Ltd.

1. Harry Levinson, "Conflicts That Plague the Family Business," HBR March-April 1971, p. 90.

2. Adolph A. Berle and Gardner C. Means, *The Modern Corporation and Private Property* (New York: Harcourt, Brace & World, 1968) and John Kenneth Galbraith, *The New Industrial State* (Boston: Houghton Mifflin, 1971.)

3. Robert Sheehan, "Proprietors in the World of Big Business," *Fortune*, June 1967, p. 178.

4. Philip H. Burch, Jr., *The Managerial Revolution Reassessed* (Lexington, Mass.: D.C. Heath, 1972.)

Should a family business stay in the family? The question now seems almost academic. It is apparent that families *do* stay in their businesses, and the businesses stay in the family. Thus there is something more deeply rooted in transfers of power than impersonal business interests. The human tradition of passing on heritage, possessions, and name from one generation to the next leads both parents and children to seek continuity in the family business. In this light, the question whether a business should stay in the family seems less important, we suspect, than learning more about how these businesses and their family owners make the transition from one generation to the next.

Inside and outside perspectives

What are the implications when the transition from one generation to the next includes both business and family change, and what are the consequences also if business and family, though separate, remain tied together in plans, arguments, and emotions? In considering these questions, it might help to examine two perspectives in addition to age difference. One is the family, the other is the business, point of view. Both of these can be viewed from either the inside or the outside.

Exhibit I shows these four different vantage points from which to observe family and business members. One viewpoint is that of the "family managers" (inside the family and inside the business) as seen by both old and young generations. When they forget or ignore the other three perspectives, they can easily get boxed into their own concerns. This kind of compulsion includes hanging onto power for the older generation and getting hold of it for the younger. To both generations, it implies the selection, inclusion, and perpetuation of family managers.

A second perspective comes from "the employees," again older and younger, who work inside the business but who are outside the family. Understandably, they face different pressures and concerns from those of the family managers, even though many are treated as part of the larger corporate family. The older employees want rewards for loyalty, sharing of equity, and security, and they want to please the boss. Younger employees

Exhibit I
Pressures and interests in a family business

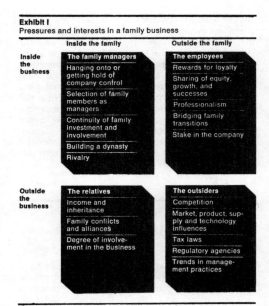

	Inside the family	Outside the family
Inside the business	**The family managers** Hanging onto or getting hold of company control Selection of family members as managers Continuity of family investment and involvement Building a dynasty Rivalry	**The employees** Rewards for loyalty Sharing of equity, growth, and successes Professionalism Bridging family transitions Stake in the company
Outside the business	**The relatives** Income and inheritance Family conflicts and alliances Degree of involvement in the business	**The outsiders** Competition Market, product, supply and technology influences Tax laws Regulatory agencies Trends in management practices

generally want professionalism, opportunities for growth, equity, and reasons for staying. Both age groups worry about bridging the family transition.

A third perspective comes from "the relatives," those family members who are not in the active management of the business. The older relatives worry about income, family conflicts, dividend policies, and a place in the business for their own children. The younger, often disillusioned brothers and cousins feel varying degrees of pressure to join the business. Both generations may be interested, interfering, involved, and sometimes helpful, as we shall see later on.

Finally, the fourth perspective comes from "the outsiders." These are persons who are competitors, R & D interests, creditors, customers, government regulators, vendors, consultants, and others who are connected to the business and its practices from the outside. They have various private interests in the company which range from constructive to destructive in intention and effect.

A curious irony is that the more "outside" the family the perspective is, as shown in *Exhibit I*, the more legitimate it seems as a "real" management

problem. Yet the concerns in the left column boxes are typically just as important as, and more time consuming than, the outside-the-family problems on the right. These inside-the-family problems tend to be ignored in management books, consultant's reports, and business school courses. Ignoring these realities can be disastrous for both the family and the company.

Our studies show that the transfer of power from first to second generation rarely takes place while the founder is alive and on the scene. What occurs instead during this time is a transition period of great difficulty for both older and younger generations. For the founder, giving up the company is like signing his own death warrant. For the son or successor, the strain may be comparable. As one of these said:

"I drew up the acquisition papers to buy my father out, because for a long time he has been saying he did not care about the business anymore. However, when it was all taken care of, and we presented him with the papers, he started to renege. Everything was done the way he would like it. Yet he would not sign. He finally told me he did not think he could do it. He felt it awfully hard to actually lose the company. He said he felt he still had something to give."

And another commented:

"I can't change things as fast as I would like to. It is absolutely clear to me that things need to be changed. However, it is not easy. First of all there is the function of age and experience as well as being the boss's son. Every other officer in the company is in his fifties. What I am talking about now are deep sources of dissatisfaction. I would like more ownership. Now I have only 7%, my father has 80% and my family another 13%. In my position, I just cannot move the company fast enough. We argue a lot, but nothing seems to change. I have set a goal for myself. If I cannot run the company within two years, I am leaving. I'll do something else."

5. George Strauss, "Adolescence in Organization Growth: Problems, Pains, Possibilities," *Organizational Dynamics*, Spring 1974, p. 3; Robert B. Buchele, *Business Policy in Growing Firms* (San Francisco: Chandler Publishing Co., 1965); Theodore Cohn and Roy A. Lindberg, *Survival and Growth: Management Strategies for the Small Firm* (New York: AMACOM, 1974); Lawrence L. Steinmetz, "Critical Stages of Small Business Growth," *Business Horizons*, February 1969, p. 29; Bruce L. Scott, "Stages of Corporate Development—Part 1," Harvard Business School Note 9-371-294, BP 798.

6. Larry E. Greiner, "Evolution and Revolution as Organizations Grow," HBR July-August 1972, p. 37.

The company transition

While family managers feel the multiple strains as the generations overlap during periods of transition, another related process is occurring as the company grows and develops. Various authors have tried to describe this process.[5] But, where one describes a smooth procedural development, another sees a series of difficult crises. For some, a series of growth stages is important. For others, it is the merging of functions with processes that count. Most writers do not tie business growth or decline to family transitions. However, the following points stand out for us in relation to company transitions.

1
Organizational growth tends to be nonlinear. Organizations grow in discrete stages, with varying growth rates in each stage.
2
Periods of profound organizational development often occur *between* periods of growth. These slower periods often are viewed with alarm, but they force managers to examine what the company has grown toward or into. These periods of development are the transition periods which appear less dramatic (i.e., there is less growth) but may be most crucial to a company's preparations for its own future.[6] The apparent floundering can provoke useful learning once management begins to adopt and encourage new practices and procedures.
3
A typical management response to transitional strains is a total or partial reorganization of the company. This sometimes helps shake up old habits but rarely resolves a transition crisis. What is needed is time for the social and political systems of the company to realign themselves into new norms and relationships.

Exhibit II shows how a later growth stage differs from and builds on the earlier ones. The first stage is characteristic of an entrepreneurial company with direct management. The second is typified by a rapidly growing product line and market situation with second-level management set up in specialized functions. The third stage has divisional operations with a diverse line of products and markets. Whereas the management style of the first stage is highly personal and direct, the second tends to become the more collaborative style of a boss and special-

Exhibit II
Characteristics of company growth

Organizational characteristic	Patterns of the first stage	Patterns of the second stage	Patterns of the third stage
Core problem	Survival	Management of growth	Managerial control and allocation of resources
Central function	Fusion of diverse talents and purposes into a unified company	Fission of general authority into specialized functions	Fusion of independent units into an Inter-dependent union of companies
Control systems	Personal (inside); survival in marketplace (outside)	Cost centers and policy formulation (inside); growth potential (outside)	Profit centers and abstract performance criteria (inside); capital expansion potential (outside)
Reward and motivation	Ownership, membership in the family	Salary, opportunities and problems of growth	Salary, performance bonus, stock options, peer prestige
Management style	Individualistic; direct management	Integrating specialists; collaborative management	Integrating generalists; collective management
Organization:			
Structure	Informal	Functional specialists	Division organizations
CEO's primary task	Direct supervision of employees	Managing specialized managers	Managing generalist managers
Levels of management	Two	At least three	At least four

ized peers. The third stage typically involves a looser, impersonal, collective style, with the chief executive managing generalists as well as functional specialists. Under the patterns of the first stage, the core problem for a small company is survival. The patterns of the roughly defined second stage show a size and scope requiring such specialized functions as finance, production, marketing, and engineering.

As the company's size continues to increase, it is likely to evolve toward third-stage patterns of growth: At this point, different product lines become separate companies or divisions, while, in multinational firms, the separation may also be on an area basis (e.g., Europe, North America, Latin America, Middle East, Far East) as well.

In between the box-like stages of growth shown in *Exhibit II* appear the transition phases which help to prepare an organization for its next stage. To cross the broken lines separating one growth stage from another in *Exhibit II* requires time, new interaction patterns, and an awkward period of overlap.

In effect, the broken vertical lines of *Exhibit II* represent widened time zones of varying and irregular width.

As we have seen, family transitions and company transitions can occur separately and at different times. However, we found that they usually occur together. As a company moves from the problem of survival to one of managing rapid growth, it must develop new control, motivation, and reward systems. It also requires a management style that can integrate specialists and their functions. This development cannot occur without a top management that wants to take the extra step beyond survival thinking. That is where an eager younger generation comes in. He, she, or they are more likely to want to go beyond traditional practices. This pent-up energy seemed to be a major factor in getting beyond company transitions in 27 out of 32 businesses we studied where the company had gone beyond the first growth stage.

Another kind of transition occurs between the second and the third growth stages. Company and division units in stage three had general managers in both the head office and the decentralized units who had learned to work with both other general managers and functional specialists. This meant that they had to have or develop a sense of the complex interdependence that characterizes most major companies today.

These dual transitions seemed best catalyzed when the old management forces somehow helped to pave the way for the new. The following case is a good example:[7]

□

When Max Krisch came to America in 1851, he brought an expertise in baking and an old family recipe for bread. Soon after settling, he established a small bakery. The business grew, and Max got help from his three sons as soon as they were old enough to operate the ovens after school and on weekends. When Martin, the oldest, graduated from college in 1890, he joined the business and soon started suggesting changes which he was convinced were good for the company's growth. His father refused, and the two men would often end up in disagreement. Sometimes the arguments were long and bitter.

Eventually, Max's wife abandoned her role of neutrality and intervened on Martin's behalf. She begged Max to give Martin a chance to implement

his ideas. Reluctantly, Max agreed and let Martin take the first step.

Martin's idea was to sell bread to milk peddlers who would offer it for sale to their milk customers. It was a new concept at the time, and it worked. The demand for Krisch's Bread increased sharply.

At this time, too, the second brother, Peter, was ready to join the company. Martin realized that the company's production capability would soon be unable to keep up with the increasing sales. He hoped that Peter could take over, modernize, and expand production, but again Max reacted strongly. He argued that the baking of Krisch's Bread could not be done in volume without ruining the quality. Martin and Peter eventually promised their father that if the new methods harmed the bread's quality they would discontinue them. Over time, Max again agreed to go along with the change, and Peter worked closely with his father to increase production while still maintaining quality. Again, too, the mother was behind the scenes trying to keep peace in the family.

When the third brother, Kurt, joined the firm, Martin gave him the responsibility for bookkeeping and financial affairs. Fortunately, Kurt had a good head for figures and did the job well.

As Max became less active in the business, Martin was in charge, with Peter heading production, while Kurt handled the financial end of the business. The business flourished. Occasionally, the three sons felt hampered by Max's continuing strong opinions on some aspects of the business. At these times, the boys' mother would often referee the disagreements. Partly because she was a sensitive person and a good listener, she was usually able to help the father and sons arrive at some mutually satisfactory solution to their problems.

Our studies show that when the familial and organizational transitions occurred together, as in the Krisch case, they typically took place in an atmosphere of strain and uncertainty. Quite often, a mother was a behind-the-scenes influence. More often, though, the transitions were not managed well either inside the family or inside the business. In the Krisch case, Martin guided the company into its second growth stage. But it was his mother's sensitive management of the family relationships that eased that process and eventually permitted the brothers to achieve an outstanding growth record for the firm. Although Max's time-tested ways and methods fell by the wayside as his sons took over, he became a useful adviser once both he and his sons accepted Martin as head of the business though not head of the family. The transfer of power inside the business took place when Max moved into a new working relationship with his sons and a new family relationship with his wife. With Martin managing the business transition and his mother helping to hold the family together, Krisch's Bakeries made both transitions.

The second transition period for Krisch Bakeries is also instructive. After an impressive growth record over a 30-year period, Martin Krisch and his brothers set the wheels in motion for the transition to the third generation. Martin's son, Max Krisch II, was the most obvious successor.

By 1925, the company had established an executive committee of both family and nonfamily managers who made decisions by consensus. The brothers believed that such an arrangement helped keep the family together and provided valuable inputs from nonfamily members on the executive committee.

In preparation for the transition, Martin, who was then 55, hired an outsider who suggested that a new role of coordinator be set up for the committee which he took on initially and then passed on to Max II, who had just been brought onto the committee as a member. Soon after, Martin was advised by the outsider that he should get off the committee and out of the company as much as possible.

Thus Martin began to spend more and more of his time away from the company in civic, volunteer, outside boards, and other business activities. At times, he was frustrated and unhappy over not being in the mainstream of the business, but he gained some satisfaction in watching Max II develop into a manager who set new wheels in motion for the company's expansion and diversification into new areas of business. New product lines were developed, the company was broken into divisions and a chain of other businesses was started. All seemed to be going well until the company was hit by an antitrust suit which restricted and delayed some of its most ambitious plans.

Though the Krisch Bakeries' plans for wider ownership, diversification, and expansion were stalled for a number of years, it seemed to again make the dual transition on both the family and the business levels.

7. This and all following cases are based on real circumstances, but fictitious names and industries are used.

The single transition

Even though most of the companies we studied changed top management and growth stages together, other companies showed one transitional change at a time. A stagnant company can get that way when the older generation gives way to the younger without any company transition. The Quinn Company was one of these.

☐

In the Quinn family business harmony had been difficult to achieve. The founder, Josiah Quinn, established his industrial supply company in 1911. He began the business with a partner, and it grew steadily. As business improved, the partner took a less active role, and Quinn soon began to resent the partner's equal salary and taking of the profits.

When his wife suddenly died, Quinn impulsively sold the business to his partner and took his five children West. After several years there, he returned home and began a new business, remarried, and had two children by his second wife.

Eventually, Quinn's oldest children joined the firm. They worked well together, and the company prospered. When his second set of children also joined the company, however, jealousy and resentment increased. Conflict began to disrupt operations daily. The problems flowed over into family life, where his wife took the side of "her" children against "his." Finally, Quinn decided to set up a separate company for his wife's children. He founded it under another name, brought customers from the other company, and enjoyed helping it get started.

When World War II broke out, Quinn's most capable son in the first company was drafted. He was sent out West, married, and eventually set up his own company in San Francisco. This left the first company without a really capable successor, though the departed son's brothers and brothers-in-law worked to keep the company going. Again, dissension increased. While the company continued to operate after Quinn died, its performance levels never rose over the next 30 years.

The Quinn Company's transition from first to second generation was influenced by a major split within the family, by the loss of its key young successor, and the divisive role taken by Quinn's second wife. The family conflicts seemed to keep Quinn and his heirs from dealing with company transition problems, since all their energies were spent on inside-the-family problems. The result was a family transition without a simultaneous company transition. Such single transitions were even harder for those inside the family and the company than when the two transitions occurred together. Today the Quinn Company is heading painfully into another transition, its second generation having apparently suffered much, but having learned little from the first one. The older family managers find it hard to let go as the 66-year-old president steps aside uneasily, only to be replaced by a 68-year-old in-law whose sons wait impatiently and sometimes irresponsibly for their turn. Meanwhile, the company suffers.

Another type of single transition occurs when a company moves from one growth stage to the next within one management generation. Such growth occurs rarely, it seems, in the first generation, partly because entrepreneurs tend not to be reorganizers, and growth requires reorganization along with a shift in management styles. We found these company transitions without a family transition to occur more often during the second generation. Whereas first generation entrepreneurs had trouble shifting to high growth strategies and more collaborative styles, the sons were more flexible, possibly because the shift from a second to a third stage growth pattern involves letting go of less personal ties or possibly because they had more help in making the shift. Here is an example of such a transition:

□

When Wells Thomas died, his hardware supply business passed on to his two sons, Paul and Bing. Paul handled production, and Bing worked in sales. The two brothers built the family firm into a major hardware supply house. Paul became chief executive officer, and he and Bing eventually diversified the business into retail hardware stores, medium equipment companies, an electrical manufacturing company, and several unrelated businesses. Along the way, they brought in six third-generation members of their own and their sister's families. But these younger family members never quite made the grade. Paul, with Bing's approval, fired five of the six and handed the presidency of the corporation over to a man who had been president of one of the acquired companies.

His justification for discharging his sons, nephews, and sons-in-law was the good of the family business,

and therefore in the long run the interests of all family members. Nevertheless, he had created a split in the family that never healed. Meanwhile, the new company president admitted that Paul had become like a father to him, and it was apparent that the father-son parallel was very strong for both of them. There was still one nephew in the company, and although he had an important position, it was clear that he had no inside track on succession plans.

Thomas Enterprises moved faster than most companies do in its growth cycle, possibly because Paul Thomas was willing to sacrifice family harmony for what seemed to be business efficiency. Ironically, though, the fired family members each went on to successful careers in outside jobs, most of them pleased in retrospect to get out from under Paul's reign. Whether any one of them could have taken over the sprawling company is hard to judge at this stage. What is clear is that Paul found another "son" who became heir apparent. In an artificial way, the "succession" transition actually came along only slightly behind the company transition.

The three patterns shown in the Krisch, Quinn, and Thomas cases suggest some overall advantages of family and business transitions occurring at the same time. The Quinn and Thomas cases also show what happens when family managers, relatives, employees, and outsiders cannot form a power coalition to protect either the family or the business transition, whichever is jeopardized by family conflicts. In the Quinn case, the family managers withdrew in the face of destructive family pressures typified by Quinn's second wife. She not only divided the family but had a strong hand in dividing the company into two separate enterprises, each also competing with the other. In effect, the microcosm of family conflict became replicated in the macrocosm of the two companies. Without capable second generation managers, the original Quinn business never got beyond the first growth stage.

In the Thomas case, the opposite occurred. The relatives retreated "for the good of the family business" as Paul Thomas put it. They helped to destroy the family by abdicating in favor of the dominant older family managers, Paul and Bing Thomas. In the process, some competent family managers were lost. However, the point is not whether Paul and Bing were right or wrong, it is only that they made sure that they were never really tested or questioned by the intimidated relatives. Neither employees nor outsiders found a way to help either.

Under the distorted dominance of either family managers or relatives, not only crippled transitions but regression can set in. Consider one more case:

☐

In the Brindle Company, a father had handed the business over to a son-in-law, did not like the results, and reclaimed the company, even though the son-in-law had done an impressive job of managing the company in terms of growth and expansion. Several years later, with the son-in-law out of the business, but still with a small ownership stake, Mr. Brindle sold the company at a fraction of the price that the same buyer had offered while the son-in-law was running the business. The business' growth had stalled and declined. The company had gone from second generation back to first generation, and the family was shattered to the extent that the two youngest grandchildren born to the son-in-law and his wife had never been permitted to meet their grandparents.

Managing the two transitions

If, as in the Brindle case, a single dominant power force tends to cause lopsided transitions or regression, how can a constructive pattern be built for creating and managing both transitions? The answer seems to lie in a power balancing setup that prevents polarized conflict. Only in the Krisch case, of those described earlier, was this power balancing done effectively. Yet it also happened in at least some of the other companies we studied. It may help to look at some of the assumptions and mechanisms that were used to encourage and manage the two transitions.

The company will live, but I won't

The key assumption for growth was an almost explicit decision by senior managers that "the company will live, but I won't." This assumption, so often avoided by older family managers, is almost built into the forced retirement programs of established companies. But an entrepreneur or even his sons, as they get older, must somehow consciously face and make the decision that, even though they will die, the company will live. Often, that decision occurs not because they are pushed into it, or out of the

company by the younger family managers, but because of the intervention of relatives, noncompeting employees, or trusted outsiders, who may find a way of helping to pull the old family manager into a new set of activities.

At some point, a critical network of family managers, employees, relatives, and outsiders must begin to focus upon the duality of both family and business transitions. Such talks should, in our opinion, begin at least 7 to 8 years before the president is supposed to retire. Even though the specific plans may change, the important assumptions behind those plans will not.

Mediation vs. confrontation

Time after time we saw cases in which an entrepreneur's wife played an important role in bridging the growing gap between father and sons, as happened in the Krisch case. It also happened that an entrepreneur's widow would step in as a peacemaker for the younger generation. But when it came to helping make both transitions occur, the wife was more important than the widow. As in the Krisch case, she would help or persuade her husband to look toward the (children's) future instead of his own past. In effect, she provided a relative's outside-the-business perspective. Such outside perspectives turned out to be crucial in transition management, because they helped to heal and avoid the wounds of family conflict.

In some management circles over recent years, a cult of confrontation has been built. Confrontation is regarded as calling a spade a spade, not in anger, but as a way to move beyond conflict toward problem solving. The approach is reasonable and works in many business situations.

As we pointed out earlier, though, families and their businesses are not necessarily reasonable. The primary emotions tend to be close to the surface, so that conflicts erupt almost without reason. Attempts at confrontation by one party often fail, because they are seen as open or continuing attacks by the other.

When such nerve ends are raw, partly because of family jealousies and partly because of historical sensitivities, a third party or outside perspective can provide mediation and help to soften hardened positions. Relatives, outside directors, friends, and key employees all take this role in family companies. But they do something else that is equally important.

They can help to begin a practice of open dialogue that cuts not only across age levels, but across the different perspectives of family managers, relatives, employees, and outsiders. The dialogues can aid in manpower planning and in managing the transitions. The question is how to develop such dialogues so as to include all the relevant perspectives.

Mechanisms for dialogue

None of the dialogue mechanisms we observed or heard of is a cure-all. But each brought different important combinations of people together. One company management had periodic family meetings for family managers and relatives. Another combined family managers and employees into project teams and task forces. Outside boards of directors, executive committees, and nonfamily stock ownership (to be sold back to the company at the owner's death or departure) brought together family managers, employees, and outsider consultants on major policy problems in a number of companies. One family company had in-company management development programs, but invited outside participants and also gave periodic progress reports to the financial and civic community for comment and review. At one extreme, family managers and key employees did set up a series of confrontation sessions, but only after detailed planning. The ground rules were carefully worked out and over the years both family and company transitions made good progress. At the other extreme, companies would hold various lunches or social events where the open dialogue opportunities were limited but sometimes possible in an informal setting.

Future role building

Unwillingness to face the future stalls both family and business transitions, since in one sense the future can only mean death for an older family manager. But in a more limited sense it implies new but separate lives for the manager and his company. If some of the above assumptions and mechanisms begin to take hold, they will lead to the building of new roles. The older managers learn how to advise and teach rather than to control and dominate. The younger managers learn how to use their new power potential as bosses. Family managers take steps to learn new roles outside the business as directors, office holders, and advisers. Employees learn new functional management skills as well as new general

management skills. Relatives learn how to take third party roles to provide an outside perspective.

Beginning near the end

We have been describing one of the most difficult and deep-rooted problems faced by human organizations. Family owned and managed concerns include some of the largest as well as most of the smallest companies in the United States and possibly the world. It seems pointless to talk about separating families from their businesses, at least in our society. Families are in business to stay.

However, as one management generation comes near its end, the life of the business is also jeopardized. Meanwhile, critics, scholars, and managers like to pretend that the "real" business problems lie outside of the family's involvement. This may be true in some cases, but it can also lead to and perpetuate four sets of tunnel vision. Family managers, relatives, employees, and outsiders adopt separate perspectives and separate paths.

Our studies, however, suggest that the healthiest transitions are those old-versus-young struggles in which both the family managers and the business change patterns. For this to happen, "the old man" must face the decision of helping the company live even though he must die. If he can do this, the management of transitions can begin. In effect, a successful family transition can mean a new beginning for the company.

Writers like to think that their work and words will have a lasting impact upon the reader. However, the history of the topic we are discussing provides little cause for such optimism. In fact, a truly lasting solution may come only from experience such as that described by an entrepreneur, who said:

"I left my own father's company and swore I'd never subject my own children to what I had to face. Now my son is getting good experience in another company in our industry before coming in to take over this one. Within five years of the day he walks in that door, I walk out. And everyone knows it—even me."

[29]

The Chinese Family Business Enterprise

Murray Weidenbaum

The most important innovations in business management are occurring in the fastest-growing part of the world—Southeast Asia. Recent growth rates in that part of the world dwarf those elsewhere (see Table 1). The pacing element in both the business firm and the macroeconomy is the ethnic Chinese business firm.

Unlike the prevailing situation in the West, the family enterprise is the basic economic unit of the typical overseas Chinese community. Examples of great success are frequent. Nine out of every ten billionaires in Southeast Asia are ethnic Chinese. The overseas Chinese, numbering approximately 55 million, hold assets of about $2 trillion and generate annual economic output estimated at more than $500 billion.[1] (See Table 2 for the impressive available data on a portion of the overseas business groups.)

The Chinese business enterprise family differs in fundamental ways from the usual Western business firm. The head of an expatriate Chinese company typically is a "paterfamilias," all-powerful in both social and economic spheres. He delegates key activities and positions to members of the family. Within the family, confidence in his judgment borders on the absolute. Women are only beginning to be given some of the key subordinate positions, although a few conspicuous exceptions already exist.[2]

Liem Sioe Liong, founder and head of the Salim Group, the largest ethnic Chinese business enterprise in Indonesia, avoids designer clothes and still speaks

This article draws heavily from Murray Weidenbaum and Samuel Hughes, *The Bamboo Network: How Expatriate Chinese Entrepreneurs Are Creating a New Superpower in Asia* (New York, NY: Free Press, 1996).

The Chinese Family Business Enterprise

TABLE 1. Comparisons of Southeast Asian Growth Rates with Other Areas, 1994

Asian GDP Percent Change		Western GDP Percentage Change	
China	10.5%	United States	3.3%
Malaysia	9.2	Europe	2.5
Singapore	8.9	Japan	0.3
Thailand	8.8	Latin America	– 0.6
Indonesia	7.6		
Taiwan	6.8		
Philippines	6.0		
Hong Kong	5.0		

Source: Morgan Stanley & Co. Economics Staff, January 1996.

TABLE 2. 500 Largest Overseas Chinese Public Companies, 1994

Location	Number of Companies	Market Capitalization (in billions)	Total Assets (in billions)
Hong Kong	123	$155	$173
Taiwan	159	111	89
Malaysia	83	55	49
Singapore	52	42	92
Thailand	39	35	95
Indonesia	36	20	33
Philippines	8	6	8
Total	500	424	539

Source: Friedrich Wu and Sin Yue Duk, (Overseas) China, Inc., *International Economy* (January/February 1995), pp. 33-35.

like a village elder. He appears very poised, consummately wise, and of few words, as though he has never left the Sumatran bazaar, even for a day.[3] Nevertheless, Liem's Salim Group alone accounts for 5 percent of Indonesia's gross domestic product.

Most if not all of the top management positions in the typical Chinese family business are filled by family members. Other strategic posts are usually reserved for close relatives and for those who have worked for the family for long periods of time. The fortunate few in the latter category become "honorary" family members. The authoritarian leadership style seems to work because of the moral authority inherent in "the boss" as founder of the business group and his resultant unrivaled experience. The combination of owners and managers avoids many of the "agency" problems that Western businesses face in getting executives to promote the interests of the shareholders. Within this framework, the Chinese family firm provides a high degree of flexibility accompanied by intense managerial effort. These desirable traits are encouraged by ties of mutual obligation.

The ethnic Chinese business groups have maintained strong family control despite holdings that on occasion total billions of dollars and range over a wide variety of industries as well as countries of operation. They often show a near fanatical reluctance to admit professional outsiders into the senior management of their firms. A fascinating example of this phenomenon occurred when Y.K. Pao, the Hong Kong shipping and property magnate, arranged for succession prior to his death in 1992. Because he had no sons, Pao divided the management of his businesses among his four sons-in-law: a Chinese doctor, a Japanese architect, a Shanghai banker, and an Austrian lawyer. Despite their unusually diverse backgrounds, apparently he had no thought of turning over the businesses to professional management. Not too surprisingly, the Shanghai-born banker, Peter Woo, has become the leader of the key Pao family enterprise, Wharf Holdings.[4]

The Pao case is not an unrepresentative example of the power of family ties. In a more recent case, a neurosurgeon in St. Louis took a one-year leave of absence to straighten up outstanding business affairs resulting from the death of his father in Taiwan. Shi Hui Huang found the management of the family's enterprises so challenging that he stayed and changed careers. He is now chairman of Ching Fong Global Corporation, a group of 35 industrial and investment businesses in Taiwan and other countries around the world.[5]

On occasion, the overseas Chinese business enterprise takes on some of the trappings of a modern corporation, such as the recruitment of professional managers and a degree of public ownership, including listing of some of the family's companies on a major stock exchange. But even then, the most desirable assets are kept in a maze of private businesses and trusts controlled by the family. Family members continue to make the strategic decisions, whether formally or behind the scenes. The tendency of these firms is to engage in as many of their business relationships as they can with people of similar culture—those from the same clan or village in China or those who speak the same dialect.

There are serious disadvantages associated with the family-run business. Keeping control within the family almost inevitably restricts the size, and especially the complexity, to which it can grow. This is less a problem for low-tech firms than it is for high-tech companies which require sophisticated organizational structures and innovative experts. Family ties can be so strong that incompetent and untrained relatives are preferred over outside professionals.

Sociologist Peter Berger notes that Chinese businesses are almost always family firms because, within traditional Chinese culture, you can only trust close relatives. After interviewing people in many Chinese businesses, he concluded that managers who were not family members were the most unhappy individuals he encountered. The reasons were interrelated: nobody trusted them; they knew they were not going anywhere, and their constant thought was to leave the business as soon as possible and start their own.[6] In practice, professional managers of these enterprises may be well paid. However, they quickly encounter the limits of their authority, especially when they deal with family members who nominally report to them. According to Simon Murray, then managing director of a major enterprise in Li Ka-shing's multi-billion dollar family group, "I'm just the guy driving the truck. Li's in the back, telling me which way to go."[7] Murray has since left the company.

The modest consumption and resultant high rates of saving (and hence reinvestment) of expatriate Chinese entrepreneurs are legendary. A former student of mine tells of his grandfather who migrated from the mainland of China to the United States. He worked in a traditional Chinese hand laundry. After many years of ironing shirts, he managed to save a very large sum from his modest earnings. He then moved to Hong Kong where he was able to invest 50,000 Hong Kong dollars in the rice business. That gutsy move was the original basis of the current family fortune, which is now diversified in enterprises across Southeast Asia and into Australia.

Despite their migration to other Asian countries and beyond, the individuals involved remain Chinese in a deep and significant sense. The Confucian tradition is remarkably persistent, especially the common core of values such as loyalty to a hierarchical structure of authority, a code of defined conduct between children and adults, and trust among relatives and friends. The closely related virtues of pride in the work ethic and a disdain for conspicuous consumption are especially beneficial to rapid growth of the family enterprise.[8]

Frugality is a very durable characteristic. Li Ka-shing, the Hong Kong billionaire, still lives in an unassuming house on the unfashionable south side of Hong Kong Island. He sports a well-worn inexpensive electronic watch. Wang Yung-Ching, the head of the $11 billion Formosa Plastics Group, is notoriously reluctant to buy new clothes. His wife waits until he is away so she can sneak an old suit out of the house and quickly commission a replacement which is set in place before her husband returns.

Organizational Structure

Overseas Chinese firms have eschewed the sophisticated business structures of Western corporations in order to adapt to the weak system of contracting and law throughout Southeast Asia. By U.S. standards, the structures are painfully simple, based on either production or sales or service. Core business groups obtain varying degrees of ownership in dozens, and sometimes hundreds, of small- to medium-sized businesses (see Table 3 for a representative listing of overseas Chinese business leaders and a sampling of their key companies).

The Chinese Family Business Enterprise

TABLE 3. Representative Overseas Chinese Business Leaders and Companies

Name	Principal Location	Estimated Family Wealth	Key Companies
Dhanin *Chearavanont*	Thailand	$5 billion	Charoen Pokphand Group CP Pokphand CP Merchandising CP Northeastern CP Feedmill Bangkok Agro-Industrial CP International Trading Ek Chor Motorcycle
Cheng Yu-tung	Hong Kong	$3 billion	New World Development Ramada Hotels Regent Hotels
Stanley *Ho*	Hong Kong and Macao	$2 billion	Sociedade de Turismo de Macau Shun Tak Holdings
Robert *Kuok*	Malaysia and Hong Kong	$2 billion	Kuok Group South China Morning Post Shangri-La Hotels Pacific Carriers Kerry Group Perlis Plantation
Lee Shau Kee	Hong Kong	$6 billion	Henderson Land Development
Li Ka-shing	Hong Kong	$6 billion	Cheung Kong Hutcheson Wampoa Hong Kong Electric Husky Oil of Canada
Liem Sioe Liong	Indonesia	$3 billion	Salim Group Indocement Indosteel Bogasari Flour First Pacific Group United Industrial Corp. Hagemeyer Hibernia Bank
Pao family	Hong Kong	$3 billion	Wheelock & Co.
Mochtar *Riady*	Indonesia and Hong Kong	$4 billion (assets of Lippo Group)	Lippo Group Lippo Bank Hong Kong Chinese Bank Lippo Insurance Group Asia Securities
Chartsiri *Sophonpanich*	Thailand	$2 billion	Bangkok Bank Asia Trust Group Bangkok First Investment and Trust
Henry *Sy*	Philippines	$2 billion	Shoe Mart Stores SM prime Holdings
Tsai Wan-lin	Taiwan	$8 billion	Cathay Life Insurance

The Chinese Family Business Enterprise

TABLE 3. Representative Overseas Chinese Business Leaders and Companies *(continued)*

Name	Principal Location	Estimated Family Wealth	Key Companies
Yung-ching *Wang*	Taiwan	$2 billion	Formosa Plastics Group Formosa Plastics Corp. Nan Yu Plastics Formosa Chemical & Fibre Co.
Peter Kwong-ching *Woo*	Hong Kong	$12 billion (assets of Wharf)	Wharf Holdings
Gordon Y.S. *Wu*	Hong Kong	$1 billion	Hopewell Holdings

Note: Family name is italicized.
Source: Murray Weidenbaum and Samuel Hughes, *The Bamboo Network* (New York, NY: Free Press, 1996), pp. 23-59 *et passim*; company annual reports; "The Business Week Global 1000," *Business Week*, July 10, 1995, p. 56; "Fortune's Global 500," *Fortune*, August 7, 1995, pp. F-30–F-40; Andrew Tanzer and Philippe Mao, "The World's Best-Kept Secret," *Forbes*, July 17, 1995, pp. 112-184.

There is no Chinese equivalent of such complex corporations as Japan's Sony, South Korea's Daewoo, or the United States's Procter & Gamble. The Salim Group consists of about 75 companies in 24 countries. Almost all of the 100 largest companies in Taiwan are owned by a single individual, a family, or very close partners.[9] The absence of the equivalent of an ethnic Chinese "Fortune 500" helps to explain why so few Americans are aware of the existence of the extensive network of ethnic Chinese businesses. The lack of publicity is often intentional. Especially at times and in places where the financial success of the ethnic Chinese arouses the envy of the native population, low visibility is an asset rather than a liability. Frequently, a family-held business maintains cross-ownership with other firms controlled by the family. The result is a web of holdings, which is reinforced by placing family members in key management positions.

This procedure allows the family to maintain ultimate, albeit circuitous, control over a large array of business activities. The resultant convoluted organizational structure provides necessary secrecy in a region where the threat of expropriation is still pervasive. Even within the organization, the flow of information is tightly controlled. The amount of company knowledge given to a specific subordinate depends on the degree of trust that the leader has in the individual. Finances especially are considered a family secret. Planning consists primarily of family discussions, with the family head making the key decisions.

The great successes of the large overseas Chinese conglomerates are forcing some fundamental changes to be made. When a family-owned corporation is listed on a stock exchange in an effort to bring in new capital and diversify risk, the Chinese group is required to adopt new procedures. For example, disclosure laws require legal documents and not just a handshake, and public financial reporting rather than informal tallies. Nevertheless, most successful ethnic Chinese business families hide much of their investor identities by retaining a large

The Chinese Family Business Enterprise

FIGURE I. Partial Cross-Holdings of the Charoen Pokphand Group

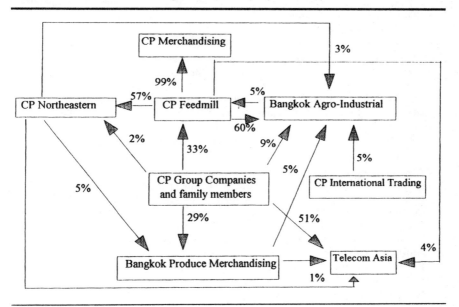

portion of their wealth in private companies through family trusts and networks of cross-holdings.

Most U.S. family business dynasties, in contrast, grew out of a solitary firm's dominance in a single market. For example, despite its enormous size and public ownership, Henry Ford's Ford Motor Company retains to the present time its "core competence" as a motor vehicle manufacturer. Likewise, Sam Walton's Wal-Mart is limited to retailing. In contrast, the typical Chinese counterpart maintains varying percentage interests in a galaxy of small to medium-sized firms, some of which have little relationship to the parent company's core competency. The ascension of Thailand's Charoen Pokphand (CP) Group from Chia Ekchor's modest seed outlets to feedmills to poultry farming is not exceptional. But its diversification to motorcycle manufacturing and joint ventures in telecommunications is quite far afield.

Figure 1 shows some of the cross-holdings of CP, the largest ethnic Chinese business group in Thailand. It can be seen that the CP Group owns 33 percent of CP Feedmill which, in turn, holds 57 percent of CP Northeastern (in addition, the Group owns directly 2 percent of CP Northeastern). CP Feedmill also owns 60 percent of Bangkok Agro-Industrial (in addition to the 9 percent interest held directly by CP and the 3 percent interest of CP Northeastern).

The Chinese Family Business Enterprise

Bangkok Agro-Industrial holds a 5 percent interest in CP Feedmill, the company that holds the majority interest in it.

In making overseas investments, CP's organizational and financial arrangements are also quite complicated. In penetrating the China market, the CP Group operates through partially owned CP Pokphand of Hong Kong. CP of Hong Kong, in turn, owns 70 percent of Ek Chor China Motorcycle, the holding company for its motorcycle business in China. Ek Chor itself operates through a series of joint ventures with companies in mainland China. For example, it shares the ownership of Shanghai Ek Chor with the Shanghai Automobile Company.[10]

The vast network of enterprises controlled by the Charoen Pokphand Group is typical of the more successful ethnic Chinese business organizations. A variation on that theme is provided by the Li Ka-shing group, headquartered in Hong Kong.[11] As shown in Figure 2, the family operates mainly through the Cheung Kong company. That firm, in turn, holds a controlling (44 percent) interest in Hutcheson Whampoa, one of the largest ex-British "hongs" that traditionally dominated Hong Kong. Hutcheson Whampoa owns Cavendish International, the holding company for Hong Kong Electric and is part owner, along with the Li family and Cavendish, of Canada's Husky Oil Company. Cheung Kong also has entered into joint ventures with Gordon Wu's Hopewell Holdings and Mochtar Riady's Lippo, two other major ethnic Chinese conglomerates, as well as with a variety of smaller enterprises.

Financial capital moves throughout the network of ethnic Chinese businesses in circuitous ways. When Taiwan had strict exchange controls, it was possible to deposit a large sum with a gold shop in Taipei and for a relative to withdraw the equivalent sum on the next day from an affiliated gold dealer in Hong Kong. Bankers speak of transactions that involved six or seven countries, with the funds flowing back to their original source at the end of it all.

The typical overseas Chinese conglomerate is privately held, or at least relatively few of its constituent enterprises are listed on stock exchanges and thus available for public ownership. Frequent asset flows between constituent members of each family group further complicate if not foil any attempt to analyze their operations. According to Kent Chan, an analyst at Salomon Brothers, "They are too complicated [to analyze]."[12] As a byproduct of the reluctance to release conventional financial data, only limited amounts of information of all types are available on the detailed operations of the overseas Chinese enterprises. Their attitude becomes more understandable when we consider the common saying among the older Chinese business leaders, "Keep your bags packed at all times."[13]

The Chinese Family Business Enterprise

FIGURE 2. Li Ka-Shing's Holdings of Business Enterprises

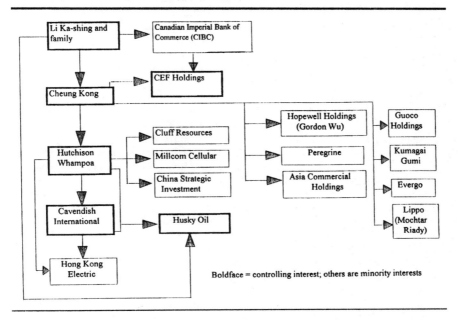

Operating Methods

Special benefits—as well as disadvantages—accompany the ethnic Chinese management style. Family control allows for a less bureaucratic management structure than Western companies use, one that permits rapid decision making. Informal networks have become the preferred vehicle for many complex transactions. The financing for a $100 million property deal can be arranged in a matter of days, compared to the many weeks or months required in the West. Personal trust replaces formal—as well as more expensive and time-consuming—"due diligence" reviews of proposed projects and investments.

The Chinese attach great importance to developing and maintaining *guanxi* (connections or relationships), which may result in missing opportunities to use the low-cost supplier or otherwise achieve greater economy and efficiency. *Guanxi* binds people through the exchange of favors rather than by means of expressions of sympathy or friendship. The relationship, at least as viewed by Westerners, tends to be more utilitarian than emotional.[14] The Chinese business leaders are more interested in long-standing commitments to working together than in the Western notion of a seemingly perfect contract that appears to contain no loopholes. In Chinese business relationships, a signed contract merely marks the end of the first stage in business dealings. Changes in specifics are expected to be made over the years as unanticipated problems arise. As an indication of the lesser role of formal contracts in the Chinese business world, about one-third of the subcontracting relationships of Hong Kong firms are based on oral understandings. Victor Fung, Chairman of the Hong Kong investment bank Prudential Asia, notes that, for an investor being considered for a partnership, "a personal reference from a respected member of the Chinese business community is worth more than any amount of money you could throw on the table."[15]

People who work with or observe overseas Chinese businesses over long periods of time are convinced that their special ability at deal making and developing transnational networks gives them a substantial competitive edge. This is strikingly the case in such industries as real estate, hotels, entertainment, banking, shipping, and foreign trade. Most overseas Chinese firms rely on a combination of centralized control and informal transactions to minimize paperwork and staff bureaucracy. Key information is obtained in conversation and retained in the memory of the senior managers, which eliminates much of the need for formal reporting. The resultant rapidity of actions allows opportunities to be seized as they arise. Other advantages are apparent. In the words of Robert Elegant, who has studied the phenomenon in depth, "ledgers are intended for the tax collector and true accounts are kept in the head."[16]

Considering the tremendous flow of studies, reports, and memos in the typical Western business, the implicit economies of time and effort are impressive. Few of these companies set up large staff departments, such as labor relations, public relations, or research which require specialized expertise. These responsibilities in a general way are assumed by each of the key family executives. The resultant level of specialization is low, with few routine work procedures and rarely any described in a formal company manual. When the two forces conflict, personal relationships take precedence over organizational efficiency.

Transactions of great size are often dealt with by common understanding and a note jotted in a diary. Fundamental business decisions are made on the basis of experience, intuition, and informal exchanges, rather than detailed statistical reports or the expensive advice of external consultants. The leading ethnic Chinese business leaders know each other personally and do deals together, with information spreading through an informal network rather than through more conventional channels. Long-time Asian analyst Louis Kraar points out that *xinyong*—having both a good reputation and a solid credit rating—is the most treasured asset of any Chinese entrepreneur.[17]

As a result of the informality of key dealings, the overall cost of doing business is lowered substantially. The transnational trading networks developed by the overseas Chinese allow for the flexible and efficient transmission of information, finance, goods, and capital in what are rarely formal agreements. In a region such as Southeast Asia, where capital markets are rudimentary and

The Chinese Family Business Enterprise

financial disclosure limited, interpersonal networks can often be critical for moving economic resources across political boundaries.

Boards of directors typically are of the rubber-stamp variety, merely meeting the legal formalities required of a listed company. One such director laments, "Our agenda arrives scribbled on the back of a Cathay Pacific in-flight menu."[18] Perhaps the most informal family-oriented decision-making and coordinating mechanism is that used by ethnic Chinese billionaire and shopping mall magnate Henry Sy of the Philippines. All six of his children are managers in the family businesses. On a typical Sunday, Sy cooks lunch for his children and grandchildren, which provides a great opportunity for coordinating the family's social and business activities. As a limited sign of modernization, however, it appears that Sy is giving his daughter Teresita (and not one of his sons) the major responsibility in running the family enterprise.

Joint ventures, especially of a cross-border nature, are common among the overseas Chinese business groups. The Salim Group in Indonesia has teamed up with the Kuok family of Malaysia to develop a hotel and golfing resort in Indonesia and a cement factory in Wuhan, China. On occasion, both groups team up with Thailand's CP Group. Stakeholders in the New China Hong Kong Group include Indonesia's Lippo Group, Hong Kong's Li Ka-shing's Group, Taiwan International Securities, Singapore's Trade Development Board, and ten mainland Chinese companies and ministries.

The transnational aspect of the overseas Chinese business firm underscores the very practical nature of its operations. The sentimental ties to the ancestral homeland are strong but, when necessary, sentiment gives way to business needs. Thus, the overseas Chinese led the foreign investment surge into the China mainland in the 1980s, when the welcome mat was out. But, in the 1990s, when the People's Republic of China is flexing its military muscles rather ostentatiously, the expatriate Chinese are often focusing their financial attention elsewhere in Southeast Asia—as well as in Australia and North America.

The ethnic Chinese entrepreneurs, although occasionally fabulously successful, do stub their toes from time to time. Gordon Y.S. Wu, the prosperous Hong Kong developer, has hit a few bumps in the road while pursuing infrastructure projects beyond his home market. His superhighway project linking Shenzhen, adjacent to Hong Kong, to Guangzhou (formerly known as Canton) is costing more than twice the originally estimated cost. Wu's Hopewell Group project to build an elevated mass transit system for Bangkok is several years behind schedule. He is trying to sell off some of his enterprises in order to generate the added liquidity required to keep his basic operations going during this difficult period. Surely, all is not sweetness and light in the bamboo network of ethnic Chinese entrepreneurs. On an earlier occasion, Wu stated laconically that there were more sharks on the land [in Hong Kong] than in Victoria Harbor.[19]

The Nature of the Product Line

Most overseas Chinese take a low profile in the commercial world, and shy away from advertising and publicity. As a result, there are few if any examples of well-known consumer goods with a Chinese brand name. Instead, we find these entrepreneurs operating in the interstices of the business world. They make components, manufacture for others, and perform subassembly work. They are also heavily involved in wholesaling, financing, sourcing, transporting, and providing other services. Most of these operations are behind the scenes, minimizing the need to market products to end-users. An example of this specialization is the activities of the Kuok Group of Malaysia, which include shipping, commodity trading, iron ore mining, and the operation of sugar plantations. None of these activities involves products marketed via the Kuok name. The Group's most consumer-oriented enterprise, its luxury hotels, bear the name, "Shangri-La."

The Salim Group is a good example of the orientation to services, as well as the convoluted organizational structure that is used. Salim manages two ports in China in a joint venture with a company linked to the government of Singapore. This activity is conducted through a three-times-removed unit—the Netherlands-listed Hagemeyer Group which, in turn, is owned by a Hong Kong–listed corporation, First Pacific Company, which is a key part of the Salim Group, headquartered in Indonesia.

The flagship of the powerful Sophonpanich family of Bangkok is the Bangkok Bank, the premier banking institution of Southeast Asia. The Bank does not bear the family name, nor do the family's other holdings, which are mainly financial institutions. The strategic interrelationships among the various family businesses are quite typical. The Bangkok Bank provides 10 percent of the capital and 30 percent of the premiums of the Bangkok Insurance Company. The insurance company, in turn, has a 9 percent interest in Bangkok First Investment & Trust Company, whose chairman is a key member of the Sophonpanich family. The Bangkok Bank, the Bangkok Insurance Company, and the Sophonpanich family together own a controlling interest (31 percent) of Krungdhep Warehouse Company, which is chaired by another senior member of the family.

The Sophonpanich family has been instrumental in aiding other overseas Chinese entrepreneurs to get started, most notably Indonesia's Liem Sioe Liong and Malaysia's Robert Kuok. Liem, in turn, arranged the initial financing for a former key employee of his, Mochtar Riady, who as noted above now manages a multinational business empire.

Forces for Change

Two related forces are pressing the traditional Chinese family business to change in fundamental ways: the growing importance of high technology

The Chinese Family Business Enterprise

products and services in global markets; and the rise of a new generation of Western-educated overseas Chinese business leaders. Designing and producing items embodying the fruits of advances in science and technology require many of the characteristics of the Western business firm, such as extensive laboratories and a host of staff analysts. Few ethnic Chinese business firms can compete effectively in this type of market.

Connections and crony networks, so useful in emerging economies in many parts of Southeast Asia, are often anachronisms in dealing with the high-tech global marketplace. Going public is often the key to obtaining large-scale financing required for the extended process of designing, developing, and producing new products based on the latest advances in science and technology. However, much of the secretiveness of the family firm, especially in the financial area, has to be sacrificed in order to meet the listing requirements of major stock exchanges. A comfortable middle ground, under these new circumstances, consists of joint ventures with American or European firms. This may be the most feasible method of successfully marketing both high-tech products and consumer services in China and Southeast Asia.

The CP Group has entered into joint ventures with NYNEX to install two million new phone lines in Bangkok and with Wal-Mart to establish retail stores in Hong Kong and the China mainland. The Lippo Group has entered into extended arrangements, at different times, with such electronics giants as Japan's Mitsubishi and the Netherlands' Philips as well as the American insurance brokers, Alexander & Alexander. Li Ka-shing's companies from time to time have joined forces with AT&T, Lockheed, and Britain's Cable & Wireless. The Salim Group has partnered with Amoco Oil and Radisson Hotels. However, the Asian emphasis on personal relations can clash with the legalism so endemic in the United States. Dhanin Chearavanont, the head of the CP Group, laments that U.S. lawyers can destroy the chemistry needed between partners to make a deal work.[20]

The second challenge may be even more formidable for the Chinese business family—to utilize the talents and skills of the sons, and increasingly the daughters, who have been educated in the West and often have gained some "alien" work experience there before returning home. At times, the combination of the Confucian work ethic and the Western training has turned out well. The transition from the entrepreneurial family firm to the modern, professionally managed corporation, although not universal, can be successful.

Ronnie Chan returned from 16 years in the United States with an MBA from the University of Southern California to take control of his father's Hang Lung Development. Since 1990, when Chan took on the chairmanship, the Group's market capitalization has more than tripled to $6 billion. A less successful blend of East and West occurred in the Acer Group in Taiwan. In 1988, the chairman brought in a senior executive from IBM to streamline operations. The effort to force consensus on the local management failed quite thoroughly. Acer is now experimenting with a middle-ground approach. Meanwhile, some entrepreneurs in the United States claim that nepotism is making a comeback here. According to Jim McCann, founder of 1-800 FLOWERS, "In today's free agent, deal-based world, only family is forever."[21]

The older generation of Chinese entrepreneurs frequently describe, albeit with some reluctance, what is in effect a three generation model: the first generation works very hard, saves and invests most of its earnings, and creates a substantial business. The second generation expands the business substantially, increasing both risk and profitability in the process. The third generation, taking the accomplishments of the past for granted, enjoys the fruits of the labors of its ancestors, and dissipates the family fortune. Judging by events thus far, the more realistic and less dramatic model of the Chinese business firm is to generate third or fourth generation leadership which attempts to shift the focus of the firm while maintaining its financial strength. In the future, that is likely to require consolidating or even selling off some of the hundreds of individual enterprises that characteristically are now controlled by a single overseas Chinese family—and often in the process raising the enterprise's level of technology.

Findings and Conclusions

The ethnic Chinese family-oriented business firm is a force that Western companies dare not ignore. Given their unique strengths and special knowledge, these Asian businesses can be valuable colleagues or partners in penetrating markets in the most rapidly growing parts of the world, notably China and Southeast Asia. Indeed, some of the best known U.S. companies have teamed up with major overseas Chinese firms in their initial efforts to develop a business presence in those exotic regions.

Yet, these same ethnic Chinese enterprises can be most formidable competitors, given their unique understanding of the governments, people, and culture of China and Southeast Asia.[22] They do not have to downsize or flatten hierarchies to become competitive because they have started with lean management structures. Perhaps their most important contribution to economic success is the long-term investment in the key people who own and run the business and the development of long-term personal relationships within and across ethnic Chinese companies. Those are difficult traits for Westerners to match.

In the long-run, the overseas Chinese companies themselves face very serious limitations. Their most noticeable weakness is very little if any experience in the worlds of brand-name goods, mass-marketing, and high-technology. Inevitably, family businesses face size limitations that restrict the range of activities that can be managed outside their boundaries.[23] They need the design, manufacturing, and marketing capabilities that Western companies can offer. Well-structured alliances between Western and overseas Chinese firms can prove beneficial to both parties, yielding a marriage of high-technology and modern marketing with regional business savvy.

The Chinese Family Business Enterprise

TABLE 4. Contrasts Between U.S. and Chinese Family Firms

Characteristic	Traditional Western Corporation	Chinese Family Firm
Ownership	Public	Private
Succession	Seniority	Family
Organizational Structure	Large Unitary Firm	Cross-Ownerships of Many Medium-Sized Firms
Nature of Control	Decentralized	Centralized
Decision Making	Analytical	Intuitive
Markets Served	Consumer and Industrial	Industrial
Product Line	Narrow	Broad
Level of Technology	High to Low	Low to Medium
Internal Reporting	Substantial and Formal	Limited and Informal
Due Diligence of Mergers and Investments	Detailed	Nil to Modest
Interfirm Relationships	Contractual	Informal
Financing	Internal and External	Mainly Internal
Public Profile	High	Low

However, attempts to transform the informal, loosely structured (but tightly controlled) Chinese enterprise into a more bureaucratic, Western-style corporation will fail. Table 4 highlights the differences between the two types of business firms. It can be seen that the variations cover so many fundamental aspects of business, ranging from ownership and succession to organizational structure and decision making to products, markets, and financing. Moreover, Westerners who analyze the Chinese business enterprise should be chastened by an old Mandarin proverb, "If you think you understand, you don't really understand."

Although many of the ethnic Chinese business families have begun to hire Western professional managers for top-level corporate slots, the family itself remains the basic coordinating mechanism—and the fundamental strength. American business managers have much to learn from the less formal, more intuitive and adaptive, and less bureaucratic approach of the ethnic Chinese family-oriented business enterprise—while avoiding the cronyism and secretiveness that seem to accompany the Confucian tradition. The American-educated younger generation of Chinese business leaders can provide a special link between the East and West in responding to the rapidly changing threats and opportunities of the global marketplace and in developing a successful managerial style for the twenty-first century.

The Chinese Family Business Enterprise

Notes

1. Min Chen, *Asian Management Systems* (London: Rouledge, 1995), p. 69; see also "The Chinese Diaspora," *Conjoncture* (November 1992), pp. 155-160.
2. For a vivid discussion of the role of Nina Wang, the "chairlady" of the Chinachem Group in Hong Kong, see Edward A. Gargan, "Asia's Unlikely Tycoons," *New York Times*, January 14, 1996, p. F11.
3. Amitabha Chowdhury and Barun Roy, "Fortune Shall Not Weary Them, Nor Fame Stale Their Infinite Wisdom," *Asian Finance* (October 1991), p. 35.
4. James McGregor, "Hong Kong Tycoon Aims to Help Bring Foreign Capital to China's Heartland," *Wall Street Journal*, January 26, 1993, p. A8.
5. Steve Givens, "Best of Both Fields," *Washington University Magazine* (Spring 1995), pp. 24-26.
6. Peter Berger, "Our Economic Culture," in T. William Boxx and Gary M. Quinlivan, eds., *The Cultural Context of Economics and Politics* (Lanham, MD: University Press of America, 1994), p. 72.
7. Andrew Tanzer, "Li Breaks Out," *Forbes*, November 25, 1991, p. 100.
8. S. Gordon Redding, *The Spirit of Chinese Capitalism* (Berlin: Walter de Gruyter, 1990).
9. Chen, op. cit., p. 94.
10. *Ek Chor China Motorcycle* (New York, NY: Bear, Stearns & Co., 1993), pp. 6-7; Gary Hamilton and Tony Waters, "Chinese Capitalism in Thailand," in Edward Chen and Peter Drysdale, eds., *Corporate Links and Foreign Direct Investment* (New York, NY: Harper Collins, 1995), pp. 104-105.
11. Lynn Pan, *Sons of the Yellow Emperor* (Boston, MA: Little, Brown & Co., 1990), pp. 364-365.
12. Quoted in Edward A. Gargan, "An Asian Giant Spreads Roots," *New York Times*, November 14, 1995, p. C3.
13. John Kao, "The Worldwide Web of Chinese Business," *Harvard Business Review* (March/April 1993), p. 25.
14. Chen, op. cit., p. 53.
15. Quoted in Louis Kraar, "The Overseas Chinese," *Fortune*, October 31, 1994, p. 92.
16. Robert S. Elegant, *The Dragon's Seed* (New York, NY: St. Martin's Press, 1959), p. 8.
17. Kraar, op. cit., p. 96.
18. "Inheriting the Bamboo Network," *The Economist*, December 23, 1995, p. 79.
19. Patrick Tyler, "Hong Kong Tycoons' Road to China," *New York Times*, December 3, 1993, p. C-1 et ff; Edward Gargan, "Hong Kong Tycoon Moves to Head Off Debt Crisis," *New York Times*, November 25, 1995, pp. 17-18; Frank Gray, "Cracking a Lucrative Market," *Financial Times*, September 26, 1995, p. 3.
20. Marcus Brauchli and Dan Biers, "Ethnic-Chinese Family-Owned Businesses in Asia Break With Tradition to Court Foreign Partners," *Wall Street Journal*, April 24, 1995, p. 2.
21. Joyce Barnathan, "Asia's New Giants," *Business Week*, November 27, 1995, p. 70; Jim McCann, "10 Business Rules and How to Break Them," *Wall Street Journal*, February 22, 1996, p. A14.
22. Louis Kraar, "Importance of Chinese in Asian Business," *Journal of Asian Business*, 9/1 (Winter 1993): 87-93.
23. Redding, op. cit.

Part VIII
Future Challenges

[30]

Socialist Entrepreneurship in Hungary: Reconciling the "Irreconcilables"

Jacob Naor
Peter Bod

This paper explores the emerging concept of socialist
entrepreneurship, stressing in particular its organic link
to the 1968 measures, as well as the apparent progress
that has been made towards resolving the complex issue
of entrepreneurship under conditions of social (or state)
ownership of means of production. Major proposals
concerning micro and macro restructuring needs are
examined, as well as relevant steps already taken, in an
attempt to demonstrate that there do not appear to be
insurmountable obstacles to the introduction of entrepreneurship into Hungarian economic life.

"He who owns everything often has nothing." Thomas
Jarkoy, Professor Karl Marks University of Economics,
Budapes.

HUNGARIAN ECONOMIC suc-
cesses, particularly in the aftermath of
the economic reforms of 1968, have
long intrigued Western observers and
continue to do so to the present. Yet,
even prior to 1968 Hungarian reformers were able to chalk up impressive gains. The Hungarian experience in the area of agriculture has
often been cited as a case in point.
The approach followed there is illuminating. Several unsuccessful attempts
at forced collectivization had, by
1959, been replaced by a voluntary
system of producers' cooperatives,
providing for meaningful self-admini-
stration and for a unique payment of
ground-rent for land owned prior to
joining (Renyi 1983). By employing
"democratic and tolerant" methods,
the Hungarian authorities claimed to
have been able to accomplish the
voluntary collectivization of ninety-
five percent of all privately owned
land in the brief span of two years
(Renyi p. 51).

After 1968, particularly until the
mid-1970s, the reform measures led
to such results as rapid improvements
in the supply of consumer goods,
steadily improving living standards,
and noticeable increases in the sensitivity of enterprises to market conditions (Antal 1983). A unique economic system, combining socialist
principles, national planning and some
features of a market economy, had
been introduced and implemented
with considerable success, through
what were generally conceded to be
non-coercive economic methods
(Portes 1972; Balassa 1973; Granick
1975).

Within this context, new developments have taken place since the
early 1980s. One of the more radical
and unique new notions introduced
was that of socialist entrepreneurship
This notion has since received wide-

Jacob Naor is a Professor of Marketing
at the University of Maine at Orono.
Peter Bod is the Scientific Secretary of
the Institute of Economic Planning in
Budapest, Hungary.

spread attention in Hungary and has been hailed by some Hungarian observers as signaling the introduction of radical changes in the awareness of managers and workers, in enterprises as well as in "organs of economic management" (Kozma 1982). It is thus clearly one of the more significant developments to emerge from the Hungarian reforms.

It is the purpose of this paper to analyze the meaning currently attributed to socialist entrepreneurship, and establish the concept's centrality to ongoing reform efforts in Hungary. In the process, the Hungarian authorities will be shown to be evolving novel approaches to achieve desired aims within the context of an economy functioning on the basis of socialist principles.

Specifically, the paper will attempt to show that the attention currently paid to entrepreneurship represents a clear shift of emphasis from that of stimulating "enterprise self-interests" to that of stimulating individual and small-group self-interests. While continuing on the one hand the central "guidance" of enterprises through applications of economic levers, the authorities' emphasis centers now on aiding the unfolding of what were believed to be strong and widely scattered latent entrepreneurial tendencies, which had been hampered by the absence of a suitably structured micro and macro environment. Such tendencies should, however, find expression as part of a "fusion" of private and public interests (utilizing for this purpose "self-regulating" markets to the extent possible), keeping within fundamental ideological constraints in a non-rigid fashion (Renyi 1983, p. 43). A wide range of institutions, practices and even theoretical underpinnings were affected. The materials presented will hopefully prove relevant to Western students of socialist systems, as well as to practitioners engaged in East-West trade, and contribute to a better understanding of entrepreneurship under various institutional settings.

THE 1968 REFORM AND RECENT PRESSURES FOR CHANGE

The 1968 reform measures, whose objective was to decentralize the economic planning and management mechanism, while concurrently increasing the role of market forces and market stimuli in economic decision making, may be seen as providing the essential backdrop for entrepreneurial activity in Hungary.[1] The reform extended the decision-making power of enterprises in such areas as purchasing, investment, production and marketing. In essence, they were freed from obligatory plan assignments and were allowed to develop autonomous production and distribution plans. The role of ministries was formally reduced to that of coordination and preparation of such plans. The reform covered a wide array of complementary measures pertaining to pricing, tax rates, investments, interest rates, and the like that would allow ministries to exercise indirect control over enterprises through appropriate financial incentives or disincentives. "Indicative planning" thus largely replaced "command planning," while the influence of "unguided" market forces saw a significant expansion as well.

One major structural problem retarded the movement towards more self-regulating markets and market-based decision making. This was the retention of the pre-1968 system of hierarchical relations between enterprises and central ministries and control organs (Antal 1982). As the structure of a command economy was largely retained, central control, characteristic of a command economy, tended to be retained as well. Commands were now replaced by "expectations" of central organs and single channel dependence (on the branch or sectoral ministry) was now replaced by an often contradiction-prone dependence on multiple control organs (banks, price administration office, etc.). As a consequence, large enterprises found it often advantageous to "bargain" and even attempt to influence expectations of central bodies, a situation far removed from that of a self-regulating market (Antal p. 203). Notwithstanding the fact that considerably more decentralized decision making was now taking place, excessive interference by central organs tended to distort economic decision making (Antal p. 203). Profitability and price considerations often yielded to administratively imposed considerations of priority tasks (such as the saving of manpower, increase of exports, etc.) (Antal p. 204). The challenge to the authorities would now be to allow market forces a freer reign in dealing with such tasks.

By the late 1970s, pressure to provide outlets for entrepreneurial behavior began to build due to the emergence of new problems. Severe external shocks buffeted the Hungarian economy, involving in particular the worsening of the terms of trade both with the East and the West. This coincided with marketing

TABLE 1

Growth Rates and Rates of Accumulation *
(percents)

Annual Growth rates (National Income)		Rate of accumulation (Net accumulation as percentage of National Income)
1978	4.2	31.9
1979	1.9	25.7
1980	− 0.2	19.6
1981	2.5	17.8
1982 (expected)	2.6.	15.8
1983	0.3	12.8
1984	2.5	12.0
1985	2.3 –2.8 **	10.6

* In comparative prices.
** Planned

Sources: Statisztikai Evkonyv, 1984; Statistical Yearbook, Budapest, 1985; Nepszabadsag, December 23, 1984.

crises in major Western export markets, as well as with a halt in growth of the much needed supply of raw materials and energy from the CMEA (Council for Mutual Economic Assistance) bloc (Tardos 1983). In the face of mounting difficulties drastic action was needed.

By the early 1980s it became urgent to mobilize hitherto unutilized or underutilized resources, both human and material, in order to overcome the stagnant economic growth (Table 1).

Entrepreneurial behavior seemed to be a particularly promising means for management as well as for work-bench level units to bring about much needed productivity gains. Hungarian reformers had clear proof of the potential of entrepreneurship in the resounding success of private plot production in agriculture, where, by 1975, work done on a mere 14 to 15 percent of total cultivated land resulted in nearly 40 percent of gross agricultural production (Tardos 1983, p. 83). The objective was to achieve similar gains in the industrial sector, without violating fundamental ideological precepts in the process.

THE EVOLVING MEANING OF ENTREPRENEURSHIP

Hungarian writers readily admit that there is as yet no consensus on the meaning of socialist entrepreneurship. Some, drawing on the widespread public perception, view entrepreneurs as "uninhibited go-getters," and oppose the concept entirely (Scientific Society of Organization and Management 1982). To others, it provides a welcome contrast to a management style characterized as "plodding along in production," "directive implementing" and "yielding to the pressure of regulators" (Kozma, p. 1). While no estimates are available on how widespread such a managerial style is, its existence must have proven sufficiently mettlesome for planners to search for alternatives. One such alternative is the stimulation of self-interest centered entrepreneurial behavior that would, by unfolding in an appropriately structured environment, bring about accelerated economic growth.

From the authorities' point of view, entrepreneurial behavior should optimally result in a "fusion" of individual, group, and public interests. This continues the principal notion underlying Hungarian "indicative" planning since 1968, in which economic levers are used to motivate enterprises to act in accordance with national plans because their own self-interest would be best served in this fashion (Granick 1975, p. 321). The difference would now be that individual and small-group self-interests would be increasingly harnessed towards this goal.

Not surprisingly, the stimulation of individuals' financial self-interests would now receive increased attention. For example, newly introduced legislation concerning top managers of large state-owned enterprises aimed at "invigorating the initiative and enterprising ability" of such managers (Bossanyi 1982). Incentives would be more differentiated depending on managerial performance, based on enterprise profitability. In a significant move, upper limits on managerial bonuses were eliminated, while less efficient managers would "fare worse than before" (Bossanyi, p. 100). Clearly, financial self-interest based behavior, often actively discouraged or severely limited in the past, would now be relied on increasingly to achieve the desired improved enterprise profit performance. Similar appeals were made to the financial self-interest of small groups, which will be explored later.

While explicit references to the term self-interest are seldom to be found in Hungarian sources, "financially responsible" risk taking and competence, manifestaitons of such behavior, often appear. One influential participant in the debate refers to the emerging concept of entrepreneurship as an "independently acting style of management that not only takes and accepts risks and responsibility but also, demands them and confidently knows its field" (Kozma 1982, p. 1).

Financial self-interest provides therefore but a part of the profile of the Hungarian entrepreneur. A study conducted in 1981 by the Hungarian Labor Research Institute on mana-

gerial interests and behavior sheds considerable light on the issue by presenting composite profiles of managerial styles to be found in Hungary (Molnar 1982). Table 2 presents a condensed version of the findings (which are unfortunately only sketchily reported on in available sources) under the headings "entrepreneurial managers" and "organizational managers." While admittedly based on a small sample, the study does suggest perseverance, initiative and risk taking as major characteristics differentiating the two managerial styles. The study appeared to suggest that as of that time but "a few" managers in their sample fit the entrepreneurial description provided (Molnar p. 50).

The desire of such entrepreneurs for an unrestricted and little regulated work environment should be underlined here, as well as their need for "internal motivation." Externally influenced motivations (which could presumably include altruistic motivations of all kinds) would apparently be operative only in the case of the organizational manager. Self-motivation, based on the satisfaction of personal interests, only partially financial (Molnar p. 50), appears central to the behavior of entrepreneurs profiled by the study. Despite the limitations of the evidence, such findings are nevertheless essential to any consideration of the kind of environment needed for entrepreneurial behavior to unfold. An exclusive reliance on financial incentives to motivate current or prospective managers would thus be insufficient.

The profile provided may or may not be the one that will finally emerge as that of the "true" socialist entrepreneur. However, based on available evidence, entrepreneurship such as that profiled appears to be viewed positively by the authorities at the present time. Under these circumstances, the state could best stimulate such behavior through the provision of an appropriately structured environment, channeling it to the desired economic spheres. The state would thus become in effect what some writers coined the "coordinator of entrepreneurship" in the interest of society at large (Kozma 1982, p.

TABLE 2

Profiles of Current Hungarian Managerial Styles

	Entrepreneurial manager	Organizational manager (specialists and experts)
Background		
career	broad experience	narrow experience
education	heterogenous	homogenous
Behavior	perseverence	accommodation
	resilience	N.A.
	initiative	"bounded" initiative
	risk taking	N.A.
	reliance on luck and intuition	strong sense of reality and precision
Mode of operation	desires unrestricted and little regulated work environment	conforms and accommodates to regulations, knows them well
	reliance on personal contacts	knows how to utilize "the system"
	ability to choose good employees that complement his personality	N.A.
	reliance on key personnel, ability to keep and motivate employees by appealing to their "interests"	N.A. N.A.
Motivation	mostly internal personal satisfaction, satisfaction of "interests"	"honorable acceptance of responsibilities"
	little reliance on outside acknowledgment	heavy reliance on external acknowledgment

Source: Based on Molnar, J.V., "Managerial Types-Professional Careers", **Nepszabadsag,** June 1982, (JPRS 81479, August 1982, pp. 50-3).

2). The study cited adds the significant conclusion (qualified by the authors as preliminary) that the system of economic regulation in place in Hungary at that time (1981) required organizational managers, while actively discouraging entrepreneurial management. The authors state that only a ". . . change in the economic environment and improvements in the selection system [of managers] will bring change in this area" (Molnar 1982, p. 53).

This view appears to have been adopted widely by Hungarian reformers. In their view, which is shared by this writer, the key to the problem of reconciliation of private and public interests would lie in a basic restructuring of environmental conditions, (providing, among other things, for an expansion of the workings of a self-regulating market system) in order to permit and encourage the emergence of entrepreneurial behavior that would be both effective and "socially desirable."

ENTREPRENEURSHIP AND OWNERSHIP

An examination of the relationship between ownership and entrepreneurship under socialism is clearly crucial for establishing the meaning of the latter. As will be seen, this involves on the one hand some highly complex considerations, while on the other hand, it appears paradoxically to be of limited practical importance. Thus, one sees practical measures involving new forms of ownership being currently implemented (such as those involving the small-business sector, discussed subsequently) while the juridical status of such forms remains as yet unsettled.

Such a state of affairs is not unique to the socialist system. Ambiguity characterizes the relationship between ownership and entrepreneurship in Western thought as well. Thus while ownership and management of the business are generally considered to be prerequisites of entrepreneurship (Brockhaus 1980, p. 509), some writers, like McClelland (1961), do not insist on the ownership characteristic, extending thereby the concept to include corporate management. Indeed, Funk and Wagnall's *Standard Dictionary* (1958) definition of entrepreneurship excludes ownership, as does Webster's *New Twentieth Century Dictionary, Second Edition* (1976) while ownership is included in its *Third New International Dictionary* (1961) definition of the term. Unresolved ambiguities are thus to be found on both sides of the ideological divide. In both cases practical needs appear to have considerably overtaken and outdistanced needed conceptual clarifications.

The wide ranging debate currently taking place in Hungary attempts to break fresh ground within the socialist community by tackling the problem in all its complexities. One of the best examples of such treatment is provided by Sarkozy (1982) who maintains that "ownership" embodies at least four basic aspects: legal, economic, sociological and socio-psychological (Sarkozy p. 225). While linked and interrelated, these aspects have not as yet been adequately addressed in socialist theory building (Sarkozy p. 231).

Some new notions along these lines have nevertheless already been advanced. While the basic notion of state ownership has persisted to date, various economic, legal, and sociological "partial ownership" notions, pertaining to enterprise ownership, have been advanced in the post-1968 period and have achieved wide usage (Sarkozy p. 236). Indeed, Hungarian legislation reflects such evolution in legal thought. A somewhat ambiguous enterprise ownership concept was introduced in 1977 as an amendment to the Hungarian Civil Code (Sarkozy p. 237). It describes the state ownership of enterprises as consisting of a separable internal and external legal relationship. In its external relationships (involving the "trade in commodities") the enterprise "appears" as owner. Regarding its "internal" legal relationship of control the enterprise is "no-owner towards the state" (Sarkozy p. 237). Yet significant contradictions remain unresolved here. According to the amendment, state enterprises "are not organs of the state," plan indicators can not be applied to them, they have "rights and duties" to take risks and "every right not prohibited or restricted by legal rule" is due to them "in connection with their management" (Sarkozy p. 240). Yet important strategic (sociological) ownership elements, such as the right to found other enterprises or to select executives, were retained by sectoral ministries, acting as supervisory organs (Sarkozy p. 240). Significantly, it is precisely such elements that some current proposals, to be discussed subsequently, aim to remove from ministerial jurisdiction.

RESTRUCTURING THE ECONOMIC ENVIRONMENT

Hungarian reform experience had shown that comprehensive, mutually complementary reform measures were needed if desired changes were to take place. This lesson has been learned and applied elsewhere in the Eastern Bloc as well (Naor 1983). Hungarian authorities were now even more acutely aware of this requirement, and attempted to introduce measures pertaining to entrepreneurship which would deepen and broaden the reform domain of 1968.

Basic decisions were now required regarding a wide range of options that were being proposed. The ownership problem needed to be addressed. In line with the basic criticism of the 1968 reform referred to above, it appeared reasonable to expect that large scale organizational changes, involving the still powerful branch or sectoral ministries would have to be made. A continuation of price reforms to better reflect resource scarcities was clearly needed as well. The competitive environmental and organizational structure of decision making in large enterprises needed reexamination. The growth of small businesses also had to be encouraged, and its nature changed, to introduce much needed competition and to develop a "hothouse" for entrepreneurial spirit.

Such and similar questions facing Hungarian decision makers are currently subject to broad based scrutiny in Hungary, with entrepreneurship clearly at the center of the debate. While some conclusions have already been reached and implemented, much remains to be resolved. The following sections will deal with some of the steps that have already been taken in various institutional settings, as well as with some of the proposals that are currently being advanced.

CHANGES EVOLVING AT THE MACRO LEVEL

Ownership Related Changes

A flood of proposals dealing with various aspects of ownership, emanating surprisingly from ministry sources as well as others, is currently forthcoming. Most involve the division between proprietary and operational functions in Hungarian industry (Kopatsy 1982, p. 1). Thus the emphasis is on the previously referred to *sociological* aspect of ownership, which following Sarkozy, deals with organizational and functional aspects of ownership. (1982, p. 228). The functional aspect in particular, dealing with the strategic and tactical ownership of enterprises, is emphasized in these proposals.

In the Hungarian setting, strategic enterprise ownership has traditonally been at the ministry level. This function includes decisions involving capital flows (direction of business policy and use of income), the choice of executives, and organizational control (creation of enterprises, liquidation, reorganization, etc.) (Sarkozy 1982, p. 229). In order to enhance entrepreneurial behavior, it is proposed that such decisions be handled at an "intermediate ownership" level, between the enterprise and the ministry. Important ownership functions would thus be transfered to new, intermediate, ownership organs other than a ministerial body. "Ownership" (which precise form of ownership was not specified) of the means of production, still to be "anchored" in the state, does not appear to be necessary in this view, for making the "owner's strategic decisions" Sarkozy 1983, p. 44). The state could thus continue as the "primary" owner, devoid however of strategic decision-making power exercised heretofore through its "representative," the ministry. Entrepreneurial behavior could now presumably be linked directly to the strategic ownership function without violating the primary ownership rights of the state. This would appear to provide a solution to the ownership-entrepreneurship dilemma that could be sanctioned on ideological grounds.

The social-psychological aspect of ownership, involving the proprietary consciousness of ownership, received some attention as well. For example, workers entrepreneurial ownership consciousness, would be strengthened through participatory management, involving increased workers' participation in the making of stratgic proprietary decisions (Sarkozy 1982, p. 230). Proposals were advanced to increase the financial interest of workers through such devices as workers' bonds or the offer of part ownership through "cooperative" ownership in the social or enterprise property (Sarkozy p. 231). Much work remains to be done in this area however.

What emerges from such proposals is that the ownership issue, which appeared at first glance to be insurmountable, may not prove to be so, given an approach that considers ideology, as well as all else, to be subject to evolutionary change. On all counts of the complex ownership issue, Hungarian reformers have been able to advance proposals that seem to be implementable from this perspective.

The Changing Role of the State

While the role of the state has received considerable attention since 1968 the intense debate on entrepreneurship brought renewed attention to the subject. The "commanding" role of the state has been mainly replaced by that of "indicative guidance." Some current proposals go considerably further however.

The state, once the effective carrier of entrepreneurial risk, is now in the process of reducing the subsidization of unprofitable enterprises and should become in effect the prime coordinator of enterprises' entrepreneurial activity. Beyond that, an active "entrepreneurial" role for the state is foreseen as well. It should initiate entrepreneurial activity and participate ·in it, in the role of a partner, not that of superior (Kozma 1982, p. 2). Partnership arrangements involving, for example, the state bank and enterprises would thus be stepped up, with the state in the role of "sleeping partner." Resources, as well as entrepreneurial initiative, could thus be channeled to areas targeted for priority development (such as various high-technology areas). The state would thus coordinate and "reconcile interests" (aiming at the "fusion" of interests, as referred to earlier) rather than dictate and enforce, while enterprises would be responsible for all intiatives for which they have "necessary and sufficient" information (Kozma p. 2).

This view suggests a significantly broader scope of activities for enterprises than before, since entrepreneurial management (which, as will be seen later, could now surface through changes in the managerial selection system) could be expected to solicit and acquire such information as would be needed for the undertaking of promising activities.

While basically agreeing with such views, government officials still maintained the necessity to retain for ministries the ability of "effective guidance." This would, however, be achieved mainly through cooperation and consultation, not through commands (Rabi 1982, p. 45). An ongoing "lowering of ministerial spheres of authority to the enterprise level" would continue as well (Rabi p. 48). Cooperation and consultation with enterprises would presumably be added to indicative planning as the means through which the state would attempt to guide enterprises. Enterprise independence would be strengthened as the state continued contracting its administration of economic activities.

The Changing Role of Ministries, Central Planning, and Related Structural Changes

In line with such reductions in state activities, branch or sectoral ministries were largely abolished at the start of 1981 and replaced by a single Ministry of Industry. This aimed at abolishing the "steering" function of such ministries, establishing the new ministry in the role of an "advisor" to the government (Antal 1983, p. 69). The pre-1981 and post-1981 organizational structures of the economy are presented in Charts 1 and 2. While the discussion of some of the details of these changes is promised at this point, it is evident that the scope for entrepreneurial activities at all levels of economic management has increased considerably since 1981. This is underlined by the move from an "orders down-reports up" structure to one that relies instead heavily on horizontal business information flows between enterprises, reducing the function of most vertical flows to that of information exchange and post-operative control. At the enterprise level, the formerly close supervision and guidance of enterprises was reduced considerably. The Hungarian Chamber of Commerce was now re-organized to represent the interest of state enterprises (Sarkozy 1983). The intent of these and similar measures was to give freer reign to enterprises and allow them to rely much more heavily on market-based

signals as a basis for demand and supply relationships.[2]

In line with the view of the state as "coordinator of interests," central economic planning should, according to top government planners, be confined to the tasks of organization, coordination, reconciliation and synthesis of macro-economic plans (Hoos 1982). Such planning would reflect macro-economic strategy, social policy and society-level consideration, and serve as a basis for the coordination of entrepreneurial activities by the state (Kozma 1982, p. 2). Central planning, it was hoped, would guide entrepreneurship, not stifle it, since it would only act to direct public funds to priority areas of economic development without specifying how such funds should be spent.

The Changing Role of Prices and Financial Institutions

In addition to structural changes, there was a need for changes in the pricing system that would permit a larger proportion of producer prices to reflect relative resource scarcities. While this had been one of the aims of the 1968 reform, most producer prices by 1982 still did not accurately reflect scarcity due to an excessive monopolization of the economy and administrative interference (Tompe 1982). Yet progress had been made, and the proportion of goods freely subject to the law of demand and supply had increased.[3] In addition, the latest price system revision of 1980 attempted to introduce the effects of world market supply and demand conditions to domestic markets. Major categories of producer prices (in particular those in which energy constituted a high proportion of total cost) were now to be linked to world market prices. (Tompe p. 53). The effects of demand and supply, both domestic and to a growing extent international, were increasingly reflected in domestic prices. By freeing prices, more efficient resource use would thus become a prerequisite for entrepreneurial decisions.

In line with the changing role of the state, its institutions such as finance and banking underwent change as well. Banks could now form partner-

CHART 1

The Pre-1981 "Pyramid"—Fashion Organizational Structure of the Economy

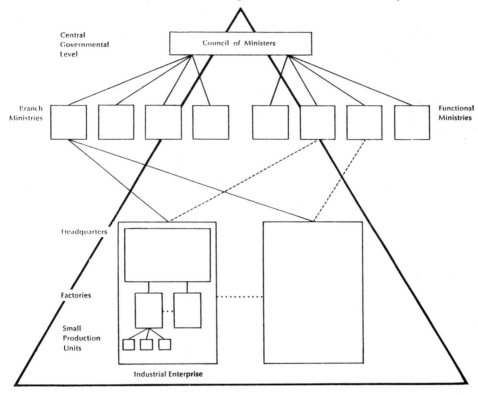

----- hierarchical channels (orders down, reports up)
- - - Information exchange or economic control (down)
. . . Business information flows (market-originating signals)

ships, participate in other enterprises or form enterprises of their own. This applied particularly to the State Development Bank (Sarkozy 1983, p. 41). The macro environment thus underwent much needed changes to facilitate the emergence of entrepreneurial activity.

CHANGES EVOLVING AT THE MICRO LEVEL

Invigorating Small Businesses

At the micro level, the small business was seen as providing a potentially ideal breeding ground for entrepreneurship which, while intro-

ducing competitive pressures, could spread from there to the larger, more bureaucratic enterprises. Clearly more was need than the previously detailed changes in the macro environment to enable Hungary to overcome the post-1980 pattern of stagnation evident in Table 1. The much neglected small

CHART 2

**The Emerging Post-1981 "Multi Channel" Organizational Structure
of the Economy**

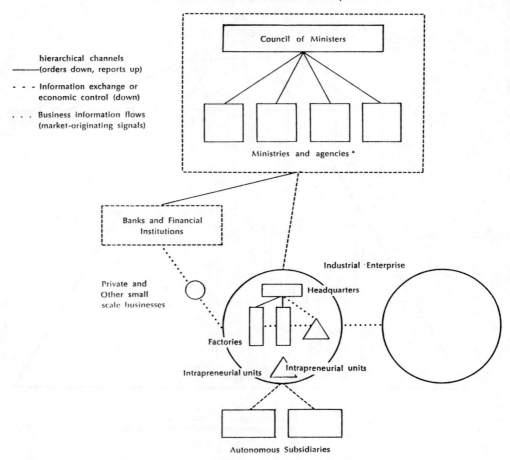

hierarchical channels
————(orders down, reports up)

- - - Information exchange or
economic control (down)

. . . Business information flows
(market-originating signals)

* Such as the Ministry of Industry which replaced several branch ministries, and agencies
such as the Planning and Price Offices.

business sector was a prime candidate for reforms which, it was hoped would emulate successes of similar small-scale operations in agriculture, that of the so-called "complementary or auxiliary" plots. It appeared tempting to unleash unutilized or underutilized initiatives and resources in small industry, which was free of the bureaucracy of large organizations. Furthermore, there appeared to be no reason for permitting the unfolding of entrepreneurial initiative in one sector while not providing similar outlets in other sectors of the economy.

By the beginning of 1982 nine new entrepreneurial forms of small business organizations, not previously available, were introduced for this purpose. Table 3 presents the forms, which have been analyzed in detail elsewhere (Naor 1985).

A brief examination of the scope of activities now permitted reveals the unmistakable entrepreneurial focus. Small enterprises could now be formed by state administrative organizations (ministry, local councils) or other enterprises, to be run as full risk bearing organizations, liable to be liquidated in the event of losses. Entrepreneurs, involving either enterprise employees or outsiders, could now run sections of enterprises at their own responsibility and risk, entitled to any profits remaining after the satisfaction of contractual arrangements. The motivation for entrepreneurial behavior is clearly extended here down to the work-bench or work-group level. Similar arrangements are available now for cooperative organizations, both inside and outside the agricultural area. Numerical limitations on participation in such groups were established, however, reflecting presumably ideological considerations. While some exploitation of "man by man" was condoned, it appeared desirable to constrain it within "tolerable" limits.

TABLE 3

Small Business Organizations Available in Hungary Since 1982

Framework	New Organization	Characteristics
State enterprise	Small independent enterprise	can be created and liquidated by ministry, national authority or local council, but operates on its own risk.
	Subsidiary enterprise	can be created and liquidated by another state enterprise, operates on its own risk backed by enterprise as guarantor.
	Independent operation of part of existing enterprise	maximum 15 people can be employed, fee established by contract with enterprise.
Cooperative	Small non-agricultural cooperatives	minimum 15 to maximum 100 members, work participation and capital contribution required.
	Industrial and service cooperative team	minimum 5 members, team works independently on basis of agreement with cooperative.
	Agricultural teams	in existence since 1972, extended now to state farms, etc.
	Self-accounting lump-sum sections	maximum 15 members, lump-sum contracts negotiated by members with cooperative.
Single proprietor	Licensed artisans	maximum 3 employees and six family members, no territorial restrictions, mostly in handicrafts.
Partnerships	Business-work partnership (BWP)	two to 30 people, private association, mostly for professional services
	Enterprise-business-work partnership (EBWP)	two to 30 members, enterprise may provide or lease equipment or premises to team on contractual basis.

Source: Adapted from Marton Tardos, "Small Firms in Hungary," **The New Hungarian Quarterly**, Vol. XXIV, No. 91, Autumn 1983, pp. 88-91.

TABLE 4

Adoption of New Small Business Forms Since 1982 *
(at year end)

Form	1982 Units	1982 Participants (in 1000)	1983 Units	1983 Participants (in 1000)	1984 Units	1984 Participants (in 1000)
Small Enterprises	23	2.2	204	19.3	285	30.0
Small Cooperatives	145	6.0	255	9.8	368	16.1
Self-Accounting Sections	477	N.A.	1243	41.4	2253	78.7
Enterprise-Business Work Partnerships	2775	29.3	9192	98.0	17377	196.0
Business-Work Partnerships	2341	11.1	4741	23.7	7397	42.5

* Source: Statisztikal Evkonyv 1984, Statistical Yearbook, Budapest, 1985, p. 326.

Table 4 presents the available record of adoption of EBWPs and that of all forms introduced. Of all forms introduced, the business-work-partnerships (BWP), and in particular those partnerships acting as subcontractors to existing firms (EBWP), turned out to be the most popular forms.

Hungarian authorities appeared pleased with such initial successes and expected continued and increasing growth in the small-business sector, as experience with the new forms accumulated and as obstacles in the way of the new forms were overcome (Naor 1985). The rapidity with which the new forms spread appears to indicate that there had indeed been a need for outlets of entrepreneurial behavior. It appeared to confirm the authorities' assumption that latent entrepreneurial tendencies did exist and that the introduction of suitable organizational structures would permit their emergence. To Hungarian authorities such findings were undoubtedly of paramount importance.

Last, the utilization of the new forms appeared to be in line with economic development objectives as well, as it led to more intensive resource utilization, increased productivity and lower overall production costs, particularly in the area of subcontracting (Naor 1985).

Decision-Making Changes at Large Enterprises

In addition to providing the framework for the introduction of entrepreneurship at the small business-enterprise level, there remained the concern with bureaucratic decision making at large enterprises, referred to earlier. Such enterprises occupied, and continue to occupy, a dominant position in Hungarian economic life. It was clearly recognized that the "solution of the Hungarian economy's problems can be based only on improving the operation and activity of the large scale plants" (Report 1983, p. 38). Such improvements ranged, by 1985, from attempts to limit or reduce the often overly-large and economically unjustified size of enterprises, to managerial reforms to select and retain more entrepreneurially minded managers for top positions. Managerial decision making at large firms was changed both in inter- and intra-organizational relationships.

The previously provided profile of the organizational manager (Table 2) provides a convenient backdrop to the discussion of emerging trends in entrepreneurial decision making at top managerial ranks. Traditionally such managers tended to exhibit limited initiative, conforming and accommodating to regulations emanating from central regulatory agencies, attempting in the process to utilize the system to the advantage of their

enterprise. Striving to build "good connections" upward with economic guidance organs had high priority in their efforts (Covacs 1983, p. 62), a tendency that clearly resulted from the institutional system in place. The 1968 reforms, as pointed out earlier, while loosening ties binding the enterprise to the top (such as regards central planning) still retained a host of formal and informal bonds tying enterprise decision makers to the central authorities. Thus, top enterprise executives continued (till the managerial reforms of 1985) to be nominated to their posts by their respective sectoral ministries or the Ministry of Industry. They continued to be "ministerial employees," dependent in large measure on their "bosses" in the ministry. It is not surprising that their style of management tended to assimilate the bureaucratic style of the central organ, conserving in the process features of the pyramid-like organizational structure which had seemingly been eliminated. Only in exceptional cases, due to pronounced business skills, professional expertise or political ties, were managers able to operate in a relatively independent manner vis-a-vis the ministry. In general, however, as succinctly stated by one authoritative Hungarian source, "sociological research has pointed out that in the present system of relationships, enterprise managers become civil servants and bureaucrats, and this keeps them back from making entrepreneurial decisions from the outset" (Pulai and Vissi 1984).

One promising point of attack on such well-entrenched bureaucratic tendencies appeared to be the large size of these enterprises.[4] One measure taken was the dismantling of a number of economically unjustified large enterprises, creating nearly two hundred new smaller autonomous enterprises (Antol 1983. p. 69), which presumably were more amenable to entrepreneurial management. State subsidies available for the expansion of enterprises were reduced as well, down by 1983 to about 40 percent of their 1978-79 level (Antal, p. 70). The authorities clearly recognized that modernization of the management system to ". . . better serve social and economic policy re-

quirements . . ." was essential (Deak 1982, p. 45). The often excessive centralization of functions at headquarters of large enterprises was decried. Subsidiaries were now to be given more independence and responsibility (Deak, p. 46). The Ministry of Industry itself was arguing for the expansion of subsidiaries' rights of entrepreneurship, opinion, determination and independent acceptance of responsibility and risk (Deak p. 48). Operational independence or decentralization, involving production-directing functions, which had been stressed previously, was considered inadequate (Deak p. 48). "Unbureaucratic" methods should now be stressed to allow more flexible operations (Deak p. 49). Significant here is that such sentiments are expressed by top ministry officials who could have been expected to oppose, or at least attempt to slow down, developments that could bring about reductions in their power and influence. This did not appear to have been the case.

Several highly significant organizational and procedural changes affecting managerial decision making were introduced, starting in 1983, designed to achieve the twin objectives of interest reconciliation and enhancement of entrepreneurial decision making.

As to the first objective, collective decision making and supervision at the enterprise level were strengthened. The workings of enterprise management committees (which included now as voting members top management, experts and blue collar representatives) assumed increased importance (Oroszi 1982, p. 5). Long-term enterprise development strategy would henceforth be decided by majority vote, with members individually and collectively responsible for strategic decisions (Oroszi p. 7). New enterprise boards of supervision were formed as well with the responsibility of comprehensive supervision, and a new right to "express opinions and present proposals" regarding long-term strategy (Oroszi p. 8). It was not intended, however, to "affect the director's specific decisions and personal responsibility" (Racz 1983, p. 8). Management committees, which functioned till then as advisory organs

64

would now assume decision-making authority in strategic matters, leading hopefully to "better-substantiated" (Racz, p. 9) and farsighted decisions, in addition to meeting the reconciliation aims (Racz, p. 11). It is too early to tell how such collective decision making involving strategic matters will affect entrepreneurial behavior. It may constrain such behavior and reduce risk taking or it may lead to better prepared, concensus-based decisions. The likelihood of managers acting as "uninhibited-go-getters," referred to earlier, would presumably be reduced. It will be highly interesting to follow the Hungarian experience in this area.

Regulations encompassed both the 1985 regulations covering the election and retention of top managers within enterprises, and the selection of top managers from the outside through open competition, rather than by ministry appointment as before (Ministerial Guidelines 1983). With regard to competitive selection, successful competitors would serve for limited periods (5 years at most), at the end of which renewal or cancellation, depending on performance, would take place. Directors, rather than the ministry, would be empowered to appoint deputy directors, thus "harmonizing" the top management team. Competitive selection and performance-based tenure were intended to replace bureaucratic meddling and non-merit based choice criteria so enterprising, risk taking managers could now compete to be chosen and to gain reappointments. Since interference by central organs has been effectively reduced, the potential for more widespread entrepreneurial behavior at top managerial levels of of large enterprises can be anticipated.

The more recent set of regulations, the management reform of 1985, similarly enhanced entrepreneurial decision making. Employees of small (and to a lesser extent) medium and large firms would now, in addition to an expansion of other rights, vote to elect, retain or recall the top management of the enterprise, increasing thereby the accountability of such managers to the work force (Table 5). The aim of conferring what

amounts to effective employer's rights to the Employee's General Assembly or, in the case of large enterprises to the Enterprise Council, is clear. Top management must consider themselves now as "enterprise employees" rather than as "ministry employees." Indications are beginning to emerge that the formerly close bonds between top enterprise executives and ministerial administrators are weakening, since directors' responsibilities for balanced and profitable enterprise management are now primarily to the enterprise council or employees' self-management organs.

In addition, the former "bosses" in the ministry have less to offer, since most of the profit impinging regulations emanate now from such functional agencies as the Price Office, the Finance Ministry and the Ministry of Foreign Trade (See Chart 2). Since such agencies tend to be less intimately linked to industry than branch ministries, it appears highly unlikely that enterprise executives

will be able to establish ties to them that would be as close as those that had existed between top executives and the branch ministries.

Another change that appears to be occuring due to the new pattern of accountability is the need to spend more time and attention on in-company affairs. No longer can unpleasant conflicts or risky decisions be avoided by passing them up the state hierarchy. The scope for an indecisive management style appears reduced. Directors aspiring for success must now acquire the ability to "sell" their ideas to a wider internal audience representing differing interests. Not least amongst those are trade union representatives who, together with representatives of the enterprise party organization, will now have a voice, but no vote, on the management committee. Their links to their respective central organizations will remain a major factor influencing the committee's deliberations. Nevertheless, such deliberations were hoped to

TABLE 5

Main Features of the 1985 Managerial Reform *

Small Firms	Organizational Unit	Scope of Authority
(Under 500 employees)	Employees' General Meeting	• Election, selections and dismissal of director and members of enterprise management • Approval of Business Plans, Balance sheet and P&L statements • Approval of bond issues • Approval of establishment or liquidation of self-accounting intra-enterprise units • Approval of mergers, split-ups, reorganization or liquidation, or founding of subsidiaries
Medium and most large enterprises	Enterprise Council Composed of elected delegates of the employees, (at least half the membership) the rest are representatives of management.	As above, except that the council elects a chairman from amongst its members. The council's decision on the appointment or dismissal of its chairman-enterprise director, requires the agreement of the founder of the enterprise **. The chairman, exercises employer's rights on behalf of the council.
Other large Enterprises ***	Managed as before	No change

* Based on "Further Development of the Economic Control and Management System," Ministry of Finance, Budapest, April 1984, pp. 25-27, and personal communication provided by the co-author.
** Relevant ministry or other central or local authority.
*** Such as public utilities communal services, or other large "state interest" involving enterprises.

permit the emergence of better-substantiated decisions through "the open confrontation of technical, financial, marketing and investment considerations" (Racz 1983, p. 9). The strength of extra-economic influences on decision making exercised within the newly constituted bodies may continue to be substantial. Still, such matters as sensitive wage related decisions, which formerly were often made at higher ministerial or trade union levels would now increasingly be made at the enterprise level. This, coupled with enhanced accountability to the work force, could spur management and work-groups towards greater entrepreneurial efforts.

In addition, the managerial reward system would become more responsive to the growing need to reward success. Since late 1982, regulations were introduced that make it easier for enterprises showing above-average profitability to increase wages and salaries, providing thereby incentives for better performance (Balazsy 1981, pp. 28-9). Managerial remunerations were increasingly differentiated depending on managerial performance, as indicated by enterprise profitability, with no upper limits on managerial bonuses. Risk taking, if it is to occur, must clearly be rewarded and Hungarian enterprises are attempting to do so. Risk shifting to higher organs appears to have declined due, no doubt, both to the severing of linkages to ministerial bodies as well as to the increased incentives of the reward system.

Last, the impetus towards entrepreneurial decision making emanating from the intrapreneurial sub-units discussed previously must not be overlooked. Newly available in-company partnerships, or in-house lease or licensing arrangements, could not fail to influence decision making at the "core" or headquarters level. Such operations could set efficiency and success (profit) standards that core management might feel compelled to emuate. On the other hand they could be, and in some cases already are, sources of conflict and discontent for managers and workers not able or willing to take part in such ventures. Such discontent can now find expression in enterprise

management councils through trade union activists, that could in turn lead to restrictions on entrepreneurial activities. Clearly the extra income earned by intrapreneurial groups would, particularly in periods of falling real wages as is the case in Hungary since 1980, provide an easy target for assorted opponents of entrepreneurship. Such issues, and a host of equally thorny problems remain to be ironed out. However, Hungarian authorities and decision makers are alert to the problems at hand and appear committed to the course of continued and accelerated diffusion and acceptance of socially acceptable entrepreneurship.

CONCLUSION

What emerges from the preceding is the view of a system in the midst of comprehensive and far reaching changes. While largely continuing the course chartered since 1968, the emphasis on entrepreneurship appears new. It provides the "integrating concept" for the wealth of emerging provisions and proposals.

While the envisioned future characteristics of such behavior appear as yet unclear, steps are already being taken to aid what are recognized as some desirable current manifestations. These include risk taking propensity, initiative and perseverance, self-motivation, self-reliance and a desire for a relatively restriction-free work environment. It is to the credit of the Hungarian authorities that they recognize the need for far reaching environmental restructuring efforts, that the issues involved enjoyed and are enjoying broad public discussion, and that bold steps were taken to implement some of the major proposals. This appears to be in line with the approach followed in the course of earlier reforms. Having largely met with success, the Hungarian authorities anticipate similar results from the current reform phase.

Indeed, attempting to introduce entrepreneurship at a number of economic activity levels corresponds with the key objectives of the 1968 reforms. The active economic role of government through centralized planning, investment, and subsidiza-

tion of industry, has been drastically reduced since then and continues to see reductions. The business environment has thus become progressively less regulated and less "guided," particularly so since the demise of the branch ministries. The macro environmental climate has fewer obstacles to entrepreneurial behavior than before. Producer prices have been more deregulated and reflect in better measure changes in international price levels. Also public funds are presumably being increasingly channeled to profitable enterprises which respond in large measure to internal and external market conditions.

Revamping the selection process for managers allows the selection and retention of entrepreneurs in top positions, as well as the timely removal of ineffective managers. Financial incentives are now increasingly differentiated. Risk taking is actively encouraged and supported, and is shifting to individuals, work-groups, and enterprises, as well as to soon-to-be-created "holding" or "stock" corporations. New forms of small businesses, partnerships, cooperatives, or even single-proprietary "artisanships" were introduced to fill the void between the operations of large enterprises and to encourage small-scale entrepreneurship and competition. These developments, as pointed out, could be sanctioned on ideological grounds by the adoption of an evolutionary stance on ideological matters. "Secondary" forms of ownership are thus beginning to emerge as well as the delegation of "strategic" ownership functions to bodies, other than ministries, which are more entrepreneurial and more flexibly attuned to market conditions than were bureaucratic ministries.

Yet, as pointed out, problems still abound. The overall structure of industry, despite some measures to the contrary, is still excessively monolithic, thus conducive to the retention of a bureaucratic style of management. The temptation to "guide" such enterprises administratively, rather than allow the market to do so, may prove overwhelming, particularly in periods of economic stress such as Hungary is experienc-

66

ing currently. Such interference may indeed be unavoidable, as is often the case under similar conditions in Western systems. A desire to curb "socially undesirable" manifestations of entrepreneurship, such as excessive earnings, or excessive influence or power, may well bring forth new restrictions in the future. Similarly, ideological purists may attempt to at least ameliorate the effects of "excessive" ideological flexibility that seem to threaten ideological fundamentals. Any constraints on the strategic decision-making power of management at large enterprises may reduce the attractiveness of such positions to entrepreneurially inclined executives. Yet, the direction of the reform has been set and first steps have been taken. It is hard to see how such developments, once set in motion, could see radical reversals, particularly as they appear to be outgrowths of the reforms of 1968. The coming period, therefore, will most likely see the introduction of some of the major proposals advanced and the continued implementation of the steps already taken. Based on the Hungarian reform record to date, it appears that the authorities' expectations regarding the adoption and diffusion of entrepreneurial behavior, both within the domain of small business and beyond, are likely to be met (given sufficient time and allowing for likely delays due to the various internal and external obstacles discussed). Hungary may thus provide an example that other Eastern Bloc members will be tempted to emulate.

NOTES

1. The following is based on a description of the reform measures provided in Granick (1975) pp. 240-4.

2. One example given by the authorities of a case where interference was still needed concerned the iron metallurgy industry, which required urgent help due to depressed world market conditions. In this critical situation the ministry "initiated and achieved central measures" (Rabi, 1982, p. 47). In general the ministry attempts to help "wherever it is justified" and whenever it is able to do so (Antal p. 46).

3. Thus, for example, food and consumer articles officially priced dropped from 86% to 72% of the total of such articles between 1968 and 1980, and from 87% to less than one-third of articles in the metal-technical sector. "The Area of Prices," in *OTLET*, March 1983, translated in EER No. 2408, JPRS 83633, p. 22.

4. The ratio of Hungarian enterprises employing over 1,000 persons was (by 1982) still "unjustifiably" high (73 percent). It is 17-41 percent in the most developed capitalist countries (Tompe, 1982, p. 54). Since 1972, despite the 1968 reform, the size of large enterprises had continued to grow. Thus while the state sector comprised 812 such enterprises averaging 1374 employees per enterprise in 1970, that number had shrunk to 699 enterprises averaging 1,569 employees per enterprise by 1980 (Tardos, 1983, p. 82).

REFERENCES

L. Antal, "Thoughts on the Further Development of the Hungarian Mechanism," *Acta Oeconomica*, Vol. 29(3-4), 1982.

L. Antal, "Carrying on with the Economic Reform," *The New Hungarian Quarterly*, Vol. XXIV, No. 91, Autumn 1983.

B. Balassa, *Plan and Market*, M. Bornstein, ed., Yale University Press, New Haven and London, 1973, pp. 347-72.

S. Balazsy, "Enterprise on a Reducing Diet?", *Heti Valaggazdosag*, December 1981, translated in EER No. 2227, JPRS No. 80012, pp. 28-9.

K. Bossanyi, "What Will Change in the Regulations?" *NEPSZABADSAG*, December 1982 translated in East-Europe Reports (EER): Economic and Industrial Affairs No. 2359, Joint Publication Research Service (JPRS) No. 82687 p. 100.

R. H. Brockhaus, Sr., "Risk Taking Propensity of Entrepreneurs," *Academy of Management Journal*, Vol. 23, No. 3, 1980, pp. 509-20.

D. Covacs, "The Socialist Enterprise," NEPSZABADSAG, May 1983, translated in EER 2414, JPRS No. 83759, pp. 60-63.

J. Deak, "Modernization of the Internal Direction System at Industrial Enterprises," *PARTELET*, July 1982, translated in EER No. 2327, JPRS No. 82039, p. 45.

Funk and Wagnall's Standard Dictionary, International Edition, New York Funk & Wagnall Co., 1958.

D. Granick, *Enterprise Guidance in Eastern Europe*, Princeton University Press, Princeton, New Jersey, 1975, pp. 234-316.

J. Hoos, "Debate on Future Economic Measures Ends" *HETI VILAGGAZDASAG*, December 1982, translated in EER No. 2359, JPRS No. 82687, p. 105.

S. Kopatsy, "Stocks—Publicly Owned," *FIGYELO*, June 1982, translated in EER No. 2293, JPRS No. 81272, pp. 1-3.

F. Kozma, "Socialist Entrepreneurship," *MAGYAR NEMZET*, December 1982, translated in EER No. 2366, JPRS No. 82804, p. 1.

D. C. McClelland, *The Achieving Society*, Princeton, New Jersey: Van Nostrand, 1961 p. 226.

"Ministerial Guidelines: Selection and Appointment of Managers," *FIGYELO*, April 1983, translated in EER No. 2410, JPRS No. 83666, pp. 54-7.

J. V. Molnar, "Managerial Types—Professional Careers," *NEPSZABADSAG*, June 1982, translated in EER No. 2301, JPRS No. 81479, pp. 50-53.

J. Naor, "Economic Reform-making in Romania—The 1978 New Economic Mechanism," Working paper, Equipe de Recherche Sur La Firme et L'Industrie, Universite de Montpellier, Montpellier, France, 1983.

J. Naor, "Recent Small Business Reforms in Hungary: A Unique Socialist Experiment," *Journal of Small Business Management*, January 1985.

I. Oroszi, "Decision, Risk, Responsibility," *NEPSZABADSAG*, December 1982, translated in EER No. 2366, JPRS No. 82804, p. 5.

M. Pulai and F. Vizsi, "Task and Problems in Developing the Hungarian Economic Control and Management System," Acta Oeconomica, Vol. 33, 1984, no. 3-4.

B. Rabi, "First Experiences in the Modernization of Industrial Management," *PENZUGYI SZEMLE*, June 1982, translated in EER No. 2301, JPRS No. 81479, pp. 45-47.

A. Racz, "Enterprise Independence, Plant Democracy," *NEPSZAVA*, January 1983, translated in EER No. 2376, JPRS No. 83030, pp. 6-11.

P. Renyi, "Socialism and Reform," in *The New Hungarian Quarterly*, Vol. XXIV, No. 91, Autumn 1983, p. 51.

Report on the Conference, "The Tasks of the New Organizational Forms and Experiences with Their Operations," *Figyelo*, May 1983, translated in EER No. 2412, JPRS No. 83698, pp. 32-38.

T. Sarkozy, "Problems of Social Ownership and of the Proprietory Organization," *Acta Oeconomica*, Vol. 29 (3-4), 1982, pp. 225-58.

T. Sarkozy, "A Contribution to the Questions of the Theory of Ownership as Applicable to the Socialist Enterprise," *TARSADALMI SZEMLE*, 1983, translated in EER No. 2373, JPRS No. 82971, p. 40.

Scientific Society of Organization and Management, "Obstacles to Entrepreneurship," *MUSZAKI ELET*, May 1982, translated in EER No. 2291, JPRS No. 81225, p. 26.

M. Tardos, "Small Firms in Hungary," *The New Hungarian Quarterly*, Vol. XXIV, No. 91, Autumn 1983, p. 87.

Z. Tompe, "The Leader's Interest," *VALOSAG*, October 1982, translated in EER No. 2353, JPRS No. 82532, p.53.

Webster's New Twentieth Century Dictionary, Second edition, Unabridged; William Collins & World Publishing Co., 1976.

Webster's Third New International Dictionary, Unabridged, Chicago: Merriam Co., 1961.

[31]

 Journal of Management
1988, Vol. 14, No. 2

Entrepreneurship: Past Research and Future Challenges

Murray B. Low
Ian C. MacMillan
University of Pennsylvania

The contributions and shortcomings of past entrepreneurship research can be viewed within the context of six research design specifications: purpose, theoretical perspective, focus, level of analysis, time frame and methodology. The authors suggest a unifying definition of the field of entrepreneurship. The recent trend toward theory driven research that is contextual and process oriented is encouraging. It is time for entrepreneurship researchers to pursue causality more aggressively. Exploratory studies that are not theory driven should be discouraged unless the topic is highly original. Implications for practicing entrepreneurs are discussed.

The past decade has witnessed a significant rise in popular enthusiasm for entrepreneurs and entrepreneurship. This enthusiasm has been matched in the academic arena, resulting in a significant increase in the amount of research effort being devoted to the subject.[1] This increased attention seems justified given the growing evidence that new firm creation is a critical driving force of economic growth, creating hundreds of thousands of new jobs (Birch, 1979; Birley, 1987; Reynolds, 1987), as well as enhancing federal and local tax revenues, boosting exports, and generally increasing national productivity *(President's Commission Report,* 1984).

As a body of literature develops, it is useful to stop occasionally, take inventory of the work that has been done, and identify new directions and challenges for the future. This reflective process is essential in order to derive the maximum benefit

---

The authors would like to thank Suzanne Low and Phil Rosenzweig for their useful comments on an earlier version of this manuscript and to acknowledge the valuable suggestions (many of which were directly incorporated) made by four anonymous reviewers. We would also like to thank the Social Science and Humanities Research Council of Canada and the Sol C. Snider Entrepreneurial Center for their support.

Address all correspondence to Murray B. Low, Sol C. Snider Entrepreneurial Center, The Wharton School, University of Pennsylvania, Philadelphia, PA 19104.

[1]There are several sources that can provide basic background for the non-specialist interested in entrepreneurship research. *The Encyclopedia of Entrepreneurship* (Kent, Sexton, & Vesper, 1982) and its recent sequel, *The Art and Science of Entrepreneurship* (Sexton and Smilor, 1986) provide comprehensive reviews under a range of entrepreneurship related subject headings. *Entrepreneurship and National Policy* (Vesper, 1983) provides an excellent discussion of the new venture process and implications for national policy. Finally, review articles by Gartner (1985a) and Wortman (1987) provide a good overview of the literature.

from future research. The purpose of this review is to provide such a reflective moment for the field of entrepreneurship research. The contributions and short-comings of past research will be examined and suggestions will be made for the direction of future research.

The organizing theme of this paper consists of six key specification decisions that we feel researchers need to address as they begin to assemble a research pro-gram in the area of entrepreneurship. These design specification decisions are in-terrelated, and cannot be made independently. However, for the purposes of this paper, we will consider each of the following research dimensions separately: **Purpose**—what is the specific as well as larger purpose of the study? **Theoret-ical Perspective**—what is the theoretical perspective adopted? **Focus**—on what specific phenomena shall the investigation be focussed? **Level of analysis**—what level or levels of analysis will be considered? **Time frame**—what length of time frame will be considered? **Methodology**—what methodology will be adopted?

Past entrepreneurship research will be reviewed within the context of these six design dimensions.[2] This organizing structure is meant to complement previous reviews that have been organized around subject categories or units of analysis. Readers who have limited familiarity with the entrepreneurship literature or those interested in specific topics may find it useful to refer to these previous compre-hensive works.

Finally, since our intention is to provide a critical review, we wish to preface our remarks by acknowledging a debt to those who have pioneered the study of entrepreneurship. Although hindsight makes it easy to identify the shortcomings of early studies, it is important to recognize that these works were necessary first steps in the exploration of the entrepreneurship phenomenon.

Decision 1: Specification of Purpose

Entrepreneurship is a multifaceted phenomenon that cuts across many disci-plinary boundaries. Studies falling under the rubric of ''entrepreneurship'' have pursued a wide range of purposes and objectives, asked different questions and adopted different units of analysis, theoretical perspectives and methodologies. This diversity is reflected in the many and varied definitions of entrepreneurship: Schumpeter (1934) defined entrepreneurship as ''carrying out new combina-tions.'' Knight's (1921) definition focussed on the ability to predict the future successfully. Leibenstein (1978) argued that firms do not necessarily operate at the outer limit of their production function; therefore, entrepreneurship is the ability to work smarter and harder than your competitor. Kirzner's (1973) concept is closely linked to arbitrage and the ability to correctly anticipate where the next market imperfections and imbalances will be. Cole (1968) defined entrepreneur-ship as purposeful activity to initiate, maintain, and develop a profit-oriented business. Stevenson, Roberts and Grousbeck (1985) suggested that entrepreneur-ship is being driven by perception of opportunity, rather than resources currently controlled. And Gartner (1985b) defined entrepreneurship as the creation of new

---

[2]Limitations of space have meant that this review has focused primarily on US literature related to new firm creation. It is important to note that there is a well defined literature on corporate venturing as well as a rapidly growing body of European literature that is not discussed in this review.

JOURNAL OF MANAGEMENT, VOL. 14, NO. 2, 1988

organizations. Empirical researchers have argued for some time that this inability to agree upon common definitions has hampered research progress (Gartner, 1985a; Vesper, 1983).

The problem with these definitions is that though each captures an aspect of entrepreneurship, none captures the whole picture. The phenomenon of entrepreneurship is intertwined with a complex set of contiguous and overlapping constructs such as mangement of change, innovation, technological and environmental turbulence, new product development, small business management, individualism and industry evolution. Furthermore, the phenomenon can be productively investigated from disciplines as varied as economics, sociology, finance, history, psychology, and anthropology, each of which uses its own concepts and operates within its own terms of reference. Indeed, it seems likely that the desire for common definitions and a clearly defined area of inquiry will remain unfulfilled in the foreseeable future.[3]

However, because of the range of approaches available for entrepreneurship research, some common ground is needed upon which to synthesize the insights of diverse approaches of inquiry. At the broadest level, there is a need for an overall, common purpose that will forge some unity among entrepreneurship researchers.

In the spirit of the challenge to define an overall, common purpose, we suggest that entrepreneurship be defined as the ''creation of new enterprise'' and propose the following: that entrepreneurship research seek to *explain and facilitate the role of new enterprise in furthering economic progress*. This fundamental purpose, or one like it, is wide in scope yet still delineates a constrained area of inquiry within which multi-disciplinary research programs may be built.[4] Furthermore, by emphasizing ''explanation'' it encourages researchers to go beyond descriptive studies and to pursue causal inference. And by emphasizing ''facilitation'' it encourages researchers to maintain relevance for practice and to consider both micro and macro perspectives.

In the past, much of the entrepreneurship research has either lacked clarity of purpose or the specified purpose was of little consequence. Many early works were of the ''census taking'' type—confined largely to documenting and reporting the occurrence of entrepreneurs or their personality characteristics, with little attempt to uncover causal relationships or to explore implications for practice. Many of these studies left the reader wondering what the authors really hoped to achieve. The failure to clearly specify the purpose of the research combined with

---

[3]It can be argued that the term *entrepreneurship* is too imprecise a concept to be of much use to researchers. In this respect, it is interesting to make a comparison with the term *leadership*. Pfeffer (1977) argues that the concept of leadership is so broad that its usefulness is called into question: ''Apparently there are few meaningful distinctions between leadership and other concepts of social influence. Thus, an understanding of the phenomenon subsumed under the rubric of leadership may not require the construct of leadership'' (p. 105). It seems that the same argument could be made about the construct of entrepreneurship.

[4]In this context, it is appropriate for us to explicitly raise our point of view regarding the outcomes of entrepreneurial effort. A comprehensive research program cannot confine itself solely to studies of entrepreneurial *success*. This is for two reasons. First, the venture's failure may be the result of established competitors' reactions to the entry of the new firm. If this competitive response enhances the industry's overall competitiveness, then economic progress has still been achieved, even if the venture fails. Second, failure is an important source of learning, and even though a specific venture may fail, the people involved may have developed skills and knowledge that will lead to future entrepreneurial success (Maidique & Zirger, 1985).

the lack of common ground for synthesizing research findings has hindered the advancement of the field. To address this problem, we suggest not only that the specific purpose of a study be explicitly stated at the outset, but that the field will best advance if this more specific purpose is explicitly linked to a generally accepted overall purpose such as "explaining and facilitating the role of new enterprise in furthering economic progress."

Decision 2: Specification of Theoretical Perspective

After the specification of purpose, the next important decision is the specification of theoretical perspective. Much of the entrepreneurship research to date has implicitly assumed a "strategic adaptation" perspective. A strategic adaptation perspective suggests that the key to entrepreneurial success lies in the decisions of the individual entrepreneurs who identify opportunities, develop strategies, assemble resources and take initiatives. Recently, this perspective has been challenged by theorists who adopt a "population ecology" perspective, which suggests that individual goal-driven behavior is largely irrelevant and that environmental selection procedures are the most powerful determining factors.

The Strategic Adaptation Perspective

Authors that adopt a strategic adaptation perspective usually start by identifying key success factors that enhance the chances of survival. Vesper (1980) suggested five key ingredients: technical knowhow, product or service idea, personal contacts, physical resources, and customer orders. Timmons (1982) reviewed the works of over two dozen authors and concluded that there are "substantial variations in content, assumptions, and emphasis, and little theory to anchor the variety of viewpoints" (p. 132). Nevertheless, he notes several recurrent ingredients in discussions of successful venture creation, such as the importance of a lead entrepreneur, building a team with complementary skills, a triggering idea for a product or service, a well developed business plan, a network of people and resources and appropriate financing.

The flip side of "key success factors" is "key failure factors." Unfortunately, the list of potential pitfalls associated with starting a new venture appears limitless. Woodruff and Alexander (1958) identified 23 causes of failure among ten small manufacturers. Vesper (1983) identified 12 "barriers" to entrepreneurship. Typical problems include lack of market knowledge, inability to delegate responsibility, lack of technical skills, lack of seed money. Rather than attempt to list all the potential pitfalls associated with new ventures, it can be argued that the seriousness of any problem depends on the extent to which it detracts from one of the key success factors identified earlier—and failure to address any *one* of the key success factors will be sufficient to kill a new venture.

In addition to key success factors, another important consideration is entry strategy. Vesper (1980) provided the most extensive compilation of entry strategies. These include new product, new service, imitative product, imitative service, franchising, geographical transfer, customer sponsored, parent company sponsored, government sponsored and acquisitions. Vesper's purpose seemed to be to make the potential entrepreneur aware of the variety of entry strategies. He suggested that a combination of strategies might be effective, but provided only anecdotal evidence about the appropriate use of a given strategy.

The most advanced strategic adaptation entrepreneurship research has come from researchers who have tried to capture the expertise of the venture capital community. The assumption here is that people who make profits from assessing new venture proposals will have developed expertise in distinguishing between winning and losing ventures. Works by Tyebjee and Bruno (1981), Roberts (1983), and MacMillan, Siegel and SubbaNarasimha (1985) all examined the factors that venture capitalists evaluate in deciding to fund entrepreneurial venture proposals. Recently, this work has been extended to studies that seek to link pre-funding characteristics with ultimate success. Roure and Maidique (1986) confirmed that experienced, well balanced venture teams improve performance and found that "successful ventures targeted product-market segments with high buyer concentration in which, through technological advantage, their products could attain and sustain a competitive edge" (p. 295). MacMillan, Zemann and SubbaNarasimha (1987) reached similar conclusions and identified two major criteria that predict success: "1) the extent to which the venture is initially insulated from early competition and 2) the degree to which there is demonstrated market acceptance of the product" (p. 124).

In the review of these studies it became clear that entrepreneurial firms are too diverse to permit simple generalization (Gartner, 1985a). Some researchers have dealt with this complexity by adopting a contingency approach that seeks to identify major contingent variables that significantly shape entrepreneurial outcomes. Sandberg and Hofer (1987), who also collected data via the venture capital route, have developed and tested a contingency model for predicting venture performance based upon characteristics of the entrepreneur, the structure of the industry being entered, the venture strategy, and the interactive effects of these three factors. Although their findings are based on a small sample and can be challenged on statistical grounds, their results are nevertheless suggestive: the entrepreneur's characteristics appear to have little effect on venture performance, whereas the interaction between industry structure and strategy appear to be strongly associated with performance. By using theory and inductive arguments to develop and test hypotheses that consider the interaction of personal, environmental and strategic variables on performance, Sandberg and Hofer take the research on strategic adaptation an important step forward. Hopefully future studies of this type will follow.

Another emerging stream of strategy research seeks to determine what repeatedly successful entrepreneurs have learned through experience. Lamont (1972) initiated the first study of this type by conducting a matched pair sample of 24 technology-based enterprises, half of which were founded by individuals with no previous entrepreneurial experience and half of which were founded by experienced entrepreneurs. He found that the experienced entrepreneurs tended to found firms with a product orientation (as opposed to a contract orientation), with larger initial financing, and with a better balance of business skills among the management team. More recently, the notion that there is much to be learned by studying repeatedly successful entrepreneurs was advocated by an individual who has himself started over 30 new businesses over a 10-year period (Executive Forum, 1986). He contends that study of one-shot entrepreneurs will inevitably focus on problems and obstacles that may simply be a product of inexperience. His argument is that only multiple entrepreneurs can provide the base for a theory of entrepreneurship since only they have developed an "experience curve."

Ronstadt (1988) argued that such multiple entrepreneurs are more common than previously supposed. In a sample of 1537 practicing and ex-entrepreneurs, Ronstadt found that 63% of the former and 40% of the latter were involved in the creation of more than one venture. He suggested that the best new venture opportunities are most often revealed only after an individual is already involved in a start-up. This is due to the fact that once the firm is initiated, greater information becomes available about relevant contacts, viable markets, product availability, competitive resources and response time.

A review of the strategic adaptation literature shows that progress is being made. The strategy conceptualizations have advanced from rather static, overly generalized "key success factor" models to contingency models that consider a range of variables under varied circumstances and take into account the learning effect of past efforts. In spite of this progress, it is still surprising that so little work has been done in the area of entrepreneurship strategy. There are very few good empirical studies, and those that exist are limited by small sample sizes.

Whether it is explicitly stated or not, the dominant assumption of the strategy oriented literature is that success is primarily dependent upon the entrepreneur's ability to develop and execute effective strategies. The literature that adopts a population ecology perspective offers a different point of view and will be discussed next.

The Population Ecology Perspective

Hannan and Freeman's 1977 article entitled "The Population Ecology of Organizations" was a provocative piece that challenged many assumptions held by organizational researchers. The authors argued that most management theory overemphasizes the capacity of an organization to adapt to a changing environment. In contrast, they viewed inertia as a dominant organizational characteristic. Employing a biological analogy, they suggested that those organizations that are well adapted to their environment will survive, and those that are not will die. Through this selection mechanism, the environment will determine the characteristics of populations of organizations. The essence of the argument is that chance variations in organizational forms that are adaptive are selected *for* whereas nonadaptive forms are selected *against*.

Perhaps that best articulation of the application of ecological thinking to entrepreneurship lies in the work of Greenfield and Strickon (1986). They argued that contemporary paradigms in social science research and thought have become static and therefore incapable of explaining dynamic social processes. As an alternative, they proposed a new paradigm that has its origins in Darwinian biology:

> With respect to entrepreneurship this means that we are no longer look-
> ing for a transcendent type—the analogue of the immutable species—

but instead recognize existing diversity of behavior within specific
populations, which at its extremes encompasses innovation and novelty. What is called entrepreneurship, from this point of view, is actually one segment of an otherwise seamless variability. (p. 14)

Population ecology theory has significantly matured in recent years, developing from a simplistic and deterministic biological metaphor into a rich theoretical
framework capable of incorporating other theoretical perspectives. There have
been many attempts to reconcile population ecology with extant organizational
theory (Hannan & Freeman, 1984; Hrebiniak & Joyce, 1985; Singh, House, &
Tucker, 1986). One such attempt is by Brittain and Freeman (1980), who developed a particularly comprehensive model of the organization creation process by
beginning with the population ecology model and incorporating elements of other
perspectives such as strategy and transaction cost economics. They argued that
new opportunities are created for the expansion of existing and founding of new
organizations through technological or demographic change. These changes result in what they call "new resource sets." Following Stinchcombe's (1965) argument, they suggested that knowledge of opportunity and access to requisite resources to exploit the opportunity are not uniformly distributed throughout the
population. Instead, opportunities are most likely to come to individuals at key
informational loci within existing organizations. Depending on the nature of the
existing organizations, the new opportunity may be best exploited by a new firm.

Brittain and Freeman's model begins to connect the insights of the seemingly
disparate perspectives of population ecology and strategic adaptation. It directly
addresses the role of chance, and by emphasizing changing resource sets and the
replacement of short-term opportunities types of firms (r strategists) with long-
term low cost producers (K strategists). it is a dynamic model that explicitly deals
with ongoing change and competition.

In their study of organizational births and deaths in the newspaper industry,
Carroll and Delacroix argued that an ecological perspective should be concerned
with both foundings and mortality, and that each will be driven by different factors (Carroll & Delacroix, 1982; Delacroix & Carroll, 1983). This research raises
an important possibility: organizational births may better be explained by macro
variables such as technological or demographic shifts, whereas survival of entrepreneurial firms may better be explained by micro variables such as strategy.

As the above studies have demonstrated, the strategic adaptation and population ecology perspectives are not irreconcilable. One promising opportunity for
combining the insights of these perspectives lies in the study of industry evolution, or the "community" level of analysis, as it has been labeled by the ecologists (Astley, 1985; Carroll, 1984). A good example is the work of Tushman and
Anderson (1986), who studied three different industries and observed that technology evolves "through periods of incremental change punctuated by technological breakthroughs" (p. 439). They defined technological breakthroughs in
Schumpeterian terms: "Major technological innovations represent technical advance so significant that no increase in scale, efficiency, or design can make older
technologies competitive with the new technology" (p. 441). They added an interesting dimension by distinguishing between two fundamentally different types

of technological discontinuity: competence-enhancing and competence-destroying. A competence-enhancing technological shift builds upon existing know-how (replacement of mechanical typewriters by electric), whereas with a competence-destroying shift, existing know-how is largely irrelevant (replacement of steam-engines by diesel locomotives).

Tushman and Anderson found that competence-destroying technological discontinuities favor the entrance of new firms into an industry because of the inability of established competitors to exploit the new technology. Competence-enhancing discontinuities, on the other hand, work to the long-run advantage of established firms who can use their resources and market position to incorporate the new technology. Thus the entrepreneurial firm that enters an industry via incremental change or via the introduction of a new competence-enhancing technology is in far greater peril from existing competitors than one that enters via the introduction of competence destroying technology.

This is an example of how the ecological perspective can provide valuable insight that can lead to more effective strategy formulation: an aggressive entry strategy is more likely to succeed under conditions of a competence-destroying discontinuity than under conditions of a competence-enhancing discontinuity, where competitors are in a strong position to retaliate.

Our review of the population ecology literature leads us to the following comment regarding future entrepreneurship research: In the past, much of the entrepreneurship research has implicitly assumed a strategic adaptation perspective. The application of ecological thinking to entrepreneurship has challenged many previously held assumptions, increased our understanding of the entrepreneurial process, and demonstrated the significant benefits of theory driven research. Ideally, the example of population ecology will encourage the exploration of other theoretical perspectives that have the potential to provide insight into the entrepreneurship phenomenon.

Whether the strategic adaptation, population ecology, or some other perspective or combination of perspectives is pursued, it is clear that the field will be better served in the future if the issue of theoretical perspective is addressed directly and unstated assumptions are avoided. Theory can then be tested and elaborated, and from this, *informed* knowledge can be developed to aid the academic and the practitioner alike.

In this section we have highlighted one set of theoretical issues by contrasting the strategic adaptation and population ecology perspectives. In the next section, on focus, we pursue a second, related set of issues by examining the trend toward more contextual and process-oriented research.

Decision 3: Specification of Focus

Early entrepreneurship studies typically focussed on the personality or cultural background of the individual entrepreneur as a determinant of entrepreneurial behavior. Over time, these approaches yielded to a recognition that meaningful research must adopt a more contextual and process-oriented focus. This section will review this progression toward richer and more dynamic approaches as a method of highlighting the challenge of "focus."

Psychological Theories

McClelland's work on "need for achievement" (McClelland, 1967) and an empirical study of 150 successful Michigan entrepreneurs by Collins, Moore and Unwalla (1964) were early works that started a prolific stream of personality-based entrepreneurship research that continues to this day. Brockhaus (1982), Gasse (1982), Martin (1984), and Sexton and Bowman (1985) have provided reviews of this psychological/personality-based literature. Most of the comments in this section are drawn from these reviews.

McClelland argued that need for achievement is culturally acquired and a key psychological characteristic of an entrepreneur. An individual with a high n-Ach is characterized as (a) taking personal responsibility for decisions, (b) setting goals and accomplishing them through his/her effort, and, (c) having a desire for feedback (McClelland, 1967). The two basic problems with need for achievement are first, the theory is as applicable to salespeople, professionals, and managers as it is to entrepreneurs, and second, subsequent research has not validated a link between a high need for achievement and the decision to start a business (Sexton & Bowman, 1985). McClelland's more recent work has gone beyond need for achievement and examined other personality characteristics such as initiative, assertiveness, efficiency orientation, systematic planning, and commitment to work contract (McClelland, 1986). As with need for achievement, these are not unique to entrepreneurs, but instead characteristics common to many successful individuals.

Internal locus of control is another characteristic that has been attributed to entrepreneurs. This concept refers to the belief held by individuals that they can largely determine their fate through their own behavior. However, internal locus of control has proved to be no more useful than need for achievement in differentiating the entrepreneur from the non-entrepreneur (Brockhaus, 1982; Sexton and Bowman, 1985; Gasse, 1982). Brockhaus concluded that although a high internal locus of control is common to both successful managers and successful entrepreneurs, it may still hold "promise for distinguishing successful entrepreneurs from the unsuccessful" (p. 45).

A high risk-taking propensity is another psychological characteristic often attributed to entrepreneurs. Although some of the empirical findings are contradictory (see Sexton & Bowman, 1985), the overall evidence is that entrepreneurs are moderate risk takers and do not significantly differ from managers or even the general population. It is perhaps more insightful to view entrepreneurs as capable risk managers whose abilities defuse what others might view as high risk situations.

One psychological characteristic that does appear to distinguish the entrepreneurial personality is the tolerance for ambiguity. Studies by Schere (1982) and Sexton and Bowman (1985) have indicated that entrepreneurs have a significantly greater capacity to tolerate ambiguity than do managers. Other personality characteristics that have been argued to distinguish between entrepreneurs and managers are a high need for autonomy, dominance, independence combined with a low need for support and conformity, and a capacity for endurance (see Sexton & Bowman, 1985).

Definitional and methodological problems associated with these past psychological studies, such as noncomparable samples, bias toward successful entrepreneurs, and the possibility that observed entrepreneurial traits are the *product* of entrepreneurial experience, make it difficult to interpret the results. Furthermore, at a more fundamental level, it can be argued that the wide variations among entrepreneurs make any attempt to develop a standard psychological profile futile. One is struck by the appropriateness of Gartner's (1985a) observation that there is as much difference among entrepreneurs as between entrepreneurs and non-entrepreneurs.[5]

Some researchers have used personality traits to identify different entrepreneurial types. Smith (1967) distinguished between crafts and opportunistic types. Stanworth and Curran (1976) specified 3 types: the artisan, the classical and the manager. Webster (1977) suggested 5 categories of entrepreneurs, Vesper (1980) listed 11 different types and Gartner developed 8 entrepreneurial archetypes (Gartner, 1983). These studies make interesting reading, but as with the other personality-based literature discussed so far, it is questionable whether these descriptive studies move us closer toward a theory of entrepreneurship.

Demographic studies of entrepreneurship suffer from some of the same problems as the psychological/personality literature. Most of the empirical work that examines the demographic characteristics of entrepreneurs suffers from small sample sizes, non-comparability of samples and static terms of reference. The most comprehensive study to date is by Cooper and Dunkelberg (1987). They collected broadly based data on 890 entrepreneurs and contrasted their findings with earlier research using smaller samples. They confirmed that entrepreneurs tend to be better educated, come from families where the parents owned a business, start firms related to their previous work and locate where they are already living and working. In other ways, however, the entrepreneurs in their sample were less different than previous research has indicated, "being no more likely to be of foreign-stock and not being particularly likely to leave school early or to drift from job to job" (p. 21) than the general population. Cooper and Dunkelberg concluded that diversity seems to be a central characteristic of their sample. This is our conclusion as well: being innovators and idiosyncratic, entrepreneurs tend to defy aggregation. They tend to reside at the tails of population distributions, and though they may be expected to differ from the mean, the nature of these differences are not predictable. It seems that any attempt to profile the typical entrepreneur is inherently futile.

More useful are recent psychological studies that focus on the entrepreneur within an organizational context. Schein (1983) examined the role of the founder in creating organizational culture. According to Schein, entrepreneurs "typically . . . have strong assumptions about the nature of the world, the role their organizations will play in that world, the nature of human nature, truth, relationships,

---

[5]There are some interesting parallels that can be made between the personality-based entrepreneurship research and the studies that sought to identify leadership traits. Theories of leadership progressed from simple "trait" theories through two-dimensional personal-behavioral approaches and on to highly complex models that considered a variety of forces at work within the leader, the situation, and the subordinate. As we shall see, entrepreneurship research has followed a similar pattern to become much more contextual and dynamic.

time and space'' (p. 17). Schein examined the process by which the assumptions and theories of the founders interacted with the organization's own experiences to determine culture. Kets de Vries (1985) focussed on dysfunctional entrepreneurial personality characteristics by examining the negative repercussions of need for control, sense of distrust, desire for applause, and psychological coping mechanisms demonstrated by some entrepreneurs. This article was the result of studies done in collaboration with Miller that sought to link executive personality with strategy and organizational structure (Kets de Vries & Miller, 1984, 1986). Kets de Vries and Miller developed a typology of pathological organizations and their most recent work examined culture as the link between personality and strategy.

The work by Schein and by Kets de Vries and Miller is important because it does not focus simply on the psychology of the entrepreneur, but focuses instead on the relationship between the entrepreneur and the organization and on the *process* by which individual characteristics affect organizational outcomes. The focus of these most recent psychological studies is clearly more contextual and process-oriented than the earlier work.

Social-cultural Theories

One of the earliest and best known attempts to link entrepreneurship to the larger social context was Weber's classic work ''The Protestant Ethic and the Spirit of Capitalism'' (1930). Weber argued that the rise of Protestantism encouraged hard work, thrift, and striving for material advancement, which in turn gave rise to capitalism. Although the causal effects of the Protestant ethic on the development of capitalism have since been hotly contested, it does seem clear that the rise of Protestantism swept away many institutional obstacles that were preventing the development of capitalism. Our conclusion is that there must be congruence between ideological constructs and economic behavior if entrepreneurship is to flourish.

The tendency of certain cultures to produce entrepreneurs has made it intuitively appealing to view culture as a determinant of entrepreneurship. Hagen (1960) explained entrepreneurial behavior as a means by which disadvantaged minorities seek to alter the status quo. Some examples are the Dissenters in England, the Protestants in France, the Samurai in Japan, the Jews in many countries, and the Parsees in India (Greenfield & Strickon, 1981). This perspective is continued today in the work of Brenner (1987), who argued that it is those groups that have lost or face the prospect of losing social status that are driven to take entrepreneurial risks. Although there may be some validity to these assertions, some contradictory evidence does exist (Shapero & Sokol, 1982). The recent entrepreneurial proliferation associated with Silicon Valley (Stanford and Berkeley graduates) and Route 128 (Harvard and MIT graduates) demonstrates that not all entrepreneurs come from disadvantaged backgrounds. The best that can be said with confidence is that *in some cases* entrepreneurship is a response to lack of social mobility through other channels.

Studies in the 1960s by Cochran (1965) and Alexander (1967) recognized the complex economic, social, and psychological factors that impact the entrepreneurial process. However, it was Glade (1967) that really set the stage for the types of contextual models currently advocated. Glade viewed the entrepreneur as a decision maker operating within a specific social and cultural setting. He termed this setting an "opportunity structure," implying both the perception and existence of an opportunity combined with the availability of resources: "Integral features of any given situation are both an 'objective' structure of economic opportunity and a structure of differential advantage in the capacity of the system's participants to perceive and act upon such opportunities" (p. 251).

More recently, Vesper (1983), Martin (1984), and Shapero and Sokol (1982) all developed models of venture initiation that build upon this idea. The Shapero and Sokol model is perhaps the most sophisticated model of entrepreneurial event formation in the Glade tradition. It identifies life-path changes, perceptions of desirability, and perceptions of feasibility as variables leading to new company formation. Their model considers the interaction of many situational and cultural factors and provides a dynamic framework that captures the range of positive pulls and negative displacements leading to the start-up of a business.

Network Theories

Recent studies that have examined "networks" are more refined attempts to place the entrepreneur within a social context. Birley (1985) studied the role of networks in the founding of new firms by sampling 160 firms in Indiana. She differentiated between two kinds of networks: informal (family, friends, business) and formal (banks, accountants, lawyers, SBA) and found that entrepreneurs rely heavily on the informal network, but seldom tap into the formal network. MacMillan (1983) argued that there is a distinct manipulative aspect of networks. In a small sample longitudinal study he identified the critical role played by deliberate network building in the launch of eight start-ups.

The importance of networks has been reflected in a growing interest in "incubators." An incubator may be a formally organized facility offering laboratory and office space, support services, technical and business consulting services, and contact with other entrepreneurs (Smilor & Gill, 1986), or may simply be the organization where the entrepreneur worked prior to launching a venture. The most famous example of a firm acting as an incubator for entrepreneurial spinoffs is Fairchild, which spawned at least 35 companies (Vesper, 1983). Studies of such incubator organizations have shown that high-tech entrepreneurs tend to locate themselves in the same area as their previous employer and develop products that are closely related to their prior organizations (Cooper, 1986).

The understanding of networks was further advanced by Aldrich and Zimmer (1986), who viewed the entrepreneurial process as embedded in a shifting network of continuing social relations that facilitate and constrain "linkages between aspiring entrepreneurs, resources and opportunities" (pp. 8-9). They contended that new business formation is part of an evolutionary processes of "variation, selection, retention, and diffusion and the struggle for existence" (p. 9). Though recognizing that individuals are intentional or purposeful in their actions, they argued that the growing evidence of cognitive limits on human behavior and the "powerful influence of social factors on cognitions and information processing" means that one cannot attribute new business formation to individual acts (p. 6). For Aldrich and Zimmer, the entrepreneurial process takes on meaning only in the context of the broader social processes that they described.

These recent studies demonstrate how the focus of entrepreneurship research has progressed to become more contextual and process oriented. Several authors have suggested frameworks for capturing this contextual complexity. Gartner (1985a) suggested a conceptual framework for describing the phenomenon of new venture creation that identified the similarities and differences between ventures. His framework "integrates four major perspectives in entrepreneurship: characteristics of the individual(s) who start the venture, the organization which they create, the environment surrounding the new venture, and the process by which the new venture is started" (p. 696). Carsrud, Olm, and Eddy (1986) suggested a similar model, one that examines the interaction between psychological, personal/demographic, organizational, and situation/environmental variables on the venture creation process.

This section has reviewed a range of entrepreneurship literature from the perspective of focus. There is strong evidence of a trend toward research with a more contextual and process-oriented focus. Research has progressed beyond deterministic personality and cultural theories toward more comprehensive and dynamic theories. The challenge for future entrepreneurship research is to continue this trend and move toward explaining rather than merely documenting the entrepreneurial phenomenon.

Decision 4: Specification of Level of Analysis

Given our earlier comments about the general purpose of entrepreneurship research, it follows that we are interested in *all* entrepreneurial phenomena that impact economic progress. This means we may be concerned with the fate of the individual entrepreneur, the progress of an entire industry, or the impact of that industry on society as a whole. Thus researchers may choose among five levels of analysis: individual, group, organizational, industry and societal levels. Most of the research to date has been at a single level of analysis. However, two recent studies illustrate just how much can be gained by attempting a richer, albeit more difficult multi-level research design.

The first is a study by Van de Ven, Hudson and Schroeder (1984) that examined the start-up of 14 educational software companies. The firms were divided into high and low performers based on a composite measure of success. Key variables from three different levels of analysis were examined for their impact on success. The three levels of entrepreneurial (characteristics of the founding individual), organizational (planning and initial development processes of the firm) and ecological (industry as a whole).

The Van de Ven et al. study is exemplary in its use of the literature to identify key variables for investigation at each level of analysis. At the entrepreneurial level, the authors concluded that success was related to education and experience, internal locus of control and risk reduction, a broad and clear business idea, and personal investment. At the organizational level, success was positively related to planning activities (although ironically, spending time on a detailed business plan seemed to result in poorer performance), small scale startup, incremental expansion, single person command, and active involvement of top management and board members in decision making. At the ecological level, the study suggested that assistance from a corporate sponsor in the form of equity capital, training, or guaranteed contracts was actually maladaptive, and that firms competing for contracts on an independent basis advanced more quickly, at least over the short run.

Aldrich and Auster (1986) provide a second example of a multi-level research design. They built upon Stinchcombe's work and argued that the "strengths of large, old organizations are often the weaknesses of small, new organizations and vice versa" (p. 165). For smaller and newer organizations they looked at various strategies such as franchising, long-term contracts, and mergers and acquisitions to overcome the liabilities of newness and smallness. For larger and older organizations, they examined strategies of franchising, mergers and acquisitions, subcontracting, and corporate venturing to overcome the liabilities of oldness and largeness. The connection between different levels of analysis was made through the observation that adaptive strategies at the organizational level result in new "forms" at the industry level that improve the viability of whole populations of organizations.

The relationships between phenomena that can be observed at different levels of analysis are important not just for academics, but for both practitioners and public policy makers as well. From the entrepreneur's perspective, the success of the individual enterprise will be affected by factors that can only be observed at different levels of analysis. To miss any one of these perspectives increases the probability that key factors will be overlooked, and that unanticipated events will take the entrepreneur by surprise. From the public policy maker's perspective, the insights generated by multi-level studies have the potential to improve targeting of government efforts to encourage successful entrepreneurship.

The two studies discussed above demonstrate that each level of analysis provides unique insight and that the synthesis of these insights yields a richer understanding than that possible from the perspective of a single level of analysis. The challenge for entrepreneurship research is to increase the incorporation of multiple levels of analysis into future research designs.

Decision 5: Specification of Time Frame

A key building block for understanding the pattern of new business formation is the notion that start-ups move through predictable stages. The fact that this pattern can only be observed through wide time frame research is the key thrust of this section. Other issues related to longitudinal research will be discussed in the final section on methodology.

Most of the studies that focus on stages in the start-up of an enterprise are variations on a theme. Although typically arranging the stages in natural order, most theorists note that the stages need not be strictly sequential, nor can they be dealt with in isolation. One of the more detailed works (Swayne & Tucker, 1973) listed 57 steps in three overall stages of concept, planning and implementation. A recent review by Gartner (1985a) of the work of eight researchers identified six common actions undertaken in the entrepreneurial process: locating a business opportunity, accumulating resources, marketing products and services, producing the product, building an organization, and responding to government and society. Stevenson et al. (1985) identified five steps in the start-up: evaluating the opportunity, developing the business concept, assessing required resources, acquiring needed resources, and managing and harvesting the business.

Block and MacMillan (1985) focussed on the planning for a launch and suggested that there are critical milestones in a start-up. They argued that a new venture is an experiment with implicit hypotheses or assumptions about the relations among product, market, and competition that can only be tested through experience. Block and MacMillan suggested that go/no-go or redirection decisions be made at each of ten milestones, based upon emerging information that becomes available as each milestone is reached.

From the point of view of advancing theory, studies that merely document the stages of a start-up are of questionable value. However, identifying the major tasks that need to be accomplished during the launch of a venture has practical value; furthermore, the notion that a start-up moves through discrete stages is an insight that must be incorporated into any theory of new venture creation.

Although the above researchers focus on the stages of start-up, other researchers use still longer time frames and focus on major stages of growth in fully launched organizations. Greiner (1972) identified five distinguishable phases of development, each characterized by ''evolutionary'' periods of relative calm followed by ''revolutionary'' periods of management crisis and realignment. This approach was furthered by Churchill and Lewis (1983), and Hambrick and Crozier (1985) and bears similarity to the ''life-cycle'' work of Kimberly and Miles (1980). These works go beyond the start-up phase and demonstrate that different management and strategic issues become paramount at different stages of development. Robinson and Pearce (1986) took the analysis one step further with a comprehensive study of the relation between venture performance at different stages of development and the attention given to strategic and operational decisions. They showed that as the firm evolves, each state calls for emphasis on different strategic activities.

Short time frame studies are simpler to design and easier to execute but clearly lack the richness of insight that results from studying a phenomenon over a longer time period. For entrepreneurship research this is extremely important, since new firms are extremely fragile and experience many changes within short periods of time. Often the seeds of future problems are sown in the early stages. Only wide time frame studies will allow us to study the development problems faced by new firms and to pursue the objective of causal inference.

Decision 6: Specification of Methodology

As entrepreneurship emerges as a recognized area of inquiry, the quality and usefulness of the theory that is developed will be tied to the ability of researchers to identify patterns of causality. Early efforts in entrepreneurship research were understandably exploratory case studies or cross sectional statistical studies of the ''census-taking'' type. However, if such exploratory studies are successful, they should be followed by more systematic studies that subject a priori hypotheses to formal testing and work toward the development of theory.

Unfortunately, the progress toward a priori hypothesis testing has been slow. The current standard appears to be data collection and a posteriori statistical testing. Still, there has been some progress in terms of building upon previous research and designing more rigorous studies. For example, in measuring the contribution of entrepreneurship to economic progress, Birley (1987) and Reynolds (1987) built upon the earlier work of Birch (1979), with their analyses characterized by much greater precision. In Reynolds' case, he used regression and discriminant analyses to distinguish between factors related to the social contribution of new firms and factors related to their survival. A further example is Khan (1987), whose study of the effectiveness of venture capital decision making went beyond simple additive regression approaches (MacMillan et al., 1987) and employed non-compensatory decision modelling.

The goal of establishing causal linkages among variables means that more longitudinal work is necessary. Longitudinal studies are inevitably more difficult and expensive than cross sectional studies, but the benefits are considerable. Two good examples of longitudinal studies are Hambrick and Crozier's (1985) examination of the difficulties of managing rapid growth firms, and Tushman, Virany and Romanelli's (1985) study of a cohort of minicomputer firms over a protracted time period. Following a group of firms over time is expensive and time consuming, but it is important to recognize that only such large scale cross sectional *and* longitudinal studies can start to provide us with enough confidence about causality to provide the basis for theoretical model building and experimental research.

To date the attempts to develop formal methods have been limited. Baumol (1982) developed a theoretical model describing the influences that determine the supply of entrepreneurship and its influence on economic growth. Kihlstrom and Laffont (1979) proposed an entrepreneurship-based theory of competitive equilibrium by building upon Knight's (1921) concept of risk. Casson (1982) developed an economic theory of entrepreneurship within the neoclassical framework. These attempts at formal model building hold promise, but pale compared to the sophistication of the models used in other fields. Until progress is made in the development of rigorous models of the entrepreneurial process, our ability to generate theory will be severely circumscribed.

If attempts at formal model building have been limited, attempts at experimentation have been rare. Worthy of note are two studies—the use of simulation techniques to study venture capital investment effectiveness by Stevenson, Muzycka and Timmons (1987) and the experimental study by Kourilsky (1980) that examined the entrepreneurial behavior of children in a simulated economy. The lack of experimental research is a further indication of slow progress in developing entrepreneurship theory.

It is interesting to note that the studies cited above stem from a variety of disciplinary backgrounds: Hambrick and Crozier from strategy; Reynolds from sociology; Kourilsky from education; Kihlstrom and Laffont, Baumol, and Casson from economics. Other disciplines that have contributed to the study of entrepreneurship include anthropology (Owens, 1978), marketing (Dickson & Giglierano, 1986), psychology (Brockhaus, 1982), history (Cochran 1965), finance (Huntsman & Hoban, 1980), and political science (Gatewood, Hoy & Spindler, 1984). This diversity of approaches and methods is to be encouraged, for entrepreneurship is as varied as it is elusive, and the range of research methods should match the complexity of the phoneomenon under study.

Our review of the literature leads us to suggest that there is a need to pursue causality more aggressively. The field must move to the stage where exploratory case analyses or cross sectional census taking studies that are not theory driven and do not test hypotheses are no longer acceptable.

Implications for Entrepreneurs

This review has focussed on issues of research design and is primarily targeted at an academic audience. This approach reflects the belief that useful knowledge for practice will only result from the pursuit of rigorous research and the development of entrepreneurship theory. For those who do not share this view, there is no shortage of anecdotal "how to" books to which they may refer.

Even though this review has focussed on research design issues, several important implications for practice have been raised. At the most general level, the design issues raised in this paper can serve as criteria for sifting through the vast amount of popular and academic literature dealing with entrepreneurship. In much of this literature the practitioner is advised to look out for the same inappropriate generalizations and misleading assumptions about causality that we caution academics to beware.

Although past attempts to stereotype entrepreneurs based upon psychological and cultural characteristics have been discredited, recent work suggests that entrepreneurs' personalities do have important influences on the organizations they create (Kets de Vries, 1985; Schein, 1983). The behaviors and values of the entrepreneur interact with the experiences of the unfolding organization to imprint its culture. In turn, organizational culture has important implications for the performance. Entrepreneurs are encouraged to be aware of how their behavior shapes the emerging culture. We by no means suggest that entrepreneurs try to change their personalities, but it may be possible for them to be alert for and avoid behaviors that have dysfunctional organizational consequences.

The literature makes it clear that opportunities do not drop from the sky. Opportunities are created within and among existing organizations as a product of ongoing networks of relationships and exchanges. Opportunities come most frequently to people located at advantageous positions within networks. Furthermore, exploiting an opportunity requires certain resources (human resources, capital, marketing and technical information, sales etc.). The same types of network relationships and contacts needed to identify opportunities are also necessary to obtain the resources required to exploit opportunities. Aspiring entrepreneurs are advised to evaluate and map their current networks. Doing so is the first step toward building an effective network, an activity that is too important to be left to chance.

It is also clear from the literature that there are no magic formulae for success.

Each venture will have its own key success factors, any one of which will be sufficient to kill the venture if overlooked. Some important items for consideration are the following: Is there an established market for the product? Is the market defensible? Is the strategy appropriate for the industry structure?

Although planning is important, spending too much time on a detailed business plan can be counterproductive. And though assistance from a corporate sponsor is usually thought to be helpful, evidence suggests that firms competing for contracts on an independent basis advance more quickly (Van de Ven et al., 1984). For technologically innovative ventures, it is important to establish whether the innovation can easily be adopted by established competitors (Tushman & Anderson, 1986). If so, a long range objective might be to be acquired by an existing firm. If not, an aggressive share-building strategy might be most appropriate.

The ecology literature suggests that success is also a matter of chance, and that one needs some luck. This is true, but it is also possible to shape luck—by building networks, by exercising parsimony of investment, by seeking competitively insulated niches, by moving incrementally, and by continually monitoring per-)formance. This approach conserves resources, heightens awareness of developing trends and maintains the flexibility needed to quickly respond to new opportunities.

Finally, start-ups move through distinct phases, with different management and strategic issues paramount in each phase. Effort must be taken to ensure that resources are spent on the areas most critical to the firm's success, given its stage of development. And care must be exercised to think through how short-term actions might be planting the seeds of future problems.

Summary and Recommendations

We have reviewed the literature in the context of the challenges faced when designing an entrepreneurship research program. In the course of this review, we came to the conclusions that are summarized in Table 1 and discussed in greater detail below:

1. Purpose. There is a need for future research programs to include a clear statement of purpose. Furthermore, we appeal to researchers to link the specific purpose of their study to the more fundamental purpose we have proposed: to explain and facilitate the role of new enterprise in furthering economic progress. It is hoped that by linking to this overall purpose, a wide variety of research activities can be brought into a broad but unifying arena.

2. Theoretical Perspective. In the past, much of the entrepreneurship literature has implicitly assumed a strategic adaptation perspective. The insights resulting from recent work using the population ecology perspective has challenged some of these assumptions and demonstrated the benefits of theory driven research. We suggest that future research should examine and clearly state theoretical assumptions and that additional theoretical perspectives should be explored.

3. Focus. Recently, there has been a trend toward more contextual and process-oriented research. This is an important advancement and moves the field closer to

Table 1
Overview of
Entrepreneurship: Past Research and Future Challenges

Research Design Decisions	Past Research	Model Research and Future Challenges
Specification of purpose	Little clarity, descriptive, lack of unity	Clearly stated, explanatory, further economic progress
Specification of theoretical perspective	Weak theory development, implicitly assuming strategic choice	Theory driven, clearly stated assumptions, variety of theoretical perspectives
Specification of focus	Focus on personality or cultural determinants	Focus on the entrepreneurial process in social context
Specification of level of analysis	Primarily single level of analysis	Multiple levels of analysis
Specification of time frame	Narrow time frame	Wide time frame
Specification of methodology	Case studies, cross sectional surveys, single method, descriptive	Theory driven, a priori hypotheses, multiple methods, explanatory

a position of being able to explain rather than merely document the entrepreneurial phenomenon. Future research should continue this trend.

4. Level of analysis. There has been a welcome initiation of studies that examined more than one of the individual, group, organization, industry, and society levels of analysis. Such multi-level studies provide a much richer understanding of the entrepreneurial phenomenon and should therefore be encouraged in future research programs.

5. Time frame. It appears that greater insights can be obtained from studies which employ wide time frames than from studies employing cross sectional "snapshots." A push towards longer time frame studies is desirable, particularly since it is becoming clear that different strategic issues become important as firm and industry evolve.

6. Methodology. There has been disappointingly slow progress in research that addresses issues of causality, perhaps reflecting the elusiveness of the entreprenurial phenomenon. Recent years have seen only limited examples of research designs that develop a priori hypotheses. Consequently, formal modelling and experimental research have lacked a foundation for development. On the positive side, the incidence of studies that are both cross sectional and longitudinal are on the rise.

In closing we wish to be realistic. Clearly it is unrealistic to expect that future research designs will incorporate all the qualities we have suggested. Very few researchers have sufficient resources to design and execute projects that are theory driven, choose a contextual and process-oriented focus, adopt multiple levels of analysis, and employ wide time frames. Indeed, although we have been arguing that entrepreneurship research needs to move in a particular direction, we accept the fact that there are unavoidable tradeoffs in research and that there is no single best approach (McGrath, 1964; Weick, 1979). However, we do suggest that more meaningful and insightful results will be forthcoming if researchers consider these design issues and eschew research program designs in which all of the easy design alternatives are selected.

References

Aldrich, H., & Auster, E.R. (1986). Even dwarfs started small: Liabilities of age and size and their strategic implications. *Research in Organizational Behavior, 8,* 165-198.

Aldrich, H., & Zimmer, C. (1986). Entrepreneurship through social networks. In D.L. Sexton & R.W. Smilor (Eds.), *The art and science of entrepreneurship* (pp. 2-23). Cambridge, MA: Ballinger Publishing.

Alexander, A.P. (1967). The supply of industrial entrepreneurship. *Explorations in Entrepreneurial History, 4*(2), 136-149.

Astley, W.G. (1985). The two ecologies: Population and community perspectives on organizational evolution. *Administrative Science Quarterly, 30,* 224-241.

Baumol, W.J. (1982). Toward operational models of entrepreneurship. In J. Ronen (Ed.), *Entrepreneurship* (pp. 29-48). Lexington, MA: Lexington Books.

Birch, D.L. (1979). *The job generation process.* Cambridge, MA: MIT Program on Neighborhood and Regional Change.

Birley, S. (1987). New ventures and employment growth. *Journal of Business Venturing, 2*(2), 155-165.

Birley, S. (1985). The role of networks in the entrepreneurial process. *Journal of Business Venturing, 1*(1), 107-117.

Block, Z., & MacMillan, I.C. (1985). Milestones for successful venture planning. *Harvard Business Review, 85*(5), 184-188.

Brenner, R. (1987). National policy and entrepreneurship: The statesman's dilemma. *Journal of Business Venturing, 2* (2), 95-101.

Brittain, J.W., & Freeman, J.H. (1980). Organizational proliferation and density dependent selection. In J.R. Kimberly & R.H. Miles (Eds.), *The Organizational Life Cycle* (pp. 291-338). San Francisco: Jossey-Bass.

Brockhaus, R.H., Sr. (1982). The psychology of the entrepreneur. In C.A. Kent, D.L. Sexton, & K.H. Vesper (Eds.), *Encyclopedia of Entrepreneurship* (pp. 39-56). Englewood Cliffs, NJ: Prentice-Hall.

Carroll, G.R. (1984). Organizational ecology. *Annual Review Sociology, 10,* 71-93.

Carroll, G.R., & Delacroix, J. (1982). Organizational mortality in the newspaper industry of Argentina and Ireland: An ecological approach. *Administrative Science Quarterly, 27,* 169-198.

Carsrud, A.L., Olm, K.W., & Eddy, G.G. (1986). Entrepreneurship: Research in quest of a paradigm. In D.L. Sexton & R.W. Smilor (Eds.), *The art and science of entrepreneurship* (pp. 153-168). Cambridge, MA: Ballinger Publishing.

Casson, M. (1982). *The entrepreneur, an economic theory.* Totowa, NJ: Barnes & Noble.

Churchill, N.C., & Lewis, V.L. (1983). The five stages of small business growth. *Harvard Business Review, 83*(3), 3-12.

Cochran, T.C. (1965). The entrepreneur in economic change. *Explorations in Entrepreneurial History 3*(1), 25-38.

Cole, A.H. (1968). Meso-economics: A contribution from entrepreneurial history. *Explorations in Entrepreneurial History, 6*(1), 3-33.

Collins, O.F., Moore, D.G., & Unwalla, D.B. (1964). *The enterprising man.* East Lansing, MI: Michigan State University Business Studies.

Cooper, A.C. (1986). Entrepreneurship and high technology. In D.L. Sexton & R.W. Smilor (Eds.), *The art and science of entrepreneurship* (pp. 153-168). Cambridge, MA: Ballinger Publishing.

Cooper, A.C., & Dunkelberg, W.C. (1987). Entrepreneurial research: Old questions, new answers, and methodological issues. *American Journal of Small Business, 11*(3), 1-20.

Delacroix, J., & Carroll, G.R. (June, 1983). Organizational findings: An ecological study of the newspaper industries of Argentina and Ireland. *Administrative Science Quarterly, 28,* 274-291.

Dickson, P.R., & Giglierano, J.J. (1986). Missing the boat and sinking the boat: A conceptual model of entrepreneurial risk. *Journal of Marketing, 50*(3), 58-70.

Executive Forum. (1986). To really learn about entrepreneurship, let's study habitual entrepreneurs. *Journal of Business Venturing, 1*(3), 241-243.

Gartner, W.B. (1985a). A conceptual framework for describing the phenomenon of new venture creation. *Academy of Management Review, 10*(4), 696-706.

Gartner, W.B. (1983). An empirical model of the business startup, and eight entrepreneurial archetypes. *Dissertation Abstracts International, 43*, 3374A.

Gartner, W.B. (1985b). *Entrepreneurs and entrepreneurship: process versus content approaches.* Unpublished manuscript, Georgetown University.

Gasse, Y. (1982). Elaborations on the psychology of the entrepreneur. In C.A. Kent, D.L. Sexton, & K.H. Vesper (Eds.), *Encyclopedia of entrepreneurship* (pp. 57-71). Englewood Cliffs, NJ: Prentice-Hall.

Gatewood, E., Hoy, F., & Spindler, C. (1984). Functionalist vs. conflict theories: Entrepreneurship disrupts the power structure in a small southern community. In J.A. Hornaday, E.B. Shils, J.A. Timmons, & K.H. Vesper (Eds.), *Frontiers of Entrepreneur Research* (pp. 265-279). Wellesley, MA: Babson College Center for Entrepreneurial Studies.

Glade, W.P. (1967). Approaches to a theory of entrepreneurial formation. *Explorations in Entrepreneurial History, 4*(3), 245-259.

Greenfield, S.M., & Strickon, A. (1986). *Entrepreneurship and social change.* Lanham, MD: University Press of America.

Greenfield, S.M., & Strickon, A. (1981). A new paradigm for the study of entrepreneurship and social change. *Economic Development and Cultural Change, 29*(3), 467-499.

Greiner, L.E. (1972). Evolution and revolution as organizations grow. *Harvard Business Review, 72*(4), 37-46.

Hagen, E.E. (1960). The entrepreneur as rebel against traditional society. *Human Organization, 19*(4), 185-187.

Hambrick, D.C., & Crozier, L.M. (1985). Stumblers and stars in the management of rapid growth. *Journal of Business Venturing, 1*(1), 31-45.

Hannan, M.T., & Freeman, J. (1984). *American Sociological Review, 49*, 149-164.

Hannan, M.T., & Freeman, J. (1977). The population ecology of organizations. *American Journal of Sociology, 82*, 929-964.

Hrebiniak, L.G., & Joyce, W.F. (1985). Organizational adaptation: Strategic choice and environmental determinism. *Administrative Science Quarterly, 30*, 336-349.

Huntsman, B., & Hoban, J.P., Jr. (1980). Investment in new enterprise: Some empirical observations on risk, return, and market structure. *Financial Management, 9*(2), 44-51.

Kent, C.A., Sexton, D.L., & Vesper, K.H. (Eds.). (1982). *Encyclopedia of entrepreneurship.* Englewood Cliffs, NJ: Prentice-Hall.

Kets de Vries, M.F.R. (1985). The dark side of entrepreneurship. *Harvard Business Review, 85*(6), 160-167.

Kets de Vries, M.F.R., & Miller, D. (1984). Neurotic style and organizational pathology. *Strategic Management Journal, 5*, 35-55.

Kets de Vries, M.F.R., & Miller, D. (1986). Personality, culture, and organization. *Academy of Management Review, 2*(2), 266-279.

Khan, A.M. (1987). Assessing venture capital investments with noncompensatory behavioral decision models. *Journal of Business Venturing, 2*(3), 193-205.

Kihlstrom, R.E., & Laffont, J.J. (1979). A general equilibrium entrepreneurial theory of firm formation based on risk aversion. *Journal of Political Economy, 87*(4), 719-748.

Kimberly, J.R., & Miles, R.H. (Eds.). (1980). *The organizational life cycle.* San Francisco: Jossey-Bass.

Kirzner, I. (1973). *Competition and entrepreneurship.* Chicago: The University of Chicago Press.

Knight, F. (1921). *Risk, uncertainty, and profit.* Boston: Houghton Mifflin.

Kourilsky, M. (1980). Predictors of entrepreneurship in a simulated economy. *The Journal of Creative Behavior, 14*(3), 175-198.

Lamont, L. (1972, July). What entrepreneurs learn from experience. *Journal of Small Business,* pp. 254-260.

Leibenstein, H. (1978). *General X-efficiency and economic development.* New York: Oxford University Press.

MacMillan, I.C. (1983). The politics of new venture management. *Harvard Business Review, 61*(6), 8-16.

MacMillan, I.C., Siegel, R., & SubbaNarasimha, P.N. (1985). Criteria used by venture capitalists to evaluate new venture proposals. *Journal of Business Venturing, 1*(1), 119-128.
MacMillan, I.C., Zemann, L., & SubbaNarasimha, P.N. (1987). Criteria distinguishing successful from unsuccessful ventures in the venture screening process. *Journal of Business Venturing, 2*(2), 123-137.
Maidique, M.A., & Zirger, B.J. (1985). The new product learning cycle. *Research Policy, 14,* 299-313.
Martin, M.J.C. (1984). *Managing technological innovation & entrepreneurship.* Reston, VA: Reston Publishing Company.
McClelland, D.C. (1967). *The achieving society.* New York: Free Press.
McClelland, D.C. (1986). Characteristics of successful entrepreneurs. In *Keys to the Future of American Business,* Proceedings of the Third Creativity, Innovation, and Entrepreneurship Symposium (Addendum, pp. 1-14). Framingham, MA: U.S. Small Business Administration and the National Center for Research in Vocational Education.
McGrath, J.E. (1964). Toward a theory of method for research in organizations. In W.W. Cooper, H.J. Leavitt, & M.W. Shelly (Eds.), *New perspectives in organizational research.* New York: John Wiley.
Owens, R.L. (1978). The anthropological study of entrepreneurship. *The Eastern Anthropologist, 31*(1), 65-80.
Pfeffer, J. (1977). The ambiguity of leadership. *Academy of Management Review, 2*(1), 104-112.
President's Commission (1984). *Entrepreneurship and its impact on the U.S. economy.* Washington, DC: President's Commission on Industrial Competitiveness.
Reynolds, P.D. (1987). New firms: Societal contribution versus survival potential. *Journal of Business Venturing, 2*(3), 231-246.
Roberts, E.B. (1983). Business planning in the start-up high-technology enterprise. In J.A. Hornaday, E.B. Shils, J.A. Timmons, & K.H. Vesper (Eds.), *Frontiers of Entrepreneurship Research* (pp. 107-117). Wellesley, MA: Babson College Center for Entrepreneurial Studies.
Robinson, R.B., Jr., & Pearce, J.A. II. (1986). Product life-cycle considerations and the nature of strategic activities in entrepreneurial firms. *Journal of Business Venturing, 1*(2), 207-224.
Ronstadt, R. (1988). The corridor principal and entrepreneurial time. *Journal of Business Venturing, 3*(1), 31-40.
Roure, J.B., & Maidique, M.A. (1986). Linking prefunding factors and high-technology venture success: An exploratory study. *Journal of Business Venturing, 1*(3), 295-306.
Sandberg, W.R., & Hofer, C.W. (1987). Improving new venture performance: The role of strategy, industry structure, and the entrepreneur. *Journal of Business Venturing, 2*(1), 5-28.
Schein, E.H. (1983). The role of the founder in creating organizational culture. *Organizational Dynamics, 12*(1), 13-28.
Schere, J. (1982). Tolerance of ambiguity as a discriminating variable between entrepreneurs and managers. *Proceedings* (pp. 404-408). New York: Academy of Management.
Schumpeter, J.A. (1934). *The theory of economic development.* Cambridge, MA: Harvard University Press.
Sexton, D.L., & Bowman, N. (1985). The entrepreneur: A capable executive and more. *Journal of Business Venturing, 1*(1), 129-140.
Sexton, D.L., & Smilor, R.W. (Eds.) (1986). *The art and science of entrepreneurship.* Cambridge, MA: Ballinger Publishing.
Shapero, A., & Sokol, L. (1982). The social dimensions of entrepreneurship. In C.A. Kent, D.L. Sexton, & K.H. Vesper (Eds.), *Encyclopedia of entrepreneurship* (pp. 72-88). Englewood Cliffs, NJ: Prentice-Hall.
Singh, J.V., House, R.J., & Tucker, D.J. (1986). Organizational change and organizational mortality. *Administrative Science Quarterly, 31,* 587-611.
Smilor, R.W., & Gill, M.D. Jr. (1986). *The new business incubator.* Lexington, MA: Lexington Books.
Smith, N.R. (1967). *The entrepreneur and his firm: The relationship between type of man and type of company.* East Lansing, MI: Bureau of Business and Economic Research, Michigan State University.

Stanworth, M.I.K. & Curran, J. (1976). Growth and the small firm—an alternative view. *Journal of Management Studies, 13,* 95-110.

Stevenson, H.H., Muzyka, D.F., & Timmons, J.A. (1987). Venture capital in transition: A montecarlo simulation of changes in investment patterns. *Journal of Business Venturing, 2*(2), 103-121.

Stevenson, H.H., Roberts, M.J., & Grousback, H.I. (1985). *New business ventures & the entrepreneur.* Homewood, IL: Irwin.

Stinchcombe, A.L. (1965). Social structure and organizations. In J.G. March (Ed.), *Handbook of organizations* (pp. 142-193). Chicago: Rand McNally.

Swayne, C., & Tucker, W. (1973). *The effective entrepreneur.* Morristown, NJ: General Learning Press.

Timmons, J.A. (1982). New venture creation: Methods and models. In C.A. Kent, D.L. Sexton, & K.H. Vesper (Eds.), *Encyclopedia of entrepreneurship* (pp. 126-138). Englewood Cliffs, NJ: Prentice-Hall.

Tushman, M.L., & Anderson, P. (1986). Technological discontinuities and organizational environments. *Administrative Science Quarterly, 31,* 439-465.

Tushman, M.L., Virany, B., & Romanelli, E. (1986). Executive succession, strategic reorientations, and organizational evolution: The minicomputer industry as a case in point. *Technology in Society, 7,* 297-313.

Tyebjee, T.T., & Bruno, A.V. (1981). Venture capital decision-making: Preliminary results from three empirical studies. In J.A Hornaday, E.B. Shils, J.A. Timmons, & K.H. Vesper (Eds.), *Frontiers of entrepreneurship research* (pp. 281-320). Wellesley, MA: Babson College Center for Entrepreneurial Studies.

Van de Ven, A.H., Hudson, R., & Schroeder, D.M. (1984). Designing new business startups: Entrepreneurial, organizational, and ecological considerations. *Journal of Management, 10*(1), 87-107.

Vesper, K.H. (1983). *Entrepreneurship and national policy.* Pittsburgh, PA: Carnegie-Mellon University.

Vesper, K. (1980). *New venture strategies.* Englewood Cliffs, NJ: Prentice-Hall.

Weber, M. (1930). *The protestant ethic and the spirit of capitalism.* New York: Scribner's.

Webster, F.A. (1977). Entrepreneurs and ventures: An attempt at classification and clarification. *Academy of Management Review, 2*(1), 54-61.

Weick, K.E. (1979). *The social psychology of organizing.* New York: Random House.

Woodruff, A.M., & Alexander, T.G. (1958). *Success and failure in small manufacturing.* Pittsburgh, PA: University of Pittsburgh Press.

Wortman, M.S., Jr. (1987). Entrepreneurship: An integrating typology and evaluation of the empirical research in the field. *Journal of Management, 13*(2), 259-279.

Name Index